The Economics of European Integration

3RD EDITION

The Economics of European Integration

3RD EDITION

Richard Baldwin and Charles Wyplosz

McGraw-Hill
Higher Education

London Boston Burr Ridge, IL Dubuque, IA Madison, WI New York San Francisco
St. Louis Bangkok Bogotá Caracas Kuala Lumpur Lisbon Madrid Mexico City
Milan Montreal New Delhi Santiago Seoul Singapore Sydney Taipei Toronto

The Economics of European Integration
3rd Edition
Richard Baldwin and Charles Wyplosz
ISBN-13 978-0-07-712163-1
ISBN-10 0-07-712163-5

McGraw-Hill
Higher Education

Published by McGraw-Hill Education
Shoppenhangers Road
Maidenhead
Berkshire
SL6 2QL
Telephone: 44 (0) 1628 502 500
Fax: 44 (0) 1628 770 224
Website: www.mcgraw-hill.co.uk

British Library Cataloguing in Publication Data
A catalogue record for this book is available from the British Library

Library of Congress Cataloging in Publication Data
The Library of Congress data for this book has been applied for from the Library of Congress

Acquisitions Editor: Natalie Jacobs
Development Editor: Hannah Cooper
Editorial Assistant: Tom Hill
Marketing Manager: Vanessa Boddington
Senior Production Editor: James Bishop

Text Design by Hardlines
Cover design by Adam Renvoize
Printed and bound in Spain by Grafo, Bilbao

ISBN-13 978-0-07-712163-1
ISBN-10 0-07-712163-5

Dedication

For Sarah, Ted, Julia and Nick – R.B.

In memory of my parents, whose sufferings inspired my yearning for a Europe at peace, and who taught me the pleasure of learning – C.W.

Brief Table of Contents

PART I

HISTORY, FACTS AND INSTITUTIONS   1
1. History   3
2. Facts, law, institutions and the budget   47
3. Decision making   110

PART II

THE MICROECONOMICS OF ECONOMIC INTEGRATION   139
4. Essential microeconomic tools   141
5. The essential economics of preferential liberalization   162
6. Market size and scale effects   189
7. Growth effects and factor market integration   211
8. Economic integration, labour markets and migration   233

PART III

THE MACROECONOMICS OF MONETARY INTEGRATION   263
9. Essential macroeconomic tools   265
10. Europe's exchange rate question   288
11. Optimum currency areas   314

PART IV

EU MICRO POLICIES   351
12. The Common Agricultural Policy   353
13. Location effects, economic geography and regional policy   381
14. EU competition and state aid policy   425
15. EU trade policy   449

PART V

EU MONETARY AND FISCAL POLICIES   469
16. The European Monetary System   471
17. The European monetary union   488
18. Fiscal policy and the Stability Pact   519
19. The financial markets and the euro   547

Detailed Table of Contents

Preface   xi
Guided Tour   xvi
Technology to Enhance Learning
and Teaching   xix
Acknowledgements   xxii

PART I: HISTORY, FACTS AND
INSTITUTIONS   1

1. History   3
   1.1 Early post-war period   4
   1.2 Two strands of European
       integration: federalism and
       intergovernmentalism   11
   1.3 Evolution to two concentric
       circles: domino effect part I   18
   1.4 Euro-pessimism   21
   1.5 Deeper circles and domino effect
       part II: the Single Market
       Programme and the EEA   25
   1.6 Communism's creeping failure
       and spectacular collapse   28
   1.7 Reuniting east and west Europe   31
   1.8 Preparing for eastern enlargement:
       a string of new treaties   32
   1.9 Summary   39
   Self-assessment questions   40
   Essay questions   40
   Further reading: the aficionado's
   corner   41
   Useful websites   42
   References   42
   Annex A. Chronology from 1948
   to 2007   44

2. Facts, law, institutions and
   the budget   47
   2.1 Economic integration in the EU   48
   2.2 EU structure: three pillars and
       a roof   59
   2.3 EU law   64
   2.4 The 'Big-5' institutions   68
   2.5 Legislative processes   77
   2.6 Some important facts   80

   2.7 The budget   83
   2.8 The Lisbon Treaty   93
   2.9 Summary   105
   Self-assessment questions   106
   Essay questions   107
   Further reading: the aficionado's
   corner   108
   Useful websites   108
   References   108

3. Decision making   110
   3.1 Task allocation and subsidiarity:
       EU practice and principles   111
   3.2 Fiscal federalism and task
       allocation among government
       levels   113
   3.3 Economical view of decision
       making   121
   3.4 The distribution of power among
       EU members   126
   3.5 Legitimacy in EU decision making   132
   3.6 Summary   133
   Self-assessment questions   135
   Essay questions   136
   Further reading: the aficionado's
   corner   136
   Useful websites   137
   References   137

PART II: THE MICROECONOMICS OF
ECONOMIC INTEGRATION   139

4. Essential microeconomic tools   141
   4.1 Preliminaries I: supply and
       demand diagrams   142
   4.2 Preliminaries II: introduction to
       open-economy supply and
       demand analysis   145
   4.3 MFN tariff analysis   149
   4.4 Types of protection: an economic
       classification   155
   4.5 Summary   159
   Self-assessment questions   159
   Essay questions   160

Further reading: the aficionado's
corner   161
Useful websites   161
References   161

5. The essential economics of
    preferential liberalization   162
    5.1 Analysis of unilateral
        discriminatory liberalization   163
    5.2 Analysis of a customs union   172
    5.3 Customs unions versus free
        trade agreements   177
    5.4 WTO rules   179
    5.5 Empirical studies   179
    5.6 Summary   180
    Self-assessment questions   181
    Essay questions   183
    Further reading: the aficionado's
    corner   183
    Useful websites   184
    References   184
    Annex A Discriminatory
    liberalization: small country case   185

6. Market size and scale effects   189
    6.1 Liberalization, defragmentation
        and industrial restructuring: logic
        and facts   190
    6.2 Theoretical preliminaries:
        monopoly, duopoly and oligopoly   192
    6.3 The BE–COMP diagram in a
        closed economy   198
    6.4 The impact of European
        liberalization   200
    6.5 Summary   204
    Self-assessment questions   205
    Essay questions   206
    Further reading: the aficionado's
    corner   206
    Useful websites   207
    References   207
    Annex A Details on the COMP and
    BE curves   208

7. Growth effects and factor market
    integration   211
    7.1 The logic of growth and the facts   212
    7.2 Medium-term growth effects:
        induced capital formation with
        Solow's analysis   218

    7.3 Long-term growth effects: faster
        knowledge creation and
        absorption   227
    7.4 Summary   230
    Self-assessment questions   230
    Essay questions   231
    Further reading: the aficionado's
    corner   231
    Useful websites   231
    References   232

8. Economic integration, labour
    markets and migration   233
    8.1 European labour markets:
        a brief characterization   234
    8.2 Labour markets: the principles   237
    8.3 Effects of trade integration   242
    8.4 Migration   248
    8.5 Summary   259
    Self-assessment questions   260
    Essay questions   261
    Further reading: the aficionado's
    corner   261
    Useful websites   262

PART III: THE MACROECONOMICS OF
MONETARY INTEGRATION   263

9. Essential macroeconomic tools   265
    9.1 Preliminaries: output and prices   266
    9.2 The aggregate demand and
        supply diagram   268
    9.3 The short run: an IS–LM
        interpretation   276
    9.4 The open economy and the
        interest rate parity condition   280
    9.5 Monetary policy and the
        exchange rate regime   283
    9.6 Summary   285
    Self-assessment questions   286
    Essay questions   286
    Further reading: the aficionado's
    corner   287
    Useful websites   287
    References   287

10. Europe's exchange rate question   288
    10.1 The impossible trinity principle   289
    10.2 Choices   291
    10.3 What Europe did   299
    10.4 Summary   311

Self-assessment questions   311
Essay questions   312
Further reading: the aficionado's
corner   312
Useful websites   313
References   313

11. Optimum currency areas   314
    11.1 The question, the problem
         and the answer   315
    11.2 The optimum currency area
         criteria   322
    11.3 Is Europe an optimum currency
         area?   329
    11.4 Will Europe become an optimum
         currency area?   341
    11.5 Summary   345
    Self-assessment questions   347
    Essay questions   348
    Further reading: the aficionado's
    corner   348
    References   349

PART IV: EU MICRO POLICIES   351

12. The Common Agricultural Policy   353
    12.1 The old simple logic: price
         supports   355
    12.2 Changed circumstances and
         CAP problems   359
    12.3 The new economic logic of CAP   366
    12.4 CAP reform   369
    12.5 Today's CAP   371
    12.6 Remaining problems   374
    12.7 Summary   377
    Self-assessment questions   378
    Essay questions   378
    Further reading: the aficionado's
    corner   379
    Useful websites   379
    References   379

13. Location effects, economic
    geography and regional policy   381
    13.1 Europe's economic geography:
         the facts   382
    13.2 Theory part I: comparative
         advantage   390
    13.3 Theory part II: agglomeration
         and the new economic
         geography   393

13.4 Theory part III: putting it all
     together   402
13.5 EU regional policy   405
13.6 Empirical evidence   412
13.7 Summary   412
Self-assessment questions   413
Essay questions   413
Further reading: the aficionado's
corner   414
Useful websites   414
References   414
Annex A Agglomeration economics
more formally   416

14. EU competition and state aid policy   425
    14.1 The economics of anti-
         competitive behaviour and
         state aid   426
    14.2 EU competition policy   440
    14.3 Summary   446
    Self-assessment questions   447
    Essay questions   447
    Further reading: the aficionado's
    corner   448
    Useful websites   448
    References   448

15. EU trade policy   449
    15.1 Pattern of trade: facts   450
    15.2 EU institutions for trade policy   456
    15.3 EU external trade policy   459
    15.4 Summary   466
    Self-assessment questions   467
    Essay questions   467
    Further reading: the aficionado's
    corner   468
    Useful websites   468
    References   468

PART V: EU MONETARY AND FISCAL
POLICIES   469

16. The European Monetary System   471
    16.1 The EMS arrangements   472
    16.2 EMS-1: from divergence to
         convergence and blow-up   475
    16.3 The EMS re-engineered   481
    16.4 Summary   485
    Self-assessment questions   486
    Essay questions   486

Further reading: the aficionado's
corner   487
Useful websites   487
Reference   487

17. The European monetary union   488
    17.1 The Maastricht Treaty   489
    17.2 The Eurosystem   495
    17.3 Objectives, instruments and
          strategy   498
    17.4 Independence and
          accountability   502
    17.5 The first decade   506
    17.6 Summary   515
    Self-assessment questions   516
    Essay questions   516
    Further reading: the aficionado's
    corner   517
    Useful websites   518
    References   518

18. Fiscal policy and the Stability Pact 519
    18.1 Fiscal policy in the monetary
          union   520
    18.2 Fiscal policy externalities   524

18.3 Principles   528
18.4 The Stability and Growth Pact   532
18.5 Summary   542
Self-assessment questions   544
Essay questions   544
Further reading: the aficionado's
corner   545
Useful websites   546
References   546

19. The financial markets and the euro   547
    19.1 The capital markets   548
    19.2 Microeconomics of capital
          market integration   553
    19.3 Financial institutions and
          markets   559
    19.4 The international role of
          the euro   572
    19.5 Summary   579
    Self-assessment questions   579
    Essay questions   580
    Further reading: the aficionado's
    corner   580
    Useful websites   581
    References   581

Preface

European integration keeps amazing its supporters and critics alike. No other region has displayed similar willingness to jettison important components of sovereignty in pursuit of shared, yet thoroughly imprecise, goals. And, in its own peculiar way, European integration keeps forging ahead at a pace that is too fast for some and too slow for others. No one would deny, though, that the transformation of the past half century is spectacular – a clean break with centuries of intra-European warfare. This integration is clearly important for the 500 or so million Europeans it directly affects, but since Europe accounts for one-quarter of the world economy, half of world trade and one-third of world capital markets, European integration also affects the lives of most non-Europeans.

A subtle interplay of strictly economic and much broader, high-minded goals has driven European integration forward along political, cultural and economic dimensions. The goal of this book is to provide an accessible presentation of the facts, theories and controversies that are necessary to understand this process. Our approach is rooted deeply in economic principles for the simple reason that economic integration has been the vanguard since the Organization for European Economic Cooperation was founded in 1948. Yet economics is not enough; historical, political and cultural factors are brought into the picture when necessary.

What this book is

This is a textbook for courses on European economic integration. Its emphasis is on economics, covering both the microeconomics and macroeconomics of European integration. Understanding European economic integration, however, requires much more than economics, so the book also covers the essential aspects of European history, institutions, laws, politics and policies.

The book is written at a level that should be accessible to second- and third-year undergraduates in economics as well as advanced undergraduates and graduate students in business and in international affairs, European studies and political science. Some knowledge of economics is needed to absorb all the material with ease – a first-year course in the principles of economics should suffice – but the book is self-contained in that it reviews all essential economics behind the analysis. Diligent students should therefore be able to master the material without any formal economics background.

What is in this book

The book is organized into five parts: essential background (Part I), the microeconomics (Part II) and macroeconomics (Part III) of European integration, and microeconomic (Part IV) and macroeconomic (Part V) policies.

Part I presents the essential background for studying European integration.

★ An overview of the post-Second World War historical development of European integration is presented in Chapter 1. The chapter should be useful to all students, even those who are familiar with the main historical events, as this chapter stresses the economic and political economy logic behind the events.

★ A concise presentation of the indispensable background information necessary for the study of European integration is presented in Chapter 2. This includes key facts concerning European economies and a brief review of the EU's legal system and principles. Chapter 2 also presents information on the vital EU institutions and the EU's legislative processes as well as the main features of the EU budget.

★ Chapter 3 presents an economic framework for thinking about EU institutions. The first part explains how the 'theory of fiscal federalism' can be used to consider the appropriateness of the allocation of powers between EU institutions and EU Member States. The second part explains how economic reasoning – game theory in particular – can be used to analyse EU decision-making procedures for their decision-making efficiency as well as their implications for the distribution of power among EU members. While these are not classic topics in the study of European integration, they are essential to understanding the current challenges facing the EU, such as the 2004 enlargement and the debates around the Lisbon Treaty.

Part II presents the microeconomic aspects of European integration.

★ An introduction to the fundamental methods of trade policy analysis is presented in Chapter 4. The chapter introduces basic supply and demand analysis in an open economy, the key economic welfare concepts of consumer and producer surplus, and uses these to study the simple economics of tariff protection.

★ An in-depth analysis of European preferential trade liberalization is given in Chapter 5. The focus is on how the formation of a customs union or free trade area affects people, companies and governments inside and outside the integrating nations.

★ A thorough study of how the market-expanding aspects of European integration affects the efficiency of European firms is presented in Chapter 6. The main line of reasoning explains how integration in the presence of scale economies and imperfect competition can produce fewer, bigger and more efficient firms facing more effective competition from each other.

★ Chapter 7 gives a detailed study of the growth effects of European integration. The emphasis is on the economic logic linking European integration to medium-run and long-run growth effects. Neoclassical and endogenous growth theory are covered, as are the basic facts and empirical evidence.

★ Chapter 8 deals with the labour markets. It recalls the basics of labour economics in order to explain unemployment and develop the notion that social requirements may have seriously negative effects in terms of jobs, wages and growth. The chapter uses these insights to study the effects of integration. It deals with many controversial issues such as social dumping and migration, trying hard to stay above the fray by presenting economic analysis as one logic, not the only one.

Part III continues the approach of Part II by providing the basic principles behind macro-economic and monetary integration.

★ The principles needed for the macroeconomic analysis are presented in Chapter 9. This chapter provides a bird's eye view of macroeconomics, with an emphasis on the role of capital movements and their implications for the role of monetary policy under different exchange rate regimes. The chapter includes a review of the Mundell–Fleming model designed for readers who need to tool up.

★ The choice of the exchange regime is the main objective of Chapter 10. It explains how to assess the desirability of each of the main possible arrangements. It includes a presentation of the two-corner strategy, which explains both why some countries have adopted the euro and others have chosen to retain their own currencies. The usefulness of this analysis is demonstrated through a brief overview of Europe's monetary history, from ancient times when Europe was a de facto monetary union under the gold standard all the way to the adoption of a single currency.

★ Chapter 11 presents the optimum currency area theory that helps to understand the main costs and benefits from sharing a common currency. The theory does not provide a black-and-white answer; rather, it develops a set of economic, political and institutional criteria to evaluate the costs and benefits of forming a monetary union. In addition, the costs and benefits may be endogenous. Europe fulfils some criteria but not others, which explains the unending debates on the merits of the European monetary union.

Part IV presents the main microeconomic policies of the EU.

★ Chapter 12 looks at the Common Agricultural Policy (CAP), presenting the economics and facts that are essential for understanding its effects. The chapter takes particular care to examine the economic forces behind recent CAP reform in the light of international trade negotiations (the Doha Round) and the 2004 enlargement.

★ Chapter 13 presents the economics that link European integration to the location of economic activities. This includes a presentation of the main facts on how the location of economic activity has shifted both within and between nations. To organize thinking about these facts – and to understand how EU regional policy might affect it – the chapter presents the location effects of integration in the light of neoclassical theories (Heckscher–Ohlin), as well as the so-called new economic geography. The chapter also presents the main features of the EU's regional policy and considers the implications of the 2004 enlargement.

★ Chapter 14 covers the basic elements of the EU's competition policy and state aid policy (EU jargon for subsidies). Instead of just describing the policies, the chapter motivates and explains them by introducing the basic economic logic of anticompetitive practices. It also presents several cases that illustrate the difficulties of applying simple economics to the complex world of international business.

★ Chapter 15 addresses EU trade policy, i.e. its commercial policies with the rest of the world. While trade policy is not as central to the EU as, say, the CAP and cohesion policies are, it is important. The EU is the world's biggest trader, and trade policy is probably the only EU 'foreign policy' that is consistently effective. The chapter covers EU trade policy by presenting the basic facts on EU trade, covering the EU's institutional arrangements as concerns trade policy, and finally summarizing the EU's policies towards its various trade partners.

Part V is the counterpart to Part IV, as it presents the main macroeconomic policies of the EU.

★ Chapter 16 deals with the European Monetary System, its now defunct first version and the new version, which is a required step towards monetary union membership. It shows that the successes of the EMS have provided a powerful incentive to go further and create a single currency, while its shortcomings have made the adoption of the euro look like the least bad of all options. Its current role is also presented.

★ The main features of the European monetary union are laid out in Chapter 17. This includes a description and an analysis of the institutions created by the Maastricht Treaty. It explains the importance attached to price stability and the measures adopted to achieve this objective. The chapter also provides a review of the first decade of the euro, assessing the performance of the ECB and current debates.

★ Fiscal policy is the last national macroeconomic instrument remaining once national monetary policy has been lost. Chapter 18 looks at the Stability and Growth Pact, designed to deliver enough budgetary discipline not to endanger the overriding price stability objective. As we suggested in the first edition of this book, the Pact had serious shortcomings, and they have forced a revision. The revision and the events that made it necessary are presented, along with remaining doubts about the chosen solution. We emphasize the economic and political difficulties inherent in preserving the last national macroeconomic instrument while ensuring fiscal discipline.

★ The last chapter deals with the financial markets. The financial services industry is being transformed by the Single European Act 1986 and by the adoption of a single currency. Chapter 19 starts with a review of what makes this industry special and then introduces the microeconomics of capital integration. This makes it possible to interpret the changes that have taken place and those that have not yet materialized. Financial markets are also important for monetary policy effectiveness, raising delicate questions: Is the single monetary policy symmetrically affecting member countries? How are financial institutions regulated and supervised? The chapter also examines whether the euro is becoming a worldwide currency, alongside the US dollar.

How to use this book

The book is suitable for a one-semester course that aims at covering both the microeconomics and the macroeconomics of European integration. If the course is long enough, the book can be used sequentially; this is how we teach, and it works well.

Shorter courses may focus on the trade and competition aspects; they can use only Parts I, II and IV. Conversely, a course dealing only with the macroeconomic aspects can use Parts III and V, and finish with labour market issues as covered in Chapter 8 (which does not really require the previous microeconomic material).

Eclectic courses that focus on theory and cover trade, competition and macroeconomics, can use only Chapters 1 to 11, or just 4 to 11.

Eclectic courses oriented towards policy issues can use, with some additional lecturing if the students are not familiar with basic theory, Chapters 1 and 2, and 12 to 19. In general, all chapters are self-contained but, inevitably, they often refer to results and facts presented elsewhere.

Each chapter includes self-assessment questions designed to help the students check how well they master the material, and essay questions which can be given as assignments. We also provide additional readings; most of them are easily accessible to undergraduate students though, occasionally, when we did not find adequate references, we point to more advanced material. Students may find some of these readings rewarding.

The third edition continues with our tradition of providing many internet links that should allow students and lecturers alike to get the latest information on the EU's many fast-developing areas. We have observed that the internet is an excellent way to stimulate students' interest by bringing classroom teaching to real issues they see every day in the media. While lecturers have long used reference to print and broadcast media for the same purpose, the links we provide go well beyond journalist treatments in a way that allows students to realize the usefulness of the basics they have learned from the text.

Guided Tour

Introduction

Each part and chapter opens with an introduction which indicates the ideas and concepts that will be presented in the following pages.

Maps and diagrams

These are provided throughout the text to show geographically the impact of changes in the EU integration across the continent.

Boxes

Each chapter provides a number of boxes that provide further examples and explanations of key facts, events or economic ideas relating to the European Union.

Clear presentation

Economic models are clearly presented to aid the interpretation of economic curves and graphs, with extra notes and explanations where appropriate.

Tables

Placed throughout the chapters, the tables provide relevant statistics and current data about the European Union and its member states.

Summaries

Placed at the end of each chapter, they recap the ideas introduced in the preceding pages and emphasize key findings.

Self-assessment questions

Useful for testing knowledge of the economic concepts and facts featured in the chapter.

Essay questions

These offer practice examples for exams or assessment, encouraging students to write full answers that explore ideas in more detail.

Further reading, websites and references

All help provide direction for further research around the topics covered in the chapter.

Annex

Where appropriate Annex sections offer further economic explanations, data or background information. The appendices enable further study to compliment the chapter, covering more advanced concepts and providing greater detail.

Technology to Enhance Learning and Teaching

Visit www.mcgraw-hill.co.uk/textbooks/baldwin today

Online Learning Centre (OLC)

After completing each chapter, log on to the supporting Online Learning Centre website. Take advantage of the study tools offered to reinforce the material you have read in the text, and to develop your knowledge of economics in a fun and effective way.

Resources for students include:

★ *Self-test quizzes*

★ *Web links*

★ *Chronology*

★ *'In the News' section*

★ *Glossary*

Also available for lecturers:

★ *Chapter Summaries*

★ *Learning Objectives*

★ *Lecture Outlines*

★ *PowerPoint Presentations*

★ *Essay Questions and Answers*

★ *Key Concepts and Terms*

Custom Publishing Solutions: Let us help make our **content** your **solution**

At McGraw-Hill Education our aim is to help lecturers to find the most suitable content for their needs delivered to their students in the most appropriate way. Our custom publishing solutions offer the ideal combination of content delivered in the way which best suits lecturer and students.

Our custom publishing programme offers lecturers the opportunity to select just the chapters or sections of material they wish to deliver to their students from a database called Primis at www.primisonline.com

Primis contains over two million pages of content from:

★ textbooks

★ professional books

★ case books – Harvard Articles, Insead, Ivey, Darden, Thunderbird and *BusinessWeek*

★ Taking Sides – debate materials

Across the following imprints:

★ McGraw-Hill Education   ★ Harvard Business School Press

★ Open University Press   ★ US and European material

There is also the option to include additional material authored by lecturers in the custom product – this does not necessarily have to be in English.

We will take care of everything from start to finish in the process of developing and delivering a custom product to ensure that lecturers and students receive exactly the material needed in the most suitable way.

With a Custom Publishing Solution, students enjoy the best selection of material deemed to be the most suitable for learning everything they need for their courses – something of real value to support their learning. Teachers are able to use exactly the material they want, in the way they want, to support their teaching on the course.

Please contact your local McGraw-Hill representative with any questions or alternatively contact Warren Eels e: warren_eels@mcgraw-hill.com.

Make the grade!

 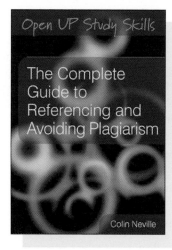 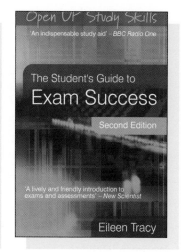

30% off any Study Skills book!

Our Study Skills books are packed with practical advice and tips that are easy to put into practice and will really improve the way you study. Topics include:

★ Techniques to help you pass exams
★ Advice to improve your essay writing
★ Help in putting together the perfect seminar presentation
★ Tips on how to balance studying and your personal life

www.openup.co.uk/studyskills

Visit our website to read helpful hints about essays, exams, dissertations and much more.

Special offer! As a valued customer, buy online and receive 30% off any of our Study Skills books by entering the promo code **getahead**

Acknowledgements

Our thanks go to the following reviewers for their comments at various stages in the text's development:

Nigel Allington, Cardiff Business School
Steven Brakman, University of Groningen
David Bywaters, University of Hertfordshire
Andreas Cornett, University of Southern Denmark
Norman Dytianquin, University of Maastricht
Finn Olesen, University of Southern Denmark
Tom Verbeke, Ghent University
Jef Vuchelen, Vrije Universiteit Brussel
Rolf Weder, University of Basel
Maurizio Zanardi, Tilburg University

We are indebted to a number of colleagues for their suggestions and help. In particular, in addition to anonymous referees, we wish to thank Antonio Barbosa, Michael Burda, Ivar Bredesen, Menzie Chinn, Rikard Forslid, Ivar Bredesen, Elena Kolokolova, Samuel Leiser, Henry Overman, Volker Pabst, Armin Riess, Frederic Robert-Nicoud, Horst Siebert and Joachim Tomaschett for catching errors, making useful suggestions or both. Thanks also go to Cristina Molina for excellent proof reading, Pierre-Loius Vezina for equally good research assistance and Roman Horvath for providing us with data on optimum currency areas. We are also grateful to Natalie Jacobs and Caroline Prodger at McGraw-Hill, who encouraged us to undertake this new edition and who have organized a panel of readers, and to Hannah Cooper and Tom Hill, the Development Editors, who worked hard to produce a high quality book. We remain responsible for any errors, of course.

PART I

History, facts and institutions

And what is the plight to which Europe has been reduced? . . . over wide areas a vast quivering mass of tormented, hungry, care-worn and bewildered human beings gape at the ruins of their cities and their homes, and scan the dark horizons for the approach of some new peril, tyranny or terror. . . . That is all that Europeans, grouped in so many ancient states and nations . . . have got by tearing each other to pieces and spreading havoc far and wide.

Yet all the while there is a remedy . . . It is to re-create the European Family, or as much of it as we can, and to provide it with a structure under which it can dwell in peace, in safety and in freedom. We must build a kind of United States of Europe.

Winston Churchill (Zurich, 19 September 1946)

Chapter contents

1.1	Early post-war period	4
1.2	Two strands of European integration: federalism and intergovernmentalism	11
1.3	Evolution to two concentric circles: domino effect part I	18
1.4	Euro-pessimism	21
1.5	Deeper circles and domino effect part II: the Single Market Programme and the EEA	25
1.6	Communism's creeping failure and spectacular collapse	28
1.7	Reuniting east and west Europe	31
1.8	Preparing for eastern enlargement: a string of new treaties	32
1.9	Summary	39

Introduction

Understanding Europe's economic integration today requires a good notion of Europe's recent past. This chapter presents the main events of European economic integration in chronological order, stressing, wherever possible, the economic and political economy logic behind the events.

1.1 Early post-war period

In 1945, a family standing almost anywhere in Europe found themselves in a nation which was, or had recently been: (a) ruled by a brutal fascist dictator, (b) occupied by a foreign army or (c) both. As a direct result of these governmental failures, tens of millions of Europeans were dead and Europe's economy lay in ruins. Worse yet, the Second World War was not an isolated historical event. If the parents were middle-aged, it would have been their second experience of colossal death and destruction; the Second World War started just two decades after the cataclysm of the First World War (1914–18). Indeed, the Second World War was the fourth time in 130 years that France and Germany were at the core of increasingly horrifying wars.

1.1.1 A climate for radical change

In 1945, it was plain to all that something was desperately wrong with the way Europe governed itself. Minds were open to radical changes.

It is hard for students born in the 1980s or later to connect emotionally with the misery and hardship that were so commonplace in Europe at the end of the Second World War. Difficult, yet it is essential. One simply cannot understand European integration without comprehending the mindset of Europeans in the late 1940s.

The miracle of the web now allows students to see photos (see Fig. 1.1), watch videos, read original documents and listen to speeches from the time. One of the best sites for all European documents is the Luxembourg-based Centre Virtuel de la Connaissance sur l'Europe. Its excellent

Figure 1.1 London 1944 and Dresden 1945
Source: National Maritime Museum, London and German Historical Museum (DHM), Berlin

and well-organized website is at www.ena.lu. Also, www.dhm.de/lemo/html/Nachkriegsjahre/ DasEndeAlsAnfang/ provides some powerful photos and videos of Germany's experience.

Table 1.1 shows some figures on the death and destruction in the Second World War. In western Europe, the war killed about 8 million people, with Germans accounting for

Table 1.1 Death and destruction in the Second World War

	Death toll	The Economic Set-Back: Pre-war year when GDP equalled that of 1945
Austria	525,000	1886
Belgium	82,750	1924
Denmark	4250	1936
Finland	79,000	1938
France	505,750	1891
Germany	6,363,000	1908
Italy	355,500	1909
Netherlands	250,000	1912
Norway	10,250	1937
Sweden	0	(a)
Switzerland	0	(a)
UK	325,000	(a)

(a) GDP grew during the Second World War.
Source: GDP data from Crafts and Toniolo (1996), p. 4; death toll from http://encarta.msn.com

three-quarters of this total. In central and eastern Europe over 9 million perished, of whom 6.3 million were Poles. The Soviet Union alone lost over 20 million. The fact that much of the killing was deliberate genocide made it even more horrifying (see www.jewishvirtuallibrary.org for information on the Holocaust).

The scale of this devastation is the key to understanding the post-1945 drive for European integration. It may, however, be difficult to imagine the mindset in 1945. To put it in perspective, note that the terrible attacks in the USA on 11 September 2001 resulted in about 3000 deaths. This event radically altered many people's and many governments' perception of the world. To approach the Second World War death toll in western and central Europe, it would have taken two '11 September' attacks on every single day between 1938 and 1945, and this excludes the 20-plus million people who perished in the Union of Soviet Socialist Republics (USSR).

The war also caused enormous economic damage. Figures are difficult to find for central and eastern Europe, but the estimates for western Europe are staggering, as Table 1.1 shows. The war cost Germany and Italy four decades or more of growth and put Austrian and French GDPs back to nineteenth-century levels.

Refugees, hunger and political instability

The economic, political and humanitarian situation in Europe was dire in the years 1945–47, especially in Germany. Food production in 1946 was low and the 1946–47 winter was especially harsh. Hunger was widespread. Food was rationed in most European nations up to the mid-1950s. At times, rations fell to just 900 calories per day in some parts of Germany (2000 calories per day is the standard today). Much of Europe's infrastructure, industry and housing lay in ruins. Many Europeans in these years were dependent on humanitarian aid, much in the same way that people in war-torn African nations are today. The UN Relief and Rehabilitation Administration (UNRRA) spent nearly $4 billion on emergency food and medical aid, helped about 7 million displaced persons return home, and provided camps for about a million refugees who did not want to be repatriated.

Politically, Western Europe suffered governmental and constitutional crises. General de Gaulle resigned as president of the provisional government in 1946 over a disagreement on France's new constitution. Italy and Belgium saw bitter internal conflicts over their monarchy. Italy abolished its monarch in a referendum that involved accusations of communist manipulation. The return of the Belgian king sparked riots. If all this seems like the plot of a B-grade apocalypse movie, you should watch some of the online audiovisual material at www.ena.lu to see just how real it was. Hunger, riots and refugee camps were commonplace all across western Europe.

1.1.2 The prime question and guiding ideologies

The horror and revulsion arising from this devastation pushed one question to the forefront in the mid-1940s: 'How can Europe avoid another war?' The solutions offered depended on beliefs about the causes of the war; three schools of thought were in evidence:

1 *Germany was to blame.* Guided by this belief, the so-called Morgenthau plan of 1944 proposed to avoid future European war by turning Germany into 'a country primarily agricultural and pastoral in character'. The same thinking guided post-First World War arrangements in

Europe. That war was blamed on Germany and the victors were rewarded with territorial gains and financial reparations. The result was a cycle of recovery, resentment and national rivalry that led to the Second World War.

2 *Capitalism was to blame.* Marxism–Leninism blamed capitalism for most of the world's evils, including both world wars. This belief suggested that communism was the solution.

3 *Nationalism was to blame.* The third school blamed the excesses of destructive nationalism for the war. The solution suggested by this belief was tighter integration of all European nations. While calls for a united Europe were heard after the 1914–18 war and during the 1939–45 war, the school's most famous post-war statement was the 1946 'United States of Europe' speech by Winston Churchill (you can listen to it at www.ena.lu).

School number 3 and the European integration solution ultimately prevailed, but this was far from clear in the late 1940s. Most European nations were either struggling to re-establish their governments and economies or were under direct military occupation. Germany and Austria were divided into US, UK, French and Soviet zones (Fig. 1.2). Soviet troops occupied all of central and eastern Europe. In western Europe, 1945 and 1946 passed with hardly any progress towards the establishment of a post-war architecture. West European governments' limited governance capacities were overloaded by the dismal humanitarian situation.

Things moved more rapidly in the east. The Soviet Union had already begun to implement its vision of a new Europe during the war. Communism was imposed on the previously independent nations of Estonia, Latvia and Lithuania, and by 1948 communist parties had been pushed to power in every Soviet-occupied country. Communists took power in Albania and Yugoslavia, and were gaining strength in Greece.

The notion that capitalism was to blame and would cause yet more suffering was widely held in western Europe. In the parliamentary elections of 1946, communists won 19 per cent of the vote in Italy and 29 per cent in France.

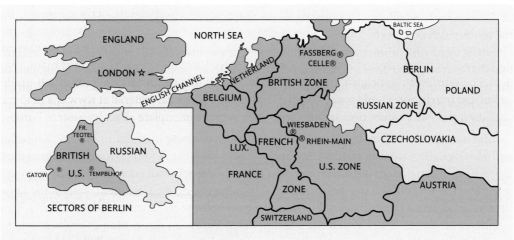

Figure 1.2 **The four-way division of Germany**
Source: www.TrumanLibrary.org

1.1.3 Emergence of a divided Europe: the Cold War

America and Britain categorically rejected the Soviet's world vision. Their wartime alliance with the USSR unravelled and the Allies-versus-Axis confrontation was replaced by an East–West confrontation, called the Cold War. By 1947, the US and Britain concluded that an economically strong Germany would be essential to the defence of liberal democracy in western Europe. They merged the UK and US zones into 'Bizonia' (September 1947), and France, which had originally favoured the Morgenthau Plan, added its zone in 1948. Germany drew up a constitution in 1948 under the leadership of Konrad Adenauer (see Box 1.1).

Box 1.1   Konrad Adenauer (1876–1967)

Born to a family of modest means, he rose to become Mayor of Cologne, a post he was stripped of by the Nazis in 1933. He was President of the 1948 Parliamentary Council that drew up Germany's constitution ('Basic Law') before becoming the first Chancellor (i.e. Prime Minister) of Germany – an office he held from 1949 to 1963. Under his leadership, Germany regained its sovereignty, joined the European Economic Community and NATO, and evolved into a cornerstone of western European democracy and economic strength. Adenauer was a key promoter of close Franco-German cooperation and of Germany's social welfare system.

Photo: © European Communities, 1995–2009

In reaction to western moves towards creating a German government in their zones, the USSR escalated harassment of western travel to Berlin. Ultimately, the Soviets imposed the famous 'Berlin Blockade' on 24 June 1948. Western powers countered with the equally famous 'Berlin air bridge' (see www.ena.lu for details and photos). In May 1949, the Federal Republic of Germany was established. The new government agreed to make a military contribution to the western defence effort.

Soviet aggressive promotion of their solution (communism for all) triggered a western reaction that narrowed the three solutions down to two with an 'iron curtain' between them. East of the iron curtain, the post-war architecture was based on communism and one-party politics. To the west, it was built on multi-party democracy, the social market economy and European integration.

The merger of the French, US and UK zones was a defining moment in Europe. Tentative and ideologically based support for European integration came to be strongly reinforced by western European nations pursuing their own interests. French leaders saw the Franco–German integration as a way of counter-balancing US–UK influence on the Continent while at the same time assuring that a reindustrialized Germany would become an economic partner rather than a military adversary. The UK and the US supported European integration as the best way to counter the spread of communism in Europe. German leaders embraced European integration as the surest route to re-establishing Germany as a 'normal' nation (Germany was recognized as an independent nation only in 1955). Italian leaders also welcomed European integration, which provided them with an ideological counterbalance to communism and helped shut the door on Italy's fascist past. The Benelux nations (Belgium, Netherlands and Luxembourg) were happy about anything that reduced the chances of another Franco–German war.

1.1.4 First steps: the OEEC and EPU

From the perspective of European integration, the most important result of the western European effort to resist communism was the so-called Marshall Plan and the Organization for European Economic Cooperation (OEEC). In reaction to the dire economic conditions in Europe and the attendant threat that communists might come to power in Greece, Italy and France, US Secretary of State (i.e. Foreign Minister) George Marshall announced that the USA would give financial assistance to all European nations 'west of the Urals', if they could agree to a joint programme for economic reconstruction.

Almost immediately, European nations gathered in Paris to study Marshall's proposal (the USSR and the central and eastern European countries eventually withdrew and never received Marshall Plan funds). The conference was intended to determine the amount of aid required and, at US insistence, to create a permanent organization (the Organization for European Economic Cooperation, OEEC) in which Europeans would cooperate in their mutual economic recovery. A joint programme and organization were duly developed by the Europeans. The US Congress, which was initially reluctant, funded the Marshall Plan in April 1948 after the communist takeover in Czechoslovakia.

The OEEC was established in 1948 with 13 members of the old EU15 (Finland was under Soviet pressure to stay neutral and Spain was under Franco's dictatorship) plus Norway, Iceland, Switzerland, Turkey and the US–UK zone of the Free Territory of Trieste until it was merged with Italy. Germany was still under occupation, but representatives from the Western Zones participated. From 1948 to 1952, Marshall Plan aid amounted to $12 billion, with half of this going to the UK, France and West Germany. The Soviet bloc's counterpart, the Council of Mutual Economic Assistance (CMEA), was set up in 1949.

Box 1.2 The Organization for European Economic Cooperation (OEEC)

The OEEC's members formed the Council of the Organization which ruled on the basis of intergovernmental decision making (unanimity). It was chaired by high-profile figures of the era (Paul-Henri Spaak, Paul van Zeeland, Dirk Strikker, Anthony Eden, Richard Heathcoat Amory). The OEEC's importance waned in 1952 as Marshall Plan aid ended and the focus of American spending shifted to more explicitly military ends in the form of the North Atlantic Treaty Organization (NATO). In 1961, the OEEC was transformed into the Organization for Economic Cooperation and Development (OECD).

Source: This box is based on the OECD's website at www.oecd.org

---

The OEEC divided American aid among its members (see Box 1.2), but a far more important role, as far as European history is concerned, was the OEEC's mandate to advance European economic integration. It did this by reducing intra-European trade barriers and improving the intra-European system of payments by establishing the European Payments Union (EPU); see Box 1.3.

Box 1.3   The European Payments Union (EPU), July 1950 to December 1958

Most European nations were bankrupt after 1945, so trade was generally conducted on the basis of bilateral agreements, often involving barter. The EPU multi-lateralized these bilateral deals. Each month, EPU members added up the deficits and surpluses in their bilateral trade accounts with other EPU members. These were offset against each other so that each nation remained with an overall surplus or deficit with respect to the EPU. The great advantage of this was that, since nations no longer owed money to each other directly, the debt-based incentives for importing from or exporting to a particular partner vanished. As a consequence, it was easy to loosen the web of bilateral trade restrictions that had been set up in the early post-war years. In its first year, the EPU removed all discriminatory trade measures among EPU members. EPU/OEEC membership also fostered overall trade liberalization via its 'Code of Liberalization'. This required members to lower trade barriers progressively by 25 per cent of their initial levels. During this time intra-European trade boomed, more than doubling in the EPU's lifetime (1950–58); imports from North America grew by only 50 per cent. The trade surplus with the US allowed European national central banks to accumulate substantial dollar reserves. This restored their financial stability and fostered trade liberalization by undermining balance-of-payments justifications for import restrictions. By 1958, the financial position of EPU members was strong enough to allow them to restore the convertibility of their currencies (prior to this, the currencies were unconvertible, e.g. it was illegal for private citizens to exchange French francs for dollars or deutschmarks without government permission).

Source: This box is based largely on Eichengreen and de Macedo 2001

In 1949, the US demanded that the OEEC make greater efforts to bring about direct European economic integration, especially intra-OEEC trade liberalization. Up to this point, Marshall Plan money was mainly used to finance European countries' dollar deficits in the EPU. In reaction to US pressure, the OEEC nations agreed to remove quantitative restrictions on private imports. While this had limited scope (at the time, much of intra-European trade was conducted by government-controlled corporations), 60 per cent of private intra-European trade was freed thanks to OEEC action by 1950, with this figure rising to 89 per cent in 1959. The OEEC's trade liberalization was important in at least two ways:

1   The liberalization fostered a rapid growth of trade and incomes. As the figures in Table 1.2 show, the 1950s were marked by a remarkable increase in GDP and the export of manufactured goods, at least on the Continent.

2   The thinking of policy makers was profoundly affected by the fact that industrial output grew at historically unprecedented rates even as European trade was being liberalized.

The second point was a critical change in policy makers' mindset – one that eventually opened the door to the Treaty of Rome's deep economic liberalization. In the decades following the First World War, especially during the 1930s, economic growth was viewed as a competition between

Table 1.2 Western European trade and output growth in manufactures, 1950–58

	GDP growth % per annum	Manufacturing export growth % per annum
Germany (West)	7.8	19.7
Italy	5.0	9.2
Netherlands	4.3	11.7
UK	2.0	1.8
France	4.4	3.8

Source: Milward 1992, Table 4.1

nations. In this competition, trade barriers played a central role as each nation sought to 'save' its market for its own industrialists.

In sharp contrast, the correlation between trade barriers and industrial growth was completely reversed in the 1940s and 1950s. Trade liberalization among west European nations went hand-in-hand with spectacular growth; intra-European imports and exports expanded even more rapidly than output. Europe's leaders came to view European integration as an idea that made as much sense economically as it did politically. As Milward (1992) put it: 'The proposals for trade liberalisation and customs unions that were made fell therefore on to a receptive soil.'

1.1.5 The drive for deeper integration

While the OEEC succeeded in economic terms, some OEEC members found it too limited to bring about the deeper integration that they felt was necessary to avoid future war and restore economic strength. The Cold War lent urgency to this drive. With East–West tensions rising steadily, Germany would not only have to be allowed to regain its industrial might, it would have to rearm in order to counter the threat of Soviet territorial aggression. Since many Europeans, including many Germans, were still uncomfortable with the idea of a Germany that was both economically and militarily strong, integrating Germany into a supranational Europe seemed a natural way forward.

1.2 Two strands of European integration: federalism and intergovernmentalism

While it was clear by the late 1940s that European integration would be the foundation of western Europe's post-war architecture, a serious schism immediately emerged over the role of nation-states. Even today, this schism defines the debate over European integration, so it is worth considering the origins of the two positions.

1 Some Europeans felt that national sovereignty and the nation-state constituted a fragile system prone to warfare. Since time immemorial, European states had been engaged in intermittent struggles for dominance – struggles that typically involved the invasion of other European nations. As industrialization made killing much more 'efficient', the cost of these

struggles rose to the point where no one could win. To these thinkers, even democracy was insufficient to prevent horrifying wars. Hitler, after all, gained his first hold on power through democratic means. To prevent another cycle of recovery and national rivalry that might lead to a third world war, nations should be embedded in a *federalist* structure – a supranational organization embodied with some of the powers that had traditionally been exercised exclusively by nations.

2   Other Europeans, led by Britain, continued to view nation-states as the most effective and most stable form of government. To them, European integration should take the form of closer cooperation – especially closer economic cooperation – conducted strictly on an *intergovernmental* basis, i.e. all power would remain in the hands of national officials and any cooperation would have to be agreed unanimously by all participants.

Not surprisingly, the federalist school was most popular in nations that experienced the greatest failures of governance – failures measured in terms of wartime death and destruction (see Table 1.1). This group included Belgium, the Netherlands, Luxembourg, France, Austria, Germany and Italy.

People from nations whose governments avoided foreign occupation and/or catastrophic loss of life tended to maintain their traditional faith in the nation-state. This included the UK, Denmark, Norway and Iceland as well as the neutrals, Ireland, Sweden and Switzerland. Spain and Portugal remained under fascist dictators until the 1970s.

1.2.1 Two early extremes: Council of Europe and the ECSC

Intergovernmentalism initially dominated the post-war architecture. In part, this was simply a matter of timing.

The only major European nation with a truly effective, democratic government before 1947 was Britain – a firm believer in intergovernmentalism. The first three organizations – the OEEC, the Council of Europe and the Court of Human Rights – followed the intergovernmental tradition. The OEEC was strictly intergovernmental (see Box 1.2), and the 1948 'Congress of Europe' established two intergovernmental structures, the Council of Europe (1949) and the Court of Human Rights (1950), both of which continue to function today and are entirely unrelated to the EU.

The first big federalist step came in 1952 with the Schuman Plan inspired by the 'father of European integration', Jean Monnet, but promoted by French Foreign Minister, Robert Schuman (see Box 1.4). Schuman proposed that France and Germany should place their coal and steel sectors under the control of a supranational authority.

This was a radical move at the time. An equivalent move today would be entirely unthinkable. The point is that coal and steel were viewed as the 'commanding heights' of an industrial economy at the time and crucial to a nation's military and industrial strength. Schuman explicitly justified his Plan as a means of rendering future Franco-German wars materially impossible.

Other European nations were invited to join this European Coal and Steel Community (ECSC), and Belgium, Luxembourg, the Netherlands and Italy actually did. This created a group of nations known simply as 'the Six' – a group that has been the driving force behind European integration ever since. See Box 1.5.

Box 1.4 Robert Schuman (1886–1963) and Jean Monnet (1888–1979)

Born in Luxembourg, **Schuman** studied and worked in Germany until the end of the First World War. He became French when Alsace-Lorraine reverted to France in 1918. He held several positions in the post-war French governments, including Finance Minister, Premier and Foreign Minister. Schuman provided the political push for the European Coal and Steel Community, which most consider to be the wellspring for the European Union. He was also the first President (1958–60) of the European Parliament.

Jean Monnet, born in Cognac in 1888, was a brilliant organizer and as such helped to organize Allied military supply operations in the First and Second World Wars. Near the end of the Second World War he joined Charles de Gaulle's provisional Free French government, and was responsible for the 'Monnet Plan', which is credited with helping France's post-war industrialization. Monnet was a convinced Europeanist and led the European movement in the 1950s and 1960s. Monnet, who is sometimes called the 'father of European integration', was the intellect behind the idea of the ECSC and the first president of its 'High Authority' (precursor of the European Commission) from 1952 to 1955. He continued to push for the European Economic Community and the European Atomic Energy Community (Euratom). He died in 1979.

Source: © European Communities, 1995–2008

Box 1.5 The European Coal and Steel Community (ECSC)

France and Germany launched the ECSC initiative, inviting other nations to place their coal and steel sectors under its supranational authority. Since coal and steel were considered the backbone of a modern industrial economy at the time, most nations declined. The ECSC's structure submerged the role of nation-states to an extent that seems unimaginable from today's perspective. It still represents the 'high-water mark' of European federalism. Crucial decisions concerning such issues as pricing, trade and production in the then-critical coal and steel sectors were placed in the hand of the 'High Authority'. This body, the forerunner of today's European Commission, consisted of officials appointed by the six Member States. The High Authority's decisions, some made by majority voting, were subject to limited control by Member State governments. See Spierenburg and Poidevin (1994) for details on the ECSC. The photo depicts the symbolic opening of the ECSC as a train bearing the flags of the Six crosses a border with coal and steel.

Source: European Commission

Times had changed

By the time the ECSC was in operation, Europe was a very different place from what it had been in 1945. The year was 1952 and Cold War tensions were high and rising. Economically, things continued to get better. As Table 1.3 shows, the Six had managed to get their economies back on track, having experienced miraculous growth.

1.2.2 Federalist track: the Treaty of Rome

The ECSC was a success, not so much in that it solved the thorny problems of Europe's coal and steel sectors, but rather as a training scheme for European integration. It showed that the Six could cooperate in a federal structure. The Six as a whole, but especially Germany, continued to grow spectacularly, while East–West tensions continued to mount. This combination made German rearmament essential.

In 1955, Germany joined western Europe's main defence organization, the North Atlantic Treaty Organization (NATO), and began to rearm in earnest. This triggered a reaction from the Soviet bloc – the USSR and the central and eastern European nations formed the Warsaw Pact to counter NATO. It also brought back the question of deeper European integration.

By 1955, it had become clear that coal and steel were no longer the 'commanding heights' of Europe's economy in economic or military terms. The ECSC might not be enough to ensure that another Franco-German war remained unthinkable. European leaders turned their minds to broader economic integration. Having failed to move directly to political or military integration (see Box 1.6), the natural way forward was broader economic integration.

Table 1.3 Post-Second World War reconstruction

	Back-on-Track Year (year GDP attained highest pre WWII level)	Reconstruction Growth (growth rate during reconstruction years, 1945 to back-on-track year)
Austria	1951	15.2%
Belgium	1948	6.0%
Denmark	1946	13.5%
Finland	1945	n.a.
France	1949	19.0%
Germany	1951	13.5%
Italy	1950	11.2%
Netherlands	1947	39.8%
Norway	1946	9.7%

Source: Crafts and Toniolo 1996, p. 4

Box 1.6 Failed integration, EDC and EPC

Encouraged by the rapid acceptance of the ECSC, Jean Monnet pressed ahead with even more ambitious plans for European unity. In the first years of the 1950s, leaders from the Six worked out plans for a supranational organization concerning defence – the European Defence Community (EDC) – as well as for deep political integration – the European Political Community (EPC). This remarkable enthusiasm for supranationality ultimately failed when the French parliament rejected the EDC. The EPC plans were subsequently abandoned.

It is worth stressing just how revolutionary the ECSC, EDC and EPC proposals are by today's standards. European governments nowadays balk at pooling their sovereignty over comparatively trivial issues such as air traffic control; the goal of political union among 25 EU members seems quixotic. In most non-European nations, advocating such massive transfers of sovereignty to supranational bodies would be unthinkable; in the USA it might even be considered treasonous. In the shadow of the death and destruction during the Second World War, it was, by contrast, mainstream thinking.

Jean Monnet formed a high-powered pressure group – bluntly called the Action Committee for the United States of Europe – whose membership included leading figures from all the main political parties in each of 'the Six'. The group's aim was nothing less than to merge European nation-states into a supranational organization along the lines of the ECSC but much broader in scope.

Foreign ministers of the Six met in Messina in June 1955 (Fig. 1.3) to start a process that soon led to the signing, on 25 March 1957, of two treaties in Rome: the first created the European Atomic Energy Community (Euratom); the second created the European Economic Community (EEC). Because the EEC eventually became much more important than Euratom, the term 'The Treaty of Rome' is used to refer to the EEC treaty. The Treaty of Rome was quickly ratified by the six national parliaments and the EEC came into existence in January 1958. (The institutions of the ECSC, the EEC and Euratom were merged into the 'European Communities', or EC, in 1965.) The Treaties of Rome were drafted by the Spaak Committee working from July 1955 to

Figure 1.3 **Messina Conference and signing of the Treaty of Rome**
Note: Left photo: Conference of Messina – the Foreign Ministers of the Six (left to right: Johan Beyen, Gaetano Martino, Joseph Bech, Antoine Pinay, Walter Hallstein, Paul-Henri Spaak). *Right photo:* Signing of the Treaties establishing the EEC and Euratom in Rome.
Source: © European Communities, 1995–2009

April 1956. The British partook in preliminary meetings of the Committee, but dropped out in October 1955. Jean Monnet and others felt the UK was trying to sabotage the Six's federalist initiatives.

The Treaty of Rome committed the Six to extraordinarily deep economic integration. In addition to forming a customs union (removing all tariffs and quotas on intra-EEC trade and adopting a common tariff on imports from non-member nations; Box 1.7), it promised free labour mobility, capital market integration, free trade in services and a range of common policies – some of which were to be implemented by a supranational body. The Treaty also set up a series of supranational institutions such as the European Parliamentary Assembly (forerunner of the European Parliament), the European Court of Justice (see Chapter 2) and most important of all – the European Commission.

Box 1.7 Formation of the EEC Customs Union and EFTA

The nascent EEC spent much of its first year of life setting up its administrative machinery in Brussels and developing an integration programme. It started with the most concrete part of the Treaty's ambitious integration scheme: the customs union.

According to the Treaty, the elimination of intra-EEC tariffs was to take place in three stages of four years each: January 1958–December 1961, January 1962–December 1965 and January 1966–December 1969. The possibility of a three-year delay was foreseen, so the maximum liberalization period was 15 years. As it turned out, no extra time was needed. Intra-EEC import quotas were abolished ahead of schedule in 1961 and tariffs were zero by July 1968 – a year and a half ahead of schedule.

Why was the EEC able to achieve their ambitious Common Market 18 months early? The formation of the customs union coincided with a period of unprecedented economic prosperity and this largely offset the political and economic costs of liberalization-induced restructuring. Indeed, during this so-called 'golden age' of growth, 1950–73, European unemployment averaged only 2.5 per cent and incomes either doubled, as in France, Belgium and the Netherlands, or tripled, as in Germany and Italy.

The new 'common external tariff' (CET) applied by all EEC members was set at the simple arithmetic average of the Six's pre-EEC tariffs. Typically this meant that France and Italy lowered their external tariffs and the Benelux nations raised theirs. Germany's tariffs were approximately at the average to begin with. Under Treaty of Rome rules, the tariff revenue was paid directly to the European Commission. This avoided discussions over a 'fair' division of the revenue (e.g. Dutch authorities collected the CET in Rotterdam even though Rotterdam was the port of entry for many German imports from the USA).

1.2.3 Intergovernmental track: from OEEC to EFTA

Formation of the EEC introduced an important new element into European economic integration. Hitherto trade liberalization in Europe had been orchestrated by the OEEC with nations liberalizing on a non-discriminatory basis.

The EEC would go much further, removing *all* trade barriers, but on a discriminatory, i.e. preferential, basis. Imports from non-member nations would not benefit from the opening. Moreover, the Six were committed to adopting a common tariff against all imports from non-member nations. The other 11 OEEC members were left on the sidelines.

Fearing the discrimination and marginalization that might occur if they faced the EEC bilaterally, seven of these 'outsiders' reacted by forming their own bloc in 1960, the European Free Trade Association (EFTA), with this move led by the UK (Box 1.8). By the early 1970s, all western European nations had forsaken bilateralism except Ireland, which was in a monetary union with its major trading partner (the UK). Greece and Turkey both applied for associate EEC membership almost as soon as the Treaty of Rome was signed, and Spain signed a preferential trade agreement with the EEC in 1970 (with EFTA in 1979).

Box 1.8 Formation of EFTA

The Stockholm Convention – EFTA's founding document – committed the EFTA nations (EFTAns) to removing tariffs on trade among themselves in tandem with the EEC's schedule and EFTA matched the EEC accelerated tariff-cutting. Importantly, EFTA was a free trade area, not a customs union, so external trade policy did not have to be decided in common. This was important if supranational decision making was to be avoided and it allowed the UK to maintain its preferential tariffs with the Commonwealth. Trade in agricultural goods was excluded from EFTA's liberalization.

1.2.4 Two non-overlapping circles: Common Market and EFTA

The trade liberalization promised by the Treaty of Rome and the Stockholm Convention (EFTA's founding document) rapidly came into effect in the 1960s. By the late 1960s, trade arrangements in western Europe could be described as two non-overlapping circles (Fig. 1.4).

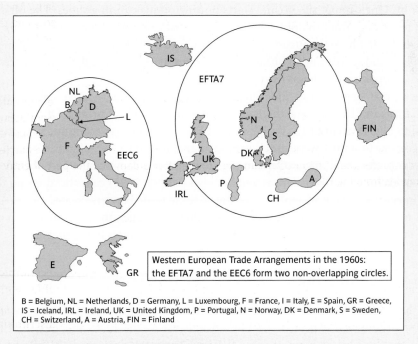

Western European Trade Arrangements in the 1960s: the EFTA7 and the EEC6 form two non-overlapping circles.

B = Belgium, NL = Netherlands, D = Germany, L = Luxembourg, F = France, I = Italy, E = Spain, GR = Greece, IS = Iceland, IRL = Ireland, UK = United Kingdom, P = Portugal, N = Norway, DK = Denmark, S = Sweden, CH = Switzerland, A = Austria, FIN = Finland

Figure 1.4 Europe of two non-overlapping circles
Source: Baldwin (1994)

The lowering of intra-EEC trade barriers had an immediate and dramatic impact on trade patterns. During the formation of the customs union (CU), the EEC's share in its own trade rose from about 30 per cent to almost 50 per cent. At the same time, the share of EEC imports coming from six other major European nations remained almost unchanged, falling from 8 per cent to 7 per cent. (More on this in Chapter 5.)

1.3 Evolution to two concentric circles: domino effect part I

At the beginning of the 1960s, EFTA-based and EEC-based firms had roughly equal access to each others' markets as the preferential tariff cutting had only just begun. As the barriers began to fall within the EEC and within EFTA (but not between the groups), discrimination appeared. This discrimination meant lost profit opportunities for exporters in both groups. Importantly, the relative economic weight and economic performance of the two circles was far from equal. The GDP – and thus the potential market size – of the six EEC nations was more than twice that of the seven EFTA nations and the EEC incomes were growing twice as fast. The EEC club was far more attractive to exporters than the EFTA club. Accordingly, the progressive reduction of within-group barriers generated new political economy forces in favour of EEC enlargement, but how did discriminatory liberalization create these forces for inclusion?

Discriminatory liberalization is studied in depth in Chapter 5, but the idea behind these new political economy forces can be illustrated with an anecdote. Two campers in Yellowstone National Park, who have just settled down in their tent, hear the roar of a hungry Grizzly bear very close by. One camper sits up and starts putting on his running shoes. The other camper says: 'Are you crazy? You can't outrun a bear!' The first camper, who continues tying his laces, replies: 'Oh, I don't have to outrun the bear. I just have to outrun you.' When it comes to out-running bears and succeeding in business, relative competitiveness is the key to success. A firm is harmed by anything that helps its rivals.

In the case at hand, closer EEC integration diminished the relative competitiveness of non-EEC firms in EEC markets, thereby harming their sales and profits. Of course, the same happened to EEC firms in EFTA, but given the EEC's much greater economic size, pressures on EFTA members to adjust were much greater than those on EEC nations. This effect helps explain why preferential integration among some nations can change the political economy attitudes of excluded nations. This is what Baldwin (1994, 1995) calls the 'domino theory' of regional integration; the preferential lowering of some trade barriers creates new pressures for outsiders to join the trade bloc and as the trade bloc gets bigger, the pressure to join grows. As history would have it, the British government was the first to react to the pressure.

1.3.1 First enlargement and EEC–EFTA FTAs

In 1961, the UK applied for EEC membership. There are many reasons for this *volte face*. In the late 1950s, Britain half expected the EEC to fail just as the EDC and EPC had before it. Moreover, the war's legacy hung heavy in the air; Clement Attlee, former UK Prime Minister, dismissed the EEC as 'six nations, four of whom we had to rescue from the other two'. Once the

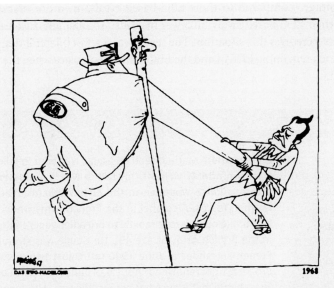

Figure 1.5 German Chancellor Willy Brandt trying to get the UK into the EEC past the objections of French President Charles de Gaulle
Source: www.ena.lu

EEC was up and working well, however, the situation was entirely different. UK industries faced the reality of rising discrimination in Europe's largest and fastest-growing markets. The British government had to react; EFTA was not a substitute for free trade access to the EEC6 markets.

Britain's unilateral decision tipped over more dominoes. If the UK was to jump from EFTA to the EEC, the remaining EFTAns would face discrimination in an even larger market (since the EEC is a custom union, the UK would have had to re-impose tariffs on imports from other EFTAns). This possibility led other nations to change their attitude towards membership. In this case, Ireland, Denmark and Norway quickly followed Britain's unilateral move. The other EFTAns did not apply for political reasons, such as neutrality (Austria, Finland, Sweden and Switzerland), lack of democracy (Portugal), or because they were not heavily dependent on the EEC market (Iceland).

While Germany was broadly in favour of UK membership, France was opposed to it (see Fig. 1.5). In a renowned January 1963 press conference, French President Charles de Gaulle (see Box 1.9) said 'non' to this first enlargement attempt (you can hear it on www.ena.lu). The four EFTAns reapplied in 1967 and de Gaulle issued another famous 'non', but after he retired, the applications were reactivated by invitation from the EEC. After many delays, membership for the four was granted in 1973. At that time, Norway's population refused EEC membership in a referendum.

The impending departure of four EFTAns to the EEC was anticipated well in advance and triggered a secondary domino effect. The 1973 EEC enlargement meant a swelling of the EEC markets and a shrinking of the EFTA markets. Firms based in the remaining EFTA states would suffer a disadvantage (compared to their EEC-based rivals) in more markets and enjoy an advantage (over their EEC-based rivals) in fewer markets. Accordingly, EFTA industries pushed their governments to redress this situation. The result was a set of bilateral free trade agreements (FTAs) between each remaining EFTAn and the EEC, which took place when the UK and company acceded to the EEC.

Box 1.9   Charles de Gaulle (1890–1970)

Charles André Marie Joseph de Gaulle was born in Lille into a family that was comfortably well off (his father was a professor of literature and history). Twice wounded in the First World War, he was captured by German forces. A colonel in the French Army when the Second World War broke out, he rose rapidly to brigadier general (the youngest general in the French Army at age 49). De Gaulle was strongly opposed to the French surrender in June 1940 (after just two weeks of combat) and broadcast his renowned 'Appeal of June 18' from London: 'France has lost a battle, but France has not lost the war.' His appeal won over leaders in some of the French Overseas Territories and he created the Free French Movement which provided an alternative to the collaborationist Vichy Republic led by Marshal Petain. After the war, he was elected to head the provisional government. He resigned in 1946, frustrated by the weakness of the President in the new Constitution. Like Adenauer, he firmly supported Franco-German cooperation but was a reluctant Europeanist, objecting to supranational organizations such as the ECSC. France, however, had already adopted the Treaty of Rome before his return to power in 1958 under crisis conditions. The General dominated political life and did much to restore French dignity and power. He resigned in 1969 and died the following year.

Photo: Deutsches Historisches Museum (DHM), Berlin.

Notice that this change of heart does need some explaining. The stance of, say, Sweden towards an FTA with the then EEC was a matter of top-level political calculation. It may seem strange, therefore, that the calculations of Sweden's political elite led them to sign an FTA in 1972 when they had not found it politically optimal to sign one in the preceding decades. The explanation, of course, is that tighter integration among a nation's trade partners (in this case between the UK, Denmark and Ireland and the EEC) alters the economic landscape facing Swedish exporters. This reshaping of the economic landscape gets translated into a new political landscape. Such forces are in operation today. The 2004 enlargement stimulates demand for free trade with nations on the EU25's new eastern border.

By the mid-1970s, trade arrangements in western Europe had evolved into two concentric circles (Fig. 1.6). The outer circle, which encompassed both EFTA and EEC nations, represents a 'virtual' free trade area for industrial products, formed by concatenation of the Treaty of Rome (for intra-EEC trade), EFTA's charter, the Stockholm Convention (for intra-EFTA trade) and individual bilateral FTAs between each EFTA member and the EEC (for EEC–EFTA trade). The inner circle, the EEC, was more deeply integrated.

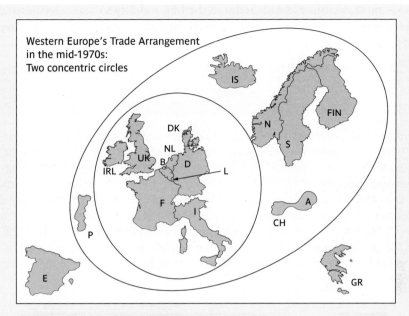

Figure 1.6 **Europe of two concentric circles**
Note: See Fig. 1.4, p. 17 for abbreviations and source.

1.4 Euro-pessimism

Although the customs union was implemented smoothly and ahead of schedule, European integration stagnated soon after its completion. The Community was rocked by a series of political crises in the 1960s soon to be followed by economic shocks in the early 1970s. This created a period known as 'Euro-pessimism' (1973–86).

1.4.1 Political shocks

The spectacularly good economic performance of Europe's economies in the 1950s and 1960s – teamed with the manifest success of European economic integration – went a long way to restoring the confidence of Europeans in their governments' ability to govern (Milward, 1984). So much so that some nations began to regret the promises of deep integration they made in the Treaty of Rome. At the head of this pro-national sovereignty charge was French President Charles de Gaulle.

The issue came to a head as the final stage in the Treaty of Rome's transition period approached (1 January 1966). At this stage the voting procedures in the EEC's key decision-making body, the Council of Ministers, were scheduled to switch to majority voting (see Section 3.3.1).

For de Gaulle, the objectionable part of majority voting was that France might have to accept a majority-backed policy even if France had voted against it. In the end, de Gaulle forced the other EEC members to accept his point of view in the so-called Luxembourg Compromise (see Box 1.10); henceforth, unanimity was the typical rule in EEC decision-making procedures.

The insistence on consensus radically reduced the EEC's ability to make decisions (see Chapter 3 on decision-making efficiency) and the problem only got worse as the EEC expanded to nine in 1973.

Box 1.10   The 'empty chair' policy and the 'Luxembourg Compromise'

De Gaulle, who had always opposed supranationality in European integration, challenged the principle in 1966. The test case came when France opposed a range of Commission proposals, which included measures for financing the Common Agricultural Policy. France stopped attending the main Community meetings (the so-called 'empty chair' policy, Fig. 1.7) and threatened to withdraw from the EEC. This marked the end of the post-war climate for radical change, but not the end of the EEC. In exchange for its return to the Council of Ministers, France demanded a political agreement – the Luxembourg Compromise – that de facto overturned the Treaty of Rome's majority voting provisions whenever a Member State announced that it felt that 'very important interests' were at stake. In short, this reversed much of the unlimited supranationality that the Six committed themselves to in the Treaty of Rome just ten years before.

Figure 1.7 Crise de la chaise vide, 1965
Photo: © European Communities, 1995–2009

Although the Luxembourg Compromise had no legal force, it had an enormous impact. It meant that unanimity was the de facto rule for almost everything. Almost all progress on deeper economic integration was blocked until the majority voting was restored in the 1986 Single European Act. The compromise in full reads: 'Where, in the case of decisions which may be taken by a majority vote on a proposal from the Commission, very important interests of one or more partners are at stake, the Members of the Council will endeavour, within a reasonable time, to reach solutions which can be adopted by all the Members of the Council while respecting their mutual interests and those of the Community, in accordance with Article 2 of the Treaty.' See Factsheet 1.3.6 on www.europarl.eu.int for further details.

1.4.2 Failure of monetary integration

The late 1960s saw the USA running an irresponsibly inflationary monetary policy – printing money to pay for the Vietnam War. Since all major currencies were linked to the dollar at the time (via the global fixed exchange rate system called Bretton Woods), US inflation was transmitted into inflation in Europe and elsewhere. This, in turn, led to the gradual breakdown of the global fixed exchange rate system (between 1971 and 1973; see Chapter 10 for details).

Exchange rate stability was widely viewed as a critical factor supporting the rapid post-war growth in trade and international investment and the rising prosperity these brought. It prevented nations from offsetting the market-opening effects of European integration with a competitive devaluation. The EEC searched for ways of restoring intra-European exchange rate stability. It established the Werner Committee which designed a step-by-step plan for European monetary union by 1980. EU leaders adopted the Werner Plan in 1971.

The economic environment for this new European monetary arrangement could not have been worse. Months after it was launched, the Yom Kippur War in the Middle East triggered an Arab oil boycott of western states. The resulting sharp rise in oil prices had a ruinous economic impact on western Europe. Just as inflationary tendencies were heating up from US actions, the oil shock severely dampened economic activity in Europe and all of its global trading partners. Most European nations adopted expansionary monetary and fiscal policies to compensate for the economic downturn and these further fuelled inflation. The result was falling incomes and rising inflation known as 'stagflation'. Just as the world was recovering from the 1973 oil shock, the Iranian Revolution produced a second massive oil price hike in 1979, aggravating stagflation. A debilitating series of exchange rate crises – caused by these massive external shocks – put the Werner Plan on hold forever. This monetary integration failure was a key feature of Euro-pessimism.

1.4.3 Failure of deeper trade integration

As tariff barriers fell, Europeans erected new trade barriers. These new barriers consisted of detailed technical regulations and standards, which had the effect of fragmenting the European markets. While these policies, called 'technical barriers to trade' (TBT), undoubtedly inhibited intra-European trade, their announced goal was to protect consumers. EEC leaders had recognized the trade-inhibiting effects of TBTs in the Treaty of Rome (Article 100 requires 'approximation', Euro-speak for harmonization, of national regulations for the 'proper functioning of the common market'). However, as European voters became richer, they demanded tighter regulation of markets and products. The usual machinery of vested-interest politics meant that many of the new standards and regulations tended to protect domestic firms.

The EU first systematically took up the removal of technical barriers in 1969 with its 'General Programme'. This launched what came to be called the 'traditional' or 'old' approach to TBT liberalization. The approach adopted relied on detailed technical regulations for single products or groups of products implemented by unanimously agreed directives. Since

Figure 1.8 Euro-pessimism
© Finn Skovgaard 2001, 2004. Used with permission: http://skovgaard.org

unanimity was required, this approach failed. Harmonization proceeded much more slowly than the development of new national barriers. For example, ten years were required to adopt a directive on gas containers made of unalloyed steel and nine and a half years was the average delay for the 15 directives adopted en masse in 1984. In the meantime, Member States were implementing thousands of technical standards and regulations a year.

Stagflation, teamed with the failure of the initiatives for deeper monetary and trade integration, created a gloom over the 'European construction'. Many inside and outside Europe suspected that the ideals that had driven European integration since the late 1940s were dying or dead; the stars, so to speak, were falling off the EU flag (Fig. 1.8).

Yet there were some bright spots in European integration during this period.

1.4.4 Bright spots

Spain, Portugal and Greece all adopted democratic governments, thus rendering them eligible for EEC membership. Greece joined in 1981 followed by the Iberians in 1986. The European Monetary System (EMS) started operation in 1978 and had good success in stabilizing intra-EEC exchange rates. EEC financing was put on a firm footing with two budget treaties (1970 and 1975, see Chapter 2 for details). The institutions of the three communities (ESCS, Euratom and EEC) were rationalized by the 1965 Merger Treaty and the EU Parliament was directly elected for the first time in 1979; previously, its members came from the members' national parliaments.

In the USA and Europe, central bankers decided to fight inflation – which had reached double-digit figures in most industrial nations. They did this by inducing a long hard recession. Between 1981 and 1983 growth was negative or only slightly positive in most of Europe. While inflation rates did decline, this was at the cost of a significant increase in unemployment.

Starting in 1984, economic growth recovered. Political attitudes also changed – in particular, a deepened belief in market economics began to spread throughout the industrialized world. US President Reagan and British Prime Minister Thatcher are often cited as vanguards, but even the Socialist French President Mitterrand adopted a much more favourable attitude towards market-based solutions. While there are many causes for this philosophical shift, the fact that highly interventionist policies had failed to prevent ten years of poor economic performance is surely one of the most important.

1.5 Deeper circles and domino effect part II: the Single Market Programme and the EEA

This favourable economic climate was matched with the arrival of a talented promoter of European integration, Jacques Delors (see Box 1.11). Delors, who was appointed to the Presidency of the European Commission in 1985, was devoted to the idea of kick-starting European integration. To this end, he pushed a programme that would complete the internal market. He dubbed this the 'Single Market Programme', although it is known by many names (the Internal Market Programme, the 1992 Programme, Completing the Internal Market, etc.). The plan was framed by Lord Cockfield's 1985 White Paper which listed 300 measures necessary to transform the Common Market into the Single Market. By July 1987, all Member States had adopted the Single European Act, which is the Community legislation that implemented the Single Market measures (along with many other changes).

Box 1.11   Jacques Delors (1925 –)

Jacques Lucien Jean Delors, born in Paris, held a series of posts in banking and the French government. He was deeply engaged in the trade union movement and a devout Catholic. After a stint in the European Parliament, he became Finance Minister under French President Mitterrand in the early 1980s. Always a committed European integrationist, he was chosen in 1985 to be President of the European Commission, a post he held for two four-year terms. This period was marked by the most important increase in European economic integration since the 1950s; most observers give much credit for this to the savvy and energy of Jacques Delors. The Single European Act, which reinstated majority voting on most economic integration issues, restored the Community's ability to act. This led to a sweeping economic integration effort known as the Single Market Programme, and while this formally ended in 1992, the programme continues to be extended and deepened even today.

Delors was also instrumental in the adoption of the Economic and Monetary Union (EMU), which led to the creation of the euro. Delors' term as Commission President was extended to help the EU to deal with the Danish rejection of the Maastricht Treaty and exchange rate crises of the early 1990s. Among Delors' many other accomplishments, the two multi-year budget deals negotiated while he was President reformed EU financing and redirected EU spending away from agriculture and towards support for disadvantaged regions. His term as President ended in January 1995.

Source: © European Communities, 1995–2009

1.5.1 The Single Market Programme: EC92

In 1985, EU firms enjoyed duty-free access to each other's markets; however, they did not enjoy free trade. Intra-EC trade was shackled by a long list of trade-inhibiting barriers such as differing technical standards and industrial regulations, capital controls, preferential public procurement, administrative and frontier formalities, VAT and excise tax rate differences and differing transport regulations, to mention just a few. Although the vast majority of these policies seem negligible individually, the confluence of their effects served to substantially restrict intra-Community trade.

Indeed, many of these barriers were introduced in the 1970s as European nations increasingly adopted standards and regulations that were aimed at protecting consumers, workers and the environment. The free movement of goods was also restricted by practices of national and local governments such as biased purchasing patterns, exclusive production or service rights, and production subsidies to national champions. Likewise, the free movement of services – which was guaranteed in principle by the Treaty of Rome – was far from being a reality, again largely due to national prudential and safety regulations. Service providers typically were required to possess local certification and the requirements for such certification often varied across nations. Moreover, the certification process was often controlled or influenced by the national service providers who had an economic interest in excluding foreign competitors via this certification process.

The key changes in the Single Market Programme were designed to reinforce the 'four freedoms' (free movement of goods, services, people and capital) promised by the Treaty of Rome. The concrete steps were:

Goods trade liberalization

★ Streamlining or elimination of border formalities.

★ Harmonization of VAT rates within wide bands.

★ Liberalization of government procurement.

★ Harmonization and mutual recognition of technical standards in production, packaging and marketing.

Factor trade liberalization

★ Removal of all capital controls.

★ Increase in capital market integration.

★ Liberalization of cross-border market-entry policies, including mutual recognition of approval by national regulatory agencies.

The Single European Act also implemented important institutional changes. To clear the decision-making log-jam that had held up similar integration initiatives in the 1970s, EC92 included a major change in the EU's decision-making procedures. Decisions concerning Single Market issues would be adopted on the basis of majority voting instead of on a basis of unanimity (see Chapter 3 for a discussion of EU decision-making procedures). This change in voting procedures was part of the so-called 'new approach' to TBT liberalization.

Focus on capital mobility

The most novel aspect of the Single Market Programme was its focus on capital mobility; other features can be viewed as deepening or extending integration initiatives already agreed. Some EU members had unilaterally liberalized capital mobility prior to EC92, but substantial pan-EU liberalization came only in the second half of the 1980s with a series of Single Market Programme directives. The opening was completed in 1988 by a directive that ruled out all remaining restrictions on capital movements among EU residents. The definitive system was codified in the Maastricht Treaty.

It is possible to think of this aspect of the Single Market Programme as unleashing a political economy process that eventually led to the euro. Simple macroeconomic logic (explained in Chapter 14) tells us that without capital controls, nations must choose between controlling their exchange rate and controlling their monetary policy. Since exchange rate stability was considered paramount, EU members slaved their monetary policy to exchange rate stabilization in the context of the EMS. But once nations were no longer actively using monetary policy, resistance to centralizing monetary policy decisions in a European central bank was greatly weakened.

1.5.2 The EEA and the fourth enlargement

Since the Single European Act promised much tighter economic integration among EU members, non-EU nations again found themselves threatened by the discriminatory effects of integration in the EU. As in the 1960s and early 1970s, this triggered a domino effect as EFTA firms prompted their governments to offset the discrimination by seeking closer ties to the EU.

In the late 1980s, EFTA governments had decided that they must react to the Single Market. Several considered applying for EU membership (Austria actually did), while others considered bilateral negotiations. Jacques Delors forced the decision in January 1989 by proposing the European Economic Area (EEA) agreement – an agreement that essentially extends the Single Market to EFTA economies (apart from agriculture and the common external tariff).

Given the political economy forces described above, it is easy to understand why EFTA nations wanted the EEA. Two aspects of the EEA, however, are extraordinary. First, the EEA is unbalanced in terms of the rights and obligations of EFTA nations when it comes to future EEC legislation. The EEA commits EFTA nations to accepting future EU legislation concerning the Single Market, without any formal input into the formation of these new laws. Second, the EEA created supranationality among the EFTA nations, a feature that they had resisted since the end of the war.

As it turned out, EFTA nations were not happy with the EEA compromises, especially in the post-Cold War environment, where the East–West political division of Europe appeared to have vanished. By the end of the EEA negotiations, Austria, Finland, Sweden, Norway and Switzerland had put in EU membership applications. For them, the EEA was a transitional arrangement. Swiss voters rejected the EEA in December 1992, effectively freezing their EU application. Accession talks with the four EFTAns were successful, so the EEA now consists of the EU25 on one hand, with Norway, Liechtenstein and Iceland on the other (Norway's voters rejected EU membership by referendum).

The Single Market, EEA and plans for monetary union were launched while Cold War politics still mattered. They came to fruition in a very different world.

1.6 Communism's creeping failure and spectacular collapse

The division of Europe into communist and capitalist camps was cemented, quite literally, in 1961 by the construction of the Berlin Wall (Fig. 1.9). While living standards were not too dissimilar to begin with, by the 1980s western European living standards far outstripped those in eastern Europe and the USSR. Anyone could plainly see that the west's economic system (free markets and an extensive social welfare system) when teamed up with its political system (multi-party democracy and freedom of the press) provided a far better way of life compared to the east's system of planned economies and one-party rule.

While this 'creeping failure' of communism was apparent to the central and eastern European countries (CEECs), Soviet leaders repeatedly thwarted reform efforts via constant economic pressure and occasional military interventions. By the 1980s, the inadequacy of the Soviet system forced changes inside the USSR itself. The USSR adopted a policy of timid pro-market reforms (*perestroika*) and a policy of openness (*glasnost*), which involved a marked reduction in internal repression and diminished intervention in the affairs of the Soviet republics and Soviet-bloc nations.

As far as European integration was concerned, the Soviet foreign policy changes were critical. Pro-democracy forces in the CEECs, which had been repeatedly put down by military force hereto, found little resistance from Moscow in the late 1980s. The first breach came in June 1989 when the Polish labour movement 'Solidarity' forced the communist government to accept free parliamentary elections (Fig. 1.10). The communists lost and the first democratic

Figure 1.9 **The Berlin Wall circa 1980**
Source: http://community.webshots.com

Figure 1.10 Solidarity movement and fall of the Wall
Source: Polish Maritime Museum and www.berlin-wall.org

government in the Soviet bloc took power. Moscow rapidly established ties with the new Polish government.

Moscow's hands-off approach to the Polish election triggered a chain of events over the next two years that revolutionized European affairs. Pro-reform elements inside the Hungarian communist party pressed for democratic elections, and, more dramatically, Hungary opened its border with Austria. Thousands of East Germans reacted by moving to West Germany via Hungary and Austria. This set off mass protests against communist repression in East Germany which culminated in the opening of the border between East and West Germany.

On 9 November 1989, thousands of West and East Berlin citizens converged on the Berlin Wall with pickaxes and sledge hammers to dismantle that symbol of a divided Europe (Fig. 1.10). By the end of 1989, democratic forces were in control in Poland, Hungary, Czechoslovakia and East Germany. In 1990, East and West Germany formed a unified Germany and three Soviet Republics – Estonia, Latvia and Lithuania – declared their independence from the USSR. By the end of 1991, the Soviet Union itself broke up, putting a definitive end to its interference in central and eastern Europe. The European Union reacted swiftly to this geopolitical earthquake by providing emergency aid and loans to the fledgling democracies.

1.6.1 Maastricht Treaty, the euro and German unification

The 'political earthquake' caused by the falling of the wall also yielded substantial changes within the EU. With the Berlin Wall gone, unification of the western and eastern parts of Germany was the natural next step, but a unified Germany would be a behemoth. With 80 million citizens and 30 per cent of Europe's output, Germany would be much larger than France, Britain or Italy. This raised many fears, ranging from a disturbed political balance in the EU to the unlikely, but still scary, spectre of German militarism. Many Europeans, including many Germans, felt that Germany would be best unified in conjunction with a big increase in the forces tying EU members together.

Riding on his success with the Single Market, Jacques Delors seized this historical moment and proposed a radical increase in European economic integration – the formation of a monetary union – a step that he believed would eventually lead to political integration.

The idea was quickly championed by French President François Mitterrand and German Chancellor Helmut Kohl. After extensive negotiations, the EU committed itself to a target of forming a monetary union by 1999 and adopting a single currency by 2002 (see Chapter 17). This commitment was made in the Treaty of Maastricht.

The Maastricht Treaty is covered in depth in Chapter 17, but for the purposes of this chapter it is important to note that the Maastricht Treaty – formally known as the Treaty on European Union – embodied the most profound deepening of European integration since the Treaty of Rome. In addition to committing members to a transfer of national sovereignty over monetary power to a supranational body (the European Central Bank), and abandonment of their national currencies for the euro, the Treaty also:

★ created EU citizenship; this included the right to move to and live in any EU state (the Treaty of Rome only guaranteed the right to work in any Member State) and to vote in European and local elections in any Member State;

★ locked in the free movement of capital;

★ strengthened EU cooperation in non-economic areas, including security and defence policy as well as law enforcement, criminal justice, civil judicial matters, and asylum and immigration policies;

★ enshrined the principle of subsidiarity that was meant to control the transfer of responsibilities from Member States to the European Union;

★ strengthened the European Parliament's power over EU legislation;

★ introduced the 'Social Chapter' which expanded the EU's social dimension by introducing policies on workers' health and safety, workplace conditions, equal pay and the consultation of employees.

Maastricht ratification difficulties

EU Treaties such as Maastricht have power because they must be part of each Member State's domestic law, i.e. EU treaties must be ratified by each and every member if they are to come into force. In many EU nations, ratification involves a vote by the national parliament, in others, a referendum. The Maastricht Treaty had great difficulties with ratification.

During the negotiations, the British insisted on a formal opt-out from the common currency (the idea was that all other members would have to adopt the euro once they met the criteria) and from the Social Chapter. Even with these provisos, Euros-sceptics from his own party nearly brought down British Prime Minister John Major's government during the UK Parliamentary ratification vote. French President François Mitterrand put the Treaty to a referendum expecting a massive 'yes' vote that would bolster the Treaty's prospects (referendums are not mandatory in France), but only 51.4 per cent of the French voted 'yes'. The Treaty was challenged as unconstitutional, but Germany's High Court ultimately judged it to be compatible with Germany's constitution. The Treaty came into force in November 1993.

More problematic was the fact that Danish voters narrowly rejected the Treaty in a 1992 referendum. After EU leaders agreed to grant Denmark opt-outs on the single currency and defence matters, a second vote on Maastricht was held and the Danes reversed their own veto by voting 'yes'.

1.7 Reuniting east and west Europe

Given that almost every other nation in the region had free trade access to the enormous EU market, free trade agreements with the EU were a commercial necessity for the newly free central and eastern European countries (CEECs). Their strategic goal, however, was EU and NATO membership; bilateral free trade deals with the EU were viewed as stepping stones. CEEC leaders felt unsure that the new situation was permanent. If things went wrong in Russia and the iron curtain re-descended, each CEEC wanted to be sure that the curtain would, this time, come down east of its border. Russia's recent actions (e.g. military incursion into Georgia and cutting off of energy supplies to the Ukraine) have shown that CEEC leaders' geo-strategy worries were well placed.

1.7.1 First steps: the Europe Agreements

Each CEEC announced that its goal was to join the EU. The EU, by contrast, was reluctant in the early 1990s. Sidestepping the membership issue, the EU signed Association Agreements (also called Europe Agreements) with Poland, Hungary and Czechoslovakia in 1991. Europe Agreements for other CEECs followed progressively. By 1994, such deals had been signed with Romania, Bulgaria, Albania, Estonia, Latvia and Lithuania. EFTA negotiated similar bilateral agreements. Some CEECs also signed trade arrangements among themselves, the most important being the 1991 Central European Free Trade Agreement among Czechoslovakia, Hungary and Poland (subsequently extended to Slovenia, Bulgaria and Romania).

The Europe Agreements established bilateral free trade between the EU and each individual CEEC. They committed the EU to removing tariffs and quantitative restrictions on most industrial products by the end of 1994. Substantial EU protection remained for a group of 'sensitive' industrial products, including some textiles, some coal and steel products, and almost all agricultural trade. Beyond the removal of tariffs on most industrial goods, a further goal was to make progress towards 'realizing between them the other economic freedoms on which the Community is based'. The adoption of EU laws and practices (competition policy, harmonized standards, etc.) helped the CEECs establish functioning market economies faster than they could have on their own.

By committing the CEECs to adopt the main elements of EU economic integration and regulation, the Europe Agreements were crucial in guiding these nations' economic transitions from planned to market economies. The goal of EU membership provided an important political anchorage that kept the pro-market reforms on track.

The Europe Agreements stopped short of offering EU membership. This reflected the profound ambivalence that many west Europeans initially felt towards eastern enlargement of the EU. For instance, slow action of the parliaments of EU Member States meant that the Europe Agreements signed with Hungary and Poland in December 1991 entered into force only in February 1994. Most of the hesitation was due to the economic nature of the CEEC. The CEECs were poor, populous and agrarian. Since the EU spends 80 per cent of its budget on farms and poor regions, eastern enlargement was viewed as a threat to special interest groups in the EU15.

1.7.2 Copenhagen to Copenhagen: from 1993 accession criteria to EU membership

The EU officially ended its hesitancy in June 1993. In Copenhagen, the EU's key political body – the European Council – decided 'the associated countries in Central and Eastern Europe that so desire shall become members of the European Union . . . The Union now looks forward to welcoming these States as members from 1 May 2004.' (The timing, May 2004, was aimed at allowing the new members to participate in the elections for the European Parliament and in the formation of the new European Commission.) The Council also defined the so-called Copenhagen Criteria for EU membership, which continue to be applied today to nations like Croatia and Turkey. These are:

★ political stability of institutions that guarantee democracy, the rule of law, human rights and respect for and protection of minorities;

★ a functioning market economy capable of dealing with the competitive pressure and market forces within the Union; and

★ acceptance of the Community 'acquis' (EU law in its entirety, including all the Treaties and subsequent rules) and the ability to take on the obligations of membership, including adherence to the aims of political, economic and monetary union.

1.8 Preparing for eastern enlargement: a string of new treaties

Once the EU15 leaders confirmed that the CEECs would eventually join, the next order of business was to reform EU institutions. In the mid-1990s, institutions designed for six members were groaning under the weight of 15; adding ten or more newcomers would surely bring down the house. This realization started a long chain of events – a chain that continues right up to the end of 2008 when this edition went to press.

The quest for enlargement-linked reform of EU institutions began formally in December 1993. A new treaty-writing exercise (an IGC) had already been agreed in the Maastricht Treaty; it was scheduled for 1996 and meant as a check-up halfway into the timetable for monetary union. The 1993 Brussels European Council added EU institutional reform to its agenda.[1] To prepare the IGC 1996, the EU established a 'Reflection Group' whose job was to study institutional reforms necessary to keep the EU on track after enlargement. In setting up the group, EU leaders explicitly mentioned two issues to be addressed: Council of Minister voting (specifically, weighting of votes and the threshold for qualified majority decisions), and the number of members of the Commission.

The Group's report (the Westendorp Report) presented a consensus on the problems facing an enlarged EU – a clear statement of the 'whys' of EU institutional reform.[2] It also describes

---

[1] For a detailed account, see the essay at http://shop.ceps.eu/downfree.php?item_id=1332.

[2] See www.ena.lu for a copy of the Westendorp Report and all the other reports mentioned in this chapter.

a thorough lack of consensus on solutions. From the perspective of 2008, it is stunning that the list of problems is so close to mandates for the Amsterdam, Nice, Constitutional and Lisbon Treaties. Moreover, the disagreements it highlights – big member vs. small members, federalists vs. intergovernmentalists, etc. – are exactly the ones that plagued every step of the decade-long process of reforming EU institutions.

The deep problems that required EU institutional reform concerned the Union's decision-making machinery on the one hand, and the changing nature of the EU's role in the world on the other.

★ The decision-making problems are complex (see Chapter 3) but the need for reform is easy to understand. Every student will have observed that taking a group decision – like rescheduling a workshop or lecture – is fairly easy in a group consisting of a handful or fewer members. It becomes almost impossible when the group gets much beyond a dozen. The same logic applies to the EU decision-making bodies such as the Council of Ministers and the European Commission.

★ Changes in EU external policy, by contrast, were forced by external events. The end of the Cold War – and the attendant demise of the two-superpower system – made international politics a much more complex affair, one in which the EU could play a role. Moreover, events in the former Yugoslavia convinced many Europeans that the traditional hands-off approach was no longer justified. Given their modest size, however, effective action would typically require some coordination among at least a subset of EU members.

1.8.1 Amsterdam Treaty: cleaning up the Maastricht Treaty

In 1996, the EU started a Treaty-writing exercise – called an Intergovernmental Conference (IGC) in EU jargon. This produced the Amsterdam Treaty in 1997. Ambitions for the Amsterdam Treaty were high – the mandate was to agree all the necessary enlargement-related reforms that the Westendorp Report highlighted. By this yardstick, the Treaty failed.

The Amsterdam Treaty is best thought of as a tidying up of the Maastricht Treaty. The substantive additions included a more substantial role for the EU in social policy (UK Prime Minister Tony Blair cancelled the British opt-out). The European Parliament powers were modestly boosted, and the notion of flexible integration, so-called 'closer cooperation', was introduced (see Chapter 2 for details).

Since the key enlargement-related reforms were not settled, EU leaders agreed to a list of issues that had to be solved before the enlargement – the so-called Amsterdam leftovers – and then agreed to launch a new IGC in 2000. These must-do topics were the same as those mentioned in 1993: Council of Ministers voting rules and the number of EU Commissioners. To this was added the composition of the EU Parliament.

1.8.2 Nice Treaty: failed attempt to reform EU institutions

After the year-long preparation of the IGC 2000, EU leaders met in the French city of Nice in December 2000 to wrap up a new treaty that was supposed to deal with the Amsterdam leftovers and thus prepare EU institutions for the impending enlargement. At four o'clock in the morning after the longest EU summit in history, EU leaders announced political agreement on a new treaty.

The result – the Treaty of Nice – was not a success. The critical Amsterdam leftover issues – the size and composition of the Commission, extension of majority voting in the Council of Ministers, and reform of Council voting rules – were not fully solved (see Chapter 3 for details). Nevertheless, these flawed reforms are the ones in force in 2008 and will continue so unless the Lisbon Treaty enters into force.

Nice Treaty ratification difficulties

The Treaty had some trouble with ratification but not nearly as much as the Maastricht Treaty. The Nice Treaty touched on highly sensitive political issues – e.g. it implied an important redistribution of decision-making power among EU members. However, EU leaders had an easy way of selling the reforms to European voters. They simply argued that enlargement made the painful reforms necessary. Most EU electorates thought eastern enlargement was worth it. Eastern enlargement would be a historic achievement that would fulfil the aspirations of 100 million Europeans who chose freedom, democracy and markets. It would ensure political and economic stability in Europe by burying the last remnants of pre-1945 Europe that had fostered intolerance, destructive nationalism and war.

In the end, only the Irish refused the Nice Treaty (in a referendum; Fig. 1.11). Since a new treaty cannot come into force until all EU members have ratified it, the Irish 'no' had to be addressed. The solution was to make a number of political commitments guaranteeing Irish neutrality and to have all 14 other members ratify the Treaty. Irish voters were then asked to vote again; the second time they said 'yes'.

Figure 1.11 The Irish 'No' to the Nice Treaty

Note: Sinn Féin opposed the Nice Treaty, but most political parties supported it. Irish voters reversed themselves after EU assurances on military issues.

Photo: www.sinnfein.ie

Incomplete reform

EU leaders at the Nice Summit knew that the Treaty did not fully adjust the EU to the new realities of the coming enlargement. As part of the final political deal on the Treaty, they agreed to commit themselves to another IGC in 2004 in order to complete the reform process. This 'Declaration on the future of the Union' highlighted four themes:

1 defining a more precise division of powers between the EU and its members;
2 clarifying the status of the Charter of Fundamental Rights proclaimed in Nice;
3 making the Treaties easier to understand without changing their meaning;
4 defining the role of national parliaments in the European institutions.

1.8.3 2004 enlargement and the Constitutional Treaty

One year after the Nice Summit, the European Council met in the Belgian city of Laeken to adopt the 'Declaration on the Future of the European Union'. This provided an outline for thinking about the new treaty to be written by the IGC in 2004.

In light of the difficult Nice Summit, the Laeken Council also decided on a novel working method. It convened the 'Convention on the Future of Europe', which came to be known as the European Convention, consisting of a large number of men and women representing current and prospective Member States, the national parliaments, the European Parliament and the Commission. The Convention's output was to be the point of departure for the IGC 2004 that would draft the actual treaty (as required by EU law).

As far as its contents are concerned, the 'Laeken Declaration' contains a list of issues that is surprisingly close to that of the 1995 Westendorp Report; 56 questions grouped under the four themes of the Nice Declaration. The Laeken Declaration, however, included two crucial novelties. First, the Declaration implicitly admits that the Nice reforms were insufficient. One question is: 'How we can improve the efficiency of decision-making and the workings of the institutions in a Union of some 30 Member States?' Since this was the main goal of the Nice Treaty, EU leaders essentially admitted that the Nice reforms would not be enough. In effect, it asks the Convention to reform the Nice Treaty reforms even before the Nice reforms had been implemented (most Nice Treaty changes only took effect after 2004). Second, while the Nice Declaration made no mention of a constitution, the word does appear in the Laeken Declaration.

The Laeken Declaration did not instruct the Convention to write a constitution. It included the question: 'The question ultimately arises as to whether this simplification and reorganization might not lead in the long run to the adoption of a constitutional text in the Union. What might the basic features of such a constitution be? The values which the Union cherishes, the fundamental rights and obligations of its citizens, the relationship between Member States in the Union?'

The European Convention, February 2002 to July 2003

The European Convention was run by former French President Valéry Giscard d'Estaing with the assistance of two Vice-Chairmen (see Fig. 1.12). It started slowly and many early observers expected its large size and ill-defined objectives to result in a muddled outcome.

By mid-2002, President Giscard d'Estaing had redefined the Convention's purpose. The 'Convention on the Future of Europe' was transformed into a constitution-writing convention. The new goal was to present the EU heads of state and government with a fully written constitution. This changed everything. From that point forward, EU members started sending heavy-weight politicians in place of low-level representatives. All arguments over the need for a constitution were dropped; discussion turned instead to its content.

The Chairman Valéry Giscard d'Estaing was firmly in charge. The Convention's decision-making procedure involved no voting by representatives and indeed no standard democratic procedure of any kind. The Convention adopted its recommendations by 'consensus', with Giscard d'Estaing defining when a consensus existed. The representatives of the candidate countries participated fully in the debate, but their voices were not allowed to prevent a consensus among representatives of the then 15 members of the EU.

Figure 1.12 The European Convention was run by its presidium

Note: Presidential podium at the plenary session debate on institutional questions, January 2003. From the left, Jean-Luc Dehaene (Vice-Chairman, Belgium), Giuliano Amato (Vice-Chairman, Italy) and Valéry Giscard d'Estaing (Chairman, France).

Source: European Commission

These unusual features of the Convention working method go a long way to explaining the many problems that the Constitutional Treaty was soon to face.

The IGC's failure and the Irish compromise

The process of turning the Convention's draft into an EU treaty (see Fig. 1.13) did not start well. Although the draft was presented in July 2003, the Italian Presidency (in the hands of Italian Prime Minister Silvio Berlusconi) did not convene the IGC until October. Differences that had been papered over in the Convention emerged immediately – especially the critical Council voting question which had not been openly discussed in the Convention. The deal-breaking issue turned on the fact that new voting rules shifted a great deal of voting power (compared to the Nice Treaty rules) to Germany and away from Spain and Poland (see Chapter 3 for details). The Italian Presidency failed to bridge the differences.

All EU members – including the ten members that joined in January 2004 – agreed that institutional reform was a must, so the Irish government, which took over the EU Presidency from the Italians, made a new attempt to rewrite the European Convention's rejected draft. Skilful diplomacy by the Irish Presidency and a change of government in Spain permitted a grudging and difficult but ultimately unanimous acceptance of a new draft at the June 2004 summit of EU25 leaders. With this high-level political compromise in hand, the IGC completed its work and the Constitution was signed in Rome in October 2004.

Figure 1.13 **Toast at the Convention's last Plenary Session, 13 June 2003**
Source: European Commission

Constitutional Treaty ratification difficulties

For a variety of reasons, five EU nations that would normally have ratified the Constitutional Treaty by parliamentary vote opted for referendums: France, the Netherlands, the UK, Luxembourg and Spain. Two of these – France and the Netherlands – turned in 'no' votes in mid-2005 that derailed the whole process.

The French and Dutch 'nos' were quite a different problem for EU leaders from the Danish and Irish 'nos' on the Maastricht and Nice Treaties. Apart from the fact that the Dutch and French were founding members, the number of no-voters was entirely different. In the first Irish poll on the Nice Treaty, less than a million people voted and only 530,000 said 'no'. In the French referendum, 16 of 29 million French voters said 'no' (see Fig. 1.14). Three days later, 4.7 out of 7.6 million Dutch rejected the Treaty. While EU leaders could 'work around' 530,000 Irish no-sayers, it was impossible to ignore over 20 million nos.

EU leaders decided to suspend the formal ratification timetable and declared a 'period of reflection'.

1.8.4 The Lisbon Treaty

Two inadequate reform attempts (Amsterdam and Nice Treaties), a decade of on-and-off negotiations and four rejections by European voters made it clear that EU institutional reform was not easy and not popular with EU voters. Why didn't EU leaders just abandon the project?

The answer lies in the factors that had been obvious since the 1993 Westendorp Report. The numerical enlargement of EU membership and the EU's evolving role on the world stage made certain reforms essential. Europe had to reform its institutions if it was to continue functioning effectively and legitimately, and the Nice Treaty reforms were not good enough. These points were obvious to the men and women most deeply involved in keeping the EU running,

Figure 1.14 Posters for French Constitutional Treaty referendum
Source: © European Communities 1995–2009

although they proved difficult to explain to EU voters – especially the inadequacy of the Nice reforms.

Germany re-launches the institutional reform process

The process was re-launched when Germany took the reins of the EU Presidency in 2007, announcing that the period of reflection was over. After some high-level and high-pressure bargaining, EU leaders declared the Constitutional Treaty to be dead and agreed on the basic outlines of its replacement, the Reform Treaty, which came to be known as the Lisbon Treaty.

As EU leaders had been talking about institutional reform since the mid-1990s, there were no magic solutions left undiscovered. The reforms in the Constitutional Treaty were the best reforms that were politically acceptable to all EU members. The plan therefore was to include the main Constitutional Treaty reforms in the Lisbon Treaty but to package them very differently.

All the grandiloquent language and gestures that the European Convention added to the essential institutional reforms were stripped away. All references to symbols of statehood were jettisoned – the flag, the anthem, the Foreign Ministers and the like. There was to be no mention of the word 'constitution'. The only federalist token was to change the formal name of the Treaty of Rome from 'The Treaty Establishing the European Community' to 'The Treaty on the Functioning of the Union' and to replace the word 'Community' with 'Union' throughout.

The technical drafting of the new Treaty and haggling over the exact wording required more time than the German Presidency had, so the task fell to the Portuguese Presidency. After a few last-minute concessions to the ever-reluctant Polish government, the new Treaty was signed in Lisbon on 13 December 2007. EU leaders hoped to have it ratified and in force in time for the 2009 European Parliament elections.

Lisbon Treaty ratification difficulties

The idea behind the German repackaging strategy was to avoid referenda in as many nations as possible. By making it more of a technocratic amendment of the existing legal structure, most EU governments felt they would be justified in ratifying the Lisbon Treaty by a vote of the national parliament – the procedure adopted for most Treaties by most members since the very beginning.

By and large, the strategy worked. The Irish constitution, however, requires a referendum on any law that changes the relationship between Irish law and EU law. Since the Lisbon Treaty certainly meets this criterion, a vote was held in July 2008. The no-voters won by a solid margin, a result that has thrown the whole reform project back into doubt.

Many analysts foresee a re-run of the Nice Treaty manoeuvres where the Irish would be asked to vote again on a slightly modified text, or the same text with new political commitments. The mood in other EU nations, however, is nowhere near as conducive to this tactic as it was for the Nice Treaty. Ratification of the Nice Treaty was a precondition for eastern enlargement. As enlargement was a strategy goal for all EU members, extraordinary machinations were viewed as necessary. This driving force is now lacking since enlargement has already happened. Moreover, the governments of some members, such as Poland and the Czech Republic, seem less than fully committed to the Lisbon Treaty.

It is a clear comment on the state of European idealism that the third edition of this section ends with the same sentence as the second edition: 'The future course of action remained undefined as this edition went to print.'

1.9 Summary

It is impossible to summarize 50 years of European integration in a few paragraphs. But it is possible to highlight the main events and lessons as far as the economics of European integration are concerned.

European integration has always been driven by political factors, ranging from a desire to prevent another European war to a desire to share the fruit of integration with the newly democratic nations in central and eastern Europe. Yet while the goals were always political, the means were always economic.

There have been basically three big increases in European economic integration. Formation of the customs union from 1958 to 1968 eliminated tariffs and quotas on intra-EU trade. The Single Market Programme implemented between 1986 and 1992 (although elements are still being implemented today) eliminated many non-tariff barriers and liberalized capital flows within the EU. Finally, the Economic and Monetary Union melded together the currencies of most EU members.

Each of these steps towards deeper integration – but especially the customs union and the Single Market Programme – engendered discriminatory effects that triggered reactions in the non-member nations. Just as the knocking down of one domino triggers a chain reaction that leads to the fall of all dominoes, the discriminatory effects of EU integration have created a powerful gravitational force that has progressively drawn all but the most reluctant Europeans into the EU. If there is a lesson to draw from this for the future, it is that the 2004 enlargement is likely to greatly magnify the pro-EU membership forces in the nations further east and south.

Self-assessment questions

1. Draw a diagram (or diagrams) that graphically shows the major steps in European economic integration, along with dates and the names of the countries involved. Be sure to discuss explicitly the removal of various barriers to the movement of goods, labour and capital.

2. Draw a diagram like Fig. 1.4 that shows the current state of trade arrangements in Europe, including all European nations west of the Urals.

3. Make a list of all the EU treaties (with dates) and provide a ten-words-or-less explanation of each treaty's major contribution to European integration.

4. Make a list of the dates of the major stages in the Common Agricultural Policy and its reforms (see europa.eu.int/comm/agriculture/index_en.htm for details).

5. Make a list of the dates of the major stages in the EU structural spending programmes (see europa.eu.int/comm/regional_policy/index_en.htm for details).

6. What were the main challenges posed by eastern enlargement of the European Union and how was the Nice Treaty meant to address these challenges?

7. Some European integration experts subscribe to the so-called bicycle theory of integration, which asserts that European integration must continually move forward to prevent it from 'falling over', i.e. breaking down. List a sequence of events from 1958 to 1992 that lends support to the theory.

8. Explain how Cold War politics accelerated European integration in some ways but hindered it in others, such as geographic expansion of the EU.

9. Explain when and by which means the organization that is known as the European Union has changed names since its inception in 1958.

10. Make a table showing the dates of all changes in EU and EFTA membership.

Essay questions

1. What role has the Council of Europe, which is a non-EU institution, played in pan-European integration?

2. How important was the USA's role in promoting European integration? Do you think Europe would have formed the EEC, or something like it, if the USA had not made the creation of the OEEC a condition for aid?

3. Describe the evolution of the various British governments' attitudes towards European integration in the 1945 to 1975 period. In the early years Labour opposed membership

while Conservatives supported it, but recently the roles have reversed. Why do you think this is so?

4. Provide an explanation for why only six of the EU15 nations joined in 1957. You should list specific reasons for each non-member.

5. Write an essay on the work towards deeper European integration that was done in the context of the OEEC. Why did this fail?

6. Write an essay on whether Charles de Gaulle promoted or hindered European integration. Chapter 8 of Urwin (1995) is a good place to start.

7. Why did the EPC and EDC plans fail when the ECSC succeeded?

8. Explain why economic integration can promote peace.

9. Explain why some countries organize referenda before ratifying European treaties.

10. In a historical perspective, has the enlargement of the EU made reforms more difficult?

11. What would be the political and economic reasons for Georgia to join the EU?

12. Why was de Gaulle against UK membership of the EEC?

13. Why was it important to the USA for Germany to be economically strong?

14. In a historical perspective, do you think opt-outs facilitate or hinder further integration?

15. What were Churchill's arguments for the creation of the 'United States of Europe'? Listen to or read his 1946 Zurich speech at www.ena.lu to answer this question. Why did he exclude the UK from this proposed union?

16. Why were the Benelux countries the first in Europe to form a custom union?

17. State which countries you would like to see join the EU in the future and give the reasons why they would want to do so.

18. Would you say it was economic forces that brought democracy throughout Europe?

Further reading: the aficionado's corner

For a good, general description of the development of European integration, see:

Urwin, D. (1995) *The Community of Europe*, Longman, London.

Two books that challenge the traditional view that federalist idealism was important in the development of Europe are:

Milward, A. (1992) *The European Rescue of the Nation-state*, Cambridge University Press, Cambridge.

Moravcsik, A. (1998) *The Choice for Europe: Social Purpose and State Power from Messina to Maastricht*, Cornell University Press, Ithaca, NY.

A detailed description of post-war growth can be found in:

Botting, D. (1985) *From the Ruins of the Reich: Germany 1945–1949*, New American Library, New York.

Crafts, N. and G. Toniolo (1996) *Economic Growth in Europe since 1945*, Cambridge University Press, Cambridge.

Jackson, J. (2003) *The Fall of France*, Oxford University Press, Oxford.

Lamfalussy, A. (1963) *The UK and the Six: An Essay on Economic Growth in Western Europe*, Macmillan, London.

Moravcsik, A. (1998) *The Choice for Europe: Social Purpose and State Power from Messina to Maastricht*, Cornell University Press, Ithaca, NY.

Tsebelis, G. (2005) 'Agenda Setting in the EU Constitution: From the Giscard Plan to the Pros Ratification(?) Document', paper presented at the DOSEI conference, Brussels, http://sitemaker.umich.edu/tsebelis/files/giscardagenda.pdf.

Useful websites

The European Parliament's 'factsheets' provide an excellent, authoritative and succinct coverage of many historical institutions, policies and debates. For example, it has pages on the historical development of the Parliament's role, on historical enlargements, and on every Treaty. See www.europarl.eu.int/factsheets/default_en.htm.

The EU's 'Easy Reading Corner' is not very well organized and the search engine is useless (instead try Google with site:europe.eu.int added to your keyword) but it has a lot of material and will eventually lead you to very detailed information on any topic concerning the EU; many brochures are oversimplified and not much use to students at the level of this textbook. See http://europa.eu.int/comm/publications/index_en.htm.

A good glossary can be found at http://europa.eu.int/abc/eurojargon/index_en.htm.

Details on specific Treaties (including handy summaries) can be found at http://europa.eu.int/abc/treaties_en.htm.

For Marxist–Leninist thinking on capitalism, imperialism and war, see this tract by Leon Trotsky at www.marxists.org/archive/trotsky/works/1939/1939-lenin.htm.

The Truman Library website www.trumanlibrary.org/teacher/berlin.htm is a good source for early post-war background documents online.

The Centre Virtuel de la Connaissance sur l'Europe provides a complete and well-organized website for documents, photos, videos, etc. on virtually every aspect of European integration at www.ena.lu.

The German Historical Museum (DHM) provides photos and videos of Germany's wartime experience at www.dhm.de/lemo/html/Nachkriegsjahre/DasEndeAlsAnfang/.

References

Baldwin, R. (1994) *Towards an Integrated Europe*, CEPR, London. Freely downloadable from http://heiwww.unige. ch/ Baldwin/papers.htm.

Baldwin, R. (1995) 'A domino theory of regionalism', in R. Baldwin, P. Haaparanta and J. Kiander (eds) *Expanding European Regionalism: The EU's New Members*, Cambridge University Press, Cambridge.

Crafts, N. and G. Toniolo (1996) *Economic Growth in Europe since 1945*, Cambridge University Press, Cambridge.

Eichengreen, B. and J.B. de Macedo (2001) 'The European Payments Union: history and implications for the evolution of the International Financial Architecture', in A. Lamfalussy, B. Snoy and J. Wilson (eds) *Fragility of the International Financial System*, P.I.E.-Peter Lang, Brussels.

Milward, A. (1984) *The European Rescue of the Nation-state: 1945–51*, Routledge, London.

Milward, A. (1992) *The European Rescue of the Nation-state*, Cambridge University Press, Cambridge.

Spierenburg, D. and R. Poidevin (1994) *The History of the European Coal and Steel Community*, Weidenfeld & Nicolson, London.

Urwin, D. (1995) *The Community of Europe*, Longman, London.

Annex A Chronology from 1948 to 2007

Year	Date	Event	Explanation
1948	16 April	OEEC	Organization for European Economic Cooperation (OEEC) established.
1950	9 May	Schuman Plan	French Foreign Minister Robert Schuman proposes the establishment of the European Coal and Steel Community (ECSC). Schuman was inspired by Jean Monnet's vision of building Europe step by step. 9 May is celebrated as the Day of Europe.
1952	1 January	ECSC	The ECSC is established for 50 years; expired 23 July 2002.
1952	27 May	EDC	'The Six' sign the Treaty establishing the European Defence Community (EDC). The project fails as the French National Assembly rejects the Treaty in 1954.
1953	9 March	EPC	A plan for the European Political Community (EPC) is published.
1957	25 March	EEC	The Six sign Treaties in Rome establishing the European Economic Community (EEC) and the European Atomic Energy Community (Euratom). EEC begins 1 January 1958.
1959	21 July	EFTA	European Free Trade Association (EFTA) is established by the Stockholm Convention among Austria, Denmark, Norway, Portugal, Sweden, Switzerland and the United Kingdom. EFTA begins 3 May 1960.
1962	1 January	CAP	Common Agricultural Policy starts.
1968	1 July	CU completed	Customs Union is completed within the EEC and a common external tariff is established.
1969	1–2 December	Failed monetary integration launched	At the Hague Summit, EC leaders agree to establish a single market, to accelerate integration, and to introduce Economic and Monetary Union (EMU) by 1980.
1972	22 July	EC-EFTA FTAs	Free trade agreements (FTAs) signed with Austria, Iceland, Portugal, Sweden and Switzerland.

Year	Date	Event	Explanation
1973	1 January	First enlargement	The Six become the Nine as Denmark, Ireland and the United Kingdom join the EC. Accession Treaties were signed 1 January 1972. EEC signs free trade agreements with Norway (May) and Finland (October).
1974	9–10 December	European Council formalized	At Paris Summit, EC leaders agree to meet regularly as a European Council.
1978	6–7 July	EMS founded	Bremen European Council establishes the European Monetary System (EMS) and the European currency unit (ECU).
1981	1 January	Second enlargement	Greece joins.
1985	14 June	EC92 White Paper	Commission presents the Cockfield White Paper on the completion of the single market (blueprint for economics in Single European Act).
1986	1 January	Third enlargement	Spain and Portugal join.
1986	17, 28 February	Single European Act	Single European Act is signed. Treaty enters into force on 1 July 1987.
1990	1 July	EMU stage 1	First stage of Economic and Monetary Union (EMU) begins.
1990	10 October	Germany unites	Germany is united as the former German Democratic Republic länder join the EEC.
1991		First Europe Agreements	EC signs Europe Agreements with Poland, Hungary and Czechoslovakia; Europe Agreements for other CEECs signed by 1995.
1992	7 February	Maastricht Treaty	Treaty on European Union is signed in Maastricht, creating the EU. Treaty enters into force 1 November 1993 after a difficult ratification process in Denmark.
1992	2 May	EEA	EC and EFTA sign an Agreement establishing the European Economic Area (EEA).
1993	21–22 June	CEECs can join when ready	EU leaders decide CEECs with Europe Agreements can join when they meet the 'Copenhagen criteria'.
1994	1 January	EMU stage 2	The second stage of EMU begins.
1994	9–10 December		Essen European Council agrees strategy on eastern enlargement.
1995	1 January	Fourth enlargement	Austria, Finland and Sweden join the EU.
1997	2 October	Amsterdam Treaty	Treaty of Amsterdam is signed; comes into force 1 May 1999.
1998	1–2 May	The euro	EU leaders decide 11 to join Eurozone (Austria, Belgium, Finland, France, Germany, Ireland, Italy, Luxembourg, the Netherlands, Portugal and Spain).
1998	1 June	ECB	The European Central Bank (ECB) is established.
1999	1 January	EMU stage 3	Euro becomes a currency in its own right; only electronic currency until January 2002.

Year	Date	Event	Explanation
2000	7–9 December	Nice Treaty	Treaty of Nice is signed; comes into force on 1 February 2003 after a difficult ratification process in Ireland.
2002	1 January	Euro cash	Euro notes and coins circulate.
2002	February	European Convention	Following Laeken Declaration (15/12/01), the Convention starts; it finishes June 2003.
2003	20 June	Draft Constitution	EU leaders accept the Giscard d'Estaing's draft Constitution as starting point for IGC.
2003	October	Constitutional IGC	The IGC begins under Italian Presidency.
2003	13 December	Draft Treaty rejected	European Council fails to adopt the Italian draft of the Treaty; IGC continues.
2004	1 May	Eastern enlargement	Ten new members join (Poland, Hungary, Slovakia, Czech Republic, Slovenia, Estonia, Latvia, Lithuania, Malta and Cyprus).
2004	18 June	Constitutional Treaty signed	EU heads of state and government sign the Constitutional Treaty. Ratification begins.
2005	30 May	French reject Constitution	French referendum on Constitution results in 55% no with 69% participation.
2005	1 June	Dutch reject Constitution	62% of Dutch voters reject Constitution; turnout was 63%.
2005	17 June	Ratification suspended	EU leaders decide to suspend the November 2006 deadline for ratifying the Constitution. Each Member State decides whether to continue ratification process.
2007	1 January		Bulgaria and Romania join the EU. Croatia, the Former Yugoslav Republic of Macedonia and Turkey are also candidates for future membership.
2007	13 December	Treaty of Lisbon	Signed by 27 member countries, the Treaty is planned to be ratified before the end of 2008 but the rejection of the Treaty by the Irish electorate puts it on hiatus.
2007	12 June	Treaty of Lisbon	Irish voters reject the Lisbon Treaty in a referendum.

Note: These chronologies are based on the excellent and succinct chronology on the website of the 1999 Finnish Presidency of the EU (http://presidency.finland.fi/doc/eu/eu_5chro.htm), and the extremely detailed chronology on the European Commission's website (http://europa.eu.int/abc/history/index_en.htm).

Chapter 2

Facts, law, institutions and the budget

In the infancy of societies, the chiefs of the state shape its institutions; later the institutions shape the chiefs of state.

Baron de Montesquieu

Chapter contents

2.1	Economic integration in the EU	48
2.2	EU structure: three pillars and a roof	59
2.3	EU law	64
2.4	The 'Big-5' institutions	68
2.5	Legislative processes	77
2.6	Some important facts	80
2.7	The budget	83
2.8	The Lisbon Treaty	93
2.9	Summary	105

Introduction

The members of the European Union are economically and politically integrated to an extent that is historically unprecedented. In many ways, the EU is already more integrated than loosely federated nations such as Canada and Switzerland. This integration is maintained and advanced by a cocktail of economic, political, historical and legal forces shaped by European institutions, laws and policies. This chapter presents the background information on these institutional features that is essential to the study of European economic integration.

The chapter starts by detailing the extent of European economic integration, before turning to more institutional issues – EU organization (the three pillars), EU law, EU institutions and the legislative process. The chapter then presents basic facts on EU members (population, incomes and economic size), which is essential for understanding the subsequent topic, the EU budget. The final section covers the Constitutional Treaty and how it would change EU institutions.

2.1 Economic integration in the EU

If markets are so integrated, you can't cook a different soup in one corner of the pot.
       Andres Sutt, deputy governor of the Bank of Estonia, on why Estonia wanted to join the Eurozone

The post-war architects of Europe had radical goals in mind when they established the European Economic Community with the 1957 Treaty of Rome. The Treaty's main architect, Jean Monnet, headed an influential pan-European group that was bluntly called the Action Committee for the United States of Europe. Having failed with their plans for a European Political Community and a European Defence Community in the early 1950s (see Chapter 1), they switched to economic integration as the means of achieving their lofty goal.

Indeed, the Treaty of Rome cannot be fully understood without reference to the founders' intentions. The various elements of economic integration in the Treaty were not subject to individual cost–benefit calculations. The idea was to fuse the six national economies into a unified economic area.[1] This fusion was expected to launch a gradual process that would draw the nations into an ever-closer union. Economic integration was to be the means of achieving the 'finalité politique'.

This section reviews economic integration in today's European Union, organizing the main features according to the logic of a unified economic area.

2.1.1 Treaty of Rome – fountainhead of EU economic integration

The Treaty of Rome was a far-reaching document. It laid out virtually every aspect of economic integration that Europe has implemented over the past half-century; it is, in a

---

[1] A clear statement of this can be found in the so-called Spaak Report, 'Rapport des chefs de délégation aux ministres des Affaires étrangères', Bruxelles, 21 avril 1956, the outcome of the experts group set up by the Messina Conference. See www.ena.lu.

sense, the bud whose leaves unfolded over 50 years into today's European Union. Written from scratch by highly literate and relatively idealistic politicians and diplomats, it is easy to read; motivated students should at least read the three-page 'PART ONE – Principles' (www.ena.lu?lang=2&doc=3800).

The Treaty's first article establishes the European Economic Community. Articles 2 and 3 set out the main economic goals and integration initiatives among the original six members (see Box 2.1 for the text verbatim).

Box 2.1   Articles 1, 2 and 3 of the Treaty of Rome

ARTICLE 1. By this Treaty, the High Contracting Parties establish among themselves a EUROPEAN ECONOMIC COMMUNITY.

ARTICLE 2. The Community shall have as its task, by establishing a common market and progressively approximating the economic policies of Member States, to promote throughout the Community a harmonious development of economic activities, a continuous and balanced expansion, an increase in stability, an accelerated raising of the standard of living and closer relations between the States belonging to it.

ARTICLE 3. For the purposes set out in Article 2, the activities of the Community shall include, as provided in this Treaty and in accordance with the timetable set out therein:

(a) the elimination, as between Member States, of customs duties and of quantitative restrictions on the import and export of goods, and of all other measures having equivalent effect;

(b) the establishment of a common customs tariff and of a common commercial policy towards third countries;

(c) the abolition, as between Member States, of obstacles to freedom of movement for persons, services and capital;

(d) the adoption of a common policy in the sphere of agriculture;

(e) the adoption of a common policy in the sphere of transport;

(f) the institution of a system ensuring that competition in the common market is not distorted;

(g) the application of procedures by which the economic policies of Member States can be coordinated and disequilibria in their balances of payments remedied;

(h) the approximation of the laws of Member States to the extent required for the proper functioning of the common market;

(i) the creation of a European Social Fund in order to improve employment opportunities for workers and to contribute to the raising of their standard of living;

(j) the establishment of a European Investment Bank to facilitate the economic expansion of the Community by opening up fresh resources;

(k) the association of the overseas countries and territories in order to increase trade and to promote jointly economic and social development.

Note: Articles 2 and 3 of the current version of the Treaty of Rome, more formally known as the Treaty Establishing the European Community (TEC), are quite similar. Article 2 includes a number of new goals (environment protection, etc.) and Article 3 includes some new activities (strengthening of consumer protection, etc.). You can download a scanned version of the original and current, i.e. consolidated, version from http://eur-lex.europa.eu/en/treaties/index.htm.

2.1.2 How to create a unified economic area

As far as economics goes, the Treaty of Rome's intention was to create a unified economic area: an area where firms and consumers located anywhere in the area would have equal opportunities to sell or buy goods throughout the area, and where owners of labour and capital should be free to employ their resources in any economic activity anywhere in the area. The steps necessary to establish this are presented below, along with references to the relevant articles in the current consolidated version of the Treaty of Rome (formally known as the Treaty establishing the European Community, or TEC for short).

Box 2.2 Treaty or Treaties of Rome?

Study of European integration is plagued by duplicate names. Many authors use the term the Treaty of Rome, others use Treaties of Rome. The facts are that two Treaties were signed on 25 March 1957 in the Capitol in Rome – The 'Treaty establishing the European Economic Community', which set up the basic economic integration, and another treaty (of special interest to France), the 'Treaty establishing the European Atomic Energy Community (Euratom)'. Together they are known as the Treaties of Rome, but since the first turned out to be vastly more important than the second, 'Treaty of Rome' is a short name for the 'Treaty establishing the European Economic Community'.

The 'Treaty establishing the European Economic Community' changed names in 1993 to the 'Treaty establishing the European Community' (the renaming was done by the Maastricht Treaty). The Lisbon Treaty, if it comes into force, will change the name from the 'Treaty establishing the European Community' to the 'Treaty on the Functioning of the European Union'.

As the full Treaty names are unwieldy, the abbreviations TEC (**T**reaty **E**stablishing the European **C**ommunity) and Euratom are frequently used.

Box 2.3 What was really signed in Rome on 25 March 1957?

The Treaty of Rome took nine months to write, which seems like lightning speed compared to today's treaty-writing negotiations. Writing and ratifying, however, are quite different things – a fact that was as true for the Treaty of Rome as it is for the Lisbon Treaty. The particular problem in 1957 was the staunch opposition of Charles de Gaulle to supranationality; France was in the midst of a political crisis and many believed that de Gaulle would return to power and kill the European project (see Chapter 1).

In the rush to get the ratification process done under a favourable French government, the signing ceremony in Rome was scheduled even before the agreement was fully fleshed out (e.g. additional Protocols were signed in April 1957). As Allan Little, the BBC's World Affairs Correspondent, wrote: 'The treaty – still being argued over and translated into four languages until the last minute – was not printed. The six went ahead with the ceremony anyway.' The source for this remarkable piece of historical trivia is Pierre Pescatore, a former EU Court Judge, who was there on 25 March 1957. He told a BBC programme to mark the 50th anniversary of the event: 'They signed a bundle of blank pages. The first title existed in four languages, and also the protocol at the end. Nobody looked at what was in between.' (You can hear Pescatore's remarks, in French, at www.ena.lu?lang=2&doc=23776; also see Fig. 2.1)

Figure 2.1 Is the pile on the right just blank paper?
Source: Signature des traités de Rome. Rome: Photothèque Parlement européen

Free trade in goods

The most obvious requirement is to remove trade barriers. Article 3a removes all tariffs and quantitative restrictions among members, thus establishing a free trade area for all goods. Tariffs and quotas, however, are not the only means of discriminating against foreign goods and services. Throughout the ages, governments have proved wonderfully imaginative in developing tariff-like and quota-like barriers against foreign goods and services. To remove such 'non-tariff' barriers, and to prevent new non-tariff barriers from offsetting the tariff liberalization, the Treaty rules out all measures that act like tariffs or quotas (in Article 3a).

Common trade policy with the rest of the world

Trade can never be truly free among nations if they do not harmonize their trade policy towards non-members. If members have different external tariffs, trade among the Six will have to be closely controlled to prevent 'trade deflection', i.e. imports from non-members pouring into the area through the member with the lowest external tariff. Since such controls would themselves be barriers to intra-EU trade, Article 3b requires the Six to adopt a 'common commercial policy', in other words, identical restrictions on imports from non-members. With these in place, every member can be sure that any product that is physically inside the European Union has paid the common tariff and met any common restrictions on, for example, health and safety standards. Tariffs are one of the most important restrictions on external trade, so a common commercial policy with respect to tariffs is referred to with the special name 'customs union'.

Ensuring undistorted competition

Even a customs union is not enough to create a unified economic area. Trade liberalization can be offset by public and private measures that operate inside the borders of EU members. For example, French companies might make a deal whereby they buy only from each other. The Treaty therefore calls for a system ensuring that competition in the area is undistorted (in Article 3g). This general principle is fleshed out in a series of articles that: (i) prohibit trade-distorting subsidies to national producers, (ii) create a common competition policy, (iii) harmonize national laws that affect the operation of the common market, and (iv) harmonize some national taxes. Why are all of these necessary to ensure undistorted competition?

★ **State aid prohibited**. Perhaps the most obvious distortions to competition stem from production subsidies or other forms of government assistance granted to producers located in a particular nation. Such subsidies (called 'state aid' in EU jargon) allow firms to sell their goods cheaper and/or allow uncompetitive firms to stay in business. Both effects put unsubsidized firms in other nations at a disadvantage. Most forms of 'state aid' are prohibited by the Treaty, although a list of exceptions is specified.

★ **Anti-competitive behaviour**. Discrimination from a private agreement operating within a Member State – e.g. a cartel or exclusive purchasing deal – can distort competition. The Treaty prohibits any agreement that prevents, restricts or distorts competition in the area. The focus is on restrictive business practices and abuse of a dominant position (see Chapter 14). Restrictive business practices include a host of unfair practices undertaken by private or state-owned firms. For example, the Treaty explicitly outlaws price-fixing agreements, controls on production, marketing, R&D or investment, and allocation of exclusive territories to firms in order to reduce competition. The Treaty also requires government monopolies of a commercial character to avoid discrimination based on the nationality of suppliers or customers.

★ **Approximation of laws** (EU jargon for harmonize). Another source of discrimination stems from product standards and regulations since these can have a dramatic impact on competition and indirectly favour national firms. Moreover, since many product standards are highly technical, so national firms are typically involved in writing a nation's rules. These firms, quite naturally, advise the government to adopt rules that discriminate in favour of their products.

★ **Taxes**. Taxes applied inside Member States can distort competition directly or indirectly by benefiting national firms. On countering this type of discrimination, the Treaty is weak, requiring only that the Commission consider how taxes can be harmonized in the interest of the common market. Of course, if a particular tax provision clearly benefits a well-identified firm or sector within one Member State, then it could be considered as a subsidy and thus directly forbidden.

Unrestricted trade in services

Right from the Treaty of Rome, the principle of freedom of movement of services was embraced, although fleshing this into reality has been hard. Services are provided by people and governments have to regulate the qualifications of service providers (e.g. medical doctors). The problem has been to separate prudential regulation of qualifications from protectionist restrictions. Box 2.4 provides the example of ski instructors where the roles of protecting consumers and protecting French ski instructors are thoroughly intermingled.

Box 2.4   British ski instructors arrested on French slopes

To flesh out the free movement of people and services, the EU adopted a general system for the recognition of professional education and training in 1992. This ensured that people who got their training in one EU nation could get a job in another EU nation without having to re-do their training. The system is based on the principle of mutual trust. If a Briton who has the diploma necessary to teach skiing in Britain wants to teach in France, then France should recognize the British diploma since they should trust the British government's ability to certify ski teachers, just as Britain trusts France to certify its doctors.

French ski-instructor training, however, is difficult and good jobs are relatively scarce in mountainous regions, so the French government faced pressure to protect the jobs of its ski instructors. Indeed, France used to arrest ski instructors teaching in France without a French diploma. Pressure from the European Commission forced France to justify this practice by asking for an exception from the general system for five jobs: ski instructors, high-altitude mountain guides, diving instructors, parachuting instructors and potholing instructors. French authorities claimed that due to the dangerous nature of the activities concerned, they should have the right to require prospective instructors to pass a test (based on French standards). The effect of such a test could, of course, be equivalent to forcing people to re-do their training in France.

The Commission's decision was to allow France to impose the test for two more years, but to cease the practice thereafter. An independent website for snowboarding fans wrote this in 2004: 'EU nationals won't need a visa to work in France, however France is the worst country in the world to get a job as a snowboard instructor. The authorities are very protective of their own. If you're caught teaching on the slopes and don't hold the French ski instructor's certificate, you will be arrested and jailed. However, more mundane forms of work such as bar work are permitted'.

Figure 2.2 **Ski Instructors and the free movement of services**
Source: www.worldsnowboardguide.com

Labour and capital market integration

If it works properly, a customs union with undistorted competition allows firms and consumers to buy and sell goods throughout the area without facing discrimination based on nationality. This is sufficient to create a unified economic area as far as the trade in goods is concerned. It is not, however, sufficient to fuse national economies into a unified economic area. Accomplishing this also requires integration of capital and labour markets.

Article 3c extends integration to factor markets by instituting a common employment and investment area. It does this by abolishing barriers to the free movement of workers and capital. The basic principles of labour and capital mobility are elaborated in subsequent articles. For instance, the freedom of movement for workers means the elimination of any form of discrimination based on nationality regarding hiring, firing, pay and working conditions. The Treaty also explicitly allows workers to travel freely in search of work.

As for capital mobility, the Treaty focuses on two types of freedom. The first is the right of any Community firm to set up in another Member State. These 'rights of establishment' are essential to integration in sectors with high 'natural' trade barriers, e.g. in sectors such as insurance and banking, where a physical presence in the local market is critical to doing business. The second type concerns financial capital and here the Treaty goes deep. It states that all restrictions on capital flows (e.g. cross-border investments in stocks and bonds, and direct investment in productive assets by multinationals) shall be abolished. It applies the same to current payments related to capital flows (e.g. the payment of interest and repatriation of profits). Very little capital-market liberalization, however, was undertaken until the 1980s since the Treaty provided an important loophole. It allowed capital market restrictions when capital movements create disturbances in the functioning of a Member State's capital market. Moreover, it did not set a timetable for this liberalization. Capital market liberalization only became a reality 30 years later with the Single European Act and the Maastricht Treaty.

Exchange rate and macroeconomic coordination

Fixed exchanges rates were the norm when the Treaty of Rome was written, and throughout the late 1940s and 1950s nations occasionally found that the level of their fixed exchange rate induced their citizens to purchase a value of foreign products and assets that exceeded foreigners' purchases of domestic goods and assets. Such situations, known as balance-of-payments crises, historically led to many policies – such as tariffs, quotas and competitive devaluations – that would be disruptive in a unified economic area. To avoid such disruptions, the Treaty of Rome called for mechanisms for coordinating members' macroeconomic policies and for fixing balance-of-payments crises. This seed in the Treaty of Rome eventually sprouted into the euro, the Stability Pact and the European Central Bank. See Chapters 17 and 18 for details.

Common policy in agriculture

From a logical point of view, it might seem that a unified economic area could treat trade in agricultural goods the same way as it treats trade in services and manufactured goods. From a political point of view, however, agriculture is very different and the EU has explicitly recognized this right from the beginning.

In the 1950s, Europe's farm sector was far more important economically than it is today. In many European nations, a fifth or more of all workers were employed in the sector. Moreover, national policies in the sector were very important and very different across nations. In reaction to the great economic and social turmoil of the 1920s and 1930s, most European nations had adopted highly interventionist policies in agriculture. These typically involved price controls teamed with trade barriers (Milward, 1992). Moreover, in the 1950s, the competitiveness of the Six's farm sectors differed massively. French and Dutch farmers were far more competitive than German farmers. If the Six were to form a truly integrated economic area, trade in farm goods would have to be included. However, given sharp differences in farm competitiveness among the Six, free trade would have had massively negative effects on many farmers, although, as usual with free trade, the winners would have won more than the losers would have lost.

These simple facts prevented the writers of the Treaty of Rome from including more than the barest sketch of a common farm policy. They did manage to agree on the goals, general principles and a two-year deadline for establishing the common policy. The Common Agricultural Policy came into effect in 1962 (see Chapter 12).

2.1.3 Omitted integration: social policy and taxes

The Treaty of Rome was enormously ambitious with respect to economic integration, but it was noticeably silent on two politically sensitive areas that might naturally be thought of as subject to the same logic as competition policy. The first was the harmonization of social policies (the set of rules that directly affects labour costs such as wage policies, working hours and conditions, and social benefits). The second was harmonization of tax policy.

Subsequent treaties have pushed social integration further but not anywhere near as deep as economic integration. Harmonization of taxes has advanced only slightly since the 1950s. This section considers the economic and political logic behind these omissions.

Social policy

Social harmonization is very difficult politically for at least two reasons. First, nations – even nations as similar as the original six members of the EEC – held very different opinions on what types of social policies should be dictated by the government. Moreover, social policies very directly and very continuously touch citizens' lives, so these opinions are strongly held; much more strongly, than, for example, opinions on the common external tariff or the elimination of intra-EEC quotas. The second reason concerns the difficulty of viewing social harmonization as an exchange of concessions.

With tariffs, all Six lower their tariffs against each other's goods. Although the tariffs might not have been identical to start with, there is a certain balance to the notion that we eliminate our tariffs and they eliminate theirs. With social policy, harmonization tends to be viewed as either an upward harmonization (e.g. all adopt a 35-hour week) or a downward harmonization (e.g. all have to allow stores to open on Sundays). Since social policies in each nation are the outcome of a finely balanced political equilibrium, changes that are 'imposed' by the EU are easy to characterize as undue interference by foreigners, rather than two-way exchange. For instance, it would be hard to view as 'balanced' a demand that Germans allow Sunday shopping in the name of social policy harmonization. The same could be said if France were forbidden from imposing the 35-hour week in the name of European integration.

In addition to social harmonization being significantly more difficult politically, there are economic arguments suggesting that it is not necessary.

The economics: two schools of thought

Does European economic integration demand harmonization of social policies? This question has been the subject of an intense debate for decades. It arose when the Benelux nations formed their customs union in 1947, when the OEEC was established in 1948, when the European Coal and Steel Community was created in 1953, and when the Treaty of Rome was negotiated.

From the very beginning of this debate there have been two schools of thought. One – the harmonize-before-liberalizing school – holds that international differences in wages and social conditions provide an 'unfair' advantage to countries with more laissez-faire social policies. In contrast, the no-need-to-harmonize school argues that wages and social policies are reflections of productivity differences and social preferences – differences that wage adjustments will counter. This school rejects calls for harmonization and notes that, in any case, social policies tend to converge as all nations get richer.

The harmonize-before-you-liberalize school is easier to explain. If nations initially have very different social policies, then lowering trade barriers will give nations with low social standards an unbalanced advantage, assuming that exchange rates and wages do not adjust.

The other school of thought – i.e. the school whose ideas prevailed in the Treaty of Rome – points out that wages do adjust. The economics of this is explained in depth in Chapter 8, but here it is in a nutshell. Roughly speaking, firms hire workers up to the point where the total cost of employing workers equals the value they create for the company. As far as the firm is concerned, it is not important whether the cost of the worker stems from a social policy or from wages paid directly to the worker. Different nations have different productivity levels and this is why wages can differ. Now if one nation has more expensive social policies, the workers in that nation will end up taking home (in the form of wages) a lower share of the value they create for the firm. The reason is that the firm pays the costs of the social policy out of the value that workers themselves create for the firm. In short, French workers in our example would be implicitly trading off lower take-home pay for workplace rules that made their lives better. This line of thinking requires an understanding of how markets work, so it is less easily grasped.

Tax policy

Like social policies, tax policy directly touches the lives of most citizens. This means that a nation's tax policy is the outcome of a hard-fought political compromise between broad groups of citizens, firms and labour unions, all of whom are well informed and fully engaged. Given this, EU leaders have always found it difficult politically to harmonize taxes.

The political difficulties are clear in the drafting of the Treaty of Rome's main mention of tax harmonization, Article 99: 'The Commission shall consider in what way the law of the various Member States concerning turnover taxes, excise duties and other forms of indirect taxation, including compensatory measures applying to exchanges between Member States, can be harmonised in the interest of the Common Market. The Commission shall submit proposals to the Council which shall act by means of a unanimous vote.'

The contrast between this weak language and the muscular language on, say, tariffs is striking. Here is the whole of Article 16 on 'customs duties' (i.e. tariffs): 'Member States shall abolish as between themselves, not later than at the end of the first stage, the customs duties on exportation and charges with equivalent effect.'

The general versus specific distinction

As with social policy, the difficult politics is matched with an economic argument that harmonization is not necessary, at least for broadly applied taxes – such as corporate taxes paid by all firms, taxes taken from worker's salaries (so-called social charges) and income taxes. When it comes to taxes, this logic is known as the general vs. specific distinction.

If a tax applies only to a specific sector, then the idea that national wages difference will adjust to offset national tax rate differences does not hold, so the tax differences may affect competitiveness and thus be viewed as unfair (see Chapter 8 for details). If the tax is applied quite broadly across the economy, then the economic offset-mechanism should be enough. In practice this distinction has guided the Commission's supervision of unfair taxes right from the EU's inception.

2.1.4 Additions and the Lisbon Treaty changes

The original Treaty of Rome Articles 2 and 3 (Box 2.1) set out the EU's first order of business – establishing a unified economic area (a 'common market' or, more recently, 'the internal market'). Since this was the foundation of the whole European construction, subsequent Treaties have done little to modify the *content* of the original Articles.

The current state of affairs: Pre-Lisbon

Roughly speaking, the Treaty of Rome's Article 2 says that the EU should promote the 'economic good life'; Article 3 lists the areas of action where the EU should work towards this goal. None of this has changed over the years, but the definition of the good life has evolved, so the various Treaty revisions have updated Articles 2 and 3. As it currently stands in 2008 (i.e. pre-Lisbon Treaty), the economic-good-life-Article-2 list has been expanded beyond the 1957 list to include items which most Europeans would consider as essential, namely:

★ a high level of employment;

★ equality between the sexes;

★ a high degree of competitiveness and convergence;

★ a high level of protection and improvement of the quality of the environment; and

★ a rising standard of living and quality of life.

To achieve these expanded economic-good-life goals, the Article-3-list-of-EU-activities has been correspondingly expanded to include:

★ visa and immigration policies for non-EU citizens;

★ coordination of members' employment policies;

★ strengthening of economic and social cohesion;

★ environmental policies;

★ strengthening of EU industrial competitiveness;

★ promotion of R&D;

★ encouragement of trans-European networks;

★ cooperation on overseas development policies;

★ promotion of health protection and consumer protection;

★ measures in the spheres of energy, civil protection and tourism.

Lisbon Treaty changes

The Lisbon Treaty would change everything in terms of form, but little in terms of content. Discussion of the reorganization is best postponed to Section 2.8, where it can be dealt with systematically.

The substantive change is easily summarized. Instead of the EU promoting the 'economic good life', it is to promote the 'good life' more generally. The first sentence in the corresponding text (Article 3 of the TEU as amended by the Lisbon Treaty) is: 'The Union's aim is to promote peace, its values and the well-being of its peoples.'

The amended text then expands on this by including a list of EU activities that is essentially the same as the pre-Lisbon list with two exceptions: there is an explicit mention of safeguarding Europe's rich cultural and linguistic diversity and heritage; and there is an explicit discussion of the EU's relations with the wider world.

On the second point, the Lisbon Treaty says that the Union 'shall uphold and promote its values and contribute to the protection of its citizens. It shall contribute to peace, security, the sustainable development of the Earth, solidarity and mutual respect among peoples, free and fair trade, eradication of poverty and the protection of human rights, in particular the rights of the child, as well as to the strict observance and the development of international law, including respect for the principles of the United Nations Charter.'

In a nutshell, the Lisbon Treaty amendments would mean that economics is no longer the 'core business' of the EU but rather one element in the broader goal of promoting peace and well-being.

2.1.5 Quantifying European economic integration

Research by economic historians permits us to quantify the progress of European economic integration. A careful reading of the timing with which various policies were implemented allows the economic historian to quantify (somewhat subjectively) the extent of integration. The indices developed by two different groups are shown in Fig. 2.3. Although the two indices differ in details, they show that European economic integration has been a 'work in progress' for half a century. The DFFM index, which has finer detail on EU integration, clearly shows the main phases:

★ Customs union formation, 1958–68;

★ Euro-pessimism, 1973–86;

★ Single Market, 1986–92;

★ Economic and Monetary Union (EMU), 1993–2001.

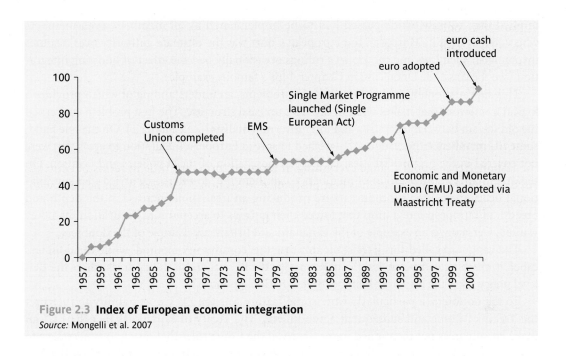

Figure 2.3 Index of European economic integration
Source: Mongelli et al. 2007

2.2 EU structure: three pillars and a roof

Late 2008, when the third edition went to print, is an awkward time to write about EU organization, institutions and the like. Since the Irish voted against the Lisbon Treaty in June 2008, no one really knows what will happen (see Chapter 1).

While awkward, this does not greatly complicate the task of this chapter. Almost no one expects the Lisbon Treaty to be in place in time for the June 2009 European Parliament elections, so those will be held under current rules. Moreover, many of the most important Lisbon Treaty changes were scheduled to take effect in 2014 or beyond.

This means that students have to learn about the current system, regardless of the Lisbon Treaty's fate. With this reality in mind, the third edition follows the practice of the second edition (when the uncertainty concerned the now abandoned Constitutional Treaty). It discusses the Lisbon Treaty changes in a separate section (Section 2.8) and the current situation in Sections 2.2, 2.3 and 2.4.

2.2.1 Ever closer? Creeping competencies

The five decades since 1958 produced a steady stream of new EU laws. Most of these strengthened integration in areas where integration had already begun. Others, however, spread EU integration to new areas, such as immigration policy, environmental policy, police cooperation, and foreign and defence policy.

Up to the 1992 Maastricht Treaty, all of this integration was subject to the Treaty of Rome's supranational decision-making procedures; for example, majority voting on EU laws which implied that any law which passed had to be implemented by all members, even members who voted against it. Moreover, the European Court was the ultimate authority over disputes involving all such laws and the Court's rulings occasionally had the effect of boosting integration (see the Cassis de Dijon case in Chapter 4 for a famous example).

This supranationality created two related problems, an understanding of which provides a logical framework that makes sense of the EU's unusual structure. The first problem concerned the old schism between federalists and intergovernmentalists (see Chapter 1). On the one hand, some EU members – the 'vanguard' – wished to spread European integration to areas that were not covered in the original Treaties, such as harmonization of social policies and taxation. On the other hand, another group of members – call them the 'doubters' – worried that supranational decision-making procedures were producing an irresistible increase in the depth and breadth of European integration that forced their citizens to accept more integration than they wanted. Germany is an example of the vanguard and Britain an example of the doubters.

The vanguard called this irresistible increase the 'community method' while the doubters called it 'creeping competencies' ('competency' is the EU jargon for policy areas where the EU-level policy takes the lead over Member States' national policies).

To the doubters, a particularly worrisome feature was the EU Court's ability to interpret the Treaty of Rome and subsequent amendments. The Treaty of Rome says that the EU can make laws in areas not mentioned in the Treaty, if the Court rules that doing so is necessary to attain Treaty objectives. The Treaty objectives, however, are extremely far reaching; the first line of the Treaty of Rome's Preamble says that the members are 'determined to lay the foundations of an ever closer union among the peoples of Europe'. Doubters worried that the Treaty's ambitious objectives combined with the Court's ability to sanction law-making in areas not explicitly mentioned in the Treaties opened the door to essentially unlimited transfers of national sovereignty to the EU level.

The second problem concerned integration that was taking place outside of the EU's structure due to differences between the vanguard and the doubters. The Schengen Accord is the classic example (Fig. 2.4). While the free movement of people is an EU goal dating back to 1958, some members (e.g. Britain) held up progress towards passport-free travel. In 1985, five EU members signed an agreement ending controls on their internal frontiers. This was completely outside of the EU's structure and many observers feared that such ad hoc arrangements could undermine the unity of the Single Market and possibly foster tensions among EU members. A more recent example is the 2005 Prüm Treaty on police cooperation, which was signed outside the EU umbrella by seven EU members.

Both problems were addressed when EU members adopted a second keystone treaty – the Treaty on European Union (Maastricht Treaty).

2.2.2 Maastricht and the three pillars as fire breaks

The Maastricht Treaty drew a clear line between supranational and intergovernmental policy areas by creating the 'three-pillar' organizational structure. The deeper integration that took place up to the Maastricht Treaty, i.e. took place under the terms of the Treaty of Rome, is the 'first pillar'; this integration continues to be subject to supranationality. The intergovernmental policies – foreign and defence matters (second pillar) and police, justice and other 'home

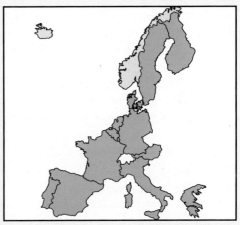

Figure 2.4 Schengen Accord, deeper integration outside the EU framework

Note: The passport-free travel zone of Schengen includes two non-EU nations, Iceland and Norway, and two EU members are not in it, Britain and Ireland.

Photo: © European Communities, 1995–2009; Map: Swedish airport services

affairs' (third pillar) – are under the European Union 'roof' but not subject to supranationality in terms of decision making and EU Court rulings (Fig. 2.5).

The three-pillar structure solved the two problems mentioned above. The clear distinction between supranational and intergovernmental cooperation allowed initiatives like Schengen to be brought under the EU's wing without forcing every member to join. This greatly reduced the resistance of Britain and other doubters to further discussion of closer integration in areas like police cooperation and foreign policy cooperation.

The key, as far as the doubters were concerned, is that Maastricht puts Member States clearly in control in second- and third-pillar areas. There is no possibility of the Court or Commission using their authority to force deeper integration on reluctant members in pursuit of the duties assigned to them by the Treaty of Rome.

Details of the three pillars

The first pillar, which encompasses the vast majority of EU activity, is called the European Community (formerly known as the European Economic Community and for a while as the European Communities). It includes the Internal Market with its four freedoms (free movement of goods, services, workers and capital), the Single Market Programme (including harmonization of members' health, safety and environment regulations and standards), competition policy and the control of 'state aids' (i.e. government handouts to businesses), the Common Agricultural Policy, spending on EU disadvantaged regions, etc. The legal foundation for all these policies, laws, institutions and practices is the Treaty establishing the European Community (i.e. the Treaty of Rome as amended by subsequent treaties). The first pillar also includes the Economic and Monetary Union (EMU) and thus comprises the European Central

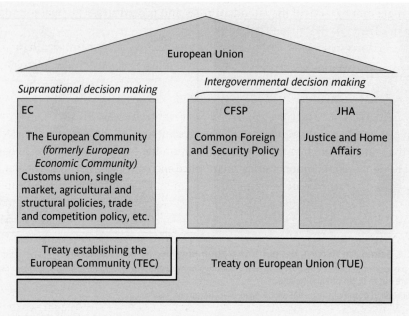

Figure 2.5 The three-pillar structure

Note: The first pillar also includes the highly specialized European Atomic Energy Community which was set up by the Treaty establishing the European Atomic Energy Community; it is often called Euratom.

Box 2.5 Supranationality in the EU

Supranationality arises in the EU in three main ways:

1 The Commission can propose new laws that are then voted on by the Member States (in the Council of Ministers) and the European Parliament. If passed, these new laws bind every member state, even those that disagree with them.

2 The Commission has direct executive authority in a limited number of areas – the most prominent being competition policy. For instance, the Commission can block a merger between two EU companies even if their governments support the merger. (See Chapter 14 for details.)

3 The rulings of the European Court of Justice can alter laws, rules and practices in Member States, at least in limited areas. (See the Factortame case discussed in Section 2.3 for an example).

The Maastricht Treaty states that these forms of supranationality continue to apply to first-pillar issues. It also defines quite precisely the limited role of the Commission, Court and Council in the second and third pillars. Reflecting concerns such as the internationalization of crime, international terrorism, human trafficking, etc., EU leaders agreed in the Amsterdam and Nice Treaties to apply first-pillar supranationality to certain Justice and Home Affairs issues.

Bank, the single money, and all the attendant rules and procedures. The legal foundations for these are in the Treaty on European Union.

Integration efforts in second- and third-pillar areas are intergovernmental in the sense that such efforts are undertaken by direct negotiation among Member States and any agreement requires unanimity.

The second pillar consists of the Common Foreign and Security Policy.

The third pillar comprises Justice and Home Affairs. Much of the EU's third-pillar policy has its origin in the 1985 Schengen Agreement. That agreement gradually removed border controls. To replace the controls that had previously relied upon the border check, the Schengen members agreed to tighter cooperation among their police and court systems. In particular, the issue of non-EU citizens required coordination of asylum and immigration policies. Much of this cooperation was transferred to the EU level by the Maastricht Treaty, although Britain famously opted out of Schengen's no-passport control rules (and many other areas). The Maastricht Treaty's introduction of EU citizenship is also usually considered a third-pillar issue.

The 'Europeanization' of today's Europeans forced even the doubters to recognize the need for additional integration on matters like international transfers of pension schemes, divorce procedures and contract law. Since it proved all but impossible to make progress on these concerns without some form of supranational decision making, many third-pillar issues have been shifted into the first pillar by Amsterdam and Nice Treaty amendments.

Specifically, the Amsterdam Treaty assigned a new task to the EU, that of creating an 'area of freedom, security and justice'. The idea was to ensure freedom of movement for individuals between all EU members and bolster members' fight against organized crime and fraud. Specially, asylum, immigration and judicial cooperation in civil matters were moved to the first pillar. The third pillar now contains only police cooperation and judicial cooperation in criminal matters. All first- and third-pillar justice and home affairs issues are grouped under the general heading of AFSJ (Area of Freedom, Security and Justice).

The EU also established cooperating agencies such as Europol (police matters), Eurojust (cooperation between national prosecutors) and Frontex (cooperation among border officials). One important and practical element of this is the Schengen Information System, which helps members fight crime, terrorism and illegal immigration.

The Lisbon Treaty (which is unlikely to come into force before 2010 and maybe never) would remove the three-pillar structure; see Section 2.8.

EU or EC?

In one of the muddles that make the EU so hard to study, saying 'EU' logically implies all three pillars. However, European Union sounds better than European Community, so the term EU, or 'the Union', is used almost universally in the media and by politicians even when they are really talking about purely the EC (first-pillar) issues. The only place that the EU/EC distinction really matters is when it comes to European law (see Section 2.3).

2.2.3 The two key treaties: TEC and TUC

Today's European Union is based on two main treaties – the 'first-pillar' treaty, the Treaty establishing the European Community (also called the TEC or Treaty of Rome) and the 'encompassing treaty', the Treaty on European Union (also called the TEU or Maastricht Treaty). There is a raft of other treaties, but these either modify the two main treaties (Single European Act, Amsterdam Treaty, Nice Treaty, etc.), or are important only in very specific areas (Treaty establishing the European Atomic Energy Community, etc.). As usual, the full picture is more complex. Interested readers will find Borchardt (1999) very helpful in filling in the details. Also the European Parliament's factsheets provide a detailed but highly readable history of the Treaties' developments; in particular, factsheets 1.1.1 to 1.1.3. (The 2004 vintage factsheets are easier, so go to www.europarl.europa.eu/facts_2004/default_en.htm.)

2.3 EU law

One of the most unusual and important things about the EU is its supranational legal system. This is a direct implication of the EU's usual degree of economic integration. Implementing and maintaining a unified economic area requires a legal system of some kind since disputes over interpretation and conflicts among various laws are inevitable.

By the standards of every other international organization in the world, the European legal system is extremely supranational. For example, even the highest courts in EU Member States must defer to decisions by the EU's Court of Justice on matters concerning the interpretation of EC law. The EU is very much like a federal state in this respect. Just as the decisions of lower courts in France, Germany and Italy can be overturned by those nations' supreme courts, the EU's Court of Justice has the ultimate say on questions concerning European law.

The topic of EU law is as intricate as it is fascinating. This section presents the barest outlines of the subject, focusing on the elements that are essential for understanding the decision-making process in particular, and the economics of European integration more generally. Note that this section is largely based on the freely downloadable book by Borchardt (1999), *The ABC of Community Law*, with some updates (use Google to find it since the Commission occasionally reorganizes its website). This book is still the best online *introduction* to the subject as the essentials have not changed.

2.3.1 'Sources' of EU law

Where did the EU's legal system come from? The legal systems of most democratic nations are based on a constitution. The EU does not have a formal constitution, so where did these principles come from? As is true of so many things in the EU, a complete answer to this question would fill a book or two, but the short answer is easy: the Treaty of Rome created the Court and the Court created the EC legal system.

The Treaty of Rome commits Member States to a series of general economic and political goals, and it transfers important elements of national sovereignty to the European level; for example, after 1958 Member States no longer had the right to control their external trade policy. The Treaty was meant to be a dynamic and adaptive agreement, so it also created ways of making new laws and modifying old ones. Most importantly for the subject at hand, it established a Court to adjudicate the disputes and questions of interpretations that were bound to arise.

The Treaty was not very specific when it came to setting up the legal system. The Treaty establishes the Court of Justice (Fig. 2.6) and states that its general task is to 'ensure observance

Figure 2.6 **Working session of the Court of Justice**
Source: European Parliament

of law and justice in the interpretation and application of this Treaty' (Article 164 in the original Treaty). It then goes on to define the Court's composition and to assign the Court a few specific tasks.

The Treaty was not specific enough to deal with the many issues that came before the Court. The Court reacted to the lack of specificity in the Treaty by creating the Community's legal system via case law. That is to say, it used decisions relating to particular cases to establish general principles of the EC legal system.

EC law is now an enormous mass of laws, rules and practices that has been established by Treaties (primary law), EU laws (secondary law) and decisions of the Court (case law). See Box 2.6 for further details on the types of secondary legislation.

Box 2.6   Secondary law: EU legislation

There are five main types of EU legislation other than the Treaties.

A regulation applies to all Member States, companies, authorities and citizens. Regulations apply as they are written, i.e. they are not transposed into other laws or provisions. They apply immediately upon coming into force.

A directive may apply to any number of Member States. However, directives only set out the result to be achieved. The Member States decide for themselves, within a prescribed time frame, what needs to be done to comply with the conditions set out in the directive. For instance, one Member State may have to introduce new legislation, while another may not need to take any action at all if it already meets the requirements set out in the directive.

A decision is a legislative act that applies to a specific Member State, company or citizen.

Recommendations and opinions are two other types of legislative act. They are not legally binding. See further details in Section 2.5.

2.3.2 EC legal system: main principles

Since the EC legal system was not created by any single document, its principles have never been officially proclaimed. The 'principles' of EC law are thus general patterns that various jurists have discerned from the thousands of pages of primary, secondary and case law, and different jurists list different principles. Three principles that always are mentioned are 'direct effect', 'primacy of EC law' and 'autonomy' of the EC legal system. These were first established in two landmark cases in 1963 and 1964 (see Box 2.7).

Box 2.7 Two cases that established the EC legal system

The EC legal system was not explicitly established in any Treaty, so the Court used some early cases to establish three key principles. Since these principles arose in the course of real-world cases, it can be difficult to precisely distinguish among the three principles in the two cases.

Van Gend & Loos v. Netherlands, 1963. In this case, the Dutch company Van Gend & Loos brought an action against its own government for imposing an import duty on a chemical product from Germany which was higher than duties on an earlier shipment; the company claimed that this violated the Treaty of Rome's prohibition on tariff hikes on intra-EC trade. The Dutch court suspended the case and asked the EC Court to clarify. The EC Court ruled that the company could rely on provisions in the Treaties when arguing against the Dutch government before a Dutch court.

Plainly, this case has an element of direct effect and primacy. The Dutch government had one rule – the higher tariff rate – while the Treaty had another (no increase allowed). The EC Court said the Treaty provision trumped the national provision. Moreover, the EC Court said that the Dutch court should consider the Treaty directly rather than, for example, the Dutch Parliament's transposition of the Treaty's principles into Dutch law. In effect, the Court said that the Treaty was Dutch law as far as the Dutch court was to be concerned. This was new, since normally a national court can consider only national law when judging a case.

The European Court also took the opportunity to write down its thoughts on the fundamental nature of the EC legal system. In Van Gend & Loos v Netherlands decision, it wrote: 'The Community constitutes a new legal order of international law for the benefit of which the States have limited their sovereign rights, albeit within limited fields, and the subjects of which comprise not only Member States but also their nationals.'

Costa v. ENEL, 1964 decision by the Court of Justice. The next year, the Court expanded its view of the EC legal system in a case involving a dispute over one euro! In 1962, Italy nationalized its electricity grid and grouped it under the National Electricity Board (ENEL in Italian). Mr Flaminio Costa, a shareholder of one nationalized company, felt he had been unjustly deprived of his dividend and so refused to pay his electricity bill for two thousand lira. The non-payment matter came before an arbitration court in Milan but since Mr Costa argued that the nationalization violated EC law, the Milan court asked the European Court to interpret various aspects of the Treaty of Rome.

The Court took the opportunity to go way beyond the question at hand. In its judgement, the Court stated the principle of autonomy and direct effect:

★ 'By contrast with ordinary international treaties, the EEC Treaty has created its own legal system which . . . became an integral part of the legal systems of the Member States and which their courts are bound to apply.'

★ 'Member States have limited their sovereign rights, albeit within limited fields, and have thus created a body of law which binds both their nationals and themselves.'

Relying on the logic of what the Treaty of Rome implied – at least implicitly – the Court established the principle of primacy:

★ '[T]he law stemming from the Treaty, an independent source of law, could not, because of its special and original nature, be overridden by domestic legal provisions, however framed, without being deprived of its character as Community law and without the legal basis of the Community itself being called into question. The transfer by the States from their domestic legal system to the Community legal system of the rights and obligations arising under the Treaty carries with it a permanent limitation of their sovereign rights, against which a subsequent unilateral act incompatible with the concept of the Community cannot prevail.'

The Court's justification was that if EC law were not supreme, the objectives of the Treaty could not be met: 'The executive force of Community law cannot vary from one State to another in deference to subsequent domestic laws, without jeopardising the attainment of the objectives of the Treaty.'

'Direct effect'

'Direct effect' is simple to define – it means that Treaty provisions or other forms of EU law such as directives can create rights which EU citizens can rely upon when they go before their domestic courts. This is radical. It means that EC laws must be enforced by Member States' courts, just as if the law had been passed by the national parliament. A good example is the case of a Sabena air stewardess (as they called female flight attendants in the 1970s) who claimed that she was paid less and had to retire earlier than male flight attendants. Although this was not a violation of Belgian law at the time, the EC Court ruled in 1976 that the Treaty of Rome (which provides for equality of pay between the sexes) had the force of law in Belgium, or in legal-ese it had direct effect. The stewardess won the case.

The principle of direct effect is quite unique. For example, when New Zealand ratifies the Kyoto Protocol, it is agreeing to certain obligations, but New Zealand courts ignore these obligations unless they are implemented by a law passed by the New Zealand parliament. Even more unusual is that this 'direct effect' notion applies to EU laws passed by majority voting, e.g. directives. This means that even if a Member State government votes against a particular law, that law automatically has the force of law, so its national courts must treat the EU law as if it were a national law. Importantly, there are complex conditions for a Treaty provision to have direct effect, so not everything in every Treaty is automatically enforceable in Member States.

The logical necessity of this principle is straightforward. If laws agreed in Brussels could be ignored in any Member State, the EU would fall into a shambles. Each member would be tempted to implement only the EU laws it liked. This would, for example, make it impossible to create a single market or ensure the free movement of workers.

Primacy of EC law

This principle, which means that Community law has the final say, is not in the Treaty of Rome and indeed appears explicitly for the first time only in the Constitutional Treaty. It is, nonetheless, a principle that is now generally accepted by all EU members. It has repeatedly been used to overturn Member State laws.

One classic example of this is the 1991 Factortame case which confirmed the supremacy of EC law over UK law. The UK's Merchant Shipping Act of 1988 had the effect of forbidding a Spanish fishing company called Factortame from fishing in UK waters. Factortame asserted in UK courts that this violated EC law, and asked the UK court to suspend the Merchant Shipping Act until the EC Court could rule on the matter (this often takes a couple of years). Under UK law, no British court can suspend an Act of Parliament. The EC Court ruled that under EC law, which was supreme to UK law, a national court could suspend laws which contravened EC law. Subsequently, the highest UK court did strike down the Merchant Fishing Act.

The logical necessity of this principle is just as clear as that of direct effect. Simplifying for clarity's sake, 'direct effect' says that EC laws are automatically laws in every Member State. Primacy says that when EC law and national, regional or local laws conflict, the EC law is what must be enforced.

Autonomy

Most European nations have several layers of courts – local, regional and national. The lower courts, however, do not exist independently of the higher courts, and often the higher courts depend upon the lower courts (e.g., in some nations, the high court can rule only after the case has been tried at a lower level). The EC legal system, however, is entirely independent of the Member States' legal systems according to the principle of autonomy.

2.4 The 'Big-5' institutions

There are many EU agencies, bodies and committees, but one can achieve a very good understanding of how the EU works by knowing only the 'Big-5': the Council of the European Union (often called by its old name, the Council of Ministers), the European Council, the European Commission, the European Parliament and the EU Court. (On the other institutions, see europa.eu/institutions/inst/index_en.htm.)

The Lisbon Treaty will change the Big-5 in important ways, but not for the most part before 2014 or even later, and that is assuming the Treaty comes into force. This section covers the facts on the Big-5 as they stand in 2008 (pre-Lisbon Treaty). The Lisbon Treaty changes for all five are considered in Section 2.8.

2.4.1 Council of the European Union

The Council of the European Union – also known as the Council of Ministers or 'the Council' for short – is the EU's main decision-making body (Fig. 2.7). Almost every piece of legislation is subject to approval by the Council. The Council consists of one representative from each EU member. The national representatives must be authorized to commit their governments to Council decisions, so Council members are the government ministers responsible for the relevant area – the finance ministers on budget issues, agriculture ministers on farm issues and so on.

The Council is where the Member States' governments assert their influence directly. Since all EU governments are elected (democracy is a must for membership) and the Council

Figure 2.7 Meeting of the Council of Ministers in Brussels
Source: © European Communities, 1995–2009

members represent their governments, the Council is the ultimate point of democratic control over the EU actions and law-making. Although the European Parliament is elected directly, very few Europeans know the name of their Member of the European Parliament. European voters do know the name of their Prime Minister – and will hold him or her accountable if something goes seriously wrong in the EU.

The Council has responsibilities in all first-pillar areas. To meet these responsibilities, it has the following powers:

★ To pass European laws (jointly with the European Parliament for many matters, see Section 2.5). Most of the laws passed concern measures necessary to implement the Treaties, or simply to keep the EU vital parts running smoothly (the Internal Market, the Common Agricultural Policy, etc.).

★ To coordinate the general economic policies of the Member States in the context of the Economic and Monetary Union (EMU). The famous 3 per cent deficit rule, which has caused Germany and France so much trouble in the past, is part of this effort.

★ To conclude international agreements between the EU and other countries or international organizations.

★ To approve the EU's budget, jointly with the European Parliament.

In addition to these 'first-pillar' tasks, the Council takes the decisions pertaining to Common Foreign and Security Policies (CFSP) and measures pertaining to police and judicial cooperation in criminal matters, the AFSJ. To the average European, these are some of the most visible actions of the Council. For example, the EU has a mission in Chad and the Central African Republic to protect civilians, facilitate delivery of humanitarian aid and ensure the safety of UN personnel (Fig. 2.8). The commander of the 4300-strong EUFOR is Irish Lt. General Patrick Nash. This military operation was approved by the Council on 15 October 2007.

Figure 2.8 **EUFOR in Chad, meeting with village chiefs, 2008**
Source: © European Communities, 1995–2009

Although the Council is a single institution, it follows the somewhat confusing practice of using different names to describe the Council according to the matters being discussed. For example, when the Council addresses EMU matters it is called the Economic and Financial Affairs Council, or 'ECOFIN' to insiders.

Decision-making rules

The Council has two main decision-making rules. On the most important issues – such as Treaty changes, the accession of new members and setting the multi-year budget plan – the Council must decide unanimously. However, on most issues (about 80 per cent of all Council decisions), the Council decides on the basis of a form of majority voting called 'qualified majority voting' (QMV). These rules are extremely important for understanding how Europe works, so they are the subject of extensive analysis in Chapter 3.

Presidency of the EU

One EU Member State at a time holds the Presidency, with this office rotating every six months. The Presidency nation sets the EU basic agenda and chairs the Council of Ministers meetings. There is no president per se, although the Prime Minister of the Presidency nation can come close to this; the job – which is enormous – is assumed by the entire national government. France has the Presidency up to December 2008 and is then followed by the Czech Republic, Sweden, Spain, Belgium, Hungary and Poland (ending December 2011). To reduce disruptions, a three-nation group consisting of the members that are the past, present and future presidents cooperate.

The Council (i.e. Council of Ministers) can easily be confused with the European Council. One way to remember the difference is to note that the European Council is a meeting of the 'bosses' of the Council members, i.e. the Prime Ministers and heads of state (European Council) rather than the relevant Ministers (Council of Ministers).

2.4.2 The European Council

The European Council consists of the leaders of each EU member plus the President of the European Commission – the EU phraseology is the 'heads of state and government' (Fig. 2.9). The European Council provides broad guidelines for EU policy and thrashes out the final compromises necessary to conclude the most sensitive aspects of EU business, including reforms of the major EU policies, the EU's multi-year budget plan, Treaty changes and the final terms of enlargements. This body is by far the most influential institution because its members are the leaders of their respective nations.

The European Council is chaired by the country that has the Presidency of the EU. This position can be powerful since it gives the President some power to set the agenda. However, since the Council operates on a basis of consensus, the agenda-setting power can be quite limited.

The European Council meets at least twice a year (June and December), but has been meeting at least four times in recent years. The highest-profile meetings are those held at the end of each six-month term of the EU Presidency. These June and December meetings are important, high-profile media events – the one aspect of the EU that almost every European has seen on television. There is good reason for this attention. European Council's decisions at their summits determine all of the EU's major moves. For example, the decision to bury the Constitutional Treaty was taken at the June 2007 Summit, and the final compromises on the Lisbon Treaty were taken at an October 2007 Summit.

Figure 2.9 European Council group photo, March 2008
Source: © European Communities, 1995–2009

The 'Conclusions' and lack of formal power

The most important decisions of each Presidency are contained in a document, known as the 'Conclusions of the Presidency', which is published at the end of each European Council meeting. Students who want to track the EU's position on a particular topic – be it the need for a constitution or its position on Zimbabwe – will do well to start from the Conclusions. The Council's website posts Conclusions (www.consilium.europa.eu), but since it is poorly organized a direct internet search may be easier.

One peculiarity of the EU is that the most powerful body by far – the European Council – has no formal role in EU law-making. The political decisions made by the European Council are translated into law following the standard legislative procedures involving the Commission, the Council of Ministers and, in most areas, the European Parliament.

Confusingly, the European Council and the Council of Ministers are often both called 'the Council'. Moreover, the Council of Ministers and the European Council should also not be confused with the Council of Europe (an international organization entirely unrelated to the EU).

2.4.3 Commission

The European Commission is at the heart of the EU's institutional structure. It is the main driving force behind deeper and wider European integration. The body, based in Brussels, has three main roles:

1 to propose legislation to the Council and Parliament;
2 to administer and implement EU policies;
3 to provide surveillance and enforcement of EU law in coordination with the EU Court.

As part of its third role, it is the 'guardian of the Treaties', i.e. the body that is ultimately charged with ensuring that the Treaties are implemented and enforced.

The Commission also represents the EU at some international negotiations, such as those relating to World Trade Organization (WTO) trade talks. The Commission's negotiating stances at such meetings are closely monitored by EU members.

Commissioners and the Commission's composition

The European Commission is made up of one Commissioner from each EU member. This includes the President and two Vice-Presidents. The current Commission President, Jose Manuel Barroso, is a former Prime Minister of Portugal. Commissioners, including the President of the Commission, are appointed all together and serve for five years. This is why people often refer to each Commission as being the 'Barroso Commission' (Fig. 2.10) or the 'Prodi Commission'. The appointments are made just after European Parliamentary elections and take effect in the January of the following year. The current Commission's term ends in January 2009.

Commissioners are effectively chosen by their own national governments, but the choices are subject to political agreement by other members. The Commission as a whole, and the Commission President individually, must also be approved by the European Parliament.

Commissioners are not supposed to act as national representatives. They are forbidden from accepting or seeking instruction from their country's government. In practice, Commissioners

Figure 2.10 The 27-member Barroso Commission
Source: European Commission

are generally quite independent of their home governments, but since they have typically held high political office in their home nations, they are naturally sensitive to issues that are of particular concern there. This ensures that all decisive national sensitivities are heard in Commission deliberations.

The Commission has a great deal of independence in practice and often takes views that differ substantially from the Member States, the Council and the Parliament. However, it is ultimately answerable to the European Parliament since the Parliament can dismiss the Commission as a whole by adopting a motion of censure. Although this has never happened, a censure motion was almost passed in 1999, triggering a sequence of events that ended in mass resignation of the Commission led by President Jacques Santer.

Each politically appointed Commissioner is in charge of a specific area of EU policy. In particular, each runs what can be thought of as the EU equivalent of a national ministry. These 'ministries', called Directorate-Generals or DGs in EU jargon, employ a relatively modest number of international civil servants. The Commission as a whole employs about 17 000, which is fewer than the number of people who work for the city of Vienna. Just as in national ministries, Commission officials tend to provide most of the expertise necessary to administer and analyse the EU's vastly complex network of policies since the Commissioners themselves are typically generalists.

Legislative powers

The Commission's main law-making duty is to prepare proposals for new EU legislation. These range from a new directive on minimum elevator safety standards to reform of the Common Agricultural Policy (CAP). Neither the Council nor the Parliament can adopt legislation until the Commission presents its proposals, except under extraordinary procedures. This monopoly on the 'right to initiate' makes the Commission the gatekeeper of EU integration. It also allows the Commission occasionally to become the driving force behind deeper or broader integration. This was especially true under the two Delors Commissions that served from 1985 to 1994.

Commission proposals are usually based on general guidelines established by the Council of Ministers, the European Council, the Parliament or the Treaties. A proposal is prepared by the relevant Directorate-General in collaboration with other DGs concerned. In exercising this power of initiative, the Commission consults a very broad range of EU actors, including national governments, the European Parliament, national administrations, professional groups and trade union organizations. This complex consultation process is known in EU jargon as 'comitology'.

Executive powers

The Commission is the executive in all of the EU's endeavours, but its power is most obvious in competition policy. Chapter 14 explains in more detail how the Commission has the power to block mergers, to fine corporations for unfair practices and to insist that EU members remove or modify subsidy to their firms. The Commission also has substantial latitude in administering the Common Agricultural Policy, including the right to impose fines on members that violate CAP rules.

One of the key responsibilities of the Commission is to manage the EU budget, subject to supervision by a specialized institution called the EU Court of Auditors. For example, while the Council decided the programme-by-programme allocation of funds in the EU's current multi-year budget (Financial Perspective in EU jargon), it was the Commission that decided the year-by-year indicative allocation of Structural Funds across members.

Decision making

The Commission decides, in principle, on the basis of a simple majority. The 'in principle' proviso is necessary because the Commission makes almost all of its decision on the basis of consensus. The reason is that the Commission usually has to get its actions approved by the Council and/or the Parliament. A Commission decision that fails to attract the support of a very substantial majority of the Commissioners will almost surely fail in the Council and/or Parliament.

2.4.4 The European Parliament

The Parliament has two main tasks: sharing legislative powers with the Council of Ministers and the Commission; and overseeing all EU institutions, but especially the Commission. The Parliament, on its own initiative, has also begun to act as the 'conscience' of the EU, for example condemning various nations for human rights violations via non-binding resolutions.

Organization

The European Parliament (EP) has 732 members who are directly elected by EU citizens in special elections organized in each Member State. The number of Members of European Parliament (MEPs) per nation varies with population, but the number of MEPs per million EU citizens is much higher for small nations than for large. For example, in the 1999–2004 Parliament, Luxembourg had six MEPs and Germany had 99, despite the fact that Germany's population is about 160 times that of Luxembourg.

MEPs are supposed to represent their local constituencies, but the Parliament's organization has evolved along classic European political lines rather than along national lines (Noury and

Roland, 2002). The EP election campaigns are generally run by each nation's main political parties and MEPs are generally associated with a particular national political party. Although this means that over a hundred parties are represented in the Parliament, fragmentation is avoided because many of these parties have formed political groups. As in most EU Member States, two main political groups – the centre-left and the centre-right – account for two-thirds of the seats and tend to dominate the Parliament's activity. The centre-left grouping in the EP is called the Party of European Socialists, the centre-right group is called the European People's Party.

National delegations of MEPs do not sit together. As in most parliaments, the European Parliament's physical, left-to-right seating arrangement reflects the left-to-right ideology of the MEPs. In the 1999–2004 Parliament, the left flank was occupied by the radical left (communist, former communist, extreme left parties and the Nordic Green Left parties). Continuing left to right, the next was the Party of the European Socialists, the Greens and allies (e.g. regional parties from Spain), the European Liberal Democrat and Reformists group, and the European People's Party. On the far right flank were the Eurosceptic Gaullists and other rightist groups. Details on the size and national composition of the European Parliament can be found on www.europarl.eu.int. These party groups have their own internal structure, including Chairs, secretariats, staffs, and 'whips' who keep track of attendance and voting behaviour. The political groups receive budgets from the Parliament.

Statistical analysis of MEPs' voting patterns shows that they vote more along party lines than they do along country lines. Indeed, cohesion within European political groupings is comparable to that in the US Congress, while cohesion of country delegations is significantly lower and is declining, as Noury and Roland (2002) show.

Location

The Parliament is not located in Brussels, the centre of EU decision making, but rather in Strasbourg (Fig. 2.11) owing to France's dogged insistence (the Parliament's predecessor in the European Coal and Steel Community, the Common Assembly, was located in Strasbourg since it was near to the heart of the coal and steel sectors). Equally determined insistence by Luxembourg has kept the Parliament's secretariat in Luxembourg. Since Brussels is where most of the political action occurs, and is also the location of most of the institutions that the Parliament is supposed to supervise, the Parliament also has offices in Brussels (this is where the various Parliamentary committees meet).

The staffs of the Parliament's political groups work in Brussels. It is not clear how much this geographic dispersion hinders the Parliament's effectiveness, but the time and money wasted on shipping documents and people among three locations occasionally produces negative media attention. This shifting location may also help to account for the fact that many MEPs do not attend all sessions. In the third Parliament, an average of 17.6 per cent of the MEPs were absent and 35.5 per cent were physically present but did not vote; this improved in the fourth Parliament, where the respective figures were 16.8 per cent and 21.6 per cent (Noury and Roland, 2002).

Democratic control

The Parliament and the Council are the primary democratic controls over the EU's activities. The MEPs are directly elected by EU citizens, so European Parliamentary elections are – in principle

Figure 2.11 **The European Parliament's building in Strasbourg (it also has buildings in Brussels and Luxembourg)**
Source: wikimedia.org

– a way for Europeans to have their voices heard on European issues. In practice, however, European Parliamentary elections are often dominated by standard left-versus-right issues rather than by EU issues. Indeed, European Parliamentary elections are sometimes influenced by pure national concerns, with the voters using the elections as a way of expressing disapproval or approval of the ruling national government's performance. Moreover, in many Member States, participation in European Parliamentary elections tends to be fairly modest. By contrast, the elections by which national governments are chosen have very high levels of popular participation.

2.4.5 European Court of Justice

In the EU, as in every other organization in the world, laws and decisions are open to interpretation and this frequently leads to disputes that cannot be settled by negotiation. The role of the European Court of Justice (ECJ, or sometimes known as the 'EU Court' or EC Court) is to settle these disputes, especially disputes between Member States, between the EU and Member States, between EU institutions, and between individuals and the EU. As discussed above, the EU Court is the highest authority on the application of EU law.

As a result of this power, the Court has had a major impact on European integration. For example, its ruling in the 1970s on non-tariff barriers triggered a sequence of events that eventually led to the Single European Act (see Chapter 4 for details). The Court has also been important in defining the relations between the Member States and the EU, and in the legal protection of individuals (EU citizens can take cases directly to the EU Court without going through their governments).

Figure 2.12 Headquarters of the European Court of Justice in Luxembourg
Source: European Commission

The European Court of Justice, which is located in Luxembourg (Fig. 2.12), consists of one judge from each Member State. Judges are appointed by common accord of the Member States' governments and serve for six years. The Court also has eight 'advocates-general' whose job is to help the judges by constructing 'reasoned submissions' that suggest what conclusions the judges might make. The Court reaches its decisions by majority voting. The Court of First Instance was set up in the late 1980s to help the EU Court with its ever-growing workload.

2.5 Legislative processes

The European Commission has a near monopoly on initiating the EU decision-making process. It is in charge of writing proposed legislation, although it naturally consults widely when doing so. The Commission's proposal is sent to the Council for approval. Most EU legislation also requires the European Parliament's approval, although the exact procedure depends upon the issue concerned. (The Treaties specify which procedure must be used in which areas.)

The main procedure, called the codecision procedure, gives the Parliament equal standing with the Council. This procedure is used for about 80 per cent of EU legislation, including that dealing with the free movement of workers, creation of the single market, research and technological development, the environment, consumer protection, education, culture and public health.

The codecision procedure is highly complex but, simplifying for clarity's sake, it starts with a proposal from the Commission and then goes through two readings by the Council and the Parliament. Passing the act requires a 'yes' vote from the Council and Parliament. The Council decides by qualified majority, while the Parliament decides by a simple majority. If the Council and Parliament disagree after the second reading, a conciliation procedure is started. If this does not produce agreement, the act is dropped. For details, see Box 2.8.

Box 2.8   The codecision procedure in detail

The procedure starts with a Commission proposal. The Parliament then gives its 'opinion', i.e. evaluates the proposal and suggests desired amendments, by simple majority. After seeing the Parliament's opinion, the Council adopts a 'common position' by a qualified majority, except in the fields of culture, freedom of movement, social security and coordination of the rules for carrying on a profession, which are subject to a unanimous vote. The Parliament then receives the Council's common position and has three months in which to take a decision. If the Parliament expressly approves it, or takes no action by the deadline, the Act is adopted immediately. If an absolute majority of Parliament's Members rejects the common position, the process stops, and the Act is not adopted. If a majority of MEPs adopts amendments to the common position, these are first put to the Commission for its opinion and then returned to the Council. The Council votes by a qualified majority on Parliament's amendments, although it takes a unanimous vote to accept amendments that have been given a negative opinion by the Commission. The Act is adopted if the Council approves all Parliament's amendments no later than three months after receiving them. Otherwise the Conciliation Committee is convened within six weeks.

The Conciliation Committee consists of an equal number of Council and Parliament representatives, assisted by the Commission. It considers the common position on the basis of Parliament's amendments and has six weeks to draft a joint text. The procedure stops and the Act is not adopted unless the Committee approves the joint text by the deadline. If it does so, the joint text goes back to the Council and Parliament for approval. The Council and Parliament have six weeks to approve it. The Council acts by a qualified majority and the Parliament by an absolute majority of the votes cast. The Act is adopted if Council and Parliament approve the joint text. If either of the institutions has not approved it by the deadline, the procedure stops and the Act is not adopted.

The other common legislative procedures include:

★ The consultation procedure. This is used for a few issues – e.g. the Common Agricultural Policy's periodic price-fixing agreements – where the Member States wish to keep tight control over politically sensitive decisions. Under this procedure, the Parliament must give its opinion before the Council adopts a Commission proposal. Such opinions, when they have any influence, are intended to influence the Council, or the shape of the Commission's proposal.

★ The assent procedure is another procedure in which the Parliament plays a subsidiary role. For example, on decisions concerning enlargement, international agreements, sanctioning Member States and the coordination of the Structural Funds, the Parliament can veto, but cannot amend, a proposal made by the Commission and adopted by the Council.

★ The cooperation procedure is a historical hangover from the Parliament's gradual increase in power. Specifically, before the codecision procedure was introduced in the Maastricht Treaty, the cooperation procedure was the one that granted the most power to the Parliament. It is best thought of as a codecision procedure, in which the Parliament's power to amend the proposal is less explicit. Also, the Council can overrule an EP rejection by voting unanimously.

2.5.1 Enhanced cooperation

The tension between the 'vanguard' members, who wish to broaden the scope of EU activities, and the 'doubters', who do not, led to the introduction of a new type of integration process called 'closer cooperation' in the Amsterdam Treaty and renamed 'enhanced cooperation' in the Nice Treaty. This allows subgroups of EU members to cooperate on specific areas while still keeping the cooperation under the general framework of the EU.

Subgroups of Member States have long engaged in closer intergovernmental cooperation. What the Amsterdam Treaty did by creating 'closer cooperation' was to allow such subgroups to proceed while at the same time keeping them under some form of EU discipline and coordination.

However, the conditions for starting new closer cooperations were so strict that no new closer cooperation was established under the Amsterdam rules. The Nice Treaty made it easier to start such subgroups and relabelled them as 'enhanced cooperation' arrangements (ECAs). Although this form of integration has not yet been used, the increased diversity of members and difficulty of decision making that came with the 2004 and 2007 enlargements may make it more important in coming years. The point is that the diversity of members' preferences for integration will become even more diverse, so subsets of members may well find that starting an ECA is the only way to get things done. See Baldwin et al. (2001) for an analysis of this possibility. The first 'enhanced cooperation' may concern divorce law (Box 2.9).

Box 2.9 Divorce and the first enhanced cooperation

Divorce is never an easy thing, but it can get nightmarishly complicated with a mixed nationality couple with children. Even within the EU, divorce laws vary widely – from the no-fault, automatic policy of secular Sweden to devotedly Catholic Malta's lack of recognition of divorce – and it is not always clear which laws should apply.

The EU tried to simplify things and avoid spouses engaging in a trying and costly search for the 'best' set of divorce laws by agreeing a regulation (known as Rome III) that would have specified which laws apply. The absolute refusal of Sweden and Malta to agree to the regulation (which must be agreed unanimously since such legal cooperation is a third-pillar issue) induced a subset of nations to proceed by requesting an enhanced cooperation on the matter. The group included Austria, France, Greece, Hungary, Italy, Luxembourg, Romania, Slovenia and Spain from the beginning; Germany, Belgium, Portugal and Lithuania are considering joining the initiative.

There are potentially serious risks involved in integration led by such clubs-within-the-club schemes. For instance, we may see calls for an ECA with respect to tighter police and intelligence cooperation, especially with respect to terrorism and organized crime. Given the uneven quality of governments in the new Member States, the ECA may seek to exclude nations whose intelligence services are not up to standard. This, of course, would be devisive. By allowing a separation of members into groups, it risks fragmenting the EU politically. Moreover, ECAs could result in an erosion of existing integration, and in so far as ECAs create diversity in integration, they might erode the consistency of European economic and social integration.

Another example can be found in the meeting of finance ministers of the Eurozone nations. Just before the standard Council of Ministers meeting for finance ministers (ECOFIN), the

Eurozone nations gather to discuss issues. Since these 12 constitute a substantial majority in terms of voting power, the non-Eurozone nations can sometimes feel that decisions have been sewn-up in advance by the Eurozone-12.

To guard against these twin risks, the Nice Treaty gives the Commission a central role in the decision to create and enlarge any enhanced cooperation. Specifically, the Commission can veto ECAs covering deeper economic integration (i.e. first-pillar areas) and it controls subsequent membership enlargements of these. In other areas, the Commission has a strong voice in the process of setting up and expanding ECAs, but less so in the Security and Foreign Policy area (second pillar) than in Justice and Home Affairs areas (third pillar). It can also be the administrator of such groups.

2.6 Some important facts

EU nations are very different, one from another. This simple fact is the source of a large share of the EU's problems, so it is important to understand it in detail. This section covers the facts on populations, incomes and economic size.

2.6.1 Populations and incomes

There are about 497 million EU citizens, a figure that is substantially larger than the corresponding US and Japanese figures (305 and 130 million, respectively).

The EU27 nations and the 'candidate countries' (Croatia, the Former Yugoslav Republic of Macedonia and Turkey) vary enormously in terms of populations, as the upper panel of Fig. 2.13 shows. The differences are easier to remember when the nations are grouped into big, medium, small and tiny – where these categories are established by comparison with the population of well-known cities.

★ The 'big' nations are defined here as having 35 million people or more – clearly more people than even the largest city in the world (Mexico City's population is about 20 million). In the EU27 there are six of these – Germany, the UK, France, Italy, Spain and Poland. Germany is substantially larger than the others, more than twice the size of the smallest in the group. The total population of the 'Big-6' accounts for about three-quarters of the 497 million people in the EU27 nations. Turkey, with whom the EU started membership negotiations in October 2005, has over 70 million inhabitants. This exceeds the population of all EU nations except Germany and, given the projected decline in German population and rapid population growth in Turkey, the ordering is likely to be reversed within ten years.

★ The 'medium' nations are defined as having populations of between 8 and 11 million, something like that of a really big city, say Paris with its surroundings. There are eight medium nations in the EU27 (Greece, Portugal, Belgium, the Czech Republic, Hungary, Sweden, Austria and Bulgaria).

★ The 'small' nations have populations along the lines of a big city, ranging from Barcelona (4 million) to Lyons (1.4 million). These are Denmark, Slovakia, Finland, Ireland, Lithuania, Latvia, Slovenia and Estonia.

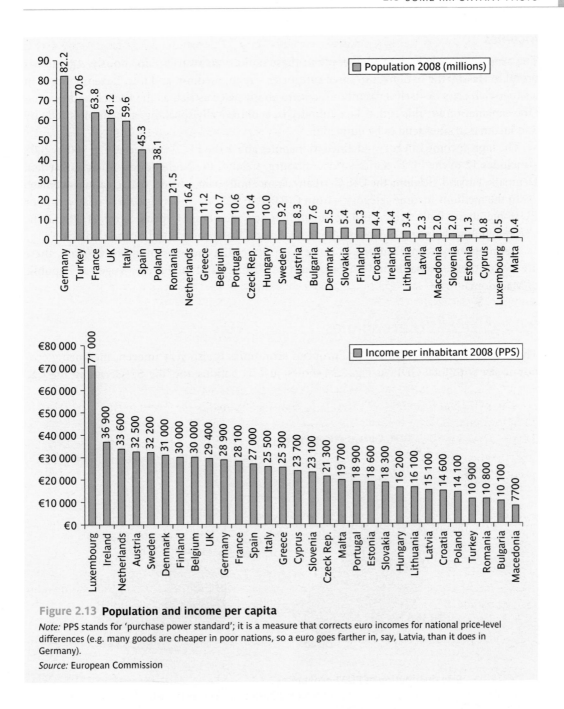

Figure 2.13 Population and income per capita

Note: PPS stands for 'purchase power standard'; it is a measure that corrects euro incomes for national price-level differences (e.g. many goods are cheaper in poor nations, so a euro goes farther in, say, Latvia, than it does in Germany).

Source: European Commission

★ The 'tiny' nations have populations that are smaller than those of a small city like Genoa. The list is Cyprus, Luxembourg and Malta.

★ The only nations that fall between these categories are the Netherlands, with its 16 million people, and Romania, with its 21.8 million.

Incomes

The average income level of the people in these nations also varies enormously. Again, it is useful to classify the nations into three categories – high, medium and low. Luxembourg is in a super-rich class by itself; Luxembourgers are about twice as rich as the French and Swedes. One explanation for this is that Luxembourg is, economically speaking, a medium-sized city and incomes in cities tend to be quite high.

The high-income category – defined as incomes above the EU27 average of €25 900 in 2008 – includes 12 of the EU27 nations (Luxembourg, Ireland, the Netherlands, Austria, Sweden, Denmark, Finland, Belgium, the UK, Germany, France and Spain, in order of decreasing incomes).

In the medium-income category – from €10 000 to €25 500 – there are three relatively poor EU15 members (Italy, Greece and Portugal), ten new members (Cyprus, Slovenia, Malta, the Czech Republic, Hungary, Slovakia, Lithuania, Poland, Latvia and Estonia) and Croatia.

Defining low-income nations as those with per capita incomes of about €10 000, there are two of them: Romania and Bulgaria, and also Turkey and the Former Yugoslav Republic of Macedonia.

2.6.2 Size of EU economies

The economic size distribution of European economies is also very uneven, measuring economic size with total GDP. As Fig. 2.14 shows, just six nations, the 'Big-5' (Germany, the UK,

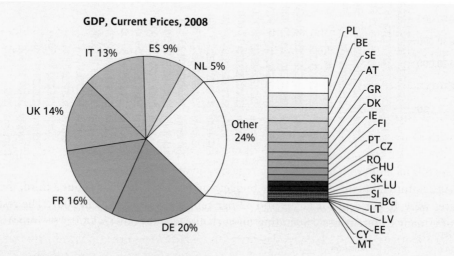

Figure 2.14 Size distribution of EU27 economies

Note: Data for 2008 not adjusted for national cost of living differences since we are interested in the relative size of economies rather than individual income levels.

Abbreviations: 'Big nations': Germany (DE), the UK (uk), France (FR), Italy (IT), and Spain (ES) and the Netherlands (NL). 'Small nations' (1 to 3 per cent of total EU27 GDP): Sweden (SE), Belgium (BE), Austria (AT), Denmark (DK), Poland (PL), Finland (FI), Greece (GR), Portugal (PT) and Ireland (IE). 'Tiny nations' (1 to 0.1 per cent): Czech Republic (CZ), Hungary (HU), Slovak Republic (SK), Luxembourg (LU), Slovenia (SI), Lithuania (LT) and Cyprus (CY). 'Miniscule nations' (less than one-tenth of 1 per cent): Latvia (LV), Estonia (EE) and Malta (MT).

Source: http://epp.eurostat.ec.europa.eu © European Commissions, 1995–2009

France, Italy and Spain) and the Netherlands, account for more than 80 per cent of the GDP of the whole EU27. The other nations are small, tiny or minuscule, using the following definitions:

★ 'Small' is an economy that accounts for between 1 and 3 per cent of the EU27's output. These are Sweden, Belgium, Austria, Denmark, Poland, Finland, Greece, Portugal, Ireland and Romania.

★ 'Tiny' is one that accounts for less than 1 per cent of the total. These are the Czech Republic, Hungary, the Slovak Republic, Luxembourg, Slovenia, Lithuania, Bulgaria and Cyprus.

★ Minuscule is one that accounts for less than one-tenth of 1 per cent; Latvia, Estonia and Malta are the nations in this category.

Figure 2.14 also shows that the 2004 enlargement had very little impact on the overall size of the EU economy; the ten newcomers' economies amount to only about 5 per cent of the EU15's GDP, with Poland alone accounting for about half of this 5 per cent.

2.7 The budget

The EU budget is the source of a great deal of both solidarity and tension among EU members, so a full understanding of the EU requires some knowledge of the budget. This section looks at the following questions in order. What is the money spent on? Where does it come from? Who gets the most on net? How does the budget process work?

2.7.1 Expenditure

Total EU spending is now about €100 billion (€114 billion in 2007). While this sounds like a lot to most people, it is really fairly small – only about 1 per cent of total EU27 GDP – just €230 per EU citizen. The first priority here is to study how this money is spent. We look first at spending by area and then spending by EU member.

Expenditure by area

As with so many things in Europe, understanding EU spending in all its detail would take a lifetime, but understanding the basics takes just a few minutes. Starting at the broadest level, the EU spends its money on farming, poor regions and other things.

Agriculture takes up about half the budget and poor regions take about a third; the precise figures were 48 per cent for farms and 32 per cent for poor regions in 2007. The rest is split among many different uses. Spending on agriculture and poor regions is so important that we have written separate chapters dealing with each, so we do not go into further detail here (see Chapter 12 on agriculture and Chapter 13 on poor regions). Figure 2.15 shows spending priorities graphically for the year 2007.

At a slightly finer level of analysis, we break the 'other things' category into four areas:

1 Internal policies (7 per cent of budget). This refers to policies where the money is spent inside the EU but not on agriculture and poor regions. This category is very diverse and includes spending on research and development (R&D), spending on trans-European transport, energy and telecommunications networks, spending on training and student mobility, the environment, culture, information and communication, etc.

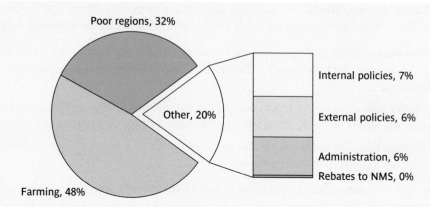

Figure 2.15 **The EU's 2007 budget: Spending**

Note: Since the EU's new long-term budget plan (called a Financial Perspective in EU jargon) for the 2007–13 period started, the main budget areas have been given new-century names that make them sound more forward looking, although the actual policies have changed little. The new names are: 'Preservation and management of natural resources' (farming and fishing), 'Cohesion for growth and employment' (poor regions). The various other internal policies are called 'Competitiveness for growth and employment' and 'Citizenship, freedom, security and justice', while the various external policies are called 'The EU as a global partner'.

Source: General budget of the EU for the financial year 2005

2   External policies (6 per cent of budget). This money is spent mainly on humanitarian aid, food aid and development assistance in non-member countries throughout the world. Small amounts are also spent on the Middle East peace process, the reconstruction of Kosovo, the European initiative for democracy and human rights worldwide, international fisheries agreements, and the Common Foreign and Security Policy.

3   Administration (6 per cent of budget). This concerns the cost of running the European Commission, the European Court of Justice, and all other European institutions. Taken together, they employ surprisingly few people (about 30 000).

4   Rebates to new Member States (NMS). This money goes to the newcomers to ensure that they are not net contributors in their first years of membership. It is spent on things like modernizing agriculture, establishing transport and environmental structures, and improving government administrations.

Historical development of EU spending by area

The EU's spending priorities and the level of spending have changed dramatically since its inception in 1958. This is shown graphically in Fig. 2.16.

As the top panel shows, the budget grew rapidly, but started at a very low level (just 8/100ths of 1 per cent of the EEC6's GDP). EU spending was negligible until the late 1960s, amounting to less than €10 per EU citizen. This changed as the cost of the Common Agricultural Policy (CAP) started to rise rapidly in the 1960s and Cohesion spending started to rise in the 1980s. From the early 1970s to the early 1990s, the budget grew steadily as a fraction of EU GDP,

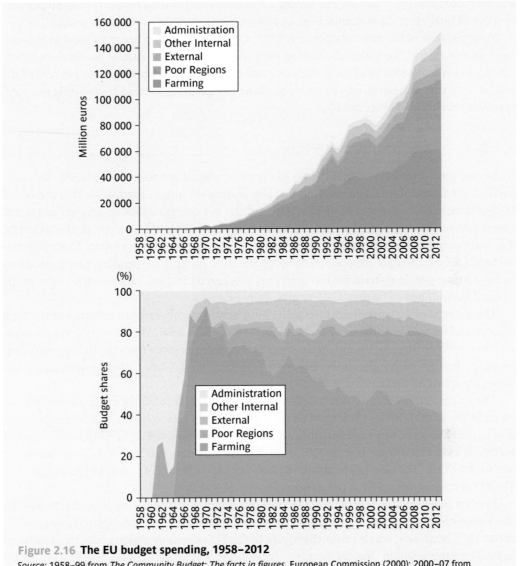

Figure 2.16 The EU budget spending, 1958–2012

Source: 1958–99 from *The Community Budget: The facts in figures*, European Commission (2000); 2000–07 from *EU Budget 2007 – Financial Report*, European Commission (2008); you can download these figures in an Excel spreadsheet format from DG Budget's website http://ec.europa.eu/budget/; 2008–13 from most recent adjustment to the Financial Perspective for 2007–13, COM(2008) 152 final, 14 March 2008

starting from about 8/10ths of 1 per cent and rising to 1.2 per cent in 1993. Since the 1994 enlargement, the budget as a share of GDP has remained quite stable at about 1 per cent.

The bottom panel of the figure depicts the spending by area in shares to illustrate how the EU's budget priorities have changed over the past half century. Until 1965, the budget – tiny as it was – was spent mainly on administration (this was the period when all the European institutions were set up and the customs union was being implemented). CAP spending began in 1965 and soon dominated the budget. For almost a decade, farm spending regularly took 80 per cent or more of total expenditures; at its peak in 1970, it made up 92 per cent of the budget!

From the date of the first enlargement, 1973, Cohesion spending began to grow in importance, pushing down Agriculture's share in the process. Indeed, the sum of the shares of these two big-ticket items has remained remarkably steady, ranging between 80 and 85 per cent of the budget. In a very real sense, we can think of Cohesion spending as steadily crowding out CAP spending over the past three decades.

2.7.2 Expenditure by member

By far the most important benefit from EU membership is economic integration. By comparison, the financial transfers involved in EU spending are minor. Remember that the whole budget is only about 1 per cent of EU GDP and the net contributions (payments to the EU minus payments from the EU) are never greater than a one-tenth of 1 per cent. Be this as it may, it is interesting to see which members receive the largest shares of EU spending. Many disputes in the EU are over budget allocations, although the basic outlines of spending have been set up to 2013 in the new long-term budget plan that was agreed in 2005 (after a bitter fight at the Council summit hosted by then UK Premier, Tony Blair).

The amount of EU spending varies quite a lot across members, both in terms of the total amount and its nature, as the top panel of Fig. 2.17 shows. In 2007, France was the number one recipient, with Spain close behind. Most of the French receipts come from the EU's spending on farming (the Common Agricultural Policy, or CAP for short), while Cohesion spending is the more important for Spain.

The figures, however, are entirely different when we look at receipts per capita (see bottom panel of the figure). By far the largest receiver per capita is Luxembourg (€2650 per person); this sounds like a lot, but since incomes are so high in the Grand Duchy, about twice the EU average at over €70 000 per year in 2007, this EU spending does not have as large an impact as one might think. The Greeks are also very large per capita recipients, about €750 per person. The EU average is around €230 per person.

Readers may find the figures in the second panel rather strange. Why should rich nations like Luxembourg, Belgium, Denmark, Finland and France be above-average recipients of EU spending? The answer, which lies in the nature of the EU's decision-making process, is pursued in much greater depth in Chapter 3.

2.7.3 Revenue

The EU's budget must, by law, be balanced every year. All of the spending discussed above must be financed each year by revenues collected from EU members or carried over from previous years.

Up to 1970, the EEC's budget was financed by annual contributions from the members. A pair of Treaties in the 1970s and a handful of landmark decisions by the European Council established the system we have today in which there are four main sources of revenue. (See Box 2.10 for further details.) According to the EU Treaties, the Union is legally entitled to this revenue, so it is known as 'own resources' in EU jargon.

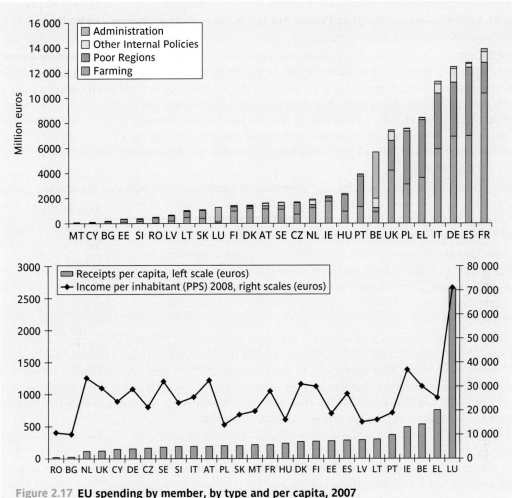

Figure 2.17 **EU spending by member, by type and per capita, 2007**
Source: Financial Report, 2007, European Commission, http://ec.europa.eu/budget/index_en.htm

Box 2.10   **Milestones in the EU budget procedure**

1958–70. The EU's budget was financed by contributions from its members.

April 1970. The Luxembourg European Council. The 'own resources' system is introduced. These included customs duties, agricultural levies (i.e. variable tariffs) and a share of VAT revenue collected by EU members. The Treaty of July 1975 refined and reinforced the system, establishing the European Court of Auditors to oversee the budget and giving the European Parliament the formal right of rejection over annual budgets.

1975–1987. This period was marked by sharp disputes over the budget contributions and ever-expanding CAP spending. The UK's Margaret Thatcher in particular complained repeatedly about the UK's position as the largest net contributor.

▶ *1984*. The Fontainebleau European Council. The VAT-based revenue source was increased and the UK was awarded its famous 'rebate'.

1988. Delors I package. This reform established the basis of the current revenue and spending system. It introduced a fourth 'own resource' based on members' GNPs, established an overall ceiling on EU revenue as a percentage of the EU's GNP, and started reducing the role of VAT-based revenue. The package, decided at the Brussels European Council in June, also established the EU's multi-year budgeting process whereby a Financial Perspective sets out the evolution of EU spending by broad categories. Substantively, the Financial Perspective adopted provided for a major reorientation of EU spending from the CAP to Cohesion spending; Cohesion spending was doubled and CAP spending growth was capped.

1992. Delors II package. The Edinburgh agreement of December 1992 increased the revenue ceiling slightly to 1.27 per cent, and further reduced the role of VAT-based revenue. It also adopted a new Financial Perspective for 1993–99, which amplified the shift of EU spending priorities away from the CAP and towards Cohesion.

1999. Agenda 2000 package. The Berlin European Council adopted the 2000–06 Financial Perspective. There were no major changes on the revenue side and the only major change on the spending side was the creation of a new broad category, 'Pre-accession' expenditures, meant to finance programmes in central and eastern European nations and provide a reserve to cover the cost of any enlargements in this period.

2005. After a failure to reach agreement at their June 2005 Summit, the issue of setting the seven-year Financial Perspective for the 2007–2013 period fell to the UK Presidency. The basic idea was to move spending slowly away from agriculture, to make the spending on poor regions more coherent and concentrated, and increase spending on competitiveness measures such as R&D. The 2004 and 2007 enlargements, however, added 12 new members with below-average incomes and many farmers, so large changes in budget priorities proved politically impossible.

There are four main types of these own resources and Fig. 2.18 shows how their relative importance has varied over the years. Two of the four have long been used, and indeed in the early days of the Union they were sufficient to finance all payments. These so-called 'traditional own resources' are:

★ Tariff revenue stemming from the common external tariff (CET). Although trade within the EU is tariff free, tariffs are imposed on imports from non-member nations. This money accrues to the EU rather than to any particular member.

★ 'Agricultural levies' are tariffs on agricultural goods that are imported from non-members. Conceptually, these are the same as the previous category (they are both taxes on imports from third nations), but are viewed as distinct since the levies are not formally part of the CET. Historically, the level of these tariffs has fluctuated widely according to market conditions (they were part of the CAP's price support mechanism; see Chapter 12).

The importance of these two revenue items has fallen over the years to the point where they are no longer major items (together, they make up only one-seventh of the revenue needs). This reduced importance stems from the way that the level of the CET has been steadily lowered in the course of World Trade Organization (WTO) rounds (e.g. the 1986–94 Uruguay Round). Moreover, EU enlargement and the signing of free trade agreements with non-members means

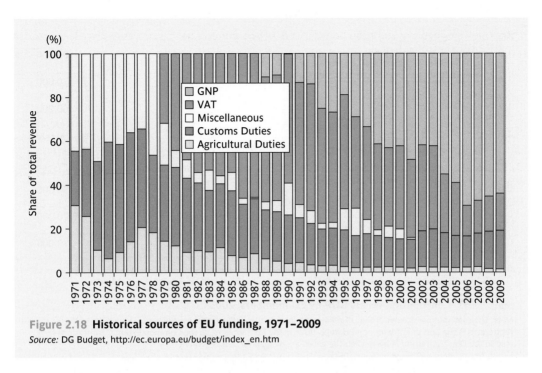

Figure 2.18 Historical sources of EU funding, 1971–2009
Source: DG Budget, http://ec.europa.eu/budget/index_en.htm

that a very large fraction of EU imports from non-members is duty free. The level of the agricultural levies has also been reduced in the context of CAP reform. The third and fourth types of 'own resources' provide most of the money. They are:

★ 'VAT resource'. As is often the case when it comes to tax matters, the reality is quite complex, but it is best thought of as a 1 per cent value added tax. The importance of this resource has declined and is set to decline further.

★ GNP based. This revenue is a tax based on the GNP of EU members. It is used to top up any revenue shortfall and thus ensures that the EU never runs a deficit.

The other revenue sources – labelled 'miscellaneous' in the diagram – have been relatively unimportant since 1977. Now, they include items such as taxes paid by employees of European institutions (they do not pay national taxes), fines, and surpluses carried over from previous years. Until the 1970s budget treaties came fully into effect, 'miscellaneous' revenue included direct member contributions, which were a crucial source of funding in the early years.

Budget contribution by member

On the contribution side, EU funding amounts to basically 1 per cent of each member's GDP. Some observers find this anomalous since taxation in most nations, especially in Europe, is progressive, i.e. the tax rate that an individual pays rises with his or her income level.

The precise figures are shown in Fig. 2.19. Here we see that the contributions as a share of GDP do not vary much from the median figure of 0.9 per cent. The highest figure in 2003 was 1.3 per cent for Greece. The lowest figure was the UK's 0.7 per cent due to the UK rebate; see Box 2.11 for details on the rebate. The precise contribution rate varies from year to year by Member State due to the complexities of the system.

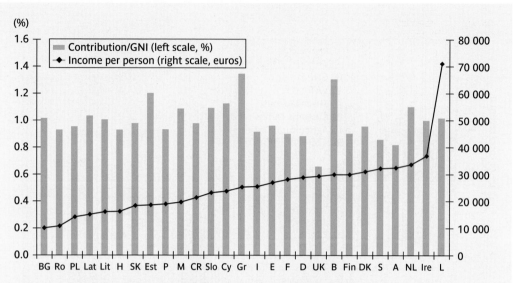

Figure 2.19 Contribution versus GDP by EU members, 2003

Note: The contributions are net of the UK rebate and include the Netherlands' usually large payment of tariffs (Rotterdam is the port of entry for non-EU imports for many EU members, so the Common External Tariff is often paid to the Dutch government even when the goods are headed for, e.g., Germany).

Source: Financial Report, 2007, European Commission, http://ec.europa.eu/budget/index_en.htm

For comparison, the nations are ordered by increasing income (the line in the figure shows the national GDP per capita). The figure makes it clear that the EU's 'tax' system is not progressive like that of most of its members. In other words, nations that have higher incomes do not pay a higher proportion of their income. The 'tax rate' is approximately 1 per cent for all members, ranging from the Bulgarians with their average income of €10 000 per year and the Luxembourgers with their €70 000 per year.

2.7.4 Net contribution by member

Putting together the receipts by member and the contributions by member allows us to show the net financial contributions in Fig. 2.20. Ten of the EU27 were net contributors in 2007 (i.e. they pay more to the budget than they receive from it). Germany is by far the largest net contributor. Other net contributors are the UK, the Netherlands, France, Sweden, Austria, Italy, Denmark, Finland and Austria. The net recipients, those with negative net contributions, are led by Greece, Poland, Spain and Portugal, followed by Belgium, Luxembourg, Ireland, the Baltic states and the other new members.

Note that the net transfers are much smaller than the overall budget. In other words, most of the EU budget can be thought of as staying inside each nation. France paid €17 billion to the budget and received €14 billion in 2007, so we can think of the French government as spending €14 billion on EU programmes that directly benefit its own citizens, with Brussels getting only €3 billion on net from Paris.

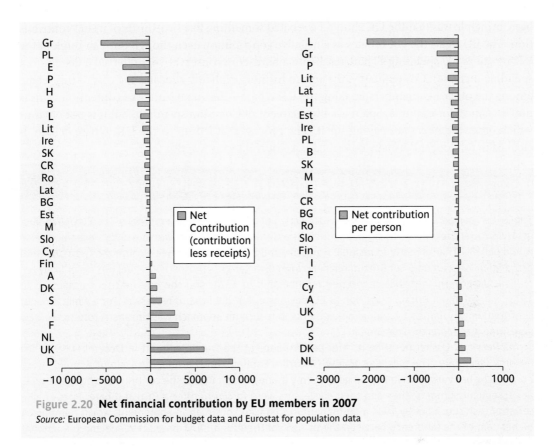

Figure 2.20 Net financial contribution by EU members in 2007
Source: European Commission for budget data and Eurostat for population data

The UK rebate

The basics of the EU spending and contributions were set in 1970, prior to the UK's entry. When the UK joined in 1973 it faced a situation in which it funded a disproportionate share of the EU budget while receiving a less than proportionate share of EU spending. The UK's agricultural situation was the cause of both imbalances. The British agricultural sector was a relatively small share of its economy compared to other members, so the UK got little of the EU's spending on agriculture (this accounted for three-quarters of the budget at the time). The UK also imported a larger share of its food from non-member nations. Since the import taxes charged on such imports are turned over to the EU budget, the UK faced a situation where it was a large net contributor to the budget.

According to some, the 1970 funding system was intentionally aimed at disfavouring the UK once it entered (the UK's application was first put in 1961 and renewed in 1967). For example, Peet and Ussher (1999) state: 'To an extent the original Own Resources Decision, adopted before Britain joined, was deliberately skewed to Britain's disadvantage.' The budgetary imbalance worsened as CAP spending continued to rise and when a new source of EU funding was added in 1979 – the levy on value added tax (VAT) income.

After years of dispute and complaints from the UK over this imbalance, EU leaders decided at their June 1984 meeting in Fontainebleau to give the UK back part of its contribution. The basic principle was that the UK should be rebated something like two-thirds of its net contribution. The EU treats the UK rebates as a negative contribution even though one can think of the UK rebate as EU spending (Thatcher, being a hard-core conservative, preferred a tax cut to a spending increase). Consequently, the agreed formula explicitly allocates the cost of this rebate among the other EU members, making the UK rebate a continual source of contention. This is unusual since, for example, Spain is a big recipient of Cohesion spending, but it is not obvious which other members are paying for it. The process that led up to the UK 'rebate debate' is cloaked in folklore and usually described in colourful terms; see Box 2.11.

Box 2.11   Lady Thatcher's 'handbagging' and the UK rebate

The British perspective on the budget is succinctly put by Peet and Ussher (1999): 'The European budgetary picture after 1973 was simple enough: the Germans and British would pay, but everybody else would benefit. Thanks partly to residual war-guilt, and also to their relative wealth, the Germans were prepared to live with this. But Britain, relatively low down Europe's prosperity league, was never likely to.'

The UK government that negotiated membership in 1971, and the one that renegotiated it in 1973, worried about Britain's position as EU paymaster but did little to redress it. For a while, the net contribution was limited by annual adjustments, but such an approach was unsatisfactory to the new government of Margaret Thatcher.

As Peet and Ussher describe it, 'Her performance at the Dublin summit in December 1979 has become legendary. The patrician Valéry Giscard d'Estaing and the haughty Helmut Schmidt were horrified by her vulgar insistence on getting "my money back". But as she continued to bang the table at subsequent summits, they and their successors were forced to offer a British rebate. First of all a series of cash sums, but by 1984 a permanent mechanism known as an abatement, which reimbursed 66 per cent of the difference between the British contribution to VAT-based revenue and the amount of EU expenditure in the UK.'

Newspapers described the event in more flamboyant terms, asserting that the rebate was won through Thatcher's handbag diplomacy. 'The former British prime minister, now Lady Thatcher, is remembered for slamming her handbag on the table and yelling at the other leaders, "I want my money!"' (*International Herald Tribune* article by Barry James, 8 October 1998).

The exact procedure for calculating the rebate is complex and results in a fairly wide fluctuation in the UK's net contribution.

There was little change in the rebate for the current 2007–2013 Financial Perspective, but the UK has signalled that it is willing to consider modifying it as part of a thorough budget review in 2008/2009. The entry of many low-income members has made the argument that the UK was paying too much given its modest income level untenable.

2.7.5 Budget process

The EU's annual budget is guided primarily by a medium-term agreement on spending priorities, called 'Financial Perspectives' as mentioned above. The current Financial Perspective sets out broad spending guidelines for the annual budgets from 2007 to 2013 (you can download this from http://ec.europa.eu/budget/index_en.htm). Since the Financial Perspective is adopted by all the institutions involved in budgeting (the Commission, the European Parliament and the Council), its existence reduces dispute over each annual budget.

The procedure for drawing up the annual budget (as laid down in the Treaties) calls for the Commission to prepare a preliminary draft budget. The Commission's draft is presented to the Council for amendments and adoption. Once it has passed the Council, the budget goes to the European Parliament which has some power to amend the budget. According to the Treaties, the Parliament cannot touch so-called 'compulsory' expenditures (basically agriculture spending), which accounts for about 40 per cent of the budget, but it can amend the rest. After two readings in the Council and the Parliament, it is the European Parliament which adopts the final budget, and its President who signs it. This formal procedure has been augmented by inter-institutional arrangements between the Parliament, the Council and the Commission that are meant to improve cooperation. For more information, see http://ec.europa.eu/budget/index_en.htm.

2.8 The Lisbon Treaty

The Lisbon Treaty (negotiated under the name 'Reform Treaty') was signed by EU leaders in Lisbon on 13 December 2007. The Treaty takes effect only if it is ratified by all EU members. Irish voters rejected it in mid-2008 (see Chapter 1), so it seems unlikely that the Treaty will take effect before 2010.

This section reviews the main changes implied by the Lisbon Treaty. Such changes are important even if the Treaty is abandoned. First, many changes can be implemented even without a new Treaty; these may be put into place in coming years if the Treaty is long delayed. Second, since some changes are necessary but can only be implemented by a new treaty, EU leaders will find a way to replace the Lisbon Treaty if it is abandoned as the Constitutional Treaty was.

Box 2.12 Plus ça change, plus c'est la même chose

The EU institutional reform process which began in the mid-1990s (see Chapter 1) has stagnated. Here is the first paragraph of this section from the second edition of our textbook (published in 2006):

'The Constitutional Treaty, formally the Treaty establishing a Constitution for Europe, was signed by EU leaders in Rome on 29 October 2004. The Constitution takes effect only if it is ratified by all EU members. French and Dutch voters rejected it in mid 2005 (see Chapter 1), so it seems unlikely that the Treaty will take effect in coming years, if ever.'

The 2008 'no'; *Source:* Flickr

The 2005 'no'; *Source:* Flickr

2.8.1 Basic constraints and the 'virtual' constitution

The Lisbon Treaty is an awkward document – 350 pages of legalese. It reads like clues to a crossword puzzle, because that is exactly what it is. The Lisbon Treaty contains amendments and additions to the two EU founding treaties – the Treaty of Rome (formally, the Treaty establishing the European Community, or TEC for short) and the Maastricht Treaty (officially known as the Treaty on European Union, or TEU). The first 145 pages of the Lisbon Treaty present amendments to the TEC and TEU; the last 150 list protocols to be added (protocols and treaty text have exactly the same legal value). As part of this, the official name of the Treaty of Rome changes to Treaty on the Functioning of the European Union, which we refer to here as the TFEU.

The Treaty is also extremely complex. It is probably fair to say that most law professors, even those specializing in European law, do not really understand the Treaty as a whole, nor its full implications for Europe. The UK House of Lords held an extensive inquiry into the Treaty's impact, receiving testimony from dozens of EU legal, political and organization experts. Its 300-page report points out numerous important areas where experts disagree on what would be the Treaty's impact. Students who want to learn more about the Treaty should read House of Lords (2008) as it is both thorough and even handed, unlike most analyses which are either anti- or pro-Lisbon Treaty.

The Treaty's complexity, however unfortunate, was unavoidable. French and Dutch voters rejected the notion of a single document laying out the EU's constitutional framework. This posed a huge problem for EU leaders. They had agreed to the essential institutional reforms, such as Council voting and Commission size, in the context of a deal establishing a constitution. To some EU members, creating a constitution was an important element of the package. To avoid undoing the painfully negotiated deal, EU leaders re-created a 'virtual' constitution by amending the existing pair of foundational treaties (TEC and TEU).

On the bright side, this means that readers familiar with the rejected Constitution have an easy task. All the abandoned Constitution's articles – with the exceptions of the word 'constitution' and symbols traditionally associated with statehood (the EU flag, anthem, etc.) – are in the Treaties. All you have to do is find where the Lisbon Treaty put them (Open Europe 2008a provides for an equivalence table). Of course, there are a few additional changes, e.g. the words 'climate change' now appear, but from the perspective of European economic integration, the Lisbon Treaty and the Constitution are functionally equivalent.

Readers might wonder why EU leaders did not replace the rejected Constitution with a short, clear statement of purposes and basic institutions – something that almost all Europeans would approve. The sad answer is that legal logic makes this impossible (Box 2.13).

Box 2.13   Why the EU cannot have a 'real' constitution

Why did EU leaders not react to the French and Dutch nos by proposing a simpler document – something that reads like the French constitution or the German Basic Law?

Unfortunately, the EU cannot have a Constitution in the traditional sense of the word – i.e. a succinct statement of goals and a description of the allocation of power among decision-making institutions. The problem turns on legal logic.

Such a constitution would create a new level of European law. The existing Treaties (TEC and TEU) are the highest level of law currently, with Directives and the like forming secondary law. The new top level of law would pose a threat to legal certainty throughout the EU legal system. The problem is that one could never be sure when a judicial interpretation of ambiguities between the Constitution and other Treaties might alter existing law. As the European Convention noted at its start, a real constitution, they concluded, 'might well prove a permanent source of conflict'.

While a 'real' constitution is the easiest way to arrange the affairs of an organization like the EU, such a document would have had to have been written at the beginning. Legal logic tells us that writing a constitution is basically impossible for an organization that has been making laws for 50 years without one.

This is why the Lisbon Treaty had to be so long, so complex and so legalist. It had to include, or refer to, every existing Treaty, Protocol and Annex so as to keep all the 'primary law' at the same level. The Constitutional Treaty did this by reproducing all the TEC and TEU articles and then repealing the TEC and TEU. The Lisbon Treaty does it by amending the TEC and TEU.

2.8.2 Organization: two pillars in a single organization

The three-pillars-and-a-roof organization is replaced. The Lisbon Treaty abolishes the European Community, replacing the term 'Community' with 'Union' throughout the TEU and TFEU as amended by the Lisbon Treaty (henceforth 'the amended Treaties' for short). Some writers refer to this as the removal of the pillar structure because there is now just one organization and it has what lawyers call 'legal personality' (it can sign agreements with nations and organizations).

From the perspective of European economic integration, a deeper and more insightful way of thinking of the organizational change is as the integration of the third pillar into the first pillar. 'Justice and Home Affairs' (third-pillar) policies – with a few exceptions and wholesale opt-outs for Britain and Poland – are placed under the old first-pillar supranational institutions and practices. New laws in third-pillar areas will be made by majority voting instead of unanimity (as is currently the case for first-pillar issues and some third-pillar issues). The Commission will have a monopoly on the right of initiative (with a few exceptions). The EU Court will have jurisdiction and its rulings will be supreme to those of national courts. This new pillar includes most internal policies but also some external policies such as trade, aid and humanitarian assistance.

Second-pillar issues – foreign and external security policies – continue to be subject to the intergovernmental procedures and practices. The amended Treaties are explicit on this point:[2]

★ 'The common foreign and security policy is subject to specific rules and procedures. It shall be defined and implemented by the European Council and the Council acting unanimously . . .'

★ 'The adoption of legislative acts shall be excluded.'

★ 'The Court of Justice of the European Union shall not have jurisdiction with respect to these provisions . . .'

---

[2] Students interested in knowing more should read House of Lords (2008). For the Eurosceptic view, see Open European (2008c).

In short, the post-Lisbon Treaty EU will have a roof and two pillars – one for supranational issues and one for intergovernmental issues (foreign, military and defence policies).

2.8.3 The EU's founding principles

Much of the Lisbon Treaty presents clarifications and restatements of things that have already been agreed on and practised for years. This is true of the founding principles that are clarified by Lisbon, although there are some changes in wording, emphasis and, in the case of the Charter of Fundamental Rights of the European Union, in legal status.

The founding principles are spread around the amended Treaties. Table 2.1 shows where the various elements are found, including:

★ the goals and values of the Union;

★ fundamental rights and citizenship of the Union;

★ EU institutions, their powers and interrelationships;

★ details of EU legal instruments and the procedures for adopting them;

★ procedures for joining and quitting the EU.

As far as values go, there is no substantial change in practice. The objectives are changed somewhat. The goals of 'a highly competitive social market economy' and promotion of 'social

Table 2.1 The founding principles of the Union

Topic	Location (with Lisbon)	Article number in abandoned Constitution
Establishment of the Union	TEU 1	I-1
The values of the Union	TEU 2	I-2
The objectives of the Union	TEU 3	I-3
Fundamental freedoms and non-discrimination	TEFU 18	I-4
Relations between the Union and Member States	TEU 4	I-5
Union law	Declaration 17	I-6
Legal personality	TEU 47	I-7
The symbols of the Union	Omitted	I-8
Fundamental rights	TEU 6	I-9
Citizenship of the Union	TEU 20	I-10
Accession to the Union	TEU 49	I-58
Suspension of Union membership rights	TEU 7	I-59
Charter of Fundamental Rights of the Union	TEU 6 (UK & Polish opt-outs)	Part II
Accession to the ECHR		Declaration on Article I-9

Note: The Location column gives the Treaty with article number. The content is arranged more logically in the abandoned Constitution, so the corresponding articles are listed for reference.

justice and protection' are added, and the commitment to ensure 'competition in the internal market is not distorted' is moved from the main text to a protocol with no change in its legal value.

The Charter of Fundamental Rights of the Union was agreed in the Nice Treaty, but the Lisbon Treaty makes it binding on all members except Britain and Poland, who insisted on opt-outs. The Charter only applies to the institutions and to the Member States when they are implementing EU law. The Charter does not transfer new powers to the European Union.

The major institutional changes concern the Commission and Council but they will not take effect until 2014, or later. See Section 2.8.5.

Apart from an important change in Council voting (which comes into effect in 2014), the law-making procedures are little changed. There is, by contrast, an important expansion of the range of policy areas where the Council and Parliament are equal partners in law-making, especially in third-pillar issues.

The criteria and procedures for joining the EU are not changed in practice, although they are for the first time mentioned in the amended Treaties. Before Lisbon, they were merely listed in the 1994 Conclusions of the European Council, so they did not have the 'force of law', although of course they were taken as thus by everyone except the EU Court.

Exit procedures are introduced for the first time. However, even without the Lisbon Treaty, it is possible to leave the EU under general principles of international law (sovereign nations have the right to quit treaties). One territory, Greenland, has left the EU already, although it switched to being associated as one of the overseas countries and territories and it is a dependency of Denmark rather than a fully sovereign state.[3]

2.8.4 Competences

The amended Treaties spell out the EU's competences more clearly and more explicitly, but there is little change in substance (Table 2.2). The treaty makes it clear that Member States confer authority over policy areas to the EU (i.e. the members confer competences, not the EU itself) and the EU should only act proportionally to meet its objectives in its areas of competence. Both of these principles (conferral and proportionality) are well established in practice but it is useful to have the principle spelt out.

Lisbon names three categories of competence: exclusive competence, shared competence and supporting, coordinating or complementary competence. The first two are well established and their economic logic is discussed in Chapter 3. The third category is less well recognized, although the practice of the EU supporting and coordinating certain members' policies in certain areas is well established.

Increases in EU competences are fairly minor, limited mostly to third-pillar issues where ever-tighter integration of markets and the Europeanization of Europeans' behaviour in things

---

[3] Greenland, formerly a colony of Denmark, became part of the Danish Kingdom in 1953 and thus a member in 1973 when Denmark joined. Given Greenland's heavy dependence on North American imports and its economy's dependence on fishing, the EU's customs union and its poorly designed Common Fisheries Policy made membership irksome. Granted Home Rule by Denmark in 1979, it held a referendum in 1982 where the majority opted for withdrawal. Greenland left the EU on 1 February 1985 with the 'Greenland Treaty' (officially, The Treaty amending, with regard to Greenland, the Treaties establishing the European Communities) which declared Greenland to be a special case. See http://eu.nanoq.gl/.

Table 2.2 Classification and exercise of competences

Topic	Location	Article in CT
Union competences	TEU 2–6 & 24	I-11 to I-18
Principle of conferral, subsidiarity and proportionality	TEU 5	I-11
Categories of competence	TEU 2	I-12
Exclusive competence	TEU 3	I-13
Shared competence	TEU 4	I-14
Supporting, coordinating or complementary competences	TEU 6	I-17
Flexibility clause	TFEU 352	I-18
Enhanced cooperation	TEU 20	I-44
Primacy of Community law	Declaration 17	I-6
Ordinary treaty revision procedure	TEU 48	IV-443
Simplified revision procedure for decision-making procedures	TEU 48	IV-444
Simplified revision procedure for any provision related to internal policies and action	TEU 48	IV-445

Note: The Location column gives the Treaty with article number. The content is arranged more logically in the abandoned Constitution, so the corresponding articles are listed for reference.

like marriage, retirement, house buying, etc. have led to calls for more harmonization at the European level.

The power to extend EU powers: passerelle and flexibility

Some of the most important rules in a constitution are those that determine how the constitution is amended. The Lisbon Treaty introduces changes in the ways the EU's virtual constitution can be amended. The first change is minor from the perspective of European economic integration. The current procedure is maintained as one possibility, although Lisbon mentions holding a 'convention' like the 2002 European Convention unless the European Council decides it is not necessary.

Lisbon also introduces a simplified treaty revision procedure for the Union's internal polices and action (basically first-pillar measures) that allows the European Council, acting unanimously, to amend first-pillar provisions without holding an IGC and without facing a vote by the European Parliament (although it and the Commission must be consulted). Such amendments, however, still have to be ratified by all the members according to their own constitutional requirements, i.e. referenda cannot be avoided.

One big change is the Treaty's introduction of a new, easier way to amend specific but important treaty provisions. Specifically, this clause allows the European Council to switch the law-making procedure from unanimity (intergovernmental) to majority voting (supranational) in all areas except defence and any area with military implications. This so-called 'passerelle' clause is important since it concerns ways in which the EU's degree of supranationality can be increased without a referendum or other national ratification procedures.

Switching from unanimity to majority voting in the Council would require unanimous agreement in the European Council. Any national parliament or the European Parliament can veto the switch. However, the leaders on the European Council include all the leaders of national parliaments and the European Parliament gains power under majority voting so it is unclear how much additional constraint the parliamentary vetos imply. The same possibility exists for the few areas where unusual decision-making procedures apply (i.e. leftovers from the 60 years of treaty revisions).

For example, EU laws on corporate taxation now must be decided by unanimous vote in the Council of Ministers. Under current practices, this could be changed only with a new Treaty that would have to be ratified by all members. The passerelle clause would allow the European Council to change this permanently, making all future laws on corporate taxation subject to majority voting.

This clause is one of the main reasons why proponents of an ever-deeper EU are strongly in favour of Lisbon (e.g. the German government and the European Commission). They fear that getting a new treaty ratified by all members will prove increasingly difficult as the EU enlarges; the passerelle allows for more supranationality without this. The clause is also why opponents of an ever-deeper EU are strongly against it (*The Economist* magazine and British Conservatives, for example). Note that special passerelle clauses apply to social policy and environmental policy; in these, national parliaments have no veto.

The flexibility clause is the second big innovation, not in terms of its existence but rather in terms of the breadth of its application. 'Flexibility' is the principle that grants the EU the power to give itself the power necessary to attain its objectives, even if that power is not granted by the amended Treaties. The clause exists in the Treaty of Rome and was the source of 'creeping competency', i.e. why the Maastricht Treaty set up the pillar structure. (The pillars limited 'flexibility' since flexibility is currently only a principle of the TEC which governs only first-pillar issues; second- and third-pillar issues are dealt with in the Maastricht Treaty.) Lisbon would apply flexibility to every area mentioned in the Constitution, except those where it is explicitly excluded, notably second-pillar issues (CFSP), defence policy and the Charter of Fundamental Rights.

The procedure for using this flexibility requires a unanimous vote by the Council and it can be vetoed by the European Parliament.

In truth, no one can know what the full implications of the passerelle and flexibility clauses would be. Europhiles have faith that the new powers would be used wisely. Eurosceptics fear that they would be abused by out-of-touch elites to force through more integration than many EU citizens want.

2.8.5 Institutional changes

The Lisbon Treaty contains important changes for the Big-5 institutions. The largest changes by far are for the Commission, Council voting and creation of a new post: the Representative for Foreign Affairs. The key facts are listed in Box 2.14.

Commission

Fierce debate surrounded the Commission reform proposals. Almost everyone realized that a Commission with too many members would be ineffective, but who should sacrifice the right to have a Commissioner? Small members – who view the Commission as a key protector of their rights – felt a Commissioner was critical. Since the six big members account for three-quarters of the EU population, large members felt it only fair that they each have a Commissioner at all times.

Box 2.14 Summary of Lisbon Treaty changes for Big-5 institutions

Commission. Commission size: current practice until 2014 after which the number equals two-thirds the number of members with slots rotated equally regardless of member size (each member will be without a Commissioner for five out of every 15 years).

Commission President powers reinforced along with Parliament's oversight of the Commission.

Council of Ministers. QMV rules: Current practice up to 2014 after which 'double majority' applies, i.e. at least 55 per cent of members representing at least 65 per cent of EU population;* blocking minority must include at least four members. During transition period (2014 to 2017) any member can request that the current (i.e. Nice Treaty) QMV rule be applied instead of double majority.

Council meetings continue to be chaired by nation with rotating presidency, except Foreign Affairs Council, which will be chaired by new 'High Representative of the Union for Foreign Affairs and Security Policy' (see below).

European Council. New post: 'European Council President'. Full-time position for person that does not hold a national office, elected by the European Council (QMV rules) for two and a half years (renewable once).

European Council becomes an official EU institution, making it subject to Court jurisdiction.

European Parliament. Joint decision-making powers with the Council are expanded concerning the EU budget (including power of CAP spending for the first time) and third-pillar issues (Justice and Home Affairs).

Also increased role in Treaty revisions and the selection of senior EU leaders.

The number of Members of European Parliament (MEPs) is capped at 750.

European Court. Significant expansion of Court's jurisdiction to include third-pillar issues (excluding Britain).

No major organizational changes, but easier to set up specialized courts (e.g. trademark law).

* The Lisbon Treaty voting reform article is anachronistic since it was taken verbatim from the abandoned Constitutional Treaty that was written in 2004 when there were 25 members. It adds a proviso to the 55 per cent criterion that a majority must include at least 15 members. This was relevant when there were 25 members; now there are 27 so one cannot get to 55 per cent with fewer than 15 members.

The compromise in the Lisbon Treaty is to remain with one Commissioner per member up to 2014, after which the number is capped at two-thirds the number of EU members. Members' right to have a Commissioner will rotate on an equal basis among Member States (i.e. regardless of size).

Importantly, the whole reform may never occur, even if the Treaty comes into effect:

★ By 2014, the Commission will have had a decade of experience with 25+ members; surely it will have found effective work methods by then. The boosted powers of the Commission President should help.

★ Lisbon grants the European Council the power to change the number of Commissioners with a unanimous vote (i.e. without a new Treaty). The European Council might well decide to stick with the one-per-member rule for the next Commission (2014–19).

Only time will tell, but the fact that the loss of a Commissioner played an important role in the Irish 'no' vote suggests that the status quo may be maintained for the foreseeable future.

Beyond the size issue, the Treaty contains some vague language about the choice of Commission President that might have a big impact on the person chosen to head the Commission. The basics of the appointment procedure are unchanged (the Council nominates and the Parliament approves) but Lisbon includes language that suggests Parliament's influence could be much larger than it is now. The European Council will 'propose' a candidate (rather than 'nominate') and Parliament 'elects' (rather than 'approves'). The European Parliament has been quite aggressive in the past about claiming more power via interpretations of vaguely worded treaty articles. Will they be in this case? Experts disagree on the matter, but many suggest that the choice of Commission President, High Representative and European Council President will be handled as a package by the Member States consulting with Parliament. All this is rather academic since the Irish-no delays imply that the President of the 2009–14 Commission (very likely to be Barroso again) will be elected under current rules. Lisbon's reforms would apply to the choice in 2014 for the 2014–19 Commission.

Council of Ministers

The Council voting changes are and have been since the 1990s the single most contentious institutional reform, but also the most necessary. Fights over voting rules started in IGC 1996 leading up to Amsterdam, and continued in IGC 2000 which produced the failed Nice Treaty reforms. The job of fixing the Nice voting rules led to a revival of the disputes in the new century. These were suppressed during the European Convention, but led to the rejection of the Convention's draft Constitution by the Council in December 2003. The Irish Presidency finally brokered a deal for the Constitutional Treaty after a great deal of pressure was applied to Poland. When the Constitution was rejected, the Poles reopened the fight over Council voting rules in 2007. The German Presidency managed a compromise after a very long summit.

The resulting compromise, however, may never be implemented. At Polish insistence, the old Nice Treaty rules apply until 2014, officially. Unofficially the old rules are likely to apply for all the most controversial and difficult decisions until 2017. As part of the compromise with Poland, there is a 'transition' period (2014 to 2017) where any member can request that the Nice Treaty QMV rules be applied instead of Lisbon Treaty's double majority. A member who would lose a vote they care about under the double majority system would have a strong incentive to invoke the old rules, so it is likely that Treaty of Nice QMV rules will apply to controversial decisions up to 2017.

High Representative of the Union for Foreign Affairs and Security Policy

One of the most important institutional innovations is the creation of a post that can be understood as Minister for EU Foreign Affairs, but which will be called 'High Representative of the Union for Foreign Affairs and Security Policy'. The High Representative would:

★ conduct Common Foreign and Security Policy (CFSP, i.e. the old third pillar) including common security and defence policy;

★ be one of the Vice-Presidents of the Commission;

★ represent the EU on CFSP issues;

★ conduct political dialogue on the Union's behalf with third nations;

★ express the Union's position in international organizations and at international conferences;

★ participate in the work of the European Council;

★ chair Council meetings on foreign, security and defence matters;

★ refer to the Council any question relating to the common foreign and security policy;

★ submit initiatives or proposals to the Council (with or without the Commission's support; and

★ convene an extraordinary Council meeting in the event of a crisis.

In essence, the new High Representative combines the jobs now performed by the Commissioner for External Affairs (currently Benita Ferrero-Waldner) and the High Representative of the Union for Foreign Affairs (currently Javier Solana), but adds a great many more rights and responsibilities.

The President of the European Council will also represent the EU in external matters. The Treaty does not clearly define the overlap between this and the High Representative's job.[4] This overlap may produce conflict depending upon the personalities chosen. Only time will tell how this overlap resolves itself.

European Council

A new post, European Council President, is created to boost stability and coherence of the European Council's work compared to the current practice where the chair is held by the head of the Member State that has the six-monthly rotating EU presidency. The President's job is to:

★ chair European Council meetings and drive forward its work;

★ ensure the preparation and continuity of the work of the European Council in cooperation with the President of the Commission;

★ facilitate cohesion and consensus within the European Council;

★ report to the European Parliament after every meeting.

This reform is very pragmatic. Men and women familiar with the situation all note that the rotating Presidency is inefficient. In testifying on the impact of this reform, British Minister for Europe, Jim Murphy, said: 'the European Union is the single biggest rules-based market in human history and yet we have tolerated a system where there is a rotating leadership every 26 weeks. You would not run a bowling club . . . on a rotating presidency of 26 weeks' (House of Lords, 2008, p. 27). There is also the problem of the micro members, who find the financial and personnel burden of the Presidency to be onerous.

This is one of the Lisbon Treaty changes that could be implemented before the Treaty is ratified. The European Council is now a group of national leaders. There is nothing in the world to stop them from appointing someone to chair their meetings. In the EU, many things go

---

[4] On the President of the European Council, Lisbon says: 'The President of the European Council shall, at his or her level and in that capacity, ensure the external representation of the Union on issues concerning its common foreign and security policy, without prejudice to the powers of the High Representative of the Union for Foreign Affairs and Security Policy.' On the High Representative it says: 'The High Representative shall represent the Union for matters relating to the common foreign and security policy. He (sic) shall conduct political dialogue on the Union's behalf and shall express the Union's position in international organisations and at international conferences.'

on outside the Treaties, based on the legitimacy implicit in the fact that they are organized by democratically elected governments of sovereign nations. The whole European Council, for instance, was created in 1974 and led the EU for decades before it was first mentioned in a Treaty (the Single European Act).

Another example showing that Lisbon Treaty changes can be implemented before the Treaty is ratified is the Eurogroup. Eurozone Finance Ministers have been meeting under the name of the 'Eurogroup' for years and recently elected Jean-Claude Junker to be the group's President. The Lisbon Treaty recognizes all this and puts that election rules in writing. In this case, the Lisbon Treaty reform is actually a codification of existing practice.

European Parliament

Lisbon boosts the Parliament's powers, most importantly its joint decision-making powers, with the Council being expanded to a wider range of areas such as the EU budget, in particular CAP spending where previously the Parliament had little say, and third-pillar issues (Justice and Home Affairs). The European Parliament also gets an increased role in Treaty revision and an increased role in the selection of senior EU leaders.

To keep the Parliament's size manageable in the face of future enlargements, the number of Members of European Parliament (MEPs) is capped at 750; the national allocation of MEPs changes little. Given the almost inevitable delay implied by the Irish 'no' vote in summer of 2008, the next Parliament (2009–14) will almost surely be elected under the current rules (implying 785 MEPs).

European Court

No major organizational changes are implied for the Court, although it will be easier to set up specialized courts (what used to be called 'judicial panels'), e.g. in the area of trademark law. The Lisbon Treaty, however, significantly expands the role of the ECJ since the Court gains jurisdiction over third-pillar issues, i.e. Justice and Home Affairs (Britain and Poland have opted out of this). The Treaty explicitly says that the Court has no jurisdiction over second-pillar issues (Common Foreign and Security policy).

2.8.6 Role of national parliaments

Since the 1997 Amsterdam Treaty, national parliaments have had a role in ensuring that the principle of subsidiarity is respected by EU law-making. The Lisbon Treaty boosts the role of the EU national parliaments by setting up a 'yellow card' system whereby the national parliaments can warn the Commission, Council and European Parliament that they feel a particular piece of legislation violates the subsidiarity principle. Lisbon also gives the national parliaments eight weeks to react and it clarifies the documentation that must be provided to the national parliaments.

The 'yellow card' system means that EU law-makers must review their proposal if at least one-third of the national parliaments argue that it violates subsidiarity. The threshold is one-quarter for third-pillar issues. The EU law-makers are free to decide to maintain, amend or withdraw the proposal, but they must provide a reason for their decision. Thus national parliaments' role is to force a second round of consideration; they cannot block a proposal.

The 'orange card' system kicks in when at least half the national parliaments object. In this case the same reconsideration process starts, but if the EU law-makers want to continue, they have to take an explicit vote on whether the proposal violates the subsidiarity principle. As with the 'yellow card', the national parliaments do not have absolute blocking power.

In practice, such national parliament oversight is unlikely to be important. Member State governments usually have a majority in their parliament. If one-third of the parliaments objected to a proposal, it would almost always be the case that enough Member State governments would vote against it in the Council to kill the proposal in the usual way.

2.8.7 Citizens' right of initiative

The Lisbon Treaty writes down the 'right of citizens' initiative', but this is unlikely to have much impact. Lisbon states that citizens who gather at least one million signatures from a significant number of Member States can ask the Commission to introduce specific legislation.

There is nothing new here, however. EU citizens do not need a Treaty provision to send petitions to EU law-makers. Indeed, they already send many such petitions. You can see the long list of such initiatives that EU citizens have sent to Commission President Barroso and his responses on the internet.[5] Sometimes they have effect, for example the well-known petition concerning trade in cat and dog fur, but usually they do not. The situation would be quite different if petitions could trigger mandatory referendums or laws as is the case in California and Switzerland, but these are completely at odds with the democratic traditions of most EU members.

2.8.8 Legislative processes

The changes here are mainly cosmetic. The Constitution re-labels what is the Codecision Procedure into the 'Ordinary Legislative Procedure'. It eliminates a number of minor legislative procedures that are holdovers from the increasing powers of the European Parliament. This would make it a little easier to understand the EU, but little will change in practice, apart from the Council's new voting rules when/if they come into effect in 2014/2017. The basic principle remains that the Council and Parliament are equal partners in EU law-making for most issues.

2.8.9 Charter of Fundamental Rights

The removal of the pillars and the formal inclusion of the European Council in the EU's institutional framework might or might not have important effects. The crux of the matter is that the Constitution, like any political document, is filled with messy political compromises, but the EU Court works on the basis of legal logic. More than once in EU history, the Court's application of logic has had unforeseen consequences (classic examples of this are the Costa v ENEL and Cassis de Dijon cases).[6]

---

[5] See ec.europa.eu/commission_barroso/president/contact/petitions/index_en.htm.

[6] One of many hypotheticals runs as follows. The fact that it is called a Constitution and explicitly includes the primacy principle, might, logically speaking, make the EU Constitution supreme to national constitutions. While such a conclusion is far-fetched, it is not extremely far from the reasoning the Court used in Costa v ENEL to establish primacy. The Court will eventually have to decide cases where the issue is a conflict between a Member State's constitution and the EU Constitution.

Norman, P. (2005) 'The accidental constitution', EuroComment, Brussels.

Noury, A. and G. Roland (2002) *European Parliament: Should it have more power?*, Economic Policy.

Open Europe (2008a) 'The Lisbon Treaty and the European Constitution: a side-by-side comparison', January 2008. Download from www.openeurope.org.uk/research/comparative.pdf.

Open Europe (2008b) 'A guide to the constitutional treaty', Second edition February 2008 (Open Europe considers the Lisbon Treaty to be equivalent to the abandoned Constitution). Download from www.openeurope.org.uk/research/guide.pdf.

Open Europe (2008c) 'Open Europe parliamentary briefing #5: Foreign policy and defence'. Download from www.openeurope.org.uk/research/cfspbriefing.pdf.

Peet, J. and K. Ussher (1999) *The EU Budget: An Agenda for Reform?*, CER Working Paper, February.

Peterson, J. and M. Shackleton (2002) *The Institutions of the European Union*, Oxford University Press, Oxford.

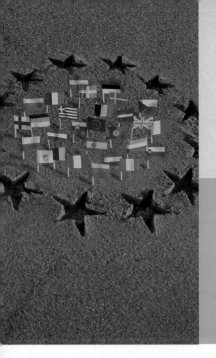

Chapter 3

Decision making

In any moment of decision the best thing you can do is the right thing, the next best thing is the wrong thing, and the worst thing you can do is nothing.

Theodore Roosevelt

Chapter contents

3.1   Task allocation and subsidiarity: EU practice and principles   111
3.2   Fiscal federalism and task allocation among government levels   113
3.3   Economical view of decision making   121
3.4   The distribution of power among EU members   126
3.5   Legitimacy in EU decision making   132
3.6   Summary   133

Introduction

Chapter 2 described how EU institutions work and how they make their decisions. This chapter presents a framework for thinking about EU decision making at a more abstract and more analytical level. The discussion is organized around two major questions:

1   Who should be in charge of what? That is, which decisions should be taken at the EU level and which should be taken at the national or sub-national levels?

2   Is the EU-level decision-making procedure efficient and legitimate?

In answering these questions we shall examine the EU's actual practice and develop a number of specific analytic tools. Moreover, we shall look at proposed reforms of the system since eastern enlargement challenges the EU's decision-making structure.

3.1 Task allocation and subsidiarity: EU practice and principles

Governments set policies in many areas – everything ranging from the speed limit on local roads and national policy on nuclear weapons to the restrictions on imports of Chinese-made shirts. Not all of these policies are made by the same level of government. Most European nations have at least three levels of government (local, provincial and national) and EU members have a fourth level of government, the EU. Typically, local speed limits are set by the local government, but motorway speed limits are determined at the national level, as are questions concerning nuclear arms. Why are various policies set at different levels of government? This is the main question addressed by the first two section of this chapter.

This section begins by covering the existing EU principles guiding the allocation of policies between the EU and Member States. The section briefly covers the actual allocation of tasks in the EU. The next section presents an analytic framework to organizing thinking about the appropriate allocation of tasks among the various levels of government.

3.1.1 EU practice

Some tasks and decisions are assigned to the EU level, some are shared between the EU and Member States, and others are set exclusively by national governments. In EU jargon, this task allocation is called the question of 'competences'. Areas where the EU alone decides are known as 'exclusive competences' or 'Community competences'. Those where responsibility is shared between the EU and Member States are called 'shared competences', and tasks where national or sub-national governments alone decide are called 'national competences'.

There are some clear examples of national competences, such as the secondary school curriculum; and there are clear examples of exclusive competences, such as competition policy where the European Commission has the final say on, for example, mergers that affect the European market. However, as is true of so many things in the EU, the exact dividing lines are unclear. The European Parliament's factsheet on subsidiarity explains (www.europarl.europa.eu/facts/1_2_2_en.htm):

> The demarcation of the areas of exclusive Community competence continues to be a problem, particularly because it is laid down in the Treaties not by reference to specific fields but by means of a functional description.

The task allocation is further blurred by the fact that the Treaty says that the Community's areas of competence can be extended if necessary to attain Treaty objectives. As Chapter 2 pointed out, the Treaty of Rome's objectives are enormously ambitious, so this proviso puts a great many tasks in the grey area between Community competence and national competence. Often, the dividing line must be established by the EU Court. As the factsheet notes:

In a number of decisions stemming from the Treaties, for example, the Court has defined and recognized certain competences (which are not explicitly regulated in the Treaties) as exclusive, but it has not laid down a definitive list of such competences.

Clarifying the allocation of tasks was one of the main jobs that EU leaders assigned to the writers of the Lisbon Treaty. More on this below.

3.1.2 Subsidiarity and proportionality

To help reduce the blurriness of the task allocation, the EU embraced the so-called subsidiarity principle in the Maastricht Treaty. The word 'subsidiarity' has a distinct meaning in the EU. Subsidiarity basically means that decisions should be made as close to the people as possible, that the EU should not take action unless doing so is more effective than action taken at national, regional or local level.

The amended Treaty of Rome defines subsidiarity as:

> The Community shall act within the limits of the powers conferred upon it by this Treaty and of the objectives assigned to it therein.
>
> In areas which do not fall within its exclusive competence, the Community shall take action, in accordance with the principle of subsidiarity, only if and in so far as the objectives of the proposed action cannot be sufficiently achieved by the Member States and can therefore, by reason of the scale or effects of the proposed action, be better achieved by the Community.
>
> Any action by the Community shall not go beyond what is necessary to achieve the objectives of this Treaty.
>
> (Article 5 TEC)

The last paragraph is called the principle of proportionality, i.e. even when the objective can be better achieved at the EU level, the EU should undertake only the minimum necessary actions. For example, some VAT harmonization is necessary for the smooth functioning of the Internal Market, but not complete harmonization. In keeping with the principle of proportionality, the EU agreed to minimum and maximum VAT rates but let members decide their own rates within the band.

3.1.3 Three pillars

Another step towards clarity came with the EU's three-pillar structure, established by the Maastricht Treaty (see Chapter 2). This explicitly delimited the range of Community competences and shared competences by defining areas (second and third pillars) where the EU would not normally be able to make policy, i.e. where cooperation would be of the more standard inter-governmental type where all the members have to agree unanimously on any common policy.

The first pillar (the EC, or Community pillar) includes policy issues relating to the single market, the free movement of persons, goods, services and capital among EU members, and cooperation in the areas of agricultural, environmental, competition and trade policies. It also encompasses Economic and Monetary Union (EMU). The second pillar consists of the Common Foreign and Security Policy (CFSP). The third pillar covers Justice and Home Affairs, i.e. police cooperation and criminal matters.

The first pillar is where EU members have allocated decision making to the EU level, in effect transferring parts of their national sovereignty by empowering EU institutions to draw up and interpret laws and regulations. Specifically, the Commission has a monopoly on the right to initiate proposals for new laws. The Council and (usually) the European Parliament decide whether to adopt them, often by majority voting. It is exactly this majority-voting element that tells us that Member States have transferred sovereignty to the EU level. An EU member can be outvoted on a particular law, but it still must accept the adopted policy. In many first-pillar areas, the laws are directly enforceable in member countries and the EU Court of Justice can overrule any national court on such matters.

Although the details are complex, the basic rule in second- and third-pillar areas is that members can pursue cooperation, but they do not transfer sovereignty to the EU level. That is, members will not be bound by decisions with which they disagree. This does not mean that they do not cooperate. EU members and even non-members do cooperate in initiatives such as the Schengen Accord.

3.1.4 Reform

As Chapter 2 discussed, the past 50 years have seen a progressively wider range of areas transferred to the EU level. In fact, this outcome – an ever-closer union – is what the EU's founders intended. The objectives of the Treaty of Rome are hugely ambitious, and the Treaty allows for an expansion of competences to attain these objectives (the principle of 'flexibility'). There are thus no hard limits as to what tasks the EU should be assigned. In recent years an increasingly wide range of Europeans have questioned whether the EU should continue to expand its list of competences. Recognizing this line of thinking, EU leaders said that one of the tasks of the European Convention was to develop a clearer definition of the 'task allocation' between EU, national and sub-national governments (more on this below). Both the rejected Constitutional Treaty and the Lisbon Treaty propose several clarifications (see Chapter 2).

3.2 Fiscal federalism and task allocation among government levels

Most would agree that it is appropriate for national authorities to set speed limits on motorways, while municipal authorities set the various speed limits within their city. But why is this task allocation so natural?

This section presents a framework for thinking about which is the most appropriate level of government for each type of task. A complete consideration of this question, however, would take us into subjects (political science, sociology, national identity, etc.) that are too far afield for this book. The main line of thinking presented here is called the theory of 'fiscal federalism'. Even though this provides only an incomplete approach to the question, it proves to be a very useful framework for organizing one's thinking about the basic trade-offs.

3.2.1 The basic trade-offs

We focus on five important considerations when thinking about the appropriate allocation of policy-making tasks to the various levels of government. In the real world, the five blend together in complex ways. To clarify our thinking, however, we consider each in isolation. The first concerns local diversity.

Diversity and local informational advantages

When people have very different preferences, centralized decision making creates inefficiencies. There is an obvious aspect and a subtle aspect to this point.

The obvious aspect is that a single, centrally chosen policy will typically be a compromise. By definition, a compromise will not be the right policy for everybody. Take the example of road speed limits. Suppose the German federal government could choose only one speed limit for the whole country. The result would be a limit that was too slow for the autobahn but too fast for residential neighbourhoods. (Of course, for some policies, choosing one policy for the whole nation might reduce costs but we put that aside for clarity's sake and deal with it below under 'scale economies'.)

The subtle aspect concerns local information about diverse situations and preferences. The speed limit example seemed strained since the federal government could set different speed limits for different roads. The subtle point is that, if many different limits are to be set, local governments are probably better at determining which limit to apply to which roads in their localities. This is basically an issue of the cost of acquiring the information necessary to adapt policies to local conditions and preferences. As a general principle (to which there are many exceptions), local governments can acquire such information more cheaply and so the decision-making task should be allocated to the local level.

The general idea is more concretely illustrated in Box 3.1.

Box 3.1   Economic inefficiency of a one-size-fits-all policy

To illustrate this general idea more concretely, we turn to Fig. 3.1. (The figure employs supply and demand analysis and the notion of consumer surplus; see Chapter 4 if you are unfamiliar with this type of reasoning.)

The panel shows demand curves for a particular public service. One is for an individual located in region 1 (marked as D_1) and the other for a person in region 2 (marked as D_2). We assume that, for some reason, people in the two regions have different preferences for public services. For example, if we are talking about the density of public bus service, people in region 2 might live in a city where commuting by car is difficult, so they prize bus service more highly than the people in region 1. These relative preferences can be seen from the fact that D_1 is below D_2; from the consumer surplus analysis in Chapter 4, this means that the marginal value of a slight increase in the density of bus service is lower for individuals in region 1 than it is in region 2.

To start the analysis, we work out the level of bus service that would be provided if the levels were chosen separately by the region 1 and region 2 governments.

The region 1 government would best serve its citizens by choosing the level where a typical region 1 person's marginal value of a denser bus service (i.e. more buses per day and/or more routes) was just equal to the per-person cost of providing the extra service. In the panel, this optimal level is Q_{d1} for region 1 (the 'd' stands for decentralized and '1' for region 1). Region 2's government would choose a higher level, namely Q_{d2}. (This assumes, for simplicity, that the marginal cost is constant at all levels of service and identical across regions.)

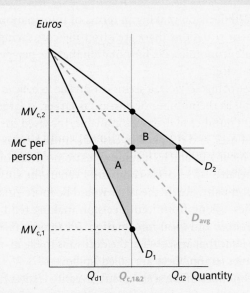

Figure 3.1 Diversity of preferences and decentralization

Note: The diagram assumes that individuals in each region are identical and the governments are 'benevolent'.
Technical note: the *MC* per person = *MV* criterion is identical to Samuelson's famous sum of MV condition since
$MC/N = MV$ implies $MC = N*MV$, where N is the number of people in the region.

Contrast this with the situation where the policy decision is centralized so that the same level is chosen for both regions. In this case, the central government would look at the average preference for bus services as reflected by the average demand curve marked as D_{avg}. Using the same reasoning as with local governments, the optimal average provision is shown by $Q_{c,1\&2}$.

How do these two situations compare in terms of people's welfare? Taking the decentralized choice as the initial situation, the figure shows that people in both regions are made worse off by centralizing the decision. The people in region 1 are forced to pay (via their taxes) for a level of bus service that is too high for their preferences. The loss to a typical region 1 person is given by the triangle 'A' since this measures – for each extra increase in Q – the gap between the marginal value of the denser service and the marginal cost. The marginal value is given by the demand curve D_1 and the marginal cost is given by the *MC per person* line. Region 2 residents also lose, but for them the loss stems from the fact that they would like a denser service than is provided when decision making is centralized. In particular, area B shows their losses since it measures, for each unit reduction of Q, the gap between their marginal value (given by D_2) and the marginal cost (given by *MC per person*).

Choosing a one-size-fits-all policy leads to an inferior outcome when people have diverse preferences.

If the Qs are chosen separately for the two regions, there is no reason to centralize the decision. It will typically be cheaper for local authorities to determine what is optimal for their region. More specifically, suppose it costs X euros more for the central authorities to get the information than it would cost local authorities. Since the decision would be the same in both cases (Q_{d1} and Q_{d2} are chosen), the centralized decision making is worse since taxpayers will have to pay the extra information-gathering cost, X.

Scale economies

The advantage of localized decision making in terms of information efficiency is really quite a robust result. Yet in many situations there are offsetting cost savings from a one-size-fits-all policy that arise from scale economies, i.e. the notation that the per-person cost of a service falls as more people use the service.

For example, in the case of bus services, it seems reasonable to believe that the cost per kilometre of bus service tends to fall as the number of buses gets larger. A large bus company can more easily ensure that the right number of drivers is available, the fixed cost of a maintenance centre can be spread over more buses, and the per-bus cost of administration may fall – at least up to a point – when the bus company is larger. Imagine an extreme situation where every bus in, say, Paris was owned and operated by separate companies versus the situation where all the buses were owned by a single company. Surely the latter would be more efficient in terms of costs.

To sum up, economies arising from joint decision making tend to favour centralization, while diversity of preferences and local information advantages favour decentralization. We turn next to another key issue that arises when the decisions made in one region affect people in other regions. In economics jargon, these are called 'spillovers'.

To understand the economics of the scale versus diversity trade-off, see Box 3.2.

Box 3.2   Economic gains from scale vs. losses from one-size-fits-all

The widespread presence of scale economies in the provision of public services – transport services, medical services, etc. – tends to favour centralization. To see this point, we refer to Fig. 3.2. The diagram focuses only on the impact of centralization on the typical region 1 individual. In the

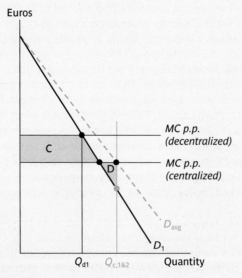

Figure 3.2 **Scale economies and centralization**

decentralized situation the marginal cost per person of a denser bus service is shown by the line marked *MC p.p. (decentralized)*. In the case of centralized service, the marginal cost is lower, namely *MC p.p. (centralized)* due to scale economies.

The figure shows that there is a trade-off between having the level of service precisely adjusted to local preferences and having a lower service cost due to scale economies. When the decision is local, the optimal provision is – as in Fig. 3.1 – Q_{d1}. When it is centralized, the marginal cost is lower so the intersection of marginal value of the average citizen (D_{avg}) and marginal cost is at $Q_{c,1\&2}$. As before, the level that is optimal for the average citizen is not right for region 1 people, so there is inefficiency; again, this is measured by a triangle, marked D in Fig. 3.2. This inefficiency, however, is offset by the gain from scale economies. That is, the region 1 person faces a lower marginal cost; the benefit of this is shown by the four-sided area, C. (The gain is just like a price reduction in standard consumer surplus analysis; see Chapter 4 for details.)

It appears, from the figure, that the gain from scale economies outweighs the loss from one-size-fits-all decision making. But, of course, if the scale economies were less important (i.e. the *MC* fell by less), or preferences were more diverse (i.e. the D_{avg} curve was further from the D_1 curve), then decentralization would be the superior outcome. The analysis for region 2 is quite similar and so it is omitted for the sake of brevity.

Spillovers

The next major consideration guiding task allocation is 'spillovers', i.e. an economic side-effect, known in economics jargon as an 'externality'.

Many public policy choices involve multi-region effects. National defence is one extreme. The presence of an army almost anywhere in the country deters foreign invasion for the country as a whole, so all the nation's citizens benefit from the army. It would be silly in this case to have taxpayers in each city decide separately on the army's size since, in making their decision, each set of taxpayers is likely to undervalue the nationwide benefit of a slightly bigger army. This is why the size of the army is a decision that is made at the national level in almost every nation. This is an example of what are called 'positive spillovers', i.e. where a slightly higher level of a particular policy or public service in one region benefits citizens in other regions.

A similar line of reasoning works when there are negative spillovers, i.e. when one region's policy has a negative effect on other regions. A good example of this is found in taxation. The value added tax (VAT) rate is set at the national level in all EU nations, so consider why this is so. If the VAT were chosen by each region, regions might be tempted to lower their VAT rate in an attempt to lure shoppers. For example, if the VAT in the centre of Frankfurt were 25 per cent, one of its suburbs might set its VAT at, say, 15 per cent in order to draw shoppers to its shops. In fact, if this tax undercutting were effective enough, the suburb would actually see its tax collection rise. (If the rate reduction was more than matched by an increase in local sales, the total VAT collected by the suburb would increase.) Of course, if the suburb's tax cutting worked, Frankfurt would probably have to respond by lowering its rate to 15 per cent. In the end, both Frankfurt and the suburb would charge VAT rates below what they would like, but neither would gain shoppers by doing so. This negative spillover is so famous it has a name: 'race to the bottom'. Again, the solution that is adopted by most nations is to set the VAT rate at the national level, but this time it is done to avoid negative spillovers.

As it turns out, cross-border shopping is not much of a problem in most parts of the EU, so there is little incentive to completely harmonize VAT rates at the EU level. The EU does, however, require VAT rates to fall within a wide band so that the maximum difference between VAT rates cannot be massive.

In summary, the existence of important negative or positive spillovers suggests that decisions made locally may be suboptimal for the nation (or EU) as a whole. The very existence of spillovers, however, does not force centralization. First, it may be possible to take account of the spillovers via cooperation among lower-level governments. This does not work for all policies, however, since cooperation is very difficult to sustain when the policies are difficult to observe directly and the spillovers are difficult to quantify. Moreover, even if decentralized cooperation does not work well, one may still resist centralization when there are big differences in preferences. A very interesting case study in this sort of fiscal federalism trade-off concerns the EU's different treatment of general VAT and extra sales taxes, or excise taxes on alcohol and tobacco. National preferences within the EU vary enormously when it comes to alcohol and tobacco, so although there is at least as much an argument for partly harmonizing these taxes as there is for harmonizing general VAT rates, the EU has never been able to do so. See Box 3.3 for details.

Box 3.3 Beer, cigarettes and VAT harmonization

Since 1 January 1993, EU travellers have been allowed to buy unlimited quantities of alcohol and tobacco (for their own use) in any Member State, and, as long as they pay taxes due in the Member State where they bought the goods, no additional taxes are due when they return home. This has posed some problems for British fiscal authorities since Britain has some of the highest 'sin' taxes in Europe.

While there has been some progress towards the harmonization of excise duties across the EU (incorporated into EC directives adopted on 19 October 1992), this effort consists of establishing specific minimum rates that are quite low. As Commons (2002) notes: 'The sheer variation in duty rates between countries made any closer form of harmonization politically infeasible.' For example, in the UK beer duty is 34p per pint (5p in France, 3p in Germany and 7p in the Netherlands), duty on a 70 cl bottle of spirits is £5.48 (£2.51 in France and £1.19 in Spain), duty on a 75 cl bottle of wine is £1.16 in the UK (2p in France and 0p in Spain), and the total excise duty on a packet of 20 cigarettes is £2.80 in the UK (£1.22 in France, £1.00 in the Netherlands and 99p in Belgium).

Such differences could, of course, lead to massive tax fraud, if, for example, all British publicans stocked up in France, claiming that their truck load of beer was for personal use. To prevent this, Britain sets indicative levels for how much alcohol and tobacco constitutes 'for personal use'. These levels are rather generous: 10 litres of spirits, 20 litres of fortified wines, 90 litres of wine, 110 litres of beer, 200 cigars, 400 cigarillos, 800 cigarettes and 1 kg of smoking tobacco. The problem has become so severe that the UK has begun to seize the vehicles used in this sort of fiscal smuggling – taking over 10 000 vehicles in 2000–01.

The Commission felt this was too harsh and referred Britain to the EU Court. As Frits Bolkestein, European Commissioner for taxation and customs union said: 'I understand any member state's need to fight fraud but the Commission simply cannot accept penalties that are so disproportionate that they interfere with the rights given to EU consumers by the EU single market to go shopping in other member states.' In 2006, the dispute was settled out of court. The UK modified its seizure policy and clarified its laws. For example, first-time offenders can choose between forfeiting the goods and paying a penalty.

Source: This box is based on Commons (2002) and www.cec.org.uk

Democracy as a control mechanism

The analysis up to this point has assumed that governments are only interested in the well-being of their citizens. The next major consideration in task assignment takes a more cynical view of governments' motives.

There are perfect public servants in this world, but not all government officials and politicians are totally selfless. For example, it is quite common for politicians to systematically favour politically powerful special-interest groups – e.g. granting them tax breaks, subsidies and favourable laws – even when this is bad for the average citizen.

Because of this divergence of interests between voters and decision makers, all European nations have adopted arrangements that check the power of politicians and force governments to stay close to the interest of the people. Democracy is the most powerful of these mechanisms.

Since politicians must win approval of the citizens on a regular basis, they are reluctant to misuse their decision-making power. From this perspective, democracy can be thought of as a control mechanism. The importance of this observation is that it helps to inform the allocation of policy making among levels of government. To understand this, however, we need to think more carefully about how elections discipline politicians.

Although democratic procedures vary across European nations, the following is a stylized version that fits many instances. When a politician runs in an election, the politician or his or her party presents a package of promises to the voters. The voters choose between packages and hope that the winner will actually do what he or she promised (deviations without good reason can be punished in the next election). The fact that issues are packaged together and that voters face a limited range of packages gives politicians some leeway. That is to say, their package does not have to fully represent the best interest of the voters; it only has to be good enough to get elected. This means that parties and politicians have room to slip in policies that favour small but influential special-interest groups. Because special-interest groups tend to provide money and other support in election campaigns, skewing the package in favour of these groups tends to increase the likelihood of winning an election.

Given this logic, voters' control over their elected decision makers depends upon the breadth of the package of promises. If democracy consists only of electing national officials once every four or five years, the package of promises must include a vast range of things. This gives politicians and parties a great deal of room to undertake policies that are not in the interest of the general public. By contrast, if the election is for a town mayor, the package will be quite specific and this tends to reduce the room for special-interest politics.

This logic is important. It underpins the basic presumption that decisions should be made at the lowest practical level of government. Or, to put it differently, decisions should be made as close to the voters as possible. As mentioned in the previous chapter, the EU's 'subsidiarity principle' does just this.

Jurisdictional competition

The final element to consider also favours decentralized decision making. It is called 'jurisdictional competition'. Voters can influence the sort of government they live under in two main ways, 'voice' and 'exit'. Voice is what we just discussed – the ability to control politicians and parties by speaking up, in particular by voicing one's opinion at the ballot box. The other way is to leave the jurisdiction that imposed the policy. This is exit.

While exit is not an option for most voters at the national level, it usually is at the subnational level. For example, if someone strongly objects to a lack of, say, parks and green areas in a particular town, they could move to a different town. This is called jurisdictional competition since the fact that people can move forces decision makers to pay closer attention to the wishes of the people. By contrast, if all decisions are centralized, voters do not have the exit option. This reduces the pressure on local governments to be efficient in the provision of public services. To put this differently, even if voters rarely move, the fact that they could move if things got bad enough goes some way to ensuring that politicians keep things from going terribly wrong.

To recap, decentralization tends to improve government since it allows (or forces) regions to compete with each other in providing the best value for money in local services. In the marketplace, competition usually improves quality and reduces prices; in local government, competition provides the same sort of benefits.

3.2.2 From theory to practice

The five points discussed above provide principles rather than precise guidelines. The situation with respect to particular policies can be extremely complex, making it difficult or impossible to determine the 'correct' level of government for each task. Such debate inevitably turns on personal judgements and so takes us into an area where economists have no particular advantage. Be that as it may, it is interesting to speculate briefly on how our framework helps us to think about the EU's actual allocation of tasks between the EU level and national level.

The one thing that is clear is that subsidiarity is probably a good idea. When in doubt, allocate the task to the lowest practicable level since higher-level decisions are less subject to democratic control via voice and exit. Going further is trickier.

In the European Union, the main area of centralization has been economic policies (EC pillar), especially policies affecting the Single Market. As the discussion of the Treaty of Rome in Chapter 2 showed, virtually every policy that directly affects the competitiveness of particular industries is subject to control at the EU level. For example, import taxes, government subsidies (called state aid in EU jargon), exceptional tax benefits, and anticompetitive behaviour by firms are subject to EU-wide rules that are enforceable in the EU Court. The thinking here is that such policies are marked by important and systematic negative spillovers. When one EU nation subsidizes its firms in a particular industry, firms in other EU nations suffer from the artificially intensified competition. As in the tax example above, a likely outcome is a Prisoners' Dilemma – all EU nations end up providing subsidies, but the subsidies cancel each other out. Likewise, each nation might be tempted to introduce idiosyncratic product regulation in an attempt to favour local firms, but the end result would be a highly fragmented European market with too many small firms (see Chapter 6 for an analysis of the economics of this).

The exceptions to centralization in economic policy can also be understood in the light of our five principles. The EU does not attempt to harmonize most social policies or general labour market policies. Nor does it centralize decision making on general taxes, such as income taxes and corporate taxes. As explained in Chapter 1, general policies like these do not necessarily affect the competitiveness of particular firms and so are subject to a much lower level of negative spillovers. Moreover, national preferences for such policies are very diverse. In Spain, for example, the primary form of labour market protection for workers is employment protection legislation, i.e. laws that make it difficult to fire workers. Germany relies much more on unemployment benefits. Given this divergence of nation preferences, the losses from a one-size-fits-all policy would be likely to outweigh any gains in efficiency or avoidance of negative spillovers. Of course, one can argue with this and it is impossible to settle the argument scientifically. For example, German labour unions insisted that nationalized, one-size-fits-all wage bargaining should also apply to the Eastern Länder despite the great diversity of economic conditions, and they insisted on the same homogeneity of labour market laws.

Most non-economic policies are decided at the national level. For example, most foreign policy, defence policy, internal security and social policies are made at the national level. Of course, various nations cooperate on some of these policies – a good example is the agreement between France, Germany, Spain and the UK to produce a common military transport plane – but the decision making is allocated to the national level and cooperation is voluntary.

Roughly speaking, first-pillar policies are where there are important spillovers, where national preferences are not too great and common policies tend to benefit from scale economies. The theory of fiscal federalism thus helps us to organize our thinking about why such policies are centralized.

Second-pillar policies – Common Foreign and Security Policies – are marked by enormous scale economies. For example, unifying all of Europe's armies would result in a truly impressive force and allow Europe to develop world-class weapon systems. However, second-pillar policies are also marked by vast differences in national preferences. Some EU members – France and the UK, for example – have a long history of sending their young men to die in foreign lands for various causes. Other EU members – such as Sweden and Ireland – shun almost any sort of armed conflict outside their own borders. Given this diversity of preferences, the gains from scale economies would be more than offset by adopting a one-size-fits-all policy. Because of this, the only common EU policies in these areas are those arrived at by common consent, i.e. by cooperation rather than centralization.

Third-pillar policies lie somewhere between first- and second-pillar policies, both in terms of the gains from scale economies and in terms of the diversity of preferences.

3.3 Economical view of decision making

The previous sections looked at factors affecting the allocation of tasks between the EU and its Member States. This abstracted from the actual process by which EU-level decisions are made. In other words, we simplified away the question of how decisions were made at the EU level in order to study the issue of which decisions should be made at the EU level.

In this and subsequent sections we reverse this simplification, focusing on the question of how the EU makes decisions. In particular, we shall concentrate on how the decision-making mechanisms affect the EU's ability to act, how they affect the distribution of power among EU nations, and how they affect democratic 'legitimacy'.

Efficiency, power and legitimacy are inherently vague concepts. To make progress, we adopt the tactic of progressive complexity. That is, we start by taking what may seem to be a very shallow view of political actors and their motives. These simplifying assumptions allow us to develop some very precise measures of efficiency, legitimacy and national power in EU decision making. The benefit is that these precise measures permit us to comment on how efficiency and legitimacy have evolved in the EU and how they will evolve with the 2004 enlargement and the Constitutional Treaty, if it becomes law.

Before turning to the measures, however, we consider the decision-making rules in detail.

3.3.1 Qualified majority voting (QMV)

The EU has several different decision-making procedures; however, about 80 per cent of EU legislation is passed under what is called the 'Codecision Procedure'. This requires the Council of Ministers to adopt the legislation by a 'qualified majority voting' (QMV) and the European Parliament to adopt it by a simple majority. As the Parliament's voting is straightforward – the usual 50 per cent majority threshold with one vote per Member of Parliament, we focus on the Council's voting rules.

The current rules: Nice Treaty QMV

The rules governing Council of Minister voting since 2004 are those adopted by the Nice Treaty. The Lisbon Treaty would simplify these rules (more on this below), but not before 2014.

Under current QMV rules, each Member State's minister casts a certain number of votes in the Council of Ministers. More populous members have more votes, but fewer than population-proportionality would suggest. For example, Sweden has 10 votes and 9 million citizens while France has six times more citizens but only 29 votes; Cyprus has about 10 per cent of the Swedish population but 40 per cent as many votes (4 versus 10). See Fig. 3.3. If a proposal is to pass the Council, it must receive yes votes for members that have at least 255 of the 345 total votes, i.e. about 74 per cent. But that is not all. There are two additional thresholds – one concerning the number of yes-voters and the other concerning the share of EU population that they

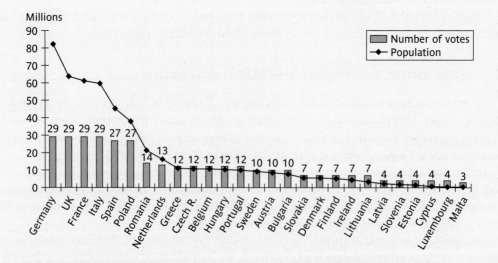

Figure 3.3 Number of Council votes, digressively proportional to population

Note: Passing a proposal in the Council by QMV requires yes votes from a group of members that have at least 74 per cent of the votes, 50 per cent of the membership and 62 per cent of the population.

represent. The number-of-members threshold is 50 per cent and the population threshold is 62 per cent.

3.3.2 EU ability to act: decision-making efficiency

EU leaders have been trying to reform EU institutions in preparation for eastern enlargement since the mid-1990s. The process is still not complete and with the Irish 'no' on the Lisbon Treaty, it may take many more years (see Chapter 1). The goal of this long series of reform attempts has been to keep the EU's decision-making procedures 'efficient' and democratically legitimate. We deal first with decision-making efficiency.

In economics, 'efficiency' usually means an absence of waste. In the EU decision-making context, the word has come to mean 'ability to act'. While 'ability to act' is more specific than efficiency, it is still a long way from operational. For instance, on some issues the EU finds it very easy to make decisions, yet on other issues it finds it impossible to find a coalition of countries that would support a particular law. The perfect measure of efficiency would somehow predict all possible issues, decide how the members would line up into 'yes' and 'no' coalitions, and use this to develop an average measure of how easy it is to get things done in the EU. Such predictions, of course, are impossible given the uncertain and ever-changing nature of the challenges facing the EU.

An alternative approach, which we shall study here, sounds strange at first, but is really the best way of thinking systematically about the issue. Rather than trying to predict details of decision making on particular topics, we adopt a 'veil of ignorance'. That is, we focus on a randomly selected issue – random in the sense that no EU member would know whether it would be for or against the proposition.

A quantitative measure of efficiency: passage probability

The specific measure we focus on is called the 'passage probability'. The passage probability measures how easy it is to find a majority under a given voting scheme. Specifically, it is the number of all possible winning coalitions divided by the number of all possible coalitions. The idea is that if each conceivable coalition of voters is equally likely, then the measure tells us the likelihood of approving a randomly selected issue; that is why it is called the passage probability. The idea behind assuming all coalitions are equally likely is that, on a randomly selected issue, each voter is as likely to say 'yes' as he or she is to say 'no'.

To explain this concept, consider a simple example. Suppose there are only three voters, whom we call A, B and C. The first step is to see what all the possible coalitions are, i.e. all possible arrays of yes and no votes. With three voters, there are eight possible coalitions. All eight are listed in the first three columns of Table 3.1. To keep things really simple, suppose that the three nations all have ten votes. The fourth column show the number of yes votes for each of the eight coalitions. The fifth column checks whether each coalition would win, assuming it takes 50 per cent (i.e. at least 15 votes) to pass the proposal.

The passage probability is calculated in the second to last row. With the simple equal vote allocation #1, half of all possible coalitions pass the proposal, so the passage probability is 50 per cent.

To illustrate the usefulness of the passage probability concept, consider what would happen to this organization's ability to act if the allocation of votes became more concentrated, but

Table 3.1 **Passage probability in a simple example**

A	B	C	Vote allocation #1		Vote allocation #2	
			10 votes each	Qualified majority? (50%)	20 votes to A, 5 to B and C	Qualified majority? (50%)
Yes	Yes	Yes	30	yes	30	yes
No	Yes	Yes	20	yes	10	no
Yes	No	Yes	20	yes	25	yes
Yes	Yes	No	20	yes	25	yes
No	No	Yes	10	no	5	no
Yes	No	No	10	no	20	no
No	Yes	No	10	no	5	no
No	No	No	0	no	0	no
Passage probability (50% majority threshold)				50.0%		37.5%
Passage probability (70% majority threshold)				12.5%		37.5%

there was no change in the majority threshold. For example, say that nation A now has 20 votes and nations B and C only 5 each. Just thinking intuitively, one would be hard put to form a judgement on whether the shift from 10 votes each to the 20, 5, 5 allocation would make it harder or easier to pass a random proposal. With the passage probability, however, we see that the second allocation of votes leads to fewer ways of forming a winning coalition and so the change in vote allocation reduces the decision-making efficiency.

The second thing that affects the passage probability is the majority threshold. It is intuitively obvious that raising the threshold makes it harder to find a coalition. Comparing the last two rows confirms this intuition. For vote allocation #1, raising the threshold from 50 per cent (i.e. 15 votes) to 70 per cent (21 votes) lowers the passage probability from 50 to 12.5 per cent. However, the details matter. Note that under allocation #2, the higher threshold does not make it any harder to find winning coalitions. The point is that there are no coalitions with a number of votes that lies between the old threshold (15 votes) and the new higher threshold (21 votes).

When looking at the real EU Council of Ministers, the principle is the same, but the calculations are much, much more tedious. The main point is that the number of possible yes/no coalitions among 27 votes is 2 raised to the power of 27 – which is a very big number, over 134 million. To find the passage probability, one needs a computer and the right software.

The level of the passage probability is affected by the number of members, the distribution of votes and, above all, the majority threshold. It is important to note, however, that the exact level of the passage probability is not very important. As Chapter 2 explained, most EU legislation is proposed by the European Commission and the Commission often refrains from introducing legislation that is unlikely to pass.

Historical efficiency and Treaty of Nice reforms

It is interesting to see how the EU's efficiency has changed over time. Above all, it is interesting to see how the 2004 enlargement will affect the EU's decision-making efficiency.

The five leftmost bars in Fig. 3.4 show the passage probability for qualified majority voting (QMV) in the historical EUs with 6, 9, 10, 12 and 15 members. These indicate that, although efficiency has been declining, past enlargements have only moderately hindered decision-making efficiency. The 1994 enlargement lowered the probability only slightly, from 10 to 8 per cent, and the Iberian expansion lowered it from 14 to 10 per cent. The figures also hide the fact that the Single European Act, which took effect in 1987, greatly boosted efficiency by shifting many more decisions from unanimity to qualified majority voting.

Notice that the 2004 enlargement greatly reduces the passage probability. This is true even with the Nice Treaty voting reforms (which were supposed to maintain the enlarged EU's ability to act). In fact, the Nice Treaty's complex rules made matters slightly worse than they would have been with no reform at all. The results show that accepting in 12 newcomers without reform would dramatically reduce efficiency, cutting the current passage probability by something like a third, from 7.8 to 3.6 per cent.

This point, which became widely accepted after 2001, was why EU leaders asked the European Convention to reconsider the EU's decision-making rules – the request that eventually led to the Lisbon Treaty's new double majority rule for the Council. Note that the decision-making rules in the Parliament and Commission were not viewed as problematic and thus were not reformed in the Constitution or the Lisbon Treaty.

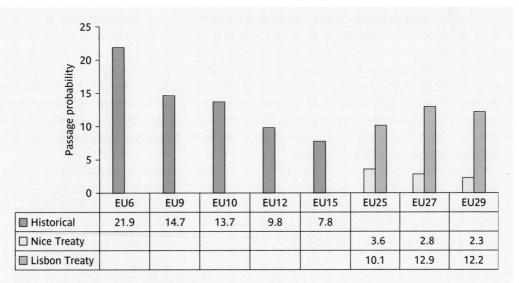

	EU6	EU9	EU10	EU12	EU15	EU25	EU27	EU29
■ Historical	21.9	14.7	13.7	9.8	7.8			
☐ Nice Treaty						3.6	2.8	2.3
▨ Lisbon Treaty						10.1	12.9	12.2

Figure 3.4 **Enlarged EU's ability to act**

The role of the Commission and Parliament

In the mainstay legislative process, the Codecision Procedure, both the Commission and the Parliament play critical roles. But they do not really affect the decision-making efficiency.

The Commission proposes legislation and drafts the first version. This gives it a good deal of power, as will be discussed in more depth below. But it has always had this power, so the increasing difficulty of passing EU legislation is not related to the Commission's role. A more plausible link would be with the enlargement of the European Parliament. After all, if enlarging the Council makes it harder to pass laws, doesn't enlarging the Parliament do the same thing?

To address this, it is necessary to realize a special feature of the 50 per cent majority rule that the Parliament uses. When the winning coalition needs only half the votes, the passage probability is unrelated to the number of voters. Upon reflection, this is obvious. There is an almost unfathomable number of possible yes/no coalitions in the Parliament with its 785 members (2 raised to the power of 785 is something like 2 with 236 zeros after it), but when you only need half to win, it is clear that half of all coalitions will be winners. Thus the passage probability is always 50 per cent regardless of the number of voters.[1] This is why we can ignore the Parliament when considering the passage probability.

Of course, in the real world things are much more complex than the passage probability, but this concept provides a good point of departure for judging how various things like enlargement and voting reform can affect the EU's capacity to act.

3.4 The distribution of power among EU members

The next aspect of EU decision making that we address is the distribution of power among EU members. As with efficiency, there is no perfect measure of power. The tactic we adopt relies on the Law of Large Numbers. That is, we look to see how likely it is that each member's vote is crucial on a randomly drawn issue. Before turning to the calculations, however, we lay out our specific definition of power.

For our purposes, power means influence, or, more precisely, the ability to influence EU decisions by being in a position to make or break a winning coalition in the Council of Ministers. Of course, no one has absolute power in the EU, so we focus on the likelihood that a Member State will be influential. On some things Germany's vote will be crucial, on others it will be irrelevant, and the same goes for all other members. What determines how likely it is that a particular nation will be influential?

The most direct and intuitive measure of political power is national voting shares in the Council of Ministers. Under current EU rules, each Member State has a fixed number of votes in the Council of Ministers. Up to the 2004 enlargement, 87 Council-of-Minister votes were divided among the 15 EU nations, with large nations receiving more votes than small ones (see Chapter 2 for details). It seems intuitively plausible that nations with more votes are more likely to be influential on average, so the first power measure to try is a nation's share of Council votes. But how can we tell if this power measure captures anything real? See Box 3.4.

---

[1] This is not exactly true with an odd number of voters but the difference is negligible.

Box 3.4 Why Parliament reform does not affect national power distributions

Most EU legislation these days must be approved by both the Council and the Parliament. As it turns out, the allocation of seats in the European Parliament does not affect national power, per se. The reason rests on three facts: (i) the national distribution of Council votes and MEP seats is quite similar, as Fig. 3.5 shows; (ii) to pass the Council, a proposal must garner at least 71 per cent of votes; and (iii) to pass the Parliament, a proposal needs to win only half the MEP votes.

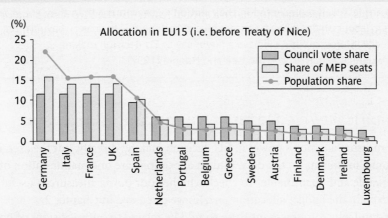

Figure 3.5 Share of MEPs, Council votes and population in the EU15
Source: Factsheets on www.europarl.eu.int/factsheets/.

   To illustrate how these three facts affect the Parliament's power from a purely national perspective, we must cover a few preliminaries. First, we start with a simple assumption – that MEPs act as national representatives and indeed that their votes are controlled directly by national governments (obviously this is false, but going to this extreme helps to build intuition for more realistic cases). Second, recall that we define power as the ability to break a winning coalition, so the question is: 'Can a nation use the votes of its MEPs to block a coalition that it cannot otherwise block?' If the answer is 'no', then the votes of MEPs do not affect a nation's power, even under the extreme assumption that MEP votes are controlled by governments. And, of course, if national power is not affected by MEP votes when they are directly controlled, national power is certainly not affected when the MEPs vote by their own conscience. Finally, we assume that each nation's share of Council votes is identical to its share of MEP votes (rather than just similar). Under these assumptions, we can think of the actual procedure as a double majority system. To pass, a proposal needs to attract the votes of Member States that have at least 50 per cent of MEP votes, and 71 per cent of Council votes.

   Now here is the main point. The first criterion is redundant since the Council vote threshold is higher than the MEP threshold. That is, since the distributions of Council and MEP votes are assumed to be identical, any coalition that has 71 per cent of Council votes will automatically have 71 per cent of MEP votes, which is plainly more than the 50 per cent necessary. Some careful thought and a little mental gymnastics reveal the implications of this for national power; there are no instances when a nation's MEP votes increase its power to block. In every instance where it can block on the basis of MEP votes, it can also block on the basis of Council votes.

▶ Even under a more realistic view of the process, the same conclusion holds. The fact that the distribution of MEP votes is similar to the distribution of Council votes, teamed with the fact that the Council threshold is much higher than the Parliament's threshold, means that MEPs' votes could never increase a nation's ability to block, even if the MEPs voted on strictly national lines.

Interestingly, this suggests one indirect reason why the Parliament has tended to form cross-national coalitions. If they acted on purely national lines, MEPs would, on typical issues (i.e. where the national government accurately represents the national view), act as rubber-stampers. If they form cross-national coalitions, they may bring something new to the process.

An important caveat to all this is the fact that EU nations are made up of diverse groups. Since some groups are less well represented in their nation's government than they are in the European Parliament (e.g. labour unions when a conservative government is in power), having more seats means that these special interest groups will have a larger say in EU decision making.

For a more detailed analysis, see Bindseil and Hantke (1997).

3.4.1 Empirical evidence on power measures' relevance

One cannot measure a nation's power in EU decision making directly, but the exercise of power does leave some 'footprints' in the data. Budget allocations are one manifestation of power that is both observable and quantifiable. To check whether our power measure is useful, we see if it can help to explain the budget allocation puzzles we discussed in Chapter 2.

To understand why our power measure should be related to outward signs of power such as the budgetary spending allocation, we need to briefly review the budget process explained in detail in Chapter 2 and then discuss 'back scratching' and 'horse trading'.

The annual budget must be passed by both the Council of Ministers and the European Parliament (EP). These annual budgets, however, are constrained by medium-term budget plans called 'Financial Perspectives' (the current one covers 2007–13). The Financial Perspectives require unanimity in the Council, but the annual budgets are passed on the basis of a qualified majority. For both the Financial Perspectives and the annual budgets, EP decision making is on the basis of a simple majority. As it turns out, the EP does not matter from a national power perspective. This notion is explained in detail in Box 3.4. For this reason, we focus solely on vote shares in the Council of Ministers.

As already pointed out, about 80 per cent of Council decisions are made on the basis of qualified majority voting. Since the Council decides many issues each year, and members do not care dearly about all of them, countries tend to trade their votes on issues that they view as minor in exchange for support on an issue that they view as major, even if the two issues are totally unrelated. This sort of natural activity is referred to by the colourful names of 'back scratching' and 'horse trading'.

Now that we have discussed the background, we can turn to the main reasoning. Citizens in EU nations, or at least some citizens, benefit when EU money is spent in their district. Successful politicians, responding to the desires of their citizens, use their political clout to direct money homewards. For example, suppose that countries ask for a little 'gift' each time they find themselves in a position that is critical to a winning coalition. In the data, the 'gift' ends up as EU spending, but the actual mechanism could be subtle, say a more favourable treatment in the allocation of EU subsidies to hillside farmers, a more generous allocation of milk quotas or inclusion of reindeer meat in the CAP's price support mechanism. In this light, it seems natural that a country's power measure would equal its expected fraction of all special gifts handed out. If one goes to the cynical extreme and views the whole EU budget as nothing more than a pile of 'gifts', then our power measures should meet the EU's budget allocation perfectly. If high-minded principles such as helping out disadvantaged regions also matter, then the power measure should only partially explain the spending pattern.

As it turns out, voting power goes a long way towards solving the 'puzzle' of EU budget allocation discussed in Chapter 2. Statistical evidence by Kauppi and Widgrén (2004) shows that, although standard elements do matter – such as a member's dependency on farming and its relative poverty – voting power always turns out to be an influential determinant of budget allocations.

3.4.2 Vote shares as a power measure: the shortcomings

While voting shares are a natural measure of power, they have problems. To illustrate the potential pitfalls of vote weights as a power measure, consider a 'toy model' of the Council. Suppose there are only three countries in this toy model – imaginatively called A, B and C – and they have 40, 40 and 20 votes, respectively. Decisions are based on a simple majority rule (+50 per cent to win). If we used voting weights as a measure of power, we would say that countries A and B, each with their 40 votes, were twice as powerful as C with its 20 votes. This is wrong.

With a bit of reflection you can convince yourself that all three nations are equally powerful in this toy Council. The point is that any winning coalition requires two nations, but any two nations will do. Likewise, any pair of nations can block anything. As a consequence, all three nations are equally powerful in the sense that they are equally likely to make or break a winning coalition.

The level of the majority threshold can also be important for power. For example, continuing with our toy model, raising the majority rule from 50 to 75 per cent would strip nation C of all power. The only winning coalition that C would belong to is the grand coalition A&B&C, but here C would not be able to turn it into a losing one by leaving the coalition. Therefore C's vote can have no influence on the outcome. Again, vote shares in this example would give a very incorrect view of power.

More generally, power – i.e. the ability to make or break a winning coalition – depends upon a complex interaction of the majority threshold and exact distribution of votes. Indeed, the useless vote-situation in which nation C found itself in our second example actually occurred in the early days of the EU. See Box 3.5 for details.

Box 3.5 Luxembourg's useless vote, 1958–73

The 1958 Treaty of Rome laid down the rules for qualified majority voting in the EEC6. The big three – Germany, France and Italy – got 4 votes each, Belgium and the Netherlands got 2 each, and Luxembourg got 1. The minimum threshold for a qualified majority was set at 12 of the 17 total votes.

A little bit of thought shows that the Treaty writers did not think hard enough about this. As you can easily confirm, Luxembourg's 1 vote never matters. Any coalition (group of 'yes' voters) that has

▶

▶ enough votes to win can always win with or without Luxembourg. According to formal power measures, this means that Luxembourg had little power over issues decided on a QMV basis. As Felsenthal and Machover (2001) write: 'This didn't matter all that much, because the Treaty of Rome stipulated that QMV would not be used until 1966; and even in 1966–72 it was only used on rare occasions. Still, it seems a bit of a blunder.' All changed from 1973 on when the weights were altered to allow for the accession of Britain, Denmark and Ireland. Indeed, since then Luxembourg's votes have turned out to be crucial in a surprisingly large number of coalitions. Maybe that is why Luxembourg has the highest receipt per capita in the EU despite being the richest nation by far.

Source: This box is based on the excellent webbook, Felsenthal and Machover (2001), which provides a much better in-depth look at voting theory

Simple counterexamples such as these led to the development of several more sophisticated power indices. We shall focus on the 'Normalized Banzhaf Index'.

3.4.3 Power to break a winning coalition: the Normalized Banzhaf Index

In plain English, the Normalized Banzhaf Index (NBI) gauges how likely it is that a nation finds itself in a position to 'break' a winning coalition on a randomly selected issue. By way of criticism, note that the set-up behind the NBI provides only a shallow depiction of a real-world voting process. For instance, the questions of who sets the voting agenda, how coalitions are formed and how intensively each country holds its various positions are not considered. In a sense, the equal probability of each coalition occurring and each country switching its vote is meant to deal with this shallowness. The idea is that all of these things would average out over a large number of votes on a broad range of issues. Thus, this measure of power is really a very long-term concept. Another way of looking at it is as a measure of power in the abstract. It tells us how powerful a country is likely to be on a randomly chosen issue. Of course, on particular issues, various countries may be much more or much less powerful.

The easiest way to understand this concept more deeply is to calculate it for our simple example in Table 3.1. To make it interesting, we take the uneven vote allocation case (#2) and assume a 70 per cent majority threshold, so winning takes 21 votes. As before, we line up all eight possible coalitions and decide which are the winning ones. These are the first three. Then we ask who the critical players are in these winning coalitions – critical in the sense that they would turn the winning coalition into a losing coalition if they changed their vote. In the first coalition, only A is critical since the defection of either B or C would not change the outcome; nation A and the remaining other nation would have enough votes to win. In the second and third coalitions, where the majority is narrower, both nations are critical, namely A and C in the second and A and B in the third.

Thus there are five situations where a nation would find itself critical. Nation A finds itself in this situation three of the five times, while B and C are critical in only one of the five times. Thus, in this sense, A is more powerful than B and C. The NBI for A is three-fifths, while it is one-fifth for B and C.

A	B	C	Yes votes	70% majority?	Critical player(s)
Yes	Yes	Yes	30	yes	A
Yes	No	Yes	25	yes	A, C
Yes	Yes	No	25	yes	A, B
Yes	No	No	20	no	
No	Yes	Yes	10	no	
No	No	Yes	5	no	
No	Yes	No	5	no	
No	No	No	0	no	

The calculation of NBI for all EU members is a topic that may fascinate some readers, but it is not essential to our study of EU decision making, so we relegate its discussion to Box 3.6.

Box 3.6   Calculating the Normalized Banzhaf Index (NBI)

The mechanical calculation of the NBI is easy to describe and requires nothing more than some patience and a PC with lots of horsepower. To work it out, one asks a computer to look at all possible coalitions (i.e. all conceivable line-ups of yes and no votes) and identify the winning coalitions. Note that listing all possible coalitions is easy to do by hand for low numbers of voters; in a group of 2 voters there are only 4, in a group of 3 there are 8. However, the general formula for the number of all possible coalitions for a group of n voters is 2^n, so determining which coalitions are winners by hand quickly becomes impractical; in the EU15, 32 768 coalitions have to be checked. In the EU27, the number is over 134 million. The computer's next task is to work out all the ways that each winning coalition could be turned into a loser by the defection of a single nation. Finally, the computer calculates the number of times each nation could be a 'deal breaker' as a fraction of the number of times that any country could be a deal breaker. The theory behind this is that the Council decides on a vast array of issues, so the NBI tells us how likely it is that a particular nation will be critical on a randomly selected issue.

For the EU15, it turns out that the theoretically superior power measure (NBI) is not very different from the rough-and-ready national vote-share measure. The measures also are quite similar for EU27. Readers who distrust sophisticated concepts should find their confidence in the Banzhaf measure bolstered by this similarity – and the same applies to readers who distrust rough-and-ready measures.

If you like this sort of reasoning, see the excellent website, http://powerslave.val.utu.fi, which is devoted to power indices of all types.

3.4.4 Power shifts if the Lisbon Treaty comes into force

The fate of the Lisbon Treaty was uncertain as this edition went to press, so it is unclear whether the Council voting reforms will ever come into effect. Indeed, even if the Lisbon Treaty is adopted, the new voting rules will not come into effect until 2014.

The NBI is a useful tool for understanding many of the struggles among Member States over EU institutional reforms – past, present and future. A good example can be found in the switch between the Nice Treaty rules (which are in effect today) and the Lisbon Treaty voting rules.

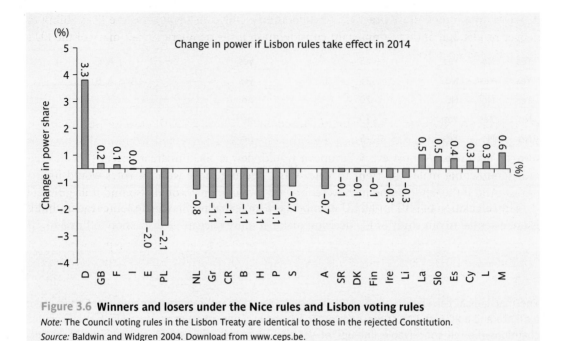

Figure 3.6 **Winners and losers under the Nice rules and Lisbon voting rules**
Note: The Council voting rules in the Lisbon Treaty are identical to those in the rejected Constitution.
Source: Baldwin and Widgren 2004. Download from www.ceps.be.

As pointed out in Chapter 1, the Nice, Constitutional and Lisbon Treaties all had a very hard time getting accepted by EU leaders. Much of the difficulty turned on the voting rules in the Council of Ministers. Specifically, the voting rule proposed by Giscard d'Estaing was included in the Italian President's draft presented to the European Council in December 2003. This was rejected for many reasons, but the main sticking point was the power changes implied, especially for Spain and Poland. Council voting rules were also one of the hardest issues in the 2004 discussions that finalized the Constitutional Treaty. Finally, after the Constitution had been abandoned, the deal on its replacement (Lisbon Treaty) was hung up on the Council voting issue right until the end.

Switching from the current rules in place (those in the Nice Treaty) to the Lisbon Treaty rules changes the power distribution between large and small nations. The Lisbon Treaty would grant some additional power to the smallest states, but it would provide a huge boost to Germany's power. Since power is measured by shares and shares must add to 100 per cent, the German and tiny-nation power gains must be paid for by the other members. As Fig. 3.6 shows, Spain and Poland will be the big losers, but the middle-sized EU Member States will also suffer from the Lisbon rules.

3.5 Legitimacy in EU decision making

The EU is a truly unique organization. Nowhere else in the world has so much national sovereignty been transferred to a supranational body. As Chapter 1 pointed out, the massive death and destruction of two world wars is what led the EU's founders to contemplate this transfer, but the continual willingness of the current generation of Europeans to accept it depends upon much more practical considerations. One consideration is the EU's ability to deliver results, but another important consideration is the democratic legitimacy of the EU's decision-making process.

3.5.1 Thinking about democratic legitimacy

What makes a decision-making system legitimate? This is a difficult question so it helps to start with an extreme and obviously illegitimate voting scheme and to think about why it seems illegitimate. Almost every European would view as illegitimate a system that allowed only landowning males the right to vote. Why? Because those without votes would find it unjust. And if the landowning men were forward looking, they would also find it illegitimate since they or their male offspring might one day lose their land. In short, a good way to think about legitimacy is to apply the 'in the other person's shoes' rule. A system is legitimate if all individuals would be happy with any other individual's allocation of voting power, which, if you think about it, requires equality. Equal power per citizen is thus a very natural legitimacy principle.

But what constitutes a citizen? In the EU there are two answers: nations and people. The EU is a union of states, so each state is a citizen and should thus have equal voting power. The EU is also a union of people, so people are citizens and so each person should have equal voting power. This makes it impossible to apply the equality principle in a simple manner. Note that there is a more classical way to phrase this same point. Democracy, it has been said, is the tyranny of the majority. To avoid this tyrannical aspect, democracies must have mechanisms that protect the rights and wishes of minorities. Indeed, many nations provide mechanisms for giving disadvantaged groups larger than proportional shares of power, but the starting point for such departures is one vote per person. In the EU, the over-weighting of small nations' votes was one such mechanism. For example, equality of power per person would grant Germany 2000 per cent more power than Ireland; equality per member would grant Luxembourgers 160 times more power per person than Germans. Given the dual-union nature of the EU, neither extreme is legitimate.

Using the NBI described above, we have a very precise (albeit crude) measure of 'power per person' and 'power per nation'. The 'fair' power distribution for the Union-of-States view is trivial; in the EU25, each member should get 1/25th of the power. For the Union-of-People view power should be distributed such that each EU citizen has equal power regardless of nationality. As it turns out, the Nice Treaty voting rules favoured the equal-power-per-person view (since it shifted power to big nations). The Constitutional Treaty rules had a less clear-cut impact since it greatly boosted Germany's power, but also boosted the power of EU members with populations below that of a medium–large city.

3.6 Summary

Just to continue to operate, the EU must make a steady stream of decisions to adjust to the ever-changing economic and political landscape. This chapter looked at the EU decision-making process from two perspectives. First, it considered the EU current allotment of 'competences' between the EU level and national governments of its members. In terms of actual practices and principles, the key points were:

★ Policy making is categorized into areas where the EU has 'exclusive competence', i.e. where the decision is made only at the EU level; areas where competence is shared; and areas where the EU has no competence, i.e. where decisions are made only at the national or sub-national level.

★ The allocation of policy areas to these three categories is determined by the Treaties and decisions of the EU Court of Justice. This allocation, however, is blurred since the Treaties do not refer to specific fields; they refer only to areas by functional description. To clarify the allocation, the EU operates on the principle of subsidiarity, which says that unless there is a good reason for allocating a task to the EU level, all tasks should be allocated to national or sub-national governments. The three-pillar structure of the European Union also helps to clarify the allocation. First-pillar (Community pillar) issues are under EU competence while second- and third-pillar issues are not.

The chapter also presented a framework for thinking about how tasks should be allocated between various levels of government (theory of fiscal federalism). This framework stresses four trade-offs that suggest whether a particular decision should be centralized or not:

★ Diversity and information costs favour decentralized decision making.

★ Scale economies favour centralization.

★ Democracy-as-a-control-device favours decentralization.

★ Jurisdictional competition favours decentralization.

The second part of the chapter considered the EU decision-making process in more detail, focusing on efficiency (i.e. the EU's ability to act), national power shares and democratic legitimacy. These three concepts are inherently vague, but the chapter assumes a series of simplifications that enable us to present precise measures of all three. Of course, the necessary simplifications mean that the resulting measures provide only shallow measures of efficiency, power and legitimacy, but at least the measures permit a concrete departure point for further discussion. These measures were:

★ *Efficiency*. We measured efficiency by the 'passage probability', i.e. the likelihood that a randomly selected issue would win a 'yes' vote in the Council of Ministers. We showed that enlargement has continually lowered the EU's passage probability, but that the 2004 enlargement lowered it by a large and unprecedented amount. We also saw that the voting reforms in the Treaty of Nice will make matters worse, even though they were intended to maintain decision-making efficiency.

★ *National power distributions*. We showed that the vote shares of small nations far exceed their population shares. Interpreting vote shares as a measure of power, this says that power in the EU is biased towards small nations. We also showed that this allocation of power goes a long way to explain why actual EU spending patterns may seem strange, i.e. that several rich nations receive above-average receipts per capita. This section also presents a more sophisticated measure of power called the Normalized Banzhaf Index; it measures the probability that a given nation will find itself in a position where it can break a winning coalition.

★ *Legitimacy.* This is by far the vaguest of the three concepts. The approach we adopt is to check whether the allocation of votes in the EU's Council of Ministers lines up against two notions of legitimacy. If the EU is viewed as a Union-of-People, a natural yardstick is equal power per citizen. If the EU is viewed as a Union-of-States, the natural metric is equal power per Member State. Under the principle of equal power per EU citizen, the mathematics of voting tells us that this requires that the Council's votes per country rise with the square root of the country's population. The benchmark of equal power per EU Member State requires an equal number of votes per nation. What we find is that the EU has historically been an 80–20 blend of these two, with the Union-of-States perspective dominating. The reforms in the Treaty of Lisbon will shift the blend a long way away from the historic mix, favouring the Union-of-People view.

Self-assessment questions

1. List the main trade-offs stressed by the theory of fiscal federalism. Discuss how the tension between negative spillovers and diversity can explain the fact that the EU has adopted only very limited harmonization of social policies. (Hint: See Annex A of Chapter 1.)

2. In many European nations, the trend for the last couple of decades has been to decentralize decision making from the national level to the provincial or regional level. How could you explain this trend in terms of the theory of fiscal federalism?

3. Using the actual Council of Ministers votes that came into force after the 2004 enlargement, list five blocking coalitions that you might think of as 'likely'. Do this using the Nice Treaty definition of a qualified majority. Do the same using the qualified majority definition proposed in the draft Constitutional Treaty.

4. The formal power measure discussed in the chapter assumes that each voter has an equal probability of saying 'yes' or 'no' on a random issue, and that the votes of the various voters are uncorrelated. That is, as the likelihood that voter A says 'yes' on a particular issue is unrelated to whether voter B says 'yes'. However, in many situations, the votes of a group of voters will be correlated. For example, poor EU members are all likely to have similar views on issues concerning spending in poor regions. Work out how this correlation changes the distribution of power (defined as likelihood that a particular voter can break a winning coalition). To be concrete, assume that there are five voters (A, B, C, D and E), that each has 20 votes, that the majority rule is 51 per cent, and that A and B always vote the same way.

5. Using the definition of legitimacy proposed in the text (equal power per person), try to determine whether the US Congress is 'legitimate'. Note that the US Congress has two houses; the Senate and the House of Representatives. In the Senate, each of the 50 states has two Senators, while the number of Representatives per state is proportional to the state's population.

Essay questions

1. Obtain a copy of the Constitutional Treaty produced and use the theory of fiscal federalism to discuss the appropriateness of the allocation of competencies between the EU and Member States.

2. Using the QMV voting weights in the EEC6 (see Box 3.5), calculate all possible coalitions, i.e. combinations of 'yes' and 'no' votes among the Six. (Hint: There are 26 = 64 of them.) Identify the winning coalitions and find the passage probability.

3. The 2004 enlargement greatly increased the diversity of preferences inside the EU. Use the theory of fiscal federalism to discuss how this change might suggest a different allocation of competencies between the EU and the Member States.

4. Discuss how 'enhanced cooperation' agreements (see Chapter 2 for details) fit into the theory of fiscal federalism. Do you think the increase in the diversity of preferences in the EU stemming from the 2004 enlargement will make these agreements more or less attractive to Member States?

5. The Constitutional Treaty produced by the European Convention was first released in draft form in May 2003. Download this draft and compare the Council of Minister's voting scheme to the scheme in the final version in terms of efficiency and legitimacy.

6. Comparing the Nice Treaty's Declaration on the Future of Europe and the Laeken Declaration's list of questions on the allocation of competences to the Constitutional Treaty's Title III Part I, write an essay on how well the European Convention accomplished its task on the competence issue.

Further reading: the aficionado's corner

More wide-ranging introduction to fiscal federalism applied to the European Union can be found in **Dewatripont et al.** (1995) and **Berglof et al.** (2003). The latter includes a general discussion that applies the theory to the Constitutional Treaty.

For an opinionated view of what decisions should be allocated to the EU, see **Alesina and Wacziarg** (1999), *Is Europe Going too Far?*, Carnegie-Rochester Conference on Public Policy. Although this contains several factual errors concerning EU law and policies, it contains a highly cogent application of the theory of fiscal federalism to decision making in the EU.

To learn more about formal measures of power and legitimacy, see **Felsenthal and Machover** (2001). For historical power distributions, see **Laruelle and Widgren** (1998).

See also:

Baldwin, R. and M. Widgren (2005) *The Impact of Turkey's Membership on EU Voting*, February 2005, CEPS Policy Brief No. 62. Download from www.ceps.be or hei.unige.ch/~baldwin/policy.html.

Baldwin, R. (1994) *Towards an Integrated Europe*, CEPR, London.

Baldwin, R., E. Berglof, F. Giavazzi and M. Widgren (2001) *Nice Try: Should the Treaty of Nice be Ratified?*, CEPR Monitoring European Integration 11, CEPR, London.

Begg, D. et al. (1993) *Making Sense of Subsidiarity: How Much Centralization for Europe?*, CEPR Monitoring European Integration 4, CEPR, London.

Peet, J. and K. Ussher (1999) *The EU Budget: An Agenda for Reform?*, CER Working Paper, February.

Useful websites

Extensive explanation and use of formal voting measures can be found on http://powerslave.val.utu.fi.

References

Baldwin, R. and M. Widgren (2004) *Council Voting in the Constitutional Treaty: Devil in the Details*, 23 June 2004. CEPS Policy Brief No. 53, July 2004, www.ceps.be or hei.unige.ch/~baldwin/policy.html.

Berglof, E. et al. (2003) *Built to Last: A Political Architecture for Europe*, CEPR Monitoring European Integration 12, CEPR, London.

Bindseil, U. and C. Hantke (1997) 'The power distribution in decision making among EU Member States', *European Journal of Political Economy*, 13: 171–85.

Commons (2002) 'Crossborder shopping and smuggling', House of Commons Library, Research Paper 02/40, London.

Dewatripont, M. et al. (1995) *Flexible Integration: Towards a More Effective and Democratic Europe*, CEPR Monitoring European Integration 6, CEPR, London.

Felsenthal, D. and M. Machover (2001) *Enlargement of the EU and Weighted Voting in the Council of Ministers*, LSE webbook on www.lse.ac.uk.

Kauppi, H. and M. Widgrén (2004) 'What determines EU decision making? Needs, power or both?', *Economic Policy*, 39.

Laruelle, A. and M. Widgren (1998) 'Is the allocation of voting power among EU Member States fair?', *Public Choice*, 94: 317–39.

PART II

The microeconomics of economic integration

Chapter 4

Essential microeconomic tools

Everything should be made as simple as possible,
but not simpler.

Albert Einstein

Chapter contents

4.1	Preliminaries I: supply and demand diagrams	*142*
4.2	Preliminaries II: introduction to open-economy supply and demand analysis	*145*
4.3	MFN tariff analysis	*149*
4.4	Types of protection: an economic classification	*155*
4.5	Summary	*159*

Introduction

This chapter presents the tools that we shall need when we begin our study of European economic integration in the next chapter. The tools are simple because we make a series of assumptions that greatly reduce the complexity of economic interactions. The primary simplification in this chapter concerns the behaviour of firms. In particular, all firms are assumed to be 'perfectly competitive', i.e. we assume that firms take as given the prices they observe in the market. Firms, in other words, believe that they have no impact on prices and that they could sell as much as they want at the market price. A good way of thinking about this assumption is to view each firm as so small that it believes that its choice of output has no impact on market prices.

This is obviously a very rough approximation since even medium-sized firms – the Danish producer of Lego toys or the Dutch brewer of Heineken, for example – realize that the amount they can sell is related to the price they charge. The second key simplification concerns technology, in particular scale economies. Scale economies refer to the way that average cost falls as the firm produces at higher scales of production. Almost every industry is subject to some sort of falling average cost, so considering them (in Chapter 6) will be important, but a great deal of simplification can be gained by ignoring them. This simplification, in turn, allows us to master the essentials before adding in more complexity in subsequent chapters.

4.1 Preliminaries I: supply and demand diagrams

To assess the economics of European integration it proves convenient to have a simple yet flexible diagram with which to determine the price and volume of imports, as well as the level of domestic consumption and production. The diagram we use – the 'import supply and import demand diagram' – is based on straightforward supply and demand analysis. But to begin from the beginning, we quickly review where demand and supply curves come from. Note that this section assumes that readers have had some exposure to supply and demand analysis; our treatment is intended as a review rather than an introduction. Readers who find it too brief should consult an introductory economics textbook such as Mankiw (2007).

Those readers with a good background in microeconomics may want to skip this section, moving straight on to the import demand and supply reasoning introduced in Section 4.2.

4.1.1 Demand curves and marginal utility

A demand curve shows how much consumers would buy of a particular good at any particular price. Since we assume that consumers' behaviour is driven by a desire to spend their money in a way that maximizes their material well-being, it is clear that the demand curve is based on a kind of optimization exercise. To see this, the left-hand panel of Fig. 4.1 plots the 'marginal utility' curve for a typical consumer, i.e. the 'happiness' (measured in euros) that a consumer gets from consuming one more unit of the good under study. If we are considering the demand for music CDs, the marginal utility curve shows how much extra joy a consumer gets from having one more CD. Typically the extra joy from an extra CD will depend upon how many CDs the consumer buys per year. For example, if the consumer buys very few CDs a year, say c' in the diagram, the gain from buying an extra one is likely to be pretty high, for example mu' in the diagram. If, however, the consumer buys lots of CDs, the gain from one more is likely to be much lower, as shown by the pair, c'' and mu''.

This marginal utility curve allows us to work out how much the consumer would buy at any given price. Suppose the consumer could buy as many CDs as she likes at the price p^*. How many would she buy? If the consumer is wise, and we assume she is, she will buy CDs up to the point where the last one bought is just barely worth the price. In the diagram, this level of

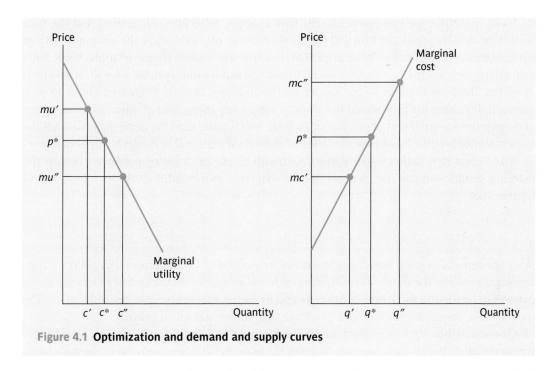

Figure 4.1 Optimization and demand and supply curves

purchase is given by c^* since the marginal benefit (utility) from buying an extra CD exceeds the cost of doing so (the price) for all levels of purchase up to c^*. At this point, the consumer finds that any further CD would not be worth the price. For example, the marginal utility from buying c^* plus one CD would be below p^*. As usual, one gets the market demand for CDs by adding all consumers' individual marginal utility curves horizontally (e.g. if the price is p^* and there are 12 000 identical consumers, market demand will be 12 000 times c^*).

A key point to retain from this is that the price that consumers face reflects the marginal utility of consuming a little more.

4.1.2 Supply curves and marginal costs

Derivation of the supply curve follows a similar logic, but here the optimization is done by firms. The right-hand panel of Fig. 4.1 shows the 'marginal cost' curve facing a typical firm (assume they are all identical for the sake of simplicity), i.e. the extra cost involved in making one more unit of the good. While the marginal cost of production in the real world often declines with the scale of production, allowing for this involves consideration of scale economies and these, in turn, introduce a whole range of complicating factors that would merely clutter the analysis at this stage. To keep it simple, we assume that firms are operating at a point where the marginal cost is upward sloped, i.e. that the cost of producing an extra unit rises as the total number of units produced rises. The curve in the diagram shows, for example, that it costs mc' to produce one more unit when the production level (e.g. the number of CDs produced per year) is q'. This is less than the cost, mc'', of producing an extra unit when the firm is producing q'' units per year.

Using this curve we can determine the firm's supply behaviour. Presuming that the firm wants to maximize profit, the firm will supply the number of goods where the marginal cost just equals the price. For example, if the price is p^*, the firm will want to supply q^* units. Why? If the firm offered one less than q^* units, it would be missing out on some profit. After all, at that level of output, the price the firm would receive for the good, p^*, exceeds the marginal cost of producing it. Likewise, the firm would not want to supply any more than q^* since, for such a level of output, the marginal cost of producing an extra unit is more than the price. Again, we get the aggregate supply curve by adding all the firms' individual marginal cost curves horizontally.

A key point here is that under perfect competition, the price facing producers reflects the marginal production cost, i.e. the cost of producing one more unit than the firm produces in equilibrium.

4.1.3 Welfare analysis: consumer and producer surplus

Since the demand curve is based on consumers' evaluation of the happiness they get from consuming a good and the supply curve is based on firms' evaluation of the cost of producing it, the curves can be used to show how consumers and firms are affected by changes in the price. The tools we use, 'consumer surplus' and 'producer surplus', are described below.

Consumers buy up to the point where the marginal utility from the last unit bought just equals the price. For all the other units bought, the marginal utility exceeds the price, so the consumer gets what is known as 'consumer surplus' from buying c^* units at price p^* (see Fig. 4.2). How much? For the first unit bought, the marginal unit was mu' but the price paid was only p^*, so the surplus is the area shown by the rectangle a. For the second unit, the marginal utility

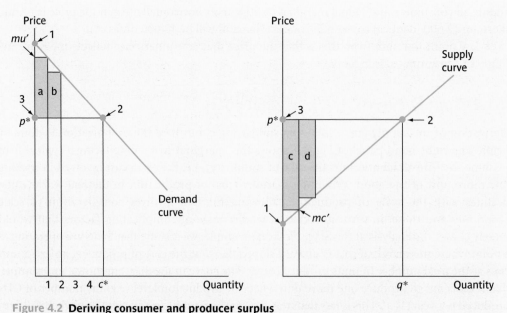

Figure 4.2 **Deriving consumer and producer surplus**

was somewhat lower (not shown in the diagram), so the surplus is lower, specifically it is given by the area b. Doing the same for all units shows that buying c^* units at p^* yields a total consumer surplus equal to the sum of all the resulting rectangles. If we take the units to be very finely defined, the triangle defined by the points 1, 2 and 3 gives us the total consumer surplus.

An analogous line of reasoning shows us that the triangle formed by the points 1, 2 and 3 in the right-hand panel gives us a measure of the gain firms get from being able to sell q^* units at a price of p^*. Consider the first unit sold. The marginal cost of producing this unit was mc' but this was sold for p^* so the firm earns a surplus, what we call the 'producer surplus', equal to the rectangle c in the right-hand panel. Doing the same exercise for each unit sold shows that the total producer surplus is equal to the triangle defined by the points 1, 2 and 3.

If the price changes, the size of the two triangles (consumer surplus and producer surplus) changes. By drawing similar diagrams, you should be able to convince yourself that a price rise increases producer surplus and decreases consumer surplus.

4.2 Preliminaries II: introduction to open-economy supply and demand analysis

This section introduces the 'workhorse' diagram in our study of the essential microeconomics of European economic integration – the open-economy supply and demand analysis. Readers who have had a good course in international trade may consider skipping this section and moving straight on to the tariff analysis in Section 4.3. The diagram, however, is used throughout this chapter and the next, so even advanced students may wish to briefly review the diagram's foundations; if nothing else, such a review will help with the terminology.

4.2.1 The import demand curve

We first look at where the import demand curve comes from; Fig. 4.3 facilitates the analysis.

The left-hand panel of the diagram depicts a nation's supply and demand curves. If imports were banned for some reason, the nation would only be able to consume as much as it produced. The normal market interactions would result in a market price of P^* since this is the price where the amount that consumers are willing to buy just matches the amount firms want to produce. Plainly, import demand is zero at P^* (for simplicity, we assume that imported and domestic goods are perfect substitutes). This zero-import point is marked in the right-hand panel as point 1.

How much would the nation import if the price were lower, say P'? The first thing to note is that the import price will fix the domestic price. Since consumers can always import the goods at P', no consumer would pay more than P' for the good. Likewise, there is no reason for domestic firms to charge anything less than P', so P' becomes the domestic price. At price P', consumption demand would be C' and domestic production would be Z'. Since consumers want to buy more of the good at P' than domestic firms are willing to produce, the excess demand would be met by imports. That is to say, imports would be the difference between C' and Z' (in symbols, $M' = C' - Z'$).

What this tells us is that import demand at P' is M'. This point is marked in the right-hand panel of the diagram as point 3. Performing the same exercise for P'' yields point 2, and doing

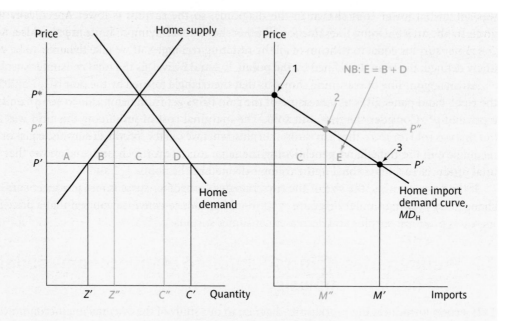

Figure 4.3 Deriving the import demand curve and welfare changes

Note: Readers who find these diagrams complicated may benefit from the step-by-step explanations available in the interactive PowerPoint presentation available on the companion website.

the same for every possible import price yields the import demand curve, i.e. the amount of imports that the nation wants at any given price of imports. The resulting curve is shown as MD_H in the right-hand panel. (For convenience, we often call the nation under study the 'Home' country to distinguish it from its trade partners, what we call the 'Foreign' nations.)

Welfare analysis: MD curves as the marginal benefit of imports

Welfare analysis is simple with this import demand curve. Consider a rise in the import price (i.e. the price faced by Home consumers and producers) from P' to P''. The corresponding equilibrium level of imports drops to M'', since consumption drops to C'' and production rises to Z''. The welfare analysis employed in the left-hand panel involves the notions of consumer and producer surpluses (see Section 4.1 for a review of these concepts). Specifically, the price rise from P' to P'' lowers consumer surplus by A + B + C + D. The same price rise increases producer surplus by A. The right-hand panel shows how this appears in the import demand diagram. From the left-hand panel, the import price rise means a net loss to the country of B + C + D, since the area A cancels out (area A is a gain to Home producers and loss to Home consumers). In the right-hand panel, these changes are shown as area C and E, where area E equals area B + D.

A powerful perspective: trade volume effects and border price effects

It proves insightful to realize that the MD_H curve shows the marginal benefit of imports to Home. Before explaining why this is true, we show that it is a useful insight. Direct reasoning showed that Home loses areas C and E from a border price rise from P' to P''. Area C is easy to understand. After the price rise, Home pays more for the units it imported at the old price. Area C is the size of this loss. (Say the price rise was €1.2 per unit and M'' was 100; the loss would be €1.2 times 100; geometrically, this is the area C since a rectangle's area is its height times its base.) Understanding area E is where the insight comes in handy. Home reduces its imports at the new price and area E measures how much it loses from the drop in imports. The marginal value of the first lost unit of import is the height of the MD_H curve at M'', but Home had to pay P' for it, so the net loss is the gap between P' and the MD_H curve. If we add up the gaps for all the extra units imported, we get the area E. The jargon terms for these areas are the 'border price effect' (area C) and the 'import volume effect' (area E).

To understand why MD_H is the marginal benefit of imports we use three facts and one bit of logic: (i) the MD_H curve is the difference between the domestic demand curve and the domestic supply curve; (ii) the domestic supply curve is the domestic marginal cost curve, and the domestic demand curve is the domestic marginal utility curve (see Section 4.1 if these points are unfamiliar); and (iii) the difference between domestic marginal utility of consumption and domestic marginal cost of production is the net gain to the nation of producing and consuming one more unit. The logical point is that an extra unit of imports leads to some combination of higher consumption and lower domestic production, and this leads to some combination of higher utility and lower costs; the height of the MD_H curve tells us what that combination is. Or, to put it differently, the nation imports up to the point where the marginal gain from doing so equals the marginal cost. Since the border price is the marginal cost, the border price is also an indication of the marginal benefit of imports.

To see these points in more detail, see the interactive PowerPoint presentations available for free on http://hei.unige.ch/~baldwin/PapersBooks/BW/BW.html.

4.2.2 The export supply curve

Figure 4.4 uses an analogous line of reasoning to derive the import supply schedule. The first thing to keep in mind is that the supply of imports to Home is the supply of exports from foreigners. For simplicity's sake, suppose that there is only one foreign country (simply called 'Foreign' hereafter) and its supply and demand curves look like the left-hand panel of the figure. (Note that the areas in Fig. 4.4 are unrelated to the areas in Fig. 4.3.)

As with the import demand curve, we start by asking how much Foreign would export for a particular price. For example, how much would it export, if the price of its exports was P'? At price P', Foreign firms would produce Z' and Foreign consumers would buy C'. The excess production, equal to $X' = Z' - C'$, would be exported. The fact that Foreign would like to export X' when the export price is P' is shown in the right-hand panel at point 2. As the price for Foreign exports (i.e. the Home's import price) rose, Foreign would be willing to supply a higher level of exports for two reasons. The higher price would induce Foreign firms to produce more and Foreign consumers to buy less. (Note that as in the case of import demand, the export price sets the price in Foreign; Foreign firms have no reason to sell for less since they can always export, and competition among Foreign suppliers would prevent any of them from charging Foreign consumers a higher price.) For example, the price P'' would bring forth an import supply equal to X'' (this equals $Z'' - C''$); this is shown as point 3 in the right-hand panel. At price P^*, exports

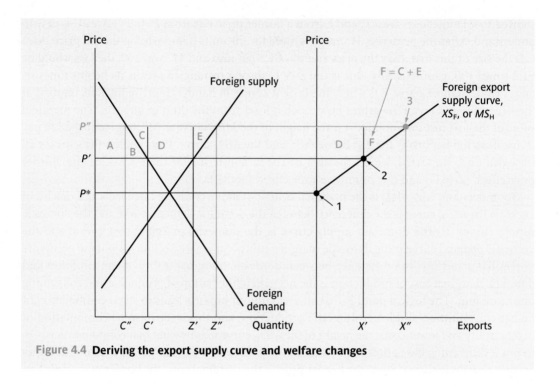

Figure 4.4 Deriving the export supply curve and welfare changes

are zero. Plotting all such combinations in the right-hand panel produces the export supply curve XS_F. We stress again the simple but critical point that the Foreign export supply is the Home import supply, thus we also label XS_F as MS_H.

Welfare

The left-hand panel also shows how price changes translate into Foreign welfare changes. If the export price rises from P' to P'', consumers in the exporting country lose by A + B (these letters are not related to those in the previous figure), but the Foreign firms gain producer surplus equal to A + B + C + D + E. The net gain is therefore C + D + E. Using the export supply curve XS_F, we can show the same net welfare change in the right-hand panel as the area D plus F. Note that the insight from the MD_H curve extends to the XS_F curve, i.e. the XS_F curve gives the marginal benefit to Foreign of exporting.

This review of import supply and demand was very rapid – probably too rapid for students who have never used such diagrams and probably too long for students who have. For those who find themselves in the first category, there are interactive PowerPoint presentations available on http://hei.unige.ch/~baldwin/PapersBooks/BW/BW.html.

4.2.3 The workhorse diagram: *MD–MS*

The big payoff from having an import supply curve and an import demand curve is that it permits us to find the equilibrium price and quantity of imports. The equilibrium price is found

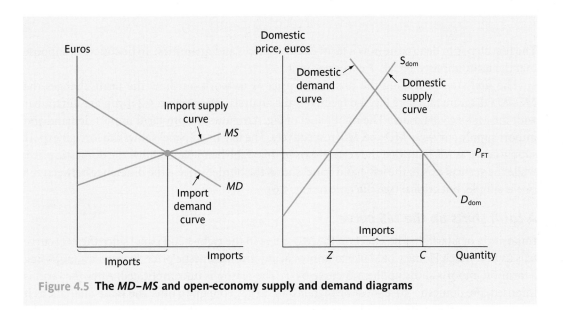

Figure 4.5 The *MD–MS* and open-economy supply and demand diagrams

by putting together import demand and supply as shown in the left-hand panel of Fig. 4.5; we drop the 'H' and 'F' subscripts for convenience.

Assuming imports and domestic production are perfect substitutes, the domestic price is set at the point where the demand and supply of imports meet, namely P_{FT} (FT stands for free trade). While the import supply and demand diagram, or *MD–MS* diagram for short, is handy for determining the price and volume of imports, it does not permit us to see the impact of price changes on domestic consumers and firms separately. This is where the right-hand panel becomes useful. In particular, we know that the market clears only when the price is P_{FT}, so we know that Home production equals Z and Home consumption equals C. The equilibrium level of imports may be read off either panel. In the left-hand panel, it is shown directly; in the right-hand one, it is the difference between domestic consumption and production.

Having explained these basic microeconomic tools, we turn now to using them to study a simple but common real-world problem – the effects of a tax change on imports from all nations.

4.3 MFN tariff analysis

The principle of progressive complexity leads us to take a detour in our drive towards the analysis of preferential trade liberalization in Europe. To introduce the basic method of analysis and gain experience in using the diagrams, we first study the impact of removing the simplest type of trade barrier – a tariff. Although discriminatory liberalization is what happened in Europe, we first look at the non-discriminatory case since it is less complex. For historical reasons, a non-discriminatory tariff is called a 'most favoured nation' tariff, which provides the handy abbreviation, MFN. We also note that all European nations have undertaken substantial MFN tariff liberalizations in the context of WTO trade negotiations, such as the Uruguay Round, so the analysis has many real-world applications.

4.3.1 Price and quantity effects of a tariff

The first step is to determine how a tariff changes prices and quantities. To be concrete, suppose that the tariff imposed equals T euros per unit.

The first step in finding the post-tariff price is to work out how the tariff changes the MD–MS diagram and here Fig. 4.6 facilitates the analysis. (See Section 4.2 if you are unfamiliar with the MD–MS diagram.) The right panel of Fig. 4.6 shows the pre-tariff import demand and import supply curves as MD and MS, respectively. The left-hand panel shows the foreign export supply curve as XS. Note that the vertical axis in this right-hand panel shows the domestic price, while the vertical axis in the left-hand panel shows the border price – the difference between the two is simple, but critical (see the note to Fig. 4.6).

A tariff shifts up the MS curve

Imposition of a tariff has no effect on the MD curve in the right-hand panel since the MD curve tells us how much Home would like to import at any given domestic price. By contrast, imposing a tariff on imports shifts up the MS curve by T. The reason is uncomplicated. After the tariff is imposed, the domestic price must be higher by T to get Foreign to offer the same quantity as it offered before the tariff. Consider an example. How much would Foreign supply before the

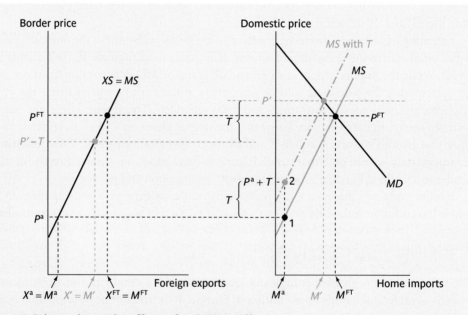

Figure 4.6 Price and quantity effects of an MFN tariff

Note: Observe the distinction between the domestic and border prices. The domestic price is the price that domestic consumers pay for the good. The border price is the price foreign producers receive when they sell the good to Home. Why can they differ? Because of the tariff (a tariff is nothing more than a tax on imports). When you buy a coffee at a café for, say, €1, the café owner does not get the full €1 because the owner has to pay a tax, called the VAT, on your purchase. As a result, the price that the café owner receives is only 80 cents (the VAT is 20 per cent in this example) even though you pay 100 cents. In exactly the same way, foreigners receive a price (the border price) that equals the domestic price minus the tariff.

tariff, if the Home domestic price before the tariff were P^a? The answer, which is given by point 1 on the MS curve, is M_a. After the tariff, we get a different answer. To get Foreign to offer M_a after the tariff, the domestic price must be $P^a + T$ so that Foreign sees a border price of P^a.

So far we see that the tariff shifts up the MS curve. Now we consider the impact on equilibrium prices and quantities.

The new equilibrium prices and quantities

Even without a diagram, readers would surely realize that a tariff raises the domestic price and lowers imports. After all, a tariff is a tax on imports and it is intuitively obvious that putting a tax on imports will raise prices somewhat and lower imports somewhat. Why do we need a diagram? The diagram helps us be more specific about this intuition; this specificity allows us to work out how much the nations gain or lose from the tariff. As we shall see, this tells us a great deal about the political economy of trade protection. Returning to our analysis, note that after the tariff, the old import supply curve is no longer valid. The new import supply curve, labelled MS with T, is what matters and the equilibrium price is set at the point where the new import supply curve and the import demand curve cross. As intuition would have it, the new price – marked P' in the diagram – is higher than the pre-tariff price P_{FT} (as already noted, FT stands for free trade). Because of the higher domestic price, Home imports are reduced to M' from M_{FT}. To summarize, there are five price and quantity effects of the tariff:

1 The price facing Home firms and consumers (domestic price) rises to P'.
2 The border price (i.e. the price Home pays for imports) falls to $P' - T$; this also means that the price received by Foreigners falls to $P' - T$.
3 The Home import volume falls to M'.

The other two effects cannot be seen in the diagram, but are intuitively obvious and could be illustrated explicitly if we included another panel in Fig. 4.6 that resembled the right-hand panel in Fig. 4.5 (this is done explicitly in Box 4.1):

4 Home production rises since Home firms receive a higher price (they see the domestic price since they do not pay the tariffs).
5 Home consumption falls in response to the higher domestic price.

There are also production and consumption effects of the tariff inside the exporting nation. Since the border price falls, Foreign production drops and Foreign consumption rises. We could see this explicitly if we put a diagram like the left-hand panel of Fig. 4.4 to the left of the diagram in Fig. 4.6.

4.3.2 Welfare effects of a tariff

Having worked out the price and quantity effects, it is simple to calculate the welfare effects of the tariffs, that is to say, who wins, who loses and by how much.

Recall that the MD curve comes from optimization by Home consumers and producers, while the $XS = MS$ curve reflects optimization by Foreign consumers and producers. What this means is that we can evaluate the Home welfare effects of the price and quantity changes using only the MD curve, and the Foreign welfare effects using only the $XS = MS$ curve, as shown by Fig. 4.7.

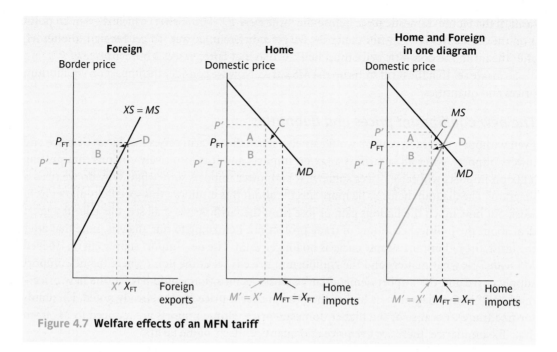

Figure 4.7 **Welfare effects of an MFN tariff**

We start with the Foreign welfare impact since it is easier. At an intuitive level, we should expect the tariff to harm Foreigners since it means they get a lower price (the border price drops) and they export less. Using the diagram we can quantify these losses. The welfare impact is shown by the areas B and D in the leftmost panel. The area B represents the direct loss from the lower price and D represents the loss from the lower level of sales. As usual, these are the trade price effect (area B) and the trade volume effect (area D).

The diagram also shows the impact of the price change on the welfare of Home residents. Intuitively, it should be clear that Home consumers will lose from the higher domestic price and Home firms will gain from the same, but that the losers will lose more than the gainers will gain since Home consumption exceeds Home production. The diagram allows us to be more precise about these welfare effects.

As we showed in Section 4.1, the loss in the 'private surplus' (i.e. the sum of the changes in consumer surplus and producer surplus) from the price rise from P_{FT} to P' is given by the area A + C in the middle panel. Since a tariff is a tax, the last thing to consider is the impact on Home government revenue. Since Home collects tariff revenue equal to the tariff times the number of units imported, this gain equals the area A + B in the middle panel of Fig. 4.7. Adding up the change in private surplus (minus A and minus C) and the gain in revenue (plus A plus B), the net effect is the area C minus the area B, which we write as C − B for short.

A useful condensation

The first time one works through these welfare calculations, it is useful to separate the Home and Foreign effects using separate diagrams (the left and middle panels in Fig. 4.7). This separation emphasizes the fact that Foreign welfare effect can be derived from the price and quantity changes using only the *XS* curve, and, similarly, the Home welfare effect can be derived from the price and quantity effects using only the *MD* curve. Yet, once one is familiar with the underpinnings of the areas A, B, C and D, it is convenient to condense the analysis into a single diagram, like the right-hand panel in Fig. 4.7.

Box 4.1 Home and foreign welfare effects: distributional consequences

The analysis in Fig. 4.7 focused on the overall welfare impact on Home and Foreign. It did not allow us to see the distributional effects of the tariffs, i.e. the impact of the tariff on different groups within Home. Since the politics of an import tariff often depend heavily on the tariff's distributional impact, it is handy to have a diagram where we can see the distributional effects and the overall effects. Figure 4.8, which is based on the open-economic supply and demand diagram, is the diagram that serves this purpose.

In both panels of the diagram, the tariff-induced changes in prices and quantities are shown. As noted in the text, the overall private surplus change – that is, the loss to Home consumers minus the gain to Home producers – is minus the areas A and C in the left-hand panel. The right-hand panel allows us to see the producer and consumer surplus components separately. The loss to consumers from the price rise (from P_{FT} to P') is minus the areas $E + C_1 + A + C_2$. The gain to Home producers is the area E. Note that the area C in the left-hand panel equals the sum of the two triangles, $C_1 + C_2$, in the right-hand panel. The gain in government revenue from the tax on imports is just equal to the areas A and B.

The gain to producers is, of course, the usual reason that governments impose a tariff – they want to help domestic producers. Despite the fact that this harms domestic consumers, governments often find tariffs to be politically attractive since domestic producers are often better organized politically than are domestic consumers.

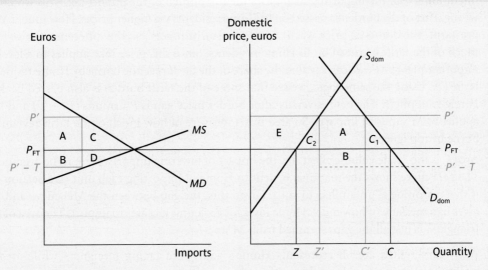

Figure 4.8 **Distributional and over welfare effects of an MFN tariff**

To summarize, using either the two-panel analysis or the condensed analysis, we find:

★ The tariff reduces Foreign welfare since it means they sell less and receive a lower price. The loss in welfare, measured in euros, equals area B plus area D.

★ The tariff creates private-sector winners and losers (Home firms gain, Home consumers lose), but the losers (consumers) lose more than gainers (firms) gain; the net impact is −A − C.

★ Home collects tariff revenue equal to A + B.

★ The overall Home welfare change, including both revenue and the net private loss, is B − C.

★ The net effect, B − C, may be positive or negative; the relative sizes of B and C depend upon the slopes of the *MD* and *MS* curves and on the size of *T*.

★ The global impact of the tariff, adding Home and Foreign welfare changes together, is definitely negative and equal to the area −C − D.

Before moving on, note that, as in Section 4.1, we can trace through the distributional effects of the welfare changes, e.g. the loss to Home consumers and the gains to Home firms, using a diagram that resembles the right-hand panel in Fig. 4.5. This is done in Box 4.1.

4.3.3 Tariffs as a way of taxing foreigners

The result that a tariff might make the Home country better or worse off is worth looking at from a different angle. The two parts of Home's net welfare impact, namely B − C, represent very different kinds of changes.

★ The area B is the 'trade price effect', i.e. the gain from paying less for imports. We can also think of it as the amount of the new tariff revenue that is borne by foreigners. This statement requires some explaining. In the real world, the importing firm pays the whole tariff, so one might think that the importing firm bears the full burden of the import tax. This would be wrong. Part of the burden is passed on to Home residents via higher prices. How much? Well pre-tariff, the domestic price was P_{FT} and post-tariff it is P', so the difference shows how much of the tariff is passed on to Home residents. Since this price hike applies to a level of imports equal to M', we can say that the share of the tariff revenue borne by Home residents is area A. Using the same logic, we see that some of the tariff burden is also passed back to Foreign suppliers. The before-versus-after border price gap is P_{FT} minus $(P' − T)$ and this applies to M' units of imports. So area B is a measure of how much of the tariff revenue is borne by foreigners.

★ Area C is the 'trade volume effect', i.e. the impact of lowering imports. Here is the argument. The *MD* curve shows the marginal benefit to Home of importing each unit (see Section 4.2 if this reasoning is unfamiliar to you). Given this, the gap between the *MD* curve and P_{FT} gives us a measure of how much Home loses for each unit it ceases to import. The area of the triangle C is just all the gaps summed from M' to M_{FT}.

To put it differently, area B represents Home's gain from taxing foreigners while area C represents an efficiency loss from the tariff.

Given all this, we can say that if *T* raises Home welfare, then it does so only because the tariff allows the Home government to indirectly tax foreigners enough to offset the tariff's inefficiency effects on the Home economy. That is, T causes economic inefficiency at Home but T is also a way of exploiting foreigners. Since the exploitation gains may outweigh the inefficiency effects, Home may gain from imposing a tariff.

4.3.4 Global welfare effects and retaliation

The global welfare impact is simply a matter of summing up effects and it turns out to be negative. The net Home welfare effect is B – C. For foreign, it is –B – D. The global welfare change is thus a loss, namely –C – D.

Put in this way, the gains from a tariff are clearly suspect. For example, if Home and Foreign were symmetric and both imposed tariffs, both would lose the efficiency triangle C and the gain to Home of B on imports would be lost to Home on its exports to Foreign. Home would also lose the deadweight triangle D on exports, so the net loss to each of the symmetric nations would be –C – D. In short, protection by all nations is worse than a zero-sum game. It is exactly this point that underpins the economics of WTO tariff-cutting negotiations. If only one nation liberalizes, it might lose. If, however, the nation's liberalization is coordinated with its trading partners' liberalization, the zero-sum aspect tends to disappear.

4.4 Types of protection: an economic classification

Tariffs are only one of many types of import barriers that European integration has removed. The first phase of EU integration, 1958–68, focused on tariff removal, but the Single Market Programme that was started in 1986 focused on a much wider range of 'non-tariff barriers'.

While there are several methods of categorizing such barriers, it proves useful to focus on how the barriers affect so-called trade rents. A tariff, for instance, drives a wedge between the Home price and the border price (i.e. the price paid to foreigners). This allows someone (in the tariff case it will be the Home government) to indirectly collect the 'profit' from selling at the high domestic price while buying at the low border price. For historical reasons, economists refer to such profits (area A + B in Fig. 4.9) as 'rents'. When it comes to welfare analysis, we must watch the trade rents closely. For some import barriers, Home residents get the rents, but for others no rents are created, or foreigners get the rents. This distinction is highlighted by distinguishing three categories of trade barriers: domestically captured rent (DCR) barriers; foreign captured rent (FCR) barriers; and 'frictional' barriers.

4.4.1 DCR barriers

Tariffs form the classic DCR barrier. Here, the Home government gets the trade rents. From a Home nationwide welfare perspective, however, it does not really matter whether the government, Home firms or Home consumers earn these rents, as long as the rents are captured domestically. What sorts of barriers other than tariffs would lead to domestically captured rents? Some forms of quotas are DCR barriers. A quota is a quantitative limit on the number of goods that can be imported per year. To control the number of foreign goods entering the country, the government hands out a fixed number of import licences and 'collects' one licence per unit imported. The price and quantity effects of a quota that restricts imports to M' in Fig. 4.9 are identical to the effects of a tariff equal to T. The point is that, if imports are limited

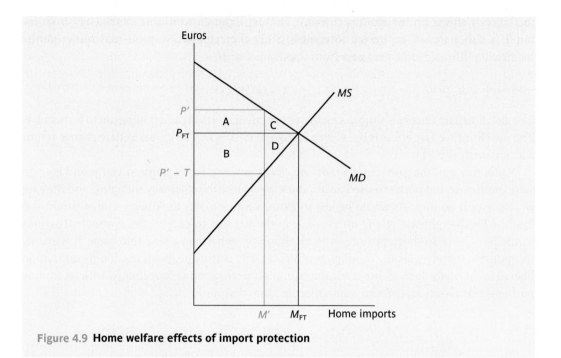

Figure 4.9 **Home welfare effects of import protection**

to M', then the gap between domestic consumption and production can be no more than M', implying that the domestic price must be driven up to P'. Another way to say this is that T is the 'tariff equivalent' of the quota. Now consider the trade rents. With a quota, whoever has the licence can buy the goods at the border price $P' - T$ and resell them in the Home market for P'. This earns the licence holders A + B. If the government gives the licences to Home residents, then the quota is a DCR barrier. If it gives them to foreigners, the quota is an FCR barrier.

4.4.2 FCR barriers

A prime example of an FCR barrier is a 'price undertaking', a trade barrier that was commonly imposed against imports from central and eastern Europe before the 2004 enlargement. In these cases, the EU strikes an agreement whereby foreign producers agree to sell their goods at a price no lower than an agreed level. For example, if the agreed level were P' from Fig. 4.9, the price undertaking would have the same price and quantity effects as a tariff T. Importantly, however, the undertaking allows foreign producers, rather than the Home government, to garner the rents A + B. Throughout the industrialized world, and in the EU in particular, it is very common for trade barriers to be arranged so that foreigners earn the rents. One reason is that trade rents are used as a kind of gift to soothe foreign companies and governments that are likely to be angered by the imposition of a trade barrier.

More recent examples of an FCR barrier are the EU's restrictions on Chinese clothing exports. The European Commission negotiated limits on how fast Chinese exports to the EU could grow. But since it is the Chinese who control the quantity (via export licences), it is the Chinese who get the trade rents. This was done on purpose to appease the Chinese government.

The USA also imposed restraints on Chinese clothing exports but it is the US that controls the quotas, so the quota rents go to US residents. No wonder the Chinese were happier about the way the EU reacted. Note that policy in this area was evolving as this edition went to print; for the latest (click through 'Textile and footwear sector') see http://europa.eu.int/comm/trade/issues/sectoral/index_en.htm.

Finally, note that an FCR barrier harms national welfare more than a DCR barrier. Specifically, the welfare cost of an FCR is always negative, i.e. $-A - C$, instead of being ambiguous, i.e. $B - C$. Moreover, the foreign welfare impact is now $A - D$, so an FCR may end up helping foreigners!

4.4.3 Frictional barriers

The main type of trade barrier remaining inside the EU consists of what are sometimes called 'technical barriers to trade' (TBTs). Western European countries often restrict imports by subjecting them to a whole range of policies that increase the real cost of buying foreign goods.

Some examples are excessive bureaucratic 'red-tape' restrictions and industrial standards that discriminate against foreign goods. One of the most famous examples is discussed in Box 4.2.

Box 4.2   Cassis de Dijon: a history-making technical barrier to trade

One very common type of frictional barrier concerns health and safety regulations that have the side-effect of hindering trade. Perhaps the most famous of these was a German regulation that forbade the importation of certain low-alcohol spirits, including the sweet French liqueur, Cassis – used in making the famous white wine drink, 'Kir'. This regulation was challenged before the EU's Court of Justice as a barrier to trade. When challenged on this regulation, the German government argued that the prohibition was necessary to protect public health (since weak spirits more easily promote alcohol tolerance) and to protect consumers (since consumers might buy weak spirits, thinking they were strong). In 1979, the Court ruled that the measure was not necessary since widespread availability of low-alcohol drinks (e.g. beer) in Germany made the prohibition ineffective in furthering public health. It also found that putting the alcohol content on the label was sufficient to protect consumers, so the import ban was not necessary for the protection of consumers. This Court ruling resulted in the frictional barrier being removed. More importantly, it established the basic principle known as 'mutual recognition' whereby goods that are lawfully sold in one EU nation shall be presumed to be safe for sale in all EU nations. Exceptions to this principle require explicit motivation. By the way, the formal name for this Court case is 'Rewe-Zentral AG v. Bundesmonopolverwaltung für Branntwein'; no wonder it is called Cassis de Dijon.

Such barriers raise the cost of imports by increasing the difficulty and thereby the cost of selling to the Home market. Nobody gets the rents with such barriers since no rents are created. From the Home perspective, frictional and FCR barriers have identical effects; using the areas in Fig. 4.9, Home loses $A + C$. From the Foreign perspective, an FCR barrier is superior. Specifically, the Foreign welfare change is $A - D$ for FCR, but $-B - D$ for a frictional barrier.

Since frictional barriers are bad for a nation, one may ask why they are so prevalent. Box 4.3 provides one explanation.

> ## Box 4.3   Why do frictional barriers arise so often?
>
> Government agencies charged with formulating and enforcing standards are often 'captured' by special-interest groups from the regulated industries. Moreover, the Home firms that are to be subjected to the standards often play an important role in setting the standards. For example, when regulating a highly technical field such as elevators, the government (which probably does not employ many full-time elevator experts) naturally asks the opinions of domestic firms that produce elevators. With an eye to their foreign competitors, they quite naturally push for standards that raise the cost of imported goods more than the cost of locally produced goods.
>
> An example can be found in the paper industry. Sweden and Finland produce paper mainly from new trees, while French and German paper producers use a lot of recycled paper and rags. In the early 1990s, the EU was considering a regulation that would require all paper sold in the EU to contain a certain fraction of recycled paper. This sounds like a 'public interest' regulation. However, it also would have had the effect of eliminating the resource-based advantage of Swedish and Finnish firms, much to the joy of French and German firms. In other words, it would have raised the real cost of imports (since the Nordic producers would have had to switch to less efficient techniques). As it turns out, it is not clear which production method is 'greener'. Recycling paper requires lots of chemicals that may be released into the environment, while setting up more tree farms is, well, green – a point that was not raised by French and German paper producers.
>
> Since Finland and Sweden joined the EU, the regulation was not adopted, but this shows the subtle mixing of public interest and protectionism that inevitably arises when nations adopt regulations and standards. Of course, nations do need health, safety, environmental and industrial standards, so we cannot eliminate frictional barriers by just abolishing all regulation. This is one of the things tackled by the EU's 1992 programme.

One important class of frictional – i.e. cost-creating – barriers involves industrial and health standards that are chosen at least in part to restrict imports. For example, some countries refuse to accept safety tests that are performed in foreign countries, even in highly industrialized nations. This forces importers to retest their products in the local country. Beyond raising the real cost of imported goods, this sort of barrier delays the introduction of new products. While this clearly harms consumers, Home producers may benefit since it may give them time to introduce competing varieties. Another example involves imposing industrial, health, safety or environmental standards that differ from internationally recognized norms. It is often difficult to objectively know whether an unusual regulation or standard represents a valid 'public interest' concern or whether it is just a protectionist device. In fact, both motives are usually behind the adoption of such measures.

Regardless of why such policies are adopted, they have the effect of protecting Home producers or service providers. Home firms design their products with these standards in mind, while foreign firms, for whom the Home market may be relatively unimportant, are unlikely to do so. Bringing imported products into conformity raises the real cost of imports.

For example, all cars sold in Sweden must have wipers for the headlights. While this policy may have some merit as a safety regulation (in the old days Sweden had lots of dusty rural roads), it also has the effect of raising the price of imported cars more than it raises the price of Swedish cars. From the drawing board onwards, all models of Volvos and Saabs – and their production facilities – are designed with these headlight wipers in mind. For other car makers, take Renault as an example, the Swedish market is far too small to really matter. The design of Renaults and Renault's mass production facilities are not optimized for the installation of headlight wipers. Consequently, while it is expensive to put headlight wipers on both Swedish and French cars, it is much more so for French cars. This gives the Swedish car makers an edge in Sweden. Similar sorts of barriers give the French an edge in their domestic market.

Such barriers are extremely common (Box 4.3 explores why). In fact, the EU initiated the 1992 Single Market Programme with the express intent of eliminating such barriers via the mutual recognition of product standards (with minimum harmonization).

With the MFN case as background, we are ready to turn to the following chapter, namely the analysis of discriminatory trade liberalization of the types undertaken in Europe.

4.5 Summary

This chapter presented the essential microeconomic tools for trade policy analysis in the simplified world where we assume there is no imperfect competition and no scale economies. The two most important diagrams are the open-economy supply and demand diagram (right-hand panel of Fig. 4.5), and the *MD–MS* diagram (left-hand panel of Fig. 4.5). The *MD–MS* diagram provides a compact way of working out the impact of import protection on prices, quantities and overall Home and Foreign welfare. The open-economy supply and demand diagram allowed us to consider the distributional impact of import protection, i.e. to separate the overall effect into its component effects on Home consumers, Home producers and Home revenue.

The chapter also discussed types of trade barriers in Europe and classified them according to what happens to the trade 'rents'. Under the first type, DCR barriers, the rents go to domestic residents. For FCR barriers, the rents go to foreigners, and with frictional barriers the rents disappear. European integration consisted primarily of removing DCR barriers up until the mid-1970s. Subsequent goods-market liberalization has focused on frictional barriers.

Self-assessment questions

1. Using a diagram like Fig. 4.8, show the full Foreign welfare effects of imposing a Home tariff equal to T, i.e. show the impact on Foreign producers and Foreign consumers separately.

2. In August 2005, EU clothing retailers such as Sweden's H&M complained about the new EU restrictions on imports from China that were imposed after complaints from EU clothing producers based in Italy, France, Spain, Portugal and Greece. Use a diagram like Fig. 4.8 to explain the positions of the various EU interest groups.

3. One way to think about the slope of the *MS* curve is in terms of the 'size' of the home nation. The idea is that the demand from a very small nation has a very small impact on the world price. For example, Switzerland could probably increase its oil imports by 10 per cent without having any impact on the world oil price. Using a diagram like Fig. 4.7, show that the

welfare costs of imposing an MFN tariff are larger for smaller nations, interpreting this in terms of the *MS* curve's slope. Show that when the *MS* curve is perfectly flat, the welfare effects are unambiguously negative.

4. Using a diagram like Fig. 4.7, show that a country facing an upward-sloped *MS* curve can gain – starting from free trade – from imposing a sufficiently small tariff. (Hint: The rectangle gains and triangle losses both increase in size as the tariff gets bigger, but the rectangle gets bigger faster.) Show that any level of a frictional or FCR barrier lowers Home welfare.

5. Using the results from the previous exercise, consider the impact of Home imposing a tariff on Foreign exports and Foreign retaliating with a tariff on Home's exports. Assume that the *MS* and *MD* curves for both goods (Home exports to Foreign and Foreign exports to Home) are identical. Starting from a situation where Home and Foreign both impose a tariff of T, show that both unambiguously gain if both remove their tariffs, but one nation might lose if it removed its tariff unilaterally. By the way, this exercise illustrates why nations that are willing to lower their tariffs in the context of a WTO multilateral trade negotiation are often not willing to remove their tariffs unilaterally.

6. Using a diagram like Fig. 4.5, show that an import tariff equal to T has exactly the same impact on prices, quantities and welfare as a domestic consumption tax equal to T and a domestic production subsidy equal to T. (Hint: A production subsidy lowers the effective marginal cost of domestic firms and so lowers the domestic supply curve by T.)

7. Using a diagram like Fig. 4.7, show the impact on quantities, prices and welfare when Home has no tariff, but Foreign charges an export tax equal to T.

8. Using a diagram like Fig. 4.5, show the impact on quantities, prices and welfare when Home has no tariff, but Foreign imposes an export quota with a tariff-equivalent of T.

9. Using a diagram like Fig. 4.7, show that the welfare effects of a quota that restricts imports to M' are exactly the same as a tariff equal to T; assume that each quota licence (i.e. the right to import one unit) is sold by the government to the highest bidder.

Essay questions

1. The concepts of consumer surplus, producer surplus and tariff revenue are meant to capture the key welfare effects of trade policy. Discuss two or three aspects of socio-economic well-being that are not captured by these concepts.

2. The welfare analysis in this chapter assumes that governments weigh one euro of consumer surplus and producer surplus equally. Find an account in a newspaper of a real-world trade policy change and summarize the analysis in the article (the basic facts, the points of view reported, etc.). Does the newspaper article make it seem as if the government cares equally about consumers and producers?

3. Go on to the European Commission's website and find an example of a frictional barrier that the Commission is trying to remove. Explain what the barrier is, how it is justified by Member States and why it was not removed during the 1992 Single Market Programme. One URL to try is: europa.eu.int/comm/internal_market/en/index.htm.

4. Write an essay describing the events that led up to the EU's and USA's imposition of new protection against Chinese clothing exports. Be sure to mention the role of the Uruguay Round agreement on the elimination of the Multifibre Agreement, the surge of exports, the Chinese export tax and reactions of buyers and makers of clothing in the EU and the USA. Use the diagrams developed in this chapter to explain the positions taken by the USA, EU and Chinese governments as well as the positions of EU and US buyers and makers of clothing.

Further reading: the aficionado's corner

Every undergraduate textbook on international economics has a chapter on tariff analysis that covers the same material as this chapter. One particularly accessible treatment can be found in **Krugman and Obstfeld** (2005). For much more on the economics of trade protection, see **Vousden** (1990).

Useful websites

The World Bank's website provides extensive research on trade policy analysis. This includes many papers on non-discriminatory trade policy but also a very large section on preferential trade arrangements under the heading of 'regionalism'. See www.worldbank.org.

The Commission's website on trade issues can be found at http://ec.europa.eu/trade/. It has lots of information on the latest EU trade policy changes.

References

Krugman, P. and M. Obstfeld (2005) *International Economics*, 7th edition (or earlier), Harper Collins, New York.

Mankiw, G. (2007) *Principles of Economics*, 4th edition (or earlier), South Western Publishing, New York.

Vousden, N. (1990) *The Economics of Trade Protection*, Cambridge University Press, Cambridge.

Chapter 5

The essential economics of preferential liberalization

. . . the ideas of economists and political philosophers, both when they are right and when they are wrong, are more powerful than is commonly understood. Indeed the world is ruled by little else. Practical men, who believe themselves to be exempt from any intellectual influences, are usually the slaves of some defunct economist.

John Maynard Keynes, 1935

Chapter contents

5.1	Analysis of unilateral discriminatory liberalization	*163*
5.2	Analysis of a customs union	*172*
5.3	Customs unions versus free trade agreements	*177*
5.4	WTO rules	*179*
5.5	Empirical studies	*179*
5.6	Summary	*180*

Introduction

This chapter begins our progressive study of the microeconomics of European integration, focusing on the preferential, i.e. discriminatory, aspects. The discriminatory effects are important since they played a central role in the political economy of European integration, as was discussed in Chapter 1. The main goal of this chapter is to provide a framework for analysing the essential economics of preferential liberalization.

5.1 Analysis of unilateral discriminatory liberalization

The non-discriminatory liberalization studied in the previous chapter assumed that Home imposed the same tariff against imports from all nations since all trading partners were lumped into one nation called 'Foreign'. While useful for pedagogical purposes, all European countries, and indeed most countries in the world, maintain different barriers against imports from different nations. Studying such discriminatory liberalization is the topic of the present chapter.

The organization of our study of the economic impact of discriminatory liberalization is directed by the principle of progressive complexity. In this section, we look at what happens when a nation removes its tariff on imports from only one of its trading partners. Of course, European integration has always involved two-way reductions in tariffs (e.g. France and Germany lowered their tariffs against each other's exports at the same time during the 1960s), but we postpone consideration of changes in partner tariffs until the next section for the sake of clarity.

Again, we continue with the last chapter's simplifying assumptions of no imperfect competition and no increasing returns (NICNIR). While these assumptions are both monumentally unrealistic, they are pedagogically convenient (see Box 5.1), and – more importantly – they allow us to study the main economic logic of discriminatory liberalization without having to invest a lot of time in learning new tools (that is postponed until the next chapter).

Box 5.1   Why use the NICNIR framework?

There are good reasons for starting our study of the economics of European integration in the highly simplified no imperfect competition and no increasing returns (NICNIR) framework.

NICNIR is the simplest framework that allows us to understand the discriminatory effect of preferential liberalization – an effect that plays a central role in understanding the economic forces driving the spread of European integration. In the early 1960s, in the mid-1970s and again in the mid-1980s, EU members embarked on liberalizations that created discriminatory effects that induced non-members to react (see Chapter 1 for details). In the 1960s, the UK reacted by forming a parallel free trade area, the European Free Trade Association (EFTA), and, in the following year, by putting in an application for EU membership. That application received a curt '*non*' from French President Charles de Gaulle, but when it was renewed and eventually accepted in the early 1970s, the EFTA members that did not follow the UK into the EU reacted by signing FTAs with the enlarged EU. The NICNIR framework allows us to present the core logic behind these reactions in a setting that is as intellectually uncluttered as possible.

Because the NICNIR framework is so simple, it is a good tool for illustrating a variety of effects and studying a variety of policies that would be too complex to study in more realistic frameworks – at least too complex for the sort of diagrammatic analysis employed in this book.

Before starting, we note that the theory of preferential liberalization is often taught using an additional simplifying factor called the 'small economy' assumption. While this simplifies the analysis from the perspective of the Home country, it also assumes away the critical impact that preferential liberalization has on excluded nations. Interested readers can find this case in Annex A at the end of the chapter.

5.1.1 The PTA diagram

Consideration of discriminatory liberalization requires at least three countries – at least two integrating nations and at least one excluded nation. Our first task is to extend the workhorse *MD–MS* diagram from Chapter 4 to allow for two sources of imports. Figure 5.1 shows how.

Free trade equilibrium

The two leftmost panels of Fig. 5.1 show the export supply curves for two individual countries, which we call Partner and Rest of World (RoW) for reasons that will become obvious. To minimize complications, we assume that Partner and RoW are identical; interested readers may want to work out how the diagram and analysis change when the foreign countries are asymmetric.

To find the free trade price in equilibrium, we need to find the intersection between the *MD* curve and the *MS* curve, as in Chapter 4. But what is the *MS* curve? Here there are two potential suppliers of imports, so we must aggregate their supply curves. As in standard microeconomics, the total supply of imports to Home is the horizontal sum of the two export supply curves. This summed curve is shown as *MS* in the right-hand panel (it is flatter than XS_P and XS_R since a given price increase will raise supply from both Partner and RoW). The equilibrium price,

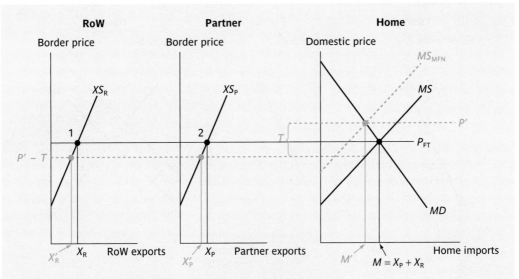

Figure 5.1 The PTA (Preferential Trade Arrangement) diagram

Note: Readers who find the diagrams in this section somewhat involved may benefit from the step-by-step explanations available in the interactive PowerPoint presentation on the companion website.

when no tariff is imposed, is where MS and MD cross, namely P_{FT}. Total imports are M. To find the imports from both Partner and RoW, we use each supplier's XS curve to see how much would be offered at the price P_{FT}. The answers are given by the points 1 and 2 in the diagram, namely Partner and RoW export X_P and X_R, respectively.

MFN tariff with two import suppliers

In order to investigate the impact of removing a tariff on a preferential basis, we need to establish the baseline where a tariff, equal to T, is applied to both nations. To this end, we first work out the effects of Home imposing a tariff of T on both RoW and Partner. As always, the first task is to find how the tariff affects the MS curve. As we saw in Chapter 4, an MFN tariff shifts the MS curve up by T since the domestic price would have to be T higher to elicit the same quantity of imports after the tariff is imposed. The new MS curve is shown in the diagram as the curve marked MS_{MFN}. As before, tariff protection does nothing to the MD curve.

The intersection of MS_{MFN} and MD tells us that the post-tariff equilibrium domestic price for imports is P' and the new import level is M'; with P' as the new domestic price, the new border price is $P' - T$. At this border price, both import suppliers are willing to supply less, namely X_R and X_P, as shown in the diagram.

5.1.2 Price and quantity effects of discriminatory liberalization

What happens when Home removes T but only for imports from Partner, i.e. when Home unilaterally liberalizes on a preferential basis?

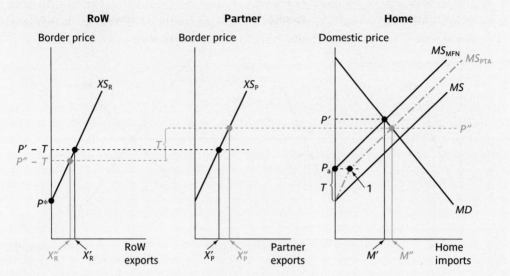

Figure 5.2 **Price and quantity effects of unilateral, discriminatory tariff liberalization**

The first step in answering this question is, as always, to see how the preferential liberalization alters the MS curve. The new MS curve, which we will call MS_{PTA}, where PTA stands for 'preferential trade arrangement', is shown in Fig. 5.2.

The position of the MS_{PTA} is quite intuitive. After the preferential tariff liberalization, half of Home's import suppliers get duty-free access; the other half pays T. It seems natural therefore that MS_{MFN} lies between the free-trade and MFN-protection MS curves. In fact, MS_{PTA} is halfway between the import supply curve with no tariffs, namely MS, and the import supply curve with tariffs on all imports, namely MS_{MFN}. One small qualification, however, is necessary, and considering this helps us see how MS_{PTA} is constructed.

The tariff prevents RoW firms from exporting until the domestic price in Home rises above the price marked P_a in Fig. 5.2. When Home's domestic price is below P_a, we have that the border price faced by RoW exports is below their zero-supply price (marked as P^* in the diagram). Partner-based firms, by contrast, would export when Home's domestic price is slightly below P_a since they face Home's domestic price (not the Home price minus the tariff). As a consequence, Partner firms – but only Partner firms – will supply imports at the domestic price P_a and this corresponds to the point marked 1 in the diagram. Thus the MS_{PTA} curve is Partner's XS curve up to point 1. After that, both foreigners supply imports, so the MS_{PTA} resumes its normal slope.

The domestic price change and conflicting border price changes

The MS_{PTA} and MD curves intersect at P'', so this is the new, post-PTA domestic price. As expected, the new domestic price is lower than the old MFN tariff price since imports from Partner can now enter duty free.

The impact on the border price is a bit more complex. For Partner-based firms, the liberalization means that they now face Home's domestic price, P'', so for them the liberalization means that their border price *rises* from $P' - T$ to P'' (since they no longer pay the tariff, they get the full price paid by Home consumers). For RoW, however, the border price falls from

$P' - T$ to $P'' - T$. One way to think of the RoW border price effect is to note that, in order to stay competitive with Partner firms' exports, RoW firms must cut their border price so that Home consumers see the same price for imports from RoW and Partner in the Home market.

Supply switching

Given that Partner firms see a price rise, they increase exports from X'_P to X''_P. RoW exports fall from X'_R to X''_R because their border price has fallen. This combination of higher Partner sales and lower RoW sales is known as the 'supply switching', or 'trade diversion' effect of discriminatory liberalization. Defining it directly, supply switching occurs when a discriminatory liberalization induces the Home nation to switch some of its purchases to import suppliers who benefit from the PTA and away from suppliers based in nations that did not benefit from the PTA.

Did this sort of supply switching actually occur in Europe? When the EEC eliminated tariffs on a discriminatory basis during the formation of its customs union between 1958 and 1968, Box 5.2 shows that supply switching did occur.

Box 5.2 The supply-switching effects of the formation of the EEC customs union

Figure 5.3 shows the trade volume effects that occurred when the EEC6 removed their internal tariffs between 1958 and 1968. In the left-hand panel, the columns show the import shares broken down into intra-EEC6 imports, imports from six other European nations (the ones who joined in the EU's first three enlargements), and the rest of the world.

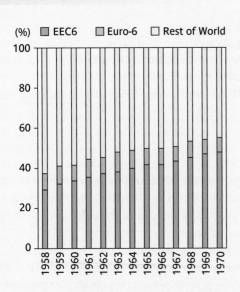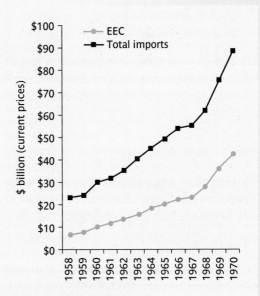

Figure 5.3 Supply switching and formation of the Common Market, 1958–70

Note: Left-hand panel shows share of EEC6's imports from the three regions. Euro-6 are the six countries that joined the EU by the mid-1980s: the UK, Ireland, Denmark, Spain, Portugal and Greece.

Source: European Commission

▶   Note that as the EEC6 share of exports to itself rose from about 30 per cent in 1958 to about 45 per cent in 1968, the share of EEC imports from other nations had to fall. Part of the displacement occurred with respect to imports from other non-EEC European nations. As the dark bars show, the import share from six other western European nations (UK, Ireland, Portugal, Spain, Denmark and Greece) fell during this period by a small amount, from 8–9 per cent to 7 per cent. The main displacement came from the rest of the world, mainly imports from the USA. The right-hand panel, however, shows that imports from all sources were in fact growing rapidly. Thus we have to interpret the 'supply switching' as a relative thing. That is, if the customs union had not been formed, imports from non-EEC6 members would have risen even faster.

These price and quantity effects may seem strange at first. The preferential tariff cut raises the price that Partner exporters receive but lowers the price faced by RoW exporters. Moreover, Home buys more from the nation whose border price has risen and less from the nation whose border price has fallen. This strangeness is simple to understand. The discriminatory liberalization distorts price signals so that Home consumers are not aware of the fact that Partner goods cost the nation more than RoW goods. To the Home consumer, imports from the two sources cost the same, namely P''. To summarize, the price and quantity effects are:

★ Home's domestic price falls from P' to P''.
★ The border price falls from $P' - T$ to $P'' - T$ for RoW imports.
★ The border price rises from $P' - T$ to P'' for Partner imports.
★ The RoW exports fall.
★ The Partner exports rise.
★ Total Home imports rise from M' to M''.

Interested readers may want to add a fourth panel to the diagram by drawing a standard open-economy supply and demand figure for Home to the right of the MD–MS panel. Doing so allows you to see that Home production falls and Home consumption rises due to the domestic price drop.

5.1.3 Welfare effects

Showing the welfare implications in the same figure as the price and quantity effects would complicate the diagram too much. Figure 5.4 reproduces the previous figure, omitting unnecessary lines to reduce its 'clutter factor'. All the welfare effects stem from the price and quantity changes, so these are all that we really need to keep track of.

The welfare effects on foreigners are straightforward. Partner gains D since it gets a higher price and sells more. In other words, Partner experiences a positive border price effect and a positive trade volume effect. RoW's losses are E for the reverse reasons; it gets a lower price and sells less (a negative border price effect and a negative trade volume effect).

Home's welfare effects are slightly more complex due to the two-fold impact on the border price. The direct way of gauging Home's net welfare effect is to use the concepts of 'trade volume effects' and 'border price effects' that were introduced in Chapter 4. This direct approach is also

for good 1, which Home imports and Partner exports. The diagram is based on the two right-most panels of Fig. 5.7 but we have added further detail to the areas. In particular, the trade price loss associated with area C is here split into two parts, C_1 and C_2, for a good reason.

Recall that Home loses $C_1 + C_2$ because the tariff cut raised the price it paid for imports from Partner (from $P' - T$ to P''). The first area, C_1, identifies how much it pays for the units it continues to import from Partner ($M' - X'_P$). Home's loss of C_1, however, is exactly matched by a gain to Partner of the same size; the higher price for the X'_P units transfers C_1 from Home to Partner. The key point is that, because C_1 is just a transfer between CU members, Home's loss of C_1 on its imports of good 1 will be offset by a gain of $D_1 = C_1$ on its exports of good 2 to Partner. After all, Partner also lowers its tariff against Home exports, so we know that Home will gain an area exactly equal to C_1 in its exports of good 2. In addition, Home will gain D_2 in its export market.

Area C_2 is quite different. It identifies the direct cost of the supply switching (trade diversion), so there is no offset gain on the export side. More specifically, recall that from pre-CU symmetry, we know that RoW exports to Home pre-CU were equal to X'_P. After the CU, RoW exports are X''_R, so the difference, $X'_P - X''_R$, measures the amount of supply switching. This quantity is multiplied by the price change ($P' - T$ to P'') to get the welfare cost of the supply switching.

In summary, using the fact that $D_1 = C_1$, the net gain to Home is $+A + B + D_2 - C_2$. This net welfare effect may still be negative, but it is clear that the welfare change from a CU is more positive (or less negative) than the welfare change from a unilateral discriminatory liberalization with Partner.

The losses to RoW from the CU are twice the size of their losses shown in Fig. 5.7, since they lose E both on the exports of good 1 to Home and on their exports of good 2 to Partner. Readers who find this reasoning a bit complex may benefit from the step-by-step explanations in the interactive PowerPoint presentations that can be freely downloaded from http://heiwww.unige/ch/~baldwin/BW/BW.htm.

Second-order terms of trade changes

Lastly, we must consider the indirect or second-round implications of the CU.

RoW experiences a reduction in the value of its exports, yet has not reduced the value of its imports from Home and Partner. While this sort of trade deficit may be sustainable in the short run, eventually RoW must turn the situation around. In the real world, this is usually accomplished by a real depreciation of its currency (or a terms of trade worsening if it is in a monetary union). This makes all RoW exports to Home and Partner cheaper and simultaneously makes imports from those two countries more expensive. Both changes have positive welfare implications for the Home and Partner countries; they earn more on their exports to RoW and pay less for their imports from RoW. This is a further negative trade price effect for RoW stemming from general equilibrium effects of the CU between its trading Partners. Such effects, however, are likely to be small.

5.2.3 Frictional barriers: the 1992 Programme

Hereto we have dealt with tariff liberalization, which was an important aspect of European integration up to the mid-1970s (see Chapter 1 for details). The next task is to study the economics of frictional-barrier liberalization (see Chapter 4 if this terminology is not familiar), the type of liberalization that has dominated European economic integration over the past three decades. Fortunately, the tools we developed while looking at tariff liberalization make this simple.

Price and quantity effects

The removal of frictional barriers was a critical element of the EU's programme to complete the Single Market by 1992. Although several important aspects of the Single Market Programme (EC92 for short) cannot be understood in the uncomplicated framework used in this chapter, the most basic points can. To keep things simple, suppose that initially all three nations, Home, Partner and RoW, impose a frictional barrier whose tariff equivalent is T (i.e. it drives a wedge equal to T between the border price and the Home price). The specific policy change to be studied is a lowering of T to zero on all trade between Home and Partner with no change in the barriers on RoW–Home or Partner–RoW trade.

The price and quantity effects of the preferential liberalization are very similar to those discussed in Fig. 5.2. The only change concerns the border price. With frictional barriers the domestic price is the border price for the importing nation, so the liberalization lowers Home's border price. At the same time, the exporter that benefits from the liberalization receives a higher price for its exports, so the exporter's border price rises.[1] For example, using the Fig. 5.2 terms, the price and quantity effects in the good-1 market are: (i) Home imports of good 1 rise, (ii) the domestic price of good 1 in Home falls from P' to P'', (iii) the border price of good 1 for Partner exporters rises from $P' - T$ to P'', (iv) the border price of good 1 for RoW exporters falls from $P' - T$ to $P'' - T$, and (v) as usual, we get supply switching since Partner exports rise and RoW exports fall.

Welfare effects

The welfare effects on Home are simple. As with tariffs, the change in Home private surplus equals areas F + A in Fig. 5.9. This is not offset by a loss in tariff revenues, as was the case in Fig. 5.4. Removing frictional barriers, even on a preferential basis, always lowers the price that the nation pays for its imports. Although both Partner and RoW exporters see changes in the prices they receive for exports to Home, and this leads to supply switching, this 'trade diversion' has no welfare consequences for Home.

In the good-2 market, where Home is an exporter to Partner, the welfare effect is also positive. Home exporters get a higher price and sell more, so they gain the area D. The overall welfare effect of the FTA is thus +D + F + A.

Non-applicability of trade creation and trade diversion concepts

Notice that Viner's ambiguity has disappeared. With frictional barriers, any kind of liberalization will lead to positive border price effects and positive trade volume effects since the border price equals the domestic price with frictional barriers.

---

[1] As discussed in Chapter 4, the importer's and exporter's border prices differ with a frictional barrier; the importer's border price is higher than that of the exporter by T.

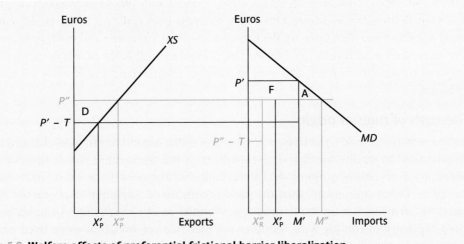

Figure 5.9 **Welfare effects of preferential frictional barrier liberalization**

5.3 Customs unions versus free trade agreements

The 1957 Treaty of Rome committed the six original EU members to eliminating all tariffs and quotas on trade among themselves but it also committed them to completely harmonizing their tariffs on imports from non-member nations. In reaction to this customs union, other western European nations formed another trade bloc – known as the European Free Trade Association (EFTA) – in 1960. This was not a customs union, only a free trade area since EFTA members did not adopt a common external tariff.

What are the key differences between a customs union and a free trade area? Why did the EEC go for a customs union while EFTA went for an FTA? We address these questions in order, starting with the main economic differences.

5.3.1 Stopping tariff cheats: 'trade deflection' and 'rules of origin'

When tariffs between two nations are zero, yet they charge two different tariffs on imports from third nations, firms have an incentive to cheat on tariffs. Take our three-nation example. If all Home–Partner trade is duty free, yet Home charges a 10 per cent tariff on imports from RoW while Partner charges only a 5 per cent tariff on goods coming from RoW, Home-based buyers of RoW goods would be tempted to import the goods first into Partner (thus paying only a 5 per cent tariff) and then to import them duty free from Partner to Home. To thwart this practice – known as trade deflection – Home and Partner have two choices. They can eliminate the temptation by harmonizing their external tariffs (thus turning their FTA into a customs union), or they can stay with the FTA but restrict duty-free treatment to goods that are actually *made* in Home or Foreign. The set of rules that enforce the latter option are called 'rules of origin'.

One problem with rules of origin, and thus with FTAs, is that it can be difficult to know where a product is made in today's highly globalized markets. Personal computers made in, say,

Switzerland will contain components from all over the world. The Swiss company may be doing little more than customized assembly of parts from the USA and Asia. In the extreme, it may be doing nothing more than opening the box of a US-made computer and putting in an instruction manual translated into, say, Norwegian. Should the full value of this computer be given duty-free treatment when it is exported to Norway? (Switzerland and Norway are both EFTA members.)

The costs of rules of origin

For manufactured goods, the basic rule of origin is that a good has to have changed its 'tariff classification' to qualify for duty-free treatment. If the component comes into Switzerland under 'TV and computer monitors', for example, but the good to be exported to Norway is classed as 'Office equipment', then the good is considered Swiss and thus granted duty-free access to Germany. But for many products, the rules can be much more complex and much more expensive to comply with. Another popular rule requires that some fixed percentage of the product's value-added be done in the exporting nation. Owing to the high cost of compliance with these rules, many non-EU firms who could in principle qualify for duty-free treatment (e.g. Swiss firms) decide instead to pay the EU's CET (common external tariff).

An additional problem with rules of origin is that they can end up as hidden protection. Since rules of origin are specified at the product level, they can be difficult for non-experts to evaluate – just as is the case with technical barriers to trade. As a consequence, rules of origin are usually written in consultation with domestic firms who have an incentive to shape the rules into protectionist devices.

One great advantage of a customs union like the EU is that firms do not have to demonstrate the origin of a product before it is allowed to cross an intra-EU border duty free. Any good that is physically in Germany was either made in Germany or paid the CET when it entered. In either case, the good deserves duty-free passage into France, or any other EU member, without any documentation at all.

The EU has greatly simplified the problem of rules of origin by adopting the Pan-European Cumulation System. See Chapter 14 for details.

5.3.2 Political integration and customs unions

Most preferential trade arrangements in the world are free trade agreements rather than customs unions, like the EU. The reason is simple – political integration. Getting a group of nations to agree on a common external tariff at the launch of a customs union is difficult, but the real problems begin as time passes. For instance, if one member nation believes its industry is being undercut by some non-member nation which is exporting its goods at a price that is below cost (so-called dumping), it may want to impose tariffs to offset the dumping. In a customs union, all nations must agree on every dumping duty since external tariffs must always remain constant. Likewise, nations typically reduce their tariffs in the context of GATT/WTO negotiations. For a customs union, this requires all members to agree on a common negotiating position on every single product.

In practice, keeping the CET common requires some integration of decision making. In the EU, the Commission formally has the power to set tariffs on third-nation goods (even though it naturally consults with Member States before doing so), but very few groups of countries are willing to transfer that amount of national sovereignty. As a result, most trade blocs, including EFTA and the North American Free Trade Agreement, are free trade areas rather than customs unions.

Another way to 'solve' the decision-making problem is for the members to let one nation decide everything. This is the case in all the successful customs unions in the world apart from the EU. For example, South Africa is the dominant nation in the Southern African Customs Union (see www.dfa.gov.za/for-relations/multilateral/sacu.htm) and Switzerland is the dominate nation in the Swiss–Liechtenstein customs union.

5.4 WTO rules

The world trading system is governed by a set of rules, known as the General Agreement on Tariffs and Trade (GATT), and an organization, known as the World Trade Organization (WTO). The most important guiding principle of the WTO/GATT is non-discrimination in trade policy, i.e. the so-called most favoured nation principle, or MFN for short. This says that nations should, in principle, impose tariffs on a non-discriminatory basis. Of course, all of the preferential liberalization discussed above contradicts this principle, so why is it allowed? As it turns out, the GATT created an explicit loophole for FTAs and customs unions. Allowing this loophole was important for some of the early GATT members since they wished to maintain existing preferential arrangements (especially Great Britain's Commonwealth Preferences).

The loophole, formally known as Article 24, specifically allows preferential liberalization, subject to a few restrictions, the most important of which are:

★ Free trade agreements and customs unions must completely eliminate tariffs on 'substantially all the trade' among members.

★ The phase-out of tariffs must take place within a reasonable period.

Although there are no hard definitions, 'substantially all trade' is usually taken to mean at least 80 per cent of all goods and a 'reasonable period' is taken to be ten years or less.

For a customs union, there is the additional requirement that the common external tariff (CET) 'shall not on the whole be higher or more restrictive' than before the customs union. That is, when forming the customs union, the members cannot harmonize the CET to the highest level of any member. In the case of the EEC's customs union formation, external tariff harmonization generally involved a reduction in French and Italian tariffs, a rise in Benelux tariffs and little change in German tariffs.

5.5 Empirical studies

Modern empirical analyses of European integration go far beyond the NICNIR framework we employed in this chapter. They include effects that we shall study in Chapters 6 and 7. Indeed, no major study of EU economic integration has relied solely on the NICNIR framework since the mid-1980s. There are, however, many examples of empirical studies based on NICNIR reasoning from the 1970s.

For example, the UK's entry into the EU elicited a large volume of empirical work in the early 1970s. While economists at the time knew of scale effects and growth effects, they did not have the theoretical tools necessary to handle them. Moreover, few economists had access to computers (PCs became widespread only in the 1980s), so much of the empirical work in the NICNIR framework consisted of what we would today call rough calculations, or 'back of the envelope' methods. The most popular method was to loosely associate the positive effects of CU formation with an increase in imports and the negative effects loosely with diverted imports. Since most studies at the time found little or no evidence that the EEC's formation was trade diverting (Balassa, 1975), the general conclusion was that the EEC must have been good for the EEC and not bad for the rest of the world. The main challenge in these studies was to determine what the trade pattern would have been without the EEC – a problem that is more difficult to resolve than one might think since imports from all sources were growing rapidly (see Fig. 5.3).

Since these NICNIR studies are now 20 years out of date, we do not review their findings here (see Artis and Nixson, 2001, for a summary). One thing that is worth discussing is the fact that all empirical studies using the NICNIR framework found that the EEC had a negligible impact on national welfare.

Balassa (1975), for example, concluded that the EU's customs union added only 0.5 per cent to the Six's GDP. This struck most observers as far too low, but such low estimates are inevitable in the NICNIR framework. To understand why, it helps to consider a simple example. Suppose that Home is a small country and removes all tariffs on an MFN basis. As Annex A shows, the welfare impact of this on Home will be *larger* than the welfare impact of any possible free trade area, so we know that the number we shall arrive at will be an overestimate of the true gain. The welfare impact of this is 0.5 times the change in imports times the level of the tariff. In symbols, this is $\Delta W = (\Delta M)(\Delta T)/2$, where Δ means 'the change in' and W stands for welfare, M for imports and T for the tariff. The change in imports is related to the responsiveness of imports to price changes, i.e. Home's import demand elasticity, ε, defined as $(\Delta M/M)/(\Delta P/P)$. In symbols, $\Delta M = \varepsilon(\Delta T)(M/P)$, so the welfare gain as a share of GDP is $\Delta W/\mathrm{GDP} = \varepsilon(M \times P/\mathrm{GDP})(\Delta T/2P^2)$. A typical, import-demand elasticity is something like 2.0, a typical EEC nation had an import to GDP ratio, i.e. $(M \times P/\mathrm{GDP})$, equal to about 0.2 in the 1960s, and the level of tariffs averaged less than 25 per cent. Taking all this together means that the gains would be 2(0.2)(0.625)/2, which equals just 0.0125 or 1.25 per cent of GDP – and that is an overestimate of the NICNIR effects.

The general point to learn from this back-of-the-envelope calculation is that NICNIR welfare gains just cannot be big. They inevitably involve the multiplication of several fractions and this inevitably produces small numbers. If trade liberalization is to have welfare effects that are big enough to matter, we need to consider scale effects, growth effects and location effects – the subject of the next chapters.

5.6 Summary

This chapter introduced the graphical methods necessary to study preferential trade liberalization in a NICNIR setting. After going over the preliminaries, we studied the price and quantity and welfare effects of the formation of a customs union. The main technical points are:

★ Formation of a preferential trade arrangement such as the EEC's customs union, or EFTA's free trade area, tends to lower domestic prices and raise imports overall, but the discriminatory aspects of these liberalizations also produce supply-switching, that is to say, a switch from non-member suppliers to member-based suppliers.

★ The welfare effects of any trade liberalization, including PTA liberalization, can be captured by standard public-finance concepts, which we here call trade volume effects and border price (or trade price) effects.

★ The welfare impact of preferential tariff liberalization is ambiguous for the liberalizing nations; this is called Viner's ambiguity. The deep fundamental reason is that PTAs are discriminatory liberalizations; the liberalization part – what Viner called trade creation – tends to boost economic efficiency, while the discrimination part – what Viner called trade diversion – tends to lower it. The impact on excluded nations is always negative.

★ Estimates of the welfare impact of trade liberalization in the NICNIR setting are inevitably very small. This suggests to most observers that one has to look to more complicated frameworks if one is to understand why trade liberalization in general, and European integration in particular, matter.

The bigger lessons from the chapter concern the way in which the economic analysis helps us to understand the big-think trends in European integration.

★ The NICNIR framework helped us to study the impact of discriminatory liberalization on outsiders in an intellectually uncluttered setting. This helps us to understand why outsiders always reacted to the deepening and widening of EU integration. As we showed, preferential liberalization definitely harms excluded nations since it leads them to face lower prices for their exports to the customs union and lower export sales. It seems natural, therefore, that the outsiders would react either by forming their own preferential arrangements (as happened in the 1960s with EFTA), or by deepening the integration between the outsiders and the EU (as outsiders did in the 1970s and again in the 1990s), or by joining the EU (as nine formerly outsider western European nations had done by 1994).

Self-assessment questions

The NICNIR was the backbone of 'customs union theory' for years, so quite a number of extensions and provisos were put forth in the NICNIR setting. Some of them are still insightful and the following exercises illustrate the basic points.

1. (Kemp–Wan theorem.) Starting from a situation like that shown in Fig. 5.1, where the three nations are symmetric in everything including the initial MFN tariff T, suppose that Home and Partner form a customs union *and* lower their common tariff against RoW to the point where the new, post-liberalization border price facing RoW exporters is the same as it was before the liberalization, i.e. $P' - T$. Show that this 'Kemp–Wan' adjustment ensures that Home and Partner gain while RoW does not lose from this CU-with-CET-reduction scheme.

2. (Cooper–Massell extended.) We can think of a preferential unilateral liberalization in the following roundabout manner. Home lowers its tariffs to zero on an MFN basis, but then raises it back to T on imports only from RoW. Now suppose that Home faces a flat MS

curve for imports from both Partner and RoW (this is the 'small country' case). Moreover, suppose that Partner's MS is somewhat above that of RoW's.

First work out the welfare effects on Home. (Hint: This is covered in Annex A.)

Second, show that Home would gain more from a unilateral MFN liberalization than it would from a unilateral preferential liberalization. (Historical note: Taking their NICNIR analysis as definitive, this result led Cooper and Massell to suggest that small countries must join customs unions for political reasons only. You can see that this is only a partial analysis by realizing that a customs union also lowers tariffs facing Home-based exporters.) Try to figure out how Home gains from Partner's removal on Home-to-Partner exports. After doing this, see if you can say definitely whether Home gains more from unilateral free trade, or from joining the customs union. You should also be able to show that the optimal policy for a small nation is to have unilateral free trade *and* join every FTA that it can.

3. (Large Partner rule of thumb.) Redo the FTA formation exercise from the text assuming that RoW is initially a much smaller trading partner of Home and Partner in the sense that most of Home's imports are from Partner and most of Partner's imports are from Home when all three nations impose the initial MFN tariff, T. Show that the 'net border price effect' (area $B - C_1 - C_2$ in Fig. 5.8) is smaller when RoW is initially a less important trade partner of Home and Partner nations. (Hint: Focus on the Home country and start with a diagram like Fig. 5.1. Keep the vertical intersections of XS_P and XS_R at the same height, but make the XS_R steeper and the XS_P flatter in a way that does not change P''; our thanks to Jonathan Gage for help with this problem.)

4. (Growth effects and RoW impact.) Suppose that signing an FTA between Home and Partner produces a growth effect that raises their income level and thus shifts their MD curves upwards. Use a diagram like Fig. 5.4 to show how big the upward shift would have to be to ensure that RoW did not lose from the Home–Partner FTA. (In the 1970s, this was the informal explanation for why the EEC6 formation did not lead to trade diversion.) Can you show the welfare impact of this growth on Home?

5. (Hub-and-spoke bilateralism.) Using PTA diagrams, show what the price, quantity and welfare effects would be of a hub-and-spoke arrangement among three nations. (Hub-and-spoke means that country 1 signs FTAs with countries 2 and 3, but 2 and 3 do not liberalize trade between them.) Assume that there are *only* frictional barriers in this world, that initially all import barriers have a tariff equivalent of T, and that the FTAs concern only frictional barrier liberalization. Be sure to look at the price, quantity and welfare impact on (i) a typical spoke economy (2 or 3) and (ii) the hub economy.

6. (Sapir, 1992.) Consider a situation where Home and Partner have formed a customs union but have not eliminated frictional barriers between them. Specifically assume that all trade flows among Home, Partner and RoW are subject to frictional trade barriers equal to T' and additionally the tariff on trade between the CU and RoW is equal to T''. Show that eliminating frictional barriers inside the CU might harm welfare since it leads to a reduction in the amount of tariff revenue collected on imports from RoW.

7. Suppose Home has no trade barriers, except anti-dumping measures. These anti-dumping measures take the form of price undertakings, i.e. instead of Home imposing a tariff on RoW and Partner imports, Home requires Partner and RoW firms to charge a high price for their

sales to Home. Show the price, quantity and welfare effects of imposing this import price floor (look at all three nations). Next, show the price, quantity and welfare effects of removing the price undertaking (i.e. allowing free trade) only for imports from Partner. Be sure to illustrate the impact on all three nations. (Hint: The price undertaking is a price floor, so it does not act just like a tariff; be very careful in constructing the MS_{PTA} for this situation.)

Essay questions

1. Using the analysis of a customs union in this chapter, explain how the domino theory of integration could explain the fact that virtually all nations in and around western Europe now have or want to have preferential trade arrangements with the European Union.

2. Using the economic analysis in this chapter, together with the political economy logic of special-interest groups (well-organized groups often have political weight that is far in excess of their economic weight), explain why the WTO restrictions on customs unions and free trade areas might be a good idea.

3. Using the economic analysis in this chapter and political economy logic, explain why most trade liberalizations are reciprocal rather than unilateral.

4. Some international trade experts believe that formation of the EU's customs union led to pressures from the USA and Japan for a multilateral tariff-cutting round called the Kennedy Round. Use the economic analysis in this chapter, together with the political economy logic of special-interest groups, to explain why this view might make sense. (Hint: US and Japanese exporters are a very powerful special-interest group.)

5. When Bismarck led the drive to unify the many small regions and nation-states of Germany, he used a customs union (*Zollverien*) as both a carrot and a stick to encourage unification. Use the economic analysis in this chapter (especially the impact on RoW) to make sense of this strategy.

Further reading: the aficionado's corner

The modern study of European economic integration began life under the name of 'customs union theory' with **Viner** (1950). Viner's seminal text triggered a flood of work. At the time, tariffs were the key trade barriers and theorists had few tools for dealing with imperfect competition, so the early literature focused on tariff removals in the NICNIR setting. For a highly readable survey of this literature, see **Pomfret** (1986). **O'Brien** (1975) provides a review of pre-Vinerian literature.

Following Viner's theory, which associated welfare effects with changes in trade flows, early empirical studies focused on trade creation and diversion. Surveys of this literature include **Srinivasan et al.** (1993), **Mayes** (1978) and **Winters** (1987).

A more extensively graphic presentation of pre- and post-1958 trade flows in Europe can be found in **Neal and Berbezat** (1998).

See also **Baldwin and Venables** (1995) and **Mankiw** (2000).

Useful websites

While the EU's customs union has been completed for over three decades, some policy issues occasionally arise. See the Commission's website http://europa.eu.int/comm/taxationcustoms/.

The history of EFTA's free trade area can be found on www.efta.int/.

Further information on WTO rules concerning preferential trade arrangements can be found on www.wto.org.

References

Artis, M. and F. Nixson (2001) *The Economics of the European Union*, Oxford University Press, Oxford

Balassa, B. (1975) 'Trade creation and trade diversion to the European Common Market' in B. Balassa (ed.) *European Economic Integration*, North-Holland, Amsterdam.

Baldwin, R.E. and A. Venables (1995) 'Regional economic integration', in G. Grossman and K. Rogoff (eds) *Handbook of International Economics: Volume III*, North-Holland, Amsterdam.

Cooper, C. and D. Massell (1965) 'Towards a general theory of customs unions in developing countries', *Journal of Political Economy*, 73: 256–83.

Kemp, M. and H. Wan (1976) 'An elementary proposition concerning the formation of customs unions', *Economic Journal*, 6: 95–7.

Mankiw, G. (2000) *Principles of Economics*, Thomson Learning, New York.

Mayes, D. (1978) 'The effects of economic integration on trade', *Journal of Common Market Studies*, XVII: 1–25.

Meade, J. (1955) *The Theory of Customs Unions*, Oxford University Press, London.

Neal, L. and D. Berbezat (1998) *The Economics of the European Union and the Economics of Europe*, Oxford University Press, London.

O'Brien, D.P. (1975) 'Classical monetary theory', in *The Classical Economists*, Clarendon Press, Oxford, pp. 140–69.

Panagariya, A. (1999) 'Preferential trade liberalisation: the traditional theory and new developments', University of Maryland mimeo (download from www.bsos.umd.edu/econ/panagariya/song/surveypt.pdf).

Pomfret, R. (1986) 'The theory of preferential trading arrangements', *Weltwirtschaftliches Archiv*, 122: 439–64.

Sapir, A. (1992) 'Regional integration in Europe', *Economic Journal*, 102 (415): 1491–506.

Srinivasan, T.N., J. Whalley and I. Wooton (1993) 'Measuring the effects of regionalism on trade and welfare', pp. 52–79 in K. Anderson and R. Blackhurst (eds) *Regional Integration and the Global Trading System*, Harvester Wheatsheaf for the GATT Secretariat, London.

Viner, J. (1950) *The Customs Union Issue*, Carnegie Endowment for International Peace, New York.

Winters, L.A. (1978) 'Britain in Europe: a survey of quantitative trade studies', *Journal of Common Market Studies*, 25: 315–35.

Annex A Discriminatory liberalization: small country case

This background appendix presents the classic analysis of unilateral preferential tariff liberalization for the 'small country' case. The so-called small country case means that we make the simplifying assumption that the volume of a nation's imports is unrelated to the price of those imports. In this case, we do not need the import supply and demand diagram discussed above. Rather, we can work directly with a simpler open-economy supply and demand diagram.

Fig. A5.1, which allows for two potential sources of imports (countries A and B), helps to organize the reasoning. To set the stage, suppose that Home initially imposes a tariff of T on imports from A and B. (Goods produced in the countries A, B and Home are all perfect substitutes.) The Home nation is assumed to face a flat import supply curve from both countries. The idea behind this simplification is that Home is so small that it can buy as much or as little as it wants without affecting the price. Specifically, the import supply curves from A and B are the flat curves at the levels P_A and P_B. We can see that country A producers are more efficient since they can offer the goods at a lower price. That is, importing from A costs Home

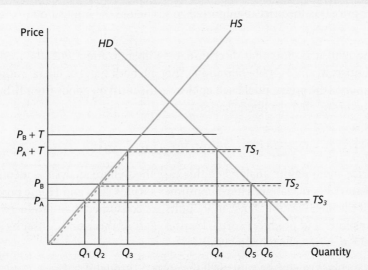

Figure A5.1 Price and quantity effects of discriminatory liberalization (small nation)

consumers $P_A + T$, while importing from B costs $P_B + T$. Plainly, all imports initially come from the cheaper supplier, namely A.

Adding together the three sources of supply (Home, A and B), we find the pre-liberalization total supply curve to be TS_1. Because it is the horizontal sum of the Home supply curve and the two import supply curves, it follows the Home supply curve up to $P_A + T$ and, beyond that, it follows A's import supply curve. The equilibrium Home price (i.e. the price facing Home consumers and producers) is $P_A + T$, since this is where total supply meets demand. The border price, namely the price that Home as a country pays for imports, is P_A.

Next, we ask what would happen if the tariff were removed on a discriminatory basis. That is to say, if it were removed on imports from only A or only B. Both cases must be considered. We turn now to the price, quantity and welfare effects of the two cases.

A5.1 Price and quantity analysis, liberalization with low-cost country

In the first case, the liberalization is applied to Home's current trading partner, namely A. The total supply curve becomes TS_3, so the Home price falls to P_A. Home consumption rises, Home production falls, imports rise and nothing happens to the border price of imports. To summarize:

★ The price in the Home market of both imports and Home import-competing goods falls to P_A.

★ Home production falls from Q_3 to Q_1.

  Home consumption rises from Q_4 to Q_6.

★ The import volume rises from the difference between Q_3 and Q_4 to the difference between Q_1 and Q_6.

★ The border price (i.e. the price of imported goods before the imposition of the tax) remains unchanged at P_A.

With some thought, it is clear that discriminatory liberalization with the low-cost country has the same impact as an MFN liberalization. After all, both types of liberalization remove the tariff on all imports (the preferential tariff cut leaves the tariff on goods from B, but no imports come from B before or after the liberalization).

A5.2 Welfare analysis: liberalization with low-cost country

As with the price and quantity analysis, in this case the welfare analysis is identical to that of non-discriminatory liberalization. Home consumer surplus rises and Home producer surplus falls because of the liberalization. Since more units are consumed than produced domestically, the sum of consumer and producer surpluses rises. Part of this gain is offset by a loss in tariff revenue. Using Fig. A5.2 to be more precise:

★ Consumer surplus rises by the sum of all the areas A through J.

★ Producer surplus falls by the area A + E.

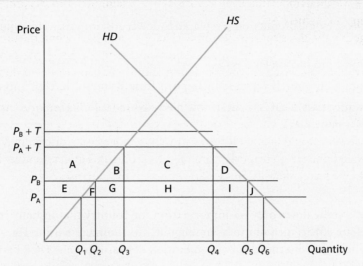

Figure A5.2 Small country welfare analysis

★ Government revenue falls by C + H.

★ The net effect is unambiguously positive and equal to (B + F + G) and (D + I + J).

A5.3 Liberalization with high-cost country: supply switching

The analysis is only slightly trickier when the preferential trade arrangement is signed with the high-cost country.

Graphically, as shown in Fig. A5.1, this results in a total supply curve of TS_2 and a Home price of P_B. Recall that since country B is the high-cost supplier (i.e. P_B is above P_A) nothing was imported from B initially. Granting duty-free access to goods from B artificially changes the relative competitiveness of goods from A and B – at least in the eyes of Home consumers. Goods from B cost P_B while goods from A cost $P_A + T$. Quite naturally, Home importers of goods will divert all their import demand from A towards B. We call this the 'supply-switching' effect of discriminatory liberalization; it is the first of two elements that arise with discriminatory liberalization but do not arise with non-discriminatory liberalization. Note, however, that discriminatory liberalization does not always lead to supply-switching. It can only do so when it is done with the high-cost country. The second novel aspect of discriminatory liberalization is the border price impact. That is, as consumers switch from the low-cost source to the high-cost source (country B), the Home border price rises. We call this the 'border price' effect, or the import-price-rising effect. The importance of this price change should be clear – such liberalization will raise the cost of imports to the country as a whole.

To summarize, there are six price and quantity effects:

1 The preferential liberalization increases competition from imports and thereby forces down the Home price of locally made and imported goods to P_B.

2 Consumption rises to Q_5.

3 Some high-cost Home production is replaced by lower cost imports. This amount is equal to $Q_3 - Q_2$.

4 The new Home production level is Q_2.

5 Imports from A are entirely replaced by imports from B and the level of imports rises.

6 The border price rises. That is to say, Home now pays more for its imports (namely, P_B) than it did before (namely, P_A).

A5.4 Welfare analysis: liberalization with high-cost country

When the tariffs come down only on imports from the country that initially sells nothing to Home, the welfare effects turn out to be ambiguous. To summarize using Fig. A5.2, there are three welfare effects of a discriminatory liberalization of a tariff (or any DCR barrier):

1 Home consumers gain the area A + B + C + D.

2 Home producers lose the area A.

3 All tariff revenue is lost. This lowers Home welfare; the change being −C − H.

The net effect is B + D − H. This may be positive or negative; discriminatory tariff liberalization therefore has ambiguous welfare effects. This is the so-called Viner ambiguity. Notice that the net welfare impact depends only on the change in the quantity of imports (which rises in this case) and the change in the price of imports (which also rises in this case).

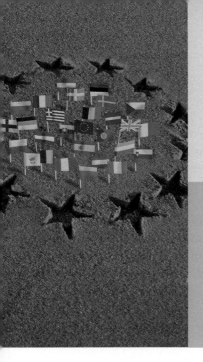

Chapter 6

Market size and scale effects

The countries of Europe are too small to give their peoples the prosperity that is now attainable and therefore necessary. They need wider markets.

Jean Monnet, 1943

By its size – the biggest in the world – the single market without frontiers is an invaluable asset to revitalize our businesses and make them more competitive. It is one of the main engines of the European Union.

Jacques Delors, July 1987

Chapter contents

6.1	Liberalization, defragmentation and industrial restructuring: logic and facts	190
6.2	Theoretical preliminaries: monopoly, duopoly and oligopoly	192
6.3	The *BE–COMP* diagram in a closed economy	198
6.4	The impact of European liberalization	200
6.5	Summary	204

Introduction

Market size matters. From its very inception in the 1950s, an important premise behind European economic integration was the belief that unification of European economies would – by allowing European firms access to a bigger market – make European firms more efficient and this, in turn, would allow them to lower prices, raise quality and gain competitiveness in external markets.

This chapter explores the economic logic of how European integration can lead to fewer, larger firms operating at a more efficient scale and facing more effective competition. The EU policy responses to these changes – notably the enforcement of rules that prohibit unfair subsidization of firms and rules restricting anti-competitive behaviour – are studied in Chapter 14. In the EU, such policies are called, respectively, 'state aids' policy and 'competition policy'.

6.1 Liberalization, defragmentation and industrial restructuring: logic and facts

We start the chapter by verbally explaining the logic that links European integration to industrial restructuring before presenting some facts on mergers and acquisitions (M&As) and the effects on competition.

Europe's national markets are separated by a whole host of barriers. These included tariffs and quotas until the Common Market was completed in 1968 and tariffs between the EEC and EFTA until the EEC–EFTA free trade agreements were signed in 1974. Yet, even though intra-EU trade has been duty free for over three decades, trade among European nations is not as free as it is within any given nation. Many technical, physical and fiscal barriers still make it easier for companies to sell in their local market than in other EU markets. While most of these barriers seem trivial or even silly when considered in isolation, the confluence of thousands of seemingly small barriers serves to substantially restrict intra-EU trade. As a result, EU firms can often be dominant in their home market while being marginal players in other EU markets (think of the European car market). This situation, known as market fragmentation, reduces competition and this, in turn, raises prices and keeps too many firms in business. Keeping firms in business is not, of course, a bad thing in itself. The problem is that this results in an industrial structure marked by too many inefficient small firms that can get away with charging high prices to cover the cost of their inefficiency. Owing to the absence of competition, poor and/or low-quality services and goods may also accompany the high prices (think of the European telephone service before liberalization).

Tearing down these intra-EU barriers defragments the markets and produces extra competition. This 'pro-competitive effect', in turn, puts pressure on profits and the market's response is 'merger mania'. That is, the pro-competitive effect squeezes the least efficient firms, prompting an industrial restructuring where Europe's weaker firms merge or get bought up. In the end, Europe is left with a more efficient industrial structure, with fewer, bigger, more efficient firms competing more effectively with each other. All this means improved material well-being for Europeans as prices fall and output rises. In some industries, restructuring may be accompanied by a sizeable reallocation of employment, as firms cut back on redundant workers and close inefficient plants and offices (a painful process for workers who have to change jobs). In other industries, however, liberalization can unleash a virtuous circle of more competition, lower prices, higher sales and higher employment.

In the remainder of the chapter we work through the logic of what was just presented informally. Schematically, the steps can be summarized as: liberalization → defragmentation → pro-competitive effect → industrial restructuring. The result is fewer, bigger, more efficient firms facing more effective competition from each other.

6.1.1 Some facts

As shown on the left of Fig. 6.1, the number of mergers and acquisitions (M&As) in the EU15 remained at a high steady level of about 10 000 operations per year until 1997, when the number started climbing steadily to a record total of 12 557 operations in 2000. In terms of the total value of deals, however, the EU figure climbed steadily and rapidly from 1991 to 2000, from about €100 billion to €2400 billion. The number and value were lower in 2001, reflecting the slowdown in economic activity, but at over 10 000 operations, it was still a considerable number.

It is interesting to note that much of this M&A activity consists of the mergers of firms within the same Member State, e.g. German firms buying other German firms. Indeed, at the end of the period, about 55 per cent of all operations were of this 'domestic' type. The remaining 45 per cent of the deals involved a non-domestic firm. This 45 per cent is split between operations where one firm was a non-EU firm (24 per cent), where one firm was located in another EU nation (15 per cent) and operations where the counterparty's nationality was not identified (6 per cent).

The right-hand panel of Fig. 6.1 shows the breakdown of firms by Member State. Two points are worth stressing. First, the distribution of M&A operations is quite varied. The big four economies (France, Italy, Germany and the UK) have the most operations; however, except for the UK, these nations' share of M&A activity is much lower than their share of the European

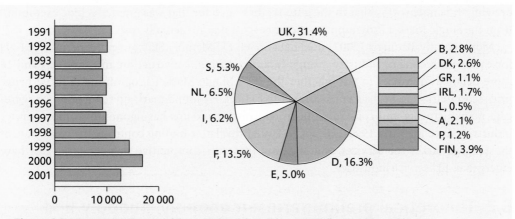

Figure 6.1 Mergers and acquisitions (M&As) involving EU15 firms, 1991–2001

Note: The left-hand panel shows the evolution of the number of mergers and acquisitions involving EU15 firms. The right-hand panel shows the distribution of all operations from 1991–2001 by Member State.

Source: Data is drawn from European Economy, Supplement A, No. 12, December 2001 downloadable from http://europa.eu.int/comm/economy_finance/publications/supplement_a_en.htm

economy. Italy, France and Germany together account for only 36 per cent of the M&As even though their economies account for 59 per cent of the EU15 economy. By contrast, many of the small EU15 members seem to have a share of M&A activity that is systematically higher than their share of the EU15's GDP. This link between domestic market size and the impact of integration on restructuring fits in with the basic logic described above. Stylizing the facts to make the point, we can say that the problem of a too-small market was most severe in the smaller EU members; integration produced the largest changes (large in proportion to their economy) in the smallest members. The second point comes from the exceptions to this rule. The EU has yet to harmonize rules on takeovers. Despite many years of trying, some members still have very restrictive takeover practices that make M&As very difficult, while others, such as the UK, have very liberal rules. The implication of this lack of harmonization is that the restructuring effects of integration have been felt very differently in the various Member States.

The sectoral composition of M&A activity (not shown in the figure) is also noteworthy. About two-thirds of all the activity in this period took place in service sectors, especially in banking. However, during the early years of the Single Market Programme (1986–92), the M&A activity was centred on manufacturing, with mergers often occurring in anticipation of liberalization that was scheduled (Commission, 1996). Interested readers can find a wealth of details on the nature of this activity in European Economy (2001).

This restructuring increased the level of concentration at the EU level. From 1987 to 1993, the share of the four largest firms in the EU's total market rose from 20.5 to 22.8 per cent, while this measure of concentration at the national level fell. In short, defragmentation resulted in fewer firms at the EU level, but even more competition at the national level.

Empirical evidence

Econometric evidence from Allen et al. (1998a, 1999b) suggests that the Single Market Programme reduced price–cost margins by 4 per cent on average. This impact varied from quite high, e.g. −15 per cent in the office machinery sector, to quite small, e.g. −0.1 per cent in brewing. It is noteworthy that in the auto sector – a sector that was granted a bloc exemption from the Single Market Programme – the price–cost margin actually rose.

More recently, Badinger (2007) used data on ten EU Member States over the period 1981–99 for each of three major industry groups (manufacturing, construction and services) and 18 more detailed industries to test whether the EU's Single Market Programme reduced firms' price–cost mark-ups, i.e. had a pro-competitive effect. He found mark-up reductions for aggregate manufacturing and construction. In contrast, mark-ups have gone up in most service industries since the early 1990s. He suggests that this latter finding confirms the weak state of the Single Market for services and suggests that anti-competitive defence strategies have emerged in EU service industries.

6.2 Theoretical preliminaries: monopoly, duopoly and oligopoly

To study the logic of European integration's impact on scale and competition we need a simple yet flexible framework that allows for imperfect competition. The framework we employ below – the *BE–COMP* diagram – assumes a knowledge of simple imperfect competition models, so by way of preliminaries, we briefly review the simplest forms of imperfect competition – monopoly, duopoly and oligopoly. Advanced readers may want to skip this section and move directly to the *BE–COMP* diagram in Section 6.3, but since it introduces notation and basic concepts, even advanced readers may find it useful.

Box 6.1   Joan Robinson (1903–83)

Joan Robinson, one of the most prominent economists of the twentieth century, made many fundamental contributions to various areas of economics, including what is widely recognized as the seminal contribution on imperfect competition in her 1933 book, *The Economics of Imperfect Competition*. Robinson, who taught at Cambridge University, was a colleage of Keynes and a prominent socialist. She actively spoke out against the social and economic injustices in the developing world. Other works by Robinson include *An Essay on Marxian Economics* (1942) and *The Accumulation of Capital* (1956).

Many economists feel that she should have been awarded the Nobel Prize, but she worked at a time of blatant sex discrimination. For instance, despite her monumental contributions to economic theory in the 1930s and 1940s, she became a full professor only in 1965.

As usual, we start with the simplest problem – namely, the decision faced by a firm that has a monopoly. The monopoly case is easy because it avoids strategic interactions. When a firm is the only seller of a product, it can choose how much to sell and what price to charge without considering the reaction of other suppliers. The only restraint a monopolist faces is the demand curve. A downward-sloping demand curve is a constraint because it forces the monopolist to confront a trade-off between price and sales; higher prices mean lower sales. When considering the impact of European integration on imperfectly competitive firms, we need to determine how various policy changes will alter prices and sales. The first step in this direction is to see what determines a monopolist's price and sales in a closed economy. The natural question then is: 'What is the profit-maximizing level of sales for the monopolist?'

An excellent way to proceed is to make a guess at the optimal level, say, Q' in the left-hand panel of Fig. 6.2. Almost surely this initial guess will be wrong, but what we want to know is whether Q' is too low or too high. To this end, we calculate the profit earned when Q' units are sold at the highest obtainable price, namely P'. The answer is A + B, since the total value of sales is price times quantity (area A + B + C) minus cost (area C).

Would profits rise or fall if the firm sold an extra unit? Of course, to sell the extra unit, the firm will have to let its price fall a bit to P''. The change in profit equals the change in revenue minus the change in cost. Consider first the change in revenue. This has two parts. Selling the extra unit brings in extra revenue (represented by areas D + E), but it also depresses the price received for all units sold initially (lowering revenue by an amount equal to area A). The net change in revenue – called 'marginal revenue' for short – is given by the areas D + E minus the area A. The change in cost – called marginal cost for short – is area E. Plainly, profit only increases if the extra revenue D – A exceeds the extra cost E. As it is drawn, D – A + E appears to

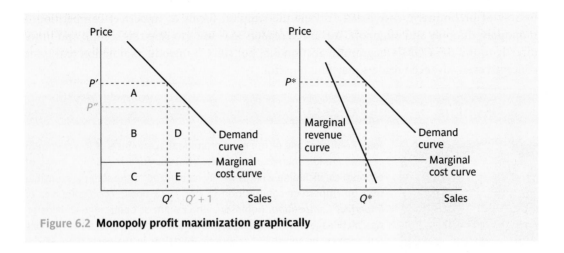

Figure 6.2 **Monopoly profit maximization graphically**

be negative, so marginal revenue is less than marginal cost at $Q' + 1$. This means that raising output from Q' would lower profits, so the initial guess of Q' turned out to be too high.

To find the profit-maximizing level using this trial-and-error method, we would consider a lower guess, say Q' minus 4 units, and repeat the procedure applied above. At the profit-maximizing level, marginal revenue just equals marginal cost. This level must be optimal since any increase or decrease in sales will lower profit. Increasing sales beyond this point will increase cost more than revenue, while decreasing sales would lower revenue more than cost. Both would reduce profit.

The right-hand panel of Fig. 6.2 shows an easier way to find the point where marginal revenue equals marginal cost. The diagram includes a new curve, called the marginal revenue curve. This shows how the marginal revenue (measured in euros) declines as the level of sales rises. (It declines since area A from the left-hand panel gets very small for low levels of sales.) At the sales level marked $Q*$, marginal revenue just equals marginal cost. The firm charges the most it can at this level of sales, and this is $P*$. These are the profit-maximizing levels of sales and price.

6.2.1 Lessons

Several deep aspects of imperfect competition come through even in the monopoly case. First, in setting up the problem, we had to assume things about the firm's beliefs concerning the behaviour of other economic agents. In this case, the monopolist is assumed to believe that consumers are price-takers and that the trade-off between prices and sales depends only on the demand curve (rather than, for example, on the reaction of firms in other markets). Second, the critical difference between perfect and imperfect competition comes out clearly. As part of the definition, perfectly competitive firms are assumed to take the price of their output as given (a classic example is a wheat farmer who cannot set his own price; he just sells at the current market price). This means that such firms are assumed to be ignorant of the fact that selling more will depress the market price. In terms of the diagram, perfectly competitive firms ignore the area A, so they maximize profits by selling an amount where price equals marginal cost. Of course, any increase in sales would have some negative impact on price, so it is best to think of perfect competition as a simplifying assumption that is close to true when all firms have market shares that are close to zero. By stepping away from this simplification, imperfect competition allows firms to explicitly consider the price-depressing effect – area A – when deciding how much to sell.

6.2.2 Duopolist as monopolist on residual demand curve

The monopoly case is instructive, but not very realistic – most European firms face some competition. Taking account of this, however, brings us up against the strategic considerations discussed above. The convention we adopt to sort out this interaction is the so-called Cournot–Nash equilibrium that won John Nash a Nobel prize (see Box 6.2). That is, we assume that each firm acts as if the other firms' outputs are fixed. The equilibrium we are interested in is where each firm's expectations of the other firms' outputs turn out to be correct, i.e. no one is fooled. This no one-fooled notion proves to be somewhat difficult to comprehend in the abstract but, as we shall see below, it is easy in specific applications.

Box 6.2   John Nash (1928–)

Source: www.nobel.se

Early work on imperfect competition (see Box 6.1) was hampered by the problem of strategic interactions among firms. The 'Nash equilibrium' was the concept that cleared away confusions and opened the door to thousands of books and articles on imperfect competition.

The brilliant but troubled creator of the Nash equilibrium concept is a mathematician whose career has attracted an unusual amount of public attention. Since Nash's path-breaking publications have been interspersed with periods of paranoid schizophrenia, Hollywood found it easy to cast him in the cherished stereotype of a mad genius, making his life the subject of a big-budget film entitled *A Beautiful Mind* in 2001. The basis of the Nash equilibrium concept was his 1950 article entitled 'Non-cooperative games'. Just 27 pages long, it earned him the Nobel Prize in economics in 1994. An autobiographical account of his life is on www.nobel.se/economics/laureates/1994/index.html.

The residual demand curve shortcut

Since firms take as given the sales of other firms, the only constraint facing a typical firm is the demand curve shifted to the left by the amount of sales of all other firms. In other words, each firm believes it is a monopolist on the shifted demand curve (we called the shifted demand curve the 'residual demand curve'). This realization is handy since it means that we can directly apply the solution technique from the monopolist's problem; the only change is that we calculate the marginal revenue curve based on the residual demand curve instead of the demand curve.

This trick is shown in Fig. 6.3 for a competition between two firms producing the same good – a situation that economists call 'duopoly'. For simplicity, we assume that the firms have the same marginal cost curves. Taking firm 2's sales as given at Q_2, firm 1 has a monopoly on the

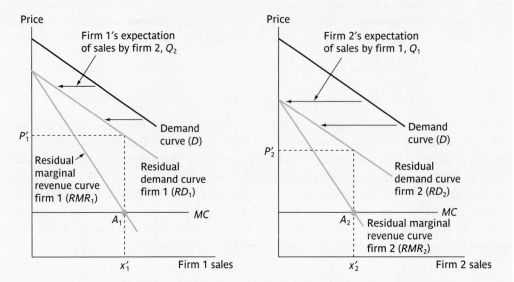

Figure 6.3 Duopolist as monopolist on residual demand: example of a non-equilibrium

residual demand curve labelled RD_1. Firm 1's optimal output in this case is x_1' (since at point A_1, the residual marginal revenue curve, RMR_1, crosses the marginal cost curve MC). The right-hand panel shows the same sort of analysis for firm 2. Taking firm 1's output as fixed at Q_1, firm 2's optimal output is x_2'.

Note that the situation in Fig. 6.3 is not an equilibrium. To highlight the importance of the difference between expected and actual outcomes, the diagram shows the solutions of the two firms when their expectations about the other firm's output do not match the reality. The consistent-expectations outcome, i.e. the Nash equilibrium, is shown in Fig. 6.4, but we first consider why Fig. 6.3 is not an equilibrium.

As drawn, x_1' and x_2' are not a Cournot–Nash equilibrium since the firms' actual output levels do not match expectations; firm 1 produces x_1', which is greater than what firm 2 expected (namely, Q_1), and likewise, firm 2 produces x_2', which is greater than what firm 1 expected (namely, Q_2). We can also see the problem by observing that the implied prices are not equal. If x_1' and x_2' were actually produced by the firms, then firms would not be able to charge the prices they expected to charge. In other words, this is not an equilibrium because the outcome is not consistent with expectations.

Finding the expectations consistent equilibrium

How do we find the expectation-consistent set of outputs? The easiest way is to use the assumed symmetry of firms. In the symmetric equilibrium, each firm will sell the same amount. With this fact in mind, a bit of thought reveals that the residual demand curve facing each firm must be half of the overall demand curve. This situation is shown in the left-hand panel of Fig. 6.4 for a duopoly. Some facts to note are that: (i) the optimal output for a typical firm is x^*, given by the intersection of RMR and MC; (ii) the total sales to the market are $2x^*$ and at this level of sales the overall market price (given by the demand curve, D) is consistent with the price

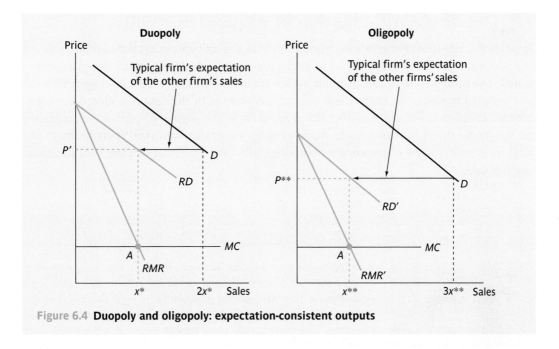

Figure 6.4 **Duopoly and oligopoly: expectation-consistent outputs**

each firm expects to receive given the residual demand curve, *RD*; and (iii) the outputs of the identical firms are equal in equilibrium.

6.2.3 Oligopoly: Cournot–Nash for an arbitrary number of firms

While allowing for two firms was more realistic than just allowing for only one firm, studying the impact of European integration on mergers and acquisitions requires us to allow for an arbitrary number of firms. In economists' jargon, this situation is called an oligopoly. As it turns out, this situation is straightforward to deal with when firms are symmetric. The right-hand panel of Fig. 6.4 shows the argument for the case of three firms.

As more firms are competing in the market (here we consider three instead of two), the residual demand curve facing each one shifts inwards, so the residual marginal revenue curve also shifts inwards; the new curves are shown in the right-hand panel as *RD′* and *RMR′*. The implication of this shift for prices is clear. The new *RMR* = *MC* point occurs at a lower level of per-firm output and this implies a lower price. In equilibrium (i.e. where outcomes match expectations), each of the three firms produces an identical amount, identified as *x*** in the diagram, and charges an identical price, *p***.

Given that we have worked through the 1, 2 and 3 firm cases, readers should be able to see what would happen as the number of firms continues to rise. Each increase in the number of competitors will shift inwards the *RD* facing each one of them. This will inevitably lead to lower prices and lower output per firm.

Of course, this analysis is just formalizing what most readers would expect. If one adds more competitors to a market, prices will fall along with the market share of each firm. As is so often the case, the brilliant concepts are simple.

6.3 The *BE–COMP* diagram in a closed economy

To study the impact of European integration on firm size and efficiency, the number of firms, prices, output and the like, it is useful to have a diagram in which all of these things are determined. The presentation of this diagram, which actually consists of three sub-diagrams, is the first order of business. To keep things simple, we begin with the case of a closed economy. Advanced readers may find the mathematical appendix to this chapter helpful in understanding the diagrams (freely downloadable from www.hei.unige.ch/~baldwin/PapersBooks/). The diagram is an extensive elaboration of one originally used by Nobel Laurate Paul Krugman (see Box 6.3).

Box 6.3 Paul Krugman (1953–)

Source: www.princeton.edu/
~paw/web_exclusives/more/
more_06.html

Building on the work of John Nash (see Box 6.2), Paul Krugman introduced imperfect competition and increasing returns to international trade theory. This introduction profoundly changed the way we think of international trade, so much so that the literature started is now called the 'new trade theory' (even though Krugman did his early work on this in 1979!).

The *BE–COMP* diagram, which is inspired by a diagram that Krugman called the *PP–CC* diagram, is most closely related to his work with James Brander, a professor at the University of British Columbia (Brander and Krugman, 1983), which focuses on imperfect competition as a cause of trade.

In recent years, Krugman has been widely known for his opinion pieces published in the *New York Times* and his blog at http://krugman.blogs.nytimes.com/.

You can read more about why he got the Nobel Prize at www.voxeu.org/index.php?q=node/2463 or on the Nobel site at http://nobelprize.org/nobel_prizes/economics/laureates/2008/press.html.

The heart of the *BE–COMP* diagram is the sub-diagram in which the number of firms and the profit-maximizing price–cost margin are determined. As usual, the equilibrium will be the intersection of two curves, the *BE* curve and the *COMP* curve. We start by presenting the *COMP* curve.

6.3.1 The *COMP* curve

It is easy to understand that imperfectly competitive firms charge a price that exceeds their marginal cost; they do so in order to maximize profit. But how wide is the gap between price and marginal cost, and how does it vary with the number of competitors? These questions are answered by the *COMP* curve.

If there is only one firm, the price–cost gap – what we call the 'mark-up' of price over marginal cost – will equal the mark-up that a monopolist would charge. If there are more firms competing in the market, competition will force each firm to charge a lower mark-up. We summarize this 'competition-side' relationship between the mark-up and the number of firms as the '*COMP* curve' shown in Fig. 6.5. It is downward sloped since competition drives the mark-up down as the number of competitors rises, as explained above. We denote the mark-up with the Greek letter μ, pronounced mu, since 'mu' is an abbreviation for mark-up. We call it the *COMP* curve since the size of the mark-up is an indicator of how competitive the market is.

While this intuitive connection between price and marginal cost may suffice for some readers, extra insight is gained by considering the derivation of the *COMP* curve in more detail. This is done in Annex A.

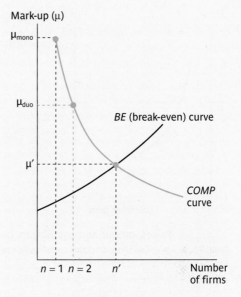

Figure 6.5 The *COMP* and *BE* curves

6.3.2 The break-even (*BE*) curve

The mark-up and number of firms are related in another way, summarized by the *BE* curve.

When a sector is marked by increasing returns to scale, there is only room for a certain number of firms in a market of a given size. Intuitively, more firms will be able to survive if the price is far above marginal cost, i.e. if the mark-up is high. The curve that captures this relationship is called the 'break-even curve', or zero-profit curve (*BE* curve, for short) in Fig. 6.5. It has a positive slope since more firms can break even when the mark-up is high. That is to say, taking the mark-up as given, the *BE* curve shows the number of firms that can earn enough to cover their fixed cost, say, the cost of setting up a factory.

Again, this intuitive presentation of the *BE* curve will suffice for many readers, but might well raise questions in the minds of more advanced readers. These questions are addressed in Annex A.

6.3.3 Equilibrium prices, output and firm size

It is important to note that firms are not always on the *BE* curve since they can earn above-normal or below-normal profits for a while. In the long run, however, firms can enter or exit the market, so the number of firms rises or falls until the typical firm earns just enough to cover its fixed cost. By contrast, firms are always on the *COMP* curve since firms can change prices quickly in response to any change in the number of firms.

With this in mind, we are ready to work out the equilibrium mark-up, number of firms, price and firm-size in a closed economy using Fig. 6.6. The right-hand panel combines the *BE*

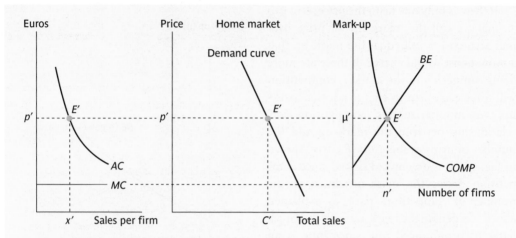

Figure 6.6 Prices, output and equilibrium firm size in a closed economy

Note: Readers who find these diagrams complicated may benefit from the interactive Power Point presentations on http://heiwww.unige.ch/_Baldwin/BW/BW.htm

curve with the *COMP* curve. The intersection of the two defines the equilibrium mark-up and long-run number of firms. More specifically, the *COMP* curve tells us that firms would charge a mark-up of μ' when there are n' firms in the market, and the *BE* curve tells us that n' firms could break even when the mark-up is μ'. The equilibrium price is – by definition of the mark-up – just the equilibrium mark-up plus the marginal cost, *MC*. Using the *MC* curve from the left-hand panel, we see that the equilibrium price is p' (this equals μ' plus *MC*). The middle panel shows the demand curve and this allows us to see that the total level of consumption implied by the equilibrium price is C'.

The left-hand panel helps us to find the equilibrium firm size, i.e. sales per firm, which we denote as x'. This sub-diagram shows the average and marginal cost curves of a typical firm. As a little bit of reflection reveals, a typical firm's total profit is zero when price equals average cost (when price equals average cost, total revenue equals total cost). Since we know that total profits are zero at the equilibrium and we know the price is p', it must be that the equilibrium firm size is x' since this is where the firm's size implies an average cost equal to p'.

In summary, Fig. 6.6 lets us determine the equilibrium number of firms, mark-up, price, total consumption and firm size all in one diagram. With this in hand, we are now ready to study how European integration has sparked a wave of industrial restructuring.

6.4 The impact of European liberalization

European integration has involved a gradual reduction of trade barriers. The basic economic effects of this gradual reduction can, however, be illustrated more simply by considering a much more drastic liberalization – taking a completely closed economy and making it a completely open economy. To keep things simple, we suppose that there are only two nations, Home and Foreign, and that these nations are identical. Since they are identical, we could trace through the effects looking at either market, but we focus on Home's market for convenience.

6.4.1 No-trade-to-free-trade liberalization

The immediate impact of the no-trade-to-free-trade liberalization is to provide each firm with a second market of the same size and to double the number of competitors in each market. How does this change the outcome?

The competition aspect of the liberalization is simple to trace out. The increased number of competitors in each market makes competition tougher. In reaction, the typical firm will lower its mark-up in each market to point A in Fig. 6.7.

The doubling of the market size facing each firm also has an important effect. The liberalization adds a new market for each firm, so it makes sense that more firms will be able to survive. To see how many more firms can survive, we work out the impact of the liberalization on the BE curve. As it turns out, the liberalization shifts the BE curve to the right, specifically to BE_{FT}, as shown in the diagram. Why? Shifting BE to the right means that at any given mark-up more firms can break even. This is true since as the market size increases the sales per firm increases, thus providing a higher operating profit per firm at any given level of mark-up.

The size of the rightward shift is determined without difficulty. If there were no changes in the mark-up (there will be in the new equilibrium, but ignore this for the moment), then double the number of firms could break even since each firm would be selling the same number of units. In other words, the new BE curve must pass through the point marked '1' in the diagram; at point 1, the mark-up is μ', the number of firms is $2n'$, and logic tells us that this combination of μ and n would result in all firms breaking even. Point 1, however, is merely an intellectual landmark used to determine how far out the BE curve shifts. It is not where the economy would be right after liberalization since the mark-up would immediately be pushed down to μ_A.

Because the increase in competition would immediately push down the mark-up to μ_A, the two newly integrated markets will initially be at a point that is below the BE curve. We know

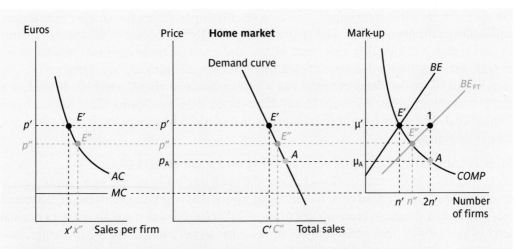

Figure 6.7 Prices, output and equilibrium firm size with integration

that all firms will be losing money at point A since the actual mark-up (μ_A) is less than what would be needed to have all $2n'$ firms break even. Now, this loss of profit is not a problem in the short run since firms only need to break even in the long run. Indeed, the profit losses are what would trigger the process of industrial restructuring that will eventually reduce the number of firms.

The corresponding effect on prices is shown in the middle diagram as the move from E' to A and then to E''. Before explaining this, observe that the middle panel shows the demand curve for Home only, so the no-trade-to-free-trade liberalization does not shift the demand curve. The Foreign market has an identical demand, but since exactly the same thing goes on in Foreign, we omit the Foreign demand curve to reduce the diagram's complexity.

As mentioned above, the initial impact of the extra competition ($2n'$ firms selling to the Home market instead of n') pushes the equilibrium mark-up down to μ_A, so the price falls to p_A. Thus during this industrial restructuring phase, the price would rise to p'' (from p_A), but this rise does not take the price all the way back to its pre-liberalization level of p'.

The impact of this combination of extra competition and industrial restructuring on a typical firm is shown in the left-hand panel. As prices are falling, firms that remain in the market increase their efficiency – i.e. lower their average costs – by spreading their fixed cost over a larger number of sales. Indeed, since price equalled average cost before the liberalization and in the long run after liberalization, we know that the price drop is exactly equal to the efficiency gain. In the left-hand panel, this is shown as a move from E' to E''. Increasing returns to scale are the root of this efficiency gain. As the equilibrium scale of a typical firm rises from x' to x'', average costs fall.

To summarize, the no-trade-to-free-trade liberalization results in fewer, larger firms. The resulting scale economies lower average cost and thus make these firms more efficient. The extra competition ensures that these savings are passed on to lower prices. It is useful to think of the integration as leading to two steps.

Step 1: Short term: defragmentation and the pro-competitive effect (from E' to A)

We start with the short-term impact, that is to say, the impact before the number of firms can adjust. Before the liberalization, each market was extremely fragmented in the sense that firms in each nation had a local market share of $1/n'$ and a zero share in the other market. After the liberalization, the market share of each firm is the same in each market, namely $n'/2$. This elimination of market fragmentation has a pro-competitive effect, which is defined as a decrease in the price–cost mark-up. This is shown in the right-hand panel of Fig. 6.7 as a move from E' to A. The short-term impact on prices and sales can be seen in the middle panel as a drop from p' to p_A.

Step 2: Long term: industrial restructuring and scale effects (A to E'')

Point A is not a long-term equilibrium since the operating profit earned by a typical firm is insufficient to cover the fixed cost. We see this by noting that point A is below the BE curve and this tells us that the mark-up is too low to allow $2n'$ firms to break even. To restore a normal level of profitability, the overall number of firms has to fall from $2n'$ to n''. In Europe, this process typically occurs via mergers and buy-outs, but in some cases the number of firms is reduced by bankruptcies. As this industrial consolidation occurs, the economy moves from

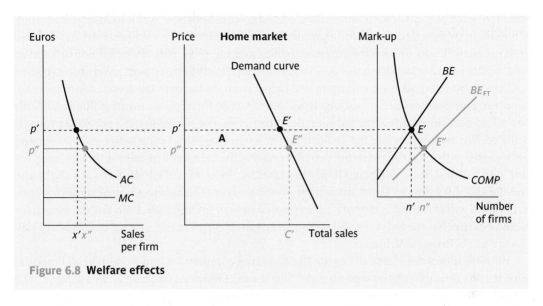

Figure 6.8 Welfare effects

point *A* to point *E″*. During this process, firms enlarge their market shares, the mark-up rises somewhat and profitability is restored.

Welfare effects

The welfare effects of this liberalization are quite straightforward. The four-sided area marked by *p′*, *p″*, *E′* and *E″* in the middle panel of Fig. 6.8 corresponds to the gain in Home consumer surplus. As usual, this gain can be broken down into the gain to consumers of paying a lower price for the units they bought prior to the liberalization, and the gains from buying more (*C″* versus *C′*). Note that the exact same gain occurs in the Foreign market (not shown in the diagram).

As it turns out, this four-sided region labelled *A* in Fig. 6.8 is Home's long-term welfare gain because there is no offsetting loss to producers and there was no tariff revenue to begin with. Firms made zero profits before liberalization and they earn zero profits after liberalization. Note, however, that this long-term calculation ignores the medium-term adjustment costs. These costs, which stem from the industrial restructuring, can be politically very important. Indeed, many governments attempt to thwart the restructuring by adopting a variety of policies such as industrial subsidies and various anti-merger and anti-acquisition policies (discussed further in Chapter 14). We should also note that the welfare gains shown can be rather substantial. Roughly speaking, the percentage gain in real GDP equals the share of the economy affected (industry in the EU, for instance, accounts for about 30 per cent of output) times the percentage drop in price.

6.4.2 Slow and fast adjustments

The discussion above has shown that the integration initially leads to big price reductions and large profit losses. These profit losses are eliminated as the number of firms falls and profits are restored to normal levels. During this industrial restructuring process, prices rise slightly.

This sequence of steps – sometimes called industry 'consolidation' or an industry 'shake-out' – is relevant to some industries, for example air travel. Here, Europe's liberalization has resulted in large profit losses for many European airlines and big price reductions for consumers. At first, airlines were reluctant to merge – largely because most airlines were government-owned and their governments were willing to use taxpayer euros to cover the losses. More recently, however, European airlines are rationalizing their costs by forming cooperative alliances. While the actual number of firms has not yet fallen, the number of planes flying a particular route is reduced. For example, before the two firms went bankrupt, cooperation between Swiss Air and Sabena meant that instead of having two planes flying the Geneva–Brussels route (one Swiss Air and one Sabena), only one plane flew. Nevertheless, Swiss Air called it a Swiss Air flight and Sabena called it a Sabena flight. Such 'code-sharing' arrangements are a way of achieving scale economies without actually eliminating a national carrier. Interestingly, both airlines eventually went bankrupt but the Swiss and Belgian governments stepped in to create replacement airlines, Swiss and SN Brussels Airlines.

In other industries, firms anticipate the increased competition and undertake the mergers and acquisitions quickly enough to avoid big losses. European banking is an example. The introduction of the euro and continuing liberalization of the banking sector mean that European banks will have to become fewer and bigger in order to break even. However, instead of waiting for profit losses to become intolerable, banks have launched a record-breaking series of mergers and acquisitions. In terms of Fig. 6.8, this would look like a move from E' directly to E''.

6.4.3 Empirical evidence

There is ample empirical evidence that European industry is marked by fewer, bigger, more efficient firms since the Single Market Programme. For example, the 1996 Single Market Review by the European Commission presents several studies illustrating these trends (see Commission, 1996, for a brief review of this multi-volume study). Unfortunately, there is little direct evidence in Europe that industry consolidation was caused by market integration, although this is what most economists believe is the obvious explanation. More direct evidence linking market size with efficiency and competition can be found in Campbell and Hopenhayn (2002). The authors study the impact of market size on the size distribution of firms in retail-trade industries across 225 US cities. In every industry examined, establishments were larger in larger cities. The authors conclude that their results support the notion that competition is tougher in larger markets and this accounts for the link between firm size and market size.

6.5 Summary

Three main points have been made in this chapter:

★ One very obvious impact of European integration has been to face individual European firms with a bigger 'home' market. This produces a chain reaction that leads to fewer, bigger, more efficient firms that face more effective competition from each other. Understanding the economic logic driving this chain reaction is the main goal of this chapter. This logic can be summarized as follows. Integration defragments Europe's markets in the sense that it removes the privileged position of national firms in their national markets. As a result, all firms face more competition from other firms in their national market, but at the same time they have better access to the other EU markets. This general increase in competition puts downward pressure on price–cost mark-ups, prices and profits. The profit-squeeze results in industrial restructuring, a process by which the total number of firms in Europe falls. The lower prices and lower number of firms mean that the average firm gets larger and this, in turn, allows firms to better exploit economies of scale. This efficiency increase, in turn, permits the firms to break even despite the lower prices.

★ The industrial restructuring is often politically painful since it often results in layoffs and the closure of inefficient plants. Governments very often attempt to offset this political pain by providing 'state aid' to their national firms. Such state aid can be viewed as unfair and the perception of unfairness threatens to undermine EU members' interest in integration. To avoid these problems, the founders of the EU established rules that prohibited state aid that distorts competition. The Commission is charged with enforcing these rules. These rules are covered in Chapter 14.

★ Industrial restructuring raises another problem that led the EU's founders to set out another set of rules. As integration proceeds and the number of firms falls, the temptation for firms to collude may increase. To avoid this, the EU has strict rules on anti-competitive practices. It also screens mergers to ensure that mergers will enhance efficiency. Again, the Commission is charged with enforcing these rules. These rules are covered in Chapter 14.

Self-assessment questions

1. Suppose that liberalization occurs as in Section 6.4 and the result is a pro-competitive effect, but instead of merging or restructuring, all firms are bought by their national governments to allow the firms to continue operating. What will be the impact of this on prices and government revenues? Now that the governments are the owners, will they have an incentive to continue with liberalization? Can you imagine why this might favour firms located in nations with big, rich governments?

2. Use a three-panel diagram, like Fig. 6.6, to show how the number of firms, mark-up and firm size would change in a closed economy if the demand for the particular good rose, i.e. the demand curve shifted out.

3. Using your findings from Question 2, you should be able to consider the impact of a no-trade-to-free-trade integration between a large and a small nation, where size is defined by the position of the demand curve (the demand curve in the large nation will be further out than the demand curve for the small nation). To do this, you will need two of the three-panel diagrams of the Fig. 6.6 type to show the pre-integration situation. Then use a three-panel diagram of the Fig. 6.7 type to show what happens to prices, firm size and the number of firms in the integrated economy. Note that you will want to show both demand curves in the middle panel. As usual, assume that all firms have the same marginal

cost. What does this analysis tell you about how integration affects firms in small nations versus large nations?

4. Consider a sequence of EU 'enlargements' where each enlargement involves a no-trade-to-free-trade addition of one more member. Specifically, suppose there are three initially identical economies, each of which looks like the one described in Section 6.3. Initially, all nations are closed to trade. Now, consider a no-trade-to-free-trade integration between two of the nations (just as in Section 6.4). Then consider a no-trade-to-free-trade integration of a third nation. (Hint: The second step will be very much like the integration between unequal-sized economies explored in Question 3.) Calculate how much the third nation gains from joining and compare it to how much the existing two-nation bloc gains from the third nation's membership. Who gains more in proportion to size: the 'incumbents' or the 'entrants'?

Essay questions

1. When the Single Market Programme was launched in the mid-1980s, European leaders asserted that it would improve the competitiveness of European firms vis-à-vis US firms. Explain how one can make sense of this assertion by extending the reasoning in this chapter.

2. Has the strategy of defragmenting Europe's markets worked in the sense of promoting bigger, more efficient firms facing more effective competition? Choose an industry, for example telecoms, chemicals, pharmaceuticals or autos, and compare the evolution of the EU industry with that of the USA or Japan. You can find information on these and many more industries at the Commission website. Search the site http://europa.eu.int/comm/enterprise/index_en.htm with Google to find specific information on specific sectors.

3. Some EU members allow their companies to engage in 'anti-takeover' practices. Discuss how differences in EU members' laws concerning these practices might be viewed as unfair when EU industry is being transformed by a wave of mergers and acquisitions.

4. Write an essay on the historical role that the scale economies argument played in the economic case for deeper European integration. Start with the Spaak Report (see www.ena.lu) and the Cockfield Report, Completing the Internal Market, White Paper, COM (85) 310 final (you can find it in French, 'Livre blanc sur l'achèvement du marché intérieur', on www.ena.lu under the subject 'The Delors White Paper').

Further reading: the aficionado's corner

Consideration of imperfect competition and scale effects was made possible in the 1980s with development of the so-called new trade theory (**Helpman and Krugman**, 1985, 1989). The new theory was naturally applied to the analysis of the Single Market Programme when it was first discussed in the mid-1980s. Many of the classic studies are contained in **Winters** (1992). **Baldwin and Venables** (1995) provide a synthetic, graduate-level survey of this literature.

Table 7.2 Growth in the post-Second World War reconstruction phase

	The setback: pre-war year when GDP equalled that of 1945	Back-on-track year: year GDP attained highest pre-war level	Reconstruction: growth rate during reconstruction years (1945 to column 2 year) (%)
Austria	1886	1951	15.2
Belgium	1924	1948	6.0
Denmark	1936	1946	13.5
Finland	1938	1945	n.a.
France	1891	1949	19.0
Germany	1908	1951	13.5
Italy	1909	1950	11.2
Netherlands	1912	1947	39.8
Norway	1937	1946	9.7
Sweden	These countries actually grew during the Second World War		
Switzerland			
UK			

Source: Crafts and Toniolo 1996, p. 4

and causality. There is, nonetheless, some general evidence – what might be called prima facie evidence in a court of law – that supports the integration-fosters-growth hypothesis.

The first element of the prima facie case concerns a country-by-country analysis of growth during the 1950–73 period. Recall from Chapter 1 that this period saw rapid integration among European nations. From 1950 to 1958, the main liberalization was common to western European nations, but from 1958 to 1968 the EEC6 integrated much faster than did EFTA members (UK, Sweden, Switzerland, Finland, Norway, Austria, Portugal and Iceland). Table 7.3 shows the growth performance of various OEEC members during this period. Focusing, first, on the third column, we note that the EEC6 (data for Luxembourg was not available) rose in the GDP per-capita rankings. Germany jumped five places, Italy jumped two, while the Netherlands and Belgium slipped slightly. By contrast, the EFTAns lost ground, with the UK and Norway dropping five and four places, respectively, with Sweden and Denmark gaining one and Austria gaining two.

The non-EEC, non-EFTA nations also lost, especially Ireland, which was tightly linked to EFTA by a bilateral free trade agreement with the UK. Note also that the average growth performance of the EEC members was almost 50 per cent better than that of the EFTAns, although much of this may be explained by a 'catching-up' phenomenon (EEC nations were poorer than EFTAns in 1950 and poorer nations tend to grow more quickly than rich nations).

What is particularly striking is the performance of the 'big four' nations: France, Germany, Italy and the UK. The first three were members of the EEC and grew between 1.7 and 2.1 times faster than the UK. Again catch-up played some role in this, but by 1973 both France and Germany were richer than the UK, so the catch-up roles were reversed by the end of the period. This suggests a correlation between integration and growth since the economic integration in the EEC was much tighter than that of EFTA during this period.

Table 7.3 GDP per capita and rankings, 1950 and 1973 (1990 international dollars)

	1950 GDP (1990 $)	European rank 1950	Change in rank 1950–1973	GDP growth rate 1950–1973
EEC average	**4825**	**8.0**	**+1.2**	**4.2**
Netherlands	5850	5	−1	3.4
Belgium	5346	6	−2	3.5
France	5221	7	+2	4.0
Germany	4281	9	+5	5.0
Italy	3425	13	+2	4.9
EFTA average	**6835**	**3.6**	**−1.4**	**3.0**
Switzerland	8939	1	0	3.1
UK	6847	2	−5	2.4
Sweden	6738	3	+1	3.1
Denmark	6683	4	+1	3.1
Norway	4969	8	−4	3.2
Finland	4131	10	0	4.2
Austria	3731	11	+2	4.9
Others average	**2401**	**14.3**	**−0.3**	**5.2**
Ireland	3518	12	−3	3.1
Spain	2397	14	+1	5.8
Portugal	2132	15	+1	5.6
Greece	1558	16	0	6.2
For comparison	**9573**			**2.4**
USA				
Japan	1873			8.0

Source: Crafts and Toniolo 1996, p. 3

Of course, not much should be read into such simple correlation, but at the time the UK's laggard growth performance in the face of the Continental growth booms played an important role in shaping British attitudes towards EEC membership. Or, to put it more bluntly, regardless of whether EEC integration was responsible for the Six's superior growth performance, political leaders at the time believed there was a connection.

Another line of indicative evidence comes from comparing the before and after growth rates of nations that have joined the EU. The facts are shown in Table 7.4. We have data for four enlargements (the 2004 enlargement is too recent). Growth picked up in half the cases (the third and fourth), but slowed in the other half. However, many things affect growth apart from EU membership. The world experienced serious growth slowdowns during the first oil shock (1973–75) and when OECD central banks decided to fight inflation with restrictive monetary policies (1981–83). One way to partially control for this is to compare the growth rate of the

Table 7.4 Growth rates five years before and five years after accession

	West Europe (%)	Britain + Denmark + Ireland (%)	Greece (%)	Spain + Portugal (%)	Finland + Austria + Sweden (%)
Pre-1968–72	18.5	12.5			
Post-1973–77	5.8	4.8			
Pre-1976–80	10.2		9.0		
Post-1981–85	7.4		0.1		
Pre-1981–85	7.4			2.7	
Post-1986–90	16.2			23.0	
Pre-1989–93	3.7				–5.0
Post-1994–98	12.7				12.4

Note: Real GDP in constant prices; 5-year average, not annualized. West Europe is all the nations that eventually ended up in the EU or EFTA, i.e. the EU15 plus Iceland, Norway and Switzerland.

Source: Penn World, Table 6.1 (RGDPL)

entrants to the average western European growth rate over the same period. We see that all the enlargements have been pro-growth by this rough measure, except Greece's.

The combined GDP of the first entrants (Britain, Denmark and Ireland) was growth much slower than the European average during the five years before accession in 1973, but only slightly less fast in the five years following membership (i.e. 18.5 versus 12.5 per cent compared with 5.8 versus 4.8 per cent). For the third and fourth enlargements, the five-year growth rates for the entrants were behind the pan-European average before but ahead of it after they joined. The one exception is that of Greece – a theme that comes out clearly in a closer examination of the data below.

Formal statistical evidence

There are better ways to isolate the impact of integration and growth than simply comparing to the western European growth average. These techniques involve statistical methods – regression analysis – that are standard in the scientific literature on trade and growth. The consensus in this literature is that economic integration is good for income growth, although the exact relationship is not fully understood. The literature on European integration per se is much less developed. A recent pair of papers by Harald Badinger suggest that, although there is no long-run (i.e. permanent) boost to growth, tighter European integration does produce a sizeable medium-run growth effect (Badinger, 2005, 2008).[1]

The point is illustrated in Figure 7.1. In reality, European integration did occur and this produced the income growth we can observe in the data. To work out the fraction of this income that was due to an integration-induced growth effect, one needs to simulate what income would have been *without* European integration. The difference is the medium-run growth effect.

---

[1] Also see Henrekson et al. (1997), Coe and Moghadam (1993) and Italianer (1994).

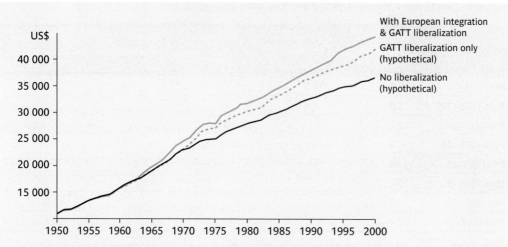

Figure 7.1 Empirical evidence on the medium-run growth effect

Note: The top line shows EU income growth. The middle and lower lines show a simulation of how much lower EU income per worker would have been under two hypothetical situations, without European integration (middle) and without any integration (lower). The difference between the middle and top line is Badinger's estimate of the medium-run growth effect.

Source: Badinger 2005, working paper version, with permission from the author

We turn now to a more careful consideration of *how* integration might affect growth. Establishing such an analytical framework is useful to understanding the growth–integration link, but more importantly, it allows us to make more pointed predictions that can be confronted with the data.

7.2 Medium-term growth effects: induced capital formation with Solow's analysis

Spain's accession to the EU in the mid-1980s was accompanied by an investment boom that raised Spain's GDP growth by several percentage points for a few years. In this section, we consider ways of understanding how EU membership could yield such a medium-term growth bonus.

The key to the medium-term growth bonus is 'induced capital formation'. That is to say, integration induces firms to raise the level of capital per worker employed. For the moment, we focus exclusively on the machine per worker (i.e. physical-capital to labour) ratio, so the first step is to identify a means of determining the equilibrium capital/labour ratio. The approach we adopt was discovered by Nobel Laureate Robert Solow in the 1950s (see Box 7.1). It assumes that people save and then invest a fixed share of their income.

7.2.1 Solow diagram

To keep things easy, we start by viewing the whole EU as a single, closed economy with fully integrated capital and labour markets and the same technology everywhere.

Box 7.1   Robert Solow (1924–)

Source: © Adephs, 2003–2005

Robert Solow, universally known as Bob, is a classic example of the Second World War generation of economists who thought that it was their duty to use their minds to improve the social situation. To this day, he remains engaged in public policy debates, for example taking an active stance against the Iraq War via Economists Allied for Arms Reduction.

His most famous contributions to economics, published in the late 1950s, revolutionized thinking about the causes of growth. Before Solow, the dominant thinking was that capital accumulation (the Harrod–Domar model) by itself was the driving force of growth. What Solow showed was that capital accumulation was driven by technological progress, so the ultimate growth driver was technological progress. This simple realization shifted the focus of governments' pro-growth policies worldwide from investment in machines to investment in knowledge.

A brilliant and precocious student (enrolled in Harvard at 16 years old and started teaching at MIT two years before finishing his PhD), Solow as a professor turned out to be an excellent teacher who devoted an inordinate amount of time to students. He is also famous for being one of the wittiest living economists. A leader of the Keynesian school (which supports active government intervention), Solow criticized his fellow economists with wit and wisdom; economists ranging from interventionists such as John Kenneth Galbraith to arch-conservatives such as Milton Friedman. Solow once wrote that Galbraith's disdain for ordinary consumer goods 'reminds one of the Duchess who, upon acquiring a full appreciation of sex, asked the Duke if it were not perhaps too good for the common people'. Of Milton Friedman, Solow wrote, 'Everything reminds Milton of the money supply. Well, everything reminds me of sex, but I keep it out of the paper' (see www.minneapolisfed.org for recent examples in an interview).

Solow was part of President Kennedy's 'Camelot', working from 1961 to 1963 on the Council of Economic Advisers. In 1961 he won the American Economic Association's John Bates Clark Award, given to the best economist under the age of 40. In 1987, he won the Nobel Prize (see his autobiography at www.nobelprize.org).

We begin our study of the logic linking growth and integration by focusing on the connection between GDP-per-worker and capital-per-worker. When a firm provides its workers with more and better equipment, output per worker rises. However, output per worker does not increase in proportion with equipment per worker. To see this, consider the example of the efficiency of your studying and your personal capital/labour ratio. The most primitive method of studying would be just to go to lectures and listen. Buying some paper and pencils would allow you to take notes and this would enormously boost your productivity in terms of both time and quality. Going further, you could buy the book and again this would boost your productivity (i.e. the effectiveness per hour of studying) but not as much as the pencils and paper. It would also be nice to have a calculator, a laptop, high-speed connection to the internet at home, and a laser printer of your own.

Each subsequent increase in your 'capital' would boost your effectiveness, but each euro of capital investment would provide progressively lower increases in productivity. As it turns out,

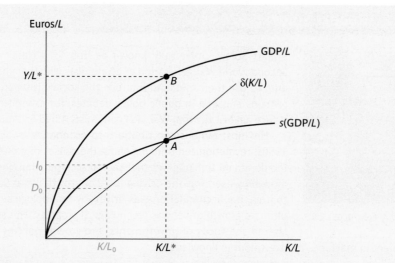

Figure 7.2 **The Solow diagram: determining the equilibrium capital/labour ratio**

this sort of 'diminishing returns' to investment also marks the economy as a whole. Raising the capital/labour ratio in the economy increases output per hour worked, but the rate of increase diminishes as the level of the capital/labour ratio rises.

This sort of less-than-proportional increase in efficiency is portrayed by the GDP/L curve. This shows that raising the capital/labour ratio (K/L, which is plotted on the horizontal axis) increases output per worker, but a 10 per cent hike in K/L raises GDP/L by less than 10 per cent. This is why the curve is bowed downwards in Figure 7.2. (Alternatively, think of the curve as rising less rapidly than a straight line.)

The GDP/L curve shows us what output per worker would be for any given K/L; but what will the K/L be? The equilibrium K/L ratio depends upon the inflow and outflow of new capital per worker. The inflow is investment – firms building new factories, buying new trucks, installing new machines, etc. The outflow is depreciation – factories, trucks and machinery break down with use and must be repaired or replaced. The equilibrium K/L is where the inflow of new investment just balances depreciation of capital. The reason is simple. If the flow of savings exceeds the depreciation of capital, then K/L rises. If depreciation outstrips investment, K/L falls. The next step is to find the inflow and outflow of capital.

Solow simply assumed that people save and invest a constant fraction of their income each year, so the inflow of capital is just a fraction of GDP/L; in the diagram, this constant savings and investment fraction is denoted as s, so the inflow-of-capital curve is marked as s(GDP/L). (In European nations, s is somewhere between 20 and 35 per cent.) The investment-per-worker curve has a shape that is similar to that of the GDP/L curve but it is rotated clockwise since the savings are a fraction of GDP/L. As for depreciation, Solow made an equally simple assumption. He assumed that a constant fraction of capital stock depreciates each year. In the figure, the constant fraction of the capital stock that depreciates each year is denoted with the Greek letter 'delta', δ. (In Europe, something like 12 per cent of the capital stock depreciates each year.)

The depreciation per worker line is shown as $\delta(K/L)$. It is a straight line since the amount of depreciation per worker increases in proportion to the amount of capital per worker.

The important point in the figure is point A, the crossing of the $s(\text{GDP}/L)$ curve and the $\delta(K/L)$ line. This occurs at K/L^*. At this capital/labour ratio, the inflow of new investment just balances the outflow. For a ratio below K/L^*, the capital/labour ratio would rise since investment outstrips depreciation. For example, if K/L were K/L_0, then the inflow would be I_0 and the outflow would be D_0. Since I_0 is higher than D_0, the amount of new capital per worker installed would be greater than the amount of capital per worker lost to depreciation. Naturally, the capital/labour ratio would rise. With more capital being installed for a ratio higher than this, depreciation surpasses investment, so K/L would fall. The last thing to work out is the output per worker implied by the equilibrium K/L. The answer, which is given by the GDP/L curve at point B, tells us that output per worker in this equilibrium will be Y/L^*.

Although it is not essential to our main line of analysis, we finish our discussion of the Solow diagram with a consideration of long-run growth. The main point that Solow made with his diagram was that the accumulation of capital is not a source of long-run growth. Capital rises up to the point where the K/L ratio reaches its equilibrium value and then stops, unless something changes. To explain the year-after-year growth we see in the modern world – about 2 per cent per year on average – Solow relied on technological progress. He assumed that technological advances would rotate the GDP/L curve upwards year after year, pulling the $s(\text{GDP}/L)$ curve up with it. As can be easily verified in the Solow diagram, such progress will lead to an ever-rising output per worker and an ever-rising capital/labour ratio. When we look at the growth effects of European integration, we shall be referring to growth that is higher than the growth that would have otherwise occurred due to technological progress.

We next use the Solow diagram to study how European integration might boost growth.

7.2.2 Liberalization, allocation effects and the medium-run growth bonus

The verbal logic of growth effects is straightforward. Integration improves the efficiency of the European economy by encouraging a more efficient allocation of European resources. Not surprisingly, this improved efficiency also makes Europe a better place to invest and thus boosts investment beyond what it otherwise would have been. The extra investment means more tools per worker, and this raises the output per worker. As workers get more tools than they would have without integration, output per worker rises faster than it would have done otherwise. To put this differently, integration produces extra growth as the capital/labour ratio approaches its new equilibrium output. This is the medium-run growth bonus introduced by Baldwin (1989). It is medium term since the higher growth disappears once the new equilibrium capital/labour ratio is reached.

Medium-run growth bonus in detail

Figure 7.3 allows us to portray the logic in more detail. The first step is to realize how 'allocation effects' of European integration alter the diagram. For all the reasons presented in Chapters 4 to 6, European integration has improved the effectiveness with which capital, labour and technology are combined to produce output. To take one concrete example, we saw that integration

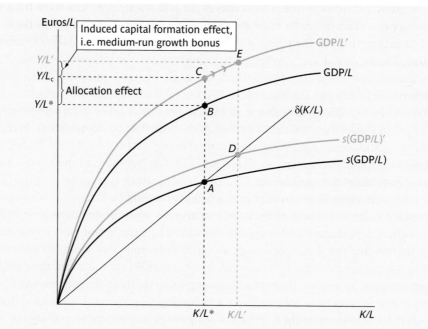

Figure 7.3 Medium-run growth bonus from European integration
Source: Baldwin 1989

can lead to fewer, more efficient firms. From the firm-level perspective, this improved efficiency means lower average cost. From the economy-wide perspective, the improved efficiency means that the same amount of capital and labour can produce more output. How can we show this in the Solow diagram?

The positive allocation effect shifts the GDP/L curve to the dashed line marked GDP/L'. The new GDP/L curve is the old one rotated up counter-clockwise since the improved efficiency means that the economy is able to produce more output, say, 2 per cent more, for any given capital/labour ratio. This is the first step. The impact of the higher efficiency on output is shown by point C. That is, holding the capital/labour ratio constant at K/L^*, output would rise from Y/L^* to Y/L_c. This is not the end of the story, however, since K/L^* is no longer the equilibrium capital/labour ratio. This brings us to the second step.

The shift up in the GDP/L curve to GDP/L' also shifts up the investment curve to $s(\text{GDP}/L)'$. After all, the fixed investment rate now applies to higher output and so generates a higher inflow of investment for any given capital/labour ratio. This is shown in the diagram by the dashed curve $s(\text{GDP}/L)'$. Since the inflow has risen, K/L^* is no longer the equilibrium. At K/L^*, the inflow exceeds the outflow, so the economy's capital/labour ratio begins to rise. The new equilibrium is at the new intersection of the inflow and outflow curves, namely point D, so the new equilibrium capital/labour ratio is K/L'. The rise from K/L^* to K/L' is called 'induced capital formation' and reflects the fact that improved efficiency will tend to stimulate investment.

What are the growth implications? As the capital/labour ratio rises from K/L^* to K/L', output per worker rises from Y/L_c to Y/L'. This is shown in the diagram as the movement from point C to point E. Since the capital stock builds up only slowly, the movement between C and E can take years. The key to the second step is to realize that the rise in output per worker between C and E would show up as faster than normal growth until the economy reaches point E. At that time, the growth rate would return to normal.

Summary in words

In words, the integration-causes-growth mechanism is: integration → improved efficiency → higher GDP/L → higher investment-per-worker → economy's capital/labour ratio starts to rise towards new, higher equilibrium value → faster growth of output per worker during the transition from the old to the new capital/labour ratio. This is the so-called 'medium-term growth bonus' from European integration.

When it comes to welfare, however, it is important to note that higher output is not a pure welfare gain. In order to invest more, citizens must save more and this means forgoing consumption today. Consequently, the higher levels of consumption made possible tomorrow by the higher K/L ratio are partly offset by the forgone consumption of today.

7.2.3 Other medium-run growth effects: changes in the investment rate

The Solow diagram relied on an extremely convenient simplifying assumption – a constant investment rate. Unfortunately, taking the investment rate as given severely limits the range of growth effects that we can study. As the introduction pointed out, the basic logic of growth rests on the decision to invest in new physical capital (machines), new human capital (skills) and/or new knowledge capital (innovations). Many growth effects operate by altering the costs and/or benefits of investing and thus by altering the investment *rate*, what we called s in the diagram. For instance, many people claim that the euro makes it easier, cheaper and safer to invest in Europe. If this turns out to be true, the extra investment would boost growth at least in the medium term, but how would we get this into the Solow framework?

If European integration raises the investment rate from, say, s to s', the inflow of capital curve, namely $s(GDP/L)$, will rotate upwards, as shown in Fig. 7.4. This change would in turn alter the equilibrium capital/labour ratio. Following the logic we considered above, the inflow of capital at the old capital/labour ratio K/L^* would exceed the outflow, so the capital stock per worker would rise to the new equilibrium shown by point C in the diagram. As before, the rising K/L would raise output per worker from Y/L^* to Y/L' (these Y/L^* and Y/L' are unrelated to those in previous figures). During this process, growth would be somewhat higher than it would have otherwise been.

This shows that it is straightforward to illustrate this second type of growth effect in the Solow diagram. We postpone our discussion of how various aspects of European integration might raise the investment rate to Section 7.3, where we consider EU capital market integration.

7.2.4 Evidence from the 'poor four'

Western Europe grew rapidly in the post-war period and experienced rapid integration. The problem, however, is that it is very difficult to separate the effects of European integration from

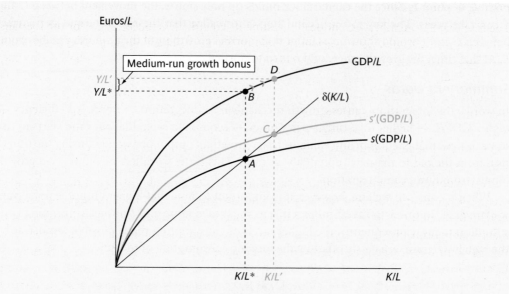

Figure 7.4 **European integration and the investment rate**

the many other factors affecting growth. One natural experiment is to look at what happened to nations that joined the EU. These nations experienced a rather sudden and well-defined increase in economic integration when they joined. Moreover, we shall study the impact that EU membership had on the four relatively poor entrants that joined the EU between 1960 and 1995: Ireland (in 1973), Greece (in 1981) and Portugal and Spain (in 1986).

The logic sketched out above explains how integration may raise a nation's steady-state capital stock. What sort of 'footprints' would this leave in the data? First, heightened efficiency makes investment more worthwhile, i.e. it tends to raise the real return to capital. Moreover, this will normally be associated with an increase in the profitability of existing capital and this, in turn, should show up in the average behaviour of the stock market (as long as the stock market reflects a broad sample of firms). An important caveat comes from the fact that liberalization usually harms some firms and sectors even when it is beneficial for the nation as a whole. If the stock market is dominated by, say, state-controlled 'white elephants' that will face increased pressure in a more liberal economy, a drop in the stock market index may accompany the enlargement. Second, the Solow diagram is too simple to distinguish between domestic and foreign investors, but we presume that an improvement in the national investment climate should attract more investment from both sources. These two effects are likely to leave four kinds of 'footprints' in the data:

1 Stock market prices should increase.

2 The aggregate investment to GDP ratio should rise.

3 The net direct investment figures should improve.

4 The current account should deteriorate as more foreign capital flows in.

Chapter **8**

Economic integration, labour markets and migration

As the extent of economic integration approaches that of the United States, labour market institutions and labour market outcomes may also begin to resemble their American counterparts. [. . .] Full and irreversible economic integration may call for harmonization of social and labour-market institutions within the European Union.

Giuseppe Bertola (2000)

Chapter contents

8.1	European labour markets: a brief characterization	234
8.2	Labour markets: the principles	237
8.3	Effects of trade integration	242
8.4	Migration	248
8.5	Summary	259

Introduction

For most people, a good job is an essential element of a good life. This is why employment is a critical political and economic issue throughout Europe. Rightly or wrongly, European citizens expect Europe to improve their lot. The failure to deliver full employment throughout Europe, therefore, is a major failure. Even though labour market policies remain a national prerogative, this failure challenges the whole integration process. The rejection of the Constitution is a symptom of a widespread discontent that does not spare Europe and its institutions. The job difficulties faced by millions of people throughout the continent are due to poor national policies and institutions, but can European integration make the situation better, or worse? This chapter explores the linkages between jobs and European integration. It covers two main topics: unemployment, and how it is related to trade integration, and migration, one of Europe's four freedoms.

The chapter starts by describing the situation of the European labour markets. It shows that in many countries unemployment is high and employment is low. We next present a simple analytical framework that explains the unemployment phenomenon. This framework shows that socially desirable features of the labour market have serious economic costs. Put differently, social protection results in labour market rigidities. With these basics in place, we next examine the impact of European integration on Europe's labour markets. We show that economic and labour market integration encourages labour market flexibility. The last section looks at migration. Migration is another form of integration. From an economic point of view, it allows for a more efficient allocation of resources. But it also helps build up a better understanding of people. In contrast to widespread fears of huge migratory movements, the evidence is that Europeans move little.

8.1 European labour markets: a brief characterization

In contrast to goods markets, each national labour market in Europe is on its own. There are two main reasons for that. First, there is not much 'trade' in labour, because migration within the EU is very limited. Second, each country has its own social customs, a historical heritage that leads to very different legislations and practices. As a result, we cannot talk of a 'European labour market' but of as many markets as there are countries. Still, on average, the EU is generally not doing well. Figure 8.1 shows two measures of labour market performance (see Box 8.1 for an explanation of these and other definitions). The employment-to-population ratio is the percentage of the working-age population (conventionally set at 15 to 64 years) that has a job. The average employment-to-population ratio in the EU27 countries is growing, but remains significantly below the US rate. In 2008, the EU27 employment-to-population ratio stood at 69 per cent. This means that 31 per cent of the working-age population does not have a proper job. Some of these people may be disabled. The others are not working for two main reasons: some cannot find a job; others are not interested in looking for work, in some cases because they are taking care of the household. The right-hand chart shows the unemployment rate, the percentage of people who want to work but do not find a job. It is higher in Europe than in the USA. It is also the case that more Europeans are apparently not keen to work. Labour is a country's most precious input, because it is its people and their talents and because each country spends considerable resources to educate its population. A non-employment rate of 31 per cent thus

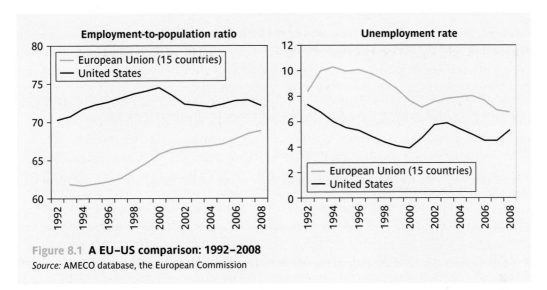

Figure 8.1 A EU–US comparison: 1992–2008
Source: AMECO database, the European Commission

represents a massive waste of talent and a huge loss in income. Just as bad is that those who do not have a job feel estranged from society.

Box 8.1 Labour market concepts

Categories

A country's total population can be broken down into several categories (Table 8.1). The first distinction is between the total population and the working-age population, conventionally defined as all valid people from 15 to 64 years old. Thus the working-age population excludes the young, the retired and the invalid.

The working-age population (N) can be decomposed into three groups: 1) those who are employed (E), 2) those who are unemployed (U) and 3) those who are out of the labour force (O):

$$N = E + U + O$$

The labour force includes the employed and the unemployed:

$$L = E + U$$

and the working-age population is the sum of the labour force and the others:

$$N = L + O$$

Table 8.1 Decomposition of the population of the EU27 countries (millions) – 2008

Employed (1)	Unemployed (2)	Labour force (3) = (1) + (2)	Out of the labour force (4)	Employment-age population (5) = (3) + (4)	Population (6)
226	16	242	93	334	497

Source: AMECO database, the European Commission

▶ People out of the labour force are those who do not want to work and those who are too discouraged even to seek a job and thus qualify as unemployed.

Ratios

The unemployment rate (u) is the ratio of the number (U) of people who declare themselves unemployed (they have no job and are actively looking for one) to the labour force (L):

$$u = \frac{U}{L}$$

The employment rate (e) is the remaining proportion of the labour force, composed of those who hold jobs:

$$e = \frac{E}{L} = 1 - u$$

The participation rate (p) is the ratio of the labour force to the working-age population:

$$p = \frac{L}{N} = 1 - \frac{O}{N}$$

The employment-to-population ratio, which is shown in Figs 8.1 and 8.2, is the proportion of people of working age who hold a job:

$$eR = \frac{E}{N} = \frac{E}{L}\frac{L}{N} = e.p$$

How are people counted?

This is not an innocuous question. Each country carries out census polls and other formal population-counting procedures. The employed, E, are identified from firms reporting taxes and various welfare contributions, and from surveys. The unemployed, U, are identified either through polls or because they are officially registered as such (the difference matters as each country has its own procedure; the International Labour Office produces harmonized data based on surveys). This leaves those out of the labour force, O, as a residual ($O = N - E - U$). Precision is not the name of the game as the black market can include 10 or 20 per cent of the working-age population.

An important distinction is between voluntary and involuntary unemployment. In principle, people who do not want to work are classified as out of the labour force (O). In practice, however, things are less clear cut: some people counted in U are really voluntarily unemployed or actually employed, whereas others counted in O are involuntarily unemployed. Three main reasons explain this discrepancy. First, some unemployed people are really working in the black market (they are counted in U whereas they should be in E). Second, being unemployed opens the door to a range of welfare payments, mainly unemployment insurance benefits. It is believed that these benefits enable workers to be choosier and to reject some job offers or to search less than would otherwise be the case; yet, they must identify themselves as involuntarily unemployed either by registering or when polled. Finally, some people who have searched for a job for a long time become discouraged and simply drop out of the labour force (i.e. they are counted in O whereas they really are in U).

Note: These concepts are further defined and explained in International Labour Organization (ILO) publications. See www.ilo.org.

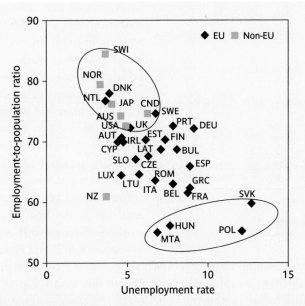

Figure 8.2 **Employment-to-population ratios and unemployment rates in 2005–08: EU27 and comparable non-EU countries**
Note: The non EU27 countries are Australia, Canada, Japan, New Zealand, Norway, Switzerland and the US.
Source: AMECO database, the European Commission

While, on average, European labour markets underperform, the situation varies considerably from one country to another. This is illustrated in Fig. 8.2, which displays the average employment-to-population ratios and the unemployment rates over 2005–08 for each EU country as well as for similar non-EU countries. The countries with the best-performing labour markets are closer to the top-left corner, while poorly performing countries appear in the bottom-right corner. With one exception (New Zealand), the non-EU countries have better-performing labour markets than the EU countries. Only two EU countries (Denmark and the Netherlands) clearly join the top league and two others (Sweden and the UK) come close. The four worst performers are among the new EU members (from left to right: Malta, Hungary, Poland and Slovakia).

8.2 Labour markets: the principles

We start with the essential tools that will guide us throughout this chapter. We look at the demand for labour by firms, at the supply of hours of work by individuals, and ask why unemployment is a general feature. This question leads us to realize that the labour market is a very special market, similar to none other.

8.2.1 Demand

Jobs exist because firms employ people. When deciding whether to hire an additional worker, a firm looks at the cost and the benefit. The cost is the wage, to which must be added the various

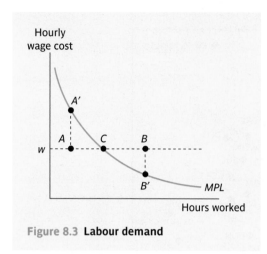

Figure 8.3 **Labour demand**

contributions that most governments impose (contributions to health, unemployment and retirement programmes). As we will think in terms of hours of work, let us call this total the hourly wage cost. The benefit is the additional output that the worker will deliver, which is called the marginal productivity of labour – because we look at the margin, the output from one more hour of work. A key feature of labour productivity is that it declines as more hours are being performed. One reason is that, at any point of time, the equipment available in the firm is given, so that more workers will have to share it. Another reason is that longer hours mean that workers get tired and equipment is used up faster and breaks down more often. The principle of declining labour marginal productivity is captured in Fig. 8.3 by the downward-sloping curve labelled *MPL*.

Now imagine a firm facing an hourly labour cost *w*. If it chooses to buy the number of hours corresponding to point *A* in Fig. 8.3, its cost is lower than its benefit, which corresponds to point *A′*. Hiring one more hour is therefore highly profitable, and there is no reason for the firm not to do so and move rightward from point *A*. How far? Imagine that the firm goes all the way to point *B*, where the hourly labour cost is now higher than the marginal productivity of labour, as point *B′* indicates. Hiring more hours would entail losses. Reducing one hour would mean saving on the wage bill by *w* and giving up output by *MPL*, hence a saving for the firm. This means that the firm does well by moving leftward from point *B*. Clearly, the best position is at point *C, on* the *MPL* curve. If *w* rises, the point corresponding to point *C* will move up the *MPL* curve. This shows that the firm will always hire the number of hours that corresponds to the marginal productivity of labour. Put differently, the *MPL* curve represents the firm's demand for labour.[1]

8.2.2 Supply

Labour is supplied by people. As we all know too well, work is tiring and less pleasurable than leisure. This is why we ask for remuneration. How much we ask will depend on our skills and personal characteristics, including our inclination to stay at home. We consider the 'average' worker, so we ignore these personal characteristics. Instead, we ask what has to happen to the wage to convince the average worker to work one more hour. If the worker is unemployed, ignoring for the time being any welfare income such as unemployment benefits, almost any salary is better than nothing. If the worker already works quite a lot, one more hour is not that attractive and it will take a fairly good salary to convince her to stay longer on the job. This

---

[1] Note that the marginal productivity is measured in units of output. To be comparable, we also need to measure wage costs in the same units, e.g. one hour of work gets you three beers or one-thousandth of a car, more generally a portion of GDP. In the terminoloy of Chapter 9, we consider here the *real* wage, which is represented as the ratio of the nominal wage *W* to the price level *P*, *w* = *W/P*.

reasoning suggests that the supply of labour can be represented by an upward-sloping curve, as shown in Fig. 8.4. The curve is steeper the choosier the worker is.

8.2.3 Equilibrium and more realism

Equipped with the demand and supply apparatus, we are tempted to conclude that the outcome occurs at point A in Fig. 8.4 where demand and supply meet.[2] Note that, in this situation, both firms and workers are perfectly satisfied with the situation. In particular, the total amount of work L_0 corresponds precisely

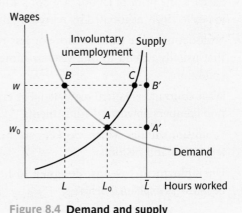

Figure 8.4 **Demand and supply**

to what workers are willing to supply at the going wage w_0. That does not mean that every worker has a job or that every employed person works full time. Such a case of full employment corresponds to $\bar{L}$. The distance AA' represents unused labour or unemployment. This is a special form of unemployment, however, for these hours are voluntarily not worked. Given the wage rate, some people do not wish to work at all or to work long hours – this is the meaning of the supply curve.

If, as Fig. 8.4 presumes, the labour markets operated like other markets, there would be no involuntary unemployment. This is why equilibrium at point A is unrealistic. Since in every country a number of people are involuntarily unemployed, we have to admit that this is not a good description of real-life labour markets. Indeed, labour markets are very special, and for a good reason. The goods that are bought and sold on this market are people's time, talent and effort. Quite obviously, these are not standard goods.

Looking at Fig. 8.4, we see that involuntary unemployment can only occur if workers are not on their supply curve. More precisely, they must be kept involuntarily somewhere to the left of the supply curve. On the other hand, firms are usually on, or close to, their demand curve. True, firms can have more workers than they want because they are forbidden to dismiss workers or, on the contrary, they may be unable to find all the workers that they need. But these are transient and limited departures, and we can safely ignore them. This all means that, in order to explain involuntary unemployment, we have to imagine that the economy lies on the labour demand curve somewhere up above point A, for example at point B. In this case, employment is L, and the distance BC measures involuntary unemployment while CB' captures voluntary unemployment.

How can point B be a lasting equilibrium? The salient feature of point B is that the wage w is above its no-involuntary-unemployment level w_0. The challenge, therefore, is to understand why such an outcome is possible. If the labour market were a market like all others, the wage rate would decline until it reached w_0. This is not what happens. Somehow, wages do not move up and down, and they very rarely move down. A number of characteristics explain this feature:

---

[2] Here we ignore the various charges that make wage costs different from what workers take home. Section 8.3.3 shows how to deal with this issue.

★ Salaries, the price of labour, are not set like the price of oil or corn, through bidding. They are collectively negotiated by representatives of employers and employees.

★ Negotiations take place at more or less regular intervals and agreements hold for periods that usually extend to one year or more. Thus labour markets react slowly to changing conditions.

★ Wage contracts are often regulated. For example, in many countries minimum wages legislation hampers downward adjustments.

★ Conditions under which workers are hired and dismissed are also the object of specific legislation and customs.

★ Unemployment benefits, designed to limit the hardship of becoming unemployed, can backfire, as explained below.

8.2.4 The economics of collective negotiations

The most crucial feature, perhaps, is the collective nature of labour negotiations. We now amend the demand–supply diagram to illustrate their economic effects. Workers resort to a collective representation – let's call it a trade union for the sake of simplicity – because it allows them to achieve better wages. If the arrangement works – if it did not, it would not have survived – the trade union's action delivers a higher wage than individual workers would achieve on their own. In Fig. 8.5 we distinguish between the individual supply curve S^{ind}, which describes how individuals trade off income from work against leisure time, and a collective supply curve S^{coll}, which lies above the previous one.

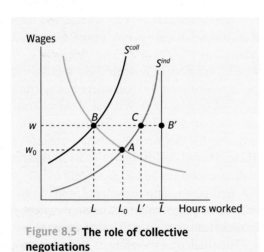

Figure 8.5 **The role of collective negotiations**

Point A shows the outcome of the free interplay of individual demand and supply in the labour market in the absence of any rigidity: employment is L_0, the real wage is w_0 and there is no involuntary unemployment. With collective negotiations, the outcome of the negotiation is now represented by point B. As collective negotiations raise the real wage to w, firms respond by aiming at production processes that are less labour intensive and employment declines to L. Note that, at the new, higher wage level w, the amount of labour that workers wish to supply increases to L', corresponding to point C. The result is involuntary unemployment represented by the distance BC. This unemployment is collectively voluntary, however.

Why is this feature of labour markets so widespread? The workers who negotiate wages are, by definition, those who hold a job. They are the insiders. Reducing their own wages would allow some of those currently unemployed, the outsiders, to find jobs. But outsiders have no voice in the negotiations and the insiders have no interest in accepting wage cuts. This is why point *B* is stable in the sense that there is no mechanism that would change the situation. From a social and political viewpoint, this is understandable. Politically, the overwhelming majority of workers are employed since the highest unemployment rates rarely exceed 10–15 per cent, at least in the developed countries. Democratically, therefore, they support an institution that delivers higher wages, even at the cost of unemployment. Socially, the insiders ask for assistance for the unemployed. Unemployment benefits are usually financed, partly at least, through taxes paid for by the employed, who then feel that the outcome is beneficial to them and fair to the unemployed. Yet, from a strict economic point of view, these arrangements can be analysed as rigidities that prevent the labour markets from being flexible enough to avoid involuntary employment, sometimes on a very large scale, as Table 8.1 shows.

Collective negotiations provide a first explanation of the involuntary unemployment phenomenon, but many other common features conspire to make things worse. This is the case of high and, especially, long-lasting, unemployment benefits. These benefits have an obvious justification. Losing a job is already a traumatic experience; at least those who face this hardship, and their families, should live decently until they find a new job. But experience shows that a by-product of these benefits is that unemployed people feel less pressure to take up new jobs, and therefore remain unemployed for longer periods of time, which further lessens the pressure on insiders to allow for more wage flexibility. Figure 8.6 shows that, in many EU countries,

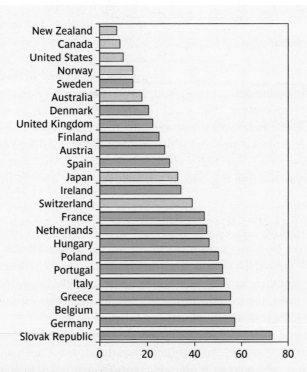

Figure 8.6 Long-term unemployment, 2006
Note: The figure reports the percentage of unemployed workers who have been unemployed for one year or more.
Source: Annual Labor Force Statistics, OECD 2008

a large number of people remain unemployed for more than one year. This is an important example of the fact that many European countries have long attached more weight to social protection than to economic efficiency. They tend to run socially generous but economically inefficient unemployment programmes. Some countries have found a way of combining both concerns. This is the case in the Scandinavian countries, which provide generous unemployment benefits coupled with the obligation to take up job offers.

8.2.5 The cyclical impact of wage rigidity

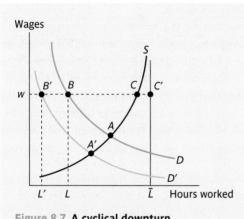

Figure 8.7 **A cyclical downturn**

An important implication of wage rigidity can be seen by considering the case of a cyclical downturn when the wage is fixed at w. We start in Fig. 8.7 from a situation where employment takes place at point B, with involuntary unemployment measured by BC. Now imagine that the economy slows down, for reasons explained in Chapter 9. Firms cannot sell all their products. Given that their equipments are in place anyway – their stock of capital cannot be reduced – the marginal product of labour declines and the demand for labour shifts down from D to D'. If the wages were perfectly flexible, we would have started at point A and moved to point A'. Employment and wages would have declined, voluntary unemployment would have risen but there would still be no involuntary unemployment. With wages rigidly maintained at w, we move to B', employment declines from L to L' and involuntary unemployment rises to $B'C$. It is easy to imagine the opposite case of an economic expansion, which would result in higher employment and lower involuntary unemployment. We see that wage rigidity explains the fact that cyclical fluctuations are accompanied by variations in involuntary unemployment.

8.3 Effects of trade integration

The previous chapters have focused on the effects of the Single Market on the goods and services markets and on overall economic growth. This section looks at the effects on the labour markets. In order to compete in the goods and services markets, producers must fight on all fronts; first and foremost, their production costs. Production costs include three main components: labour costs, the price of equipment and the price of materials.

Both equipment and material costs are largely determined internationally (since domestically produced goods must compete with imports) and therefore are not a source of comparative advantage. Labour costs, which typically amount to over 50 per cent of total production costs, on the other hand, are a key source of competitiveness. Competition in the goods market, in turn, has deep implications for the labour markets. Through goods markets, national labour markets indirectly compete against each other. This section examines some implications of this observation.

wages). The firms we consider here are competitive and so cannot bear any part of T (they earn zero profits both before and after T is imposed).

Why does the take-home wage fall when social policies are imposed? Firms hire workers up to the point where marginal labour productivity is equal to the wage cost, as explained in Section 8.2.1. This cost includes wage and non-wage costs, such as the cost of social policies. Firms cannot pay higher labour costs if they want to avoid losing money. Given this iron law of the labour market – firms hire workers up to the point where all-included employment costs equal the workers' value to the firm – everything that raises non-wage labour costs must force down the take-home pay of workers. In essence, the social policies are a way of 'forcing' workers to take part of their remuneration in the form of non-wage 'payment', e.g. four weeks of paid holiday or generous sick leave, instead of in the direct form of take-home pay.

Next, consider the impact of freeing trade in goods between France and other nations. As far as the labour market is concerned, freer trade has two main impacts:

1 As discussed at length in Chapters 4, 5, 6 and 7, trade tends to boost the productivity of an economy. It does this by allowing a nation's capital and labour to be allocated more efficiently. For example, Chapter 6 showed how freer trade produced fewer, larger, more efficient firms that faced more effective competition from each other.

2 Trade also tends to flatten the demand curve since it heightens the competition between national firms and foreign firms. For example, if real wage costs rise by €100 per week, firms will have to raise prices. The negative impact of higher prices on output, and therefore employment, is greater in the presence of foreign competition. Or, to put it more directly, greater integration of goods markets means that workers in different nations compete more directly with each other.

We begin with the second concern since this is closest to the everyday concerns of many workers in Europe. The middle panel in Fig. 8.9 shows the impact of the flatter demand curve on French labour. The way the diagram is drawn, openness per se would have no impact if there were no social policy. Without the tax T, wage and employment levels would be as in the closed economy case (i.e. w and L). The non-wage costs, i.e. T, however, change things. Since labour demand is now more responsive to total labour costs, the take-home wage of French workers will fall more, to w'' rather than w' when T is imposed. The reason is simple. Greater openness gives consumers a wider range of options; when T is imposed more of it gets paid by workers than by consumers. In other words, the greater price sensitivity forces workers to bear more of the burden of the social-policy 'tax'.

The result that greater openness reduces wages flies in the face of Europe's experience. The incomes of European workers have been growing steadily as European markets have become more tightly integrated. Moreover, as discussed in Chapter 7, some of the fastest income growth occurred in the 1960s when European trade integration was proceeding at its fastest pace. How can we explain this? The efficiency-enhancing effects of trade integration are the answer.

The third panel in Fig. 8.9 shows the labour market implications of trade-induced efficiency gains. As productivity rises, the value of workers to firms rises and this shows up as a shift up the demand curve to D'. Now we see that, even if trade integration makes the demand curve flatter, the shift up in the labour demand curve more than offsets flattening. In the figure, the take-home wage has rise to w''' and employment has increased to L'''.

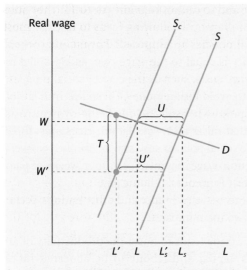

Figure 8.10 Social policy distortions with involuntary unemployment

So far we have put the issue of unemployment to the side by assuming that the labour market clears. To consider unemployment, we allow the 'collective' labour supply curve (S^{coll}) and the individual labour supply curve (S^{ind}) to differ, as in Section 8.2.4. This is done in Fig. 8.10, which corresponds to the second panel of Fig. 8.9. The initial position is characterized by unemployment U, with employment L and supply L_s. The social policy distortion reduces employment to L' and supply to L'_s. The effect on unemployment is not clear, however, and this is also the case of the trade-opening effect, as we already saw in Section 8.3.1. Here again, trade integration has no direct impact on unemployment, only on employment.

What has all this got to do with social dumping? What we have shown is that the total cost of employing workers – wage and non-wage costs – is tied to the productivity of workers. If governments raise social policy standards, the economy will adjust by lowering employment and reducing the wages (of course, wages rarely fall; what would happen is that wages would rise more slowly than productivity for a number of years, as happened in France when the 35-hour week was introduced). When an economy is more open, the wage and employment adjustments tend to be greater, other things equal. Or, to put it more colloquially, the anti-employment effects of social policies are magnified by greater openness.

This does not necessarily put pressure on social policies. The key point is that the same mechanism is at work in France's trade partners. If the other nations have lower social policy standards, their workers will have higher take-home pay than otherwise, since the foreign firms hire workers up to the point where their total labour cost matches their workers' productivity. Social harmonization would result in lower wages in these countries but would have little impact on the competitive pressures facing French employers. Turning this around, the same logic tells us that lowering French social policy standards would not boost French competitiveness in anything but the short run.

The upshot of all this should be clear. The logic of competition ties the sum of wage and non-wage costs to workers' productivity. The founders of the EU therefore believed that the division between wage and non-wage costs could be left to the choice of each Member State exactly because this division has only a moderate impact on external competitiveness.

8.4 Migration

Along with the other freedoms of movement (goods, services, capital), the free movement of workers is the cornerstone of EU integration and has been so since its inception in the 1950s. The goal is both economic and political. Allowing workers to move freely within the Community should enhance economic efficiency by allowing workers to find the jobs that best suit their skills and experience, while simultaneously allowing firms to hire the most appropriate workers. On a political level, the architects of the EU hoped that mobility would foster mutual understanding among the peoples of Europe. As many readers will know from first-hand experience, the fact that many young Europeans spend some time living, studying or working in other EU nations has had a big impact on the way Europeans view each other. This section considers European migration. We start with some facts.

8.4.1 Some facts

We start with global migration patterns. Figure 8.11 presents the net migration record – the excess of immigrants over emigrants, so that negative numbers indicate an outflow of workers while positive numbers mean an inflow – of continents since the 1950s, with forecasts for the current period, 2005–10. The figure confirms that people move from 'the South' to 'the North' and increasingly so. It also shows that Europe has switched from net emigration to net immigration. This is explained by Europe's spectacular growth during the late 1950s and the 1960s, which brought about conditions of full employment and led governments and firms to seek out foreign labour. The turnaround of Europe's economic fortunes, starting with the 1973 recession, temporarily stopped the evolution, but the trend has been resumed. This pattern reflects the

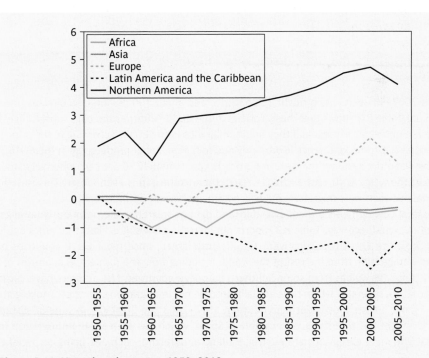

Figure 8.11 Net migration rates, 1950–2010
Note: The net migration rate is the ratio of number of net migrants (immigrants less emigrants) to the local population.
Source: World Population Prospects, UN

two basic reasons why people leave their countries: (1) they flee poverty and (2) they flee political instability and related violence. In general, political instability breeds poverty.

Global numbers should not conceal important differences within Europe. For decades, southern Europe (Italy, Spain, Portugal and Greece) and south-eastern Europe (mainly Turkey) were prime sending nations, while the northern European nations (the EEC6 less Italy plus the Nordic and Alpine countries) were big receiving nations. Since the early 1980s, with growth picking up, the southern European nations have become net importers as well. Some of this migration involves the return of Spanish, Italian and Portuguese workers who had previously emigrated, but it also reflects an increasing inflow of non-European workers from places such as Africa or Latin America. Within Europe, Turkey has been joined in its role as a provider of migrants by central and eastern European nations that dropped, by the end of the 1980s, general restrictions on emigration imposed by their previous regimes.

Migration within the EU is, in principle, free. Yet, when the EU was expanded in 2004, special provisions were temporarily imposed on the ten new members to limit migration from these countries to the incumbent 15 members. Similar restrictions were imposed on Bulgaria and Romania upon accession in 2007. We return to this issue in Section 8.4.4. Box 8.2 explains why fears of massive immigration from central and eastern Europe have been unjustified. In fact, seven out of ten foreign workers in EU Member States are from non-EU countries. The policies that govern labour flows from non-member nations are entirely national – the EU does not try to impose what might be called a common external migration policy. To put it differently, being part of the EU's common labour market does not seem to matter very much for migration.

Box 8.2 The flood that was not to be

The 2004 and 2007 enlargements brought 12 countries and about 100 million new citizens into the European Union. Table 8.2 shows that most workers in the EU12 countries are paid substantially less in their home nations than they would if they held similar jobs in the EU15. According to the principles laid out in Section 8.2.1, this difference is primarily due to higher labour productivity in the EU15. The income gap between the east and the west in Europe is approximately 50 per cent when adjusted for higher prices in the west; at current exchange rates, the income gap is even larger. This raised the prospect of massive east–west migration, but this possibility has not become reality.

Direct bilateral flow numbers are not available (and data on migration are notoriously unreliable), so we proceed in an indirect way. Table 8.3 reports net migration flows. It is likely that gross outflows from the EU12 to the EU15 countries were significantly larger, since most EU12 countries have also witnessed immigration from the rest of the world, including from the former CIS countries of the former Soviet Union, as well as from some Southern European countries. Net outflows have declined in all EU12 countries, several of which have actually become net immigration countries. Looking at the EU15 countries, net inflows mostly declined between 1997–2003 and 2004–07, in spite of sustained flows from the rest of the world. A good example is Spain, which has seen rising immigration from Latin America. The main exceptions are Austria, Finland and Ireland, each one being a special case of its own.

Why didn't the flood happen? One possible reason is that most EU15 nations negotiated long transition periods during which EU12 cannot move freely into their labour markets. But countries

Table 8.3 Net immigration before and after enlargements (thousands of people)

	Belgium	Denmark	Germany	Ireland	Greece	Spain	France	Italy
1997–2003	164	71	1146	193	302	2596	853	1197
2004–2007	202	42	237	245	162	2558	358	1753

	Luxembourg	Netherlands	Austria	Portugal	Finland	Sweden	UK	Total EU15
1997–2003	27	266	164	344	32	143	924	**6522**
2004–2007	12	−60	179	131	40	157	842	**5557**

	Bulgaria	Czech Rep.	Estonia	Cyprus	Latvia	Lithuania	Hungary	
1997–2003	−213	32	−14	41	−33	−96	97	
2004–2007	−1	174	1	52	−5	−28	71	

	Malta	Poland	Romania	Slovenia	Slovakia			Total EU12
1997–2003	17	−497	−592	18	−14			**−186**
2004–2007	7	−79	−23	29	17			**262**

Note: A positive number indicates net immigration, a negative number signals net emigration.
Source: European Communities, 1995–2009

that opened their borders, such as Ireland, Sweden and the UK, report no or little increase in net inflows. Most likely, the low migration numbers reflect the fact that the 'New Europeans' share much of the 'Old Europeans'' resistance to moving (see Chapter 11). With the prospect that the EU12 countries are likely to catch up with the EU15 countries, the incentives to leave home, family and friends, to wade into a new culture with another language, have been too limited to trigger large-scale migration.

Being part of a common labour market does not seem to be the key to determining the origin of migrants. Migrants from EU nations make up a much higher percentage of foreign workers in Norway and Switzerland than they do in France and Germany. This shows that the discriminatory liberalization implied by the free mobility of workers within the EU (i.e. workers from one EU nation are free to work in any other EU nation, but they need special permission to work in non-EU nations such as Norway) is not a dominant factor in determining migration patterns. This contrasts sharply with discriminatory liberalization of goods. As Chapter 7 shows, the composition of imports is strongly influenced by implementation of the customs union.

There is nothing really new here. We already mentioned that, in the 1950s and 1960s, nations across north-western Europe were experiencing such rapid growth that industry found itself short of workers. Individual nations responded by facilitating inward migration from many different nations. Not surprisingly, nations that wanted to 'import' workers found it easiest to induce migration from nations with low wages and relatively high unemployment. The fact that Spain, Portugal and Greece were not at the time members of the EU did little to hinder the flow of their workers into EU members such as Germany. Indeed, German immigration policy in the 1960s was at least as welcoming to Turks and Spaniards as it was to southern Italians. Moreover, nations such as Sweden and the UK, whose industries also experienced labour shortages, managed to attract migrants – including some migrants from EU nations such as Italy – even without being part of the Common Market. In short, the western European policies that fostered the big migration flows in the 1960s were basically unrelated to the policies of the Common Market.

8.4.2 Economics of labour market integration

Labour migration is probably the most contentious aspect of economic integration in Europe. In most western European nations, popular opinion holds immigrants responsible for high unemployment, abuse of social welfare programmes, street crime and deterioration of neighbourhoods. As a result, a number of explicitly anti-immigration political parties have fared well in elections. How does immigration affect the sending and receiving nations, and who gains and loses from it?

Simplest framework

We start with the simplest analytical framework that allows us to organize our thinking about the economic consequences of labour migration. We start with the case where migration is not allowed between two nations (Home and Foreign) which initially have different wages. Figure 8.12 shows a situation where workers initially earn better wages in Home than in Foreign. The length of the horizontal schedule represents total available labour available in both countries, L in Home and L^* in Foreign. For the time being, we will assume full employment, $L + L^*$ in total for both countries. The marginal productivity of labour in Home is measured on the left vertical axis. The corresponding MPL curve is downward sloping as employment in Home is measured along the horizontal axis from left to right. The foreign marginal productivity of labour is measured on the right vertical axis. The corresponding MPL^* curve seems upward sloping, but it is not, since employment in Foreign is measured in the opposite of the usual direction, from right to left. Initially, the situation in Home is represented by point Q, with wage

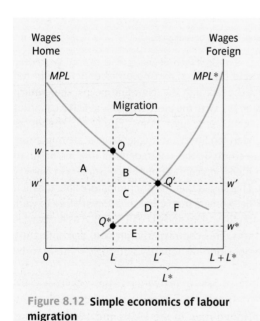

Figure 8.12 **Simple economics of labour migration**

w and employment L. Point Q^* describes the initial situation in Foreign, with wage w^* and employment L^*.

Now allow migration. Given the wage difference, labour will flow from Foreign to Home. This will push down wages in Home and thus harm the Home workers – while benefiting Home capital owners. The opposite happens in Foreign. As some Foreign labour moves to Home, Foreign wages tend to rise, making the remaining Foreign workers better off – and Foreign capital owners worse off. If there is no impediment – legal, personal reticence or other – migration will go on until wages are equalized. This is represented by point Q′, with wages w′ in both countries.

We find that, in each country, some lose and some gain from migration, but what about each country? Start with Home country. We need to understand the impact of migration on the earnings of workers and capital-owners. To that effect we look at Fig. 8.13, which enlarges the Home country situation around point Q. The area under the *MPL* curve represents total Home output. The reason follows directly from the definition of the marginal product of capital. The first unit of labour employed produces output equal to the height of the *MPL* curve at the point where $L = 1$. The amount produced by the second unit of capital is given by the level of *MPL* at the point where $L = 2$, and so on. Adding up all the heights of the *MPL* curve at each point yields the area under the curve.

The total earnings of Home labour is just the wage rate w times the amount of labour L, which is measured in Fig. 8.13 by the rectangle below and to the left of point Q. Since we are assuming that capital and labour are the only two factors of production in this simple world, capital receives all the output that is not paid to labour. Graphically this means that capital's income corresponds to the triangle between the *MPL* curve and w line.

With this in hand, we turn now to the welfare effects of capital flows. We saw that the 'native' Home workers lose. As they move from Q to Q′, their wages decline by $w - w'$. Their loss is represented by the rectangle marked 'A' in Fig. 8.12. Home capital-owners

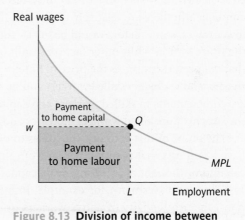

Figure 8.13 Division of income between capital and labour

increase their earnings by area A plus the triangle B. Thus the total economic impact on Home citizens is positive and equal to the triangle B. Another way of seeing that Home gains from migration is to note that the immigrant workers raise total output in Home by the areas B + C + D + E, but some of it, equal to areas C + D + E (i.e. w′ times the labour flow $L^* - L'$), does not benefit 'native' workers since it is paid out to the immigrants.

The Foreign workers who remain in their country see their wages rise from to w* to w′. The size of this gain is shown by rectangle F. With production falling, Foreign capital-owners lose by D + F. Combining all these losses and gains, the factors of production that remain in Foreign lose overall by an amount measured by triangle D. However, if we count the welfare of the emigrant workers as part of Foreign's welfare, the conclusion is reversed. Foreign workers abroad used to earn E, now they receive C + D + E, so they gain C + D. Altogether, Foreign gains by an amount equal to the triangle C.

In short, while migration creates winners and losers in both nations, collectively both nations gain. The deep reason for this has to do with efficiency. Without labour mobility, the allocation of productive factors was inefficient. For example, on the margin, Foreign workers were less productive. Migration improves the overall efficiency of the EU economy and the gains from this are split between Home and Foreign. Foreign gets area C; Home gets area B.

This all assumes that there is no unemployment to start with and therefore seems unrealistic; we return to this issue in Section 8.4.3 below.

Broader interpretation: complementarity vs. substitutability

The analysis above classifies all productive factors into two categories: capital and labour. It is important to note, however, that for most EU nations we should interpret 'capital' as including 'human capital', i.e. highly educated workers. The reason has to do with the economic notion of 'complementarity' versus 'substitutability'.

Consider the example of how productive factors combine to produce hotel services. Apart from material inputs such as food and bed linen, hotels require unskilled workers (cleaners, etc.), skilled workers (managers, marketing people, etc.) and capital (the building, furniture, etc.). In a country such as Norway, unskilled labour is very costly so hotels are very expensive; consequently there are relatively few hotels. If Norway allowed hotels to hire foreign workers at lower wages, some factors would be hurt – the unskilled workers who earned high wages before the immigration – but other factors would be helped. Skilled workers and capital would find that their rewards rise. As the price of hotel rooms fell, the hotel industry would expand, raising the demand for highly skilled workers and capital. In this situation, we say that unskilled workers are complements to skilled workers and capital: demand for skilled workers and capital rises as the supply of unskilled workers increases and their price falls.

The point of this is to put the losses to domestic labour in perspective. Immigrants often have a skill mix that is very different from that of domestic workers. Skilled domestic workers can thus be thought of as belonging to 'capital' in Fig. 8.12 and thus winning from immigration. In France and Germany, for example, immigrants often work at jobs, e.g. in factories, that boost the productivity of native workers in related fields such as management, finance, sales and marketing. Indeed, immigrants often fill jobs that no native would take, such as kitchen workers, street sweepers, etc.; this is an extreme form of complementarity in which there are no economic losers in the receiving nation.

We can look at the opposite case, when immigrants have higher skill levels than the average native worker. In these cases, the analysis of immigration is somewhat different. Instead of shifting L from Foreign to Home, migration shifts 'capital'. Graphically this raises the MPL curve in Fig. 8.12 for Home and lowers it for Foreign. The reason is that the presence of more skilled workers tends to raise the productivity of unskilled workers. If you want a mental picture of this process, think of American entrepreneurs coming into Ireland and starting businesses that hire Irish workers away from the farm sector. Again, we see that immigration can be a win–win situation for the receiving nation.

Another insight from the notion of complementarity is that of micro-level matching. Some immigrants may have very specific skills that are lacking in the receiving nation. Since these workers do not compete with native workers, or compete with very few native workers, such immigration is usually less contentious since it creates few losers. This level of matching among countries can proceed to an even lower level. For example, even within a single company, the experiences of workers vary, and free mobility of labour may make it easier to move workers into jobs that best fit their experience. Again, it is entirely possible that everyone gains from such matching. More generally, immigrants who have skills that are complementary to the skill mix in the receiving nation are typically less likely to create losers in the receiving nation.

Table 8.4 Education level and skills of recent immigrant workers in the EU15 countries in 2005 (percentage of total)

	Overall EU employed	Immigrant workers from:		
		EU15	EU10	Outside EU
Education				
Low	27	15	15	36
Medium	47	41	63	40
High	26	44	22	23
Occupation				
High-skilled white collar	40	55	16	20
Low-skilled white collar	26	24	28	25
Skilled manuals	25	12	27	21
Elementary tasks	10	9	30	35

Source: Survey of the European Union, OECD, Sept 2007

Empirical evidence

So much for the theory. What does the evidence tell us? Given the importance of immigration in the various national debates in Europe, economists have done a great deal of work estimating the impact of migration on the wages of domestic workers. Generally, these studies find that a 1 per cent rise in the supply of workers via migration changes the wages of native workers by between 1 per cent and −1 per cent, with most studies putting the figure in the even narrower range of ±0.3 per cent. There are two key points to take away from these findings. First, it is not obvious that immigration always lowers wages. Since nations tend to let in workers who have skills that are complementary to those of domestic workers, the impact is often positive. Second, whether it is slightly positive or slightly negative, the impact is quite small. Again, this outcome is due in part to the fact that countries tend to restrict the types of labour inflow that would have large negative effects on wages.

Table 8.4 provides some information regarding the complementarity/substitutability issue. It shows the education levels of workers employed in the EU15 countries, according to where they come from, in percentage of all employed workers. Immigrants from the other EU15 countries are generally better educated and occupy higher-skill jobs than the natives. This suggests micro-level matching and explains why this type of immigration is not controversial. Immigrants from outside the EU are complementary in the opposite direction: they are often less educated and fill in elementary tasks/jobs. Immigrants from the EU10 – the ten countries that acceded in 2004 – are in-between as far as education is concerned and they tend to accept less skilled jobs.

8.4.3 Unemployment

Framework

One common belief is that immigrants cause unemployment. The framework presented in the previous section cannot help us assess this view since it explicitly assumes that all workers get

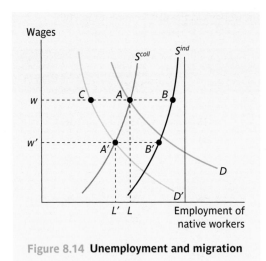

Figure 8.14 Unemployment and migration

jobs. Instead, we use the framework presented in Section 8.2.4 and apply it to the employment of native workers. In Fig. 8.14, in the absence of immigration, the labour market is at point *A* and involuntary unemployment is *AB*.

Now suppose that some immigrants enter the country. We have to imagine how the immigrants will operate in the labour market. One extreme assumption is that the immigrants are willing and able to perform the same jobs as natives but at a wage that is below the union-set wage *w*. Being cheaper, they displace the native workers. The demand curve for native workers shifts to the left from *D* to *D′*. The idea here is that firms first hire cheap immigrants and then turn to the native market to fulfil any remaining demands. The distance *AC* measures the share of employment taken over by immigrant workers. The result is that the market moves to point *A′*. The union-set wage and native employment fall to *w′* and *L′*, respectively. Two points are worth stressing. First, even in this extreme case – where firms are able to hire immigrants at below market wages – the drop in native employment (*L − L′*) is less than the number of immigrants (*AC*). As a consequence, total employment, counting both natives and immigrants, rises. This dampening is due to the drop in native wages, which allows firms to produce more output and therefore expand jobs.

Second, there may be no change in unemployment. Because unemployment is a result of the labour market's structure, immigration will affect unemployment only to the extent that it affects the structure of the labour market. In the particular example shown in the diagram, where the two labour supply curves S^{ind} and S^{coll} are drawn as parallel, there is no change in the number of unemployed natives. In that case, the drop in wages from *w* to *w′* decreases the number of native workers who want to work at the going wage by as much as the drop in native employment. If we had not drawn the two supply curves as parallel, we would have got a different answer.[5] The main point, however, is that if immigration is to affect unemployment, it must do so by altering labour market structure.

Another possible assumption is the opposite one, that immigrants participate in the labour market in exactly the same way as native workers do. In this case (not shown in the diagram), both curves S^{ind} and S^{coll} shift to the right. The results would be qualitatively identical to those shown in Fig. 8.14. There would be some drop in the wage and some increase in employment. Since the true impact of immigrants on national labour markets is probably somewhere between these two extremes, it seems reasonable to believe that the standard impact of immigration will be some increase in employment, some decrease in wages and an ambiguous effect on unemployment.

[5] How are the curves in reality? Truth is that we don't know. The proof of the pudding is in the eating, namely in the empirical evidence discussed below.

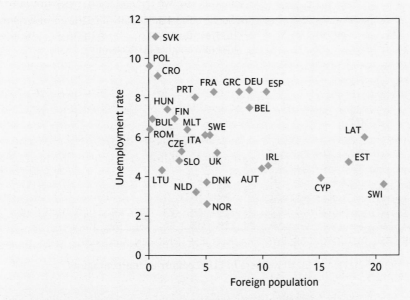

Figure 8.15 Foreign population and unemployment, 2007
Note: Foreign population as a percentage of total population and rate of unemployment.
Sources: Eurostat and AMECO, European Commission

Empirical evidence

The empirical evidence on the effect of immigration on unemployment is mixed. A visual inspection of Fig. 8.15 does not suggest any link. Some studies have found that immigrants increase the chance of unemployment for some groups of workers, but have the opposite effect on other groups of workers. This is clearly linked to the complements and substitutes analysis. Other authors find little or no effect of immigration on the risk of being unemployed. In summary, the empirical evidence we have to date does not support the notion that immigration has large, negative effects on European labour markets. As usual, this lack of convincing evidence is due in part to the fact that countries tend to pick and choose their immigrants, presumably with a view to avoiding large negative effects on employment and/or unemployment.

8.4.4 Barriers to mobility

Two key results emerge: (1) immigration is likely to raise employment and national income; and (2) immigration is unlikely to affect unemployment in either direction. These results provide a strong endorsement for the fundamental principle of freedom of movement of workers within the EU. Figure 8.16 indicates that few people take advantage of this opportunity. One reason is that EU citizens do not regard freedom of establishment as an attractive option. Another is that, in spite of the stated policy, there remain a large number of barriers, some explicit, most implicit.

The first barrier is the explicit temporary arrangement concerning the new EU members, except Cyprus and Malta. Starting in 2004, all countries may apply restrictive measures for up

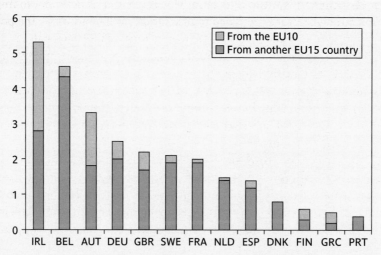

Figure 8.16 Proportion of EU15 and EU10 workers in EU15 countries (percentage of population)

Source: Survey of the European Union, OECD, Sept 2007

to seven years following accession. Except Ireland, the UK and Sweden, all EU15 countries and Hungary chose to implement this clause. In 2006, obviously reassured that migration was moderate, a number of countries allowed unrestricted entry from the 2004 acceding countries.

Other implicit barriers concern social protection. Health insurance does not raise serious difficulties since any EU worker is allowed to enter the local system upon settlement, paying local dues and receiving equal treatment. In order to simplify the transition process, a European Health Card was introduced in 2004.

The situation is more complicated as far as pension rights are concerned. The principle is simple: workers collect pension rights wherever they go; upon retirement, they apply to their country of residence to establish their pension rights on the basis of work performed anywhere in the EU. However, the rights acquired in each country of previous residence are assessed on the basis of that country's system. This 'detail' means that pension rights act as a strong barrier to mobility. The reason is that rules to accumulate rights differ widely from one country to the next. This concerns, in particular, the length of time required to receive a pension and the age at which pensions can be claimed. For example, Finns work until 67 while Italians are often encouraged to retire before age 60. A Finn who moved to Italy when she was 50 may thus be pushed into retirement at age 57, with a minimal Italian pension, and she will not receive the complement from Finland until ten years later. The situation is even worse than that. The agreement concerns general pensions, not those tied to a company or a profession. In several countries, such occupational pensions represent the larger share of retirement income.

Similarly, unemployment benefits discourage mobility. Existing agreements allow an unemployed worker who moves elsewhere within the EU to keep receiving the benefits for up to three months. Imagine the case of a worker who moves from a high to a low unemployment country after having lost his job. If he does not find a job within three months of arrival, he loses his unemployment benefit and is without income. This is a powerful deterrent to migration. The rule might seem strange, but it is designed to discourage 'welfare tourism', the possibility that people move not to seek jobs but to gain access to generous welfare payments.

A last barrier worth mentioning concerns the regulated professions. Obviously, not everyone can set himself up as a medical doctor. In principle, the EU countries recognize each other's qualifications, so doctors, architects, nurses or lawyers can practise anywhere they wish. But the rule does not apply to all regulated professions. For instance, in order to open a hairdressing salon in France, one has to satisfy surprisingly exacting conditions, which rule out all other European hairdressers.

These are examples of the many barriers that limit labour mobility within Europe. Add languages and customs, distance from home, frequent housing shortages, and you start understanding why the freedom of establishment is not delivering. The European Commission is regularly advancing proposals to beat back all regulatory barriers, but many initiatives fail because myriads of local private interests – such as French hairdressers – are opposed to the free entry of competitors.

8.5 Summary

This chapter has dealt with two related topics: the link between trade integration and labour markets and migration, and the view that the EU may be moving to a single integrated labour market. Both issues are politically sensitive but there is surprisingly little substance behind widely held fears that workers systematically get the wrong end of the stick.

Relative to comparable advanced economies, many European countries exhibit low rates of employment and high rates of unemployment. This represents a waste of our most precious resources and a source of anxiety. The situation, though, is very uneven, reflecting the diversity of labour market arrangements inherited from each country's history. Labour market regulations are needed to protect workers but many of them introduce rigidities that prevent the achievement of full employment.

European integration affects the labour markets in two main ways:

★ Trade integration indirectly leads to competition between labour markets. It affects the labour markets in two ways. It creates winners and losers and it shifts production patterns, which require labour market flexibility to avoid job losses. In general, countries with more flexible labour markets have a comparative advantage in goods markets. This has led countries with more rigid markets to complain about social dumping, as they resist economic pressure to reform their labour markets. The principle remains that labour markets and social policies are a national prerogative. Theory and evidence support this principle.

★ The EU treaty guarantees the freedom of movement of workers. Here again, many citizens fear that competition from foreign workers will lower wages and create more unemployment. The fear is commonplace in the EU15 countries where wages are much higher than in the EU12 countries. Theory and evidence suggest that these fears are largely misplaced. In fact, for a number of cultural and institutional reasons, there is too little mobility of workers in Europe, in spite of the general principle of freedom of movement.

Self-assessment questions

1. Explain what happens to a firm's profits as it moves in Fig. 8.3 from point *A* to point *B*.

2. Using the diagram of Fig. 8.4, explain what happens to voluntary and involuntary unemployment as workers individually ask for higher wages for the same amount of work. Answer the same question using Fig. 8.5, assuming that there is no change in the collective supply of labour.

3. Figure 8.17 depicts the evolution of the unemployment rate in France and in the UK, distinguishing between a trend and deviations from the trend. In the UK, the rate tends to deviate more from its trend than in France. Can you explain this pattern?

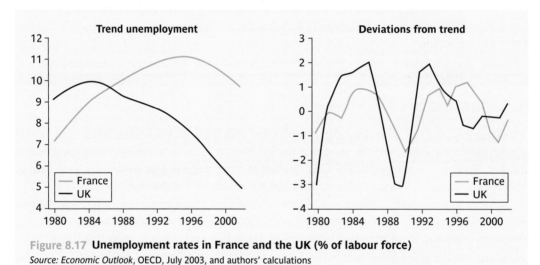

Figure 8.17 **Unemployment rates in France and the UK (% of labour force)**
Source: Economic Outlook, OECD, July 2003, and authors' calculations

4. Figure 8.8 shows the effect of trade integration in the presence of collective bargaining. How would things look like in the absence of collective bargaining but when wages are downward-rigid?

5. Same question as (4) but looking at the effects of migration in Fig. 8.14.

6. Explain why the immigration of low-skilled workers can hurt native low-skilled workers and benefit high-skilled workers.

7. Capital accumulation and technological innovations raise the marginal productivity of capital. Graphically, in Fig. 8.13 the *MPL* curve shifts up. Starting from point *Q*, consider two cases: (a) wages rise but employment remains unchanged at *L*; (b) employment increases but wages rise. Compare the changes to the income shares of capital and labour and interpret your results.

8. Looking at Fig. 8.2, there seems to be a weak inverse relationship between the unemployment rate and the employment-to-population ratio. Why? And why is this relationship not tighter?

Essay questions

1. 'Compared to Americans, Europeans care more about equity than efficiency.' Comment.

2. It is argued – and it is the case in some countries – that the minimum wage should be set at different levels for the young, for the older, for the unskilled or for particular industries. Evaluate this argument.

3. The distinction between voluntary and involuntary unemployment is not as clear-cut as presented in this chapter. Explain why, providing examples.

4. 'Hard line' trade unions push for higher wages while 'cooperating' trade unions push for more jobs. What do these differences imply for the working of the labour market and for output? (Hint: Capture the distinction in terms of the shape of the S^{coll} curve.)

5. 'Social magnets' are countries that offer generous unemployment and other welfare benefits. This is one key reason why unemployment benefits are not served to migrants for more than three months. Explain why, otherwise, this could be a serious problem in Europe in view of the freedom of movement of workers.

6. 'The poorer EU countries should reduce their welfare programmes to better take advantage of accession.' Evaluate this advice.

7. Use the distinction between complementarity and substitutability to evaluate the effects of immigration in your country from neighbouring countries.

Further reading: the aficionado's corner

For general overviews, see:

Bean, C., S. Bentolila, G. Bertola and J. Dolado (1998) *Social Europe: One for All?*, CEPR Monitoring European Integration 8, Centre for Economic Policy Research, London.

Blanchard, O. (2006) 'European unemployment: the evolution of facts and ideas', *Economic Policy*, 45: 5–60.

Boeri, T., M. Burda and F. Kramarz (2008) *Working Hours and Job Sharing in the EU and USA*, Oxford University Press, Oxford.

Freeman, R.B. (2004) 'The European labour markets: are European labour markets as awful as all that?', *CESifo Forum*, 5 (1): 34–9.

Nickell, S. (2002) *Unemployment in Europe: Reasons and Remedies*. Download from www.cesifo.de.

Portugal, P. and J.T. Addison (2004) 'The European labour markets: disincentive effects of unemployment benefits on the paths out of unemployment', *CESifo Forum*, 5 (1): 24–30.

The articles collected in: **Bertola, G., T. Boeri and G. Nicoletti (eds)** (2001) *Welfare and Employment in a United Europe*, MIT Press, Cambridge, MA.

On the trade-off between economic efficiency and social concerns, see:

Atkinson, A. (1999) *The Economic Consequences on Rolling Back the Welfare State*, MIT Press, Cambridge, MA.

On trade unions, see:

Calmfors, L., A. Booth, M. Burda, D. Checchi, R. Naylor and J. Visser (2001) 'What do unions do in Europe? Prospects and challenges for union presence and union influence', in T. Boeri, A. Brugiavini and L. Calmfors (eds) *The Role of Unions in the Twenty-first Century*, Oxford University Press, Oxford.

Checci, D. and C. Lucifora (2002) 'Unions and labour market institutions in Europe', *Economic Policy*, 35: 361–408.

On migration, see:

Boeri, T. and H. Brücker (2005) 'Why are Europeans so tough on migrants?', *Economic Policy*, 44: 629–704.

Diez Guardia, N. and K. Pichelmann (2006) *Labour Migration Patterns in Europe: Recent Trends, Future Challenges*, Economic Papers No. 256, European Commission. Download from http://ec.europa.eu/economy_finance/publications/publication644_en.pdf.

European Commission, *Job Mobility Action Plan*. Download from http://ec.europa.eu/social/main.jsp?catId=540&langId=en.

Hatton, T. (2007) 'Should we have a WTO for international migration?', *Economic Policy*, 50: 339–84.

Nickell, S. (2007) *Immigration: Trends and Macroeconomic Implications*, Nuffield College, Oxford. Download from www.nuffield.ox.ac.uk/users/nickell/papers/Immigration-Trends&MacroeconomicImplicationsDec07.pdf.

OCDE (2007) *Survey of Europe*, September.

To find a job in the EU:

The European Commission's job mobility portal EURES: www.europa.eu.int/eures/home.jsp?lang=en.

Useful websites

The website of the Rodolfo de Benedetti Foundation, dedicated to European labour market issues: www.frdb.org.

PART III

The macroeconomics of monetary integration

Chapter **9**

Essential macroeconomic tools

The fact that an economist offers a theoretical analysis does not and should not automatically command respect. What is needed is some assurance that the analysis is actually relevant.

Paul Krugman (1988)

Chapter contents

9.1	Preliminaries: output and prices	*266*
9.2	The aggregate demand and supply diagram	*268*
9.3	The short run: an *IS–LM* interpretation	*276*
9.4	The open economy and the interest rate parity condition	*280*
9.5	Monetary policy and the exchange rate regime	*283*
9.6	Summary	*285*

Introduction

This chapter presents the key concepts used in macroeconomics when studying an economy as it goes through business cycles. You will learn – or review if need be – how economic activity is measured and how its fluctuations are interpreted and explained. This short review is geared to the issues that matter for monetary integration. In particular, we look at the relationship between monetary policy and the exchange rate. As the next chapter will show, the perceived need to stabilize intra-Europe exchange rates has been a key driving force behind the long process that eventually led to the adoption of the euro.

The chapter starts with some essential definitions. It proceeds to the presentation of the two workhorses of macroeconomics: the *AD–AS* diagram, which explains the joint behaviour of output and prices in both the short and the long run; and the *IS–LM* diagram, which focuses on the short run and describes the roles of the interest and exchange rates. Having covered the main macroeconomic principles, the chapter moves on to draw implications for monetary policy and its relationship with the exchange rate regime.

9.1 Preliminaries: output and prices

We have already encountered the GDP (gross domestic product) in Chapter 7. It is the most commonly used measure of economic activity. We often call it output, as it captures the total production of an economy, all the goods and services that are available for sale. Although sales and production are not exactly equal – for example some production may be stored as inventory – we will ignore that difference. The GDP simply adds up the value, measured in euros, sterling, francs, etc., of all sales in a country over a given period of time, usually one year, sometimes one quarter. An important aspect of GDP is that it also measures all incomes earned during the same period. Incomes are equal to sales because any commercial exchange means that one person spends money and another person receives that money:

GDP = sum of all production = sum of all sales = sum of all incomes

Of course, taxes take a bite on these incomes, as VAT first, then in multiple ways (income tax, corporate tax, etc.). But taxes are the revenue of government and therefore represent a form of collective revenue.

A frequent use of GDP is to measure economic growth. This requires a bit of care. From one year to the next, GDP normally increases, but for two very different reasons:

1 More goods and services are produced: more bread, more machines, more car repairs, more visits to the doctor, and so on.

2 Some goods and services become more expensive, while some may become cheaper. This changes the value of output.

The second source of increase is inflation, the increase in the average price level. Inflation is a very different phenomenon from growth, which captures rising standards of living. These two effects must be carefully disentangled.

To that effect, we distinguish between nominal and real GDP. The previous definition, the result of adding up the value of all sales, is the way nominal GDP is *measured*. Real GDP is *computed* by estimating the average increase in prices, which is inflation. For example, over a year, the nominal GDP can increase by 6 per cent, but if prices on average rose by 2 per cent, the growth rate of real GDP is approximately 4 per cent, the difference between the nominal growth rate and the inflation rate. Because nominal GDP mixes up two different phenomena, growth and inflation, we will normally only look at real GDP on one hand, and inflation on the other.

This is exactly what we do in Chapter 7. There we see that, normally, real GDP tends to grow secularly, because more capital is put in place and because innovations make us more productive. But that does not mean that actual GDP always follows its underlying growth trend. For example, the top chart of Fig. 9.1 displays the real GDP of the Eurozone,[1] both its trend

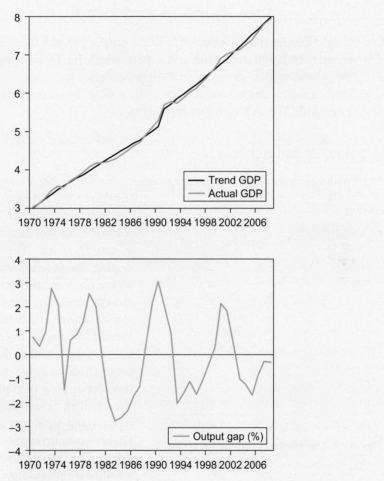

Figure 9.1 Real GDP of the Eurozone: trend, actual and the output gap (1970–2008)
Note: The jump increase in 1991 corresponds to German unification.
Source: Economic Outlook, OECD

---

[1] The area includes the original countries of the monetary union: Austria, Belgium, Finland, France, Germany, Greece, Ireland, Italy, Luxembourg, Netherlands, Portugal and Spain.

– sometimes called potential GDP – and the actual level. Over nearly 30 years, when real GDP almost tripled, the differences between actual and trend GDP looks trivial. The lower chart shows the difference between actual and potential GDP in percent of potential GDP. The output gap, as this difference is called, reveals the business cycles, uneven periods when actual exceeds trend GDP – these are boom years – followed by periods when the output gap is negative – these are slowdown years – with a total amplitude that can reach 5 per cent or more, which is not perceived as at all trivial when it occurs. These fluctuations, called business cycles, are accompanied by sensitive changes in employment, firm profitability and, more generally, individual incomes. Macroeconomics is chiefly devoted to understanding business cycles.

9.2 The aggregate demand and supply diagram

When trying to explain the evolution of both the output gap and the price level, the basic tool brings together the familiar demand and supply schedules. In contrast to microeconomics, where demand and supply refer to a particular good's price and output, in macroeconomics we deal with the average price level and total output, i.e. GDP. To prevent any confusion, we refer to aggregate demand (*AD*) and aggregate supply (*AS*).

9.2.1 The supply side

We start with aggregate supply. In microeconomics, the supply curve is upward sloping because the good's price rises to make up for increasing marginal cost as output is expanded. A similar, but not identical, reasoning applies in the aggregate. The *AS* curve is upward sloping. Producers of goods and services keep an eye on their costs, including wages. When growth weakens – the output gap declines – markets shrink and firms reduce employment. Fearful of rising unemployment, workers accept wage moderation. This means that production costs grow less fast and firms slow down their own prices. In the opposite situation, in boom periods, unemployment recedes and workers push for higher wages. Higher costs invariably translate into higher prices. This explains why in Fig. 9.2 the *AS* schedule is upward sloping.

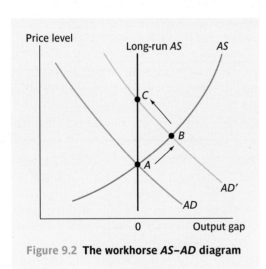

Figure 9.2 **The workhorse *AS–AD* diagram**

9.2.2 The demand side

The reason why the *AD* curve is downward sloping is presented in Section 9.3.2 below. In brief, higher prices erode the purchasing power of large segments of the population and lead the central bank to adopt a contractionary policy. It also makes domestic goods and services more expensive and therefore less able to withstand international competition on both domestic and foreign markets. Thus, while the *AS* curve says that a rising output gap is accompanied by higher prices, the *AD* curve says that a rising price level reduces the output gap. Each variable, output and the price level, drives the other until equilibrium is achieved at the intersection of both curves, point *A* in Fig. 9.2.

As an example of how this framework can be used, imagine a boom abroad. As growth in the rest of the world picks up steam, spending rises and, in principle, some of it is directed to our goods and services. This higher demand is not home-made, it is given to us. The effect is captured by a rightward shift of the *AD* curve to *AD′*. The new equilibrium occurs at point *B*, where the GDP has increased. This is how world business cycles are transmitted. The downside is that prices rise too as the economy moves along the *AS* curve.

Tighter labour markets result in wage increases and firms raise prices to cope with higher production costs. If we assume that we started at point *A* in a situation where the output gap was zero – so that GDP was on trend – at point *B* GDP is above trend. Obviously, by the very definition of trend, the economy cannot remain indefinitely at point *B*. We have found the short-run effect of higher demand, but we need to think about the long run.

9.2.3 The long run (1): neutrality of money

A key principle of macroeconomics is that, in the long run, money is *neutral*. This principle asserts that the money stock does not affect real variables such as growth, unemployment, wealth, productivity or competitiveness. Instead, increases in the nominal money supply are absorbed by a proportional increase in the price level. More generally, the evolution of real variables (quantities such as real GDP, employment, exports) is independent of the evolution of nominal variables (values expressed in units of the domestic currency, such as prices, the exchange rate, wages), and conversely.[2] Money is the fundamental nominal variable since all the other variables are measured in monetary units (euros, dollars, pounds, etc.), which explains why this is called the monetary neutrality principle.

This principle is illustrated in Fig. 9.3, which shows differences in money growth and inflation between France and Switzerland. Monetary neutrality implies that differences in inflation rates between these two countries should reflect differences in their money growth rates, and France's exchange rate should depreciate vis-à-vis the Swiss franc at an equivalent rate.[3] For the moment, we ignore the exchange rate. In the first panel, which shows year-to-year changes, it is hard to detect any link between inflation and money growth. Clearly, there is a lot of 'noise' in the short run: money growth is quite volatile while inflation moves more smoothly. The second panel goes some way towards eliminating this noise by plotting five-year moving averages. A pattern clearly emerges, but the association is not perfectly tight. The last panel takes a really long-run view by displaying ten-year moving averages. The association is

---

[2] Because of this separation, this principle is also known as the dichotomy principle.

[3] If an increase in the money stock M is matched by a proportional increase in the price level P, we expect the rate of inflation in Switzerland $(\Delta P/P)^{CH}$ to be equal to the growth rate of money in Switzerland $(\Delta M/M)^{CH}$. With the same property holding for France, we expect the inflation differential $(\Delta P/P)^{FR} - (\Delta P/P)^{CH}$ to be equal to $(\Delta M/M)^{FR} - (\Delta M/M)^{CH}$. We use differences because we also wish to show the relevance for the exchange rate ahead of the purchasing parity principle presented in Section 9.2.4 below.

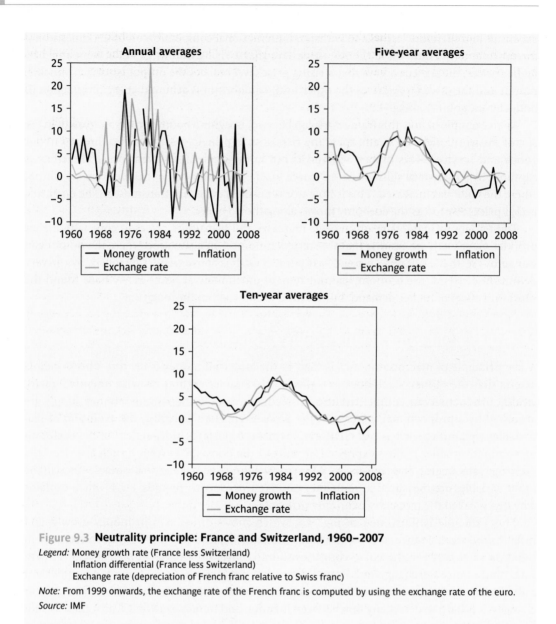

Figure 9.3 Neutrality principle: France and Switzerland, 1960–2007

Legend: Money growth rate (France less Switzerland)
Inflation differential (France less Switzerland)
Exchange rate (depreciation of French franc relative to Swiss franc)

Note: From 1999 onwards, the exchange rate of the French franc is computed by using the exchange rate of the euro.

Source: IMF

now almost perfect: the French money growth rate usually exceeds the Swiss rate, and this is accompanied by an almost equally high inflation in France. If neutrality is clearly not achieved in the short run, it is valid in the longer run, say five years and more.

Since the neutrality principle carries important implications for European monetary integration, a brief review of the underlying theory may be helpful. As explained in detail in Section 9.3, money is provided by the banking system under control of the central bank. It is held by the public at large, which needs it to carry out daily transactions. But the public is not interested in the number of zeros that figure on banknotes, it is interested in the purchasing power of money. Suppose that the price level doubles up overnight. The public will need twice as much money to hold the exact same purchasing power. Once money and the price level have both doubled up, we are back to the previous situation in real terms. Nothing has really changed, except that everything is worth twice as much in terms of the currency, which is twice more abundant. This is what money neutrality means.

How does this come about? Suppose that the central bank lets the money stock double up. At the initial price level, the public holds twice as much money as it wishes, so it will get rid of it. The way to get rid of money, as you well know, is to spend it. But if spending increases that strongly, production cannot respond, at least not fully. With demand outstripping the supply of goods and services, prices rise. Eventually, they will have doubled up as well. Because prices do not usually jump, this is a slow process. This is why the money neutrality principle is not valid in the short run, as illustrated in Fig. 9.3.

This experiment of an increase in the money stock, which prompts more spending, is illustrated in Fig. 9.2. The rise in the demand for goods and services is captured by the rightward shift of the *AD* curve to *AD′*. In the short run, say within a year or two, the economy moves from *A* to *B*. The public spends more, output responds and rises above its trend. As predicted, prices rise but, being 'sticky', are not yet in full proportion to the increase in the money supply. Consequently, at point *B* the public still has more cash at hand than it wishes, and its spending remains unusually large. In the short run, the neutrality principle does not hold and the increase in money, a nominal variable, affects real GDP. In the long run, we expect real GDP to be unaffected by the increase in money and therefore to return to trend. Put differently, in the long run, we expect the output gap to be zero and real GDP to be back on trend, as in Fig. 9.1. This conclusion is captured in Fig. 9.2 by the long-run aggregate supply schedule, a vertical line that corresponds to a zero output gap. This means that, over time, the economy moves from point *B* to point *C* where prices have increased in proportion to the money supply.

Why do we associate the vertical line with supply? The short-run *AS* curve says that the economy can produce more than its potential but that wages, and therefore production costs, rise and so do prices. As prices rise, they erode the purchasing power of wages, which are raised anew in a climate of strong economic activity. As the economy moves from *B* to *C* along the *AD* curve, prices rise and reduce demand, which gradually weakens the ability of employees to obtain ever-higher wages in response to ever-higher prices. Graphically, in Fig. 9.2, the short-run *AS* curve shifts upward until it goes through point *C*. The long-run *AS* schedule captures this result: the inflation spiral that sees wages pushing prices and prices pushing wages must eventually come to an end and the economy must return to its trend growth path. Box 9.1 provides a formal presentation of this reasoning.

Box 9.1 Aggregate supply from the short to the long run: a formal presentation

The short-run aggregate supply curve describes how wages and prices respond to market conditions. It can be formalized as follows. Firms set prices with two considerations in mind: (1) to cover costs and (2) to maximize profits.[1] Costs include labour, capital, intermediate goods, taxes and imported materials.

▶ Capital and intermediate costs for one firm are revenues for others. In the aggregate, they cancel out. Ignoring for the time being taxes and imported materials, we limit our attention to labour costs, which we represent as W (since wages represent the bulk of these costs). We can describe firms' pricing strategy as:

$$P = (1 + mk_P)\,W \tag{13.1}$$

where mk_P is the mark-up of the price level P over average labour costs W.

Wages are set through periodic negotiations. Employees seek to achieve the highest possible wage, of course, and to protect themselves against price increases during the period over which the agreement under negotiation will be valid. We describe the outcome of the strategy as:

$$W = (1 + mk_W)\,P^e \tag{13.2}$$

where mk_W is the mark-up of wages W over the price level P^e expected to prevail during the upcoming period.

Combining (13.1) and (13.2) we obtain:

$$P = (1 + mk)\,P^e \tag{13.3}$$

where mk is the combined mark-up such that $1 + mk = (1 + mk_P)\,(1 + mk_W)$.

The final step recognizes that employees are successful in raising the wage mark-up mk_W when the output gap is high, while they have to accept a limited mark-up when the output gap is low. The price mark-up mk_P is not clearly related to cyclical conditions. In the end, the combined mark-up rises with the output gap. We represent this by writing $1 + mk = f(output\ gap)$ – a function f of the output gap – so that (13.3) becomes:

$$P = f(output\ gap)\,P^e \tag{13.4}$$

This equation describes the short-run *AS* curve. Given current expectations of the future price level P^e, the actual price level moves in the same direction as the output gap. If the price level rises, sooner or later, the expected price level P^e too will rise and the *AS* curve will shift upward. This is a slow process because it is tied to wage negotiations, which only take place once a year or more.

The long run is characterized by a situation when prices have stabilized, which will also stabilize price expectations. In fact, when the situation is stable, we have $P^e = P$ and the long-run *AS* curve is defined by $f(output\ gap) = 1$. The observation that on average the GDP remains close to its trend implies that the long-run *AS* curve boils down to $output\ gap = 0$. Formally, it means that $f(0) = 1$ and the combined mark-up mk is zero.

Finally, we can recognize that, occasionally, taxes and primary commodity prices can rise or decline. These events come on top of the wage–price mechanism. They are called supply-side shocks and can simply be represented by a factor s, which is positive when they raise production costs and negative in the opposite case:

$$P = f(output\ gap)\,P^e + s \tag{13.5}$$

Note that wages rise secularly as the result of productivity gain. We ignore this aspect for the sake of simplicity.

---

[1] In Chapter 4, firms equate prices to marginal cost, which occurs when competition is perfect and firms cannot make 'extra' profits. Here, we consider that many firms have market power, which occurs when competition is not perfect. This is called monopolistic competition. For an elaboration, see e.g. Burda and Wyplosz (2009).

9.2.4 The long term (2): purchasing power parity

Monetary neutrality also carries an implication for the exchange rate. The resulting principle is known as purchasing power parity (PPP). It asserts that the rate of change of the nominal exchange rate between two countries is equal to the difference between the inflation rates in these two countries, the inflation differential:

Exchange rate appreciation = foreign inflation rate − domestic inflation rate

$$\underbrace{\text{foreign inflation rate} - \text{domestic inflation rate}}_{\text{Inflation differential}}$$

If inflation at home is durably lower than abroad, our currency should appreciate in the long run. Conversely, a country with higher inflation sees its exchange rate depreciate vis-à-vis the currency with a lower inflation rate. Since we know that inflation differentials reflect differences in money growth, the evolution of the nominal exchange rate is ultimately driven by relative money growth rates.

Figure 9.3 also plots the rate of change of the nominal exchange rate between the French franc (FRF) and the Swiss franc (CHF). This exchange rate is expressed as the number of FRF needed to buy one CHF: when the CHF appreciates vis-à-vis the FRF, the exchange rate increases. As before, over the short run, there is no visible link between the exchange rate, money growth and inflation. Indeed, we see that the nominal exchange rate is very volatile, even more than the money stock, while price differentials are much more stable. As the horizon extends to the very long run, things fall nicely into place. The rate of appreciation of the CHF – or, equivalently, the rate of depreciation of the FRF – follows a pattern very similar to those of the money growth and inflation differentials. In brief, why is the CHF typically appreciating vis-à-vis the FRF? Because money growth, and therefore inflation, is higher in France than in Switzerland. Table 9.1 confirms that over the period 1960–98 (when the FRF ceased to exist), the average annual rate of appreciation of the CHF vis-à-vis the FRF is related – but not exactly equal – to the average difference between inflation in France and in Switzerland. This is PPP.

An alternative definition of PPP leads us to define the real exchange rate. The nominal exchange rate is the one that is widely discussed and reported in newspapers. We will define it as the price in foreign currency of one unit of the domestic currency, for instance 1.3 dollars for 1 euro or 2 dollars for 1 pound. One function of the exchange rate is to translate the price of goods from one currency to another. When it changes, it affects the country's international competitiveness. The real exchange rate is designed to provide a measure of competitiveness. It is defined as the ratio of domestic to foreign good prices. But for the comparison to be meaningful, prices must be expressed in the same currency. Consider the real exchange rate of the euro in terms of dollars. The real exchange rate compares the dollar price of a basket of

Table 9.1 France vs. Switzerland, 1960–98

Average money growth: France less Switzerland	2.0%
Average inflation: France less Switzerland	2.1%
Average appreciation CHF vs. FRF	1.0%

Source: IMF

goods made in Europe to the dollar price P* of a basket of goods made in the USA. To that effect, we need to convert into dollars the basket price of domestic goods in euros P (e.g. €100):

Price of a basket of European goods in euros:	P	(e.g. €100)
Exchange rate (dollars per euro):	E	(e.g. 1.3 $/€)
Price of the same basket of European goods in dollars:	EP	(e.g. $130)

Thus we can compare EP with P*, since both are measured in dollars. The real exchange rate is the ratio EP/P*. We could instead measure the price of the US basket in euros as P*/E and compare it to the domestic price in euros as well. When we divide P by P*/E, we obtain EP/P* as before. Reassuringly, it does not matter which currency we use.

When the real exchange rate increases – we say that it appreciates – domestic goods become more expensive relative to foreign goods and our competitiveness declines. The real exchange rate appreciates when:

★ the nominal exchange rate E appreciates;

★ domestic prices P rise faster than foreign prices P*, so that P/P* increases.

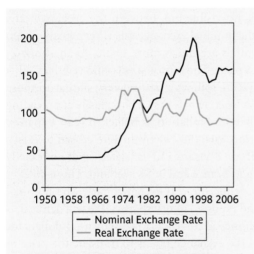

Figure 9.4 Nominal and real exchange rates (Germany vs. UK, 1950–2007)

Note: The graph shows the £/DM nominal and real exchange rate, so that an increase is a DM appreciation vis-à-vis sterling. These indices are set to 100 on average over 1950–2007. From 1999 onwards, the value of the DM is derived from the evolution of the euro.

Source: IMF

Of course, a real exchange rate depreciation – a decline in EP/P* – signals a gain in competitiveness.

The exchange rate E and prices are nominal variables. The PPP and money neutrality principles assert that whatever happens to them does not affect the real exchange rate. Thus PPP implies that the real exchange rate is constant.[4] This is illustrated in Fig. 9.4, which displays the nominal and real exchange rates between sterling and the deutschmark (the euro after 1998). Year-to-year movements in the nominal exchange rate are mirrored in similar but subdued movements in the real exchange rate. While it is not constant from year to year, the real exchange moves around a reasonably stable level. Indeed, the five-fold nominal depreciation of the pound since 1950 fails to leave a lasting impression on the real exchange rate.

The stable long-run level is sometimes called the equilibrium real exchange rate. When the real exchange rate is above equilibrium, it is said to be overvalued, and it is undervalued in the opposite case. Over- and undervaluations

---

[4] The link with the first definition of PPP can be shown mathematically. Since the rate of change (e.g. in per cent) of the real exchange rate is $\Delta(EP/P^*)/(EP/P^*) = \Delta E/E + \Delta P/P - \Delta P^*/P^*$, we have $\Delta(EP/P^*)/(EP/P^*) = 0$ when $\Delta E/E = \Delta P^*/P^* - \Delta P/P$.

Let us assume that the central bank keeps the nominal money supply constant – we will revisit this assumption shortly. This means that, given the output level, the interest rate has risen in response to the price-induced contraction in the real money stock. Graphically, in Fig. 9.6, the *LM* curve shifts up. The economy moves from point *A* to point *B* and the output level falls. We have just seen that an increase in the price level reduces output. This is exactly what the negative slope of the *AD* schedule in Fig. 9.2 reflects.[8]

9.3.3 Effects of monetary and fiscal policies

The *IS–LM* diagram not only explains the *AD* curve, it also provides many useful detailed explanations of how the economy reacts when some important changes occur. It suggests two broad reasons why demand may vary:

1 Changing conditions in the goods market. One possibility is that exports rise, presumably in response to booming conditions in the rest of the world. Another is that the government decides to spend money to hire more civil servants or build more roads. The government might also encourage private spending by cutting taxes. These are examples of an expansionary fiscal policy. At the initial interest rate, such a move strengthens aggregate demand, which implies that the *IS* curve shifts rightward to *IS'* in Fig. 9.7. As the economy moves from point *A* to point *B*, both output and the interest rate increase.

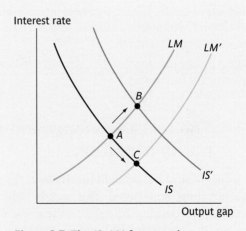

Figure 9.7 **The *IS–LM* framework**

2 Changes in monetary policy. Consider an expansionary monetary policy. For instance, we assume that the central bank controls the money supply – schedule S_1 in Fig. 9.5 – and decides to increase it. This means that S_1 moves to the right and the interest rate declines. This means that the *LM* curve shifts down, to *LM'* in Fig. 9.7. Demand expands as the economy moves from point *A* to point *C*. One reason is that borrowing costs are lower, another is that credit is more readily available. Box 9.3 provides more details on how monetary policy affects demand. As we see, in the short run, money is not neutral.

---

[8] If the central bank lets the nominal supply increase to partly compensate for the price increase, the fall in output is smaller and the *AD* curve is steeper. If the central bank increases the nominal supply in proportion to the increase in the price level, the real money supply remains constant, the interest rate does not increase, the *LM* curve does not move at all and the *AD* curve is vertical.

Box 9.3 **Loose ends: the distinction between the nominal and real interest rate and the channels of monetary policy**

Nominal and real interest rates

The nominal interest rate is the one that is routinely mentioned, for example by banks when they make loans to their clients. Assume that you borrow €1000 for one year at a 5 per cent nominal interest rate. This means that, a year from now, you will pay back €1050. But if there is some inflation, €1050 will be worth less in one year's time than today. For example, if the inflation rate is 2 per cent, €1050 will buy only what you can obtain today with €1030 (this is approximately found by taking off 2 per cent from 1050). This means that the real cost of borrowing is less than 5 per cent. In fact it is 3 per cent, approximately the nominal rate of 5 per cent less the inflation rate of 2 per cent. Thus 3 per cent is the real interest rate. (The general formula is $r = i - \Delta P/P$, where i is the nominal interest rate and r is the real interest rate.) When there is no inflation, the two rates are equal.

Channels of monetary policy

The interest rate channel. More money means lower interest rates, which is an incentive to borrow and spend more.

The credit channel. More liquidity encourages banks to compete more forcefully in offering loans.

The stock market channel. Declining interest rates are typically accompanied by higher stock prices. Firms find it interesting to issue shares and invest the proceeds. Households feel wealthier and consume more abundantly.

The exchange rate channel. The nominal depreciation is also a real depreciation and makes domestic goods more competitive.

9.4 The open economy and the interest rate parity condition

So far, we have not thought much about the international aspects of the macroeconomy, as if the economy were closed. This section remedies that deficiency by considering the case of a small open economy. Being open, the economy trades in goods and services with the rest of the world. It is also integrated into the world financial markets. Being small means that domestic events do not affect the rest of the world. The small country assumption is not just a convenient simplification, it is also a good description of nearly all countries in the world with the exception of the USA and, maybe, the European Union *as a whole*. Taking into account trade in goods, and especially in financial assets, has very strong implications for our analysis. In addition, it brings to the fore the issue of the exchange rate regime, which is central to the process of monetary integration in Europe.

Trade in goods and services means that foreign events will affect the economy in as much as they affect our exports and imports. In fact, we already considered this situation in Section 9.2.2 when we noted that such events shift the *AD* curve. An additional channel is the real exchange rate. For example, in Section 9.3.2 we looked at the effect of an increase in the price level. We ignored the fact that, if the exchange rate remains unchanged, a higher price level results in a real appreciation and a loss of external competitiveness, which should reduce world demand

(and therefore flatten the *AD* curve). Here we see, for the first time, that the evolution of the exchange rate matters.

Financial transactions have a more fundamental effect. Imagine the situation when the domestic interest rate is low relative to interest rates elsewhere in the world. International investors, always on the lookout for a good deal, are likely to borrow at home and use the proceeds to lend abroad. Given the huge size of resources available to international investors, the resulting outflows of capital and sales of the domestic currency on the foreign exchange market would have a profound impact. In fact, in this particular case, it would lead to a sharp depreciation of the nominal exchange rate. This is where the central bank must decide what it wants to see happening to the exchange rate. We return to this issue in Section 9.5.

The sheer size of these flows makes the situation unsustainable. Something has to give. In fact, the domestic interest rate will have to move to the 'world level'. In order to understand the meaning of this conclusion, we turn to Fig. 9.8, which displays long-term (ten years) interest rates on government bonds and exchange rates vis-à-vis the US dollar. Broadly, interest rates in all countries, except Poland, move closely together. Closer inspection, however, shows some differences, which are detailed in Box 9.4. The box suggests that interest rates are closer the less the exchange rates diverge. This is logical. Borrowing at home and investing abroad means initially converting the borrowed amounts into the foreign currency and, when the arrangements mature, moving funds in the opposite direction. If, in the mean time, the exchange rate changes, the profitability of the operation is altered. If, for instance, the domestic currency appreciates, the value of the foreign investment will decline – this is called a capital loss. If instead the domestic currency depreciates, the investor will benefit from a capital gain. International financial markets are in equilibrium when capital flows of this kind are unnecessary because the returns on domestic and foreign assets are equalized, taking into account likely capital gains or losses. This property of international financial markets is called the interest rate parity condition. It can be stated as:

Domestic interest rate = Foreign interest rate + Expected exchange rate depreciation

$$\underbrace{\phantom{\text{Foreign interest rate + Expected exchange rate depreciation}}}$$

Return on foreign assets

Box 9.4 Detailed analysis of interest rates in Fig. 9.8

We first focus on interest rates in Germany and Denmark, a small economy deeply linked to its neighbours. The Danish interest rate closely follows the rate in the Eurozone. The right-hand chart shows that the Danish authorities have tightly linked the krone to the euro, to the point where the evolution of their exchange rates is undistinguishable.

Comparing next three countries with large financial centres, the Eurozone, the UK and the USA, we see that the interest rates only broadly move together. Most likely they are influenced by the US rate, given the size of its financial markets. Importantly, all these currencies freely float vis-à-vis each other.

Poland appears as an outlier. Its interest rate initially diverges considerably but then, from 2004 onward, its fluctuations share some of the broad features of the other rates. The left-hand chart shows that the zloty has also been the most volatile currency of the lot. Importantly, following its accession to the EU in January 2004, Poland has eliminated nearly all its restrictions on capital movements.

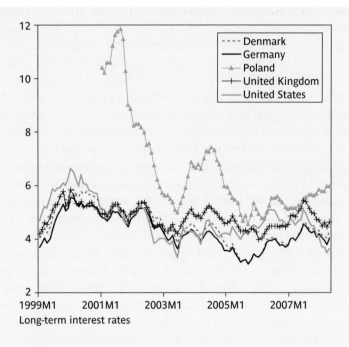

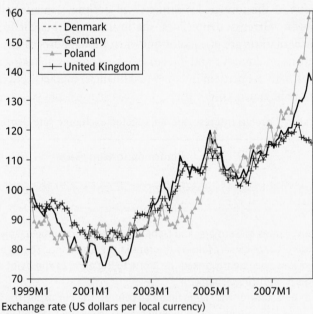

Figure 9.8 Long-term interest rates and exchange in selected countries (January 1999–April 2008)

Note: For comparison, the exchange rates vis-à-vis the US dollar are computed as an index worth 100 on average during the whole period.

Source: IMF

Note that this reasoning assumes that capital can move freely from one country to another. In countries that impose some capital controls, there is no reason for the interest rate parity condition to hold.

9.5 Monetary policy and the exchange rate regime

9.5.1 Exchange regimes

We now revisit the *IS–LM* diagram to take account of capital mobility. As we do so, we will find that monetary policy is deeply affected by the exchange rate regime. Exchange rate regimes determine the degree to which the exchange rate is allowed to fluctuate. The many varieties of exchange regime are described in Chapter 10. To keep things simple, we focus on the two generic regimes: fixed (and adjustable) and fully flexible (or free float).

When they are freely floating, exchange rates are continuously priced on foreign exchange markets. These markets do not have a physical location. Rather they operate as a network of large financial institutions that trade currencies among themselves, for their own accounts and on behalf of their customers, which include smaller financial institutions. The amounts transacted are huge (on average $3.2 trillion per day in April 2007, the date of the latest survey).

Central banks may, if they so wish, intervene in the foreign exchange markets. When they do, they buy or sell their own currencies against other currencies, chiefly the US dollar and the euro. To that effect, central banks hold sizeable amounts of foreign currencies, called foreign exchange reserves. When it adopts a fixed exchange regime, a central bank commits to keep the exchange rate within the declared band of fluctuation. In order to honour its commitment, the central bank must stand ready to intervene in whatever amount is necessary. If its currency weakens, the central bank buys it back, selling some of its foreign exchange reserves. If the currency strengthens, the central bank sells it and accumulates more foreign exchange reserves.

9.5.2 Monetary policy when the exchange rate is freely floating

Let's consider again the role of monetary policy already examined in Section 9.3.3, but now we take openness to capital flows into account.[9] The story starts the same way: an increase in the money supply is captured by a rightward shift of the *LM* schedule in Fig. 9.9. Previously, we concluded that the economy moves to point *B* where the interest rate is lower than at the initial point *A*. But we know that domestic and foreign interest rates are linked by the interest rate parity condition. For a small country, this means that the domestic interest rate is driven by the foreign interest rate (for simplicity, we ignore capital gains or losses).

At point *B*, the interest rate is below the foreign rate. This is bound to trigger capital outflows, as previously described, and therefore sales of the domestic currency. If the exchange rate is freely floating, it depreciates. As we assume that the price level is constant, both at home and abroad, a nominal depreciation translates into a real depreciation, which makes our goods and services more competitive.[10] The result is an increase in exports, which means that the

[9] An exercise asks you to do the same for fiscal policy.

[10] Formally, when P and P^* are constant, a fall in E reduces EP/P^*.

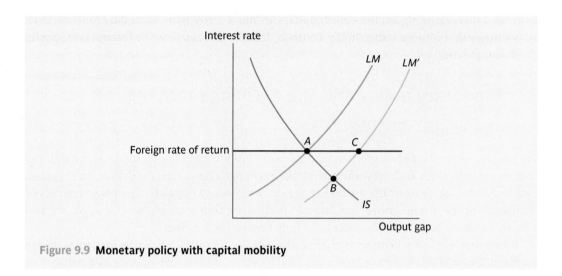

Figure 9.9 Monetary policy with capital mobility

IS curve shifts to the right and the economy starts moving from point *B* toward point *C* along the curve *LM'*. How far will it go? All the way to *C*, because this is where the interest rate is again equal to the foreign rate.

Indeed, as long as the interest rate remains lower than abroad, capital flows out, the nominal and real exchange rates depreciate, competitiveness improves and the *IS* curve keeps moving to the right. All of this stops when the *IS* curve passes through point *C* (not shown). Remarkably, at point *C* monetary policy is expansionary even though the interest rate is at its initial level. The reason is that the exchange rate has depreciated. This is a crucially important result. In a small open economy, monetary policy works primarily because it affects the exchange rate and therefore competitiveness. Put differently, monetary and exchange rate policies are two sides of the same coin.

Note that, over time, monetary neutrality will reassert itself. Indeed, the expansion fuels inflation because the *AD* curve has shifted to the right, as in Fig. 9.2. As the domestic price level rises, two things happen. First, the real money supply declines because the purchasing power of money is being eroded. Second, the real exchange rate appreciates and competitiveness declines. In Fig. 9.9, the first effect moves the *LM* curve back to the left, the second effect does the same for the *IS* curve. Eventually, both curves go back to their initial positions, just as the economy reaches point *C* in Fig. 9.2. The real money stock and the real exchange rate have returned to their initial levels, with no lasting expansionary impact.

9.5.3 Monetary policy when the exchange rate is fixed

We now look at the same experiment, but when the exchange rate is fixed. The story starts in the same way. The money supply is increased, the *LM* curve shifts to the right, the economy moves to point *B* in Fig. 9.9 and capital flows out. Now, however, the central bank will not let the exchange rate depreciate. It will intervene on the foreign exchange market, selling its reserves to buy back its currency. In doing so, the central bank re-absorbs some of the money that it has created, and the money supply shrinks. This moves the *LM* curve back to the left. In fact, to avoid a speculative attack, the central bank will have to promptly return the *LM* curve to its initial position. Indeed, as long as the domestic interest rate is below the foreign rate, capital flows out, draining the stock of foreign exchange reserves. The *IS* curve does not move because the nominal exchange rate is fixed and the domestic and foreign prices are assumed to be constant, which leaves the real exchange rate and external competitiveness unchanged. Simply put, the economy does not stay away from point *A* very long.

The striking implication is that efforts by the central bank to expand its money supply are frustrated by the need to conduct offsetting foreign exchange market operations in defence of the exchange rate. Monetary policy simply does not work when the exchange rate is fixed. Put differently, monetary policy autonomy is lost because it is entirely dedicated to the exchange rate commitment. Once again, we find that monetary and exchange rate policies are one and the same thing. A central bank can control either the money stock or the exchange rate, but not both.

In practice, exchange rates are rarely rigidly fixed, and are usually allowed to move within bands. If the band is narrow (e.g. the 4.5 per cent width in the pre-1993 ERM, see Chapter 16), the room for monetary policy independence is very limited. As the band widens, of course, monetary policy can increasingly be used, but there is then little substantive difference between a fixed exchange rate with wide bands (like the post-1993 ERM, with 30 per cent wide bands) and a floating exchange rate.

Since the central bank cannot move the *LM* curve, it cannot move the *AD* curve either. What then determines the price level in the long run? The answer is given by PPP. Since the real exchange rate remains at its equilibrium level in the long run – unless structural changes create a Balassa–Samuelson effect, which we ignore for the time being – the price level is ultimately determined by the price level in the country to whose currency the exchange rate is pegged. Indeed, when the nominal exchange rate E is fixed, the real exchange rate EP/P^* remains constant when the ratio P/P^* is unchanged. For a small economy, this means that the domestic price level must follow the foreign price level P^*.

9.6 Summary

This chapter has presented the macroeconomic tools for macroeconomic analysis. The essential tools are the *AD–AS* and *IS–LM* diagrams. The *IS–LM* diagram is relevant for the short run, the period over which it is reasonable that the price level is constant. The *AD* builds upon the *IS–LM* diagram, showing how things change on the demand side when the price level changes. The *AD–AS* diagram is designed to study in a compact way both the short and the long run, and to sketch the medium run in between. The transition from the short to the long run is driven by shifts in the *AS* curve, which correspond to reassessment of the evolution of the price level by wage negotiators.

The chapter has also presented some fundamental principles:

★ monetary neutrality, which asserts that in the long run nominal and real variables do not interfere;

★ purchasing power parity, itself an implication of the monetary neutrality principle, which asserts that the real exchange rate remains constant in the long run, unless real changes (e.g. catch-up growth) are present;

★ interest rate parity, which links the domestic interest rate to foreign returns, the latter including capital gains or losses.

Self-assessment questions

1. Examine carefully Fig. 9.4 and determine periods when the *DM* was overvalued or undervalued.

2. If the nominal exchange rate appreciates by less than the excess of foreign over domestic inflation, is the real exchange rate appreciating or depreciating?

3. Why are fixed exchange rates believed to impose discipline on monetary policy?

4. Why would the exchange rate regime be irrelevant if money were also neutral in the short run? What would make money neutral in the short run?

5. Using the *IS–LM* diagram under a fixed exchange rate regime, show the effects of an expansionary fiscal policy. How does your result differ from Fig. 9.7?

6. Using the *IS–LM* diagram under a free float exchange rate regime, show the effects of an expansionary fiscal policy. How does your result differ from Fig. 9.7?

7. Re-do the analysis of Section 9.3.2 assuming that the central bank has a policy of keeping the interest rate unchanged. What is the shape of the *AD* curve?

8. Why is it asserted that there cannot be speculative attacks against freely floating exchange rates?

9. Using the *IS–LM* diagram, study the effect of a sudden increase in the foreign price level. Distinguish between a fixed and a floating exchange rate regime.

10. The fixed-price assumption is acceptable for countries with a low inflation rate. How do things change when inflation is very high?

Essay questions

1. The real, not the nominal, exchange rate is what matters for the real side of the economy. Why don't central banks attempt to control the real rather the nominal exchange rate?

2. It is often believed that a peg encourages residents (households, firms, banks) to borrow in a foreign currency. Then, if the exchange rate is devalued, many residents face the risk of bankruptcy. Explain and comment.

3. Money is non-neutral when prices move slowly. Is this a good or a bad thing?

4. We see that monetary policy determines the price level and therefore the inflation rate. What can lead some central banks to let prices rise quickly?

5. A strong currency is a currency that is expected to appreciate vis-à-vis most other currencies. How can this status be achieved? What are the advantages and disadvantages of achieving strong-currency status?

6. About half of the dollar bills printed by the Federal Reserve circulate outside the US. Much the same applies to the euros printed by the ECB. Why, in your view? How does this affect the neutrality principle?

7. Central bankers are often described as 'conservatives', meaning that they are more concerned with inflation than growth. What could explain this feature?

8. Fixed exchange rate regimes usually allow for occasional changes of the central parity. Use the interest parity condition to explain why the reputation of the central bank – its ability to stick by its words – matters for the well-being of the economy.

Further reading: the aficionado's corner

A review of the evidence on purchasing power parity is:

Rogoff, K. (1996) 'The purchasing power parity puzzle', *Journal of Economic Literature*, 34 (2): 647–68.

The size and functioning of foreign exchange markets is surveyed every three years by the Bank for International Settlements. The latest survey is described in:

BIS, *Triennial Survey*, December 2007, available at www.bis.org/publ/rpfxf07t.htm.

Useful websites

The IMF presents up-to-date evaluations of exchange rate policies:

www.imf.org

To find out about the exchange rate regime of a particular country, visit its central bank's website. The list of all central bank websites is at:

www.bis.org/cbanks.htm

References

Burda, M. and C. Wyplosz (2009) *Macroeconomics, A European Text*, 5th edition, Oxford University Press, Oxford.

Krugman, P. (1988) *Strategic Trade Policy and the New International Economics*, MIT Press, Cambridge, MA, pp. 4–5.

Chapter 10

Europe's exchange rate question

The grass is always greener on the other side of the parity.

Jeffrey Frankel (1999)

Chapter contents

10.1	The impossible trinity principle	289
10.2	Choices	291
10.3	What Europe did	299
10.4	Summary	311

Introduction

This chapter uses the framework presented in Chapter 9 to present the debate on the choice of an exchange regime. This debate lies at the heart of the monetary integration process in Europe since exchange rate stability requires that monetary policies be coordinated. The ultimate degree of exchange rate stability is achieved when exchange rates are eliminated and monetary policies are delegated to a common central bank.

The chapter starts with the impossible trinity, a principle that determines which arrangements are durable. This principle, which is a consequence of results obtained in Chapter 9,

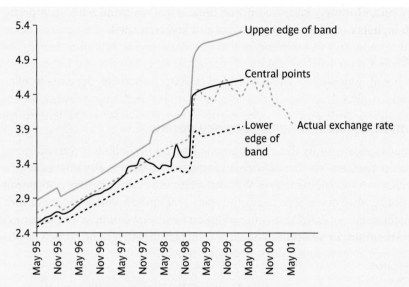

Figure 10.4 Poland's crawling band, May 1995–March 2000

Notes: The exchange rate is an index computed by the National Bank, which rises when the currency depreciates. The crawling band was introduced in March 1995 and lasted until April 2000 when the zloty was allowed to float, and soon appreciated. The anchor was a basket index whose composition was occasionally changed (in 1999 it included the euro, with a 55 per cent weight, and the US dollar, with a 45 per cent weight). The vertical scale (zloty per euro) is inverted so that an upward movement represents a nominal appreciation.

Source: National Bank of Poland

widened to ±2.25 per cent. Between 1979 and 1993, Europe's Exchange Rate Mechanism (ERM) also operated as a system of fixed and adjustable exchange rates, with a ±2.25 per cent band, which was enlarged to ±15 per cent after 1993. The current ERM-2 has retained the latter wide band. Denmark has operated this regime since its creation in 1979. Latvia is currently the only other ERM member, with Bulgaria expected to join.

Currency boards

Currency boards are a tight version of fixed exchange rate regimes. Under a pegged regime, monetary policy has to be wholly dedicated to the exchange rate target but, as we saw, the possibility to devalue or revalue and the existence of margins of fluctuations introduce some degree of flexibility. Currency boards are designed to remove this flexibility. In order to ensure that monetary policy is entirely dedicated to support the declared parity, with no margin of fluctuation, the central bank may only issue domestic money when it acquires foreign exchange reserves. If it spends its foreign exchange reserves, the central bank must retire its own currency from circulation and the money supply shrinks.[3]

Currency boards used to exist in the British Empire, and disappeared with it. They were revived by a number of Caribbean islands as they became independent and by Hong Kong in

---

[3] The study of the gold standard in Section 10.3.1 provides the logic of this rule.

1983. They became more widespread in the 1990s when countries with weak political institutions, such as Argentina, Bosnia-Herzegovina and Bulgaria, chose this rigorous arrangement to put an end to monetary indiscipline and its corollary, raging inflation. Freshly independent from the Soviet Union, with no history of central banking, Estonia and Lithuania also adopted a currency board. Argentina's system collapsed in 2002, illustrating the dangers of an inflexible arrangement.

Dollarization/euroization and currency unions

A yet stricter regime is to fix the exchange rate irrevocably, which means adopting a foreign currency, hence the term '*dollarization*' (as in Ecuador, El Salvador, Panama, Liberia) or '*euroization*' (as in Kosovo and Montenegro). Without a domestic currency, there obviously can be no monetary policy whatsoever. This regime is typically adopted by small countries with very weak political institutions. A related case is the adoption by several countries of the same currency, as in a monetary union. In addition to Europe, francophone Africa and some Caribbean islands have formed monetary unions, as described in Box 10.2.

Box 10.2   Existing monetary unions

The CFA zone was created when the former French colonies reached independence in the 1960s.[1] It includes two unions: the West African Economic and Monetary Union (Benin, Burkina Faso, Côte d'Ivoire, Guinea Bissau, Mali, Niger, Senegal, Togo) and the Central African Economic and Monetary Union (Cameroon, Central African Republic, Chad, Democratic Republic of Congo, Equatorial Guinea, Gabon). These countries never created their own currencies (Mali and Equatorial Guinea did, until they joined the CFA zone in 1985). The two monetary unions are formally independent from each other and each has its own central bank, yet both peg their currency to the French franc at the same rate, devalued once by 50 per cent in 1994. They have been pegged to the euro since 1999. The arrangement is special, a legacy of colonial times and based on a guarantee by France, but it is a true, modern monetary union.

The East Caribbean Common Market (Antigua and Barbuda, Dominica, Grenada, St Kitts and Nevis, St Lucia, and St Vincent and the Grenadines) form a monetary union. These are small islands that can hardly be compared to the European monetary union.

Brunei and Singapore also form a currency union.

Other countries have unilaterally adopted a foreign currency and therefore do not actively participate in the running of the central bank. This is the case of Kiribati, Nauru and Tuvalu, which use the Australian dollar; Lesotho, Namibia and Swaziland, which use the South African rand; and Bahamas, Liberia, Marshall Islands, Micronesia, Palau and Panama, which have adopted the US dollar. More recently, Ecuador and San Salvador have also adopted the US dollar since 2001. In Europe, Monaco uses the French franc (now the euro), Liechtenstein the Swiss franc, and San Marino the Italian lira (now the euro). These are not true monetary unions, since the centre country is not committed to take into account the interests and viewpoints of its 'satellites', and actually never does.

[1] The term CFA comes from the old colonial French designation 'Comptoir Français d'Afrique'. The Western Africa's CFA means *Communauté financière d'Afrique* (Financial Community of Africa), while the Central Africa version means *Coopération financière en Afrique centrale* (Financial Cooperation in Central Africa).

10.2.3 What drives the choice of an exchange rate regime?

The wide variety of existing exchange rate regimes indicates that there is no universally best solution and that a country may find it advantageous to choose one regime at some point in time and another regime at another point in time. Many considerations come into play:

★ Retaining monetary policy autonomy. Monetary policy is a useful instrument in the short run, but it can be mishandled and lead to long-run inflation. One consideration is the quality of domestic institution. Another one is country size: currencies of small countries are not that useful as they can only serve on a limited territory.

★ Insulating the economy from foreign disturbances. Exchange rate movements tend to offset these disturbances, but they do so by affecting external competitiveness.

★ The impact of exchange rate volatility. While some exchange rate changes are welcome reactions to domestic or foreign disturbances – others, which may be driven by purely financial considerations, can be disruptive.

A simple way of weighing these various aspects is to focus on two broadly defined regimes: (1) fixed exchange rates, which includes all the regimes where the central bank has made some explicit commitment from crawling pegs to adoption of a foreign currency; and (2) floating rates, where the central bank does not intervene on the foreign exchange market or, if it does, at its total discretion as with managed floats. Target zones belong to the middle grey zone.

The case for flexible exchange rates rests on three main considerations:

1 When shocks occur – national or worldwide recessions, oil shocks, technological change, etc. – prices must be adjusted to avoid deepening cyclical fluctuations. When prices and wages are sticky, the required adjustments may take far too long and misalignments occur. Flexible exchange rates provide the fast way to adjust relative domestic and foreign costs and prices.

2 Exchange rate changes are unavoidably enmeshed with politics. An appreciation or a depreciation affects income distribution[4] and is invariably perceived as a judgement on the government's economic competence. For example, a depreciation is often interpreted, rightly or wrongly, as a signal of government failure. More generally, any sharp change in the exchange rate provides ammunition to political opposition, which can argue that there is something wrong with government policies. Politics rarely mix harmoniously with economics, so removing the exchange rate from the realm of politics is desirable.

3 It is difficult to renounce the convenience of monetary policy autonomy in each and every circumstance. Too often, governments instruct their central banks to act in ways that lead to bruising currency crises.

In the opposite camp, the case for fixed exchange rates emphasizes the tendency of exchange markets to misbehave as well as cases where exchange rate policy is useful:

---

[4] An appreciation is good news for consumers, who find imported goods cheaper, but bad news for producers, especially exporters, who must compress profit margins – and maybe even labour costs – to remain competitive. Conversely, a depreciation hurts the consumers and benefits the producers.

★ The exchange markets are driven by a short-term financial logic, where information about the future is essential but highly imperfect. The result is fads, rumours and herd behaviour, which occasionally provoke panic.

★ Even if exchange market gyrations do not result in panic, they provoke large fluctuations. For international traders and investors, these fluctuations are a source of uncertainty which can hurt trade and foreign direct investment.

★ Harnessing monetary policy to an exchange rate target introduces discipline since foreign exchange markets are likely to immediately sanction inflationary policies by launching speculative attacks.

★ In case of serious shocks, parity realignments are always possible when the exchange rate is explicitly fixed but adjustable. Adopting a parity is not a permanent commitment; it only provides an anchor for monetary policy.

10.2.4 The two corners

The 1990s was a decade of violent currency crises. Europe's ERM was hit in 1992–93, Latin America followed in 1995–99, then it was Southeast Asia's turn in 1997–98 and Russia in 1998. These countries were operating one or another form of a peg, but countries like Hong Kong and Argentina, both with a currency board, escaped the apparently contagious wave. This has made popular the 'two-corner' view according to which the only safe regimes are the extremes ones, free floating or 'hard pegs' such as currency boards, monetary unions or dollarization. Hard pegs were seen as impregnable because the central banks have no opportunity to give in to market pressure, even if they – or their governments – wish to do so. Freely floating rates too are presumed to be immune from speculative attacks simply because there is no peg to attack; like soft pillows, they absorb any blow.

The two-corner view holds that, when capital is freely mobile, soft pegs try to combine irreconcilable objectives and are predestined to fail, possibly badly. It is yet another implication of the impossible trinity principle developed in Section 10.1. In a globalized world of full capital mobility, either monetary policy is completely free or it is entirely committed to uphold the chosen peg. The intermediate regimes, called 'soft pegs', may be seen as a reasonable compromise between fear of floating and fear of fixing, but they run against the impossible trinity principle. As the world went through a wave of capital liberalization over the 1990s, the two-corner view predicted that the middle ground of soft pegs would hollow out.

Figure 10.5 shows the percentage of countries that have adopted the corners and the 'soft middle' ground. This classification is based on actual observed behaviour, not on official announcements (since many countries do not necessarily practise what they claim). The big changes came in the early 1970s when the Bretton Woods system collapsed – the number of strictly fixed exchange rate regimes declined – and in 1999 when the euro was adopted in Europe. It may be surprising that nearly 40 per cent of countries operate de facto a hard peg. Most of them, in fact, share the same currency as part of a monetary union, see Box 10.2, and have done so for quite a long time. In Europe, therefore, the two-corner view is reasonably well vindicated: fewer fixed-but-adjustable regimes, more hard pegs with the monetary union and some currency boards (Estonia, Lithuania) and some countries (Sweden, the UK) letting their exchanges float freely. Elsewhere, however, there is little support for this view. Freely floating rates, in particular, have made limited headway.

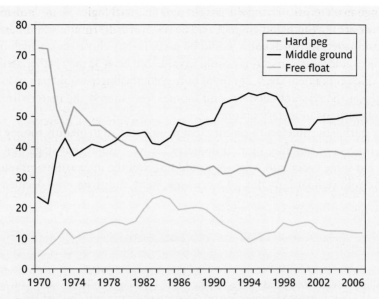

Figure 10.5 **Actual exchange rate regimes (percent of total): 1970–2007**
Source: Ilzetzki et al. (2008)

10.3 What Europe did

Europe's path to complete monetary integration is spectacular but, in many ways, it is just a return to the situation that prevailed before the introduction of paper money. This section reviews the historical record, partly for its own sake, and partly because some important lessons have been learnt and shape the current thinking of policy makers.

10.3.1 The world as a monetary union

From time immemorial until the end of the nineteenth century, money was metallic (mainly gold and silver) and a bewildering variety of currencies were circulating side by side. Each currency was defined by its content of precious metal and each local lord endeavoured to control the minting of currency in his fiefdom, chiefly because seigniorage was a key source of revenue. When public finances were under pressure, money was frequently debased, i.e. the metallic content was reduced through 'shaving' (rubbing off scraps of metal) or reminting coins to reduce the precious metal in the alloy. Exchange rates were the relative values of different coins, really measuring the weights of precious metal in each coin. With so many coins circulating in every political jurisdiction, life was not easy for shoppers:

> The multiplicity and diversity of 'sous' and 'deniers' is such that it would be nearly impossible to assess their precise values, and to sort out these various coins. It would lead to deep confusion which would increase work, trouble and other inconveniences of daily traffic.
>
> (Nicolaus Copernicus, *Monetae Cudendae Ratio*; written in 1556, first published in 1816; our translation from French)

This is why goods were priced in gold weight and the currencies were used in the reverse order of what we are now accustomed to. If a horse was worth 100 grams of pure gold, the buyer and seller would agree on which coins would be used. If they chose ecus, which included, say, 0.5 gram of pure gold, the transaction would involve 200 ecus. If they rather settled in thaler, each coin of which contained, say, 0.1 gram of pure gold, the buyer would pay 1000 thaler coins. In effect, gold was the relevant currency and monies were merely the materialization of gold. The 'world' was just one monetary union.[5]

It was only during the nineteenth century that people started to identify money and country, a part of the process of building up nation-states.[6] It was also at that stage that efforts were developed to put some order into what we would now call the international monetary system. This led to the gold standard. As Box 10.3 explains, some countries even decided to share the same currency.

Box 10.3 Early European monetary unions

By the early nineteenth century, gold and silver coins circulated side by side. The exchange rate between gold and silver fluctuated depending on discoveries. Britain was the first large country to drop silver and adopt the gold standard. On the Continent, bimetallism survived much longer, even though some countries (Germany, the Netherlands, the Scandinavian countries) favoured silver, until gold discoveries in the 1850s resulted in the disappearance of silver money on much of the Continent.

To preserve bimetallism, Belgium, France, Italy and Switzerland formed the Latin European Monetary Union in 1865 – a distant ancestor of today's monetary union. Greece joined in 1868. That effort foundered following the Franco-German war of 1870–71, when the newly established German empire shifted from silver to gold and weakened French finances by imposing war reparations to be paid in gold. When silver discoveries in Nevada depressed the price of silver, the Latin European Monetary Union was abandoned in 1878 and gold became the monetary standard.

The Scandinavian Monetary Union was created in 1873 by Denmark, Norway and Sweden, as part of the 'Scandinavianism' movement in support of the symbol of a common krona. These countries' currencies circulated widely in each other's territories. At the outbreak of the First World War, the Scandinavian Monetary Union ceased to exist, and was officially pronounced dead in 1924.

These precedents are merely of historical interest. Currencies were still based on metal, so monetary unions amounted to nothing more than harmonized coinage. They were not associated with any trade agreement and, more importantly, there was no common central bank and very little coordination among the national monetary authorities. When external conditions became difficult (the fall of the price of silver in the case of the Latin European Monetary Union, and the dislocations of war in the case of the Scandinavian Monetary Union), each country reacted in its own way to protect its own interests.

---

[5] A couple of qualifications are in order. The 'world' here refers to Europe and its colonies. In addition, as mentioned, silver was used alongside gold, so in fact there were two monies and the gold–silver price was the meaningful exchange rate.

[6] Germany and Italy achieved political unification late in that century, and many different currencies still circulated there well into the 1850s. It took Italy two decades after its political unification in 1861 to achieve monetary unification. Similarly, even after the creation of the German Reich in 1871, different monetary standards survived until the Bank of Prussia unified German monies.

The gold standard remains a fundamental reference because it had a very nice property: it automatically restored a country's external balance. This property, which got lost when we adopted paper money, is known as Hume's price–specie mechanism (see Box 10.4 for a note on Hume). The mechanism is well worth a modern visit because it applies to the internal working of a monetary union. It is based on several results from Chapter 9: the long-run neutrality of money and PPP, and the short-run effect of money on interest rates.

Box 10.4   **David Hume (1711–76)**

Born in 1711 to a well-to-do family in Berwickshire, Scotland, Hume mostly wrote on philosophy, including the *Principles of Morals* (1751) which founded, among other things, the theory of utility. His works were highly influential even though they were denounced at the time as sceptical and atheistic. His economic thinking, mainly contained in *Political Discourses* (1752), had a large impact on Adam Smith and Thomas Malthus.

Source: National Galleries of Scotland

The neutrality principle is represented in the upper-left panel of Fig. 10.6 by the upward-sloping schedule, which describes the proportionality between the money stock M and the price level P. In the same panel, we add a horizontal line meant to capture PPP. When all prices are defined in terms of gold, the exchange rate is fixed and simply equal to unity ($E = 1$). Imagine that the price of domestic goods P rises while the price P^* of foreign goods remains unchanged. The domestic economy becomes less competitive and must eventually run a current account deficit.[7] The horizontal line corresponds to the price level P at which exports equal imports and the current account is in equilibrium. Above this line, the current account is in deficit, and it is in surplus below the line. Point E represents the external equilibrium where the money stock M is consistent with price level P.

Where is the gold money stock coming from? Some of it may be dug out from the ground, but Europe has been notoriously poor in that respect and we may as well ignore this source. Gold money, therefore, has to be imported. Ignoring for the time being financial flows, it is earned through exports and spent on imports. Thus a current account surplus results in an inflow of gold money, the modern-day equivalent of the accumulation of foreign exchange reserves, the counterpart to a balance of payments surplus. Of course, gold flows out in presence of a deficit. Now consider point A, where the stock of gold money brings about a relatively high price level and, therefore, a current account deficit. The country sends more gold abroad to pay for its imports than it receives for its exports. The stock of gold money declines. This mechanism is represented by the downward-sloping schedule in the right-hand panel of Fig. 10.6. It

---

[7] It is the trade balance that changes. It is assumed that the other components of the current account remain unaffected.

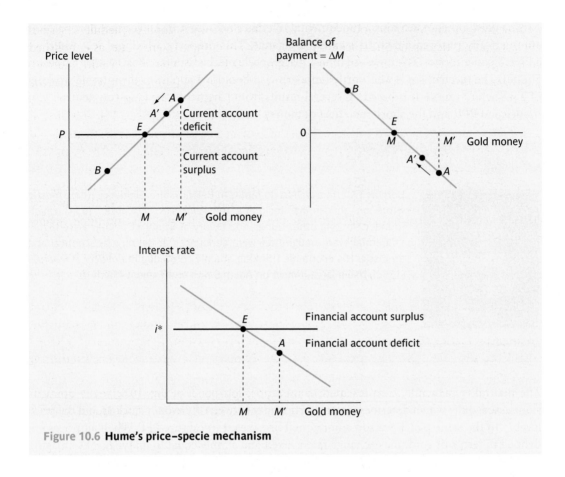

Figure 10.6 **Hume's price–specie mechanism**

says that the balance of payment deteriorates as the stock of money increases (because the price level rises, as shown in the top left-hand panel). Point A in both panels describes a situation of external deficit, which corresponds to money stock M'. The deficit means that gold is flowing out. As the money stock contracts, we move to point A' in both panels. The price level declines and the deficit is reduced. At A' the deficit is not yet fully eliminated, gold is still flowing out and the money stock keeps contracting, so we continue moving in the same direction. The process will not stop until point E is reached. At point E, the price level is just 'right', the balance of payments is in equilibrium and the money stock is stabilized. Obviously, a surplus such as point B will trigger an inflow of money (specie) and an increase in prices, bringing the economy gradually to point A. This link between money and external balance is Hume's price–specie mechanism.

The mechanism that takes us from a situation of excessively high money and price level (point A) to equilibrium (point E) involves two steps: (1) the link from the balance of payments to the money stock in the right-hand panel, which is instantaneous; and (2) the link from money to the price level in the top left-hand panel, which takes time when prices are sticky. This is a long-run mechanism, as predicted by PPP and monetary neutrality. In the shorter run, most of the action takes place in the financial sector, which has been overlooked so far. To remedy this,

Guggenheim, T. (1973) 'Some early views on monetary integration', in H.G. Johnson and A.K. Swoboda (eds) *The Economics of Common Currencies*, Harvard University Press, Cambridge, MA.

Holtfrerich, C.L. (1993) 'Did monetary unification precede or follow political unification of Germany in the 19th century?', *European Economic Review*, 37: 518–24.

On the evolution of Europe to the monetary union:

Eichengrenn, B. (2007) 'Sui Generis Euro'. Download from www.econ.berkeley.edu/~eichengr/sui_generis_EMU.pdf.

Kenen, P.B. (1995) *Economic and Monetary Union in Europe*, Cambridge University Press, Cambridge.

Padoa-Schioppa, T. (2000) *The Road to Monetary Union in Europe: The Emperor, the Kings, and the Genies*, Oxford University Press, Oxford.

On exchange rate regime choices:

Bordo, M. (2003) *Exchange Rate Regime Choice in Historical Perspective*, Working paper no. 03/160, IMF.

Frankel, J. (1999) 'No single currency regime is right for all currencies or at all times', *Essays in International Finance*, International Finance Section, Princeton University p. 215.

Tavlas, G., H. Dellas and A. Stockman (2006) 'The classification and performance of alternate exchange-rate systems', unpublished, Bank of Greece.

Two studies show the difference between the officially declared regime and what countries actually do:

Levy-Yeyati, E. and F. Sturzenegger (2005) 'Classifying exchange rate regimes: Deeds vs. words', *European Economic Review* 49 (6): 1603–35.

Reinhart, C. and K. Rogoff (2002) 'The modern history of exchange rate arrangements: a reinterpretation', *Quarterly Journal of Economics*, 119 (1): 1–48.

Useful websites

The European Parliament's factsheet on monetary integration: www.europarl.eu.int/factsheets/5_1_0_en.htm.

General resources on monetary history: www.ex.ac.uk/~RDavies/arian/other.html; www.micheloud.com/FXM/MH/Glossary.htm.

References

Ilzetzki, E.O., C. Reinhart and K.S. Rogoff (2008) 'Exchange rate arrangements entering the 21st century: Which anchor will hold?', unpublished paper, University of Maryland. Download from www.wam.umd.edu/~creinhar/Papers.html

Mitchell, B.R. (1998) *International Historical Statistics: Europe 1750–1993*, Macmillan, London.

Chapter 11

Optimum currency areas

The European countries could agree on a common piece of paper, . . . they could then set up a European monetary authority or central bank. . . . This is a possible solution, perhaps it is even an ideal solution. But it is politically very complicated, almost utopian.

Robert Mundell (1973)

Chapter contents

11.1	The question, the problem and the answer	315
11.2	The optimum currency area criteria	322
11.3	Is Europe an optimum currency area?	329
11.4	Will Europe become an optimum currency area?	341
11.5	Summary	345

Introduction

This chapter presents the optimum currency area theory, a systematic way of trying to decide whether it makes sense for a group of countries to abandon their national currencies. The theory develops a battery of economic and political criteria which recognize that the real economic cost of giving up the exchange rate instrument arises in the presence of asymmetric shocks – shocks that do not affect all currency union member countries. The chapter then examines whether Europe passes these tests. The conclusion is that Europe is not really an optimum currency area, but it does not fail all the tests either. A further consideration is that the adoption of the euro may change the situation. Over time, Europe may eventually satisfy all or most of the criteria.

11.1 The question, the problem and the answer

It is usually taken for granted that each country has its own currency. After all, like the flag or the national anthem, a currency is a symbol of statehood. National heroes or rulers are proudly displayed on coins and banknotes, much as kings, emperors and feudal lords had their faces stamped on gold and silver coins. And yet, it is worth asking whether it makes good *economic* sense for each country to have its own currency. The chapter provides answers to a simple question: If we forget about nations and focus purely on economic relations, how would we redraw the map of the world?

To start with, does the world need more than one currency? Could Zimbabwe, Peru and China share the same currency? Most likely not. At the other extreme, should each city have its own currency, as was sometimes the case a few centuries ago? No, of course not. These answers seem obvious, but exactly why? Box 11.1 presents an example that is suggestive of the issues involved.

Box 11.1   The case for a Californian dollar

In the late 1980s, something bad happened to the state of California. The Cold War ended shortly after the retirement of President Reagan who had championed the building up of the military and, in particular, massive investments in high-tech equipment. Sharp cuts in defence spending severely hurt California, home to many of the big weapon-producing firms. Even though the USA, and much of the rest of the world, suffered a severe slowdown at that time, the situation was much worse in California, where growth turned negative for three solid years and hundreds of thousands of jobs were lost. In the mid-1990s, California was the great beneficiary of the information technology (IT) revolution. Firms were desperately looking for staff as they were trying to seize on the apparently unbounded opportunities lying ahead of them. In 2001, the IT bubble burst and, once again, California was severely hit. See Fig. 11.1.

Now imagine that the state of California had its own currency. A depreciation in the early 1990s would have enhanced the battered state's competitiveness. An appreciation in the late 1990s would have moderated the boom and the accompanying job scarcities that followed when the IT mania struck. A depreciation in 2001 would, again, have softened the blow. With an economy that differs from the average US economy, California cannot use the exchange rate to insulate itself from disturbances. Yet, no one in California has seriously proposed a monetary secession. Somehow, all Californians consider that belonging to the US dollar currency area provides benefits that far outweigh the costs.

▶

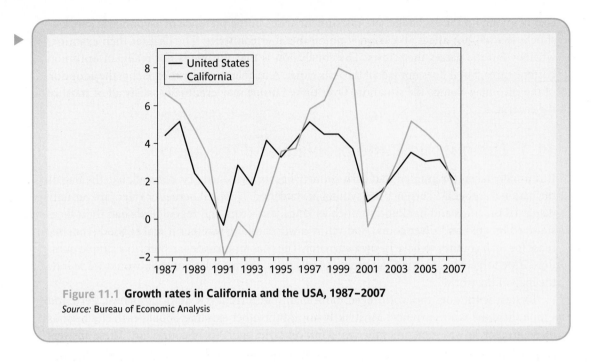

Figure 11.1 Growth rates in California and the USA, 1987–2007
Source: Bureau of Economic Analysis

11.1.1 Why is a large currency area desirable?

Money is one of humanity's great inventions. Economics textbooks tell you that its key feature is to avoid achieving the 'double coincidence of wants', i.e. barter. With money you buy what you want without bothering about simultaneously selling something. Money is useful because it makes commercial and financial transactions immensely easier than barter and also because it is immediately recognized. The more people accept a currency, the more useful it is.[1]

In that sense, the world would benefit from having just one currency that would be recognized and accepted everywhere. There would be no need to exchange money when travelling, exporting or importing. Currency exchanges are bothersome – how many unspent foreign coins lie in one of your drawers? They are costly too; as everyone painfully finds out, selling and buying rates are often 10 per cent or more apart – this is how currency dealers and credit card companies get paid for the service that they provide. In addition, currency transactions are risky as exchange rates fluctuate and seem always to go against you. This is why small currency areas – geographic zones which share the same currency – are clearly not optimum. A currency that is used in a small area is just not very useful.

Figure 11.2 symbolically represents this idea. Since the usefulness of a currency grows with the size of the area over which it is being used, its marginal benefit is positive. Yet, it is declining as the area expands because the extra benefit from adding one more country to an already large currency area is smaller than when the initial area was small.

---

[1] Technically, money is said to generate network externalities. Network externalities are studied in Chapter 18.

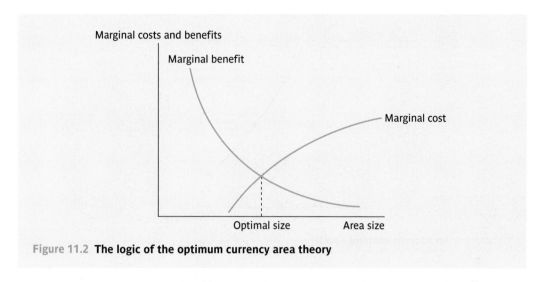

Figure 11.2 **The logic of the optimum currency area theory**

If the marginal benefit is always positive, is the world the optimal currency area? It would be if there were no costs. What can these costs be? As a currency area grows larger, it becomes more diverse – in standards of living, for instance. If more diversity means more costs when sharing a common currency, the marginal costs are positive and rising with the size of the area. This idea is depicted in Fig. 11.2 by the upward-sloping marginal cost schedule. The figure reveals the existence of a trade-off: a large currency area is desirable because it enhances the usefulness of money, but it has drawbacks. The optimal currency area corresponds to the situation where the marginal costs and benefits from sharing the same currency balance each other, as shown in Fig. 11.2. The figure is highly symbolic and there should be no pretence that we can actually draw these schedules. Yet, it summarizes what this chapter is about.

There are many ways in which diversity matters – some are economic, some are political. Diversity is costly because a common currency requires a single central bank, and a single monetary authority is unable to react to each and every local particularity. The optimum currency area (OCA) theory takes the benefits as obvious and aims at identifying more precisely these costs. The basic idea is that diversity translates into asymmetric shocks and that the exchange rate is very useful for dealing with these shocks. The intuition, brought up in Box 11.1, is made more precise in the rest of this section. We proceed in three steps:

1 First, we define and examine the effects of asymmetric shocks.
2 Second, we study the problems that arise in the presence of asymmetric shocks in a currency area.
3 Finally, we ask how the effects of asymmetric shocks can be mitigated when national exchange rates are no longer available.

11.1.2 Preview: adverse shocks

Imagine that the world demand for a country's exports declines because tastes change or because cheaper alternatives are developed elsewhere. This opens up a hole in the balance of trade. To

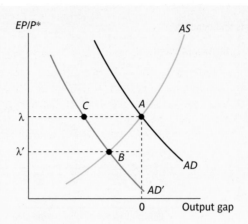

Figure 11.3 **An adverse demand shock**

re-establish its external balance, the country needs to make its exports cheaper. This calls for enhancing competitiveness. One solution would be for prices and wages to decline; but what if they do not? Chapter 10 makes the point that the exchange rate regime matters because prices and wages are sticky. In this case, a depreciation will do the trick if the country has its own currency. If, however, the country is part of a wider currency area, there is no alternative to lowering prices. From Chapter 9, we know that this requires that the economy slows down, deeply enough for long enough.

In order to examine the situation, we turn to the aggregate demand–aggregate supply diagram developed in Chapter 9, with one modification. World demand for our goods depends on their prices relative to those of competing goods. At the aggregate level, competitiveness is captured by the real exchange rate EP/P^*. This is why, in Fig. 11.3, the vertical axis represents the real exchange rate, denoted λ, rather than just the price level P. Starting from point A, where GDP is assumed to be on its trend, an adverse demand shock is represented by the leftward shift of the AD curve, from AD to AD'. If the nominal exchange rate is allowed to depreciate, or if prices are flexible, the short-run effect will be a shift from point A to point B: the real exchange rate depreciates from λ to λ'. This is a painful move, of course, but an unavoidable one given the adverse shock.

The outcome is more painful if the exchange rate is fixed and prices are rigid. In that case, the economy moves to point C, where the output decline is even deeper. At the unchanged real exchange rate λ, domestic producers continue to supply the output corresponding to point A, but point C represents the new, lower, demand. The distance AC represents unsold goods. Obviously, domestic firms will not accumulate unsold goods for ever. Something has to give and production will fall. The recession generates incentives to gradually cut prices, eventually bringing the economy to point B. But this is likely to be the outcome of a painful and protracted process.

The example illustrates why exchange rate fixity, when combined with sticky prices, makes an already bad situation worse. In a monetary union, instead of a simple once-and-for-all change in the nominal exchange rate, a real exchange rate adjustment can only come from changes in prices and wages. If prices and wages are sticky, the adjustment can take time, creating hardship along the way. Box 11.2 tells the story of Germany.

Box 11.2   Early pain for Germany

Germany joined the Eurozone in 1999 at an overvalued exchange rate. Figure 11.4, patterned after Fig. 11.3, shows the evolution of the German real exchange rate and output gap. For a while, until 2001, Germany benefited from a worldwide expansion. Once this expansion was over, it went through several years during which GDP remained below trend. This is when the magazine *The Economist* dubbed Germany 'the sick man in Europe'. With an inflation rate lower than in the rest of the Eurozone, Germany gradually recovered competitiveness until it was pronounced healthy again in 2007.

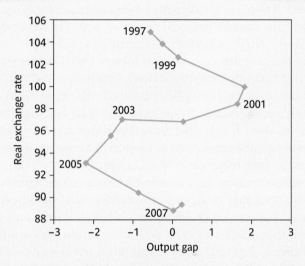

Figure 11.4 Germany: the real exchange rate and the output gap (1997–2008)
Note: The real exchange rate is the German price level relative to the average price level in the EU15 countries.
Source: AMECO, European Commission

11.1.3 Asymmetric shocks

So far we have thought of a country in isolation to set the stage for the study of the key insight from the OCA theory: diversity means that different countries face different shocks. The simplest case is a currency area with two member countries. We call these countries A and B and examine what difference it makes to share or not the same currency. Note carefully that country A has two (nominal and real) exchange rates: one vis-à-vis country B and one vis-à-vis the rest of the world. The same applies to country B, of course.

If countries A and B are hit by the same adverse shock, we know from the previous section that both have to undergo a real depreciation vis-à-vis the rest of the world. If they are similar enough, to a first approximation, there is no need for their bilateral (nominal and real) exchange rate vis-à-vis the rest of the world to change. They are in the same boat facing the same headwinds. The situation is very different, however, in the presence of an asymmetric shock. Assume, for instance, that country A is hit by an adverse shock, but not country B. Country A must now undergo a real depreciation vis-à-vis both country B and the rest of the world.

This reasoning shows that the loss of the exchange rate within a currency union is of no consequence as long as all member countries face the same shocks. In the presence of symmetric shocks, the union simply adjusts its common exchange rate vis-à-vis the rest of the world and its member countries are as well off as if they had each independently changed their own exchange rate.

With asymmetric shocks, however, monetary union membership becomes seriously constraining. What happens then? The situation is examined in Fig. 11.5. The vertical axis measures each country's real exchange rate vis-à-vis the rest of the world: EP_A/P^* and EP_B/P^*, where P_A and P_B are the price indices in country A and country B, respectively, P^* the price level in the rest of the world, and E is the common currency's exchange rate, initially equal to E_0. Points A in both panels represent the initially balanced situation, with the same real exchange rate λ_0 in both countries: $\lambda_0 = E_0/P_A/P^* = E_0/P_B/P^*$. Prices are assumed to be sticky – otherwise, the exchange rate regime does not matter, as we already know from Chapter 10.

Now let an adverse shock affect country A alone. This is represented in the left-hand chart, which describes country A, as the shift of the demand schedule from AD to AD'. If country A is not part of a monetary union and can change its own nominal exchange rate, its best course of action is to let it depreciate to E_1 such that the real exchange rate depreciates to $\lambda_1 = E_1/P_A/P^*$, which allows for a new equilibrium at point B. Country B has no reason to change its nominal and real exchange rates, which remain at E_0 and λ_0, respectively.

Things are very different when countries A and B belong to a monetary union. They cannot have different nominal exchange rates, as they would like to in this circumstance. The now-common central bank must make a choice on their behalf. If it cares only about country A, it depreciates the common exchange rate to E_1. With sticky prices, both countries must share the same real exchange rate λ_1. Figure 11.5 shows that this is not good for country B, which now faces a situation of potentially inflationary excess demand (represented by the distance $B'B''$). If the central bank favours country B, it will keep the common exchange rate unchanged. Both countries retain the initial real exchange rate λ_0, and stay at the initial point A. This suits well country B, which does not face any disturbance, but it means excess supply for country A

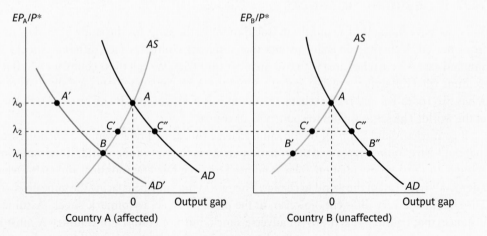

Figure 11.5 **An asymmetric shock in a currency union**

(represented by the distance $A'A$). Clearly, in the presence of an asymmetric shock, what suits one country hurts the other.

If the union's common external exchange rate floats freely, it will depreciate because of the adverse shock in one part of the area, but not all the way to E_1. It will decline to an intermediate level such as E_2, to which corresponds a real exchange rate $\lambda_2 = E_2/P_A/P* = E_2/P_B/P*$.[2] The outcome is a combination of excess supply in country A and excess demand in country B (both represented by $C'C''$). Both countries are in disequilibrium. The new exchange rate level is 'correct' on average, but it is too strong for country A, which is in recession, and too weak for country B, which is overheating.

This is the fundamental and unavoidable cost of forming a monetary union. The logic is very intuitive. With sticky prices, the nominal exchange rate is the only way of adjusting a country's competitiveness to changing conditions. If an asymmetric shock occurs, the common exchange rate cannot insulate all countries that belong to a monetary union.

Disequilibria cannot last for ever. Over time, prices are flexible and will do what they are expected to do. Consider the latest case, when the common exchange rate vis-à-vis the rest of the world is E_2. It has no reason to change any more since it has already done its job of taking into account the average situation in the union. Country A cannot sell all of its production, so its price level must eventually decline until the real exchange rate depreciates to λ_1 and country A will reach its equilibrium at point B. This will require a recession – remember, country A's goods are in excess supply – and unemployment will rise, putting downward pressure on prices. The price of country A's goods will decline until it reaches level P_A' such that $\lambda_1 = E_2 P_A'/P*$.

Country B is in the opposite situation: facing buoyant demand, the price of its goods will rise to P_B' such that its real exchange rate appreciates back to its equilibrium level, which is the original level $\lambda_0 = E_2 P_B'/P*$. Recession and disinflation in country A, boom and inflation in country B: these are the costs of operating a monetary union when an asymmetric shock occurs.

11.1.4 Symmetric shocks with asymmetric effects

The analysis has focused on asymmetric shocks, but it applies also to the case of symmetric shocks that produce asymmetric effects. There are many reasons why no two countries react in exactly the same way to the same shock. Their differing reactions may be due to their different socio-economic structures, including labour market regulations and traditions, the relative importance of industrial sectors, the role of the financial and banking sectors, the country's external indebtedness, the ability to strike agreements between firms, trade unions and the government, and so on. A good example is the case of a sudden increase in the price of oil and gas. This shock hurts oil- and gas-importing countries but benefits – or, at least, hurts less – oil- or gas-producing countries, such as the Netherlands, Norway and the UK. It is one reason why the two latter countries have not joined the European monetary union.

Another asymmetry concerns the way monetary policy operates. When a common central bank reacts to a symmetric shock, it is not a foregone conclusion that the effect of its action will be the same throughout the currency union. Differences in the structure of banking and financial markets or in the size of firms – and their ability to borrow – may result in asymmetric effects. Chapter 19 examines this aspect.

---

[2] Where exactly E_2 lies depends on a host of factors, such as the relative size of the two countries and how sensitive is their trade to changes in the real exchange rate.

When countries are sufficiently different, symmetric shocks can have asymmetric effects and the analysis carried out in the previous section fully applies. The situation is similar to the one described in Fig. 11.5. This is why, from here onwards, when reference is made to asymmetric shocks, it also includes the case of symmetric shocks with asymmetric effects.

11.2 The optimum currency area criteria

The key elements of analysis are now in place. We go back to Fig. 11.2. In Section 11.1.1, we have seen that sharing a common currency brings important benefits in the form of network externalities, the very reason why money is so convenient. In Section 11.1.3, we have seen how painful can be asymmetric shocks when different countries share the same currency. Whether or not to form a monetary union – or a currency area, as it is sometimes referred to – is a matter of trading off costs and benefits. As will soon be clear, there is no simple, black-and-white answer. The optimum currency area (OCA) theory takes the benefits as given and proposes criteria by which to judge the costs of sharing the same currency. A useful and succinct summary is provided in the British Chancellor of the Exchequer's assessment on UK membership:

> EMU membership could significantly raise UK output and lead to a lasting increase in jobs in the long term. As noted above, the assessment shows that intra-euro area trade has increased strongly in recent years as a result of EMU, perhaps by as much as 3 to 20 per cent; that the UK could enjoy a significant boost to trade with the euro area of up to 50 per cent over 30 years; and that UK national output could rise over a 30-year period by between 5 and 9 per cent.
>
> (*UK Membership and the Single Currency*, HM Treasury, London, June 2003, p. 222)

There are three classic economic criteria and an additional three which are political. The first criterion looks at a way of minimizing the costs of an asymmetric shock within a currency area. The next two economic criteria take a different approach: they aim at identifying which economic areas are likely to be hit by asymmetric shocks infrequently or moderately enough to be of limited concern. The last three criteria deal with political aspects; they ask whether different countries are likely to help each other when faced with asymmetric shocks. This section lists and explains the logic of the OCA criteria; Section 11.3 will examine whether they are satisfied in Europe.

11.2.1 Labour mobility (Mundell)

The first criterion was proposed by Robert Mundell (Box 11.3) when he first formulated the notion of an OCA. The idea is that the cost of sharing the same currency would be eliminated if the factors of production, capital and labour were fully mobile across borders. Since it is conventionally assumed that capital is mobile, the real hurdle comes from the lack of labour mobility.

Mundell criterion

Optimum currency areas are those within which people move easily.
The reasoning is illustrated in Fig. 11.6, which is based on Fig. 11.5. The adversely affected country A undergoes unemployment while non-affected country B faces inflationary pressure.

As shocks occur randomly, the country to pay out a transfer will be tomorrow's beneficiary. In effect, such transfers work like a common insurance against bad shocks.

Transfer criterion

Countries that agree to compensate each other for adverse shocks form an optimum currency area.

Transfer schemes of this kind exist across regions in every country. Sometimes they are explicit; most often they are implicit. For example, if a particular region suffers an asymmetric shock, then, as income declines, so do tax payments, while welfare support – chiefly unemployment benefits – rise. In the net, the region receives transfers from the rest of the country. These transfers are often implicit, part-and-parcel of the redistributive mechanism at work in the country. Some federal countries, such as Germany and Switzerland, operate explicit transfer systems.

11.2.5 Homogeneous preferences

Political conditions matter even for symmetric shocks. Section 11.1.2 shows that symmetric shocks do not pose any problem as long as each country reacts in the same way to the shock. But this result assumes that all countries agree on how to deal with each and every possible shock. In practice, however, there rarely exists a 'best way' to deal with a shock. For example, should we be more concerned about inflation or about unemployment? Should we favour the exporters – who wish to have weak exchange rates to buttress competitiveness – or the consumers – who wish to have strong exchange rates to raise their purchasing power? These are trade-offs, which generate the confrontation of opposing interests and are dealt with through the respective influence of political parties, trade unions and lobbies. There is no reason for the resulting decision to be the same across different countries because national preferences are not necessarily homogeneous.

If the currency area member countries do not share the same preferences over such trade-offs, each of them will want the common central bank to pursue different policies. Whatever the central bank chooses to do will be controversial and will leave some, possibly all, countries unhappy. At best, there will be resentment, at worst the currency union may not survive. Box 11.4 shows how this can play in practice. The collective preference, which shapes the policy response, thus intimately depends on domestic politics, and there is no reason for all the countries of a currency area to share the same balance of political forces. The fifth criterion states that these differences should not be too wide.

Homogeneity of preferences criterion

Currency union member countries must share a wide consensus on the way to deal with shocks.

11.2.6 Solidarity vs. nationalism

The final criterion goes deeper into political considerations. Since none of the previous criteria are likely to be fully satisfied, no currency area is ever optimum. This is even true for individual

Box 11.4   Will Italy and Portugal leave the Eurozone?

The left-hand chart in Fig. 11.7 shows that growth of per-capita GDP in Italy and Portugal has been slower than in the rest of the Eurozone since the common currency came into effect in 1999. One reason is that prices have risen faster, as shown in the left-hand chart, which displays the two countries' real exchange rate vis-à-vis the comparable EU15 countries. The 10 per cent real appreciation is likely to represent a significant loss in competitiveness.[1] There are many reasons for this evolution, but the main one seems to be important increases in wages, especially in the public sector. The implication is clear: in order to eliminate the overvaluation that holds growth back, both countries need to depreciate their exchange rates. Since they do not have exchange rates of their own, it can only be achieved through lower inflation than in the rest of the Eurozone. This, in turn, means a period of low growth, seen as an investment for a later resumption of faster growth, as happened in Germany, see Box 11.2. Meanwhile, the situation is unnerving citizens who may come to lament the lost ability of the quick fix of a nominal depreciation.

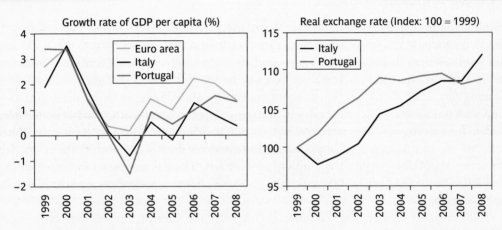

Figure 11.7 Italy and Portugal in the Euro area, 1999–2008
Source: AMECO, European Commission

It may not come as a surprise that, in June 2005, an Italian minister called for his country to leave the Eurozone and re-establish the lira. Most economists consider that such a move would be a disaster for Italy, which has never known as stable prices and low interest rates as those it has enjoyed since it adopted the euro. In addition, given its high public debt, Italy would face much-increased debt service costs if, as is nearly certain, its interest rate were to increase significantly after leaving the Eurozone. Yet some observers and financial market analysts have become quite jittery. Interestingly, the minister in question was in charge of labour markets; he might find it easier to reduce employment with an undervalued lira than through unpopular reforms. Of course, Italy's partners would not happily see one EU member play beggar-thy-neighbour inside the single market. So far, at least, no such rumour is affecting Portugal, which may have started to come to grips with overvaluation.

[1] 'Likely' because we need to remain alert to the possibility of a Balassa–Samuelson effect, as explained in Box 9.2. The fact that wage pressure originated in the public sector suggests that this may not be the case.

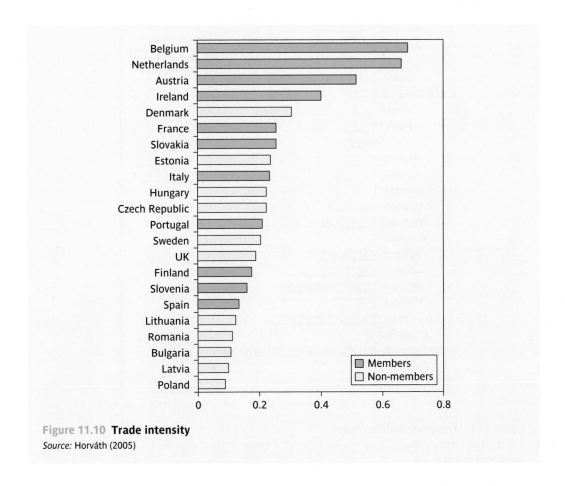

Figure 11.10 Trade intensity
Source: Horváth (2005)

As far as the McKinnon criterion is concerned, most EU economies qualify for joining a monetary union. They are very open and well integrated within Europe.

11.3.3 Diversification and trade dissimilarity

The Kenen criterion rests on the idea that asymmetric shocks are less likely among countries that share similar production patterns and whose trade is diversified. Fig. 11.11 presents an index of dissimilarity of European trade. The index looks at how each country's trade structure differs from the situation in Germany (old members) or the Eurozone (new members). The index is based on the decomposition of trade into three classes of goods: agriculture, minerals and manufacturing.

Dissimilarity is highest for Latvia and Denmark, two countries that have not joined the Eurozone, but it is also low for non-member countries such as the Czech Republic, the UK and Hungary. Of interest is the case of the Netherlands, a natural gas exporter that sets it apart and yet an enthusiastic member of the EMU. This case is a good illustration that the OCA criteria are not absolute, and that they focus on the costs of EMU membership, ignoring the economic and political benefits. The Dutch authorities believe that their economy is far too integrated

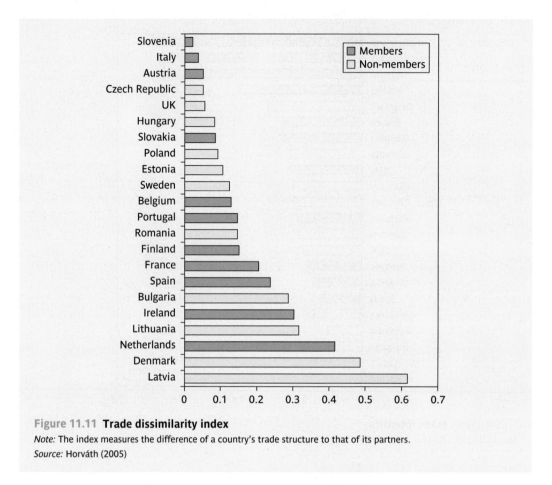

Figure 11.11 Trade dissimilarity index

Note: The index measures the difference of a country's trade structure to that of its partners.

Source: Horváth (2005)

with the European economy – a fact that Fig. 11.10 readily confirms – to afford exchange rate fluctuations and wish to be deeply involved in European integration.

11.3.4 Labour mobility

In principle, labour mobility is the key to dealing with asymmetric shocks in a currency area. To be effective, this criterion requires that workers promptly move in response to economic incentives. Here again, the criterion is a matter of degree. People always move, but full mobility is never to be seen. Full labour mobility occurs if people immediately take advantage of any difference in earnings, and move to where they can earn more. Moving, however, is a grave decision with significant risks and massive uncertainty. Migrants have to consider many issues, such as:

★ the cost of moving, possibly including the selling and buying of dwellings;

★ the prospect of becoming unemployed, both in the country of origin and in the country of immigration;

★ career opportunities, which means not only current but also future earnings;

★ family career prospects, including the spouse and children and sometimes even more distant relatives;

★ social benefits, including unemployment, health and retirement;

★ taxation of earnings from both labour and savings.

Labour mobility is also subject to non-economic incentives such as:

★ cultural differences (language, religion, traditions, possibly racism and xenophobia) in the country considered for immigration;

★ family and friendship links that can be weakened;

★ commitment to one's country of origin (nationalism).

For these reasons, labour mobility can only be relative and a natural approach is to proceed by comparison with existing, well-functioning currency areas, such as Canada and the USA. We first compare international migration. Figure 11.12 shows the percentage of the labour force

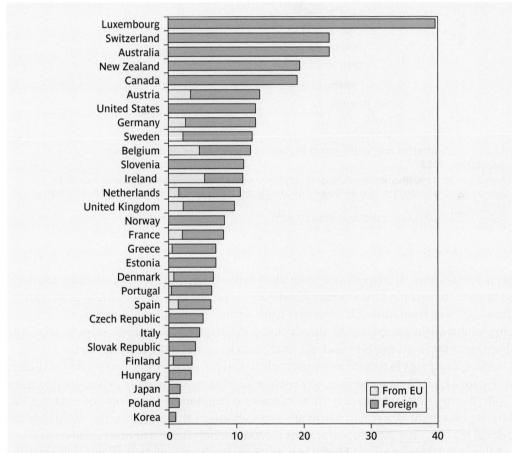

Figure 11.12 Foreign-born population as a percentage of total population, 2005

Notes: (1) For EU countries, when available, the figure shows the numbers of foreigners from other EU countries as a fraction of population; (2) Greece and Poland: 2000; (2) Estonia, Japan, Korea, Italy: foreign population instead of foreign-born population (includes locally born foreigners).

Sources: Factbook: Economic, Environmental and Social Statistics, OECD 2008 and European Union, *Economic Survey* 11, OECD 2007

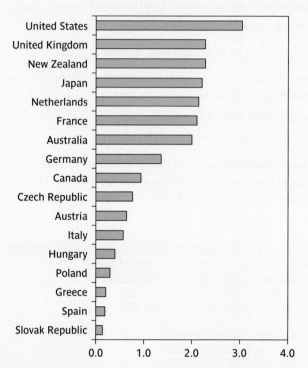

Figure 11.13 Internal migration across regions as a percentage of working-age population, 2003

Note: Migration is measured as the percentage of people who moved from one region to another in 2003, as a percentage of population aged 15 to 64. Data are not strictly comparable because the region sizes vary significantly across countries.

Source: Employment Outlook, OECD 2005, Chart 2.7, p. 89

that is foreign-born. It suggests two main observations. First, the EU countries are relatively less open to immigration than similar developed countries, Luxembourg being an exception. Second, citizens from other EU countries form a small proportion of immigrants, Belgium being a noteworthy exception. As already noted in Chapter 8, Europeans seem to take little advantage of the single market which allows them to work and settle anywhere in the EU.

In fact, Europeans in general move relatively less within their own country than US citizens do. Figure 11.13 displays the flow of people who migrated internally, when each country is spliced into several regions (e.g. three regions for Belgium or 12 regions for the UK). Yet, there are important disparities. There are also indications that Europeans move mainly for personal reasons, since professional reasons account for only 5 per cent of reported moves.

Why do Europeans move so little? There are many reasons, some obvious ones like language and traditions, others less well appreciated, such as the fact that housing tends to be more expensive in Europe than in the USA. Other reasons have to do with cracks in the integration process. For instance, moving across countries means switching from one welfare system to another, with serious difficulties regarding health and retirement benefits. In the USA, in contrast, no such difficulty arises when moving from one US state to another. Europeans, in any event, move relatively little within their own countries, where none of these barriers apply.

Low migration by European nationals could be compensated by immigration from outside the EU.[6] If immigrant workers were to move to where job offers exceed supply, some of the costs of a monetary union would be reduced. Even viewed this way, immigration – a big political issue in Europe – is relatively limited in Europe, as shown in Chapter 8.

In summary, Europe is far from fulfilling the labour mobility criterion. An important implication is that asymmetric shocks, when they occur, are likely to be met by unemployment in countries facing a loss of competitiveness. Box 11.6 reports that, indeed, when asymmetric shocks occur, migration plays a smaller role in Europe than in the USA, with the unfortunate result that employment takes most of the burden.

11.3.5 Fiscal transfers

Countries hit by a temporary adverse shock could receive transfers from better-off countries as compensation for having lost the exchange rate instrument for the common good. Within most countries, seen as currency areas, these transfers are automatic. When adversely hit, a region sees its income decline, at least relatively to the rest of the currency area, and tax payments by its residents decline. At the same time, various welfare payments (unemployment benefits, subsidies to poor people, etc.) rise. In good years, the opposite occurs and the favoured region supports less fortunate regions. In the USA, for instance, it has been estimated that any shortfall of income in a state is compensated by federal transfers that amount to between 10 and 40 per cent of the loss. There is no such system at work in the EU. The EU budget is small, slightly above 1 per cent of GDP, and almost entirely spent on three items: the Commission's operating expenses, the Common Agricultural Policy and the Structural Funds which support the poorer regions irrespective of whether they are hit by shocks. Any transfer system would need a significant increase in the EU budget, which is not likely in the near future.

On this criterion, Europe is definitely not an optimum monetary union.

11.3.6 Homogeneous preferences

Do all countries share similar views about the use of monetary policy? On the basis of past inflation rates, this does not seem to be the case. Low-inflation Germany and formerly

Box 11.6 **The effects of asymmetric shocks in Europe and the USA**

How does Europe's low labour mobility affect the response to an asymmetric shock? A study by Fatás (2000) compares Europe and the USA. Fatás looks at 51 regions in the USA (the 50 states and the District of Columbia) and at 54 regions in Europe (a decomposition of 14 countries, all EU countries with the exception of Luxembourg). He asks what happens when an adverse asymmetric shock occurs, i.e. when it affects just one region. Figure 11.14 shows the result. The figure depicts the joint

---

[6] See Chapter 8 for an analysis of immigration.

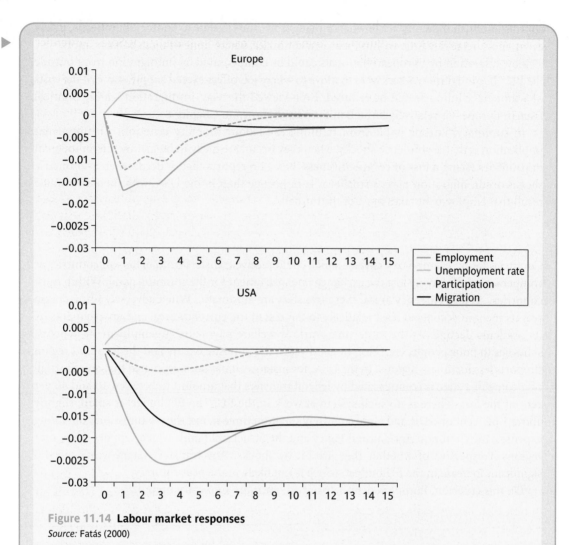

Figure 11.14 Labour market responses
Source: Fatás (2000)

behaviour of total employment, unemployment and the participation rate in each region (all compared with the overall situation in the USA and Europe, respectively).[1] Obviously, employment declines and, for the same shock size, the effect is quantitatively similar in Europe and in the USA. The difference lies elsewhere. In the USA, most of the drop in employment is met by regional emigration; people move to more fortunate parts of the country. In Europe, instead, most of the drop in employment is met by a fall in the participation rate; people withdraw from the labour force and stay at home. Interestingly, in the long run, in the USA those who leave do not return, and in Europe those who stop working remain inactive.

   This study corroborates a key element of OCA theory: labour mobility crucially affects the response to asymmetric shocks. The twist is that, with low European labour mobility, following an adverse shock, people become unemployed and many others simply give up the hope of working.

[1] Box 8.1 provides the definitions of employment, unemployment and participation rates.

by itself and ought to be related to fairness, solidarity and quality of life. Will monetary union change that?

One possibility is that the single currency increases the costs of the 'European way' and reduces opposition to measures that aim at flexing the labour markets. When each country had its own currency, workers were advocating using monetary policy and the exchange rate to boost the economy. This is now impossible, at least at the national level, and to date there are no pan-European trade unions. In addition, with prices set in euros across the Union, there is increasing transparency in goods markets, which should benefit countries where labour markets are more flexible. Thus, it is believed, economic competition will indirectly lead to competition among the welfare programmes and this will shift the trade-off between economic performance and labour protection. The opposite, a hardening of labour market rigidities, is possible as well. This possibility is based on increasing emphasis on a 'Social Europe'. Advocates of a high degree of labour protection well understand the risk of competition among the welfare programmes and they have successfully called for the adoption of Union-wide minimum standards.

There is no clear evidence yet where things are going. Figure 11.16 presents an index that evaluates the intensity of reforms in the labour markets of OECD countries. The period spans both pre- and post-euro years. Some Eurozone countries have taken important steps towards

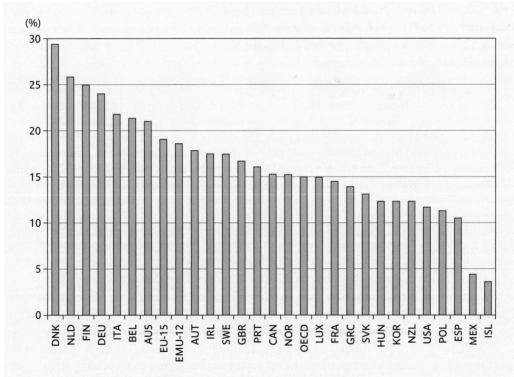

Figure 11.16 Intensity of labour market reforms over 1994–2004
Note: EU12 includes the initial Eurozone member countries *plus* Greece, EU15 the old EU member states.
Source: Duval and Elmeskov (2006)

reforming their labour markets, others not. On the other hand, on average, the Eurozone member countries do not outperform the non-Eurozone member countries.

11.4.4 Fiscal transfers

There is at present no political support for established extensive and automatic intra-European transfers, but proposals regularly surface. It has been suggested that a European tax could be established that could support a European unemployment benefit scheme, for example. Some limited funds are disbursed by the European Commission when a country is hard hit by a natural disaster. It is reasonably certain that, in the not-too-distant future, Europe will have adopted some form of transfer scheme.

11.4.5 Beyond the OCA criteria: politics

We have reached two important conclusions. First, Europe is not exactly an optimum currency area; it does well on some but not all of the criteria. Second, it is not just labour mobility that is insufficient but, more generally, the labour markets that display significant rigidity, especially in the large countries. In these countries, the monetary union may worsen an already painful situation of high unemployment.

It is natural therefore to ask why the European heads of state and governments who gathered in Maastricht in 1991 still decided to take the risk and set up a monetary union. The answer is: politics.[7] Interestingly enough, Harvard economist Martin Feldstein, a sharp critic of the single currency, sees it as a source of conflict:

> Political leaders in Europe seem to be prepared to ignore these adverse consequences because they see EMU as a way of furthering the political agenda of a federalist European political union. . . . The adverse economic effects of EMU and the broader political disagreements will nevertheless induce some countries to ask whether they have made a mistake in joining. Although a sovereign country could in principle withdraw from the EMU, the potential trade sanctions and other pressures on such a country are likely to make membership in EMU irreversible unless there is widespread economic dislocation in Europe or, more generally, a collapse of peaceful coexistence within Europe.
>
> (Feldstein, 1997, pp. 41–2)

In Feldstein's view, the EMU is not only unjustified on economic grounds (it is not an OCA) but its survival will require a major step towards a federal Europe, including common defence and foreign policies as well as a generalized harmonization of taxation and labour market regulations. Much the same view, that the EMU will trigger a bandwagon of pro-federal moves at the expense of the nation-states, was also harboured by former Prime Minister Margaret Thatcher, and underpinned her staunch opposition to the EMU. In every member country of the Union, a large number of people share this view and adamantly want to preserve the nation-state.

Indeed, political considerations have been paramount in launching the euro. It is fair to say that the political leaders who agreed on the monetary union did not think at all in terms of the

---

[7] For a detailed discussion, see the exchange between Feldstein and Wyplosz in the symposium published in the *Journal of Economic Perspectives*, 11(4): 3–42, 1997.

OCA theory (see Box 11.8). They were largely focusing on the symbolic nature of the undertaking. Precisely because money and statehood are intertwined, their intention was to move one step further in the direction of an 'ever-closer union'.

Box 11.8   The return of the OCA theory

The negotiators who prepared the Maastricht Treaty did not pay attention to the OCA theory. They were first and foremost heeding the impossible trinity principle, focusing on the need to preserve exchange rate stability in the wake of full capital movement liberalization. They were also concerned that the new currency should be as strong as the Deutschmark, hence the tough entry conditions detailed in Chapter 17. Overall they believed that, if the countries allowed into the monetary union had sufficiently converged, and if the new central bank was well protected from political interference, then the undertaking would work.

This view was at variance with many economists' opinion that the OCA criteria were more important and that due account should be paid to the difficulties that would inevitably arise because the Mundell criterion was not satisfied. The authorities are now rediscovering the importance of the OCA theory. In June 2005, for instance, the European Central Bank convened a conference – where both authors of this text were asked to present their views – which paid tribute to the OCA theory and its inventors. The picture shows the panel of the concluding session.

European Central Bank, 17 June 2005. Left to right: Charles Wyplosz, Adam Posen (IIE, Washington), Robert Mundell, Ronald McKinnon, Vitor Gaspar (Bank of Portugal) and Otmar Issing (Chief Economist of the ECB)

11.5 Summary

The OCA theory seeks to determine over what geographic area it is desirable to establish a single currency. The key insight is that the usefulness of money grows with the size of the area but that costs arise when the area becomes too diverse.

Diversity matters mostly because it is a source of asymmetric shocks. In the presence of price and wage rigidity, however, the exchange rate can be a powerful instrument to deal with shocks. This is why giving up the exchange rate can be costly. The OCA theory asks what characteristics may either reduce the incidence of asymmetric shocks or take the edge off asymmetric shocks.

The logic of OCA theory is summarized in Fig. 11.17. The first question is whether asymmetric shocks are likely to occur often enough, and strongly enough, to be a serious concern. If the answer is negative, the cost of adopting a common currency is low. The McKinnon and Kenen criteria provide the answer. The McKinnon criterion says that the exchange rate is of limited use if the countries are very open. The Kenen criterion concludes that countries that produce and trade a wide range of similar goods are unlikely frequently to face asymmetric shocks.

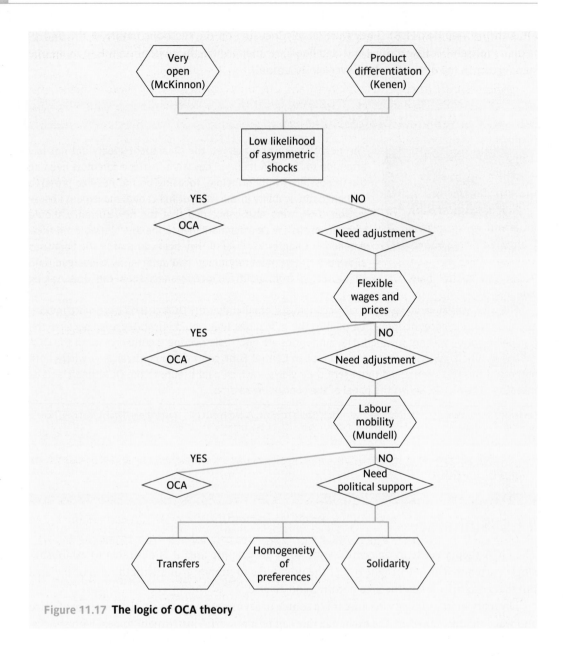

Figure 11.17 **The logic of OCA theory**

If these criteria are not well satisfied, asymmetric shocks should be expected and the next question is whether the area is well equipped to deal with them. The Mundell criterion says that, in the absence of wage and price flexibility, labour mobility provides a way of cushioning the impact of asymmetric shocks. In the absence of labour mobility, asymmetric shocks will be costly.

The next question is whether there is a way of compensating for these shocks. It takes us to the political criteria. An obvious compensation takes the form of financial transfers. Transfers offer an insurance mechanism; a country will receive transfers when adversely hit, and will support other member countries when they face a shock. These transfers can be automatic, via taxes and welfare payments, or explicit, based on formal sharing rules.

In the presence of asymmetric shocks, the common central bank will have to make hard choices. It must decide how it caters to the varied needs of individual member countries. This is bound to be a controversial decision, which can sap support for the currency area unless a common ground can be designed. Support for the central bank will be more likely if there is broad agreement on its aims, i.e. if policy preferences are reasonably homogeneous, and if there is a sense of solidarity across the currency area, i.e. if the costs are accepted because 'we are in the same boat'.

Fulfilment of the criteria is generally not black or white. It is unlikely, therefore, that several independent countries can be identified as forming an optimal currency area. In the end, some judgement must be passed on how to balance the important benefits of a common currency and the potentially severe costs of giving up national monetary policy. In addition, adopting a common currency may trigger changes that enhance the degree of satisfaction of the criteria. The degree to which the OCA criteria are satisfied could well be endogenous.

Europe does well on three criteria: openness, diversification and homogeneity of preferences. It does not pass the labour mobility and fiscal transfers conditions. A key question is whether the endogeneity assumption will become verified.

Self-assessment questions

1. Reconsider Fig. 11.5 when Country A is affected by a positive demand shock. Carefully interpret your results.

2. What happens in Fig. 11.5 if prices are perfectly flexible in Country A but rigid in Country B?

3. What happens in Fig. 11.5 if prices are perfectly flexible in Country B but rigid in Country A?

4. Imagine that wages are exogenously increased in Country A. Use Fig. 11.5 to explore the impact on a monetary union.

5. The labour mobility criterion implicitly assumes that the labour force is homogeneous, which is not the case as workers are most often specialized. How should this criterion be refined?

6. In Fig. 11.3 an adverse asymmetric shock is met by a depreciation. What does the size of the depreciation depend upon?

7. Trade increases among two countries can take two forms: each country becomes more specialized and therefore exports and imports different goods (e.g. France sells wine and Germany sells beer), or both countries compete more directly on similar goods (e.g. France and Germany sells cars to each other). How do these alternatives affect the OCA criteria?

8. The new Member States are likely to be affected by the Balassa–Samuelson effect presented in Chapter 9. What does this imply for their inflation rates once they join the Eurozone?

Essay questions

1. Could immigration be a solution to the labour immobility problem?

2. Can you imagine other regions in the world that could also adopt a common currency?

3. You are given the task of designing a transfer system to cope with asymmetric shocks within the Eurozone. Consider both how to collect and how to spend these resources.

4. 'Admission of the new Member States into the Eurozone is likely to increase the risk of asymmetric shocks.' Comment.

5. The UK Chancellor of the Exchequer has stated that the UK will join the EMU when five economic tests are passed. These five tests are:
   ★ Are business cycles and economic structures compatible so that we and others could live comfortably with euro interest rates on a permanent basis?
   ★ If problems emerge, is there sufficient flexibility to deal with them?
   ★ Would joining the EMU create better conditions for firms making long-term decisions to invest in the UK?
   ★ What impact would entry into the EMU have on the competitive position of the UK's financial services industry, particularly the City's wholesale markets?
   ★ In summary, will joining the EMU promote higher growth, stability and a lasting increase in jobs?

   Evaluate these tests.

6. Would the European Monetary Union benefit from British or Swedish membership?

7. Write a science fiction story: a severe asymmetric shock occurs and leads to such economic hardship that the European monetary union is dissolved. Carefully explain each step in the process.

8. Imagine that you are the Governor of the central bank of Poland (or Hungary, or the Czech Republic). Would you be for or against your country adopting the euro?

Further reading: the aficionado's corner

Is Europe an OCA?

In May 2003, the UK government undertook a study on EMU membership, in fact closely following the OCA criteria. This study represents an excellent way of putting to work the material presented in this chapter:

HM Treasury (2003) *UK Membership of the Single Currency*, HMSO, Norwich. Also available, with additional detailed studies, at www.hm-treasury.gov.uk.

A concise summary of the debates throughout Europe can be found in:

Wyplosz, C. (1997) 'EMU: why and how it might happen', *Journal of Economic Perspectives*, 11 (4): 3–22.

Chapter 12

The Common Agricultural Policy

There is a common misconception that the CAP is about helping small struggling farmers and looking after the European rural environment. But in reality the bulk of these funds end up in the pockets of the wealthiest farmers and processors while also doing enormous harm to developing countries.

Luis Morago, Head of Oxfam International in Brussels

In Europe the CAP has been so successful in achieving food security that consumers have come to take it for granted. But the EU has now dismantled almost every instrument that created this stability.

Pekka PESONEN, Secretary General of COPA-COGECA (EU farm lobby)

Chapter contents

12.1	The old simple logic: price supports	355
12.2	Changed circumstances and CAP problems	359
12.3	The new economic logic of CAP	366
12.4	CAP reform	369
12.5	Today's CAP	371
12.6	Remaining problems	374
12.7	Summary	377

Introduction

The Common Agricultural Policy (CAP) is a set of policies aimed at raising farm incomes in the EU. The CAP is problematic. It accounts for almost half the EU budget but farmers continue to leave the land. It accounts for many of the quarrels among EU members and between the EU and third nations, yet it is extremely difficult to reform. Given all these problems and its dominant role in the budget, a good understanding of the CAP is essential to the study of European integration. This chapter presents the essential elements and economics of the CAP.

Today's CAP is a massively complex matrix of policies, but it was not always that way.

The CAP started life in 1962 as a straightforward policy of keeping agricultural prices high and stable. This simple policy had unintended consequences that created huge problems and triggered a reform process that has been going on since the early 1980s. The need and general direction of this reform has been obvious from the beginning, but because farming is so politically sensitive in so many members, reform has been piecemeal and very, very slow. That is why the CAP is so complex. What we see today is not a well-designed policy aimed at achieving well-thought-out objectives. It is a snapshot of an ongoing adjustment process.

The radical transformation of European agriculture goes a long way to explaining why this process is so politically painful and slow. Figure 12.1 shows a three horse ploughing team in St Justin, near Montreuil. Such a world required a great deal more farm workers than today's world of tractors and high-tech production methods. This technological progress – combined with the fact that Europeans do not really eat much more food than they used to – means that numbers in the farm sector have been falling steadily for decades. To a large extent the CAP has been a programme aimed at buffering the worst pain of this inevitable downsizing. As the agricultural sector changes, so too must the CAP.

The CAP is a policy that is in the politically painful process of moving from one simple economic logic to another simple economic logic. This suggests that the best way to understand the CAP is to study the CAP's original simple economic logic before discussing the unintended problems that are driving EU leaders to reform the CAP towards its new simple economic logic.

Once we have these analytic organizing frameworks in place, we consider the details of the CAP's policy instruments and commodity regimes.

Figure 12.1 French farming in the 1950's
Source: Fox Photos/Getty

12.1 The old simple logic: price supports

The simple economic logic of the early CAP was to establish a price floor. This was enforced by a tariff, and when necessary, direct purchases. The EU set price floors for many major farm products, including grains, dairy products, beef, veal and sugar. For most of the CAP's existence, these prices were between 50 and 100 per cent higher than world prices, and even higher than this for dairy products and sugar.

These price floors were enforced by guaranteed, unlimited purchase by CAP authorities at the price floor, but such purchases were only the last resort. In the early days of the CAP, the EU was a net importer of most farm products, so it could ensure that supply and demand matched at high prices by manipulating the amount of foreign food that entered the EU market. The manipulation was done with import tariffs, so the best way to understand the early CAP is with a standard open-economy supply and demand diagram of the type we considered in Chapter 4.

12.1.1 Basic price-floor diagram for a net importer

The economics of the tariffs used to raise EU food prices above the price floor are quite similar to the standard tariff analysis presented in Chapter 4. For convenience, we briefly repeat the analysis here – pointing out the minor differences as we go (the presentation in Chapter 4 provides much more detail and explanation).

The goal of these CAP tariffs – called 'variable levies' in CAP jargon since they changed daily according to world market conditions – was to ensure that imports never pushed EU prices below the price floor.

The left-hand panel of Fig. 12.2 helps us to analyse the impact of such a price floor in cases where it is set above the world price (P_w) but below the level where the EU would import no

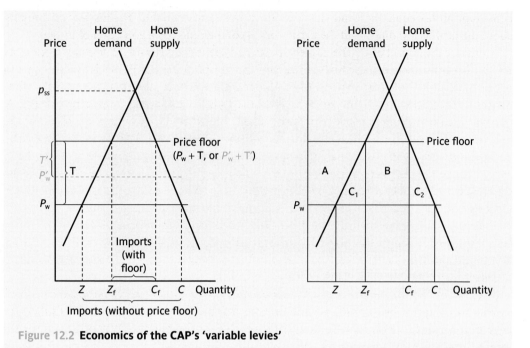

Figure 12.2 **Economics of the CAP's 'variable levies'**

food (in agricultural economics, this level is called the point of 'self-sufficiency', so we mark the level as p_{ss} in the diagram). As we saw in Chapter 4, the domestic price ends up as the world price plus the tariff. No one in the EU would pay more than $P_w + T$, and the inability of domestic producers to make enough food to satisfy the demand at $P_w + T$ means that EU farmers would never have to accept a price lower than $P_w + T$, so the EU price becomes $P_w + T$. At this price, all domestic production (equal to Z_f) is sold at the price floor. Domestic consumption is C_f and the difference between consumption and production equals the level of imports. The subscript 'f' indicates 'floor'.

What is the economic impact of having a price floor above the world price?

★ The higher price induces EU farmers to produce more (Z_f instead of Z).

★ The higher price is to discourage food consumption (C_f instead of C).

★ The EU consumption reduction and production increase move the EU towards self-sufficiency in food.

★ Since the price floor is enforced by a variable tariff, the EU receives tariff revenue equal to the area B in the right-hand panel.

The food tax and subsidy interpretation

To get at the economic fundamentals of the CAP's impact and to help understand the politics of CAP reform, it is useful to recast the economics of the tariff. As it turns out, any tariff can be thought of as an all-in-one package consisting of (i) free trade in the presence of (ii) a consumption tax equal to T and (iii) a production subsidy equal to T. This way of thinking about the tariff is less direct, but the extra work is compensated by a good deal of insight.

Consider the impact of the free trade with tax and production subsidy. The consumption tax means that consumers pay the world price plus the consumption tax T (this is exactly equal to the price floor in the left-hand panel of the diagram). EU producers sell at the world price but they also receive the production subsidy T (i.e. they sell all output at the world price but they also get a payment from the government equal to T for each unit of output they sell); thus the price they actually receive is $P_w + T$, which is just equal to the price floor. So far, so good. The tax-and-subsidy means that consumers and producers see the same price as with the tariff and so consume and produce exactly the same amounts (C_f and Z_f); as imports are just the difference between EU consumption and production, the level of imports is also exactly the same with the tax-and-subsidies package. What about the revenue implications?

The revenue from the consumption tax is the level of consumption C_f times the tax T; the cost of the production subsidy payment to farmers is production Z_f times T. What this means is that the government's receipt net of its payments is equal to $(C_f - Z_f) \times T$. This is exactly equal to revenue collected under the CAP tariff (area B).

This way of looking at the price floor is insightful since it makes it quite plain that consumers are the ones who pay for a price floor enforced with a variable levy. Part of what they pay goes to domestic farmers (area A), part of it goes to the EU budget (area B) and part is wasted (areas C_1 and C_2). This interpretation is important when we think about the distributional impact of price floors in more detail.

Aggregate welfare effects

The overall welfare effects of the tariff are familiar from Chapter 4. The right-hand panel of Fig. 12.2 recaps the analysis. The higher price ($P_w + T$ instead of P_w) means that consumer surplus falls by $A + C_1 + B + C_2$. The first part of this, $A + C_1 + B$, reflects the higher cost that consumers pay for the food they continue to consume. The second part, C_2, is what they lose from the tariff-induced drop in consumption. For producers, the gain in producer surplus is equal to area A. We can think of this impact on producers as consisting of the impact of getting a higher price for the amount they would have produced without the tariff plus the gain in producer surplus from the higher sales.

The diagram leaves out one effect that is important in the real world. Since the EU would be a large importer of food under free trade, the tariffs tend to lower the world price. This effect, not shown in the diagram for the sake of simplicity, counts as a welfare improvement for the EU. (The *MD–MS* diagram in Chapter 4 can be used to show the impact of a tariff on the world price.)

The variable levy (i.e. tariff)

Price instability is a key feature of food markets, so we also need to consider what happens when the world price changes to, say, P_w'. In this case, maintaining its price floor requires the EU to apply a lower tariff. Specifically, the tariff must be lowered to T' so that the new world price (P_w') plus the new tariff (T') equals the old price floor. The levels of EU production, consumption and imports are held constant. The only thing that varies in this simple example is the tariff.

12.1.2 Farm size, efficiency and distribution of farmer benefits

The overall welfare analysis that lumps all EU farms together is useful for some things, but it hides a very important effect of price floors – the distribution of benefits among farms. This fact is at the heart of one of the problems that continues to plague today's CAP, so it is worth studying its basic economic logic in a simple setting.

Anyone who has done much travelling in Europe realizes that a 'farm' means very different things in different places. A wheat farm in the Paris Basin and a farm on a small Greek island, for example, are very dissimilar. On the Parisian plain, farms tend to be very large and very, very high tech. They use expensive, high-yield, disease-resistant seeds to boost their 'yield' (food produced per hectare), they apply large quantities of pesticides to control bugs, large quantities of chemical fertilizers to maintain the soil's fertility, and they use massive, labour-saving machines to plant, tend and harvest. In the Greek islands, farms are smaller and less efficient. As we shall see, these differences have important implications for the distribution of gains from price floors.

The logic is best illustrated with the help of Fig. 12.3. To keep things simple, suppose there are only two farms in the EU, one large and one small. The small-farm supply curve is shown in the left-hand panel, that of the large farm in the middle panel, and the total supply curve in the right-hand panel. Note that the small farm's supply curve is above the large farm's supply curve, reflecting the large farm's greater efficiency. (Remember from Chapter 4 that the supply curve shows marginal cost, so a higher supply curve means that the small farm has higher marginal cost at any level of output.)

The world price is marked as P_w. Note that at this price only the large farm would produce anything. The small farm would stop farming with free trade since the price would be below its marginal cost of producing even a small amount. With the price floor at $P_w + T$, however, both farms produce. Specifically, the small farm produces Z_{small} and the large farm produces Z_{big}. Total output is just the sum of the two.

From Fig. 12.3 we see that the producer surplus generated by the price floor is quite unevenly distributed. The small, low-technology, high-cost family farm earns only A_{small}, while

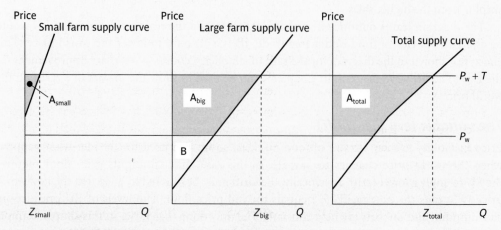

Figure 12.3 **Distribution of gains, big and small farms**

the large, modern industrial farm earns A_{big}. This should be intuitively obvious. Since a price floor helps producers in proportion to their production, big producers will benefit more from the policy.

How is this connected with income levels? The benefit from owning a farm is the producer surplus it yields, so the income generated by the small farm is A_{small} and the income for owners of the large farm is $A_{big}+ B$, since B measures the producer surplus that the large farm would have without the price floor. Plainly, the owners of big farms tend to be richer than the owners of small farms. This is the main point. Price floors help all farmers but most of the gains go to large farmers who tend to be richer; after all, they own larger farms.

This uneven-distribution point is critical – the key to many of the CAP's paradoxes – so it is worth presenting it from another angle. Few readers will be familiar with modern farming, but everyone has been to a food store. Box 12.1 presents an analogy by considering what would happen if CAP-like policies were used to support the owners of European food stores.

Box 12.1   An analogy with hypothetical support for food stores

In most European nations, there are many, many food stores, but food sales are dominated by huge supermarket chains. Simplifying to make the point, we can think of there being two types of stores: small, family-run stores and hypermarkets. The small stores are much more numerous, but since many people do their main food shopping at hypermarkets, the total sales of the many small stores is only a fraction of the hypermarkets' sales. To be concrete, suppose that the hypermarkets account for only 20 per cent of the total number of stores, but account for 80 per cent of the sales. Now suppose that small, family-owned stores experienced severe problems and that the EU decided to support them. However, instead of subsidizing only the small stores, the EU decides to subsidize the sales of *all* food stores. Plainly, 80 per cent of the subsidies would go to the hypermarkets that did not need them. Once the hypermarkets got used to the billions, you can bet that they would engage in some pretty fierce politicking to hold on to the money. Moreover, the public might support the policy in the belief that the funds are helping the millions of small, family-owned stores.

In summary, the distributional consequences of using price floors to support the EU farm sector are quite regressive:

★ The benefits of price supports go mainly to the largest EU farms because large farms produce a lot (and the support is tied to the level of production) and because large farms tend to be more efficient (so their costs are lower). Since the owners of large farms tend to be rich, the benefits of a price floor are systematically biased in favour of large, rich farmers.

★ Since price floors are paid for by consumers (they are the ones that have to pay the higher price), and food tends to be more important in the budget of poor families than it is in the budget of rich families, price floors are in essence paid for by a regressive consumption tax.

12.2 Changed circumstances and CAP problems

In its first few years of life, the CAP was a politician's dream. The price floors provided higher and stable prices to farmers, so they were happy. They also substantially raised food production and this, at the time, was viewed as a good thing, reducing EU dependence on imported food.

Higher farm incomes suited the EU's goal of fostering 'social cohesion' between rural and urban Europe. The variable tariffs even generated revenue for the EU budget. The only ones who might have objected were European consumers, since they paid for the policy via higher prices. As it turned out, consumers were also happy about the CAP:

* Average incomes in the 1950s and 1960s rose rapidly – much faster than food prices – so the share of people's income spent on food actually fell, although not as fast as it would have without the CAP.

* During the Second World War and its aftermath, food was in short supply and rationed in most European nations. The memory of this – and the hunger that came with it – was still fresh in people's minds in the early 1960s. More food and lower dependence on food imports seemed like good ideas to most Europeans.

* Consumers had a great deal of empathy with farmers. As is still the case today, most Europeans viewed agriculture as a form of economic activity unlike others.

The CAP's 'honeymoon', however, was soon to end.

12.2.1 The 'green' revolution

The post-war period saw revolutionary advances in the application of science to agriculture. Crops and farm animals were selectively bred to boost yields. A whole agro-chemical industry sprang up, producing pesticides to control insects, herbicides to control weeds and chemical fertilizers to boost soil fertility. Huge planting and harvesting machines were developed to save labour. Strange as it may seem today, this chemical-, energy- and machine-intensive technology was known as the 'green revolution'.

Since the CAP rewarded output, EU farmers – especially those with large farms – switched to these new, more intensive farming methods. The result was impressive. EU farm production rose rapidly – so much so that the EU swung from a net importer to a net exporter in most farm products.

In most sectors, this sort of rapid productivity growth would be a cause for celebration. In European agriculture, it was called the 'supply problem'. Other European sectors that have experienced rapid technological progress – e.g. telecoms – saw rapid price falls as the efficiency gains were passed on to consumers. The political power of the EU farm lobby, however, was strong enough to prevent this. EU food prices continued to be fixed far above the world price.

Cascade of unintended consequences

This combination of high, fixed prices and rapid technological progress created a whole cascade of unintended consequences. To understand these, we study the impact of a price floor in the presence of a positive supply shock. Figure 12.4 shows the situation. Technological improvements shifted the supply curve down (recall that the supply curve is marginal cost, so cost-lowering technology shifts the whole curve downwards; see Chapter 4).

Before the supply shift, the EU was a food importer and the price floor worked as in Fig. 12.2. After the shift, the EU supply curve is S_2 with the price floor in place, so the EU has surplus food production; production level Z' exceeds the consumption level, C. Since the EU is no longer a food importer, the price floor cannot be maintained with a tariff. The EU actually has to purchase the surplus food (i.e. Z' minus C). In fact, this is exactly what the CAP was doing in the late 1970s and 1980s. This supply problem set off a cascade of problems.

The budget problem

The immediate difficulty was budgetary. Instead of earning money by imposing tariffs, the EU had to dole out large sums from its budget to buy the 'excess' food. The CAP came into operation in 1962 and did not incur a positive expenditure until 1965. After this, however, its cost and share of the budget started to grow exponentially, rising from 8 per cent in 1965 to 80 per cent in 1969 (Fig. 12.5). Fights over how to pay for these hindered EU cooperation through the 1970s and early 1980s.

The disposal problem: wheat, beef and butter mountains

Apart from the cost of buying all this food, the EU faced the problem of what to do with it.

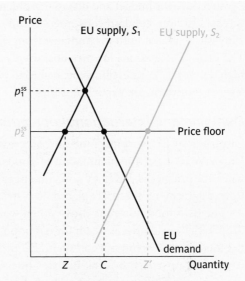

Figure 12.4 **The green revolution and price floors: EU becomes an exporter**

When the food 'surpluses' first appeared, the EU viewed them as temporary. The main solution was to store the food, hoping that market prices would rise above the price floor. This was not to be. High and stable prices teamed with steady technological progress made investment in agriculture very attractive. The supply curve continued to shift out, so the EU had to continue buying food. The EU found itself the owner of what the media called 'wheat, beef and butter mountains'. In 1985, the EU had 18.5 million tonnes of cereals stored, about 70 kilos for each of its citizens. Much of this rotted, causing a major public relations problem (it looks bad to pay high prices for food and then allow it to rot).

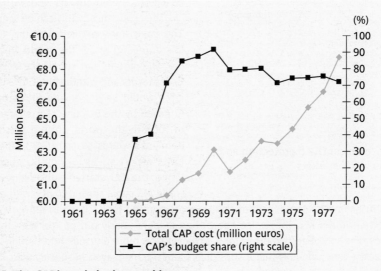

Figure 12.5 **The CAP's early budget problem**

To reduce the budget and disposal problems, the EU sold the food at subsidized prices. Some was sold to non-standard consumers within the EU. For example, a sixth of the wheat crop in 1969 was rendered unfit for human consumption and sold as animal feed at a subsidized price. The major destinations for the subsidized sales were foreign markets. This practice of buying high domestically and selling cheap abroad is called 'dumping', although the EU jargon for it is 'export restitution' or 'export subsidies'.

Dumping and international objections

Disposing of EU 'surplus' food abroad created the next problem – a foreign trade problem. Under WTO rules for manufactured goods, dumping is normally not permitted, especially when the practice is driven by government export subsidies. However, before the 1994 Uruguay Round agreement, the WTO placed no restrictions on the dumping of agricultural goods.

The EU's food dumping drove down world food prices. As we saw in Chapters 4 and 5, a drop in the world price is a gain for net importers but a loss for net exporters. While the world's net food importers did not complain, EU dumping infuriated the world's large food exporters: Argentina, Australia, Bolivia, Brazil, Chile, Colombia, Costa Rica, Guatemala, New Zealand, Paraguay, the Philippines, South Africa, Thailand, Uruguay, Canada and – most importantly – the USA. (See Box 12.2 for details.)

Box 12.2 Economics of the CAP's impact on world food markets

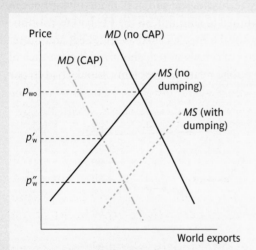

Figure 12.6 **Impact of CAP protection and dumping on world markets**

Even in the early days, the CAP's price floor policy harmed other nations. By shutting off EU markets to the exports of non-members, the CAP reduced the world price of food as well as reduced the volume of non-members' exports. As the EU's food surplus grew, and the EU started to subsidize its exports, non-members were further harmed.

The economics of this can be seen in Fig. 12.6. The solid lines marked *MD* (*no CAP*) and *MS* (*no dumping*) show the world import demand (i.e. *MD*) and import supply (i.e. *MS*) without the CAP's tariffs and without the CAP's dumping. The price would be p_{wo}. In the first stage, the tariff imposed by the EU, one of the largest importers of food in the world, shifted the world import demand inwards to *MD* (*CAP*). This resulted in lower export prices for non-EU members (to p'_w). When the EU started subsidizing exports, the world *MS* curve shifted to *MS* (*with dumping*).

Many countries impose some form of import protection on food, so while the CAP's tariffs were harmful to the world market, they were not viewed as particularly out of line with the rest of the world's practice. The subsidized export of food, however, was more unusual. Additionally, the USA and the EU were, at the time, the only major subsidizers and often engaged in subsidy wars.

Although there are few EU farmers – less than 5 per cent of the population even back in the 1970s (around 4 per cent now in the EU15; 6 per cent for the EU27 overall) – their political power was, and still is, enormous. Large commercial farmers have become used to the extra millions that the high prices brought them.[1] Just think about the numbers involved. The EU 2007–13 budget package, which was agreed by EU leaders in a stormy December 2005 summit, spends €330 billion on payments to farmers and on keeping farm prices high. There are only 12.6 million people working in the farm sector. If the money were divided evenly, that would be about €26 000 per person – certainly something worth fighting for. The money, however, is not distributed evenly. Most of the money goes to farm owners, with most of it going to the largest farm owners. For example, in 2006, the EU25 paid €33.1 billion to 7.3 million farmland owners, with about 70 per cent of the money going to just 10 per cent of these (the ones with the largest landholdings). For these large landowners, the CAP is a gold mine. Just as real gold mine owners hire armed guards to protect their investment, large farmland owners are willing to spend millions on politicking that guards their virtual gold mine – the CAP.[2]

Moreover, farmers had invested heavily in restructuring their farms to focus on the goods most heavily supported by the CAP. Small farmers earned much less from the CAP but, without the higher prices, many would be driven out of farming altogether. In a nutshell, the CAP meant loads of cash for the happy few (large farms) but it was a matter of survival for the 80 per cent of EU farmers with small operations. In addition to the cold-hearted political logic of cash, part of the farmers' disproportionate power stems from the warm-hearted feeling that the average European has towards the sector; opinion polls show that most EU citizens approve of CAP spending in general.

The farm sector's political strength meant that it was impossible to just eliminate the price floor. EU leaders had to 'bribe' the farmers into allowing them to undertake CAP reform that was good for the EU as a whole. This was done by linking the lowering or elimination of price floors to compensation payments paid directly to farmland owners. The direct payment amounts per farm were more or less linked to the amount of money each farm got under the old price-support system. To break the link between the payments and overproduction, the payments were 'decoupled', i.e. the size of the payment was not related to the amount currently produced – it was set according to historical production levels. (Note to non-native English readers: decouple is the verb one uses when a railroad car is disconnected from the train engine.)

12.3.1 Price floor liberalization and decoupled payments: the economics

This is the new simple economic logic that the CAP is heading for – market-determined prices with direct payments to farmers that are not related to production levels. Before turning to the actual reform, we study the basic economics driving the direction of the reform, namely the

---

[1] It is important to note that the EU's special treatment of farmers was not unusual. In the early 1990s, the EU's generosity was only in the middle of the OECD pack. OECD (2004) reports that the subsidy equivalent per EU farmer was $13 000, less than half the amount for EFTA members (Sweden, Switzerland, Norway, Finland and Austria) and about equal with that of the USA and Japan.

[2] See http://ec.europa.eu/agriculture/fin/directaid/2006/annex1_en.pdf for details.

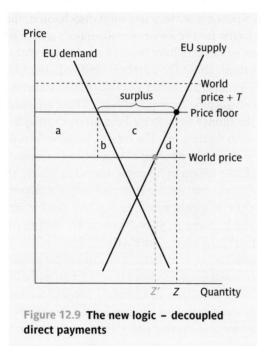

Figure 12.9 The new logic – decoupled direct payments

economics of switching from a price support system to market-determined prices with direct payments to compensate farmers for the price reduction.

Figure 12.9 considers a product, such as wheat, where the EU is a net exporter even without the CAP price floor. To keep things simple, we assume that in the pre-reform situation all the surplus food was dumped on the world market. The cost of this is the difference between the price floor (the price paid by the EU when it buys excess food) and the world price (the price the EU gets when it sells on the world market) times the surplus, namely the area b + c + d.[3] Observe that the EU still needs high tariffs to make the price floor work. Although no imports come into the EU with the tariff shown, they would if the tariff were removed. Every farmer in the world would like to sell at the EU's price floor instead of the world price; to reserve the higher price only for EU producers, the world price plus the EU tariff must exceed the price floor.

The decoupling reform lowers the price faced by EU farmers and consumers from the price floor to the world price. EU production falls from Z to Z' and consumption rises.

EU consumers gain from the lower prices by the area a + b (this is the consumer surplus gain; see Chapter 4 if you are unfamiliar with this concept). EU farmers lose the producer surplus equal to area a + b + c, and the EU budget saves b + c + d. Overall, the reform is welfare improving since the net gain is area d + b, i.e. (a + b) plus (b + c + d) minus (a + b + c).

If the farmers are to be fully compensated, the direct payments must equal a + b + c. Since this may well be larger than the cost of dumping the surplus, this policy reform is unlikely to reduce the cost of the CAP.

Notice that this reform solves most of the CAP's problems: the disposal problem, the dumping problem and the over-intensification of farming problem. The surplus disappears, so there is no disposal problem and thus no need to dump food on world markets. Overproduction is no longer being stimulated by the CAP, so, although the industrialization of EU farming may persist, it cannot be blamed on EU farm policy. Moreover, the EU's actual decoupling policy has linked the payments to greater respect for the environment and animal welfare, so the switch improves the environmental impact of EU farming.

The only problems not fixed by decouple-with-compensation reform are the budget problems and the farm income problem.

---

[3] In practice, it is not the EU that does this; the EU pays private companies – mostly multinational agro-commodity firms – to buy high in the EU and sell low on the world market. For example, the sugar multinational Tate & Lyle receives hundreds of millions of euros a year to dump EU sugar abroad.

Having laid out the basic economics of this new system, we turn to a brief discussion of the decades of reform that have moved the CAP gradually from the pure price-support system of Fig. 12.2 to the decouple-with-compensation system of Fig. 12.9.

12.4 CAP reform

Up to the mid-1980s, the primary way of dealing with higher CAP costs was to increase the contribution from the members. This changed when Spain and Portugal joined in 1986 and the politics in the Council of Ministers shifted importantly.

The CAP did little to help Spanish and Portuguese farmers since their climates prevented them from producing the goods that the CAP supported the most, i.e. dairy, sugar, wheat, rice and beef. The newcomers, who were reluctant to see their national contributions to the budget rise year after year in order to subsidize the production of rich Northern European farmers, teamed up with the two incumbent poor nations (Ireland and Greece) to shift EU spending priorities towards 'structural spending' in poor nations (see Chapter 3 for further details). One option would have been to expand the EU budget to pay for the extra structural spending, but the EU net contributors (especially Germany, Denmark and the UK) opposed this.

12.4.1 Ad hoc supply control attempts

This situation posed a reform dilemma; lowering farm prices faced a political roadblock, but buying all the excess food was too expensive. The EU's first reaction was to try to work around the problem, dealing with the surplus situation without fundamentally changing the price-floor system. As European Commission (1994) puts it, the 1983 to 1991 period were 'years of experimentation' with supply controls.

The CAP during this period became fantastically complex. Fortunately, most of these experiments have been dropped, so most students of European integration have no need to study their details. What is important is the outcome of these new policies. The CAP's share of the budget began to fall to meet the new political imperative of spending more of the EU budget on poor members and regions.

These ad hoc supply control policies, however, failed to address the supply problem. The wheat and butter mountains continued to grow along with subsidized exports, and, despite this, average farm incomes continued to fall relative to the EU-wide average.

12.4.2 The MacSharry reforms

The first really big reform was driven by pressure from the EU's trade partners who were fed up with seeing the market for their exports ruined by export subsidies (the USA also subsidized its exports). The issue came into sharp relief when the global trade talks, known as the Uruguay Round, failed in December 1991 when the EU refused to commit to phasing out its export subsidies and open its agriculture markets.

Since these global trade talks were viewed as vital to European exporters of goods, services and intellectual property, Europe's highest-powered exporters started to push for CAP reform. The political power of poor regions who wanted to use the money and European exporters who wanted the Uruguay Round to succeed was sufficient to get a major reform accepted by the Council of Ministers.

The resulting reform package (the MacSharry reforms) put the CAP on the road to the economic logic of Fig. 12.9. All subsequent reforms to date have followed its main outlines. (See Box 12.4.)

Box 12.4   The MacSharry reform

Late in 1986, the world embarked on a set of trade talks (called the Uruguay Round) that were supposed to end in four years. One of the explicit goals was to reduce protectionist farm policies such as those of the USA, the EU and Japan. While earlier world trade talks had repeatedly failed to tackle the issue, the situation in the 1980s was quite different. In particular, instead of opposing agricultural liberalization as it had done in the past, the USA backed liberalization in the Uruguay Round. Moreover, a group of food-exporting countries – called the Cairns Group – steadfastly refused any agreement that did not include important farm trade liberalization. Throughout the talks, the EU declined to agree to any substantial liberalization. When the 'final' meeting came in December 1990, the EU's refusal to liberalize led to a walk-out by the Cairns Group.

This crisis threatened the whole future of the world trading system – an outcome that most EU exporters could not accept (over 80 per cent of EU exports involve industrial goods). EU governments began to face very serious pressure from their own industrialists and export-oriented service sectors. In the end, this pressure was sufficient to force a reform of the CAP that was substantial enough to allow a Uruguay Round agreement that was acceptable to the Cairns Group. The reform package, which was called the MacSharry reforms after the EU Farm Commissioner responsible for it, was adopted in mid-1992. The Uruguay Round deal was struck 18 months later.

The main thrust of the MacSharry reforms was to cut the price floors to near-world prices. To make these acceptable to politically powerful farmers, the MacSharry reforms 'compensated' farmers with cash payments. Thus the MacSharry reforms did not substantially lower the cost of the CAP. What it did was shift the nature of the payments. Before, most of the money went on buying and then disposing of excess food. After, most of the money was handed over directly to farmers.

Another part of the MacSharry reform that continued the CAP's long history of unbelievable-but-true features was that it paid farmers to not grow food. Specifically, to get the direct payment, farmers had to agree to reduce the area they planted by 15 per cent. Similar linkages were created to foster pro-environmental and animal-welfare measures. For example, farmers received a premium per animal for keeping the number of cattle per hectare below specified limits.

Note that the politically powerful milk and sugar sectors were not reformed in 1992.

How much money did each farmer get? Since the idea of these so-called compensatory payments was to offset farmers' income losses, big productive farms got big payments and small farms got small payments. Importantly, the payments were not made to particular farmers; they were tied to the land. This detail had two significant implications:

1   The money was paid to the owner of the farmland regardless of whether the owner was a farmer or not. (This is why the CAP continues to pay money directly to Queen Elizabeth II even today.)

2   The money was only paid if the land was farmed, so the payments were still coupled to production indirectly. This detail meant that some marginal farmland was kept in production in order to collect the compensation cheque.

There have been two major CAP reforms since the MacSharry package, which pushed the basic MacSharry logic even further. Both involved further price cuts that were compensated by direct payments to landowners. The first came at the March 1999 meeting of the European Council in Berlin. The prime driver of this reform was the need to get the CAP ready for Eastern enlargement and to prepare the CAP for a falling budget share in the 2000 to 2006 Financial Perspective.

The second came in 2003. The driving force was the current WTO trade talks (the so-called Doha Development Agenda). Developing countries were reluctant to start new WTO talks and were only convinced when the EU members and other rich nations promised in November 2001 to liberalize agricultural markets as part of the Doha Round. With the crucial midterm meeting of ministers scheduled for September 2003 in Cancun, Mexico, the EU had to come up with a reform of the CAP that would allow it to fulfil its liberalization pledge. The Cancun meeting ended in failure. Although there is plenty of blame to go round, many observers believe that the meagre liberalization contained in the CAP reform was at least one major reason for the failure. The 2003 reform has been followed up by a series of sector-specific reforms in recent years.

12.5 Today's CAP

Today's CAP has two pillars. The first concerns direct payments and the cost of the remaining price supports. The second is called 'Rural Development'. We address the first pillar first.

12.5.1 CAP's first pillar

With the 2003 reform of the CAP – a reform process that is being phased in slowly (delayed up to 2014 in some sectors) – the CAP continues to approach the simple economic logic of Fig. 12.9. The backbone of the system is the 'Single Payment Scheme', or SPS as it is known in EU literature (sometimes SFP for Single Farm Payment). To explain how it works, consider an example provided by this extract from the 22 September 2003 article by Peter Hetherington in *The Guardian* (a leading British newspaper):

> The harvest has been good for Oliver Walston and many other farmers. . . . With 2000 acres (800 hectares) of prime arable land at Thriplow, near Cambridge, Mr Walston runs a medium-sized undertaking . . . Mr Walston volunteers that he gets around £165,000 annually in subsidies . . .

Since the 2003 reforms were phased in from 2005 to 2007, Farmer Walston is talking about the old system set up by the MacSharry reforms.

Under the old system, Farmer Walston's payment was linked to his historical production of particular products, say wheat. To get the £165 000 (about €230 000), he had to continue growing wheat. In this sense, payments were only partially decoupled; payment was linked to growing wheat, but the size of this year's payment was not related to the amount of wheat grown this year.

Under the new system, the Single Payments Scheme, he would get the £165 000 regardless of what he grows – he need not continue to grow wheat to get the cash. This completes the decoupling of CAP payments and production. There are exceptions, as always with the CAP, many of which sound a bit fanciful to non-specialists. (For example, farmers receiving the new Single Farm Payment can produce any commodity on their land except fruit and vegetables and table potatoes.)

The size of the single payment is based on historical payments in the old EU15. There are two methods of determining the historical payment; either it is the average amount the particular farm received in the period 2000 to 2002 (historical model) or it is based on the number of hectares farmed during the first year of the scheme and the average payment for the region (regional model). Member States choose which to apply. Since the new Member States (central and eastern European nations) entered the CAP only upon accession in 2004, they hand out money per hectare, with the amount limited by national ceilings that were agreed in their Accession Treaties.

Cross-compliance

To get the single payment, farmers are supposed to comply with the EU and national rules governing the CAP's environmental impact, European food safety and animal welfare. Importantly, these requirements were already in place. The idea is that tying the cash to compliance makes it more likely that farmers will obey the existing laws.

The rules to comply with are complex and vary somewhat from nation to nation. There are two basic categories:

1 'Good agricultural and environmental conditions'. For the UK, the first category includes things such as: soil protection, post-harvest land management, waterlogged soil, crop residue burning, overgrazing and unsuitable supplementary feeding, heather and grass burning, stone walls, protection of hedgerows and watercourses, etc.

2 'Statutory management requirements'. These include rules on: wild birds, groundwater, sewage sludge, nitrate vulnerable zones, pig identification and registration, restrictions on the use of plant protection products, restrictions on the use of substances having 'hormonal or thyrostatic action and beta-agonist' in farm animals, control of foot-and-mouth disease, certain animal diseases and bluetongue, welfare of calves, etc.

Exceptions

The political resistance to the 2003 Reform was vicious (see Box 12.5). Some Members States insisted on maintaining the link between the payment and the crop produced for some crops. Moreover, the most powerful lobby, sugar, escaped reform altogether. Political pressure also dampened reform in many sectors, such as wine, durum wheat, protein crops, rice, nuts, energy crops, starch potatoes, milk and milk products, seeds, cotton, tobacco, fruit and vegetables, and olive groves. Since 2003, most of these sectors have had to adopt reforms leading to decoupling. For example, the EU lost a WTO case against its sugar policy and was forced to reform that sector or face retaliation. That led to a reform in 2006, which goes some way towards reducing the CAP-induced waste and a long way to reducing the EU's need to dump sugar on the world market. Reform of the fruit and vegetables sector came in 2007, and for the wine sector in 2008.

Box 12.5 Name-calling and national positions

Since the CAP pays millions of euros to Europe's large, rich farmers and these farmers are extremely well organized politically, any change in the CAP is politically difficult. In particular, former French President Jacques Chirac has always counted on the political support of French farmers. He could not help but view CAP reform as a threat to his personal political base.

When it comes to direct payments based on hectares, one euro of payment ends up having a minimal impact on the earning of farm household labour. Since the payments are tied to the land, it is the land price that soaks up most of the subsidy. This is not a problem for farmers who owned their land before the area payments were instituted, but about 40 per cent of EU farmland is not owned by the people who farm it.

The OECD calculates that about 45 cents of every euro of direct payment benefits non-farming landowners instead of farmers. The other major CAP policy – market price support – does even worse. Farmers get only 48 cents on the euro, with 38 cents going to real resource costs and input supplies.

12.7 Summary

The CAP started in the 1960s as a way of guaranteeing EU farmers high and stable prices. Because agricultural technology advanced rapidly, and because the high prices encouraged farm investment, EU food production rose rapidly, much faster than EU food demand. As a consequence, the EU switched from being an importer of food to being an exporter of food. This change meant that supporting prices required much more than keeping cheaper foreign food out with high tariffs. The EU began to purchase massive amounts of food – an operation that became very expensive, consuming over 80 per cent of the EU's budget in the 1970s. Since the EU had no use for the food it bought, it disposed of the surplus by storing it or dumping it on the world market. The former was expensive and wasteful; the latter had serious international repercussions since it tended to ruin world markets for farmers outside the EU.

A combination of budget constraints and pressure from EU trade partners forced a major reform of the CAP in the 1990s, the so-called MacSharry reform. This reform lowered the guaranteed prices, and thus reduced the amount of food the EU had to buy, but it compensated farmers for the price-cut by providing them with direct payments. This type of price-cut-and-compensate reform was carried further by the so-called Agenda 2000 reforms and the June 2003 reforms.

The economic impact of the CAP is quite unusual at first glance. Despite high prices and massive subsidies, the EU farming population continues to decline because CAP support is distributed in an extraordinarily unequal way. The largest farms, which are typically owned by rich citizens or corporations, receive most of the money, while the small farms get very little. In short, CAP payments to most EU farms are too small to prevent many farmers from quitting. Yet, despite the small size of most payments, the total cost of the CAP is huge because payments to big farms are big. The MacSharry and Agenda 2000 reforms did little to change this because the direct payments are related to farm size.

The CAP was seriously reformed in 2003 with a trail of related reforms in 2005, 2006 and 2007. These moved the CAP a long way from a price-support system to an income-support system with market-determined prices. This has solved many of the trade conflicts that arose from the EU's dumping and it has eliminated the food mountains. The CAP, however, still has problems as most of the money still goes to rich landowners. Future reforms seem quite likely, but nothing important will be done before the end of the current Financial Perspective in 2013.

One likely direction will be to largely nationalize the CAP. For example, most of the CAP spending could be done by turning over the CAP payments to Member States. In this way, the French taxpayers would be free to continue handing millions to large landowners and multinationals without upsetting poor Polish farmers. In the terminology of Chapter 3, the CAP is a classic situation where local information and a lack of scale economies make national decision making the superior choice.

Self-assessment questions

1. In 2003, the world wheat price is above the CAP's target price so the price floor has become a price ceiling. (i) Using a diagram like Fig. 12.2, show how the EU could implement the price ceiling with an export tax. (ii) What are the effects of this in the EU and in the rest of the world (prices, quantities and welfare)?

2. Some developing nations accuse the EU of using technical standards for food (pesticide content, etc.) as a barrier to trade. Suppose they are correct. Use diagrams to show how you would analyse the impact of such protection on EU and RoW welfare. (Hint: See Chapter 4's analysis of 'frictional' barriers.)

3. Before the UK adopted the CAP, it supported its farmers with a system of 'deficiency payments', which is the agro-jargon for production subsidies. Using a diagram like Fig. 12.2, analyse this policy assuming that the import of food was duty free, but the government directly paid farmers the difference between the market price and a target price for each unit of food they produced. Be sure to consider the implications for world prices, UK production and UK imports as well as the welfare implications for UK farmers, consumers and taxpayers.

4. Suppose that the EU allowed free trade in food and subsidized production on small farms only. Analyse the price, quantity and welfare implications of this policy using a diagram.

5. The text mentions that since direct payments are tied to the land, it is the land price that soaks up most of the subsidy. Use a classic supply and demand diagram to demonstrate this result. (Hint: This is a standard exercise in what is known as the 'incidence of a tax' since a subsidy is just a negative tax.)

6. The European Commission has proposed putting an upper limit on the total direct payment per farm of approximately €300 000. What would be the impact of this on prices, output and the distribution of farm incomes?

Essay questions

1. Compare the EU's agricultural policy to that of the USA. The EU's policy is based on price support plus direct payments. Does the USA have the same system? Which policy provides a higher level of support to farmers? (Hint: The US Department of Agriculture has an excellent website, and the OECD annually publishes a comparison of farm policies.)

2. What sort of CAP reforms are proposed by environmental groups in Europe? Choose one group's policy recommendations and discuss its implications for the overall level of support to the farm sector, its distribution among farmers and its implications for world food markets.

3. Select a particular European nation and investigate the political influence of its farmers. In particular, identify the main farm lobby group(s) and show how they put pressure on politicians to continue the high level of support.

4. What is the overall impact of the EU's CAP on farmers in developing nations (Hint: The IMF published a study on this issue in its September 2002 *World Economic Outlook*.)

5. Using the theory of fiscal federalism presented in Chapter 2, can you argue that agricultural policy should be set at the EU level?

Further reading: the aficionado's corner

A wide-ranging and accessible consideration of the CAP can be found in: **Hathaway, K. and D. Hathaway** (eds), *Searching for Common Ground. European Union Enlargement and Agricultural Policy*, FAO, Rome.

Other useful works are those by **ERS** (1999), **EU Court of Auditors** (2000), **European Commission** (1994a, 1994b, 1999), **Farmer** (2007), **Halverson** (1987), **Milward** (1992), **Moehler** (1997), **Molle** (1997), **Nevin** (1990), **Swinnen** (2002) and **Zobbe** (2001).

Useful websites

For a non-institutional view of the CAP, and a series of readable and informative essays, see http://members.tripod.com/~WynGrant/WynGrantCAPpage.html.

The Commission's website http://europa.eu.int/comm/agriculture/ provides a wealth of data and analysis, although much of it is politically constrained to be fairly pro-CAP. The US government's Agricultural Department provides even more analysis and tends to be more openly critical of the CAP; the pages of the Economic Research Service are especially informative. See www.ers.usda.gov/briefing/EuropeanUnion/PolicyCommon.htm.

Every year, the OECD publishes an excellent report on the agricultural policy of all OECD members (this includes the CAP). For the latest figures and exhaustive analysis, see www.oecd.org.

References

DG-Ag (2006) 'Annex 1: Indicative figures on the distribution of aid, by size-class of aid, received in the context of direct aid paid to the producers according to Council Regulation (Ec) No 1259/1999 and Council Regulation (Ec) No 1782/2003 (Financial Year 2006)'. Download from http://ec.europa.eu/agriculture/fin/directaid/2006/annex2_en.pdf.

DG-Ag (2007) 'Situation and prospects for EU agriculture and rural areas', Note to file. Download from http://ec.europa.eu/agriculture/analysis/markets/prospects12_2007_en.pdf.

ERS (1999) *The EU's CAP: Pressures for Change*, US Department of Agriculture Economic Research Service, International Agriculture and Trade Reports, WRS-99 – 2. Download from www.ers.usda.gov/publications/wrs992/wrs992.pdf.

EU Court of Auditors (2000) *Greening the CAP*, Special Report No. 14/2000.

European Commission (1994) (1994a) (1994b) *EC Agricultural Policy for the 21st Century*, European Economy, Reports and Studies, No. 4.

European Commission (1999) *Agriculture, Environment, Rural Development: Facts and Figures – A Challenge for Agriculture*, DG Agriculture. Download from http://europa.eu.int/comm/agriculture/envir/report/en/.

Farmer, M. (2007) *The Possible Impacts of Cross Compliance on Farm Costs and Competitiveness*, Institute for European Environmental Policy, 21, January.

Halverson, D. (1987) *Factory Farming: The Experiment That Failed*, Animal Welfare Institute, London.

IMF (2002) *World Economic Outlook*, September. Download from www.imf.org.

JNCC (2002) *Environmental Effects of the Common Agricultural Policy and Possible Mitigation Measures*, Report prepared for the Department for Environment, Food and Rural Affairs by the Joint Nature Conservation Committee. Download from www.jncc.gov.uk.

Milward, A. (1992) *The European Rescue of the Nation-state*, University of California Press, Berkeley.

Moehler, R. (1997) 'The role of agriculture in the economy and society', in K. Hathaway and D. Hathaway (eds) *Searching for Common Ground: European Union Enlargement and Agricultural Policy*, FAO, Rome, www.fao.org/docrep/W7440E/w7440e00.htm.

Molle, W. (1997) *The Economics of European Integration*, Ashgate, London.

Nevin, E. (1990) *The Economics of Europe*, Macmillan, London.

OECD (2003) *Farm Household Income: Issues and Policy Responses*, Paris.

OECD (2004) *Analysis of the 2003 CAP Reform*, Paris.

Oxfam (2002) 'Stop the dumping', Oxfam Briefing Paper 31. Download from www.oxfam.org.uk/resources/policy/trade/downloads/bp31_dumping.pdf.

Swinnen, J. (2002) *Towards a Sustainable European Agricultural Policy for the 21st Century*, CEPS Task Force Report No. 42, Brussels.

Zobbe, H. (2001) *The Economic and Historical Foundation of the Common Agricultural Policy in Europe*, Working paper, Royal Veterinary and Agricultural University, Copenhagen. Download from www.flec.kvl.dk/kok/ore-seminar/zobbe.pdf.

Chapter 13

Location effects, economic geography and regional policy

. . . the Community shall aim at reducing disparities between the levels of development of the various regions and the backwardness of the least favoured regions or islands, including rural areas.

Treaty Establishing the European Community, 1958

Chapter contents

13.1   Europe's economic geography: the facts   382
13.2   Theory part I: comparative advantage   390
13.3   Theory part II: agglomeration and the new economic geography   393
13.4   Theory part III: putting it all together   402
13.5   EU regional policy   405
13.6   Empirical evidence   412
13.7   Summary   412

Introduction

When deeper European economic integration took off in the 1950s, rural Europe was really poor. Electricity and telephones were far from standard in rural households and many were without indoor plumbing. Europe as a whole was booming, but cities and a few industrial regions were leaving rural Europe behind. The EU's founders made a concern for rural Europe one of the key goals of European integration. As the 2004 and 2007 enlargements added large swaths of poor rural areas to the EU, helping Europe's rural communities remains a touchstone of today's EU.

This chapter looks at the facts, theory and policy connecting European integration to the location of economic activity in Europe.

13.1 Europe's economic geography: the facts

Regional incomes in the EU follow a clear pattern. Rich regions are located close to one another and form the 'core' of the EU economy. Poor regions tend to be geographically peripheral. (See Combes and Overman, 2004, for more detail.) These points are clear in Fig. 13.1. This shows a map of Europe's night-time light pollution. Since light pollution lines up very closely with economic activity at this scale, we can think of this as showing the spatial distribution of economic activity. The 'heart of Europe' is clearly made up of western Germany, the Benelux nations, north-eastern France and south-eastern England. This region contains only one-seventh of the EU's land but a third of its population and half its economic activity. It is the economic centre of Europe. Roughly speaking, the concentration of economic activity drops as one moves away from the core, although the map shows that there is also a massive concentration of economic activity in northern Italy and various hot spots in Iberian and Nordic regions.

The map also serves to make an important point about nations and regions. The focus of our analysis in the earlier chapters has been on nations' economies and the integration of nations. Looking at Fig. 13.1, it is not hard to see that national borders are not really the best way to think about economic activity in Europe. In short, regions matter.

Although distance is continuous, when we discuss the economics below we frequently refer to the 'core' and the 'periphery'. An important link between the spatial spread of economic

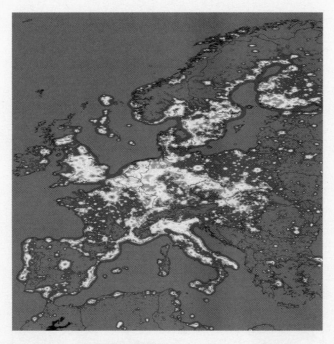

Figure 13.1 Europe at night – light 'pollution'
Source: P. Cinzano, F. Falchi (University of Padova), C.D. Elvidge (NOAA National Geophysical Data Center, Boulder). Copyright Royal Astronomical Society. Reproduced from the Monthly Notices of the RAS by permission of Blackwell Science (www.lightpollution.it/dmsp/)

activity (and thus of regional inequality) concerns the accessibility of each region to other markets – accessibility defined as the ease of shipping goods. In the EU, core regions have good access to EU markets while peripheral regions do not. This is an abstraction from the rich reality of Europe, but Fig. 13.2 gives a rough idea of these terms. The criteria for this categorization are the regions' accessibility to markets (by lorry). The idea behind this is that the peripheral regions are remote in the sense that it is costly to sell goods to the main EU markets. While this is a long way from perfect, and certainly not the only way to define peripherality, the results line up with most experts' idea of Europe's core and periphery regions (Fig. 13.2).

13.1.1 Why does peripherality matter?

Why should anyone care about the location of economic activity? There are, after all, very few people in northern Finland. Why is it a problem that there is also very little economic activity there? For reasons we discuss below, incomes tend to be lower for people living in the periphery regions – although, as always, there are exceptions, especially around key but remote cities such as Rome, Madrid, Dublin, Edinburgh, Stockholm and Helsinki (see Fig. 13.3). Note that:

★ Most regions in the 12 new members have incomes that are below those of the EU15 nations. The differences are stark. The poorest region in the EU27 is Romania's north-east,

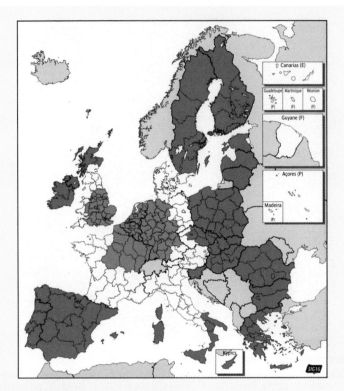

Figure 13.2 **Europe's core and periphery regions**
Source: Adapted from Schürmann and Talaat 2000

which has a per-capita income that is 24 per cent of the EU27 average while the figure for the richest region, Inner London, is 303 per cent.

★ Apart from the western-most and southern-most parts of the Continent, none of the EU15 regions have incomes below 75 per cent of the EU27 average. Although it is not shown on the map, the northern extremes of the Continent would also have very low incomes if it were not for the colossal income transfers and special programmes undertaken by Sweden and Finland. One of the most striking things about the map is how regional incomes seem to fall with the region's distance from the 'heart of Europe'.

The wide disparity in income levels is a problem from a social point of view, but it is also a problem from the political perspective. Large income gaps between regions foster bitter political disputes that can hinder cooperation on things such as European integration. Giving the poorer regions hope that they will catch up is an important role for the EU's regional policies.

The disadvantages of the poor regions range much further than low incomes. Many standard indicators of social misfortune suggest that many of Europe's poor regions have many problems. For instance, the poor regions also often have higher levels of youth unemployment, long-term unemployment and lower levels of investment and education.

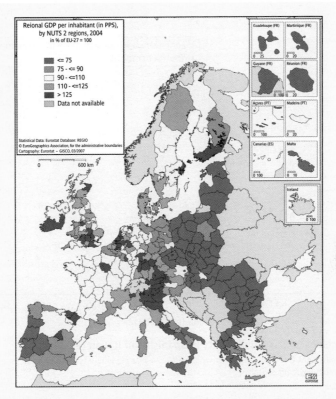

Figure 13.3 Income disparity in the EU

Note: Regional GDP per capita adjusted for prices (PPS) for 2004.

Source: European Communities 1995–2009

This point is illustrated for the regions of Italy and Spain in Fig. 13.4, which plots each region's income on the horizontal axis and the unemployment figures on the vertical axis. The incomes are measured relative to the EU27 average since we take the EU27 to equal 100; regions with low numbers are poor relative to the EU average. What the figure shows is that poor regions tend to have more problems with long-term unemployment and youth unemployment. Although the connection is far from perfect, it helps illustrate that the problems of Europe's remote regions concern more than money.

Note that the regions in the new members are different in many ways from those in the old EU15. The new member regions are almost universally dynamic, with fast-rising incomes, employment and productivity. Much of this is simply a quick catch-up to the investment and technology standards of western Europe. The poor/remote regions of the old members tend to be areas that have suffered prolonged decline in output, investment and populations as people and industry headed for the cities.

Much more detail on the state of the EU's economic and social cohesion can be found in the Cohesion reports and annual updates (http://europa.eu.int/comm/regional_policy/). This includes downloadable data at the regional level and statistical mapping software.

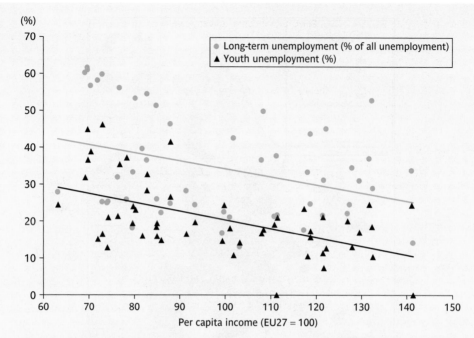

Figure 13.4 Incomes and social disparity in Spanish and Italian regions

Note: Youth unemployment is unemployment among the 15–24-year-old labour force; long-term employment is as a share of regional unemployment overall.

Source: European Communities 1995–2009

13.1.2 Evolution over time: narrower national differences, wider regional differences

While the dispersion of income levels across nations is still very high, the gaps among EU members have been steadily narrowing, as Fig. 13.5 shows. The EU15 members have on average seen a significant convergence of their incomes to the EU15 average (shown in each year as EU15 = 100). Note that Sweden, Finland and Austria only joined in 1995, but had participated in much of the economic integration with the EU even before they joined (see Chapter 1). The real success stories are Spain, Portugal, Greece and, above all, Ireland, which went from one of the poorest to the second richest Member State. The obvious exception to the convergence story is Luxembourg, which started above average and continued to diverge. The fact that it is a net recipient of EU funds (see Chapter 3) has little to do with this performance; most of it is due to the Grand Duchy's development of a highly lucrative financial service sector based in part on its low taxes and banking secrecy.

The convergence of the new Member States is also clear in the chart, although the process has been gradual and their membership in 2004 did not lead to any visible jump.

Divergence within nations

The convergence across nations, however, hides an important trend. Income inequality across regions within each EU nation has been rising steadily. We can see this clearly by taking the example of the UK. The left-hand map in Fig. 13.6 shows the distribution of per-capita income

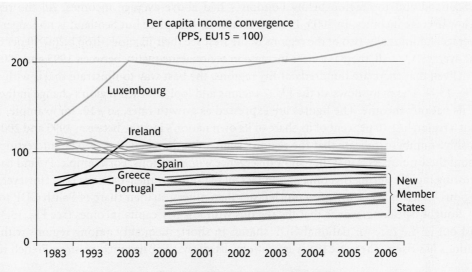

Figure 13.5 Income convergence among old EU members, 1983–2006
Source: Eurostat Yearbook (various years), and First Convergence Report
(http://ec.europa.eu/economy_finance/publications/specpub_list9259.htm)

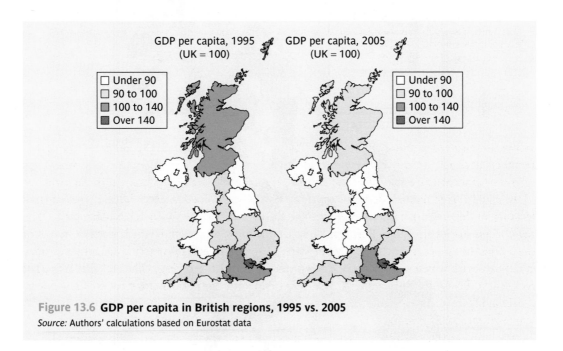

Figure 13.6 GDP per capita in British regions, 1995 vs. 2005
Source: Authors' calculations based on Eurostat data

in 1995, region by region. The right-hand map shows the same for 2005. To ease comparison between 1995 and 2005, we look at each region's per-capita income compared to the UK average. Thus a region with a per-capita income equal to 100 is just at the UK average, while those with figures below 100 have below-average incomes. In 1995, Greater London was the only region with more than 140 (i.e. more than 40 per cent above the UK average). Two other regions

– Scotland and the region below London – had above-average incomes. All the rest had below-average incomes. In 2005, London retains its first place but Scotland is no longer above average. Additionally, two of the regions in the west see their incomes drop below 90 per cent of the average. Overall, there is a clear increase in regional inequality between 1995 and 2005.

Given that there are hundreds of EU regions, the best way to illustrate this is with a map (Fig. 13.7). The map shows all the EU27 regions and looks at each region's change in the share of its nation's income. The figures are expressed as growth rates, so −10, for example, means that a region lost 10 per cent of its share of its own nation's income between 1995 and 2004. The positive numbers indicate that the region's share of national GDP rose. The interesting thing about these numbers is that they show divergence *within* nations. For example, Poland has been growing rapidly during this time and in fact all regions saw their incomes rise. However, some regions – such as Warsaw – grew much faster than others, so their share of Polish GDP rose.

Roughly speaking, we see that the regions with low per-capita incomes (see Fig. 13.3) have lost out in the race for national GDP shares. In short, inequality among regions within EU nations has risen. There are many exceptions, as always. For instance, western French regions

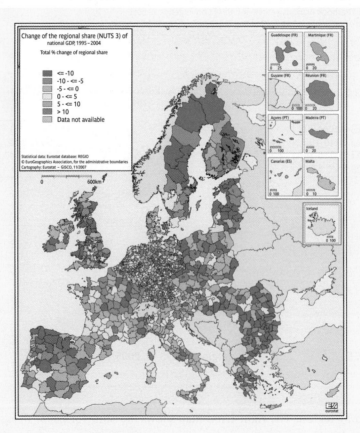

Figure 13.7 **Divergence within nations**
Source: DG Regio

have seen their GDP shares rise, as have some of the poorer parts of southern Italy, but even in equalitarian Sweden, the northern regions have shrunk relative to the rest of the nation.

13.1.3 Integration and production specialization

The evidence presented up to this point suggests that European economic integration has had only a modest impact on the location of economic activity as a whole, with the many changes occurring within nations rather than across nations. Lumping together all economic activity (i.e. measuring activity by total GDP), however, may hide changes in the composition of economic activity within each nation or region. European integration may have encouraged a clustering of manufacturing by sector rather than by region. To explore this possibility, we look at regions' and nations' industrial structures and their evolution. We focus on industry since it is difficult to get comparable data on services.

Figures for European nations

Using a particular measure of specialization – called the Krugman specialization index – we look at how different the industrial structures are in various European nations and how they have evolved. The Krugman index tells us what fraction of manufacturing activity would have to change sector in order to make the particular nation's sector-shares line up with the sector-shares of the average of all other EU15 nations.

The indices for the EU27 are shown in Table 13.1. Since almost all the changes are positive, we conclude that the industrial structures of most nations are diverging from the average EU

Table 13.1 Specialization by nations, 1980 to 1997

	1980–83 (%)	1988–91 (%)	1994–97 (%)
Ireland	62	66	78
Greece	58	66	70
Finland	51	53	59
Denmark	55	59	59
Portugal	48	59	57
Netherlands	57	55	52
Sweden	39	40	50
Belgium	35	38	45
Italy	35	36	44
Germany	31	35	37
Austria	28	28	35
Spain	29	33	34
UK	19	22	21
France	19	21	20
EU15 average (weighted)	30	33	35

Source: Midelfart-Knarvik and Overman 2002

industrial structure. In other words, taking the EU average as our standard, most European nations experienced an increase in the extent to which they specialized in the various manufacturing sectors. The only major exception is that of Spain, whose industrial structure became substantially more similar to the EU average over this period.

How important is this increase in specialization? To take one example, Ireland's index in 1970–73 was 70 per cent, which means that 35 per cent of total production would have to change sector to bring it into line with the rest of the EU. Ireland's index had increased by 8 per cent by 1997, so by 1997, 38 per cent of Ireland's manufacturing would have to change sector to get in line with the EU average. For most EU nations, the change has been fairly mild, on the order of 5 or 10 per cent.

13.1.4 Summary of facts

To summarize, the facts are:

★ Europe's economic activity is highly concentrated geographically at the national level as well as within nations.

★ People located in the core enjoy higher incomes and lower unemployment rates.

★ While the income equality across nations has narrowed steadily with European integration, the geographical distribution of economic activity within Member States has become more concentrated (taking income per capita as a measure of economic activity per capita).

★ As far as specialization is concerned, European integration has been accompanied by only modest relocation of industry among nations, at least when one lumps all forms of manufacturing together.

★ The little movement that there has been tends to lean in the direction of manufacturing activities having become more geographically dispersed across nations, not less.

★ Most European nations have become more specialized on a sector-by-sector basis.

★ At the subnational level, we see that industry has become more concentrated spatially (details on this are in Annex A).

13.2 Theory part I: comparative advantage

We now turn to the economic logic that connects European integration and the location of economic activity, focusing on two aspects in particular: specialization at the international level and agglomeration at the international level.

To keep things simple, we consider each effect in isolation, using a separate framework for each. The first framework focuses on natural differences among European nations – what economists call comparative advantage. The second framework – which is presented in the following section – focuses on the tendency of closer integration to encourage the geographic clustering of economic activity.

13.2.1 Comparative advantage and specialization

Opening up trade between nations raises economic efficiency. This is just the 'magic of the market'. When trade is very difficult, each nation has to make the most of what it consumes. Trade allows nations to 'do what they do best and import the rest'. Trade allows a nation to concentrate its productive resources in sectors where it has an edge over other nations. The jargon word for the edge is 'comparative advantage'. This effect of liberalization can have important effects on the location of industry because it encourages a nation-by-nation specialization. The main purpose of this section is to explain how comparative advantage and European economic integration help explain the type of industrial specialization that happened in Europe in the 1980–97 period and is likely to continue into the future.

An example

To see the basic idea more clearly, think about what Europe would look like without any trade. European nations have different supplies of productive factors – and different types of goods use factors in different proportions – so without trade the output of a nation would be largely determined by its supplies of factors. Focusing on labour supplies, consider the current distribution of labour among EU members, dividing labour into three types: those with little education (less than secondary), those with at least secondary education, and highly educated workers (researchers). To make the numbers comparable, we compute each nation's supply of low-education workers relative to its total supply of workers and compare this to the same ratio calculated for the EU as a whole (EU's supply of low-educated labour to overall labour) – and we do the same for the other two labour types.

The numbers are shown in Fig. 13.8. For example, we see that Portugal's supply of low-education workers (divided by Portugal's total supply of workers) is 83 per cent above the EU average. Germany's is 52 per cent below the EU average. Now consider what this means for the price of a good that uses low-education labour intensively, such as clothing. Without any trade, Germany and Portugal would have to make all their own clothes. Since the factor that is used intensively in clothes production is relatively abundant in Portugal and relatively scarce in Germany, we should expect clothing to be more expensive in Germany than in Portugal, if there were no trade.

Now think about what would happen if trade between Germany and Portugal opened up. Since clothes are relatively cheap in Portugal, we would see Portugal exporting clothing to Germany. But what would Germany export to Portugal in exchange? As Fig. 13.8 shows, Germany is relatively abundant in high-education labour. Using the same logic that told us clothing would be relatively cheap in Portugal without trade, we know that goods that are intensive in their use of high-education labour – for example, pharmaceuticals – would be relatively cheap in Germany. In this highly simplified world with trade only between Portugal and Germany, we would see Portugal exporting clothing (and other goods that are intensive in the use of low-education labour) in exchange for pharmaceuticals (and other goods that are intensive in the use of high-education labour) from Germany.

Germans would get their clothes for less and Portuguese would get the pharmaceuticals for less, so this exchange would be good for both nations (although individual workers might be hurt by the implied structural adjustment). The key to this 'gain from trade' is the way in which

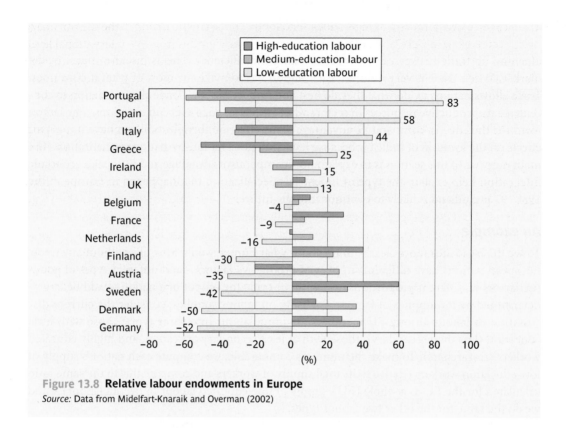

Figure 13.8 Relative labour endowments in Europe
Source: Data from Midelfart-Knaraik and Overman (2002)

trade allows for a more efficient allocation of production across countries. Instead of each nation having to make everything it consumes, trade allows production to locate in its 'natural' place. In this case, some production of low-education-intensive goods shifts to the nation that is relatively abundant in this type of labour.

Before turning to the main point – the implication of this trade liberalization for the spatial allocation of manufacturing – it is worth stressing the logical necessity of each nation having a comparative advantage in something. The way we defined our measure of relative factor abundance, each nation's labour supplies must either be exactly in line with the EU average (Belgium's is very close to this), or it must be abundant in some types of labour and scarce in others. Thus, without trade, each nation would have some goods that were relatively expensive and some goods that were relatively cheap. This type of comparative advantage, based on relative factor endowments, is known to economists as 'Heckscher–Ohlin' comparative advantage (it is named after the two Swedish economists who worked out its logic in the 1920s and 1930s).

The spatial implications of Heckscher–Ohlin comparative advantage

How does trade change the geographical pattern of production in this framework? In the example, trade induces an expansion in Portuguese sectors that are intensive in the use of low-education labour. Since the resources needed to expand output in these sectors must come from somewhere, trade also induces a contraction of other Portuguese sectors, in particular the sectors that had relatively high prices without trade, e.g. pharmaceuticals and other goods that are intensive in the use of high-education labour. In the simple example, the mirror-image shift would occur in Germany's industrial structure. If we view this from the international level, the resulting structural changes would look like a shift of clothing production from Germany to Portugal and a shift of the production of pharmaceuticals in the opposite direction. As a result, the industrial structures of both Portugal and Germany would become more specialized.

Of course, European integration is not limited to two nations. Allowing for many nations makes the analysis much more difficult, but it does not change the basic results that freer trade induces nations to specialize in producing products that they are relatively good at and importing products that they are relatively bad at producing. Consequently, trade liberalization of any type – including European economic integration – tends to lead nations to specialize on a nation-by-nation basis. Economic resources get shifted between sectors within each nation and, as a result, it seems as if production is being reallocated sector by sector across nations.

From the point of view of economic geography, this shows up as an increase in national specialization sector by sector. While this is not the only possible explanation for the increased specialization we saw in Table 13.1 (more on this below), it provides a very natural way of understanding why European integration was so systematically associated with an increase in specialization by nation.

We turn now to the logic behind the increased concentration of economic activity within European nations.

13.3 Theory part II: agglomeration and the new economic geography

The deep economic logic of the comparative advantage mechanism just discussed concerns how a nation's productive factors – i.e. its capital, skilled and unskilled labour, etc. – are employed *across sectors within the same nation*. To keep things simple, we implicitly assumed that there was only one region per nation so the issue of the geographic location of economic activity within a nation never arose.

In this section, we switch to the opposite extreme, where the key question is: 'How does European integration affect the location of economic activity *across regions within the same nation*?' To keep things simple, we assume that there is only a single industry in a nation but several regions within the nation.

The basic issues we are trying to understand in this section can be illustrated with a pair of maps – one showing the geographic distribution of economic activity (i.e. GDP) and one showing the population. Economic integration within the UK has, for decades, encouraged the shift of economic activity within Britain towards southern England. The facts for the 1995–2005 period are shown in Fig. 13.9. The left-hand map shows how each region's share of the UK's total economic activity has changed; darker colours indicate bigger increases. The right-hand map shows the same figures for regional population shares.

The dominant fact that comes out clearly from the maps is that the rise in GDP shares is closely matched by the rise in population shares. In other words, what we see here is a movement of productive factors across regions within a nation. Economic activity and population are agglomerating in southern England. Population figures are easy to obtain, but if we could find regional statistics on capital stocks and other types of productive factors, we would see the

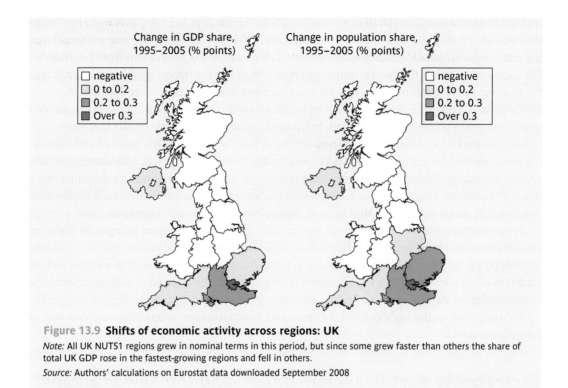

Figure 13.9 Shifts of economic activity across regions: UK

Note: All UK NUTS1 regions grew in nominal terms in this period, but since some grew faster than others the share of total UK GDP rose in the fastest-growing regions and fell in others.

Source: Authors' calculations on Eurostat data downloaded September 2008

same pattern of spatial agglomeration accompanied by a spatial agglomeration of productive factors.

But what causes what? Is economic activity clustering in southern England because this is where the workers are clustering, or is it the other way around? To organize our thinking on this question and related questions, we need to study the basic elements of economic geography. In what follows, the concepts are introduced with verbal logic alone.

13.3.1 Agglomeration and dispersion forces in general

The logic of economic geography rests on two pillars – dispersion forces and agglomeration forces. Agglomeration forces promote the spatial concentration of economic activity while dispersion forces discourage such concentration. The spatial distribution of economic activity at a moment in time depends upon the balance of the pro-concentration (agglomeration) forces and anti-concentration (dispersion) forces. The main question we want to answer is: 'How does European integration affect the equilibrium location of an industry?' To set the stage for the equilibrium analysis, we first consider dispersion and agglomeration forces in isolation.

Dispersion forces

Dispersion forces favour the geographic dispersion of economic activity. Land prices are the classic example. The price of land – and therefore the price of housing, office space, etc. – is usually higher in built-up areas, such as Central London, than it is in rural areas, such as North

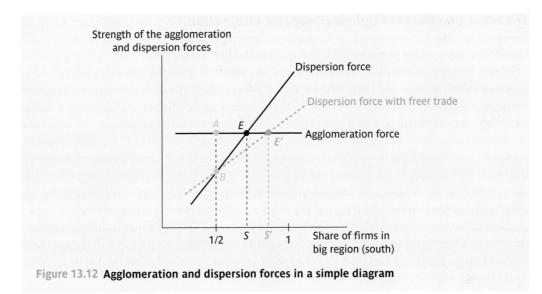

Figure 13.12 Agglomeration and dispersion forces in a simple diagram

difference between the degree of local competition in the north and in the south increases as a higher share of firms move to the south. For example, suppose there were only four firms. When they are split 2-2 between the regions, the local competition is even. When they are split 3-1, the local competition is more intense in the region with three firms (the south). Finally, if the split is 4-0, then the difference in local competition is even greater. Connecting these observations, we see that the dispersion force (i.e. the attractiveness of the small market) rises as the share of firms in the south rises. Graphically, this means that the 'dispersion force' curve is upwards sloped.

The locational equilibrium is shown by point E; this is where the share of firms in the south rises to the point where incentives to agglomerate are just balanced by incentives to disperse. It is instructive to consider why other points are not the equilibrium. For example, consider the point where half the firms are in the north. For this equal distribution of firms, the strength of the agglomeration force is shown by point A; the strength of the dispersion force is shown by point B. Because A is greater than B, we know that the agglomeration force – i.e. the force leading more firms to move to the south – is stronger than the dispersion force – i.e. the force leading firms to move to the north. As a consequence, having only half the firms in the south cannot be an equilibrium. Moreover, since the agglomeration force is stronger than the dispersion force, some firms will move from the small north to the big south.

As firms move southward, the gap between the agglomeration force and the dispersion force narrows. The location equilibrium is where the two forces just offset each other, namely point E, where the share of firms in the south is S. Although it is not shown in the diagram, readers can easily convince themselves that points to the right of point E involve a situation where the dispersion forces are larger than the agglomeration forces so the share of firms in the big region would tend to fall back to point E.

The location effects of tighter European integration

Finally, we come to the main subject of this section: How does tighter economic integration affect the location of industry inside a nation? We think of greater economic integration as lowering shipping costs. Note that here we are speaking of the trade costs among regions within a nation. Such cost reductions come with improvements in technology and improvements in transportation infrastructure and competition. All of these are fostered directly and indirectly by various elements of European integration. This is especially true for EU regional spending on roads, airports, seaports – the sort of thing we discuss below. It is worth noting, however, that such within-nation integration would proceed even without European integration. For the purposes of the diagram, we do not care about the exact reason trade costs are falling, we simply assume they do fall and trace out the impact on the spatial dispersion of firms.

How do we show the trade cost reduction in the diagram? The first point is that the agglomeration force line does not move. The agglomeration force is based on the fact that the northern market is bigger and this fact does not change when trade gets freer. Nothing happens to the 'agglomeration force' line.

Freer trade, however, has a very direct effect on the 'dispersion force' curve. The source of the dispersion force is that trade costs protect firms located in the small market from competition from firms located in the big market. It is clear, then, that something will happen to the dispersion force line. To get a handle on this, consider a very particular point on the line, the point where the share of firms in the big region is $1/2$. At this point, the level of trade costs has no influence on the relative attractiveness of the two regions. Whether trade costs are high or low, the degree of local competition in the two markets will be identical. The thrust of this is that the dispersion force line must always pass through point *B* in the diagram. Any change will be a rotation of the line around point *B*.

For points to the right, the dispersion force line must come down. The reason is that, with more firms in the south than the north, the advantage of being in the low-competition north (low competition since there are fewer firms there) is reduced by lower trade costs. In other words, the lower trade costs provide less protection against competition from south-based firms. For this reason, the local competition advantages of being in the north are reduced. Since this is true for all points to the right of $1/2$, this shows up graphically as a clockwise rotation of the 'dispersion force' line around the $1/2$ point. (See Annex A for a more detailed treatment of Fig. 13.12.)

Given that the dispersion-force curve rotates clockwise and the agglomeration-force curve stays put, the new locational equilibrium is at point *E'*. Note that this involves a higher share of firms in the big region. In other words, free trade promotes the agglomeration of economic activity in the initially big region. As we saw in Fig. 13.7, this within-nation concentration of economic activity is a widespread phenomenon in Europe.

The simplifying assumptions above made it very easy to study integration's impact on the location of economic activity in Fig. 13.12. While it assumed away many important factors affecting the location of economic activity, it is sufficient for understanding the basic economic logic of how tighter European integration can be expected to favour the location of industry in Europe's core regions. Some readers, however, will want to explore the economics of this in greater depth. Box 13.2 shows how some factors can be included in a modified version of Fig. 13.12. Annex A presents the logic more formally (i.e. using mathematics).

Box 13.2   Considering additional complicating factors

As it turns out, it is not very difficult to add back in a number of complicating factors that we assumed away to start with.

For example, we can easily allow for circular-causality in the agglomeration force. We do this by drawing the agglomeration-force line as upward sloped (Fig. 13.13). If the line slopes upward, it says that the strength of the agglomeration force rises as a larger share of firms move to the big northern region. This addition raises an extra complication concerning the impact of freer trade. Freer trade rotates the dispersion-force line as in the text; however, now it also reduces the agglomeration force for any level of firms in the north. The reason is clear; the agglomeration force stemmed from the fact that locating in the big market helps a firm reduce its shipping costs. Since lower overall shipping costs narrow this difference between the markets, the agglomeration-force line shifts down. The complica-tion is that there is now a graphical possibility that the new E' will be to the left of the old E. A careful study of the logic shows that this cannot occur (see Annex A). Roughly speaking, the free trade reduces the agglomeration forces by less than the dispersion forces so the new location equilibrium involves more spatial concentration.

We can consider other dispersion forces by shifting the dispersion-force curve up or twisting it at the ends. For dispersion forces that are not related to the share of firms in the north, the dispersion-force curve is shifted up vertically. For example, it could be that the one region is intrinsically more pleasant to live in. Since the impact of this on location does not depend upon the share of firms in the south, we allow for such forces by shifting the curve either up or down. Interested readers can easily check that a downward shift will lower the equilibrium share of firms in the south. Other dispersion forces, however, are related to the share of firms. For example, the concentration of firms in southern England drives up the wages of workers in this region. Other things equal, this acts as a dispersion force in that it discourages some firms from moving to the south. We can reflect this in the diagram by rotating the dispersion-force line counter-clockwise around the ½ point.

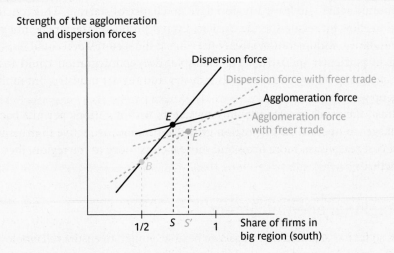

Figure 13.13 **Allowing for circular causality**

13.4 Theory part III: putting it all together

The facts presented above showed that European integration was accompanied by location effects within nations that are quite different from those between nations. European integration seems to be associated with a more even dispersion of economic activity in the sense that per-capita GDP figures tended to converge nation by nation. Within nations, however, the opposite has happened. In most Member States, regional disparities have grown as European integration has deepened. The theory presented above helps us to understand the difference. The key factor is the mobility of capital and labour.

While there are few remaining restrictions on intra-EU labour flows, workers seldom move across national borders in the EU. Labour mobility between regions within a nation is higher, but still not enormous – as we can see with the huge variation in regional unemployment rates. However, labour mobility has not always been low within nations. The post-war period, for example, saw a massive shift of the population from rural regions to urban regions and this often involved a move across regional boundaries. Moreover, other productive factors are more mobile; for example, capital and skilled workers are quite mobile between regions within the same nation.

Oversimplifying to make the point, think of all factors as perfectly mobile within nations, but perfectly immobile across nations. In this case, removing barriers to trade allows nations to specialize in the sectors in which they have a comparative advantage. The resulting efficiency gain allows all nations to increase their output. Moreover, deeper aspects of integration, such as foreign direct investment and mobility of students, suggest that European integration would also be accompanied by a convergence of national technology frontiers to the best practice in Europe, with the technological laggards catching up with the technological leaders. Both of these factors would promote a convergence of per-capita incomes across European nations. Importantly, the lack of factor mobility across nations means that agglomeration forces are not dominant at the national level. That is to say, the cycles of circular causality that might lead all economic activity to leave a region have no chance of starting. This conclusion must be modified to allow for sector-specific clusters. Even if productive factors do not move across national boundaries, agglomeration forces operating at the sectoral level could result in nations specializing in particular industries. For example, deeper integration could foster greater geographic clustering of, say, the chemicals industry and the car industry, but in the end each nation ends up with some industry.

By contrast, the much greater mobility of factors within nations permits backward and forward linkages to operate. As one region grows, it becomes attractive to firms for demand reasons and cost reasons, so more firms and more factors move to the region, thereby fuelling further growth.

13.4.1 Regional unemployment

The analysis so far has assumed that wages are flexible enough to ensure full employment of all labour. Since regional unemployment is a serious problem in Europe, we turn to the economic logic connecting delocation and unemployment. As usual, we follow the principle of progressive complexity by starting simple.

If wages were adjusted instantaneously across time and space, we would have no unemployment. The wage rate paid for each hour of work would adjust so that the amount of labour that workers would like to supply at that price just matched the amount that firms would like to 'buy' (hire). In this hypothetical world, the wages would instantaneously jump to the market-clearing level, i.e. the level where labour supply matches labour demand. Things are not that simple, however.

For many reasons, most European nations have decided to prevent the wage – the 'price' of labour – from jumping around like the price of crude oil or government bonds. (See Chapter 8 for a more formal treatment of unemployment.) All sorts of labour market institutions, ranging from trade unions and unemployment benefits to minimum wages and employment protection legislation, mean that the price of labour is systematically stabilized at a level that exceeds the market-clearing wage level. The direct logical consequence is that workers systematically want to offer more labour at the going wage than firms are willing to hire; this is the definition of unemployment. As in any market, if the price is fixed too high, the amount offered for sale will exceed the amount that is bought.

In most European nations, there is a strong spatial element to this price-fixing of labour. Take Germany, for example. For many reasons, labour productivity in the eastern Länder is lower than it is in the western Länder. Thus, firms would only be willing to employ all the eastern labour offered if wages were lower in the east. However, German labour unions have methodically prevented eastern wages from falling to their market-clearing level, either in an attempt to avoid downward pressure on their own wages, or, more charitably, in the spirit of solidarity with the eastern workers who actually do get employed. Whatever the source of regional wage inflexibility, its logical consequence is regional unemployment. Moreover, since firms can leave a region much more easily than workers, a continual within-nation clustering of economic activity will tend to be associated with high levels of unemployment in the contracting regions and low levels in the expanding regions.

Finally, it should be clear that this sort of mismatch of migration speeds (firms move faster than workers) – teamed with a lack of regional wage flexibility – has the effect of creating an agglomeration force. A little shift of industry raises unemployment in the contracting region and lowers it in the expanding region. Since unemployment is an important factor in workers' migration decisions, the initial shift makes workers more likely to migrate to the expanding region. Such migration, however, changes the relative market sizes in a way that tends to encourage more firms to leave the contracting region. (For a detailed account of geographical clustering of unemployment in Europe, see Overman and Puga, 2001).

13.4.2 Peripherality and real geography

Our theoretical discussion has intentionally simplified physical geography considerations by working with only two nations, both of which are thought of as points in space. Real-world geography, of course, is much more interesting and this matters for the location of economic activity. We can use the basic logic of demand-linked agglomeration forces to consider how one can put real geography back into the picture.

As discussed above, firms that want to concentrate production in a single location tend, other things being equal, to locate in a place that minimizes transportation costs. With only two markets, this means locating in the bigger market, but when the economic activity is spread out over real geography, the answer can be less obvious. However, the fact that economic activity is highly concentrated in Europe makes the problem easier. As the map in Fig. 13.2 showed, the core of Europe is fairly compact from a geographical point of view, i.e. it is concentrated in the northeast corner of the continent. This is why it is useful to abstract Europe's geography as consisting of two regions, the core and the periphery, what we called the north and the south in the previous section.

There are many complicating factors, however. For example, despite the Alps forming a wall between northern Italy and the big French, German and UK markets, northern Italy has quite good road access thanks to several tunnels and passes through the Alps.

Economists have a way of taking account of the various real-geography features, known as the accessibility index (also called the market potential index); see Fig. 13.14 for a recent example. The accessibility index for each region measures the region's closeness to other regions that have a lot of economic activity. For example, to calculate the accessibility of the region that contains Paris, the Ile de France, one calculates how long it would take to get from the centre of Paris to the main urban centre of every other region in the EU (the calculation varies somewhat according to the form of transport used; the map here works with road transportation). Finally, one weights

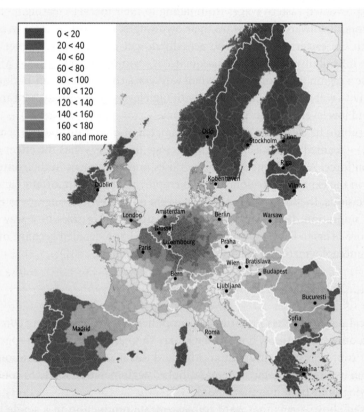

Figure 13.14 **Real geography and market accessibility**

Note: The map is scaled such that 100 equals the average accessibility in the EU27.

Source: Third Cohesion Report, European Commission. Downloadable from europa.int.eu

each of these transport times by the destination region's share of the EU's total economic activity. Adding up these weighted times gives us an idea of how close Paris is to the bulk of EU economic activity. Doing the same for every other region gives us an index of accessibility by region.

13.5 EU regional policy

As mentioned in the introduction, a concern for Europe's disadvantaged regions has always been a headline goal of the European Union. For the first three and a half decades of the EU's existence, however, the task of helping less-favoured regions was left firmly in the hands of national governments. All European nations, both inside and outside the EU, spent huge sums on rural infrastructure during the 1950s, 1960s and 1970s. They extended their electricity and telephone grids to every city, town, village and farmhouse. They built roads, rails and provincial universities in an effort to develop their less-favoured regions. In many cases, modern banking was extended to the rural community via the state-owned PTTs (Post, Telephone and Telegraph).

The EEC, as it was known at the time, did have some programmes for rural regions, but despite real poverty in some members' regions – like Italy's Mezzogiorno – the level of EU funding was negligible. Structural spending was only 3 per cent of the budget in 1970, rising to only 11 per cent by 1980. To the extent that the EEC was not involved in helping rural communities at all, it did so by artificially raising the price of agricultural goods via the Common Agricultural Policy (CAP).

Major EU funding for less-favoured regions would have to wait for a change in Community politics. When the first 'poor' member, Ireland, joined in 1973, a new fund – the European Regional Development Fund (ERDF) – was set up to redistribute money to the poorest regions, but its budget was minor. The situation changed in the 1980s when the EU admitted three new members, Greece, Spain and Portugal. These nations were substantially poorer than the incumbent members, and, importantly, their farmers did not produce the goods that the CAP supported most heavily (mainly wheat, sugar, dairy and beef). If these nations were to benefit financially from the EU's budget, EU spending priorities would have to be changed.

As it turned out, the voting power of Spain and Portugal, teamed with the votes of Ireland and Greece, was sufficient to produce a major realignment of EU spending priorities (see Chapter 3 for an analysis of how power politics shapes the EU budget). During the Iberian accession talks, the EU promised to substantially increase spending on poor regions. The official rationale for the increase was the assertion that economic integration, implied by the 1986 Single European Act, favoured Europe's industrial core (an assertion that fits in perfectly with the economics of agglomeration described in the previous section). As the Commission's website puts it, the policy was 'designed to offset the burden of the single market for southern countries and other less-favoured regions'. Whether it was caused by a new-found concern for less-favoured regions, simple power politics or a combination of the two, the fact is that EU spending on poor regions rose sharply in the mid- to late 1980s, as Fig. 13.15 shows.

When the issue of monetary union was raised in talks leading up to the Maastricht Treaty, the 'poor-4' again managed to obtain a significant increase in regional spending via the creation of a new fund (the Cohesion Fund) that could be spent only in Greece, Ireland, Spain and Portugal. Again, the justification was that tighter economic integration would mostly favour Europe's industrial core, so peripheral regions should be compensated by a big increase in EU money for poor regions, what is known as 'structural spending' in EU jargon. The practical outcome was that structural spending doubled its share of the EU budget between 1986 and 1993.

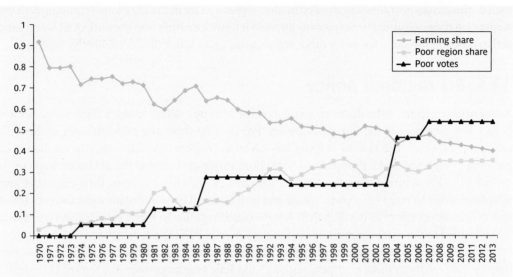

Figure 13.15 **EU budgetary expenditures, 1965–2013, CAP vs. Structural Funds**

13.5.1 Politics and the allocation of EU regional spending

This link between the political power of poor countries and the budget is clear to see in Fig. 13.15. The share of the EU budget going to poor regions rises in tandem with the share of poor countries' votes in the Council of Ministers. Up to the most recent enlargement, when Austria, Finland and Sweden joined, the correlation was remarkably good. Since 1994, however, the connection between poor nations and structural spending has been greatly diluted. Large parts of Finland and Sweden were designated as eligible, and even some Austrian regions, together with all of the former East Germany, were deemed as poor. The figure also shows the power of 'poor nations' after ten new members joined in 2004 and two more in 2007. The budget plan for 2007–13 shows that the spending share on poor regions will rise, but nowhere near in line with the poor regions' voting share. This may be in part explained by the fact that many of the new members are both poor and highly agrarian, so they may not be as clearly interested in downsizing the CAP as were Spain, Greece and Portugal (who benefited little from the CAP).

13.5.2 Instruments, objectives and guiding principles

The EU spends about a third of its budget on less-favoured regions. How is this money allocated? As mentioned above, politics plays a role, but the EU does have a set of guidelines, objectives and principles that help to channel the spending to where it will do the most good. Here we just touch upon the main points. (Interested readers can find well-written documentation of all the details at http://ec.europa.eu/regional_policy/index_en.htm.)

The EU's regional policy for the period 2007–13 has three main objectives: convergence, regional competitiveness and employment, and territorial cooperation. The main changes from the previous seven-year period are that the money is more concentrated in the poorest areas and the spending should be linked to the Lisbon goals of making the EU the most competitive economy in the world.

	% Cohesion budget	% of EU27 population covered
Convergence	82	Standard convergence regions (34), Phase-out convergence regions (3), Cohesion Fund nations (34)
Regional competitiveness and employment	16	All non-Convergence regions (66)
Territorial cooperation	2	100

Source: 'EU Cohesion Policy 1988–2008: Investing in Europe's future', InfoRegio, June 2008

Convergence

Most of the money (€283 billion, or about 80 per cent of total cohesion spending) is spent on the first objective, which is called 'convergence' since it is aimed at reducing income differences across EU regions. There are three ways to qualify for this money. The main way is to be a NUTS 2 region with GDP per capita that is less than 75 per cent of the average GDP of the EU25 (which is the reference even after the 2007 enlargement). There are 84 of these regions with a total population of 154 million (31 per cent of the EU27 population). The second is to be a so-called phasing-out region, which are regions that got this sort of money before the Eastern enlargement, but do not qualify under the new 75 per cent threshold since the newcomers, being much poorer than the EU15, lowered the threshold. This covers only 16 million people (about 3 per cent of the EU27 population), but includes some poor regions in rich nations, such as Germany, Austria, Britain and Italy.

Finally, the Cohesion Fund spending (about €70 billion of the €283 billion) is allocated by country rather than by region; all regions in the cohesion countries are eligible regardless of their wealth. This is a holdover from an earlier programme (set up in 1992); the nations that benefited from it, especially Spain, Portugal and Greece, used their political power to maintain the programme. The qualifying threshold is a national income below 90 per cent of the EU25 average. Spain, which is technically too rich as a nation to qualify, used its political power in the Council of Ministers to get itself included on a transitory basis. Since the poorest regions in Spain, Portugal and Greece already qualify under the first criterion, the Cohesion Fund allows convergence money to be spent in the richer regions of Spain, Portugal and Greece.

Regional competitiveness and employment

The second objective is called 'regional competitiveness and employment'. Under this heading, all the non-convergence regions are eligible. The goal is to strengthen the competitiveness and attractiveness of the regions, as well as regional employment. This objective approaches the problem in two ways. First, development programmes are designed to help regions promote economic change through innovation and encouragement of the 'knowledge society' as well as entrepreneurship, protection of the environment, and improvement of the regions' accessibility. It also encourages more and better jobs by helping regions to adapt their workforce.

European territorial cooperation

This objective aims to reinforce cooperation at cross-border, transnational level. It collects under one objective a handful of small programmes that already exist. The sum total budget of all these projects is just €9 billion, or 2 per cent of total cohesion spending. All EU citizens are covered by at least one of the 'transnational cooperations' and about a third live in regions that are consided to be 'cross-border areas'.

The map in Fig. 13.16 shows which regions are eligible for the first- and second-objective spending.

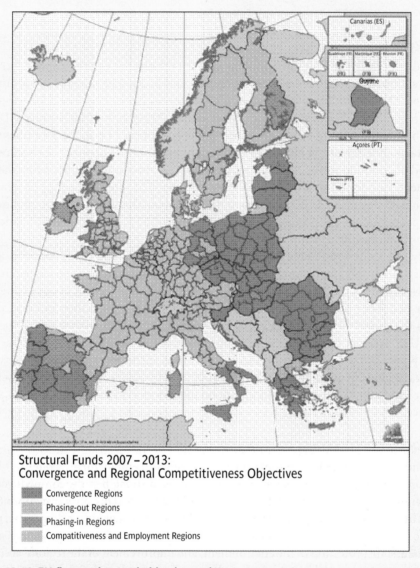

Figure 13.16 EU first- and second-objective regions

Notes: The Convergence Regions plus the 'Phasing-in Regions' are eligible for Convergence Objective spending; the rest are eligible for the Competitiveness and Employment Objective spending. The European Territorial Cooperation regions are not shown (see http://ec.europa.eu/regional_policy/).

Box 13.3 Relationship with old 2000–06 cohesion objectives

The new objectives are not a substantial reorganization of the basic programmes, although there has been additional concentration on the poorest regions, and much of the cohesion spending has to be explicitly motivated as helping regions meet the Lisbon criteria of boosting growth, jobs and innovation.

Table 13.2 shows what has happened to the old objectives and miscellaneous cohesion projects.

Table 13.2 The old and new objectives compared

2000–06	2007–13

Objective 1: Regions lagging behind in development terms
    Cohesion Fund (money set aside for Spain,
    Portugal, Greece and Ireland)
	Convergence

Objective 2: Economic and social conversion zones	

Objective 3: Training systems and employment policies
    Miscellaneous cohesion programmes
    Interreg III
	Regional competitiveness and employment

URBAN II(*) ERDF EQUAL (*) ESF	European Territorial Cooperation

Common Agricultural Policy based programmes
    Leader + EAGGF-Guidance
    Rural development and restructuring of the
    fishing sector beyond Objective 1
	CAP second pillar

Source: Derived from *Cohesion Policy 2007–13: Commentaries and Official Texts,* January 2007, DG Regio (p. 10). http://ec.europa.eu/regional_policy/sources/docoffic/official/regulation/pdf/2007/publications/guide2007_en.pdf

The many structural funds

For historical reasons, most EU regional spending is channelled through three 'funds': two 'Structural Funds' and the 'Cohesion Fund', and the CAP's second pillar which is run separately from the rest of the regional policy. Although there are three funds, they are subsumed in an overall strategy aimed at fighting unemployment and stimulating growth in poor regions. The details of the funds are only important for experts, but for the record, the two structural funds are: the European Regional Development Fund (which funds all three objectives) and the European Social Fund (which funds the first two), plus the Cohesion Fund which helps with the convergence objective. Politically and administratively, the CAP is quite separate from the EU's Regional Policy, so the second pillar of the CAP is only loosely connected with the regional policy.

Spending priorities

What is this money spent on? Although there are many types of project, a good deal goes to physical infrastructure such as roads, bridges, regional airports, etc. The 2007–13 Regional Policy programme calls for a new generation of programmes that earmark a certain proportion of the resources for projects connected to the EU's so-called Lisbon Agenda (formally, the

Strategy for Growth and Jobs). These include research and innovation, infrastructures of European importance, industrial competitiveness, renewable energies, energy efficiency, eco-innovations and human resources.

The proportion devoted to these more forward-looking projects must be at least 60 per cent of the total available funding in Convergence Regions and 75 per cent in all other regions. According to plans laid in 2007 and 2008, around €200 billion will be allocated to such projects; compared to the previous seven-year budget period, this is a €50 billion increase.

Guiding principles

The Structural Funds are not spent on projects chosen at the European level. The choice of projects and their management are solely the responsibility of the national and regional authorities. The projects, however, are co-financed from both national and Community funds. As a matter of principle, the so-called additionality principle, Community funding should not be used to economize on national funds. This principle is naturally difficult to verify. National budgetary priorities change frequently, so it is hard to know how much the members would have spent if the Community funding were not available.

Besides additionality, the structural spending is characterized by five other basic rules:

1 *Concentration.* The spending should be geographically concentrated.

2 *Coherence.* Spending should be in the context of broad development programmes that are drawn up by EU members and approved by the Commission.

3 *Coordination.* The Commission, the Member State concerned, the regional and local authorities, industry, and labour unions should cooperate in the spending.

4 *Monitoring and evaluation.* The spending should be monitored and evaluated.

5 *Consistency and complementarity.* The spending should be consistent with the provisions of the Treaties and other Community policies such as the Single Market, the CAP and the Common Fisheries Policy.

13.5.3 Political allocation

As part of its responsibilities within the framework of Structural Funds management, the European Commission takes decisions on the concrete implementation of the regulations. This includes allocating the money by objective and by EU member. The outcome of the most recent deal is shown in Table 13.3. Note that this is set in advance for the whole seven-year period.

This allocation was decided as part of the political struggle surrounding the seven-year Financial Perspective for the 2007–13 period (see Chapter 2 for details). While Poland, which is both populous and relatively poor by EU standards, gets by far the most money, well-to-do nations such as Germany, Italy and Spain are also top beneficiaries.

The last two columns show the facts on the per-capita cohesion spending and the per-capita incomes measured in PPS terms (PPS stands for Purchasing Power Standard, i.e. it is a measure that adjusts for the fact that prices tend to be higher in some nations, especially rich nations). Comparing the columns shows that there is a clear distinction between the Cohesion Countries (i.e. the 12 new members plus Portugal, Greece and Spain) and the other members. The

Table 13.3 Country allocations in the financial perspective, 2007–13 (million euros)

	Convergence Objective	Regional Competitiveness and Employment Objective	European Territorial Cooperation Objective	Total	Per capita cohesion spending (euros)	Per capita income (2008, PPS)
Poland	66 553		731	67 284	1 765	14 100
Spain	26 180	8 477	559	35 217	778	27 000
Italy	21 641	6 325	846	28 812	2 034	15 100
Czech Rep.	25 883	419	389	26 692	112	31 000
Germany	16 079	9 409	851	26 340	1 821	25 300
Hungary	22 890	2 031	386	25 307	204	36 900
Portugal	20 473	938	99	21 511	2 026	18 900
Greece	19 575	635	210	20 420	2 519	16 200
Romania	6 565		455	19 668	914	10 800
France	3 191	10 257	872	14 319	320	28 900
Slovakia	3 906	449	227	11 588	2 146	18 300
UK	177	6 979	722	10 613	173	29 400
Lithuania	6 775		109	6 885	134	71 000
Bulgaria	6 674		179	6 853	805	23 700
Latvia	4 531		90	4 620	2 045	16 100
Slovenia	4 101		104	4 205	2 076	23 100
Estonia	3 404		52	3 456	324	30 000
Belgium	638	1 425	194	2 258	897	10 100
Netherlands		1 660	247	1 907	116	33 600
Sweden		1 626	265	1 891	206	32 200
Finland		1 596	120	1 716	225	28 100
Austria	177	1 027	257	1 461	212	30 000
Ireland	0	751	151	901	483	25 500
Malta	840	0	15	855	2 082	19 700
Cyprus	213	399	28	640	2 571	21 300
Denmark		510	103	613	2 577	18 600
Luxembourg		50	15	65	175	32 500
Interregional			445	445		

Source: *Cohesion Policy 2007–13: Commentaries and Official Texts*, January 2007, DG Regio

Cohesion Countries all get substantially more per person than the richer nations. However, among the Cohesion Countries the allocation does not line up at all well with per-capita income. Chapter 3 discusses issues of power and EU decision making which may help account for these facts.

13.6 Empirical evidence

The chapter has stressed three main determinants of the location of economic activity: regional policy and two purely economic determinants (comparative advantage and agglomeration). We now consider the importance of these three forces.

To evaluate the determinants of industrial location in the EU, researchers try to explain how regional and national shares of various types of manufacturing vary with regional and national characteristics, where it is useful to divide the national characteristics into three broad groups: relative labour supplies, economic geography features, and policies affecting industrial location.

For instance, the theory section explained why we should expect nations that have a relatively high share of the EU's skilled labour also to have a relatively high share of the EU's manufacturing sectors that are relatively intensive in their use of skilled labour. The same link should be expected for relative endowments of other types of labour – low-skilled and medium-skilled workers – and sectors that use these types of labour intensively as well as regional endowments of agricultural land and industries that use agricultural inputs intensively.

The theory section also explained that the spatial allocation of demand affects the location of industry since sectors where firms tend to concentrate production in a single location (i.e. those marked by important economies of scale) will tend to favour locations that are near large markets. This so-called demand linkage (firms want to be near the demands for their goods) is complemented by so-called supply linkages – that is, firms in sectors that use lots of intermediate inputs will tend to favour locations with concentrations of their suppliers.

Finally, policy can directly encourage the location of particular types of sectors in particular locations and this effect can either amplify or dampen the impact of factor endowments and economic geography factors on the location of industry.

Although the research in this area is limited – mainly owing to a lack of data on the location of manufacturing and regional labour endowments – the results so far suggest that all three factors matter. Interestingly, it seems that labour endowments have become more important in determining location as European economic integration has become tighter. One of the two agglomeration forces – namely, supply linkages – seems to be getting stronger, while the demand linkage is getting weaker. (See Redding et al. 2001, for a survey of empirical results. This can be downloaded from http://econ.lse.ac.uk/staff/ajv/research_material.html.)

Given that EU regional policy has been operating at a significant level only since the mid-1980s, results on the impact of policy are even more tenuous. The best study in this area, Midelfart-Knarvik and Overman (2002), finds that EU policy has significantly affected the geographical location of industries. In particular, these authors find that EU structural spending did affect the location of high-skilled intensive industries. For an integrated survey of the empirical evidence, see Combes and Overman (2003).

13.7 Summary

Europe's economic activity is highly concentrated geographically at the national level as well as within nations. This is a problem for social cohesion since people located in the 'core' enjoy higher incomes and lower unemployment rates. European integration seems to have led to a narrowing of income equality across nations, but an increase in inequality within nations. Nevertheless, European integration has been accompanied by only modest relocation of industry among nations, but the little movement we have seen has been in the direction of manufacturing activities having become more geographically dispersed, not less, while most European nations have become more specialized on a sector-by-sector basis.

The chapter presented two main theories that could account for these facts. The first – the comparative advantage framework – explains why nations have become more specialized while at the same time income differences have narrowed. The second – based on the so-called new economic geography – focuses on agglomeration forces that account for the way in which tighter economic integration can foster the clustering of economic activities within nations.

The chapter also presented the main outlines of the EU's regional policy. The goal of this policy is to help to disperse economic activity to less-favoured regions. Most of the money is spent on so-called Convergence regions that typically have per-capita incomes that are less than 75 per cent of the EU average. The EU spends about a third of its budget on these policies.

Self-assessment questions

1. Draw a diagram with the extensions to the agglomeration diagram suggested in Box 13.2.

2. Download the European Commission's proposal for reforming structural spending and compare them to the principles of the system in place up to the end of 2006.

3. The educational level in all EU nations is rising. How would this affect the spatial allocation of production in the Heckscher–Ohlin framework?

Essay questions

1. EU regional policy was reformed in the context of 'Agenda 2000'. What were the major reform themes and how successfully were they implemented?

2. When the ten newcomers joined, some Objective 1 regions become 'statistically' rich. That is, the lowering of the EU average will push their incomes above the 75 per cent threshold for Objective 1 status. Referring to the two theoretical frameworks discussed in the chapter, do you think it is correct for the EU to remove their Objective 1 status?

3. Many of the ten newcomer members are both very agrarian and very poor. Some of them have agricultural land that is well suited to the production of the products that the CAP supports most. How do you think these nations will vote when the new long-term budget plan is drawn up for the post-enlargement period? (Hint: Think about special-interest group politics and the position of farmers in the political life of the newcomer countries.)

4. Using the theory of fiscal federalism presented in Chapter 2, can you argue that regional policy should be set at the EU level?

Further reading: the aficionado's corner

For a more extensive discussion of the facts concerning changes in the location of economic activity in the EU, see **Brülhart and Traeger** (2003).

Each year, the Commission produces a report on 'cohesion' in the EU. This contains a large number of maps showing things such as unemployment, declining population, share of the economy in agriculture, industry and services. It also presents a large number of indicators of social cohesion, such as youth unemployment and income distribution. See **European Commission** (1996, 2001, 2003).

For an advanced treatment of the new economic geography, see part I of *Economic Geography and Public Policy* by **Baldwin et al.** (2003), freely downloadable from http://heiwww.unige.ch/~baldwin/.

Useful websites

The webpage www.europarl.eu.int/factsheets/4_4_1_en.htm provides a wealth of information on EU regional policy.

The Commission department devoted to regional policy has an extensive website that provides masses of data and several highly readable explanations of EU policy in the area. Search the EU's main site europa.eu.int with Google using the search words 'EU regional policy' to find the site's location (it changes occasionally when the Commission reorganizes its webpages).

References

Baldwin, R., R. Forslid, P. Martin, G. Ottaviano and F. Robert-Nicoud (2005) *Economic Geography and Public Policy*, Princeton University Press, Princeton, NJ.

Brülhart, M. and R. Traeger (2003) *An Account of Geographic Concentration Patterns in Europe*, Cahiers de Recherches Economiques du Département d'Econométrie et d'Economie Politique (DEEP), Université de Lausanne. Download from www.hec.unil.ch/deep/publications-english/e-cahiers.htm.

Combes, P.-P. and H.G. Overman (2004) 'The spatial distribution of economic activities in the European Union,' in J.V. Henderson and J.-F. Thisse (eds) *Handbook of Regional and Urban Economics*, Volume 4: *Cities and Geography*, Elsevier, Oxford.

European Commission (1996) *European Cohesion Report*, so-called first cohesion report; see http://europa.eu.int/ comm/regional_policy/sources/docoffic/official/repor_en.htm.

European Commission (2001) *Second Report on Economic and Social Cohesion*.

European Commission (2003) *Communication from the Commission: Second Progress Report on Economic and Social Cohesion*, COM (2003) 34 final. Download from http://europa.eu.int/scadplus/leg/en/lvb/g24004.htm.

Midelfart-Knarvik, K.-H. and H.G. Overman (2002) 'Delocation and European integration: is structural spending justified?', *Economic Policy*, 17 (35): 321–59.

Overman, H. and D. Puga (2001) 'Regional unemployment clusters: nearness matters within and across Europe's national borders', *Economic Policy*, 17 (34): 115–47.

Redding, S., H.G. Overman and A. Venables (2001) *The Economic Geography of Trade, Production and Income: A Survey of Empirics*, CEPR Discussion Paper, London.

Schürmann, C. and A. Talaat (2000) *Towards a European Peripherality Index*, Final Report, Institut für Raumplanung Fakultät Raumplanung, Universität Dortmund.

Annex A   Agglomeration economics more formally

A13.1 The agglomeration diagram

This section provides a formal treatment of the economics behind Fig. 13.12. The underlying model is the so-called FC model (see Baldwin et al., 2003, Chapter 3 for the mathematical details). The model assumes that firms move to the region where they earn the highest profit. Simplifying assumptions in the model imply that a firm's profit is a constant fraction of its sales, so the choice of location boils down to a comparison of sales when the firm is located in the north versus the south. As firms move to the region in which they would have the highest sales, however, they increase competition in that market and reduce competition in the market they left. As a consequence, the migration of firms (sometimes called delocation) evens out the difference in the market. The equilibrium share of firms in the north is determined by the equality of sales in the two markets.

The model assumes that firms are producing differentiated varieties and competition is of the Dixit–Stiglitz type. In other words, the varieties are all symmetric in terms of demand and each firm takes as given the prices of all other firms. A final implication of Dixit–Stiglitz competition is that all firms charge the same price-to-marginal-cost mark-up. Given these assumptions, and assuming a CES demand function, the sales of a typical south-based firm are:

$$p_j c_j = \frac{p_j^{1-\sigma} E}{n p_i^{1-\sigma} + n^* (p_i^*)^{1-\sigma}} \tag{1}$$

where E is the total expenditure in the northern market on all varieties in the sector, and σ is the elasticity of substitution among varieties (we must assume that $\sigma > 1$ for the model to make sense). The denominator has two terms. The first term reflects the price of locally made varieties (of which there are n) and the second term reflects the price of imported varieties (of which there are n^*).

Notice that the denominator is a measure of how much competition there is in this market. If prices are very low and/or there are many firms, then the denominator will be very high (recall that $\sigma > 1$ so $1 - \sigma < 0$) so the sales for a typical firm will be low – i.e. the typical firm will face a lot of competition.

Note that since firms in the north and the south have the same marginal cost and use the same constant marginal cost, the only difference between the price of local and imported varieties is the trade cost raised to the power $1 - \sigma$. In other words, p_i^*/p_i equals $\tau^{1-\sigma}$, which we relabelled as ϕ, a mnemonic for the freeness of trade; when $\phi = 0$, trade costs are prohibitive and no trade occurs in this sector. When $\phi = 1$, trade is costless so $p_i^*/p_i = 1$. Using these simplifications and eqn (1), we can write the value of sales of a north-based firm in the northern market as:

$$p_j c_j = (\frac{1}{n^w}) \frac{E}{s_n + (1 - s_n)\phi} \tag{2}$$

where n^w is the number of varieties in the world (i.e. in north and south) and s_n is the share of these produced in the north.

Using similar calculations, we can calculate value of sales of a north-based firm into the southern market. Adding the sales of a north-based firm into both the north and south markets, we get that total sales of a north-based firm are:

$$Sales_{North} = (\frac{1}{n^w})\left(\frac{E}{s_n + (1 - s_n)\phi} + \frac{\phi E^*}{\phi s_n + 1 - s_n} \right) \tag{3}$$

where E^* is total expenditure in the southern market. The parallel expression for a south-based firm is:

$$Sales_{South} = (\frac{1}{n^w})\left(\frac{\phi E}{s_n + (1 - s_n)\phi} + \frac{E^*}{\phi s_n + 1 - s_n} \right) \tag{4}$$

The equilibrium location of firms – as measured by s_n – is given by the equality of eqns (3) and (4). A little algebraic manipulation shows that this difference equals:

$$Sales_{North} - Sales_{South} = (\frac{(1 - \phi)}{n^w})\left(\frac{E}{s_n + (1 - s_n)\phi} - \frac{E^*}{\phi s_n + 1 - s_n} \right) \tag{5}$$

The equilibrium s_n is the one for which this difference is zero. Since $(1 - \phi)$ is not zero unless trade is costless and location has no implication for sales, the condition that characterizes the spatial equilibrium is:

$$\frac{E}{s_n + (1 - s_n)\phi} = \frac{E^*}{\phi s_n + 1 - s_n} \tag{6}$$

This is simple to solve for s_n, but intuition is boosted by rewriting the location condition as:

$$\frac{E}{E^*} = \frac{s_n + (1 - s_n)\phi}{\phi s_n + 1 - s_n} \tag{7}$$

The left-hand side of this equation is what we called the 'agglomeration force' line; notice that it is not affected by either the level of trade freeness, ϕ, or the actual distribution of firms s_n. The larger is the left-hand side, the more attractive is the north compared to the south since, all else equal, a higher E/E^* means that a typical firm will sell more when located in the north.

The right-hand side is what we called the 'dispersion force' curve. Since the denominators in the demand functions measure the degree of competition in each market, the right-hand side is the ratio of the degrees of competition in the two markets. Namely, it captures the relative 'local competition' effect. This relative effect is affected by the level of trade freeness and the spatial distribution of firms. In particular, for any given level of ϕ, raising s_n increases the degree of local competition in the northern market and thus makes staying in the south more attractive.

To study the location condition, suppose firms were evenly divided between the regions, i.e. $s_n = \frac{1}{2}$. In this case, the right-hand side would equal 1. Since the northern market is bigger by assumption, the left-hand side is greater than one, so we know that $s_n = \frac{1}{2}$ cannot be an equilibrium. In particular, the bigger northern market would attract firms until the point that s_n rose high enough so that the advantage of the bigger northern market was offset by the higher degree of competition.

Finally, note that as trade freeness rises, the impact of s_n on the right-hand side gets stronger. Graphically, this means that the 'dispersion force' curve gets flatter as trade gets freer.

A13.2 The *EE–KK* diagram

In the first edition, we included a more complete analysis of agglomeration forces than shown in Fig. 13.12. Here we reproduce the first edition analysis.

The logic of agglomeration and dispersion forces can be illustrated more deeply with a diagram that relates relative market size to the relative number of firms. To make this diagram no more complicated than needed to illustrate the logic, it is helpful to make some simplifying assumptions.

We continue to work with only two regions, north and south, which have the same technology and factor supplies (this rules out comparative advantage effects). There will also be only two types of productive factor: labour, which is assumed to be immobile across regions (migration flows are quite small in Europe), and capital, which is assumed to be very mobile across regions. In particular, capital flows to the region with the highest rate of return, so in equilibrium the rate of return is equalized across regions (or else all capital is in the high-return region). Each industrial firm requires some capital and some workers to produce its goods, and to make counting easy we say that each industrial firm needs one unit of capital. This means that a region's share of total capital is identical to the region's share of industrial firms. Furthermore, to start with, we suppose that north and south have half of the total supply of the immobile factor, labour. We rule out cost linkages by assuming that neither sector buys intermediate inputs. Finally, since we want to focus on agglomeration, we assume that the wages paid in this sector are fixed by things going on in the rest of the economy and that the wages in both nations are the same, so there is no wage-related reason for delocating. (This assumption rules out one very important dispersion force, namely the tendency of agglomeration to drive up wage rates in the core region.)

With all these simplifying assumptions spelt out, we turn to a diagrammatic analysis.

The *EE* curve

We start with the demand linkage, i.e. the relationship between the share of industry in the north and the north's share of expenditure. Suppose industry – and thus capital – were evenly split between north and south. In this case, the two regions would have the same size markets. Why? Market size depends upon the purchasing power of local consumers. Since there is the same amount of labour in the two regions and the same amount of capital, the regional income

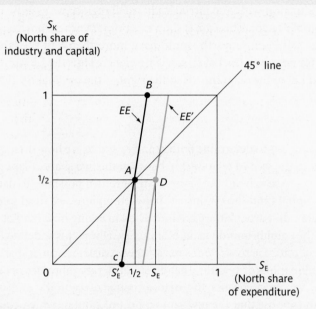

Figure A13.1 **Demand linkages: the EE schedule**

levels must be the same and thus the expenditure in each market must be the same. This case can be illustrated in Fig. A13.1 by point A, which is located at the $(^1/_2, ^1/_2)$ point. The diagram has s_E (short for 'share of expenditure') on the horizontal axis and this measures the relative market size of north. That is, if s_E is bigger than $^1/_2$, then north is the bigger market. On the vertical axis is s_K, which shows the share of industry that is in the north (share of industry and share of capital, K, are identical, as mentioned above).

Consider what the north's share of expenditure would be if all industries and thus all capital were in the north. Clearly, s_E would be greater than $^1/_2$ since north would have half the labour income and all the capital income. But s_E would be less than 1, since south still has all the income of its immobile workers (who would be working only in the service sector). This is shown as point B in the diagram. In a similar fashion, point C shows the north's expenditure share when all the industry is in the south.

There are three main points to retain:

1 *EE* is upward sloped since, as north gets a larger share of industry, its market becomes larger relative to that of the south.

2 *EE* is steeper than the 45° line since the mobile factor makes up only part of total expenditure.

3 As far as the *EE* line is concerned, the impact of s_K on s_E has nothing to do with trade costs. What matters is how much labour and how much capital is in each region.

The last point to make with this diagram is to consider what happens when south is fundamentally smaller than north, i.e. when, in the initial situation, north has more than half the immobile factor. It is important to consider this case. Much of the real-world politics of EU regional policy is driven by the fears of small regions and countries.

To consider a situation with one intrinsically small region, we assume that north has more than half the immobile factor. This case is shown as point D, where north's share of expenditure will be more than half because north would have more than half the labour and half of the capital. Likewise, for any given level of s_K, s_E will be higher. Thus the EE curve for the asymmetric size case – marked EE' in the diagram – is to the right of the original EE curve.

The *KK* line

The goal of the diagram is to determine both s_E and s_K and to see how these change as trade costs fall. This brings us to the second relationship between the two shares. Capital is mobile between regions and it moves to search out the highest rate of return possible. To determine the equilibrium division of capital (and thus industry) between regions, we need to calculate the rate of return in each region. In particular, we are interested in seeing how market size and the level of trade costs affect the equilibrium division of industry, where this is defined as the division that equalizes the rate of return across regions for any given distribution of market sizes (i.e. for any given s_E). The combinations of s_K and s_E that do equalize rates of return is called the KK curve.

To start with, we must discuss the determinants of capital's rate of return. A handy simplification is to suppose that the reward to a unit of capital (which equals the profitability of a single firm, since each firm needs one unit of capital) is proportional to sales. How can this be? Assuming that the profit margin is constant, at, say, 20 per cent, the total profitability of a firm is 20 per cent of sales. This one-to-one relationship between sales and profitability means that the rate of return is equalized between the regions when a typical firm in either region can sell the same amount (sales include both local and export sales).

It seems natural that equalizing the profitability of the two regions would require the north's share of industry to rise as the north's share of expenditure rises. As argued above, firms that must choose one location will tend to prefer location in the big market, since this would allow them to economize on trade costs. But as more firms move into the big market, competition gets fiercer in the big market and gets weaker in the small market. Consequently, not all firms will move to the big market. The division of industry, i.e. s_K, adjusts to balance the agglomeration forces and dispersion forces.

To get a better handle on this interaction, consider how the KK line would look if there were no trade between the regions, i.e. trade costs were prohibitive (although this situation is not very realistic, it provides a useful intellectual landmark). In particular, what would be the equilibrium division of industry for $s_E = \frac{1}{2}$? Remember that equalizing the rates of return requires equal sales per firm in the two regions. Since there is no trade in this simple case, equal sales means an equal number of firms in each region, i.e. that $s_K = \frac{1}{2}$. This is plotted as point A in Fig. A13.2. The same sort of equalize-sales-per-firm reasoning shows that if north has 100 per cent of expenditure then it must also have 100 per cent of firms, and if it has 0 per cent of expenditure then the equilibrium $s_K = 0$. These points are plotted as B and C, respectively. Repeating the reasoning for any s_E reveals that the equilibrium division without trade would always equal the given s_K. In short, the no-trade KK line coincides with the 45° line between B and C.

But what does KK look like in the more reasonable case when trade is possible but somewhat costly? To find the answer, it is useful to consider in depth why the no-trade KK line had a slope of 1. Start at point A in Fig. A13.2 and increase north's expenditure share by 10 per cent. This

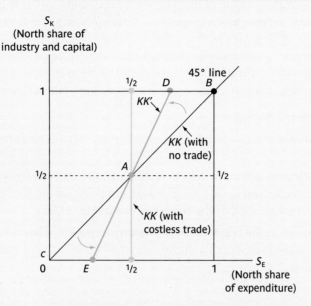

Figure A13.2 **Equalized rates of return for capital: the *KK* schedule**

automatically reduces south's expenditure share by 10 per cent. If s_K stayed at one-half when s_E was above one-half, then the firms in the north would sell more than those in the south and thus earn more. To restore equal profitability, the degree of competition in the north would have to rise by 10 per cent and the degree of competition in the south would have to fall by 10 per cent. Since there is no trade (i.e. total sales consist only of local sales), the 10 per cent increase in competition requires a 10 per cent increase in the number of firms in the north and a 10 per cent reduction in the number of firms in the south.

This reasoning was simple because there were no exports, i.e. competition was entirely local. Shifting firms from south to north has a more complex impact on the degree of competition when there is trade because each shift in firms changes the degree of competition in both markets. Specifically, if the number of northern firms rises by 10 per cent (by shifting firms from south to north), the degree of competition in the north will not rise by 10 per cent. Why not? The reason is that northern firms now face lower competition in their export market – the southern market – since there are fewer locally-based firms in the south. What this means is that restoring equal sales when there is trade will require the number of north-based firms to rise more than 10 per cent. This piece of logic is known as the 'home market effect'.

Graphically, the fact that s_K must increase by more than s_E shows up as the *KK* (with trade) line being steeper than the 45° line. In the diagram this is drawn as *KK'*, which reaches from point *E* to point *D*. Of course, it passes through point *A* since equalization of sales-per-firm with $s_E = \frac{1}{2}$ requires that $s_K = \frac{1}{2}$.

How does European integration affect the *KK* line? As it turns out, lower trade costs make *KK* steeper. The easiest way to see this is to contrast two extremes – the no-trade extreme, in which case the slope of the *KK* line is 45° as discussed above, and the costless trade case.

When trade is costless, the division of firms between north and south is entirely irrelevant – any division would result in equal earnings per firm since each identical firm would sell the same amount in each region. Graphically, this is the vertical dashed line that extends from $1/2$ to $1/2$ as shown in the diagram. In other words, if the markets were of equal size, then any division of firms would equalize sales. A vertical KK line reflects this since any s_K works for a given s_E.

There are four main points to retain from this discussion of the KK line:

1 The curve is upward sloping.
2 It is steeper than the 45° line due to the home market effect (except in the extreme case of no trade).
3 The level of trade costs affects the KK curve. In particular, as trade costs fall from prohibitive levels, KK gets steeper, but since ($1/2$, $1/2$) is always a point on the KK line, the curve rotates around point A (as indicated by the curved arrows in Fig. A13.2).
4 The share of labour in the two regions has no impact on KK. That is because all that really matters for KK is the share of expenditure, not whether this expenditure comes from labour or capital spending.

The locational equilibrium

Next we put together the EE and KK curves in Fig. A13.3. The diagram has north as the region with more than half the immobile labour (this is why EE does not pass through the ($1/2$, $1/2$) point but rather is to the right of it). The intersection of the EE and KK curves, point B, determines the equilibrium division of industry and the relative market sizes. Why?

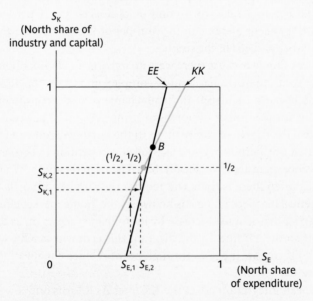

Figure A13.3 **The locational equilibrium**

EE tells us what s_E will be for any given s_K and KK tells us what s_K will be for any given s_E. At the intersection of the two lines, the rewards to capital are equalized between regions (so there is no pressure for s_K to change) and, given this equilibrium s_K, the relative market sizes are given by EE.

It is easy to see that point B is a stable outcome. For instance, suppose that for some reason, we started with s_E equal to $s_{E,1}$. Given this level of s_E, the KK lines tells us that firms would move until s_K were equal to $s_{K,1}$. But, if s_K were equal to $s_{K,1}$, then EE tells us that s_E would equal $s_{E,2}$. The iterations would continue, with s_K and s_E rising until B is reached.

A13.3 The impact of economic integration

Finally, we are ready to consider the impact of deeper European integration on the location of industry with the help of Fig. A13.4. As trade costs fall, KK rotates counter-clockwise to KK' and the new equilibrium is B'. That is, tighter integration favours concentration of industry in the market that was initially bigger. Indeed, in this very simple model – where competition is the only anti-concentration force – continued lowering of trade costs leads to the 'core–periphery' outcome. That is, a situation where all industries are in the big region (the core) and none are in the small region (the periphery).

A13.4 Adding back some elements of reality

In the EE–KK diagram, local competition is the only dispersion force so the model quite easily produces full agglomeration of capital/industry. In the real world, many things, especially land

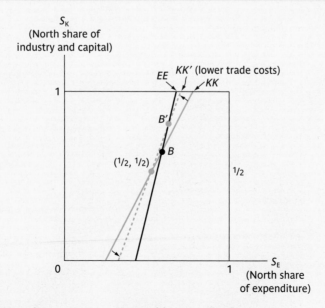

Figure A13.4 **Integration encourages geographic concentration**

prices, tend to discourage full clustering. That is, as economic activity tends to cluster in, say, Paris, Parisian land prices rise and provincial land prices fall. This geographic change in the relative price of productive factors tends to prevent all activities from moving to the biggest market.

There are many other dispersion forces. For example, some types of industries are intensive in the use of natural resources that are immobile. Steel production, for example, tends to locate near iron ore mines. Aluminium production, which requires huge inputs of electricity, tends to locate near cheap sources of electricity, such as hydroelectric dams and atomic energy plants.

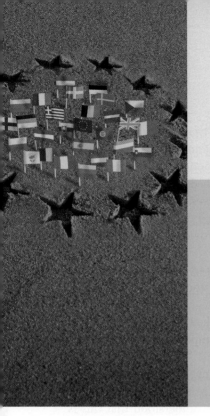

Chapter 14

EU competition and state aid policy

Competitive markets make our companies more innovative, more productive and more cost effective, and at the same time deliver lower prices, better quality, new products and greater choice for our citizens. Competitive markets require a strong competition policy, rigorously enforced, and the EU's state aid rules are an intrinsic part of this.

Neelie Kroes, 28 October 2008

Chapter contents

14.1 The economics of anti-competitive behaviour and state aid   426
14.2 EU competition policy   440
14.3 Summary   446

Introduction

Deeper European economic integration – together with more general trends such as WTO trade liberalization and globalization – has put European manufacturing and service sector firms under a great deal of pressure. As discussed in Chapter 6, the long-run outcome of this heightened competitive pressure is typically a reshaped industry marked by fewer, bigger, more efficient firms engaged in more effective competition among themselves. However, in the short and medium run firms may be tempted to collude in order to avoid or postpone industrial restructuring, and Member State governments may be tempted to provide subsidies that delay the necessary but painful restructuring.

The founders of the European Union understood that pressures to collude and subsidize would arise in the course of economic integration. They also understood that anticipation of such unfair practices could reduce political support for economic integration in all nations; an 'I will not liberalize since the others are not playing fair' feeling could halt all deeper integration, especially in the sectors where it is most critical, i.e. those marked by important scale economies and imperfect competition.

To guard against these pressures, they wrote into the Treaty of Rome broad prohibitions on private and public policies that distort competition. Of course, the Treaty of Rome has several provisions that have not been followed seriously, and the founders understood that this is frequently the fate of many provisions in many treaties. Yet, the Treaty writers felt that enforcing fair play in the Internal Market was so important that EU competition policy required special institutional arrangements – arrangements that would ensure that political expediency would not hinder the maintenance of a level playing field.

To this end, the Treaty grants the European Commission the sole power (exclusive competency in EU jargon; see Chapter 2) to regulate the EU's competition policy. The Commission's decisions can be overturned by the EU Court but they are not subject to approval by the Council of Ministers or the European Parliament. Of course, the Commission is not a 'Lone Ranger' in such matters. It continuously consults with Member States, especially via their respective competition authorities, but the Commission has the final word on whether mergers are allowed, whether particular business practices are allowed, and whether aid provided by Member States to firms is allowed. We can say that competition policy is one area where the Member States have truly transferred substantial sovereignty to a supranational level.

This chapter opens by providing an introduction to the economics of anti-competitive practices by private firms and subsidies by governments. It then proceeds to discuss the EU's actual policies.

14.1 The economics of anti-competitive behaviour and state aid

Before turning to how the European Commission regulates competition and state aid, it is important to understand the economics that lead private firms to engage in anti-competitive behaviour and what the effects of this are on the broader economy. This is the task we turn to first. Here, we study basic issues using the framework introduced in Chapter 6. The discussion here assumes readers have mastered the *BE–COMP* diagram, which is explained at length in Chapter 6.

14.1.1 Allowing collusion in the *BE–COMP* framework

As the EU's Single Market gets less fragmented, firms experience greater competition and this forces them to restructure in a way that lowers their costs. Frequently, such adjustments involve waves of mergers and acquisitions. An alternative, however, is for the firms to collude in order to avoid or postpone industrial restructuring. Or, to put it more directly, in many sectors firms face the choice between perishing and engaging in anti-competitive behaviour; some firms choose the latter. (We discuss some examples below.)

While this reaction by firms under pressure may be understandable, it is illegal under EU law and economically harmful for Europe as a whole. In a nutshell, allowing collusion among firms can result in too many, too small firms who must charge high prices to compensate for their lack of efficiency. The high prices result in lower demand and production. Thus protecting existing firms can end up reducing the overall level of industrial production.

One very clear real-world example was seen in telecoms services. Before liberalization, each European nation had its own monopoly provider, services were expensive since firms were small and as a result consumers did not spend much on telecoms. Since liberalization, competition has forced a massive industrial restructuring, a massive increase in the size of firms and a massive reduction in the price of services. The result has been a boom in the amount of telecoms services produced and consumed in Europe.

We illustrate this general point with an extended version of the *BE–COMP* framework from Chapter 6.

The BE–COMP diagram

Reviewing it briefly, the *BE–COMP* diagram, shown in Fig. 14.1, has three panels:

1 The middle panel shows the demand curve facing the sector in a typical nation (the diagram assumes that there are two identical nations; the middle panel shows the demand curve for one of them, the Home market). This panel is used for keeping track of consumer surplus and the connection between price and industry-wide production (which must equal consumption). For example, in the closed-economy case, the long-run price is P'. This means that total consumption must equal C'. This in turn means that total production must be C'.

2 The left-hand panel show the average and marginal cost curves for a typical firm (all firms are identical). The diagram assumes that firms enter or exit until all pure profit is eliminated, i.e. until price equals average cost. This panel is used to keep track of the typical firm's size, x, and its efficiency, as measured by its average cost (lower average cost means higher efficiency). The long-run equilibrium firm size is deduced from the long-run equilibrium price since we know that pure profits are zero in the long run, so the long-run price must equal the average cost of the typical firm. The average cost curve, *AC*, thus tells us how large the typical firm must be to have an average cost equal to the long-run equilibrium price. For example, if the long-run price is P', the typical firm size must be x' to ensure that price equals average cost.

3 The right-hand panel shows two equilibrium relationships between the mark-up and the number of firms. Recall that the mark-up is price minus marginal cost and that we denote it with the Greek letter 'mu', i.e. μ. The number of firms is denoted n. The *COMP* curve shows

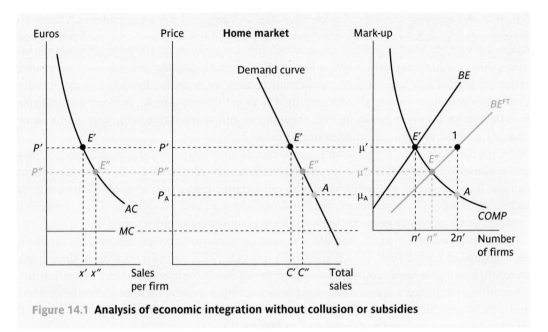

Figure 14.1 **Analysis of economic integration without collusion or subsidies**

the equilibrium combinations of μ and n assuming normal competition; as expected, more firms corresponds to more competition and thus a lower mark-up. The *BE* (break-even) curve is upward sloped since, as the number of firms rises, the sales per firm fall and so firms would need a higher mark-up in order to cover their fixed costs.

The equilibrium in the three panels identifies the equilibrium number of firms, n, mark-up, μ, price, P, firm size, x, and total output/consumption, C.

As in Chapter 6, we model European integration as a no-trade-to-free-trade liberalization between two identical nations. The equilibrium with no trade is marked by E'; the one with free trade between the two identical nations is marked E''.

There are two immediate and very obvious effects from the no-trade-to-free-trade liberalization:

1 Market size: post-integration, each firm has access to a second market of the same size.
2 Degree of competition: post-integration, each firm faces twice the number of competitors.

The market-size effect shifts the *BE* curve to the right, specifically out to the point marked '1' (see Chapter 6 for a detailed explanation). The competition aspect is the simplest to illustrate in the diagram, Fig. 14.1. Immediately upon opening the markets, i.e. before the industry has had time to adjust, the number of firms is $2n'$. Thus the typical firm will lower its mark-up in each market to point A – assuming, of course, that firms do not collude (recall that the *COMP* curve shows the mark-up under normal competition).

The extra competition forces mark-ups down to point A, and this pushes prices down to P_A. At this combination of sales per firm and mark-up, all firms begin to lose money (i.e. A is below the relevant break-even line, BE^{FT}). This 'profit pressure' forces industrial reorganization (mergers, acquisitions and bankruptcies) that gradually reduces the number of firms to the new long-run equilibrium number, n''. Note that after this long-run 'industry shake-out', firms are bigger and more efficient (the left-hand panel shows that x has increased to x'' and average cost has decreased to p''); they are also facing more effective competition than before the liberalization (the right-hand panel shows that the price–cost margins drop to μ'').

To summarize in words, deeper European integration boosts the degree of competition and this in turn requires the industry to consolidate so as to better exploit scale economies. Naturally, this consolidation involves the exit of some firms. The classic examples are telecoms, airlines, banking and autos where market integration has resulted in a wave of mergers.

The key point as far as competition policy is concerned is that deeper European integration will generally be accompanied by a long-run reduction in the number of firms. This is important for two reasons:

★ First, it means that Europe must be even more vigilant to ensure that the fewer bigger firms do not collude.

★ Second, it means that firms may be tempted to engage in anti-competitive practices in order to avoid or delay the industrial restructuring.

We turn now to showing what anti-competitive practices look like in the *BE–COMP* diagram.

Perfect collusion

The *COMP* curve in Fig. 14.1 assumes that firms do not collude. Both before and after the integration, we assumed that firms engaged in 'normal' competition in the sense that each firm decided on how much to sell, taking as given other firms' sales. In other words, each firm decided its output without any coordination among firms.

This assumption of 'normal' competition is quite reasonable for many industries, but it is not the most profitable behaviour for firms. If firms were allowed to collude, they could raise profits by reducing the amount they sell and raising prices. We consider some real-world examples in the policy section below (Section 14.2), but interested readers may wish to go to ec.europa.eu/comm/competition/cartels/cases/cases.cfm for details on the latest cases where the European Commission has caught firms colluding.

There are many, many forms of collusion in the world. The first form of collusion we consider is the simplest form to study. Instead of assuming no collusion on output, we consider the extreme opposite of perfect collusion on output.

If all firms could perfectly coordinate their sales, i.e. if they could act as if they were a single firm, they would limit total sales to the monopoly level. This would allow them to charge the monopoly price and to earn the greatest possible profit from the market. After all, the monopoly price–sales combination is – by definition – the combination that extracts the greatest profit from the market. In the diagram, this is shown by the mark-up, μ^m, that corresponds to one firm ($n = 1$). The resulting price is the monopoly price, shown as P^m.

The hard part of collusion is finding a way to divide up the monopoly level of sales among the colluding firms. The problem is that, because the price is so much higher than marginal cost, each firm would like to sell a little more than its share. To keep things simple, we assume that the firms manage the collusion by allocating an equal share to all firms. This type of behaviour can be illustrated in the *BE–COMP* diagram with the 'perfect collusion' line shown in Fig. 14.2.

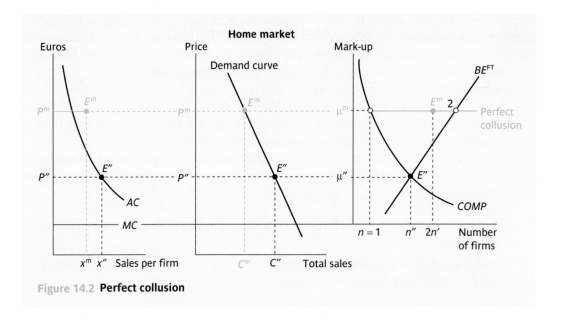

Figure 14.2 **Perfect collusion**

This line extends horizontally since it assumes that the mark-up always equals the monopoly mark-up, μ^m, regardless of the number of firms.

If all firms did charge the monopoly mark-up, then the maximum number of firms that could break even is shown by the point '2'. This would involve new entry – an outcome that we rarely observed after liberalization. Another possibility is that all $2n''$ firms would stay in business, without any new firms entering; this is shown as the point A'. Note that, at this point, all firms are making pure profits owing to the collusion (since E^m is above the AC curve in the left-hand panel and it is above the BE^{FT} curve in the right-hand panel).

This collusion is good for firms' profits, but it is bad for the society as a whole. Comparing the perfect collusion outcome to the long-run outcome without collusion (equilibrium marked with E''), we see that the price is higher, and consumption and production are lower. Moreover, since firms are smaller (since overall production is lower with collusion, the output of each firm must be smaller), average costs are higher, so the industry is less efficient.

Partial collusion

Perfect collusion is difficult to maintain since the gains from 'cheating' on other colluders are quite high. To reduce the incentive to cheat, the actual degree of collusion may be milder than perfect collusion. This sort of partial collusion restricts sales of all firms but not all the way back to the monopoly level, so the mark-up is lower than the monopoly mark-up but higher than the $COMP$ mark-up. With the mark-up lower, it is easier to sustain the collusion since the benefits from cheating are not quite as large.

But how much lower would the mark-up be under partial collusion? As it turns out, an understanding of advanced economics is needed to formalize this notion of 'partial collusion', so we do not address it here explicitly (see Mas-Colell et al. 1995, for an advanced treatment). Fortunately, the basic idea can be easily depicted in Fig. 14.3.

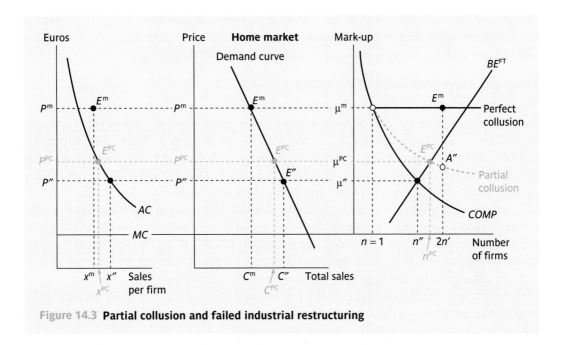

Figure 14.3 **Partial collusion and failed industrial restructuring**

The curve labelled 'partial collusion' shows a level of collusion where the mark-up is somewhere between the monopoly mark-up and the no-collusion mark-up shown by the *COMP* curve. We do not specify exactly where it lies between the two as it does not change the qualitative analysis. All we need to assume is that the partial collusion curve lies between the *COMP* curve and the perfect collusion curve as shown in the diagram.

If the $2n'$ firms all engaged in this partial collusion, then the mark-up would be shown by the point A''. This mark-up is higher than the long-run equilibrium mark-up without collusion (μ''), so we see that this partial collusion offsets, to some extent, the increase in competition induced by integration. (Recall from Chapter 6 that the size of the mark-up is an indicator of the degree of competition.)

Note, however, that although this mark-up is higher than under normal competition, it is not high enough for all the firms to break even. We can see this from the fact that point A'' is below the break-even curve (BE^{FT}). What this means is that even with partial collusion, some firms will exit the market. In the long run, the number of firms adjusts to restore zero pure profits, and this is where the partial competition curve and the break-even curve intersect, namely point E^{PC}.

Point E^{PC} is the long-run equilibrium since with n^{PC} firms the mark-up would be μ^{PC} and, with this mark-up, n^{PC} firms would all break even. As before, we can read off all the important aspects from the diagram. The level of consumption in the Home market (which is half of total consumption since Foreign is assumed to be identical) is C^{PC}. Since supply equals demand in equilibrium, we know that C^{PC} is also the total production in each nation. As usual, the equilibrium price also tells us the equilibrium efficiency, i.e. the typical firm's average cost. Using the average cost curve, we also know that the size of the typical firm is x^{PC}.

Now we study the economic implications of such collusion, comparing it to the long-run equilibrium with normal competition, i.e. equilibrium E''. To summarize the price and quantity changes, we note that, compared to the normal competition equilibrium, the partial collusion equilibrium involves firms that are smaller, less efficient and more numerous. The mark-up is higher along with the price, so consumption and total production are lower.

Long-run economic costs of collusion

The first point is that collusion will not in the end raise firms' profits to above-normal levels. Even allowing for the way that partial collusion raises prices above P'', the initial number of firms after liberalization, namely $2n'$, is too high for all of them to break even. Industrial consolidation proceeds as usual, but instead of the zero-profit level being reached when the number of firms has dropped to n'', the process halts at n^{PC}. As noted above, this is where pure profits – which started at zero in the pre-integration long-run equilibrium described in Fig. 14.1 – are returned to zero. In other words, the higher prices do not result in higher long-run profits. It merely allows more small, inefficient firms to remain in the market. The welfare cost of the collusion is measured by the four-sided area marked by P^{PC}, P'', E'' and B. This is just the consumer surplus loss, but since there is no change in pure profits (it is zero in the long run with or without collusion), the change in consumer surplus is the full welfare effect.

To summarize, collusion prevents the full benefits of restructuring from occurring. By keeping too many firms in the market, anti-competitive behaviour thwarts part of the industry's adjustment that is the key to the gains from integration.

Having presented a general analysis that suggests why deeper European integration and competition problems tend to go hand in hand, we turn now to considering four types of anti-competitive practices in more detail. We start with cartels.

14.1.2 Anti-competitive behaviour

Firms like to make money. Competition hinders this, so some firms try to limit competition. One age-old way of doing this is to form a cartel with other firms in the industry. For example, one of the best-known cartels, the Organization of the Petroleum Exporting Countries (OPEC), has been controlling the international price of crude oil since the early 1970s.

Horizontal anti-competitive practices: cartels and exclusive territories

The classic example of a cartel in Europe is the vitamins cartel (see Box 14.1). As Fig. 14.4 shows, the economic effects of cartels are rather straightforward (see Chapter 4 if you need a refresher on this sort of economics). The diagram depicts the impact of the price-raising effects of a cartel.

The diagram shows the situation for a particular market, say vitamin C, where the price without the cartel would be P. This initial

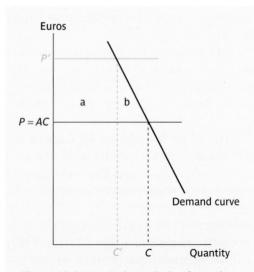

Figure 14.4 **Economic analysis of cartels**

price is shown as being equal to average costs (*AC*), which indicates zero profits even before the cartel; the analysis follows through even if the initial price were above *AC*, but this way makes it easier to see the effects. When the cartel raises the price to *P'* by reducing the volume of sales to *C'*, consumer surplus is reduced by the areas 'a' plus 'b'. The cartel's profit rises by the area 'b'.

This analysis illustrates the two main problems with cartels: the rip-off effect and the inefficiency effect.

Box 14.1 **The vitamin cartels**

In 2001, the European Commission fined eight companies for their participation in cartels that eliminated competition in the vitamin sector (vitamins A, E, B1, B2, B5, B6, C, D3, Biotin, Folic acid, Beta Carotene and carotinoids) for more than ten years. The European vitamins market is worth almost a billion euros a year since, in addition to being sold directly to consumers, vitamins are added to a wide variety of products, such as cereals, biscuits, drinks, animal feed, pharmaceuticals and cosmetics.

The European Commissioner in charge of competition policy at the time, Mario Monti, described it as the 'most damaging series of cartels the commission has ever investigated'. Mr Monti said: 'The companies' collusive behaviour enabled them to charge higher prices than if the full forces of competition had been at play, damaging consumers and allowing the companies to pocket illicit profits.'

The firms fixed prices, allocated sales quotas, agreed on and implemented price increases and issued price announcements according to agreed procedures. They also set up a mechanism to monitor and enforce their agreements and participated in regular meetings to implement their plans. This included the establishment of a formal structure and a hierarchy of different levels of management, often with overlapping membership at the most senior levels to ensure the functioning of the cartels, the exchange of sales values, volumes of sales and pricing information on a quarterly or monthly basis at regular meetings, and the preparation, agreement, and implementation and monitoring of an annual 'budget' followed by the adjustment of actual sales achieved so as to comply with the quotas allocated.

Under EU law, companies found guilty of antitrust practices can be fined up to 10 per cent of their total annual sales. Hoffman-La Roche of Switzerland received the largest fine (€462 million) for being the cartel ringleader, which also included BASF and Merck (Germany), Aventis SA (France), Solvay Pharmaceuticals (the Netherlands), Daiichi Pharmaceutical, Esai and Takeda Chemical Industries (Japan).

Source: This box is based on information from the European Commission's website; the quotes are from a *Guardian* newspaper article dated 21 November 2001, posted on their excellent website, Guardian Unlimited, www.guardian.co.uk

---

First, the fact that they allow firms to profit at the expense of customers is considered by most people (and by EU law) to be unfair – a rip-off to put it colloquially. Second, the gain to firms is less than the loss to consumers, so the cartel is inefficient from a purely technical point of view. Specifically, the net economic loss is the area 'b'. While few Europeans know or care about the efficiency loss, almost all would find that the rip-off effect was something their governments should do something about.

Another rather common way of restricting competition is for firms to agree upon so-called exclusive territories. For example, one company would agree to sell only in its local market in exchange for a similar promise by its foreign competitors. One example of this can be found in the market for video games.

Nintendo and seven of its official distributors in Europe teamed up in the 1990s to boost profits by dividing up Europe's markets and charging higher prices where consumers had a higher ability to pay. Under this practice, distributors had to prevent games being shipped from their territory to that of another EU market where prices were higher. Independent customers who allowed such sales among territories were punished by being given smaller shipments next time or by being cut off altogether. In this way, these companies managed to maintain big price differences for play consoles and games in various EU markets (e.g. Britons enjoyed prices that were 65 per cent cheaper than those faced by the Germans and Dutch). The European Commission fined Nintendo and the seven distributors €168 million.

Thinking more broadly, it is clear that such practices offset all the goals of European integration, which is exactly why the Treaty of Rome prohibited such behaviour.

Figure 14.5 shows a situation where a firm would like to charge a different price in the German and UK markets.

The diagram shows the two demand curves; the German demand curve D^D is steeper than the British demand curve D^{UK}. The steepness of a demand curve reflects a 'willingness to pay' since it tells us how much consumption of Nintendo products would drop for a given price increase. The German curve is drawn as steeper to reflect the fact that Germans have fewer options when it comes to consumer electronics and games (owing to the smaller number of people who speak German versus English worldwide, and to widespread restrictions on retail outlets in Germany). In economics jargon, German demand is more inelastic, i.e. more unresponsive to price. In this situation, Nintendo would maximize profits by selling the quantities in Germany and Britain that correspond to the intersections of the marginal revenue curves (MR^D and MR^{UK}) and marginal cost curves (MC); see Chapter 6 if this reasoning is unfamiliar. The quantities are not shown explicitly, but the resulting prices are marked as P^D and P^{UK}.

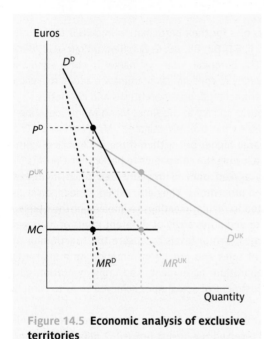

Figure 14.5 Economic analysis of exclusive territories

In an integrated market, independent firms, often called 'traders', could arbitrage the price gap by buying Nintendo goods in the UK and shipping them to Germany. Such shipments – which are known as 'parallel trade' – would lower Nintendo's profits and that of its official distributors. To preserve their profits, Nintendo and its distributors attempted, illegally, to prevent such trade.

Bullies in the market: abuse of dominant position

Business leaders and stock markets often evaluate a company's performance based on the growth of its market share, so many firms aim to conquer the market. Firms that are lucky or possess excellent products can succeed in establishing very strong positions in their market. This is not a problem if the position reflects superior products and/or efficiency – Google's triumph in the market for search engines could be one example. However, once a firm has a dominant position, it may be tempted to use it to extract extra profits from its suppliers or customers, or it may attempt to arrange the market so as to shield itself from future competitors. According to EU law, such practices, known technically as 'abuse of dominant position', are illegal.

The classic example of this is Microsoft. Most computer users are happy that Microsoft has standardized the basics of personal computing around the world – especially those that move between nations or use more than one machine on a regular basis. In other words, computer operating systems are subject to network externalities. That is, computer operating system software becomes more valuable to each user as more people use it.

To understand how and why network externalities work, just think about why the English language has spread so widely and continues to do so; more and more people learn it since so many people speak it. Just as with English, industries characterized by network externalities tend to be marked by a dominant firm, or a handful of firms.

In the case of Microsoft, which has dominated the operating system software market for decades, the question is how it came to dominate applications with products such as Word and Excel. Although it has never been proved in court, many observers believe that the company used frequent updates of its operating system to induce users to drop competing applications (as recently as ten years ago, Microsoft had real competition from rival products such as WordPerfect and Lotus). The details of Windows updates are available to engineers updating Microsoft applications but not to those updating rival applications, so new versions of rival applications often had glitches caused by incompatibilities with the latest version of Windows. Even if a user preferred the other applications, incompatibilities with successive versions of DOS and Windows meant it was easier to switch to Microsoft's applications than it was to deal with the glitches. Moreover, when competing firms came up with innovative programs, Microsoft typically responded with similar programs and gave them away for free. Today, for example, Microsoft charges a high price for Word, where it no longer has any real competitors, but it charges a zero price on software where it has significant rivals, such as media readers and web browsers. See Box 14.2 for details.

Box 14.2 **The Microsoft case**

The case against Microsoft was triggered by one of its competitors, Sun Microsystems, asserting that Microsoft refused to supply information that it needed to make its products work with Microsoft's PC operating system. Since Microsoft dominated the market, Sun could not really do business without the information, so the denial of information was a possible abuse of Microsoft's dominant position. During its investigation, the Commission found evidence of additional illegal behaviour by Microsoft and it broadened the scope of the investigation to include Microsoft's conduct with regard to its Windows Media Player product. In particular, it seemed that Microsoft was using its dominant position in the operating system market to push out rivals that had developed innovative products for playing various forms of audio and video files.

The investigation dragged on for years and, during this time, Microsoft engaged in additional practices that the Commission suspected. Finally, the Commission concluded its investigation on 24 March 2004 and issued a Decision. As Chapter 2 points out, these are EU laws that have direct effect in all Member States. The decision found that Microsoft had abused its dominant position in the PC operating system market in two ways: (1) by refusing to supply competitors with the information they needed to compete with Microsoft products – the decision ordered Microsoft to make that information available on reasonable terms, and (2) harming competition through the tying of its separate Windows Media Player product to its Windows PC operating system. The decision ordered Microsoft to provide a version of Windows without Windows Media Player. The European Commission also fined Microsoft €497 million at the time.

The problems did not stop there, however. The Commission decided in December 2005 that Microsoft was failing to comply with the ruling by not releasing information in a way and at a price that fostered competition. The Commission decided to fine Microsoft more than a million euros a day until the company complied.

The daily fine was levied in July 2006, at €1.5 million per day (16 December 2005 to 20 June 2006) for a total of €280 million. The Commission also threatened to increase the fine to €3 million a day from July 2006, if Microsoft did not comply by then. EU Competition Commissioner Neelie Kroes said, 'I regret that, more than two years after the decision . . . Microsoft has still not put an end to its illegal conduct.' Predictably, Microsoft appealed. In September 2007, it lost the appeal against the European Commission's case and was forced to pay most of the Commission's court costs.

Despite all this, Microsoft continued in its non-compliance and the Commission imposed an €899 million fine in February 2008. This was for non-compliance between 21 June 2006 and 21 October 2007, the date that the Commission determined Microsoft to be in compliance with its 2004 ruling.

Although the total fine amounted to €1.7 billion since 2004, that is only about two weeks' worth of the company's cash flow. For example, Microsoft posted a record profit of $4.7 billion in the second quarter of 2008. Moreover, Microsoft has a long history of paying antitrust fines, e.g. $750 million to AOL/Time-Warner in 2003, $1.1 billion to California in 2003, $536 million to Novell in 2004, $1.6 billion to Sun in 2004, $775 million to IBM in 2005, $776 million to Real Networks in 2005.

The story is far from over. In January 2008 the Commission launched fresh investigations into Microsoft's behaviour in the market for its Office software and its Internet Explorer. In May 2008, Microsoft announced that it would appeal the February 2008 fine.

14.1.3 Merger control

In many European industries, the number of firms is falling as firms merge or buy each other out. This sort of concentration of market power is a natural outcome of European integration, as Fig. 14.1 showed, but it may also produce cartel-like conditions. The basic trade-off can be illustrated with the so-called Williamson diagram in Fig. 14.6.

Consider a merger that allows the merged firms to charge a higher price, but which also allows them to lower average cost by eliminating redundant capacities in marketing, accounting, sales representatives, etc. The price rise is shown in the diagram by the increase in price from P to P' (the diagram assumes that the market was in long-run equilibrium with $P = AC$ to start with). The efficiency gain is shown by the drop in average cost from AC to AC'.

The gain to the firm's profitability is strongly positive. Before, $P = AC$ meant there were no profits. After, profits are the areas 'a' plus 'c'. The merger is bad for consumers, since the price hike implies a loss of consumer surplus equal to the area a + b. The overall gain to society, taking profits and consumer surplus together, is the area 'c' minus the area 'b' since area 'a' is just a transfer from consumers to firms.

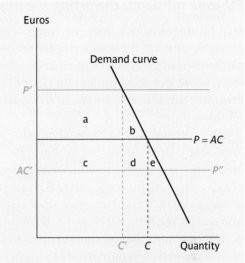

Figure 14.6 Basic economics of mergers: market power vs. efficiency gains

There is a point here that is important for understanding the EU's new rules on mergers. Notice that if entry and exit in the industry are unrestricted, and the remaining firms do not collude, then the long-run outcome of this merger will be to drive the price down to the lower average costs, $P'' = AC'$. This is essentially what happens when the equilibrium shifts from E' to E'' in Fig. 14.1. In this case, the merger-with-efficiency gain is always positive and equal to area c + d + e since the consumer surplus gain from the lower long-run price, P'', is not offset by any loss of producer surplus; profits were zero to start with ($P' = AC'$) and to end with ($P'' = AC'$). Since entry and exit in most EU industries is fairly unrestricted, there is a presumption that mergers will generally be of the type that boosts efficiency and passes on this efficiency to consumers.

Note that our treatment of competition here is highly simplified. The impact of mergers on pricing and costs can be extremely complicated and highly dependent on the nature of the industry. Examples of such reasoning can be found in the Commission's analysis of actual merger cases on their website: europa.int.eu/comp/.

14.1.4 State aid

The Fig. 14.1 logic linking integration and industrial restructuring presumes that profit-losing firms would eventually leave the industry – that they would be bought out by another firm, merged with other firms or, in rare cases, go bankrupt. All three of these exit strategies may involve important job losses in specific locations, or at the very least an important reorganization that may require workers to change jobs. Since job losses and relocations are painful, governments frequently seek to prevent them. For example, if the firm is government owned, trade unions may force the government to continue to shore up the money-losing enterprise. If it is privately owned, the government may provide subsidies through direct grants or through long-term loans that may not be repaid.

What we want to do here is to look at the long-run economics of such subsidies – called 'state aid' in EU jargon – under two distinct scenarios. The first is where all governments provide such support. The second is where only one does.

EU-wide subsidies: thwarting the main source of gains

Start by supposing that both governments provide subsidies that prevent restructuring. To be concrete, we make the additional, more specific assumption that governments make annual payments to all firms exactly equal to their losses. Under this policy, all $2n'$ firms in the Fig. 14.1 analysis will stay in business, but, since firms are not making extraordinary profits, no new firms will enter. The economy, in short, remains at point A owing to the anti-restructuring subsidies.

An insightful way to think about this subsidy policy is as a swap in who pays for the inefficiently small firms. Before integration, prices were high, so consumers paid for the inefficiency. After liberalization, competition drives down the price but this comes at the cost of extra pay-outs from the national treasuries, so now the taxpayers bear the burden of the industry's inefficiency. Moreover, since all the firms stay in business, integration is prevented from curing the main problem, i.e. the too-many-too-small firms problem. Firms continue to be inefficient since they continue to operate at a too small a scale. As a consequence, the subsidies prevent the overall improvement in industry efficiency that was the source of most of the gains discussed in Chapter 6.

Do nations gain from this liberalize-and-subsidize scheme? As it turns out, both nations do gain overall, even counting the cost of the subsidies. We shall show this with a diagram, but before turning to the detailed reasoning, it is instructive to explain the deep reason for this result. Imperfect competition is inefficient since it leads prices to exceed marginal costs. Recalling from Chapter 4 that the consumer price is a measure of marginal utility, the fact that price exceeds marginal cost implies that the gain to consumers from an extra unit would exceed the resource cost of providing the unit. In short, society tends to gain from an expansion of output when price exceeds marginal cost. Because of this, policies that increase output tend to improve welfare. In the jargon of public economics, the subsidy is a 'second-best' policy since it reduces the negative effects of market-power distortion, even if it does not solve the root of the problem.

Note, however, that this reasoning is very partial. This sort of 'reactive' subsidy turns out to be a very bad idea in the long run. The subsidies are paid to prevent firms from adapting to changed circumstances. While the government may occasionally improve things by preventing change, a culture of reactive interventionism typically results in a stagnant economy. Staying competitive requires industries to change – to adapt to new technologies, to new competitors and to new opportunities. When firms get used to the idea that their governments will keep them in business no matter what, the incentive to innovate and adapt is greatly weakened. Firms with this sort of mindset will soon find themselves far behind the international competition.

Welfare effects of the liberalize-and-subsidize policy

To explain the welfare effects of the liberalize-and-subsidize policy, we refer to Fig. 14.7. The policy we consider freezes the economy at point A in the right-hand and middle panels (this point A corresponds exactly to the point A in Fig. 14.1). We know that the price falls from p' to p^A and consumption rises from C' to C^A. Since the number of firms has not changed but total sales in each market (which must equal total consumption in each market) have increased, we know that the sales of each firm have increased somewhat, as shown in the left-hand panel from x' to x^A. At this point, firms are losing money, but the government offsets this with a subsidy.

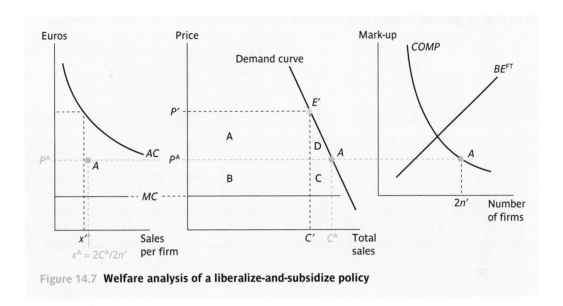

Figure 14.7 **Welfare analysis of a liberalize-and-subsidize policy**

How big will the subsidy be? The easiest way to make this comparison is to adopt a round-about approach. First, consider the total size of operating profit that the whole Home industry needs to cover all fixed cost before the liberalization. The answer is already in the middle panel. Before the liberalization, the industry broke even by selling a total of C' units at the price p'. The operating profit on this was the area A + B in the middle panel of the diagram, i.e. the gap between price and marginal cost times the units sold. After the liberalization, the industry's operating profit is area B + C (the new price–cost gap, $p^A - MC$, times the new sales, C^A). The drop in operating profit is thus area C minus area A. The subsidy we are considering would have to exactly offset the loss, so the subsidy would equal area A − C. With these facts established, we turn to the welfare calculation.

The consumer part of the welfare calculation is simple. Consumers see a lower price so consumer surplus rises by the area +A + D. To see the overall welfare effect, we subtract the subsidy, which equals A − C. The net welfare effect is A + D − (A − C), which equals D + C. We know this is right since this area is the gap between price and marginal cost summed over all the extra units consumed. Notice that this is the classic gain from partially redressing a market power distortion.

Only some subsidize: unfair competition

EU members' governments differ over how much they can or want to subsidize loss-making firms. Yet, when only some governments subsidize their firms, the outcome of the restructuring may be 'unfair' in the sense that it gets forced upon the firms in nations that do not subsidize, or stop subsidizing before the others. The real problem with this is that it may create the impression that European economic integration gives an unfair advantage to some nations' firms.

To examine this problem more closely while keeping the reasoning as tangible and simple as possible, we continue with the Fig. 14.1 example of two nations engaged in an extreme no-trade-to-free-trade integration. The integration moves each identical economy from the point E' to A. At A, all firms in both nations are losing money. Now suppose that restructuring takes, say, five years in the sense that after that time the number of firms has adjusted from $2n'$ to n''. In our simple example, there is no way of telling which of the surviving firms will be Home firms and which will be Foreign firms. Symmetry suggests that half the remaining firms would be Foreign, but nothing in the example ensures that this is the case. This is where subsidies can make a big difference.

To be concrete, suppose that prior to the liberalization there were ten firms in Home and ten in Foreign, and that after restructuring there will be 12 firms in total. Furthermore, suppose that Home provides a five-year subsidy to all of its ten firms, with the size of the subsidy being large enough to offset the liberalization-induced losses. The Foreign government, by contrast, is assumed to pursue a laissez-faire policy, i.e. it allows the market to decide which firms should survive – either because it believes in the market, or because it cannot afford the subsidies. In this situation, it is clear that eight of the ten Foreign firms will go out of business, while all ten Home firms will survive. At the end of the five-year period, the Home government no longer needs to subsidize its firms since the exit of eight Foreign firms restores the industry to profitability.

From a purely economic perspective, the Foreign nation might have been the winner since having firms in our example brings nothing to national welfare (firms earn zero profit in the best of cases). The Home nation's subsidies were merely a waste of taxpayers' money. Two comments are relevant at this stage. First, this sort of conclusion shows that our simple example is actually too simplistic in many ways. For example, we did not consider the cost of workers having to switch jobs and possibly being unemployed for some time. Second, it shows that economics is only part of the picture.

The politics of state aid disciplines: I'll play only if the rules are fair

From a political perspective, this sort of unfair competition would be intolerable. Indeed, if trade unions and business groups in Foreign anticipated that this would be the outcome, they might very well block the whole integration exercise. To avoid this sort of resistance to liberalization, the EU establishes very strict rules forbidding such unfair competition. In this sense, one of the most important effects of disciplines on state aid is the fact that it allows governments to procede with painful and politically difficult reforms.

14.2 EU competition policy

Having laid out the basic logic of collusion and subsidies, we turn now to considering actual EU policy that constrains such actions by private actors (anti-competitive practices) and governments (subsidies).

14.2.1 Institutions: The European Commission's power

The EU's founders were fully aware that integrating Europe's markets would result in restructuring and that this would produce incentives for private and public actors to resist consolidation. This is very clear, for example, in the 1956 Spaak Report which was the economic blueprint for the Treaty of Rome (*Rapport des chefs de délégation aux ministres des affaires étrangères,*

Bruxelles, 21 avril 1956). Moreover, they feared that the perception that some nations might 'cheat' in an effort to shift the burden of consolidation onto others would, in itself, make deeper European integration politically impossible. To ensure that the prevailing attitude was 'I will reform since the rules are fair' instead of 'I cannot reform since other nations will cheat', the Treaty of Rome prohibited any action that prevents, restricts or distorts competition in the common market.

Importantly, the Treaty puts the supranational Commission in charge of enforcing these strictures. Just as European leaders decided to forgo their control over monetary policy (by making central banks independent) since they knew in advance that short-run politics would lead to bad long-run policy, the Treaty of Rome grants a great deal of power on competition policy directly to the European Commission. The idea was that the politicians in the Council of Ministers might not be able to resist the short-run pressure of special-interest groups opposed to the consolidation that is necessary to obtain the long-run gains from European economic integration. In fact, competition policy is probably the area in which the Commission has the greatest unilateral power.

The Commission has considerable powers to investigate suspected abuses of EU competition law, including the right to force companies to hand over documents. Most famously, the Commission has the right to make on-site inspections without prior warning, which the media often call 'dawn raids'. With a court order, the Commission can even inspect the homes of company personnel.

The Commission has the power to prohibit anti-competitive activities. It does this by issuing injunctions against firms. To back up these demands, the Commission has the right to impose fines on firms found guilty of anti-competitive conduct. The fines vary according to the severity of the anti-competitive practices, with a maximum of 10 per cent of the offending firm's worldwide turnover. When it comes to subsidies, the Commission has the power to force firms to repay subsidies it deems to be illicit.

Unlike most other areas where the Commission acts, the Commission's decisions are not subject to approval by the Council of Ministers or the European Parliament. The only recourse is through the European Court. This is an area where Member States truly did pool their sovereignty to ensure a better outcome for all.

14.2.2 EU law on anti-competitive behaviour

EU law on anti-competitive practices is laid out in the Treaty of Rome (formally, the Treaty Establishing the European Community, or EC Treaty for short). Here we review the main provisions, but it is important to note that this gives only a hint as to actual policy. EU competition policy has been subject to many decisions of the EU Court and one must master the details of these cases in order to fully understand which practices are prohibited and why. Moreover, the Commission publishes its own administrative guidelines so that firms can more easily determine whether a particular agreement they are contemplating will be permitted by the Commission.

Article 81 of the EC Treaty outrightly forbids practices that prevent, restrict or distort competition, unless the Commission grants an exemption. This article is clearly written and worth reading in its entirety (Box 14.3).

> ## Box 14.3   Article 81 (formerly Article 85)
>
> 1. The following shall be prohibited as incompatible with the common market: all agreements between undertakings, decisions by associations of undertakings and concerted practices which may affect trade between Member States and which have as their object or effect the prevention, restriction or distortion of competition within the common market, and in particular those which:
>   (a) directly or indirectly fix purchase or selling prices or any other trading conditions;
>   (b) limit or control production, markets, technical development, or investment;
>   (c) share markets or sources of supply;
>   (d) apply dissimilar conditions to equivalent transactions with other trading parties, thereby placing them at a competitive disadvantage;
>   (e) make the conclusion of contracts subject to acceptance by the other parties of supplementary obligations which, by their nature or according to commercial usage, have no connection with the subject of such contracts.
>
> 2. Any agreements or decisions prohibited pursuant to this Article shall be automatically void.
>
> 3. The provisions of paragraph 1 may, however, be declared inapplicable in the case of:
>   ★ any agreement or category of agreements between undertakings;
>   ★ any decision or category of decisions by associations of undertakings;
>   ★ any concerted practice or category of concerted practices, which contributes to improving the production or distribution of goods or to promoting technical or economic progress, while allowing consumers a fair share of the resulting benefit, and which does not:
>   (a) impose on the undertakings concerned restrictions which are not indispensable to the attainment of these objectives;
>   (b) afford such undertakings the possibility of eliminating competition in respect of a substantial part of the products in question.

Typically, the restrictions in Article 81 are classified as preventing horizontal or vertical anti-competitive agreements. Horizontal agreements are arrangements, like cartels and exclusive territories, upon competitors selling similar goods. Vertical agreements are arrangements between a firm and its suppliers or distributors (e.g. agreements by retailers to charge not less than a certain price, and tie-in arrangements whereby goods are only supplied if the vendor agrees to purchase other products).

The first part of Article 81 is so categorical that it rules out an enormous range of normal business practices, which can in fact be good for the European economy. The final part therefore allows the Commission to grant exemptions to agreements where the benefits outweigh the anti-competitive effects. The Commission does this for individual agreements notified to the Commission for exemption, but it also has established the policy of 'block exemptions' that grant permission to broad types of agreements. These exist for technology transfer and for R&D agreements. Political pressure has also forced the Commission to grant a block exemption to the anti-competitive practices in the distribution of motor vehicles.

The second major set of policies – restrictions on the abuse of a dominant position – are found in Article 82 of the EC Treaty (see Box 14.4). A dominant position usually depends upon a firm's market share. Abuse is a general term but it includes refusal to supply, unfair prices and conditions, predatory pricing, loyalty rebates, exclusive dealing requirements, and abuse of intellectual property rights.

Box 14.4   Article 82 (formerly Article 86)

Any abuse by one or more undertakings of a dominant position within the common market or in a substantial part of it shall be prohibited as incompatible with the common market insofar as it may affect trade between Member States.

Such abuse may, in particular, consist in:

(a) directly or indirectly imposing unfair purchase or selling prices or other unfair trading conditions;

(b) limiting production, markets or technical development to the prejudice of consumers;

(c) applying dissimilar conditions to equivalent transactions with other trading parties, thereby placing them at a competitive disadvantage;

(d) making the conclusion of contracts subject to acceptance by the other parties of supplementary obligations which, by their nature or according to commercial usage, have no connection with the subject of such contracts.

14.2.3 Control of mergers

The EC Treaty does not contain specific provisions on mergers, but since mergers can affect competition the Treaty requires the Commission to oversee merger activity. The Commission realized that the 1992 programme for the completion of the Internal Market would produce a flurry of merger activity. To promote transparency and allow firms to better understand whether a particular merger will be allowed, the EU set out explicit rules in Council and Commission Regulations starting in the late 1980s. The current set of regulations are called simply 'Merger Regulation'. This regulation, which reformed a string of earlier regulations to include new thinking and various EU Court decisions, was introduced in January 2004 and entered into force with the Union's enlargement. The Regulation does not stand by itself but rather is one pillar in a merger control edifice that also includes guidelines on the assessment of horizontal mergers and on best practice in merger investigations, and reforms within the Commission.

The Merger Regulation defines anti-competitive behaviour as: 'A concentration which would significantly impede effective competition, in the common market or in a substantial part of it, in particular by the creation or strengthening of a dominant position, shall be declared incompatible with the common market.' Under the new rules, mergers that meet the relevant criteria do not have to be notified to the Commission since they are presumed to be compatible with competition.

The new rules also give a prominent role to national competition authorities and courts, under the so-called European Competition Network which facilitates coordination among EU and national competition authorities and courts. See Box 14.5 for some merger decision examples.

Box 14.5   Some merger decision examples

The European pharmaceutical sector has experienced a wave of consolidation and, as part of this, two mega-mergers were brought to the attention of the European Commission, the Sanofi and Synthélabo link-up and the Pfizer and Pharmacia fusion. The Commission determined that both would lessen competition in certain market segments by limiting the choice of some drugs. The Commission, however, recognized the need for efficiency gains and believed that the mergers could be useful. The outcome was that the Commission allowed the mergers subject to conditions. The firms were required to transfer some of their products to their competitors so as to redress potential anti-competitive effects. For example, Sanofi/Synthélabo sold off certain antibiotics, hypnotics and sedatives.

Another case involved a mainly domestic merger between TotalFina and Elf Aquitaine, which were the main players in the French petroleum sector. The Commission determined that their merger would have allowed them to push up costs for independent petrol station operators (e.g. supermarkets) and the combined company would have operated around 60 per cent of the service stations on French motorways. The combined firms would also have been the leading supplier of liquid petroleum gas. The European Commission believed that this level of market power would be anti-competitive and agreed to the merger only on the condition that TotalFina/Elf sell off a large proportion of these operations to competitors. For example, it sold 70 motorway service stations in France to competitors.

14.2.4 EU policies on state aid

The EU's founders realized that the entire European project would be endangered if EU members felt that other members were taking unfair advantage of the economic integration (see Box 14.6 for an example of unfair competition in the EU energy market). To prevent this, the 1957 Treaty of Rome bans state aid that provides firms with an unfair advantage and thus distorts competition. Importantly, the EU founders considered this prohibition to be so important that they actually empowered the supranational European Commission to be in charge of enforcing the prohibition. Indeed, the Commission has the power to force the repayment of illegal state aid, even though the Commission normally has no say over members' individual tax and spending policies.

Box 14.6   Subsidies and unfair competition in the energy market

The market for electricity was one of the few markets left largely untouched by the sweeping liberalization of the EU's Single Market Programme between 1986 and 1992. Until the 1990s, the sector was dominated by government-owned or -controlled firms, but as part of the general trend towards market-oriented policies, many EU members privatized their state-owned energy monopolies and opened their markets to foreign competition. These moves, however, were not part of a coordinated EU strategy. The resulting difficulties provide an excellent illustration of how important the EU's anti-state aid policy is to keeping European economic integration on track.

As with much of European industry, the energy sector was and still is marked by too many firms which are too small to be truly competitive. As in many other sectors, a process of consolidation and industrial restructuring has begun. Unlike other EU sectors, however, liberalization varies greatly across Member States. France is one of the most closed markets in two senses. It is difficult for foreign firms to supply French customers and the French energy monopoly Electricité de France (EdF) is tightly controlled by the government so that it cannot be bought. Moreover, EdF receives various subsidies that give it an advantage in the market.

Other EU members feared that France had embarked on a cynical campaign of ensuring that EdF would be one of the survivors of the industrial restructuring that would inevitably come when energy was eventually liberalized. For example, France consistently opposed full liberalization of energy markets, and when the EU adopted a partial opening measure in which members were bound to open up their energy markets to third-party competition, France delayed passing the necessary laws. The real trouble began when EdF launched an aggressive campaign of expanding rapidly into the power markets of neighbouring Member States (Britain, Germany, Italy and Spain) while remaining a state-owned monopoly in its home market.

Such expansion would be unremarkable in other sectors, but the perception that EdF's moves were 'unfair' led other EU members to postpone or restrict their own liberalization efforts. For example, in 2001, German economy Minister Werner Mueller threatened to prevent the French state-owned power giant EdF from importing electricity into Germany as long as France did not open up its power market to foreign companies. Italy had a similar reaction after EdF began to take over the Italian company Montedison. As Italy's treasury Minister Vincenzo Visco explained, it was 'unacceptable to let a player with a rigged hand of cards join the game'. The Italian government quickly introduced measures designed to block further takeovers.

To prevent this action–reaction chain from ruining prospects for liberalization, the Commission launched an investigation in 2002 into EdF's state aid. Following the formal investigation procedure initiated by the Commission on 2 April 2003, the French government agreed to end EdF's unlimited state guarantee by 2005. Mario Monti, the Competition Commissioner at the time, said: 'I welcome the favourable outcome reached in this highly sensitive case. . . . A competitive situation has for the first time been created for EdF, without distortions due to state aid. The introduction of conditions of fair competition and the correction of past distortions is all the more important in sectors such as energy which are in the process of being liberalized and will enable all the positive effects to be reaped from that liberalization.'

Source: This box is based mainly on BBC news stories dated 12 June 2001 and 16 October 2002 (see www.bbc.co.uk)

The EC Treaty prohibits state aid that distorts competition in the EU. The Treaty defines state aid in very broad terms. It can, for instance, take the form of grants, interest relief, tax relief, state guarantee or holding, or the provision by the state of goods and services on preferential terms.

Some state aid, however, is allowed according to the Treaty since subsidies, when used correctly, are an essential instrument in the toolkit of good governance. The permitted exceptions include social policy aid, natural disaster aid and economic development aid to underdeveloped areas. More generally, state aid that is in the general interest of the EU is permitted. For example, the Commission has also adopted a number of bloc-exemption rules that explain which sorts of state aid are indisputable. These include aid to small and medium-sized enterprises, aid for training and aid for employment. More information can be found in DG Competition's highly accessible document *Competition Policy and Consumers*, downloadable from europa.eu.int (use Google to find the exact link since the Commission occasionally reshuffles its websites).

A contentious example: airlines in trouble

The Commission is frequently in the headlines over its state aid decisions since these often produce loud protests from firms and/or workers who benefited from any state aid that the DG Competition judges to be illegal. An excellent example concerns the airline industry – an industry where there are clearly too many firms in existence and the tendency to subsidize is strong. Many European airlines are the national 'flag carrier' and as such are often considered a symbol of nation pride.

Consolidation of the European airline industry has been on the cards for years, but the problem was exacerbated by the terrorist attacks of 11 September 2001. The ensuing reduction in air travel caused great damage to airlines all around the world and led to calls for massive state aid. To prevent these subsidies from being used as an excuse to put off restructuring, the Commission restricted subsidies to cover only the 'exceptional losses' incurred when transatlantic routes were shut down immediately after 11 September. To date, the Commission has managed to resist the desire of several Member State governments to support their national airlines to the same extent that the US government has supported US airlines.

It is easy to see the logic of the Commission's stance. Low-cost airlines, such as Ryanair and easyJet, have done well without subsidies. Moreover, artificial support for inefficient national carriers hinders the expansion of low-cost airlines. As Bannerman (2002) puts it:

> No-one will benefit from a return to spiralling subsidies, which damage the industry by encouraging inefficiency. Both consumers and taxpayers would suffer as a result. As for the national carriers, they would probably benefit from some market consolidation, creating fewer, leaner, pan-European airlines – although this process would need monitoring for its competitive effects on key routes. If the airline industry can use the crisis to create more efficient carriers, it will probably be the better for it. But this long-term view cuts little ice with workers who stand to lose their jobs, or with some politicians, for whom a flag carrier is a symbol of national pride. Unfortunately, the benefits of controlling state-aids occur mainly in lower fares and taxes, and are therefore widely diffused among the population. The costs, on the other hand, take the form of job losses, which hurt a small but vocal constituency.

14.3 Summary

Three main points have been made in this chapter:

★ One very obvious impact of European integration has been to face individual European firms with a bigger 'home' market. This produces a chain reaction that leads to fewer, bigger, more efficient firms that face more effective competition from each other. The attendant industrial restructuring is often politically painful since it often results in layoffs and the closure of inefficient plants. Governments very often attempt to offset this political pain by providing 'state aid' to their national firms. Such state aid can be viewed as unfair and the perception of unfairness threatens to undermine EU members' interest in integration. To avoid these problems, the founders of the EU established rules that prohibited state aid that distorts competition. The Commission is charged with enforcing these rules.

★ Private firms may also seek to avoid restructuring by engaging in anti-competitive practices and EU rules prohibit this. Moreover, as integration proceeds and the number of firms falls, the temptation for firms to collude may increase.

★ To avoid this, the EU has strict rules on anti-competitive practices. It also screens mergers to ensure that mergers will enhance efficiency. Again, the Commission is charged with enforcing these rules.

Self-assessment questions

1. Suppose that liberalization occurs as in Fig. 14.1 and the result is a pro-competitive effect, but instead of merging or restructuring, all firms are bought by their national governments to allow the firms to continue operating. What will be the impact of this on prices and government revenues? Now that the governments are the owners, will they have an incentive to continue with liberalization? Can you imagine why this might favour firms located in nations with big, rich governments?

2. Look up a recent state aid case on the Commission's website (europa.int.eu) and explain the economic and legal reasoning behind the Commission's decision using the diagrams in this chapter.

3. Look up a recent abuse of dominant position case (Article 82) on the Commission's website (europa.int.eu) and explain the economic and legal reasoning behind the Commission's decision using the diagrams in this chapter.

4. Look up a recent antitrust case (Article 81) on the Commission's website (europa.int.eu) and explain the economic and legal reasoning behind the Commission's decision using the diagrams in this chapter.

5. Using a diagram similar to Fig. 14.2, show what the welfare effects would be following a switch from normal competition to perfect collusion. Be sure to address the change in consumer surplus and pure profits.

Essay questions

1. When the Single Market Programme was launched in the mid-1980s, European leaders asserted that it would improve the competitiveness of European firms vis-à-vis US firms. Explain how one can make sense of this assertion by extending the reasoning in this chapter, and explain why this makes EU competition policy an important part of Europe's external competitiveness.

2. While the case for strengthening European-wide competition policy in tandem with the Single Market Programme is clear, is it obvious that this task should be allocated to the EU level instead of being left in the hands of Member States?

3. Some EU members allow their companies to engage in 'anti-takeover' practices. Discuss how differences in EU members' laws concerning these practices might be viewed as unfair when an EU industry is being transformed by a wave of mergers and acquisitions.

4. Read about the EU's 'Lisbon Strategy' and use the reasoning and logic in this chapter to explain the role that EU leaders expected competition policy to play in making the EU the most competitive economy by 2010.

5. In 2008, the EU began a review of its merger regulations. Read about the various considerations posted on the Commission's website and write an essay on how you think the merger regulations should be changed.

Further reading: the aficionado's corner

For a very accessible introduction to EU competition policy, see **Neven et al.** (1996).

Every interested reader should at least skim through the most recent version of the Commission's document, *Competition Policy and the Consumer*. This presents a succinct and authoritative presentation of EU competition policy. It also presents a large number of examples of EU competition policy in action (most of the examples in this chapter are based on these).

Useful websites

The website of DG Competition has several highly accessible accounts of EU competition policy and information on recent cases; see http://europa.eu.int/comm/competition/.

References

Bannerman, E. (2002) *The Future of EU Competition Policy*, Centre for European Reform. Download from www.cer.org.uk/pdf/p297_competition_policy.pdf.

Mas-Colell, A., M. Whinston and J.R. Green (1995) *Microeconomic Theory*, Oxford University Press, New York.

Neven, D., P. Seabright and M. Nutall (1996) *Fishing for Minnows*, CEPR, London.

Chapter 15

EU trade policy

The European economy stands or falls on our ability to keep markets open, to open new markets, and to develop new areas where Europe's inventors, investors and entrepreneurs can trade . . .

Peter Mandelson, EU Trade Commissioner, European Parliament, Brussels, 19 September 2005

Chapter contents

15.1	Pattern of trade: facts	*450*
15.2	EU institutions for trade policy	*456*
15.3	EU external trade policy	*459*
15.4	Summary	*466*

Introduction

The European Union is the world's biggest trader. Counting EU exporters within the EU and with third nations, the EU accounts for about 40 per cent of world trade and its share of trade in services is even greater. Three of the EU25 are individually in the top ten trading nations in the world (Germany, Britain and France). The EU is also a leader in the world trade system, both as a key player in the World Trade Organization (WTO) and as a massive signer of bilateral trade agreements. While the EU has been one of the staunchest supporters of the WTO's trade rules, many observers view EU trade policy – especially its policy on agricultural goods – as a major roadblock to greater liberalization worldwide. For example, as this edition was going to press, disputes over EU agricultural policies were one of the biggest stumbling blocks to the worldwide talks on trade liberalization known as the Doha Round. Other critics claim that EU external trade policy is particularly harmful to the world's poorest nations since the EU puts up its highest barriers against the goods that they are best able to export.

This chapter covers EU trade policy by presenting the basic facts on EU trade, covering the EU's institutional arrangements as they concern trade policy, and finally summarizing the EU's policies towards its various trade partners. It is important to note that EU trade policy – like so much about the Union – is mind-numbingly complex. There is a whole army of specialists who do nothing but follow EU trade issues, and most of these have to specialize in one particular area in order to master all the detail. Plainly, then, this chapter cannot come even close to surveying all EU trade policy. Its goal is rather to present the broad outlines and key issues. Readers who are interested in greater detail on a particular trade partner, sector or policy should start with the European Commission's website: http://europa.eu.int/comm/trade/.

15.1 Pattern of trade: facts

The EU trades mainly with Europe, especially with itself, as Fig. 15.1 shows. The top diagram shows the share of EU exports that goes to the EU's various partners. The figures include EU sales to non-EU nations as well as exports from one EU nation to another. This gives perspective on the relative importance of intra-EU trade and external trade. The main points are:

★ Two-thirds of EU27 exports are to other EU27 nations. More than 90 per cent of this is actually among the EU15, since the ten new Member States are fairly small economically.

★ If we add in other European nations – EFTA (Switzerland, Norway, Iceland and Liechtenstein), and Turkey – the figure rises to three-quarters. In short, three out of four export euros earned by the EU27 are from sales within Europe, broadly defined.

★ After Europe, North America and Asia are the EU27's main markets, but each account for a little less than one-tenth of EU exports.

★ Africa, Latin America and the Middle East are not very important as EU export destinations; their shares are each less than 3 per cent.

Rounding off to make the numbers easy to remember, we can say that three-quarters of EU exports go to Europe. The remaining quarter is split more or less evenly among three groups of nations: North America, Asia and all other nations.

The pattern on the import side is very similar, as the bottom diagram shows. The biggest difference lies with Asia since it provides 12 per cent of the EU's imports but absorbs only 7 per cent of EU exports (i.e. the EU runs a trade deficit with Asia). The opposite is true of North America since it accounts for a larger share of EU exports than of EU imports (i.e. the EU runs a small trade surplus with North America). The EU's trade with the rest of the world is approximately in balance, although it has been in a slight surplus in recent years (not shown in the figure).

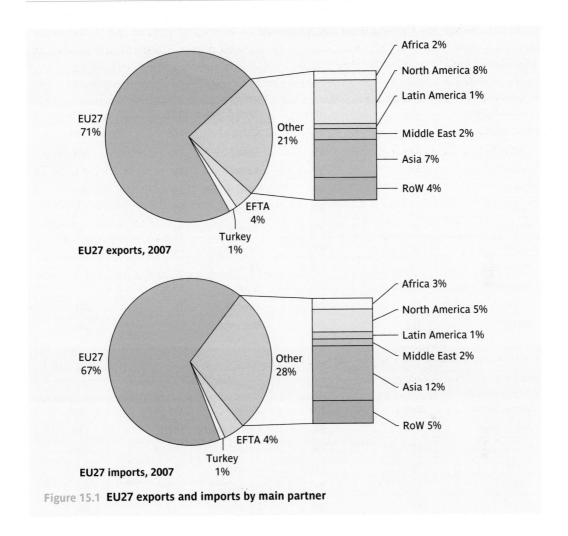

Figure 15.1 **EU27 exports and imports by main partner**

Again rounding off to make the numbers easy to remember, we can say that three-quarters of EU imports are from Europe, with the fourth quarter split into two more or less even groups of nations – Asia, and all other nations.

It can be useful to take an even closer look by separating out individual nations, as in Table 15.1. Just ten nations account for about two-thirds of EU27 *external* trade, but the list is slightly different on the import and export sides. The USA is the number one importer by a very large margin, and China is the biggest exporter. The next most important market for EU exports is Switzerland, but the Swiss buy only 30 per cent as much as Americans (still, this is a big number given that there are 7 million Swiss and 300 million Americans). China is now number three on the EU's export destination list; Chinese trade with the EU has been booming, both imports and exports, so China is set to become the EU's number two partner. Japan, the third economic powerhouse in the world after the USA and the EU, is the number four export destination and provider of imports.

Table 15.1 The EU's top ten import and export partners

	Exports (€ billion, current prices 2003)	% of all EU external exports		Imports (€ billion, current prices 2003)	% of all EU external imports
United States	226	26%	United States	157	17%
Switzerland	71	8%	China	105	11%
China	41	5%	Japan	72	8%
Japan	41	5%	Russia	68	7%
Russia	37	4%	Switzerland	59	6%
Turkey	29	3%	Norway	51	5%
Norway	28	3%	Turkey	26	3%
Canada	22	2%	South Korea	26	3%
Hong Kong	18	2%	Taiwan	22	2%
Australia	18	2%	Brazil	19	2%
United Arab Emirates	16	2%	Canada	16	2%
South Korea	16	2%	Malaysia	16	2%

	Exports (€ billion, current prices 2007)	% of all EU external exports		Imports (€ billion, current prices 2007)	% of all EU external imports
United States	261	22%	China	231.51	16%
Switzerland	93	8%	United States	181.1	13%
Russia	89	7%	Russia	143.88	10%
China	72	6%	Japan	78.1	5%
Turkey	53	4%	Norway	76.83	5%
Japan	44	4%	Switzerland	76.7	5%
Norway	43	4%	Turkey	46.86	3%
India	29	2%	South Korea	39.61	3%
United Arab Emirates	27	2%	Brazil	32.65	2%
Canada	26	2%	Libya	27.32	2%

Source: Eurostat © European Communities 1995–2009

The other nations that are both big import and export partners of the EU are Russia, Norway, Turkey, Canada and South Korea.

15.1.1 Differences among Member States

One of the things that makes EU trade policy a contentious issue is the fact that the various Member States have quite different trade patterns. Some members are landlocked and surrounded by other EU members, while others are geographically and/or culturally close to

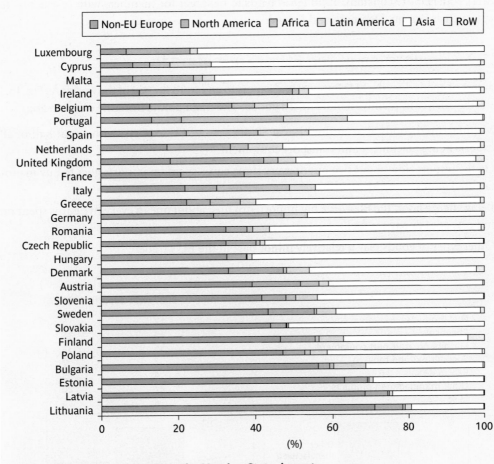

Figure 15.2 Main trade partners by Member State, imports

Source: Eurostat © European Communities 1995–2009

Africa, North America or Latin America. It is not surprising, therefore, that the importance of various trade partners varies quite a lot across the EU27.

Figure 15.2 illustrates this divergence. The reliance of Member States on imports from the various regions is shown by the 100 per cent bars. The leftmost segment shows the share of imports from non-EU Europe. This ranges from about 5 per cent for Luxembourg to almost 80 per cent for Lithuania. Geography matters a great deal when it comes to trade partners, so it is not surprising that non-EU Europe countries – which includes Ukraine and Russia – play a big role in the imports for the central European members such as Poland and the Baltic states. The importance of North America varies almost as much. North America's share in Irish external imports is about 40 per cent, while for the Baltic States it is 10 per cent or less.

The figure also shows some fairly natural linkages. The Iberians import a large share of their external trade from Latin America and Africa. Africa's share is also over 15 per cent for Italy and France.

Asia's role is more constant, although it tends to be larger for members with easy access to the sea, such as Britain, Denmark and Poland.

15.1.2 Composition of the EU's external trade

What sort of goods does the EU27 import and export to and from the rest of the world? As Fig. 15.3 shows, the answer is 'mainly manufactured goods'. The main points from the diagram are:

★ Manufactured goods account for almost 90 per cent of EU exports, with about half of all exports being machinery and transport equipment.

★ On the import side, about two out of every three euros spent on imports goes to buy manufactured goods.

★ Being energy poor, the EU27 is a big importer of fuel; about one in every five euros spent on imports goes to pay for fuel.

★ Other types of goods play a relatively minor part in the EU's trade.

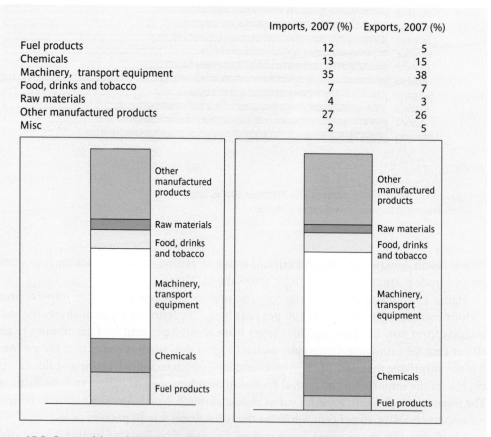

	Imports, 2007 (%)	Exports, 2007 (%)
Fuel products	12	5
Chemicals	13	15
Machinery, transport equipment	35	38
Food, drinks and tobacco	7	7
Raw materials	4	3
Other manufactured products	27	26
Misc	2	5

Figure 15.3 Composition of EU27 imports and exports, aggregate trade
Source: Eurostat © European Communities 1995–2009

About 7 per cent of EU27 exports to the rest of the world consist of food (more precisely, food, drinks and tobacco). The EU's imports of such goods account also for 7 per cent of all its imports. As the chapter on the CAP (Chapter 12) showed, Europe's trade in agricultural goods is massively distorted by subsidies to EU farmers, subsidies to EU exports, and high barriers against imports. If the CAP were fully liberalized in the direction the Commission is pushing for (see Chapter 12 for details), all trade distortions would be removed and the EU would surely become a net importer of food.

What with whom?

The situation illustrated in Fig. 15.3 aggregates all the EU's trade with all partners. This is useful since it gives us an idea of just how dominant manufactured goods are when it comes to EU trade policy, and it provides an important perspective when we turn to EU trade policy where a key fact is that the EU has almost no tariff protection on imported manufactured goods. Moreover, it illustrates quite clearly that agricultural goods play only a minor role in the EU's trade despite the dominance of agriculture in political conflicts both within the EU and with the rest of the world.

The aggregate trade pattern, however, hides a set of facts that are important to understanding the impact of the EU's external trade policy. Simply put, the commodity composition of the EU's *exports* is approximately the same for all of the EU's trade partners, but this is not true for its imports. Figure 15.4 shows the facts.

The diagram gathers EU trade partners into eight groups: North America, South America, Africa, Middle East, Asia, the EU27 itself, non-EU Europe and Oceania (Australia, New Zealand and various Pacific island nations). For each group, the diagram shows two 100 per cent bars (these are basically vertical 'pie' charts). The left bar in each pair shows the percentage of EU exports to the region made up by manufactured goods (top segment), raw materials (middle segment) and food (bottom segment). The right bar in each pair shows the same for EU imports from the region. There is a great deal of information in the diagram, but the main points are:

★ Scanning across the diagram it is easy to see that all the left bars are quite similar. That is, the shares of manufactures in EU exports to all regions are fairly similar, ranging from 85 per cent to 95 per cent. Things are much more varied, however, on the import side.

★ As might be expected, Europe tends to import a lot of primary goods – food and raw materials including fuel – from continents that are relatively abundant in natural resources. Raw materials account for over half of EU imports from Africa and the Middle East, with petroleum playing a dominant role in these particular flows.

★ Food is never a dominant import for any of the eight groups (although it is for particular nations, especially small poor nations). The highest shares are for the EU's imports from South America and Oceania (mainly Australia and New Zealand).

★ The EU's import composition from non-EU Europe has a large share of raw materials (about one-third). This group, however, combines two sets of very different nations. On one hand, it includes the nations that sell mostly manufactures to the EU (Switzerland, Bulgaria, Romania, Croatia, etc.). The trade composition with these nations is quite similar to the

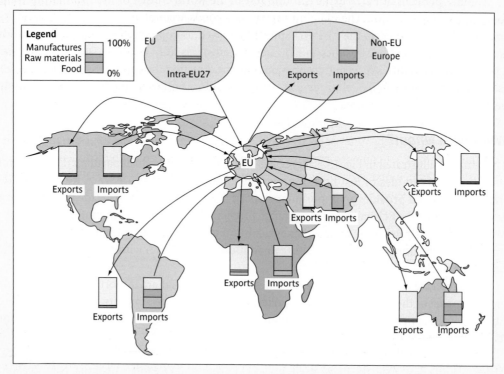

Figure 15.4 **EU27 commodity composition of imports and exports, 2007**
Source: Eurostat © European Communities 1995–2009

EU's trade itself. On the other hand, Russia and Norway are mainly natural resource exporters, with oil and gas dominating their sales to the EU.

15.2 EU institutions for trade policy

Formation of a customs union – which means the elimination of tariffs on intra-EU trade and adoption of a common external tariff – was the EU's first big step towards economic integration. A customs union requires political coordination since trade policy towards third nations is an ever-evolving issue. To facilitate this political coordination, the Treaty of Rome granted supranational powers to the EU's institutions as far as external trade policy is concerned. This section reviews the allocation of the powers among the EU institutions.

15.2.1 Trade in goods

Trade policy in today's globalized world touches on a vast array of issues. Correspondingly, EU trade policy is extremely complex since it has to deal with issues ranging from quotas on men's underwear from China to internet banking to sugar imports. A good way to tackle this complexity is to start with the most traditional aspects of EU trade policy, i.e. trade in goods.

The Treaty of Rome assigns to the European Commission the task of negotiating trade matters with third nations on behalf of the Member States (Article 133 of the EC Treaty). In practice, this means that the EU trade Commissioner (currently Lady Catherine Ashton) is responsible for conducting trade negotiations. These negotiations are conducted in accordance with specific mandates defined by the Council of Ministers (called 'Directives for Negotiation'). When it comes to very broad and very important trade negotiations, e.g. the WTO's ongoing Doha Round of trade talks – an ad hoc coordination procedure allows Member States to be involved in each phase of the Commission's negotiations.

The Council has the final say on whether to adopt the trade deals negotiated by the Commission. When it comes to agreements involving trade in goods, the Council decides on the basis of qualified majority voting. The European Parliament has no explicit powers regarding the conduct of trade policy in general but the Commission informs Parliament on a regular basis about developments in European trade policy. The Treaty also puts the Commission in charge of enforcing third countries to comply with deals they have struck with the EU. This is why the Commission is always out front in the frequent confrontations between the USA and the EU, e.g. on subsidies to Airbus and Boeing.

15.2.2 Beyond tariffs

In the EU's early days, tariffs were a key trade barrier, so tariffs were the main issue when it came to external trade policy. Indeed, although the Treaty of Rome speaks of the 'Common Commercial Policy' – a name that suggests it should be much more than just tariffs – the wording in the Article provides only a suggestive list, and this basically mentions various forms of tariff protection.

As tariffs have gradually come down through 50 years of multilateral and regional trade negotiations, other barriers have emerged as relatively more important. For example, in the last set of WTO negotiations (the so-called Uruguay Round that lasted from 1986 to 1994), the key negotiating points involved trade-offs in areas far beyond traditional trade in goods. These included: trade in services (e.g. banking and insurance), intellectual property rights (copyrights, patents, etc.) and trade-related measures concerning foreign investment (e.g. policies that require multinationals to buy a certain proportion of their inputs from local suppliers). The Commission found itself in an awkward position vis-à-vis the other major players such as the USA, Japan and Canada, since its formal negotiating mandate included only trade in goods. Moreover, the EU's economy and external trade have reduced their dependence on industrial products; the service sector is now the main source of jobs within the EU and accounts for a large and growing proportion of its trade with nations.

In reaction to these altered circumstances, the Commission has pushed for broader negotiating authority and the Court of Justice has usually backed it by interpreting very broadly the scope of the Common Commercial Policy (as defined by Article 133) – at least as far as trade in goods is concerned. (The Court explicitly ruled in 1994 that trade negotiations on services and intellectual property could not be based on Article 133 and so were not part of the EU's exclusive competency on external trade policy.) Nevertheless, the need for a coherent EU stance on external trade – at a minimum, the need for a single chief negotiator – was apparent to all. The Member States have reacted by expanding the Commission's authority in various Treaties.

The 1997 Amsterdam Treaty took the first tentative steps and the Treaty of Nice extended the coverage of the common trade policy to the fields of trade in services and the commercial aspects of intellectual property.

Since the Treaty of Nice, agreements on services and intellectual property are decided under the same qualified majority rule as applied to trade in goods. However, it introduces the principle of 'parallelism'. What this means is that decisions relating to the negotiation and conclusion of trade agreements are subject to unanimous voting in the Council, if unanimity would be required for the adoption of rules on the same subjects in the context of the Single Market. For example, unanimity is required on extra-EU immigration issues, but trade agreements very often contain clauses on the free movement of specific types of foreign workers whose physical presence in the country is a necessary component of free trade in services. To the extent that trade in services, such as banking and insurance, requires a local presence, issues surrounding investment, services and free movement of workers are becoming increasingly intertwined. The principle of parallelism determines whether such provisions are subject to unanimity or qualified majority voting.

Changes in the Constitutional Treaty

Although the Constitutional Treaty is unlikely to ever come into force as written (see Chapter 2), many of the hard-fought compromises in the Constitution are likely to re-emerge in other ways. It is important therefore to note that the Constitution extended the EU's authority on external trade matters to include foreign direct investment (Article III-217). Other notable changes included a streamlined decision-making process (although the principle of parallelism is maintained) and an expanded role for the European Parliament.

15.2.3 Anti-dumping and anti-subsidy measures

Under WTO rules, tariff liberalization is a one-way street. Once a nation has lowered its tariff in WTO talks (such talks are often called 'Rounds', the ongoing one being called the Doha Round), it is not allowed to put the tariff back up. This principle of 'binding' tariffs applies to the EU's external tariffs (the so-called Common External Tariff, CET). The principle, however, is subject to some loopholes, the most important of which are anti-dumping and anti-subsidy tariffs.

Dumping is defined as the selling of exports below some normal price. According to WTO rules, a nation, or more broadly speaking, a customs area (i.e. the EU), can impose tariffs on imports if dumping 'causes or threatens material injury to an established industry'. The EU, together with the USA, is one of the world's leading users of such measures, especially in iron and steel, consumer electronics and chemicals.

The European Commission is in charge of investigating dumping complaints. If the Commission finds that: (i) dumping has occurred (this involves intricate and somewhat arbitrary calculations), and (ii) that material injury to EU producers has or might happen, it can impose a provisional duty (that lasts between six and nine months). The Council of Ministers must confirm the Commission's decision before the tariffs become definitive (these stay in place for five years). Sometimes the Commission avoids imposing tariffs by negotiating 'price undertakings' with the exporting nation; these are promises by the exporters to charge a high price for their goods in exchange for suspension or termination of the Commission's anti-dumping investigation. In terms of EU welfare, price undertakings are worse than tariffs since the EU collects no tariff revenue. Nevertheless, price undertakings are often more expedient politically since they are a way of 'bribing' the exporting nation into not complaining too loudly about the EU's new protection. (See Chapter 4 for the economic analysis.)

Since dumping duties, like all tariffs, help producers but harm consumers and firms that buy the goods (see Chapter 4), the Commission often faces a tricky balancing act among Member States. Frequently, the EU producers are concentrated in one or a few Member States while there are consumers in every Member State. Typically the former want the Commission to impose dumping duties while the latter oppose them. For this reason, the Commission implements anti-dumping measures only when it believes that they are in the broader interest of the EU. For historical and institutional reasons, the EU rarely imposes anti-subsidy duties, preferring to deal with such behaviour as 'below normal' pricing.

Many observers believe that both the EU and the USA employ a cynical manipulation of dumping rules – especially the calculation that determines whether imports have been dumped – in order to provide WTO-consistent protection for sectors whose producers are usually powerful politically. The iron and steel industry and the chemical industry are leading examples.

15.3 EU external trade policy

The EU's external trade policy is extremely complex. For example, the EU has preferential trade agreements with all but nine of the WTO's 148 members. Moreover, each free trade agreement can contain hundreds of pages of exceptions and technical rules, and the EU often has more than one agreement with each of these partners. For example, the EU has a general agreement on trade with Ukraine (a so-called Partnership and Cooperation Agreement), as well as separate sectoral agreements on steel and textiles. On top of this, the EU unilaterally extends duty-free treatment to some Ukrainian exports. Given that the Ukrainian example is typical of the EU's bilateral agreements with over a hundred nations, it is easy to understand why it would take a lifetime to fully understand EU trade policy.

The best way to a broad understanding of EU external trade policy is by grouping the arrangements into categories. We start with the bouquet of trade arrangements that link the EU with its immediate neighbours. Readers who are interested in one or more of these agreements can find all the details on the European Commission's website; at the end of 2008 the URL was http://ec.europa.eu/trade/.

15.3.1 The European Mediterranean trade area

The EU27 encompasses almost all of western Europe and most of central and eastern Europe (Bulgaria and Romania joined in 2007). The remaining western European nations participate in the Single Market via the European Economic Area agreement (Norway, Iceland and Liechtenstein) or the EU–Swiss Bilateral Accords. Although there are a multitude of exceptions that matter to specialists, understanding is greatly boosted by thinking of European trade arrangements as being characterized by two concentric circles, the EU and the Single Market (see Fig. 15.5). That is to say, every nation in the Single Market circle enjoys the 'four freedoms' with respect to every other nation in the circle. (Trade in food products is generally excluded.)

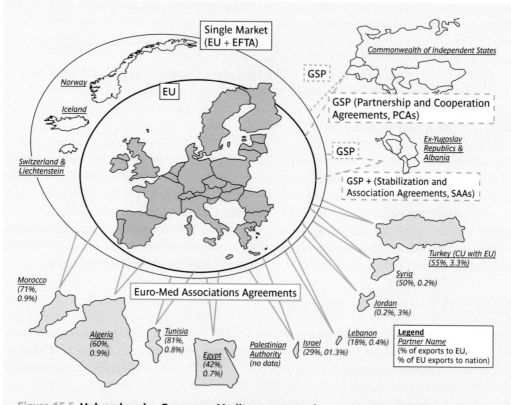

Figure 15.5 Hub and spoke: European–Mediterranean trade arrangements, 2007

Source: Authors' simplification of information on europa.eu.int/comm/trade/. Adapted from Baldwin (1994) *Towards an Integrated Europe*, CEPR, London

The nations in the EU share even deeper integration in the political, agricultural and several non-economic spheres such as foreign and defence policy.

Euro-Meds

Trade arrangements in Europe go beyond this group of four EFTAns and 27 EU members (counting Bulgaria and Romania). The next most important group of trade links are the so-called Euro-Med Association Agreements that the EU has with ten Mediterranean nations – Morocco, Algeria, Tunisia, Egypt, Israel, the Palestinian Authority, Lebanon, Jordon, Syria and Turkey – a group called the Med-10 for short. These agreements are free trade agreements in that they promise bilateral duty-free trade in industrial goods. They are asymmetric, however, in that the EU had to cut its tariffs to zero faster than did its partners. The EU has already phased out its tariffs on industrial goods and is in the process of gradually lowering trade barriers on most food products. The Med-10 have promised to eliminate their tariffs on EU industrial goods by 2010.

As usual, the full reality is more complicated and these general statements can be subject to endless qualification since each of the ten agreements is slightly different and the EU has multiple agreements with many of the Med-10. Here are several complications that are worth keeping in mind:

⭐ The EU market can be thought of as the 'hub' in a regional hub-and-spoke system of trade deals. As Fig. 15.5 shows, the exporters in each of these nations depend heavily on the EU market while each individual nation is negligible for EU exporters. Morocco is a typical case. The EU market accounts for 71 per cent of its exports while the Moroccan market accounts for less than 1 per cent of EU external exports. This massive asymmetry in market-dependency gives the EU a great deal of leverage in dealing with these nations.

⭐ Turkey unilaterally sets its tariffs on industrial imports from third nations at the level of the EU's Common External Tariff, so it can be said to be in a customs union with the EU. Turkey, however, has no voice in the setting of EU external trade policy and this customs union does not apply to trade in agricultural goods.

⭐ The EFTA nations have signed similar free trade agreements with all the Med-10 in order to ensure that their exporters compete on an equal basis with firms located in the EU (i.e. so EFTA firms face the same tariffs as EU firms do). Indeed, this is true throughout the world; whenever the EU signs an FTA with a new partner, the EFTA nations sign a similar agreement. This creates what might be called a 'virtual FTA union' between the EU and EFTA nations. Or, to put it in terms of the hub-and-spoke metaphor, EFTA's practice of shadowing the EU's FTA policy has the effect of making EFTA part of the EU's hub, at least as far as preferential tariffs are concerned. EFTA has pursued this strategy for decades; Turkey has recently followed suit since its customs union with the EU forces it to have the same external trade policy as the EU does.

⭐ The Euro-Med arrangements are more than FTAs since they contain provisions for financial and technical assistance from the EU and they address additional issues such as trade in services and foreign direct investment.

⭐ Several of the Med-10 are trying to engineer free trade deals among themselves. If they manage to do this, they would create a third concentric circle – a sort of virtual Euro-Med free trade area containing the 27 EU members, four EFTAs and Med-10; every industrial firm located in any nation within the circle would have duty-free access to every other market in the circle. As matters stand now, the 'spoke' economies typically impose relatively high tariffs on each other's industrial exports.

PanEuroMed cumulation system

In addition to removing tariffs, the PanEuroMed arrangement imposes a common set of 'rules of origin', namely the rules that customs officers use to determine whether an import is actually made in the nation from which it was shipped (as opposed to, for example, being trans-shipped from a third nation in an effort to evade tariffs). To reflect the fact that any value-added in this area counts as local content as far as rules of origin are concerned, the PanEuroMed arrangement is often called the Pan-European Cumulation System.

Former Soviet republics and the western Balkans: 'GSP treatment plus'

The EU grants trade preferences to all of the nations of the Commonwealth of Independent States (Russia, Ukraine, Georgia, Belarus, Armenia, Azerbaijan, Kazakhstan, Kyrgyzstan, Moldova and Uzbekistan) under deals called Partnership and Cooperation Agreements (PCAs). These agreements address many matters other than trade. As far as trade is concerned, the deals are asymmetric. The EU has lowered its tariffs on most exports from these nations without requiring that the PCA partners lower theirs. Thus from the trade perspective, the PCAs can be viewed as generous versions of the Generalized System of Preference. (The Generalized System of Preference, or GSP, is a loophole in the WTO's non-discrimination rule that allows rich nations to voluntarily charge lower tariffs on imports from poor nations.) As usual, the EFTAns and Turkey typically mimic the PCAs by extending the same preferences to the PCA nations.

Lastly, we come to the bilateral EU trade deals with Albania and the nations that emerged from the break-up of Yugoslavia, apart from Slovenia which acceded to the EU in 2004. These so-called Stabilization and Association Agreements (SAAa) are best thought of as GSP preferences with additional elements concerning financial assistance, trade in services, etc. Although it is never stated explicitly by the EU, most observers believe the SSA will eventually lead to EU membership, whereas the PCA nations, for the most part, are unlikely to join the EU in the foreseeable future.

15.3.2 Preferential arrangements with former colonies

Europeans were big colonisers in the nineteenth and twentieth centuries and they still had many colonies right up to the 1960s and 1970s – Britain, France and Belgium in particular. Colonial ties almost always involved important trade relations; usually the 'mother' country's market was the main export destination for the colony's traded goods. When this aberrant system came to an end with the independence movements of the 1960s and 1970s, the former colonists typically wanted to maintain preferential treatment for goods coming from their former colonies. Since the EU is a customs union (i.e. all members must have the same tariffs on imports from third nations), these pressures came to bear on the EU's external trade policy. In particular, to avoid putting the Common External Tariff (CET) on imports that had long been duty free, the Six signed agreements with many of their former colonies while they were establishing the EU's customs union in the 1960s. These trade deals were asymmetric in the sense that the EU tariffs were set to zero but the poor nations did not remove theirs.

When the UK joined in 1974, these old agreements (Yaoundé Convention and Arusha Agreement) were rolled into a comprehensive policy that was extended to the poor members of the UK's Commonwealth (this way, Britain avoided imposing the CET on these nation's exports). The combined group was labelled the ACP nations since they are located in Africa, the Caribbean and the Pacific; the new agreement was known as the Lomé Convention. This latter granted duty-free status to all industrial exports and most agricultural exports of ACP nations (with quotas on sensitive items such as sugar and bananas) without requiring that the ACP nations lower their barriers to EU exports.

The Lomé Convention was based on the now discredited belief that such unilateral preferences would help the former colonies industrialize. Experience has shown that the preferences did not encourage industrialization or growth. Most ACP nations fell further behind while many Asian and Latin American countries enjoyed rapid industrialization, booming exports to the EU and income growth without preferences. When the Lomé Convention came up for renewal in 2000, the EU and the ACP nations agreed to modernize the deal.

The result was the ACP–EU Partnership Agreement, usually referred to as the Cotonou Agreement. This is not a hard-nosed trade agreement to win EU exporters better market access. As with the Euro-Med partners, the EU is a major market for the ACP nations, but the ACP markets are marginal markets for EU exporters. The best way to understand the Cotonou Agreement is to view it as an economic and trade cooperation aimed at fostering development in the ACP nations.

The big change from Lomé was that Cotonou commits the ACP nations to eventually removing their tariffs against EU exports. The idea is that gradually phasing in two-way free trade with the EU is a good way of integrating these developing nations into the world economy and that this is a necessary step towards development in the modern, globalized world. While the Cotonou Agreement lays out principles, the actual trade bargains are struck in bilateral deals known as Economic Partnership Agreements (EPAs). These have been negotiated with all 75 ACP nations (see Table 15.2).

15.3.3 Preferences for poor nations: GSP

As mentioned above, many scholars and policy makers in the 1960s and 1970s believed that rich countries could help poor countries develop by granting unilateral preferential tariff treatment for poor nation industrial exports. This notion was formally brought into world trade rules – i.e. the WTO, or GATT as it was known at the time – in 1971 under the name 'Generalized

Table 15.2 Regional groups, ACP nations

West Africa	Central Africa	East South Africa	Southern Africa	Caribbean	Pacific
Benin	Cameroon	Burundi	Angola	Antigua, Barb	Cook Is.
Burkina Faso	Centr. Africa	Comoros	Botswana	Bahamas	Fed. Micron.
Cape Verde	Chad	Congo (Dem. Rep.)	Lesotho	Barbados	Fiji
Gambia	Congo	Djibouti	Mozambique	Belize	Kiribati
Ghana	Equat. Guinea	Eritrea	Namibia	Dominica	Marshall Is.
Guinea	Gabon	Ethiopia	Swaziland	Dominican Rep.	Nauru
Guinea Biss.	S. Tome, Princ	Kenya	Tanzania	Grenada	Niue
Ivory Coast		Malawi		Guyana	Palau
Liberia		Mauritius		Haiti	Papua N. G.
Mali		Madagascar		Jamaica	Samoa
Mauritania		Rwanda		St Lucia	Solomon Is.
Niger		Seychelles		St Vincent	Tonga
Nigeria		Sudan		St. Ch. & Nevis	Tuvalu
Senegal		Uganda		Surinam	Vanuatu
Sierra Leone		Zambia		Trinidad & Tobago	
Togo		Zimbabwe			

Source: europa.eu.int/comm/trade © European Communities 1995–2009

System of tariff Preferences', GSP for short. The EU was the first to implement a GSP scheme, in 1971, and it now grants GSP preferences to almost every developing nation in the world.

As is true of all aspects of its trade policy, the EU's GSP policy is extremely complex. It helps to categorize the various EU GSP policies into two general groups:

1 general GSP, which is available to all developing nations at the EU's discretion, and

2 super GSP, which involves extra 'generous' EU unilateral preferences for nations that the EU wishes to encourage for some reason or the other. Currently, 'super GSP' is granted to nations that comply with the EU's idea of labour rights, the EU's idea of environmental protection, the EU's idea of combating illegal drugs, and very poor nations.

The later group, which is more politely called 'least developed nations', gets the most generous form of GSP preferences – a programme called 'Everything But Arms', or EBA as it is known in EU trade jargon. On paper, EBA grants zero-tariff access to the EU's market for all products from these nations, except arms and munitions. One must say 'on paper' since the goods in which these nations are most competitive are in fact excluded from the deal. Tariffs on bananas, rice and sugar – products where these poor nations could easily expand their EU sales – are to come down only in the future. Moreover, even though all tariffs on these items will be gone by 2009, the export quantities are limited by bilateral quotas. This has led cynical observers of EU trade policy to call EBA the 'Everything But Farms' programme. (Oxfam is particularly pointed in its criticism of EBA and EU trade policy more generally; interested readers may want to consult www.oxfam.org.uk.)

Currently, 49 nations qualify for EBA in principle. The list is: Afghanistan, Angola, Bangladesh, Benin, Bhutan, Burkina Faso, Burundi, Cambodia, Cape Verde, Central African Republic, Chad, Comoros, Congo (Democratic Republic), Djibouti, Equatorial Guinea, Eritrea, Ethiopia, Gambia, Guinea, Guinea Bissau, Haiti, Kiribati, Lao PDR, Lesotho, Liberia, Madagascar, Malawi, Maldives, Mali, Mauritania, Mozambique, Myanmar, Nepal, Niger, Rwanda, Samoa, Sao Tome e Principe, Senegal, Sierra Leone, Solomon Islands, Somalia, Sudan, Tanzania, Togo, Tuvalu, Uganda, Vanuatu, Yemen, and Zambia. Note that the EU imposes restrictions on nations it deems to be insufficiently democratic, in violation of international law, or otherwise undesirable.

15.3.4 Non-regional FTAs

In recent years, a number of non-European nations have sought out FTAs with the EU. The EU is almost always open to FTAs (as long as they exclude agriculture) and so it has signed a number of these deals. In late 2008 when this edition went to print, the list included Mexico, Chile, Mercosur (Brazil, Argentina, Uruguay and Paraguay), the Gulf Cooperation Council (Bahrain, Kuwait, Oman, Qatar, Saudi Arabia and United Arab Emirates), India, the ASEAN nations (Indonesia, Malaysia, Philippines, Thailand, Singapore, Vietnam, Cambodia, Burma and Laos) and South Africa. Also, negotiations for an FTA between the EU and Colombia, Peru and Ecuador have just started. The first round was in February 2009.

15.3.5 EU's Common External Tariff

Although the EU has preferential tariffs on imports from all but nine nations in the world, those nine nations account for about a third of the EU's external trade so the tariff it charges

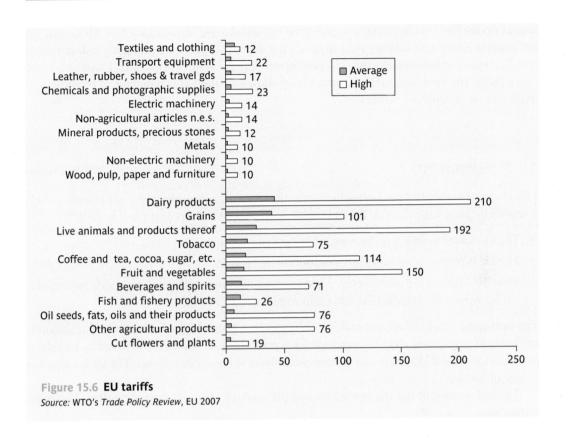

Figure 15.6 EU tariffs
Source: WTO's *Trade Policy Review*, EU 2007

these nations – the CET – matters. The CET also matters since it defines how much of an edge duty-free treatment provides under the EU's preferential trade agreements. If the CET is zero on a product, then acquiring duty-free treatment via GSP or an FTA is useless for that product.

The EU defines individual tariff rates for about 10 000 products, so we must generalize to get a handle on the EU's tariff policy. The average CET rate is 6.5 per cent, but this hides a wide variation. About a quarter of the rates on all products are set at zero (mostly industrial goods including electronics) and the average for industrial goods is 4.1 per cent. The average on agricultural imports is four times this, namely 16.5 per cent.

Figure 15.6 shows how the CET varies according to a finer disaggregation of products. The dark bars show the average tariff for all goods in the categories listed; the light bars show the maximum tariff in the category. The most obvious fact in the diagram is the enormous difference between agricultural goods and manufactured goods. Owing to the protection imposed by the Common Agricultural Policy, most food imports are subject to high tariffs, with the rate on some dairy goods rising to 210 per cent! The maximum rates on some manufactured goods are still high, but the average rate on manufactures is always below 5 per cent, except for textiles and clothing where the average is 8 per cent.

The fact that the CET is very low on industrial goods goes a long way to explaining why the EU is so ready to provide duty-free treatment to the industrial exports of its friends. To put it bluntly, granting zero-tariff status to the industrial exports of most nations has very little impact on the EU's market since the non-preferential rates are already very low. Moreover, for the imports where zero-tariffs might matter – the imports from the most highly industrialized non-European nations such as the USA and Japan – the EU is not keen to sign FTAs.

Likewise, the very high tariffs in agriculture show why the EU is reluctant to provide such treatment on agricultural imports.

15.4 Summary

This chapter provided a broad introduction to the immensely complex topic of EU trade policy. It started by presenting facts on the EU's trade pattern. The main points there were:

★ The EU trades mainly with Europe, with itself in particular.

★ The EU is primarily an exporter of manufactured goods.

★ Most EU imports are manufactured goods, although imports of primary goods are important for Africa, the Middle East and Latin America.

The next topic was EU decision making on trade. In a nutshell, the European Commission is in charge of negotiating the EU's external trade policy, but its efforts are directed by mandates from the Council of Ministers and all deals are subject to Council approval. The Parliament has a negligible role.

The last section in the chapter addressed the content of the EU's trade policy. The main points were:

★ Trade arrangements in Europe can be characterized as hub-and-spoke bilateralism. The hub is formed by two concentric circles (the EU, which has the deepest level of integration, and EFTA, which participates in the Single Market apart from agriculture). These circles form a 'hub' around which a network of bilateral agreements are arranged with almost every nation in Europe (broadly defined) and the Mediterranean. These bilateral deals fall into three groups: the Euro-Med agreements, the Stabilization and Association Agreements with western Balkan nations, and the Partnership and Cooperation Agreements with former Soviet republics in the Commonwealth of Independent States.

★ The EU has preferential trade agreements with its former colonies – the so-called ACP nations – that are currently asymmetric (the EU charges zero tariffs but the ACP nations do not) but they are aiming at establishing full-blown two-way FTAs in the coming years.

★ The EU grants unilateral preferences of various types to almost all developing nations. These typically include duty-free treatment for industrial exports from these nations, but restrictions on the goods that they could most easily sell to the EU, namely agricultural goods such as sugar.

★ The EU's common external tariff (CET) is low on average, but it is four times higher on agricultural goods than it is on industrial goods.

Self-assessment questions

1. What is the role of the Member States and the Commission when it comes to external trade policy? Be sure to distinguish between trade in goods and more 'modern' trade issues such as trade in services, trade in intellectual property rights and foreign direct investment.

2. What does the EU buy from and sell to the five continents, Europe, Africa, North America, South America and Asia?

3. What is the most protected good in the EU and which is the least protected good?

4. Why did the EU extend unilateral tariff preferences to former French and Belgium colonies, and why did it extend these to former British colonies in the mid-1970s?

5. Explain the term 'hub-and-spoke bilateralism' as applied to the EU's neighbours in Europe and around the Mediterranean.

Essay questions

1. 'In some sense, the trade policy has been the EU's most effective form of "foreign policy", and indeed up until the Maastricht Treaty it could be considered the EU's only foreign policy.' Write an essay evaluating this statement.

2. 'Some non-governmental organizations (NGOs) claim that the EU only provides developing nations with tariff preferences that are not worth much, either because the developing nations are not competitive in these goods or because the EU's CET is low on these goods so duty-free treatment is not much different from non-preferential treatment.' Write an essay evaluating this statement.

3. Select a particular European trade partner and investigate all the trade agreements the EU has with it and the EU's imports and exports to this nation. You can find trade data on http://europa.eu.int/comm/trade/, and information on trade agreements on the same site (but also check the more general site, http://europa.eu.int/comm/world/).

4. Write an essay describing the EU's trade policy in a particular sector, such as steel or textiles.

5. Write an account of the EU's recent troubles with Chinese textile exports. Be sure to explain how this illustrates the allocation of competences and the difficult politics within the EU on trade matters.

6. Do you think it would be a good idea for the EU to sign more trade agreements? If so, with which countries and why?

7. Why do you think European nations trade more with their former colonies?

Further reading: the aficionado's corner

A very lengthy and complete treatment of the EU's trade policy can be downloaded from the WTO's website, www.wto.org (follow links to the Trade Policy Reviews, or use Google with the words EU, Trade Policy Review and WTO). This is an independent review of EU trade policy which includes detailed presentation of its preferential, multilateral and sector policies. This also provides references to many academic studies of the impact of EU policies.

A very sceptical presentation of EU trade policy that includes explicit economic evaluation is **Messerlin** (2001).

For general information on the WTO, see **Hoekman and Kostecki** (2001), or the **WTO**'s website, www.wto.org.

For more on the EU trade policy with poor nations, see **Hinkle and Schiff** (2004) and **Panagariya** (2002). For more on GSP in general, see **GAO** (1994).

Useful websites

The best general site is the European Commission DG-Trade site, http://europa.eu.int/comm/trade/.

For information on preferential trade agreements worldwide, see www.bilaterals.org.

References

Baldwin, R. (1994) *Towards an Integrated Europe*, CEPR, London.

GAO (1994). *Assessment of the Generalized System of Preferences Program*, US General Accounting Office, Washington DC. Download from www.gao.gov.

Hinkle, L. and M. Schiff (2004) 'Economic Partnership Agreements between Sub-Saharan Africa and the EU: a development perspective', *World Economy*, 27 (9): 1321–34.

Hoekman, B. and M. Kostecki (2001) *The Political Economy of the World Trading System: The WTO and Beyond*, Oxford University Press, Oxford.

Messerlin, P. (2001) *Measuring the Costs of Protection in Europe: European Commercial Policy in the 2000s*, Institute for International Economics, Washington, DC.

Panagariya, A. (2002) 'EU preferential trade policies and developing countries', *World Economy*, 10 (25): 1415–32.

PART V

EU monetary and fiscal policies

Chapter **16**

The European Monetary System

It was the 1992 EMS crisis that provided the immediate impetus for monetary unification.

Barry Eichengreen (2002)

Chapter contents

16.1	The EMS arrangements	472
16.2	EMS-1: from divergence to convergence and blow-up	475
16.3	The EMS re-engineered	481
16.4	Summary	485

Introduction

Historically, the European Monetary System (EMS) served as a bridge between the dollar-centred Bretton Woods system and the monetary union. Its creation in 1979 reflected the quest for exchange rate stability within Europe. The impossible trinity principle implied that monetary policies be restricted. Failure to fully recognize this implication resulted in an agitated history. Yet, paradoxically, the EMS's shortcomings made the adoption of a single currency seem a natural and desirable step.

The currency crises that plagued the arrangement also led to changes. Along with the adoption of the euro, the revamped EMS now serves as the entry point for the countries that join the monetary union.

The chapter first presents the rules that govern the EMS. Next, it describes the evolution of the system from a fully symmetric arrangement to what has been called the 'greater Deutschmark area'. It also presents the changes that followed the speculative crises of 1993 and led to the current EMS. The last section describes the present situation.

16.1 The EMS arrangements

The decision to create the EMS was taken in 1978 by German Chancellor Helmut Schmidt and French President Valéry Giscard d'Estaing. They were alarmed by the monetary disorders that had followed the end of the Bretton Woods system and by the inability to sustain the Snake arrangement, described in Chapter 10. In line with a view long held in Europe, they saw large exchange rate movements as a direct threat to the Common Market. They wanted a stronger, more resilient arrangement.

Political sensitivities were important, however. Germany would never take the risk of weakening its star currency, the Deutschmark, while France could not be seen to be playing second fiddle to Germany. Additionally, the smaller countries had to be brought along, while the UK was staunchly opposed to a fixed exchange rate regime. The solution came close to squaring the circle. The chosen arrangement was explicitly symmetric, without any currency at its centre, and it established a subtle distinction between the European Monetary System (EMS), of which all European Community countries were de facto members, and the Exchange Rate Mechanism (ERM), an optional but operational scheme. The ERM was the only meaningful part of the EMS. It rested on four main elements: a grid of agreed-upon bilateral exchange rates, mutual support, a commitment to joint decision of realignments and the European Currency Unit (ECU).

16.1.1 The ERM's parity grid

All ERM currencies were fixed to each other, with a band of fluctuation of ±2.25 per cent around the central parity (Italy was initially allowed a margin of fluctuation of ±6 per cent, in recognition of its higher rate of inflation and internal political difficulties). The arrangement was represented by the parity grid, a matrix-like table collecting all pairwise central parities and their associated margins of fluctuations.

The arrangement carried a number of interesting features. First, the system was entirely European, with no reference to the dollar or to gold. Never before had European countries built an exchange rate system standing on its own. Second, the system was fully symmetric: no currency played any special role, in contrast to the dollar in the Bretton Woods system. Third, the responsibility for maintaining each bilateral exchange rate within its margin was explicitly shared by both countries,[1] thus removing the stigma of one weak and one strong currency.

---

[1] Since all arrangements were bilateral, it would always be the case that the threat to break through a band of fluctuation would simultaneously affect two currencies, a strong one and a weak one.

16.1.2 Mutual support

The Snake had failed because the weak currencies had to fend for themselves. In contrast, the ERM included an agreement to automatically provide mutual support. By construction, exchange market pressure would simultaneously hit two countries. For example, the bilateral exchange rate between the Danish krone and the Dutch guilder could be pressed against one of its 2.25 per cent margins where, say, the krone was weak and the guilder strong. The ERM agreement stipulated that, in this case, the Danish and Dutch central banks were both obliged to intervene on the foreign exchange market. The Dutch would sell guilders to make them more abundant and therefore cheaper, and the Danish central bank would buy krone to raise its value. These interventions could be carried out with any currency: for example, the Dutch central bank would sell guilders against US dollars, Deutschmarks, etc., including the krone.

Crucially, in principle, this commitment was *unlimited*. Each concerned central bank was committed to keep intervening as long as its parity vis-à-vis any other member currency was pressed against one of its limits. But what if it ran out of ammunition? In the above example, the Dutch central bank could never be in that position since it would be accumulating foreign exchange reserves while selling its own currency, which it could produce in unlimited amounts. The Danish central bank, on the other hand, could run out of foreign exchange reserves, having spent all it had to buy back krone. In that case, the central bank of the Netherlands would also be committed to making a loan to its Danish colleague, allowing for continuing interventions as long as necessary. Other ERM central banks, even if they were not directly involved, could decide to give a helping hand, by also intervening on the foreign exchange markets, buying krone, or lending directly to the Danish central bank.

16.1.3 Joint management of exchange rate realignments

How long should this game be pursued? Clearly, if markets remained unimpressed by the artillery lined up against them, the central banks providing theoretically unlimited support could become concerned that no end was in sight. In that case, the solution would be to throw in the towel, acknowledge the market pressure and realign exchange rates. How was that done?

Allowing any central bank to change its exchange rate as it pleases would have made little contribution to the establishment of a level playing field. The founding fathers of the EMS were concerned that individual countries might try to achieve unfair trade advantage through recurrent devaluations, the infamous beggar-thy-neighbour practice of the inter-war period perceived to have been a source of economic and political disintegration. This is why the ERM stipulated that any change in any bilateral exchange rate had to be jointly decided by all members. The consensus rule implied that, in effect, each country gave up exclusive control of its own exchange rate. Realignments, as the exercise came to be known, turned out to involve tough but ultimately successful bargaining, usually concluded by multiple bilateral parity changes. The history of realignments is shown in Table 16.1.

16.1.4 The ECU

The EMS included the mostly symbolic creation of the European Currency Unit, or ECU. The ECU was a basket of all EMS-country currencies, including those of EC countries that did not

Table 16.1 **ERM realignments**

Dates	24.9.79	30.11.79	22.3.81	5.10.81	22.2.82	14.6.82
No. of currencies involved	2	1	1	2	2	4
Dates	21.3.83	18.5.83	22.7.85	7.4.86	4.8.86	12.1.87
No. of currencies involved	7[a]	7[a]	7[a]	5	1	3
Dates	8.1.90	14.9.92	23.11.92	1.2.93	14.5.93	6.3.95
No. of currencies involved	1	3[b]	2	1	2	2

[a] All ERM currencies realigned.
[b] In addition, two currencies (sterling and lira) leave the ERM.

Table 16.2 **The ECU basket**

	Amount in ECU 1	Weight (%)
Belgian franc	3.43100	8.71
Danish krone	0.19760	2.71
Deutschmark	0.62420	32.68
Dutch guilder	0.21980	10.21
French franc	1.33200	20.79
Greek drachma	1.44000	0.49
Italian lira	151.80000	7.21
Irish punt	0.00855	1.08
Portuguese escudo	1.39300	0.71
Spanish peseta	6.88500	4.24
UK pound sterling	0.08784	11.17

participate in the ERM. Each currency entered with a weight meant to represent the country's size and importance in intra-European trade. These weights, which were revised every five years, were initially chosen so that ECU 1 was worth US$ 1. The latest weights are shown in Table 16.2.

Formally, the ECU was designated the official unit of account of the European Community, used for all official transactions and accounts. Yet, any resemblance to a monetary union was then unacceptable. For this reason, it was explicitly designed not to be a currency: there were no physical ECUs and central banks did not carry out transactions in ECUs. The private markets, however, adopted the ECU and started to issue debt instruments using this unit. Technically and legally, these were currency baskets. When the euro was started on 4 January 1999, it was set to be worth exactly ECU 1 at its first quotation on that day, and the ECU ceased to exist.

16.1.5 Assessment: a flexible and cohesive arrangement

Overall, the EMS was built as a flexible yet cohesive arrangement. It allowed membership *à la carte*, permitting countries unhappy with fixed exchange rate regimes, chiefly the UK, not to

Table 16.3 **The impossible trinity at work**

	Early EMS	Late EMS	UK	Netherlands
1. Fixed exchange rate	✓	✓		✓
2. Monetary policy autonomy	✓		✓	
3. Full capital mobility		✓	✓	✓

join the ERM. Even within the ERM, the margins of fluctuation, normally set at ±2.25 per cent, could be temporarily set at ±6 per cent, an option exercised by Italy from 1979 to 1990, and by Spain and Portugal following their entry in 1989 and 1992, respectively.

On the other hand, the arrangement implied a deep commitment from member central banks. According to the impossible trinity principle presented in Chapter 10, as long as the exchange rate peg was being adhered to, there was little policy autonomy left. In return, mutual support, the agreement that interventions ought to be bilateral, automatic and unlimited, represented an unusually strong collective commitment.

Table 16.3 uses the impossible trinity principle to interpret the various situations in Europe before the adoption of the euro. During the early EMS period, many countries restricted capital movements; they could award themselves some degree of monetary autonomy even though they were part of the ERM. The UK dismantled its capital controls in the early 1980s and retained monetary policy independence by staying out of the ERM. The Netherlands, which removed its capital controls early, soon tied the guilder rigidly to the Deutschmark, effectively giving up any pretence at monetary policy autonomy. The trinity proved to be a curse to those countries that were in the ERM and were gradually allowing increased capital mobility, and yet were reluctant to give up the monetary policy instrument. Many of the ERM crises can be directly traced back to failed attempts at breaking this iron law.

16.2 EMS-1: from divergence to convergence and blow-up

The response to the challenge of the impossible trinity has varied over time. During the first period, which continued until the mid-1980s, ERM members had opted for exchange rate stability and policy independence, with capital controls in place in the devaluation-prone countries. Monetary independence mainly allowed each country to operate with a different inflation rate. As a result, realignments were frequently needed to re-establish competitiveness, an implication of the PPP principle presented in Chapter 9. In a second stage, bringing down inflation became the priority assigned to monetary policy. Within the ERM, it meant that countries with high inflation rates endeavoured to converge to the lowest rate. In effect, monetary policy independence was being surrendered. This is when Germany, the perennial low-inflation country and now the standard to emulate, established its dominance – an evolution that ultimately prompted the next move to monetary union.

16.2.1 The first version of EMS: agreeing to disagree (1979–85)

The EMS was initially conceived to avoid large fluctuations in intra-European real exchange rates. Building a robust ERM was one thing; the constraints implied by the impossible trinity

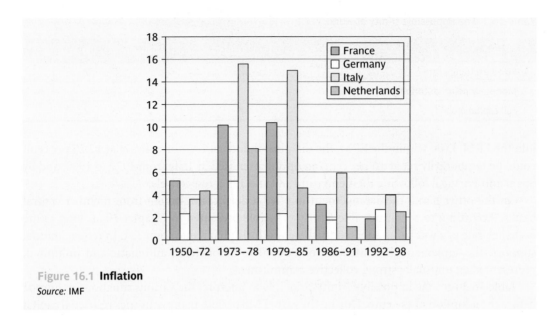

Figure 16.1 **Inflation**
Source: IMF

were something else. After the first oil shock of 1973, inflation rates started to diverge markedly, and the second oil shock did nothing to improve the situation. Once committed to a system of fixed but adjustable exchange rates, the ERM countries faced a choice between two strategies. Plan A was to dedicate monetary policies to the exchange pegs. This required similar inflation rates, for any lasting difference would inexorably hurt the competitiveness of high-inflation countries relative to that of low-inflation countries. Plan B was to accept lasting divergences in inflation and adjust the exchange rates as frequently as needed to avoid competitiveness problems and trade imbalances. As Fig. 16.1 clearly shows, Plan B was chosen in the initial period and Table 16.1 confirms that realignments occurred frequently.

The economic interpretation of this choice is quite straightforward. It is based on the relationship between money and inflation established in Chapter 10. Because, in the long term, inflation depends on money growth, Plan A would have required that all countries adopt similar rates of money growth. However, it was not easy to decide what should be the common inflation rate target. Low inflation is better than high, of course, but money is not neutral in the short term. Aiming at low rates of money growth and inflation would have led to contractionary policies and rising unemployment in high-inflation countries. Conversely, low-inflation countries were unwilling to accept higher rates. France, a country traditionally committed to low unemployment, would not agree to adopt contractionary measures, whereas Germany, a country deeply attached to low inflation, would not countenance any monetary policy relaxation. The inability to resolve this conflict, as well as considerations of national prestige, explains why Plan B was chosen by default.

16.2.2 The second version of EMS: towards a greater Deutschmark area (1986–92)

Plan B did not function without problems, however. Two main difficulties emerged. First, between realignments, high-inflation countries would see their real exchange rate appreciate

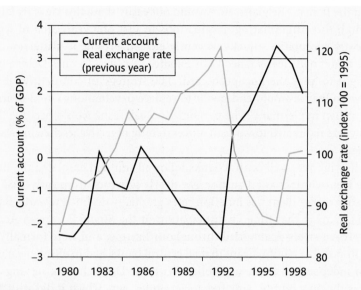

Figure 16.2 **Italy in the EMS**
Source: OECD and IMF

and, therefore, their trade accounts deteriorate. Inevitably, there would come a time when a remedial nominal depreciation would be needed, and it would have to be agreed upon by all ERM members. Low-inflation countries, which enjoyed a trade surplus, were quite reluctant to allow deep depreciations. The bargaining usually resulted in a depreciation that corrected for the accumulated difference in inflation, but no more. As a result, high-inflation countries were more or less permanently in external deficit while the low-inflation countries exhibited surpluses. This is illustrated in Fig. 16.2, which shows Italy's current account and real exchange rate vis-à-vis Germany's (the figure shows the previous year's exchange rate since it takes time to affect the current account). The Italian account's see-saw behaviour closely mirrors the evolution of the real exchange rate: between realignments the real exchange rate appreciates and the current account deteriorates, and devaluations are soon followed by an improvement in the current account.

Another serious problem with Plan B was that realignments were easily foreseen. The precise date could be in doubt – although shrewd observers often correctly identified many of them by looking at the timing of elections and other important political events – but the need to ultimately realign was plain for all to see. Looking at Fig. 16.2, it is quite obvious that the Deutschmark could only be revalued and the lira could only be devalued. To make the bet even easier, the gradually deepening external imbalance unambiguously signalled when this would happen. Speculators did not miss these signals and played what came to be called 'one-way bets': they speculated against the currencies of high-inflation countries and accumulated the currencies of low-inflation countries. As a result, most realignments took place in the midst of acute speculative pressure, hardly the 'island of monetary stability' promised by the founding fathers of the EMS. Plan B quickly exhausted its charms.

A key problem with Plan A had always been the difficulty of agreeing upon a standard in terms of monetary policy. Germany never had any doubt that the Bundesbank had it right, but the French (and the Italians, Belgians, etc.) would not easily share this view. By late 1983, France had gone through three humiliating devaluations in just one year, each of which had been preceded by costly speculative attacks. Recently elected President Mitterrand had tried his leftist medicine and it had clearly failed.[2] His Finance Minister, Jacques Delors, convinced him that France ought to 'play the European card'. The strategy of competitive disinflation was born: from now on France would endeavour to replace devaluations with low inflation, hopefully lower even than in Germany. The perennially weak franc would become the 'franc fort'. Monetary policy was redirected towards that overarching objective, eschewing short-term gains from easy money.

Over the following years, all central banks followed suit and emulated the Bundesbank, in effect using the Deutschmark as an anchor. For nearly six years, from early 1987 to September 1992, there was no realignment,[3] as inflation rates gradually declined towards the low German level (Fig. 16.1). During that time, in anticipation of the Single European Act 1992, capital controls were progressively dismantled throughout Europe, and were formally banned as of July 1990. The impossible trinity meant that all central banks had in effect given up their ability to carry out an independent monetary policy. With the Deutschmark serving as anchor, the Bundesbank was the only central bank free to act on its own, which it did with two important consequences: the other countries became eager to move to a monetary union as a way of recovering some influence on their monetary policies, and the EMS exploded.

16.2.3 The crisis of 1992–93

The long period of complete exchange rate stability that followed the adoption of the Deutschmark anchor convinced many that it could last for ever. This proved to be terribly wrong, as the impossible trinity should have forewarned. Trouble accumulated slowly. To start with, the absence of any realignment might have looked good, but inflation rates did not quite fully converge. Figure 16.3 shows that, while countries such as Denmark and France indeed moved towards the German inflation rate, others, such as Italy (or Portugal and Spain, not shown in the figure), had failed to get any closer by 1991. For these countries, the fixed exchange rate strategy meant a dangerous loss of competitiveness.

As it turned out, this is when the Berlin Wall collapsed. Germany's unification was a complex operation: taking over an impoverished country of 16 million inhabitants imposed a heavy burden on West Germany's public finances. In addition, to prevent East German workers from moving to the more prosperous West – which they were instantaneously entitled to do as unification occurred – wages were brought up to levels that were inconsistent with the productivity of East German firms. The result was a surge of inflation in Germany, clearly visible in Fig. 16.3. Predictably, the Bundesbank responded by tightening up monetary policy, sharply raising the interest rate.

---

[2] Soon after his election, Mitterrand relaxed monetary and fiscal policies, significantly raised minimum wages, reduced the working week and proceeded to nationalize several banks and large corporations.

[3] The 1990 realignment (Table 16.1) was not really a realignment. It was merely a technical adjustment prompted by Italy's decision to switch to the narrow ±2.25 per cent band of fluctuation, a consequence of the 'strong lira' policy. Parity was brought closer (from 6 per cent to 2.25 per cent) to its weak margin.

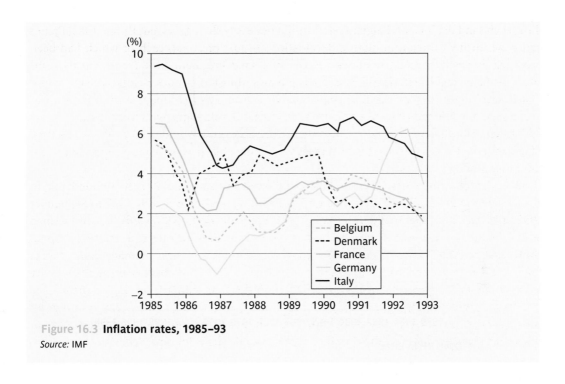

Figure 16.3 **Inflation rates, 1985–93**
Source: IMF

What could the other ERM members do? One solution would have been to let the Deutschmark appreciate. Blinded by the stability of ERM exchange rates and recent successes in bringing inflation down, and bent on achieving strong currency status, they rejected what they saw as a humiliating depreciation vis-à-vis the Deutschmark. This meant that they had to stick with the strategy of blindly following the Bundesbank and its tight policy imposed by the unification shock. This policy was much too tight for the other ERM members but the Bundesbank, reasonably enough, saw no reason to adjust its stance to the needs of the other countries. Bad luck played its part, too. Outside Germany, the early 1990s were years of slow growth, the wrong time for tight monetary policies. The ERM started to look fallible.

The last stroke came from the EMU project itself. The Maastricht Treaty had been signed in December 1991 and was to be ratified by each member country during 1992. The first country to initiate the ratification process was Denmark, where law mandates that international treaties be submitted to referenda. For a variety of reasons, the Danes voted down the Treaty by a few thousand votes. The Treaty included one provision which stated that it would be void unless ratified by all EU countries. Thus, before the other countries even had a chance to ratify it, the Treaty was technically dead by mid-1992. This alarmed the exchange markets, which had bought into the authorities' excessive confidence in both the ERM and the monetary union project. Speculative attacks started immediately, initially targeting Italy (the lira was seriously overvalued by then) and the UK. The UK had finally joined the ERM a year earlier, soon after John Major had replaced Margaret Thatcher as Prime Minister (largely because her opposition to ERM membership appeared anachronistic in the midst of a wave of Euro-optimism), yet the central rate chosen for the pound was seen to be overvalued.

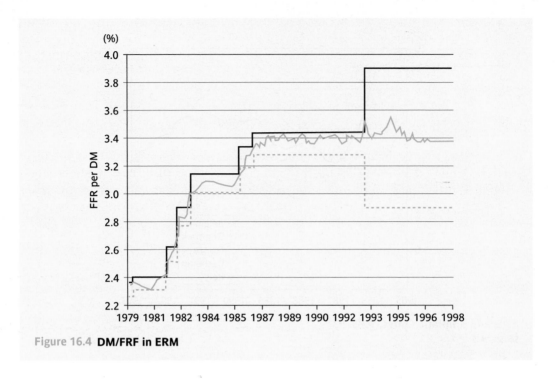

Figure 16.4 **DM/FRF in ERM**

In response to the speculative attacks, the strong currency central banks initially intervened in support of the embattled Banca d'Italia and Bank of England. By mid-September 1992, the attacks had become massive; a frightened Bundesbank decided that truly unlimited interventions were not reasonable and stopped its support. Left to themselves, with foreign exchange reserves falling rapidly, the lira and the pound withdrew from the ERM and the markets concluded that the ERM was considerably more fragile than hitherto admitted. Speculation shifted to the currencies of Ireland, Portugal and Spain, which twice had to be devalued. Contagion then spread to Belgium, Denmark and France, even though inflation in these countries had converged to below the German level and their currencies were not overvalued. By the summer of 1993, huge amounts of reserves had been thrown into the foreign exchange markets and speculation was still going strong. In order to uphold the principle of the ERM, and save face at the same time, the monetary authorities adopted new ultra-large (±15 per cent) bands of fluctuations. Figure 16.4 shows the ERM history of the DM/French franc parity. The tight ERM was dead.

It was not only that monetary integration seemed to be a failure, but also bad blood had been spilled, which complicated any reconstruction efforts. The Bundesbank's reneging of the principle of unlimited interventions offended Italy and the UK. After a decade of hesitation, the UK had finally shed its traditional Euro-scepticism and joined the ERM; its forcible departure left a scar that would not heal easily.

16.2.4 The lessons

A number of features of the experience remain controversial. Inflation was successfully reduced among ERM countries. This has been seen as a proof that tying the hands of central banks through an exchange rate peg is the way to get rid of inflation. However, a comparison with non-ERM countries does not indicate that inflation has declined more quickly or less painfully. At the same time, the sharp turnaround of France in 1983 – away from a go-it-alone approach that would have been inflationary – took the form of retaining ERM membership and maintaining exchange rate stability, but these were side benefits of a wider political decision not to turn its back on Europe. A possible interpretation is that, lacking adequate domestic economic and political institutions, an external arrangement like the ERM has a useful substitution role to play.[4] This interpretation also applies to Italy, a country with a history of chronically high inflation, which could explain why, despite the 1993 setback, it has made a major effort to be a founding member of the Eurozone. The debate of 2005 about whether Italy would be better off outside the monetary union evokes similar consideration.

On the other hand, a number of lessons seem to be generally accepted:

★ The impossible trinity requires that domestic monetary policy independence be abandoned if the exchange rate is rigidly fixed. This is a tall order when economic conditions differ across countries (Germany was too different as it went through unification).

★ As long as the weaker-currency countries imposed restrictions on capital movements, speculative attacks were manageable. Once full capital mobility was achieved, central banks soon realized that even large stocks of foreign exchange reserves are too small, and that unlimited interventions are practically impossible.

★ In particular, once a speculative attack has started, attempting to defend a parity implies offering the market one-way bets: either the peg is abandoned and the speculators win, or it is upheld and they lose nothing. One-way bets are too good to be turned down: this is why speculative attacks are part-and-parcel of a system of fixed exchange rates in the presence of full capital mobility.

★ Consequently, monetary integration with separate currencies is a very risky endeavour, possibly a hopeless quest. Monetary union is one response.

16.3 The EMS re-engineered

16.3.1 A softer ERM

The post-crisis ERM agreed upon in 1993 differed little from a floating exchange rate regime. Bilateral parities could move by 30 per cent, a very wide margin. Unsurprisingly, therefore, the (non)system worked well. Figure 16.4 shows that the DM/FRF fluctuated slightly outside of its earlier narrow ±2.25 per cent range for a few years and then gently converged to its ultimate EMU conversion rate.

---

[4] A similar argument concerns the Stability and Growth Pact presented in Chapter 18.

One precondition set by the Maastricht Treaty for joining the monetary union is at least two years of ERM membership (the other conditions are presented in Chapter 17). This is why Italy returned to the ERM in 1997, as did two new members of the EU, Austria and Finland. The UK, not interested in joining the monetary union, has not returned and argues that this condition should not be interpreted literally since the wide bands have little practical relevance. This position is supported by Sweden, which has also decided to stay out of the monetary union after joining the EU at the same time as Austria and Finland.

16.3.2 EMS-2

The adoption of the euro in January 1999 was accompanied by the launch of a new EMS. EMS-2, as it is called, is described in Box 16.1. It incorporates most of the features of its predecessor, yet differs in some key aspects:

★ While EMS-1 was a symmetric system based on a grid of bilateral parities, in EMS-2, parities are defined vis-à-vis the euro, which is clearly the centre currency. There is no grid, just a table. The margin of fluctuation is less precisely defined. De facto, the 'standard' band is 15 per cent as in the latter version of EMS-1, but a narrower band is also possible.

★ Interventions are still automatic and unlimited, but there is a clear signal that the European Central Bank (ECB) may decide to suspend this obligation.

Box 16.1 The Amsterdam Resolution of the European Council on the establishment of an exchange rate mechanism in the third stage of economic and monetary union (June 1997) – excerpts

'A central rate against the euro will be defined for the currency of each Member State outside the Eurozone participating in the exchange-rate mechanism. There will be one standard fluctuation band of plus or minus 15 per cent around the central rate. Intervention at the margins will in principle be automatic and unlimited, with very short-term financing available. However, the ECB and the central banks of the other participants could suspend intervention if this were to conflict with their primary objective.'

'On a case-by-case basis, formally agreed fluctuation bands narrower than the standard one and backed up in principle by automatic intervention and financing may be set at the request of the non-Eurozone Member States concerned.'

'The details of the very short-term financing mechanism will be determined in the agreement between the ECB and the national central banks, broadly on the basis of the present arrangements.'

The full text is available on, for example, the website of the Danish central bank at: www.nationalbanken.dk/nb\nb.nsf/ alldocs/Fthe_erm_ii_agreement.

Thus the system is more flexible and less committal than EMS-1, no doubt a consequence of the 1992–93 crisis. In addition, it is *à la carte*, allowing different margins of fluctuation. Two countries joined when EMS-2 came into force, at the same time as the monetary union was launched in January 1999: Greece, with the standard ±15 per cent band, until it joined the monetary union in January 2001, and Denmark, which has adopted the narrow ±2.25 per cent that prevailed in EMS-1. Sweden and the UK have decided to stay out 'for the time being' and continue to argue that ERM membership is not a prerequisite should they wish to join the monetary union.

16.3.3 New EU Member States

The Amsterdam Resolution of 1997 specifies the position of the new EU members regarding ERM membership:[5]

> Participation in the exchange-rate mechanism will be voluntary for the Member States outside the Eurozone. Nevertheless, Member States with a derogation can be expected to join the mechanism. A Member State which does not participate from the outset in the exchange-rate mechanism may participate at a later date.

This establishes a presumption that they will be asked to join the ERM, but the UK and Swedish examples mean that joining is not an absolute obligation. In practice, the new member states see the ERM as an entry condition to the Eurozone. Four countries promptly joined the ERM (Slovenia in 2004; Cyprus and Malta in 2005; Slovakia in 2006) and left it when they adopted the euro. Table 16.4 shows that, as of September 2008, in addition to Denmark, the ERM includes the three Baltic States. Estonia and Lithuania joined soon after they acceded to the EU, in effect ratifying the previous currency board arrangement that tied their currencies to the German mark first and the euro afterwards.[6] All three Baltic States are keen to adopt the euro but they have not fulfilled the entry conditions presented in Chapter 17.

In many respects, the new Member States behave like the previous ones. The majority of them value exchange rate stability. They want to adopt the euro, and many have done so. When they cannot, at least they have joined the ERM. They are typically small and very open. Others are lukewarm, especially the larger and less open ones. Yet, officially at least, all are committed to join the Eurozone and will pass through the ERM, as required. Box 16.2 discusses the situation in more detail.

Table 16.4 **ERM membership as of September 2008**

Country	Date of ERM membership	Band of fluctuation (%)
Denmark	1 January 1999	± 2.25
Estonia	27 June 2004	± 15
Lithuania	27 June 2004	± 15
Latvia	2 May 2005	± 15

[5] The text of the Amsterdam resolution, which sets up EMS-2, is available at: http://europa.eu.int/comm/economy_finance/euro/documents/resolution_erm2%20_amsterdam_en.pdf.

[6] Currency boards are explained in Chapter 10.

Box 16.2 Life outside the Eurozone

According to the impossible trinity, adopting a fixed exchange rate implies the loss of the monetary policy instrument. For ERM members that peg their currencies to the euro, in effect this means importing the ECB's policy. The principles developed in Chapter 9 suggest that ERM members should have inflation rates similar to those in the Eurozone. Conversely, the countries that retain monetary policy autonomy, staying outside the Eurozone and the ERM, may well end up with different rates. Figure 16.5 shows that things are not that simple.

One country that closely conforms to the principle is Denmark. The exchange rate vis-à-vis the euro is the key anchor of monetary policy, the Danish Central Bank closely follows the ECB, and inflation is nearly identical. More surprising is the case of Sweden, which carries out an independent monetary policy. Yet, inflation differs very little from that in the Eurozone. The Swedish Riksbank and the ECB seem to follow similar strategies so, in the absence of significant asymmetric shocks, they end up carrying out similar policies, which deliver similar inflation rates. The Bank of England too

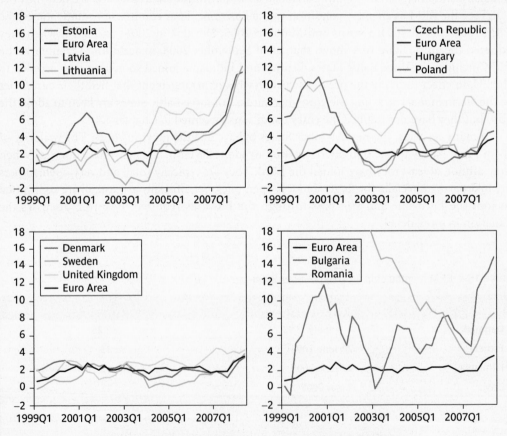

Figure 16.5 **Inflation rates in the non-Eurozone members (1999Q1–2008Q2)**

Source: IMF

follows a similar approach but the UK economy is less open and is an oil producer. The shocks affecting the Eurozone and the UK are less symmetric, leading to different policy decisions and, eventually, to somewhat different inflation rates.

The real surprise in Fig. 16.5 comes from the Baltic States. Even though they are ERM members, inflation is very different from that in the Eurozone. All three countries are going through a rapid catch-up process, which triggers the Balassa–Samuelson effect presented in Chapter 9. Yet, this does not explain the explosion of inflation since late 2006. Fast growth and rising standards of living have prompted a boom, powered by rising housing prices and generous public spending in what has been dubbed 'EU-phoria'. Absent monetary policy autonomy, the central banks cannot exercise restraint and prevent prices from accelerating. It is likely that overvaluation will soon drag the economy down. A concern is the vulnerability of ERM members to speculative attacks, as discussed in Section 16.2.3.

The five remaining new EU members have so far decided not to join the ERM. As EU members, they have eliminated all restrictions to capital mobility and concluded that they wish to retain monetary policy autonomy. As they undergo deep structural changes, conditions differ from those of the Eurozone – asymmetric shocks are sizeable – so monetary policies differ and so does inflation. Three of them (the Czech Republic, Hungary and Poland) have indicated that they intend to join the ERM by the end of the decade. The newest EU members (Bulgaria and Romania) have yet to fully stabilize their economies (Bulgaria operates a currency board).

16.4 Summary

The EMS was adopted in 1979 in an effort to preserve exchange rate stability within Europe following the end of the Bretton Woods system. Initially created to shield Europe from international monetary disturbances, its success made the monetary union look almost like the natural next step. A new arrangement has been set up following the adoption of the euro. All EU members are members of the EMS but the active part of the system, the ERM, is optional in the sense that some countries (Denmark and the UK) have a derogation while Sweden and three of the new EU members are postponing membership.

The ERM was based on a grid specifying all bilateral parities and the corresponding margins of fluctuation, normally ±2.25 per cent. ERM members were committed to jointly defend their bilateral parities, if necessary through unlimited interventions and loans. Realignments were possible, but required the consent of all members. This amounted to a tight and elaborate arrangement.

The EMS went through three phases. During the first period, inflation differed quite widely from one country to another and realignments were frequent. Then, all countries decided to adopt the Bundesbank's low inflation strategy, in effect adopting the Deutschmark as an anchor and avoiding further realignments. Finally, the 1992–93 crisis – which saw two currencies, the Italian lira and the British pound, exit – ended with the adoption of wide margins of ±15 per cent, allowing the ERM to nominally survive until the launch of the euro.

The 1992–93 crisis provides an example of the impossible trinity. The liberalization of financial markets and the fixity of exchange rates were incompatible with divergent monetary policies. For a while, during the late 1980s, most countries did follow the Bundesbank and achieved low inflation. But when Germany went through its unification shock, the Bundesbank adopted a tight policy stance that was incompatible with the low growth situation in the other ERM member countries.

With the adoption of a single currency, a new EMS was established. EMS-2 differs from EMS-1 mainly in that the euro is now the reference currency and the unlimited intervention obligation no longer exists. As a result, the ERM is asymmetric and its members must rely on their own resources to maintain the declared parities within the standard ±15 per cent band. EMS-2 remains a prerequisite for joining the Eurozone.

Nowadays, the ERM is one of the requirements to join the Eurozone. Of the 12 countries that joined the EU in 2004, four have joined the ERM until they adopt the euro, three are currently part of the mechanism and five have delayed ERM membership.

Self-assessment questions

1. What is the difference between the EMS and the ERM?
2. How does EMS-2 differ from EMS-1?
3. What are the margins of fluctuation? What role do they play?
4. Explain the principle of mutual support within the ERM.
5. Estonia and Lithuania simultaneously operate a currency board arrangement and are ERM members. Is there a contradiction?
6. Imagine three ERM countries. Compute a fictional parity grid linking their three currencies pairwise.
7. In Fig. 16.5, compare inflation in the UK and Sweden on the one hand, and the Czech Republic, Hungary and Poland on the other. These countries have in common that they did not join the ERM and that their central banks pursue strategies quite similar to that of the Eurosystem. Why are the inflation outcomes so different?
8. What do we mean by saying that the EMS-1 had become a 'Deutschmark area'? How did that happen and could it have been foreseen?

Essay questions

1. In retrospect it is claimed that the 1992–93 crisis of the EMS could have been anticipated. Why and why not? Once the crisis started, could Italy and the UK have stayed in the system, and if so under what conditions?
2. Would the Bretton Woods system have survived had it been patterned after the ERM?
3. The EU new members have to operate for at least two years within EMS-2's ERM. What problems can you envision? What alternatives would you suggest?
4. 'The EMS turned out to be a successful transition to the establishment of the monetary union.' Comment.

5. 'Mandatory capital mobility – as part of the Single Market – turns out to be a hindrance to ERM membership by the new Member States.' Comment.

Further reading: the aficionado's corner

A very useful description of the EMS is given in Chapter 1 of **P. Kenen** (1995) *Economic and Monetary Union in Europe*, Cambridge University Press, New York.

On the history of the EMS and its evolution towards EMU, see **D. Gros and N. Thygesen** (1998) *European Monetary Integration*, 2nd edn, Addison Wesley Longman, London.

A study of the exchange rate regime treatment of accessing countries can be found in **D. Begg et al.** (2003) *Sustainable Regimes of Capital Movements in Accession Countries*, Policy Paper 10, Centre for Economic Policy Research, London. Download from www.cepr.org/pubs/books/PP10.asp.

A Swedish view on the ERM can be found in L. Heikensten (2003) 'Euro entry before reforms or reforms before euro entry?' Download from www.riksbank.se/templates/speech.aspx?id=8544.

A consideration of the choice faced by new members can be found in S. Schadler, P. Drummond, L. Kuijs, Z. Murgasova and R. van Elkan (2005) 'Adopting the euro in central Europe: challenges of the next step in European integration', Occasional paper 234, IMF, Washington, DC.

Useful websites

For a concise summary of the EMS, access the European Parliament's factsheet at www.europarl.eu.int/factsheets/5_2_0_en.htm.

The European Commission publishes annual Convergence Reports that evaluate each country's position relative to the EU: http://ec.europa.eu/economy_finance/publications/specpub_list9259.htm.

Reference

Eichengreen, B. (2002) *Lessons of the Euro for the Rest of the World*, December. Download from http://repositories.cdlib.org/cgi/viewcontent.cgi?article=1005&context=ies.

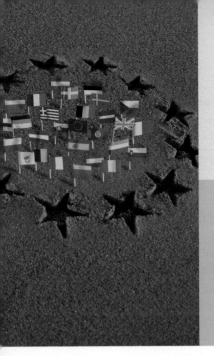

Chapter **17**

The European monetary union

A normal central bank is a monopolist. Today's Eurosystem is, instead, an archipelago of monopolists.

Tommaso Padoa-Schioppa (Executive Board of the ECB)

Chapter contents

17.1	The Maastricht Treaty	489
17.2	The Eurosystem	495
17.3	Objectives, instruments and strategy	498
17.4	Independence and accountability	502
17.5	The first decade	506
17.6	Summary	515

Introduction

The European monetary union did not come as a surprise. It was carefully mapped out in the Maastricht Treaty, which specified how and when the single currency would be launched and laid down a precise set of institutional arrangements, which are presented in Section 17.1. Section 17.2 describes how the European Central Bank interacts with the national central banks. The Treaty also prescribes the essential elements of the monetary policy doctrine; Section 17.3 explains how these principles are implemented to guarantee price stability. Section 17.4 explains why price stability can only be preserved if the central bank enjoys a high degree of independence and describes how this is done; it also examines the related issue of democratic accountability. The last section reviews the first years of the single currency and discusses the next enlargement of the Eurozone.

17.1 The Maastricht Treaty

17.1.1 Main components

Maastricht – unpronounceable by non-Dutch natives – is a picturesque Dutch town. In December 1991, the 12 heads of states and governments of the EU gathered there to sign a treaty that replaced the European Community (EC) with the European Union (EU). The change of name was symbolic. It was meant to signal that the treaty was not just about economics but also included political considerations. Two new pillars – foreign and defence policies, justice and internal security – were added to the first, economic pillar. The power of the European Parliament was enhanced and it was also agreed to substitute 'qualified majority' for 'unanimity' for Council decisions on a number of issues. Many of these ambitious-looking steps were incomplete, which called for the subsequent treaties of Amsterdam, Nice and Lisbon.[1] The monetary union part of the Treaty, however, was fully worked out. It included an irrevocable decision to adopt a single currency by 1 January 1999. The Treaty described in great detail how the system would work, including the statutes of the European Central Bank (ECB) and the conditions under which monetary union would start.

The Maastricht Treaty marks the end of a long road – three decades of attempts to achieve a monetary union, summarized in Table 17.1. It was ratified by all signatories over the next year and a half, as recalled in Box 17.1. In many ways, the adoption of the euro has changed the nature of the integration process. At the symbolic level, the official name of the European

Table 17.1 EMU timetable

Towards Maastricht		Between Maastricht and the single currency		The single currency	
1970	Werner Plan	1994	European Monetary Institute (precursor of ECB)	1999	Monetary union starts
1979	European Monetary System starts	1997	Stability and Growth Pact	2001	Greece joins
1989	Delors Committee	1998	Decision on membership	2002	Euro coins and notes introduced
1991	Maastricht Treaty signed	1998	Conversion rates set	2007	Slovenia joins
1993	Maastricht Treaty ratified	1998	Creation of ECB	2008	Cyprus and Malta join
				2009	Slovakia joins

---

[1] Chapter 1 provides more details.

Community (EC) was changed to European Union (EU) to recognize that the Treaty was meant to be wider than economic issues.

Box 17.1   Ratification of the Maastricht Treaty

Any international treaty must be ratified by the signatories. The ratification procedure varies from one country to another: some countries require a referendum, others must obtain parliament's approval, yet others can decide between these two alternatives.

The first country to undertake ratification of the Maastricht Treaty was Denmark, and it had to be by referendum. The Danish people chose to reject the Treaty by a small margin. A clause stipulated that, to enter into existence, the Treaty must be ratified by all the signatories. Thus the Treaty looked dead before the other countries even had a chance to consider it. Yet, hoping that a legal solution would be found, it was decided to continue with the ratification process.

France offered to be the second country to consider ratification. In the hope of reversing the bad impression created by Denmark's popular rejection, President Mitterrand chose the referendum procedure at a time when polls indicated strong support. As the campaign went on, support gradually eroded. When some polls reported a majority against the Treaty, fearing a collapse of the whole project, the exchange markets became jittery and speculation gained momentum. In the event, Italy and the UK were ejected from the ERM and several currencies had to be devalued, some of them many times, as described in Chapter 16. Meanwhile, the French approved the Treaty by a narrow margin.

The Danes were asked to return to the polls, after the Danish government committed itself to invoke the right not to adopt the single currency, a right included in a special protocol to the Treaty, as is explained below. This time, the Danes approved the Treaty. Just when the road seemed clear, the German Constitutional Court was asked by opponents to decide whether the Treaty was compatible with Germany's constitution. The Court took several months to deliver its opinion, keeping the process hanging. The Court finally decided that the Treaty did not contradict the German constitution. This allowed Germany to ratify the Treaty in late 1993, the last country to do so.

17.1.2 Convergence criteria

In the early 1990s, the macroeconomic situation differed widely from one country to another. Germany, deeply attached to price stability, was concerned that some countries were not quite ready to adopt the required monetary discipline. It insisted that admission to the monetary union would not be automatic. A selection process was designed to certify which countries had adopted a 'culture of price stability', meaning that they had durably achieved German-style low inflation. In order to join the monetary union, a country has to fulfil the following five convergence criteria, which remain applicable to all future candidate countries.

Inflation

The first criterion deals directly with inflation. To be eligible for monetary union membership, a country's inflation rate should not exceed the average of the three lowest inflation rates achieved by the EU Member States by more than 1.5 percentage points. Figure 17.1 shows how the 'Club Med' countries of southern Europe managed to bring their inflation rates below the acceptable limit by 1998. Greece (not shown) failed (actually it did not even try and decided to join later, which it did in 2001).

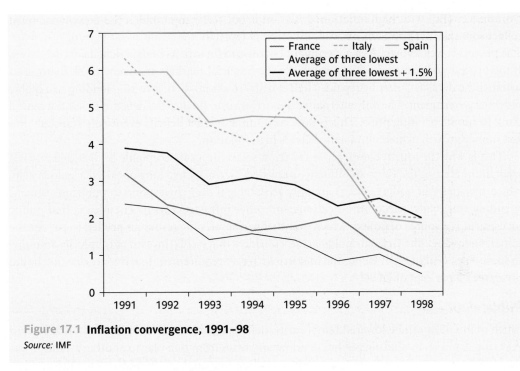

Figure 17.1 Inflation convergence, 1991–98
Source: IMF

Long-term nominal interest rate

An inflation-prone country could possibly squeeze down inflation temporarily, on the last year before admission – for example, by freezing administered prices (electricity, transports) – only to relax the effort afterwards. In order to weed out potential cheaters, a second criterion requires that the long-term interest rate should not exceed the average rates observed in the three lowest inflation rate countries by more than 2 percentage points. The reasoning is shrewd. Long-term interest rates mostly reflect markets' assessment of long-term inflation.[2] Achieving a low long-term interest rate therefore requires convincing naturally sceptical financial markets that inflation would remain low 'for ever'.

ERM membership

The same concern about a superficial conversion to price stability lies behind the third criterion. Here, the idea is that a country must have demonstrated its ability to keep its exchange rate tied to its future monetary union partner currencies. The requirement is therefore that every country must have taken part in the ERM for at least two years without having to devalue its currency.[3]

Budget deficit

The three previous criteria aim at demonstrating a country's acceptance of permanently low inflation, but it makes sense to eradicate the incentives to tolerate high inflation. Why do some

---

[2] This is based on the Fisher principle: nominal interest rate = real interest rate + expected inflation. Since the real interest rate is reasonably constant and set worldwide, the main driving force determining the long-term interest rate is the expected long-term inflation rate. See Box 17.5 for an elaboration.

[3] The exchange rate mechanism is presented in detail in Chapter 16.

countries end up with high inflation? Inflation is not really desirable, so its acceptance must reflect some deeper problem. Indeed, inflation is typically the result of large budget deficits. The process is well known. As a government borrows to finance its budget deficits, its debt rises. If the process goes on unchecked, eventually the financial markets are likely to ask themselves whether the debts will ever be repaid. Their normal reaction, then, is to stop lending to a highly indebted government. The only alternative to borrowing to finance the deficit is to ask the central bank to run its printing press. This is how continuing budget deficits eventually translate into fast money growth, which ultimately delivers high inflation.

This is why the fourth convergence criterion sets a limit on acceptable budget deficits. But what limit? Here again, German influence prevailed. Germany had long operated a 'golden rule', which specifies that budget deficits are only acceptable if they correspond to public investment spending (on roads, telecommunications and other infrastructures). The idea is that public investment is a source of growth which eventually generates the resources needed to pay for the initial borrowing. The German 'golden rule' considers that public investment typically amounts to some 3 per cent of GDP. Hence the Maastricht Treaty requirement that budget deficits should not exceed 3 per cent of GDP.[4]

Public debt

Much as inflation can be lowered temporarily, deficits can be made to look good on any given year (for example, by shifting public spending and taxes from one year to another). Thus it was decided that a more permanent feature of fiscal discipline ought to be added. The fifth and last criterion mandates a maximum level for the public debt. Here again, the question was: which ceiling? Unimaginatively perhaps, the ceiling was set at 60 per cent of GDP because it was the average debt level when the Maastricht Treaty was being negotiated in 1991. An additional reason was that the 60 per cent debt limit can be seen as compatible with a deficit debt ceiling of 3 per cent, as explained in Box 17.2.

Box 17.2   **The arithmetic of deficits and debts**

Debts grow out of deficits, but how does the debt/GDP ratio relate to the deficit/GDP ratio? A little arithmetic helps. If total nominal debt at the end of year t is Bt, its increase during the year is $B_t - B_{t-1}$, and this is equal to the annual deficit D_t:

$$B_t - B_{t-1} = D_t \tag{1}$$

The two fiscal convergence criteria refer not to the debt and deficit levels, but to their ratios to nominal GDP Y, denoted as b_t and d_t, respectively. Divide the previous accounting equality by the current year GDP to get:

$$\frac{B_t - B_{t-1}}{Y_t} = \frac{D_t}{Y_t} \quad \text{or} \quad b_t - \frac{B_{t-1}}{Y_t} = d_t \tag{2}$$

---

[4] This entry condition is somewhat distinct from the same limit prescribed by the Stability and Growth Pact, which is studied in Chapter 18. There is a link between the two limits, though: having joined the monetary union, a country is not allowed to let its budget deficits rise again.

Then note that $\dfrac{B_{t-1}}{Y_t} = \dfrac{B_{t-1}}{Y_{t-1}}\dfrac{Y_{t-1}}{Y_t} = \dfrac{b_{t-1}}{1+g_t}$

where $g_t = \dfrac{Y_t - Y_{t-1}}{Y_{t-1}} = \dfrac{Y_t}{Y_{t-1}} - 1$

is the growth rate of GDP in year t. We can rewrite the debt growth eqn (2) as:

$$b_t - b_{t-1} = (1 + g_t)d_t - g_t b_t \qquad (3)$$

If the debt to GDP ratio b is to remain constant, we need to have $b_t = b_{t-1}$, which from eqn (3) implies:

$$d_t = \frac{g_t}{1 + g_t} b_t \qquad (4)$$

The fiscal convergence criteria sets $d_t = 3$ per cent and $b_t = 60$ per cent. If nominal GDP grows by 5 per cent, eqn (4) is approximately satisfied. The implicit assumption is therefore that real GDP annual growth is about 3 per cent and inflation is 2 per cent, hence a nominal GDP growth rate of 5 per cent.

If the debt level is constant, the debt/GDP ratio declines as the result of GDP growth, the more so the faster nominal GDP grows. This means that some debt increase, and therefore some deficit, is compatible with a constant debt/GDP ratio, and the tolerable deficit is larger the faster nominal GDP grows.

However, by definition of an average, some countries had debts in excess of 60 per cent of GDP, and some much larger. In particular, Belgium's public debt stood at some 120 per cent of GDP. Yet, by 1991, Belgium had overhauled its public finances and was adamant that it was now committed to adhere to a strict budgetary discipline. However, it would take a long time to bring its debt to below 60 per cent.[5] As a founding member of the Common Market in 1957, an enthusiastic European country and a long advocate of monetary union, Belgium argued that it could not be left out because of past sins now firmly repudiated. At its request, the criterion was couched in prudent terms, calling for a debt to GDP ratio either less than 60 per cent or 'moving in that direction'.

Figure 17.2 shows the deficits and debts in 1998, the last year before the launch of the monetary union, which was used to determine which country fulfilled the criteria. All countries managed to bring their deficits below the 3 per cent threshold, sometimes thanks to accounting tricks.[6] Few, however, could report debts below 60 per cent of GDP. In the end, all were saved by the 'Belgian clause'.

17.1.3 Two-speed Europe

An important aspect of the Maastricht Treaty is that it introduced, for the first time, the idea that a major integration move could leave some countries out. Initially, the intention was to

---

[5] In 2008, the Belgian public debt was down to 82.6 per cent of GDP.

[6] France privatized part of its state-owned telecommunications corporation, which provided the revenues needed to achieve the deficit target. Italy collected at the end of 1998 some taxes which would normally have been due in early 1999. Even the German government considered selling gold to pay back its debt but backed off as the Bundesbank publicly attacked the idea.

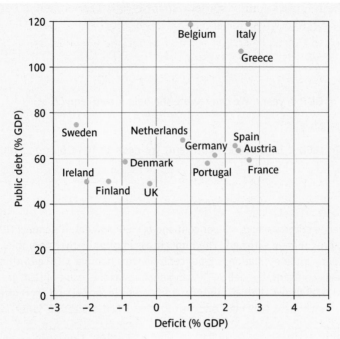

Figure 17.2 Deficits and debts in 1998
Source: European Commission

protect price stability and not let the inflation wolf enter into the den. Then things turned out differently.

Prime Minister Thatcher's Britain was firmly opposed to the monetary union. For a while, Thatcher stonewalled the discussions, which went ahead without her. The view in London was that this was a bizarre idea with no future at all, a sort of conventional exercise that no one really intended to bring to fruition. When it realized that the other European countries were in fact serious, the UK found itself cut off from a major negotiation that would powerfully shape Europe's future. Partly because of her unwillingness to engage her partners on the issue, Thatcher was dismissed and replaced by John Major. Unable to scuttle the project, the best he could achieve was to obtain an opt-out clause, which stated that the UK, alone, was not bound to join the monetary union. This further confirmed that Europe could move at different speeds. A similar opt-out clause was given to Denmark after a first rejection of the Treaty by Danish voters (see Box 17.1).

In 1995, Sweden joined the EU. The Swedish authorities made it clear that they were less than enthusiastic regarding the monetary union. They asked for an opt-out clause, which was denied. The diplomatic solution was a gentleman's agreement whereby Sweden did not enter the ERM and was therefore disqualified for monetary union membership. De facto, Sweden is treated as Denmark, with the right to decide when to apply for membership to the Eurozone.

In the end, the monetary union started on time with 11 members. The 'outs' included Greece, which did not meet the convergence criteria, the UK and Denmark, which invoked the opt-out clause, and Sweden. Greece converged later and joined in January 2001. The story started anew when the EU expanded in 2004. By 2009, the Eurozone included 16 members thanks to the admission of four new members: Cyprus, Malta, Slovakia and Slovenia.

17.2 The Eurosystem

17.2.1 *N* countries, *N* + 1 central banks

With a single currency there can be only one interest rate, one exchange rate vis-à-vis the rest of the world, and therefore one monetary policy. Normally this implies a single central bank, but this is not quite the way the EMU was set up. Each member still comes equipped with its own central bank, the last remaining vestige of lost monetary sovereignty. No matter how daring the founding fathers of the EMU were, they stopped short of merging the national central banks into a single institution, partly for fear of having to dismiss thousands of employees. In fact, as Table 17.2 shows, national central banks have hardly downsized their staff.

The solution was inspired by federal states like Germany and the USA where regional central banks coexist with the federal central bank. But the EU is not a federation, and the word 'federation' is highly politically incorrect in Europe. Inevitably, therefore, the chosen structure is complicated. The newly created European Central Bank (ECB) coexists with the national central banks, one of which did not even exist prior to 1999 since Luxembourg, long part of a monetary union with Belgium, only established its own central bank to conform to the new arrangement.

On the other hand, in many respects the euro was meant to be a continuation of Europe's most successful currency, the Deutschmark. The structure of the Bundesbank was used as a blueprint for the monetary union. This inspiration is visible not only in the new institution but also in the policy objective and framework, and in the location of the ECB in Frankfurt, only a few kilometres from the Bundesbank.

Table 17.2 Staff in national central banks and the ECB in 2007

	Total	Per population 1 million		Total	Per population 1 million
Austria	918	110	Luxembourg	219	469
Belgium	2 032	194	Malta	314	772
Finland	490	93	Netherlands	1566	95
France	12 828	208	Portugal	1707	161
Germany	11 160	135	Slovenia	425	212
Greece	3 086	280	Spain	2719	61
Ireland	991	230			
Italy	7 400	126	ECB	1342	4

Note: Data refer to 2002.
Sources: Central banks' Annual Reports and IMF

17.2.2 The system

The European System of Central Banks (ESCB) is composed of the new, specially created European Central Bank (ECB) and the national central banks (NCBs) of all EU Member States. Since not all EU countries have joined the monetary union, a different term, Eurosystem, has been coined to refer to the ECB and the participating NCBs.[7] The Eurosystem implements the monetary policy of the Eurozone, as described below. If needed, it also conducts foreign exchange operations, in agreement with the Finance Ministers of the member countries. It holds and manages the official foreign reserves of the EMU Member States. It monitors the payment systems and it is involved in the prudential supervision of credit institutions and the financial system.

As shown in Fig. 17.3, the ECB is run by an Executive Board of six members, appointed by the heads of state or governments of the countries that have joined the monetary union, following consultation of the European Parliament and the Governing Council of the ESCB. It comprises the six members of the Executive Board and the governors of the NCBs of monetary union Member States. The Governing Council is the key authority deciding on monetary policy. Its decisions are, in principle, taken by majority voting, with each member holding one vote, although it seems to operate by consensus. A transitory body, the General Council, includes the members of the Governing Council and the governors of the NCBs of the countries that have not joined the monetary union. The General Council is in essence fulfilling a liaison role and has no authority.

While decisions are taken by the Governing Council, the ECB plays an important role. Its president presides over the meetings of the Governing Council and reports its decisions at press

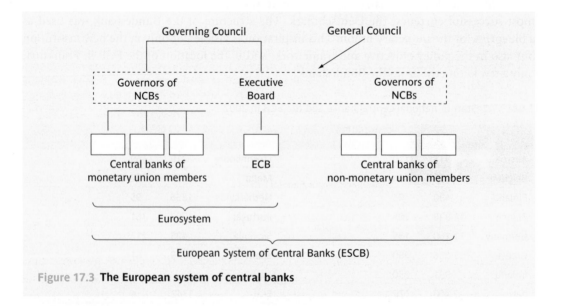

Figure 17.3 The European system of central banks

---

[7] For a full and formal description, see the July 1999 issue of the ECB's *Monthly Bulletin*, pp. 55–63.

conferences. The ECB prepares the meetings of the Governing Council and implements its decisions. It also gives instructions to the NCBs to carry out the common monetary policy. An important characteristic of the ECB is that its Executive Board members are not representing any country: they are appointed as individuals, even though the large countries (France, Germany, Italy and Spain) all had a national sitting in the first Board. The first president was Dutch, Wim Duisenberg, and his successor is French, Jean-Claude Trichet, both having previously served as governors of their own NCBs (see Box 17.3). Thus the ECB is of a federal nature while the Eurosystem is a hybrid, partly federal (the ECB) and partly including national institutions (the NCBs).

Box 17.3   ECB Presidents, 1998–2011

Wim Duisenberg (1998–2003)
Wim Duisenberg, the first president of the ECB, was born in 1932. He holds a PhD in economics, worked at the IMF and was professor of macroeconomics at the University of Amsterdam before entering politics in the Labour Party and serving as Minister of Finance. Later on, he joined De Netherlandsche Bank and became its governor in 1982. In 1997, he was appointed President of the European Monetary Institute, in charge of preparing the introduction of the single currency.

Source: www.ecb.int

Jean-Claude Trichet (2003–11)
His successor, **Jean-Claude Trichet**, was also a central bank governor prior to taking over the ECB. Born in 1942, he studied economics and civil engineering before attending the elite Ecole Nationale d' Administration. He capped a distinguished career in the French Finance Ministry by becoming head of the Treasury and, in 1993, Governor of the Banque de France. While at the Treasury, he designed the 'franc fort' policy of disinflation.

Source: www.banque-france-fr

The size of the Governing Council is seen by external observers as a source of difficulty. With $6 + N$ members, where N is the number of countries that have joined the monetary union, the Council is large. It will become larger as new members join the union by the end of the decade, although some change will be introduced to ensure that the decision-making committee's size is, and remains, efficient (see Box 17.4).

> ## Box 17.4   Changing the rules of the Eurosystem

Monetary policy choices are often delicate, with many pros and cons to be balanced. For this kind of decision, smaller committees are more efficient than larger ones. The expansion of the EU challenges the Eurosystem decision-making process as the size of the Governing Council could eventually grow to 30 or more members – a small parliament. The Nice Treaty of 2000 includes an enabling clause which calls upon the Eurosystem to make a recommendation to the Council on how to prevent an unwieldy situation. After long internal deliberations, the Eurosystem made its position known in December 2002. It suggests capping the number of NCB Governors exercising a voting right at 15. While all Council members will be attending the meetings, NCB Governors will exercise a voting right on the basis of a rotation system. The frequency at which every NCB Governor will rotate will depend on the size of the financial market of his/her country, following a complex procedure.[1] This proposition has been approved by the EU Council. It should take effect in 2009 with the admission of Slovakia but it was to be ratified by all EU member countries as part of the newly proposed Constitution. Rejection of the Constitution leaves the situation open.

[1] For a complete description, see the May 2003 issue of the ECB's *Monthly Bulletin*, pp. 73–83, and the decision at http://europa.eu.int/scadplus/leg/en/lvb/l25065.htm.

17.3 Objectives, instruments and strategy

17.3.1 Objectives

The Maastricht Treaty specifies that the main task of the Eurosystem is to deliver price stability, but the formulation is both vague and ambiguous:

> The primary objective of the ESCB shall be to maintain price stability. Without prejudice to the objective of price stability, the ESCB shall support the general economic policies in the Community with a view to contributing to the achievement of the objectives of the Community as laid down in Article 2.
>
> (Article 105)

The Treaty does not give an exact definition of price stability. The Eurosystem has chosen to interpret it first as follows: 'Price stability is defined as a year-on-year increase in the Harmonized Index of Consumer Prices (HICP)[8] for the Eurozone of below 2 per cent. Price stability is to be maintained over the medium term.' In 2003, with fears of deflation rising, 'the Governing Council agreed that in the pursuit of price stability it will aim to maintain inflation rates close to 2 per cent over the medium term'. Thus, while many central banks typically announce an admissible range for inflation, the Eurosystem indicates only an imprecise target. It does not specify either the meaning of 'the medium term'.

The Treaty considers price stability a 'primary objective'. Secondary objectives are described in Delphic terms, referring to Article 2 which states the objectives of the EU as including 'economic and social progress, and a high level of employment'. Price stability clearly takes

[8] The Harmonized Index of Consumer Prices is an area-wide consumer price index. The same method is also used to compute national HICPS.

precedence over these secondary objectives, but leaves the Eurosystem with quite some leeway to decide its strategy. Over its first ten years, the Eurosystem has displayed flexibility as it emphasizes price stability but is quite sensitive to growth.

17.3.2 Instruments

Like most other central banks, the Eurosystem uses the short-term interest rate to conduct monetary policy. The reason is that very short-term assets – 24 hours or less – are very close to cash. As central banks have a monopoly on the supply of cash, they can control very short-term rates. On the other hand, longer-term financial instruments can be supplied by both the public and private sectors, making it nearly impossible for central banks to dominate the market and control the rate. In fact, longer-term rates incorporate market expectations of future inflation and future policy actions. These expectations are beyond the control of the central bank, and therefore long-term interest rates cannot be steered with any degree of precision. By concentrating on short-term rates, central banks can achieve greater precision.

The problem is that central banks control the short maturity whereas it is the long-term interest rate that affects the economy because households and firms borrow for relatively long periods, typically from 1 to 20 years or more. Stock prices and exchange rates, which are the other channels through which monetary policy affects the economy,[9] also incorporate longer-term expectations, similar to those that move the long-term interest rates. Thus central banks act indirectly on the economy. They affect the long-term interest rates through their influence on future short-term rates and inflation. Being clear about longer-run aims and intentions is part of the art of central banking.

The Eurosystem focuses on the overnight rate EONIA (European Over Night Index Average), a weighted average of overnight lending transactions in the Eurozone's interbank market). Control over EONIA is achieved in two ways:

1   The Eurosystem creates a ceiling and a floor for EONIA by maintaining open lending and deposit facilities at pre-announced interest rates. The marginal lending facility means that banks can always borrow directly from the ECB (more precisely, from the NCBs) at the corresponding rate; they would never pay more on the overnight market, so the marginal lending rate is in effect a ceiling. Similarly, since banks can always deposit cash at the ECB's deposit rate, they would never agree to lend at a lower rate, and this rate is the floor. Figure 17.4 shows that, indeed, EONIA moves within the corridor thus established.

2   The Eurosystem conducts, usually weekly, auctions at a rate that it chooses. These auctions, called main refinancing operations, are the means by which the ECB provides liquidity to the banking system and the chosen interest rate serves as a precise guide for EONIA.

How does liquidity flow from the Eurosystem to all the corners of the Eurozone banking system? As noted above, the Eurosystem organizes auctions on a regular basis. Each NCB collects bids from its commercial banks and passes the information to the ECB. The ECB then decides which proportion of bids will be accepted and instructs the NCBs accordingly. The

---

[9] Box 9.3 presents the channels of monetary policy.

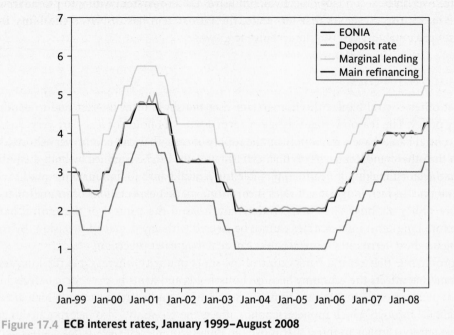

Figure 17.4 **ECB interest rates, January 1999–August 2008**
Source: Monthly Bulletin, ECB

commercial banks can then disseminate the liquidity on the interbank market. It does not matter where the initial injection is made: since there is a single interest rate throughout the Eurozone, the area-wide interbank market ensures that money is available where needed.

17.3.3 Strategy

How does the Eurosystem go about using its instrument (the short-term interest rate) to achieve its objective (inflation close to 2 per cent)? It announced its strategy in October 1998, a few months before starting its operation. In spring 2003, it conducted a strategy review to take stock of the experience accumulated so far.[10] As stated, the strategy relies on three main elements: the definition of price stability, as presented in Section 17.3.1, and two 'pillars' used to identify risks to price stability.

The first pillar is what the Eurosystem calls 'economic analysis'. It consists of a broad review of the recent evolution and likely prospects of economic conditions (including growth, employment, prices, exchange rates and foreign conditions). The second pillar, the 'monetary analysis', studies the evolution of monetary aggregates (M3, in particular) and credit which, in the medium to long term, affect inflation, in line with the neutrality principle developed in Chapter 10. In the Eurosystem's words, 'these two perspectives offer complementary analytical

---

[10] The initial strategy is presented in the ECB's *Monthly Bulletin*, January 1999. The strategy review is presented in the ECB's *Monthly Bulletin*, June 2003.

frameworks to support the Governing Council's overall assessment of risks to price stability. In this respect, the monetary analysis mainly serves as a means of cross-checking, from a medium- to long-term perspective, the short- to medium-term indications coming from economic analysis' (ECB, 2003).

What does this mean in practice? The Governing Council is presented by its Chief Economist with a broad analysis, including forecasts of inflation and growth. Monetary conditions are then used to qualify the forecasts and allow the Council to form a view of where inflation is heading. Then the real debate starts: What should happen to the interest rate? Should it be raised because inflation is perceived as excessive? How much weight should be attached to other considerations, such as growth and employment, or the exchange rate and stock markets? Officially, the Eurosystem is only dealing with inflation, but it has visibly adjusted its actions when it has felt the need to smooth the edges of what it considers to be secondary concerns. Importantly, the Eurosystem does not take any responsibility for the exchange rate, which is freely floating.

Is the Eurosystem's strategy special? Over the past decade, many central banks have adopted the inflation-targeting strategy. In Europe, this is the case of most non-monetary union member central banks (including the Czech Republic, Hungary, Norway, Poland, Sweden and the UK). Inflation targeting comprises announcing a target, publishing an inflation forecast at the relevant policy horizon (usually one to two years ahead), and adjusting the interest rate according to the difference between the forecast and the target. For example, if the forecast exceeds the target, the presumption is that monetary policy is tightened, i.e. that the interest rate is raised.

The Eurosystem has resisted this approach, along with the US Federal Reserve and the Bank of Japan. One reason is that the Eurosystem wants to claim the Bundesbank heritage, and the Bundesbank did not target inflation; it targeted money growth, which explains the second pillar. On the other hand, the Eurosystem's strategy resembles inflation targeting: there is an implicit target (the 2 per cent definition of price stability) and an inflation forecast is published twice a year. What the Eurosystem seems to reject is giving the impression that it acts mechanically. Box 17.5 examines this question in more detail.

Box 17.5   How different is the ECB?

Inflation-targeting central banks set the short-term interest rate with one eye on inflation forecasts and the other eye on the expected activity level, measured as the deviation from actual GDP from its 'normal' level. The Eurosystem too tries to steer inflation in the medium run towards 'close but less than 2 per cent' but does not ignore the output gap.[1] So, beyond the rhetoric, does the Eurosystem really act differently from inflation-targeting central banks? A simple way to check is to ask whether the actual interest rate is indeed driven by the deviation of inflation from its (implicit or explicit target) and by the output gap. This representation of interest rate decisions is called the Taylor rule. It involves choosing weights to be applied to the inflation and output gaps; these weights reflect the relative importance attached by the central bank to its two objectives.

Figure 17.5 looks at the record of the Eurosystem (and its predecessor, the Bundesbank), of the Swedish Riksbank and of the Bank of England. It displays two short-term interest rates: the actual one and the one that would have been chosen if the central banks had followed the same Taylor rule.[2] We

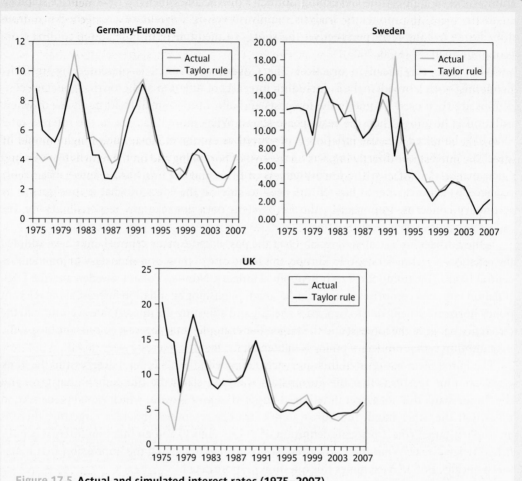

Figure 17.5 Actual and simulated interest rates (1975–2007)
Sources: IMF and *Economic Outlook*, OECD

see that central bank behaviour has increasingly conformed to the Taylor rule formulation. This applies to the Bundesbank until 1999. Despite all of its tough rhetoric, it was an early practitioner of the Taylor rule. We also see that the Eurosystem followed suit and that its actions do not differ from those of the Riksbank or the Bank of England.

[1] The output gap is defined in Chapter 9.
[2] The weights are 1.5 on inflation and 0.5 on the output gap. The Taylor rule involves expected inflation and output gaps. In the simulation that follows, we use actual inflation and output gaps. The Taylor rule is presented in Burda and Wyplosz (2009).

17.4 Independence and accountability

Current wisdom is that a central bank should be primarily entrusted with the task of delivering price stability. To that effect, it must be free to pursue this task without outside interference. While, in principle, everyone approves of price stability, some important actors occasionally have second thoughts. As noted in Section 17.1.2, financially stressed governments may come to see the printing press as the least bad option. Exporters like low exchange rates and are frequently asking their central banks to relax their policies, with the support of trade unions concerned with employment. Debtors like inflation for it erases the value of their (non-indexed) liabilities. Financial institutions often make larger profits when liquidity is plentiful. In any democracy, these are formidable coalitions, and this is why the modern trend of focusing monetary policy on price stability also argues in favour of central bank independence from all segments of society and, in particular, from the political powers.

On the other hand, monetary policy affects citizens of the monetary union in a number of ways. The interest rate directly impacts on the cost of borrowing and on the returns from saving; the exchange rate affects the competitiveness of firms and the purchasing power of citizens; and both of these factors indirectly influence wealth. In effect, by granting independence to their central bank, the citizens delegate a very important task to a group of individuals who are appointed, not elected, and who cannot be removed unless they commit grave illegal acts. In a democratic society, delegation to unelected officials needs to be counterbalanced by democratic accountability. This section examines how these two goals are dealt with in the EMU.

17.4.1 Independence

The Eurosystem is characterized by a great degree of independence; it is probably the world's most independent central bank. Both the ECB and the NCBs are strictly protected from political influence. Before joining the Eurozone, each country must adapt the statutes of its NCB to match a number of common requirements. In particular, the EU Treaty explicitly rules out any interference by national or European authorities in the deliberations of the Eurosystem:

> When exercising the powers and carrying out the tasks and duties conferred upon them by this Treaty and the Statute of the ESCB, neither the ECB, nor a national central bank, nor any member of their decision-making bodies shall seek or take instructions from Community institutions or bodies, from any government of a Member State or from any other body. The Community institutions and bodies and the governments of the Member States undertake to respect this principle and not to seek to influence the members of the decision-making bodies of the ECB or of the national central banks in the performance of their tasks.

(Article 108)

In addition, to guarantee their personal independence, the members of the Executive Board are appointed for a long period (eight years) and cannot be reappointed, which reduces the opportunity for pressures.[11] Similar conditions apply to the NCB governors, although they differ slightly from one country to another, but their mandates must be for a minimum of five years. No central bank official can be removed from office unless he or she becomes incapacitated or is found guilty of serious misconduct, with the Court of Justice of the European Communities competent to settle disputes.

The independence of the Eurosystem applies to the choice of both policy objectives and instruments. The Treaty sets the objectives in terms vague enough to allow the Eurosystem to decide what it tries to achieve, as explained in Section 17.3.1. The Treaty further leaves the

---

[11] In order to ensure a smooth rotation, the first members received mandates of staggered length, from four to eight years. Subsequent appointments are always for eight years.

Eurosystem completely free to decide which instruments it uses, and how. Other central banks sometimes have only instrument independence. This is the case of the Bank of England, which is instructed to pursue an inflation target set by the Chancellor of the Exchequer.

Finally, the ECB is financially independent. It has its own budget, independent from that of the EU. Its accounts are not audited by the European Court of Auditors, which monitors the European Commission, but by independent external auditors.

17.4.2 Accountability

Democratic accountability is typically exercised in two ways: reporting and transparency. Formally, the Eurosystem operates under the control of the European Parliament. Its statutes require that an annual report be sent to the Parliament, as well as to the Council and the Commission. This report is debated by the Parliament. In addition, the Parliament may request that the President of the ECB and the other members of the Executive Board testify to the Parliament's Economic and Monetary Affairs Committee. In practice, the President appears before the committee every quarter and the members of the Executive Board also do so quite often. In addition, the President of the EU Council and a member of the European Commission may participate in the meetings of the Governing Council without voting rights.

Transparency contributes powerfully to accountability. By revealing the contents of its deliberations, a central bank conveys to the public (the media, the financial markets and independent observers) the rationale and difficulties of its decisions. The Eurosystem does not provide detailed reports of the meetings of its Governing Council. Instead the president of the ECB holds a press conference immediately after the monthly policy-setting meeting to present its decisions in highly standardized terms. Table 17.3 shows how major central banks reveal

Table 17.3 **Provision of information on monetary policy meetings**

	Federal Reserve	ESCB	Bank of Japan	Bank of England	Bank of Canada	Swedish Riksbank
Interest-rate decision immediately announced	Yes (after 1994)	Yes	Yes	Yes	Yes	Yes
Supporting statement giving some rationale for a change	Yes	Yes	Yes	Sometimes	Yes	Yes
Release of minutes	5–8 weeks[a]	No	1 month	13 days	n.a.	2–4 weeks
Official minutes provide full details of:						
internal debate	Yes	No	Yes	Yes	n.a.	No
individuals' views						No
Verbatim records of MP meetings are kept	No Yes	Yes	No	No	No	
Verbatim records released to the public after:	5 years	n.a.	10 years	n.a.	n.a.	n.a.

[a] The minutes are released after the following FOMC meeting.
Source: Blinder et al. 2001

the work of their decision-making committee meetings. Several of them publish the committee meeting's minutes within a month, but since they can be heavily edited, minutes are not necessarily very informative. Very few (the US Federal Reserve and the Bank of Japan) publish extensive records of the discussion, but with very long delays, which makes the publication irrelevant except for historical purposes. Many central banks report on individual votes, which is a clear way of indicating how certain policy makers feel about their collective decisions. The Eurosystem is nearly alone in doing none of that. It considers that revealing individual votes could be interpreted in a nationalistic manner that does not, in fact, correspond to the thinking of members of the Governing Council who are duty-bound to look only at the Eurozone as a whole.

Box 17.6 Independence and transparency

In principle, the more independent is a central bank, the more accountable it should be, and transparency is one key element of transparency. Since there is mounting evidence that inflation tends to be lower where central banks are more independent, a good central bank should be very independent and very transparent.

A recent study has constructed scores for central bank independence and transparency. The numbers are inevitably arbitrary but Fig. 17.6, which looks at 29 countries around the world, suggests that the ECB is indeed very independent but only ranks 17th as far as transparency is concerned.

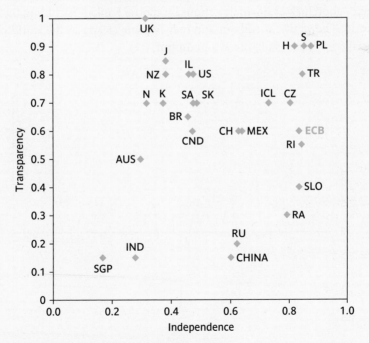

Figure 17.6 **Independence and transparency indices**
Source: Crowe and Meade (2008)

17.5 The first decade

17.5.1 Inflation and growth

When the euro was launched in January 1999, inflation was very low, partly because all member countries had been working hard at meeting the Maastricht entry criteria, as explained in Section 17.1.2. Soon thereafter, oil prices rose three-fold in 2000. An oil shock means both more inflation and less growth, a classic dilemma that all central banks fear. Simultaneously, stock markets fell worldwide, the end of a long-lasting financial bubble fed by unrealistic expectations of the impact of the information technology revolution. Within months, the US economy went into recession, and Europe's economy also slowed down. Then, the terrorist attacks of 11 September 2001 shook the world economy. There followed a mellower period until oil prices rose again to record levels and a massive financial crisis erupted in the USA in mid-2007.

The result has been an inflation rate almost always above the 2 per cent ceiling, as Fig. 17.7 shows. It would be wrong to conclude that the Eurosystem has failed to deliver price stability. Until late 2007, it has delivered an average inflation rate close enough to 2 per cent for comfort. In fact, no member country – including Germany – has enjoyed such a long period of low inflation since the Second World War. Yet, in a strange twist, a large number of citizens see that the adoption of the euro has brought inflation, as discussed in Box 17.7. On the other hand, low inflation has been a general feature of developed countries during this period, sometimes referred to as the Great Moderation. This has generated a debate on whether low inflation has been the result of good luck or of smart actions by central banks – including the Eurosystem – around the world. The verdict is still out and may become clearer as the world goes through a historic financial crisis where skills are at a premium.

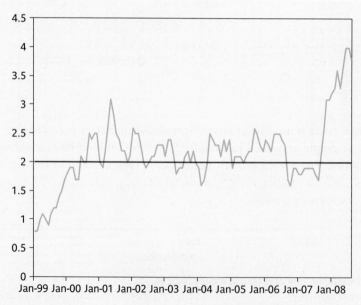

Figure 17.7 **Inflation in the Eurozone, January 1999–August 2008**
Source: Monthly Bulletin, ECB

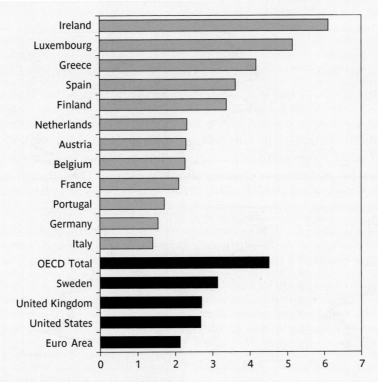

Figure 17.8 Growth rate of GDP, 1999–2008
Source: Economic Outlook, OECD

Growth, on the other hand, has been slow, which has generated much criticism, including from member governments. The criticism may be unfair. To start with, growth has been slow on average, not in every Eurozone country. Some countries have grown very fast, as Fig. 17.8 shows, looking at the old Eurozone members. The overall Eurozone's growth rate is low because some of the largest members – chiefly Germany and Italy, with France only slighter better – have achieved a disappointing performance. The Eurosystem has argued that the failure of some countries to grow faster is not due to an over-restrictive monetary policy stance. It has a point. The neutrality principle presented in Chapter 9 asserts that long-run growth is independent of monetary policy. The varied growth performances across the Eurozone point instead to country-specific features rather than to monetary policy. Indeed, the evidence presented in Chapter 8 relates the laggard countries to domestic rigidities.

Box 17.7   Public opinion on inflation

When euro coins and banknotes were introduced in early 2002, a number of retailers rounded up prices. This created a perception of a jump in the price level. The jump has been confirmed by HICP measures but its amount – about 0.5 per cent – is trivially small in comparison with public perceptions. Figure 17.9 shows actual inflation as measured by the HICP and an estimate of perceived inflation by

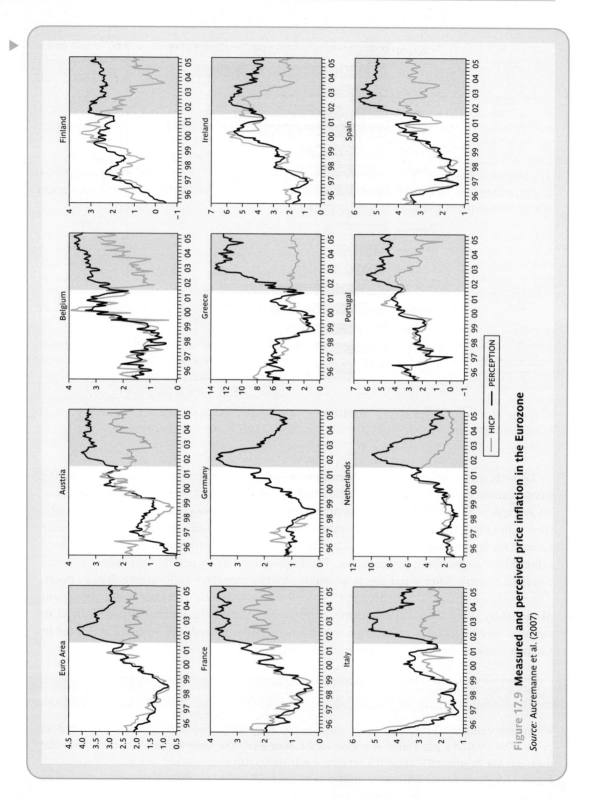

Figure 17.9 Measured and perceived price inflation in the Eurozone

Source: Aucremanne et al. (2007)

citizens. Not only is the gap large in the months following the introduction of euro notes and coins, but it has not disappeared. Public opinion polls keep revealing that Eurozone citizens believe that the euro has been a major source of high and enduring inflation. In fact, many people deeply believe that the official measure of inflation is deeply flawed since it is much lower than what 'they see'.

Many studies have been conducted to ascertain that the official index is not flawed and to try to explain why perceptions can systematically differ from 'facts'. One explanation is that rounding up has mostly affected cheap goods (an increase in €0.5 for a cup of coffee that costs $1.5 is indeed a 33 per cent increase) that people purchase frequently, which keeps reminding them of the jump. Another explanation is that people still evaluate prices by computing their value in the old currency (liras, francs, pesetas, etc.) but make their own rounding up errors as they do so. There is still no satisfactory explanation of the phenomenon.

17.5.2 The exchange rate

The Eurosystem has faced another vexing issue. Just when the euro was launched in early 1999, the dollar started to rise vis-à-vis all major currencies, including the euro and, to a lesser extent, the pound sterling. Given that the US dollar has long been the world's standard, the general interpretation was that the euro was weak. This left the impression that the Eurosystem was unable to deliver the strong currency that had been predicated upon its price-stability commitment, following the PPP logic presented in Chapter 9. Then, from late 2002 onwards, the dollar started to fall. Instead of praising the Eurosystem for having finally delivered a strong currency, critics complained that the euro was overvalued and hurting European exporters. Yet, as Fig. 17.10 shows, the movements of the dollar/euro exchange rate have not been particularly out of step with the past, at least until 2007.

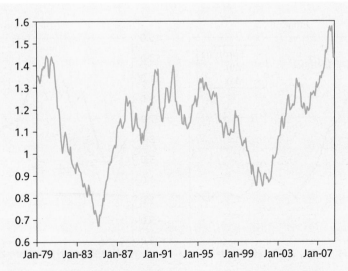

Figure 17.10 The dollar/euro exchange rate, January 1979–September 2008
Source: Monthly Bulletin, ECB

From the start, the Eurosystem clearly announced that it would take no responsibility for the exchange rate. Its view is that the euro is a freely floating currency. Noting that capital movements are completely free, it follows the logic of the impossible trinity and refuses to take responsibility for the exchange rate. The discussion of exchange rate regimes in Chapter 10 suggests that very large and closed economies, like the Eurozone, have little interest in stabilizing their exchange rates; the freely floating 'corner' is likely to be its best option, and this is where the Eurosystem has chosen to stand. 'Best option' does not mean that it does not have some unpleasant implications, however, and critics have seized on these adverse effects to blame the Eurosystem.

It is also true that the exchange rate between the euro and the dollar is as much driven by US as by European events. In that sense, it is not the euro that is too strong but the dollar that is too weak. Undoubtedly, this debate will go on for many years to come.

17.5.3 One money, one policy

Asymmetries

How about the much-feared asymmetric shocks emphasized by the optimum currency area (OCA) theory? Sure enough, there is no lack of complaints that the Eurosystem does not pay attention to economic conditions in this or that country. The fact is that with one money there can exist only one central bank, and therefore one monetary policy. The Eurosystem can only deal with the Eurozone as a whole. It would open a Pandora's Box should it ever attempt to bend its policy to a particular country. After all, a key implication of the OCA theory, presented in Chapter 16, is that joining the monetary union implies the acceptance that member countries will occasionally have to bear some costs.

Figure 17.11 documents how different economic conditions have been throughout the Eurozone, before and after monetary union (the figure displays the Eurozone inflation and

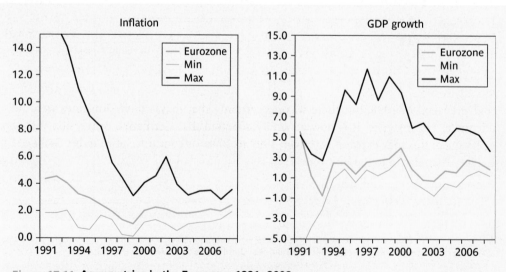

Figure 17.11 Asymmetries in the Eurozone, 1991–2008
Source: Economic Outlook, OECD

real GDP growth rates, along with the highest and lowest national rates each year). Inflation differences narrowed dramatically during 1991–98, the Maastricht-mandated convergence years. In the aftermath of the 2000 oil shock, there has been a tendency towards some divergence but it has remained subdued. Real growth dispersion, too, has tended to narrow down and has stayed that way. So far, at least, there is no evidence of any dramatic asymmetric shocks. In fact, recent evidence indicates that inflation rates do not differ any more among the Eurozone member countries than across broad regions in the USA.

Lasting inflation differentials

That, in a given year, inflation is higher in one country than in the Eurozone is normal. What matters is the possibility that, year after year, a particular country faces systematically higher (or lower) inflation. For instance, a country which faces continuously higher inflation than others is bound to face a loss in competitiveness. If this process persists, the country would then have to undergo several years of lower inflation to restore competitiveness. As the Eurosystem strives to achieve and maintain price stability, this could require deflation – negative inflation – which is usually only achieved under severe pressure in the form of a protracted recession accompanied by high unemployment. This is an implication of the self-equilibrating mechanism of Hume. As explained in Chapter 10, high inflation results in an external deficit; the implied decline in the money supply acts as a contractionary monetary policy, which eventually dampens prices and wages. Conceivably, this ugly scenario could make leaving the Eurozone an attractive option.[12]

Figure 17.12 shows that, over the first decade of monetary union, lasting inflation differentials occurred in several countries; inflation has been lower than average in Germany, Finland and France, and higher than average in Ireland, Spain, Portugal, the Netherlands and Italy. Why? The potential explanations are:

★ The Balassa–Samuelson effect. This effect, presented in Box 9.2, predicts that the real exchange rates of catching-up countries appreciate. Within a currency area, real appreciation can only be achieved through higher than average inflation.[13] This higher inflation rate does not imply a loss of competitiveness. Quite to the contrary, it is a consequence of rising productivity. This effect could be part of the explanation for the cases of Ireland, Spain and Portugal.

★ Wrong initial conversion rates. Each currency was converted into euros at the ERM parity that prevailed in 1998, but there was no certainty that these conversion rates were fully adequate. For instance, it is now generally accepted that Germany's conversion rate was overvalued; this may explain why, from 1999 to 2008, its consumer price index declined by 4.5 per cent relative to the Eurozone's HICP.

★ Autonomous wage and price pressure. Wage negotiators should understand that wage increases in excess of labour productivity gains eat into competitiveness. Wage agreements,

---

[12] From 1991 to 2001, Argentina operated a currency board arrangement vis-à-vis the US dollar (see Chapter 10 for an explanation of currency boards). For many years, however, its inflation rate exceeded the US rate. Eventually inflation turned negative, but the pain of a deep recession triggered a popular revolt that led to the end of the currency board.

[13] One Eurozone country's real exchange rate vis-à-vis the zone is EP/P^*. With a common currency the nominal exchange rate is $E = 1$, so the real exchange rate is P/P^*. A real appreciation requires that the domestic price level P increases faster than the foreign price level P^*.

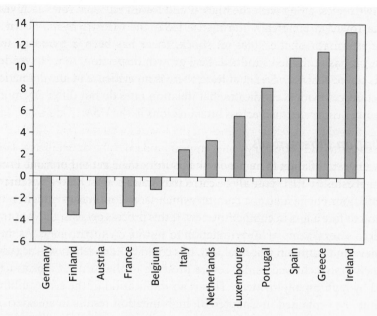

Figure 17.12 **Change in price levels relative to the Eurozone, 1999–2008**
Source: Economic Outlook, OECD

however, are driven by factors other than economics. For example, minimum wages can be raised to reduce inequality; civil servants – who do not face directly any foreign competition – may be well organized to extract wage increases; administered prices – electricity, transports – may be pushed up to avoid losses in state-owned companies. These increases filter down to all wages and prices as they raise production costs and the price level. These factors seem to have played a role in Greece, Italy, the Netherlands, Spain and Portugal.

★ Policy mistakes. Through excessively expansionary fiscal policies or public sector price and wage increases, mentioned above, governments may, temporarily at least, contribute to inflationary pressure.

★ Asymmetric shocks. This is the scenario that lies at the centre of the OCA theory. Oil shocks have not affected all Eurozone member countries to the same extent. Many other factors may have played a role, even though none has been identified so far.

Asymmetric monetary policy effects

Different rates of inflation have another, more subtle effect. The single monetary policy implies a common nominal interest rate throughout the Eurozone. Yet, monetary policy does not affect the economy through the nominal interest rate. What matters is the real interest rate, i.e. the nominal rate less expected inflation. Take the case of a country where inflation is, and is expected to remain, higher than average. Its real interest rate is lower than average, which means that monetary policy is comparatively expansionary. Conversely, a country with low growth and low inflation faces a relatively high real interest rate, which exerts a contractionary effect.

Is the single monetary policy systematically destabilizing, therefore? It all depends on the source of the inflation differential. If higher inflation is driven by productivity gains, e.g. the Balassa–Samuelson effect, the real exchange rate must appreciate through wage and price increases. In that case, the low real interest rate encourages investment, which is needed to implement the productivity gains, and its expansionary impact speeds up the rise of prices to their new equilibrium level.

If the higher inflation is due to national policy mistakes or unwarranted wage increases, possibly encouraged by a cyclical expansion, the low real interest rate adds fuel to an already overheated economy and monetary policy appears indeed to be destabilizing. How worrisome is this effect? One view is that there is no risk that things will get out of hand. Hume's mechanism ensures that excesses will eventually be corrected. Another view, however, is that the correction may be painful. As noted above, the pain may one day lead a country caught in this process to reconsider its continuing monetary union membership. There is nothing that the Eurosystem can do about it. The only policy prescription is to avoid falling into the trap of inflation and, if it happens, to use a contractionary fiscal policy to try to contain the expansionary pressure.

17.5.4 More members?

The new EU members do not have a derogation so they are required to join the Eurozone as soon as possible. To do so, they must meet the five convergence criteria described in Section 17.1.2. The earliest that a country can become a Eurozone member is two years after having joined the ERM. Slovenia joined the ERM soon after accession and could adopt the euro about two years later. Cyprus, Malta and Slovakia followed suit. The remaining countries are treated as potential applicants. Every year the European Commission and the ECB publish their *Convergence Reports* in which they assess how each of these countries performs vis-à-vis the convergence criteria. Table 17.4 summarizes the 2008 assessment by the European Commission.

Table 17.4 Non-Eurozone members: the convergence criteria in 2008

Country	Inflation	Long-term interest rate	ERM membership	Budget deficit	Public debt
Bulgaria	9.4	4.7	No	−3.4	18.0
Czech Republic	4.4	4.5	No	1.6	28.1
Estonia	8.3	N.A.	June 2004	−2.8	3.4
Hungary	7.5	No	No	5.5	66.0
Latvia	12.3	5.4	May 2005	0.0	9.7
Lithuania	7.4	4.6	June 2004	1.2	17.3
Poland	3.2	5.7	No	2.0	45.2
Romania	5.9	7.1	No	2.5	13.0
Sweden	2.4	4.2	No	−3.5	46.0
Convergence limits	3.2	6.5	> 2 years	3	60.0

Note: The countries with a derogation (Denmark and the UK) are not subject to official convergence reports.
Source: Convergence Report 2008, European Commission

None of these nine countries fulfils the five conditions. In one case, this is intentional: by not joining the ERM, Sweden does not have to join the Eurozone, which it clearly does not want to do. All the other countries miss the inflation condition, which often means that the long-term interest rate is too high, as noted in Section 17.1.2. By staying out of the ERM, several countries spare themselves the unpleasant situation of signalling a willingness to join the Eurozone only to be rebuffed, which happened to Lithuania in 2006.

Yet, Lithuania is de facto a member of the Eurozone since its exchange rate is rigidly tied to the euro via a currency board arrangement. There is no monetary policy autonomy in Lithuania and therefore no tool to reduce inflation and fiscal policy is deemed satisfactory. The same applies to Estonia. Both countries are kept out and yet cannot do anything to meet the inflation and long-term interest rate conditions. The interest rate parity principle, presented in Chapter 9, implies that the high long-term interest rate reflects the market's belief that Lithuania will not be allowed to join in the near future. This is a vicious circle that hurts the country. Indeed, adoption of the euro provides a country with a credible central bank and the promise of price stability, which immediately translates into lower interest rates. Lower interest rates mean a significant reduction in the cost of servicing the public debt. Box 17.8 recalls how Italy benefited from this effect.

Box 17.8   Italy's windfall gain from Eurozone membership

Italy joined the Eurozone with a very large public debt (see Fig. 17.2). At the time when the Maastricht Treaty was agreed upon, its government was spending some 12 per cent of GDP on debt service, about one-quarter of its total expenditures. Debt service is approximately equal to the product of the interest rate and the debt value (iB, where i is the interest rate and B the debt). This means that part of the debt burden was associated with a high interest rate. Figure 17.13 shows how the Italian interest

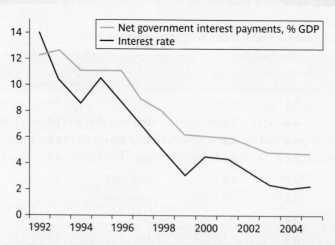

Figure 17.13 **The interest rate and net debt service as a percentage of GDP in Italy, 1992–2005**
Source: Economic Outlook, OECD

rate steadily declined in the years following the Maastricht agreement. The decline is explained by the disinflation process, as Italy strived to meet the convergence criteria. It is also explained by the credibility associated with Eurozone membership and its price-stability-oriented central bank. The remarkable feature of this evolution is the parallel decline in debt service, which has declined to about 40 per cent of what it used to be. Most of this huge windfall gain, worth 7.5 per cent of GDP, has been used by the Italian authorities to increase spending in many areas.

17.6 Summary

The monetary union is an elaborate construction carefully mapped out in the Maastricht Treaty. The treaty was signed in 1991 and the single currency started to operate, as planned, in 1999, even though the new currency was not issued until 2002. This long process was part of a careful approach that recognized the unique nature of the undertaking. It rested on a number of provisions:

★ The adoption of a common currency had to be the end of a convergence process. All member countries would have to demonstrate their acceptance of price stability and of the discipline that goes with it.

★ Monetary union membership would not be automatic. Admission is to be assessed on the basis of five convergence criteria: low inflation, low long-term interest rates, ERM membership, low budget deficits and a declining public debt.

★ While all EU members are expected to join the currency area, two countries (Denmark and the UK) were given opt-out clauses. This was the first time that the possibility of a 'two-speed Europe' was accepted.

The monetary union implies the delegation of monetary policy to a single authority. Yet, the EU is not a federal system, so it was decided to maintain the national central banks. The resulting Eurosystem thus formally brings together the newly created ECB and the national central banks of all EU countries. Decisions are taken by the Governing Council, chaired by the President of the ECB, which includes the ECB's Executive Committee and the governors of the central banks of the countries that have adopted the euro. The size of the Governing Council is considered by outside observers to be excessive, a situation that will worsen when new members join the Eurozone. A proposal has been advanced by the Governing Council; it caps the size of the Council by instituting a rotation of national central bank governors, taking into account the size of the country that they represent.

The Eurosystem has been given the primary goal of price stability, but it is free to decide what that means and how to go about it. It considers that price stability is achieved when the Eurozone's inflation rate is close to 2 per cent over the 'medium term'. It has also adopted the common practice of steering the euro short-term interest rate through three channels: the marginal refinancing facility sets a ceiling, the deposit facility sets a floor, and the interest rate is kept close to the middle of that range through regular auctions that establish the main refinancing rate.

The logic of this procedure is that the short-term interest rate affects the economy through a number of channels that operate via credit availability and the money supply, the long-term real interest rate, asset prices and the exchange rate. Thus, the effect of monetary policy on the economy, and on inflation in particular, is indirect and the Eurosystem must factor in these various effects, all of which take time to produce results. This requires a strategy. The Eurosystem's approach is to rely on two pillars: economic analysis (the medium-term impact of current conditions on inflation) and monetary analysis (the longer-term impact of monetary aggregates on inflation). In addition, the strategy recognizes that in a monetary union, there can only be one monetary policy. This is why the Eurosystem explicitly cares only about the whole Eurozone, not about individual member countries. In addition, it takes no responsibility for the exchange rate that is freely floating.

The Eurosystem constitutionally enjoys considerable independence, both in defining its objectives and in deciding how to conduct monetary policy. It is not allowed to take instructions from any other authority, be it European or national. This independence is a condition for guaranteeing price stability, but it raises an important issue: in a democracy, every authority has to be accountable to its citizens for its actions. The solution adopted by the Maastricht Treaty is to make the Eurosystem formally accountable to the European Parliament. Accountability takes the form of an annual report and of regular hearings of the ECB president and members of the Executive Board by the Parliament's Committee on Economic and Monetary Affairs. A number of observers feel that this is too weak a form of accountability and consider that the monetary union suffers from a 'democratic deficit'.

Self-assessment questions

1. What are the five convergence criteria and what is the logic behind each of them?
2. 'With one money there can exist only one central bank, and therefore one monetary policy.' What, then, is the role of national central banks in the EMU?
3. Why can inflation rates differ across the EMU member countries? What are the consequences?
4. What is the difference between Denmark and Sweden regarding monetary union membership? Which one, if any, is likely to adopt the euro first?
5. What happens to a country's interest rate when it joins the Eurozone?
6. The Eurosystem sets the money supply in the Eurozone, but what drives the money stock in each country? How does this relate to Hume's mechanism and the gold standard (Chapter 10)?
7. What is the Eurosystem's definition of price stability? What would be your own definition?
8. Why can the Eurosystem not take responsibility for national inflation rates?

Essay questions

1. The Eurosystem asserts that, in its deliberations, it never pays attention to local (i.e. national) economic conditions. The reason is that there is a single monetary policy and that 'one size fits all'. Discuss this approach and imagine alternative approaches.

2. Find on www.ecb.int the latest press conference on monetary policy decisions and interpret the text in the light of the stated strategy.

3. The Maastricht Treaty describes in minute detail the creation of the Eurozone but is silent on a possible break-up. Imagine that a country is suffering from a severe adverse shock. Could it leave? How? What could the other countries do to try to keep it in?

4. Box 17.4 presents the solution proposed by the Eurosystem to face the enlargement of the Eurozone. Evaluate this proposal and make your own suggestions.

5. Why are transparency and accountability so important for the Eurosystem? What kind of difficulties can you envision if the system is perceived as not sufficiently accountable? Not sufficiently transparent?

6. The convergence criteria are about nominal conditions (inflation, deficits and debts) but not about real conditions (GDP per capita, growth). This was understandable for the original founders but what does it mean for the upcoming wave of accession of the ten new EU members? Should the same criteria apply? Why or why not? Is the lack of real convergence problematic?

7. Make the case for and against Eurozone membership of Estonia and Lithuania.

Further reading: the aficionado's corner

The first decade of the euro as reviewed by:

★ the ECB (www.ecb.int/pub/pdf/other/10thanniversaryoftheecbmb200806en.pdf?a2a06e7f1ee81c0d42249ee63d0ce0e8)

★ independent observers:

Aghion, P., A. Ahearne, M. Belka, J. Pisani-Ferry, J. von Hagen and L. Heikesten, (2008) *Coming of Age, Report on the Eurozone*, BRUEGEL, Brussels. Download from www.bruegel.org.

Fatás, A., H. Flam, S. Holden, T. Japelli, I. Mihov, M. Pagano and C. Wyplosz (2009) *EMU at Ten: Should Denmark, Sweden and the U.K. Join?*, Stockholm: SNS-Centre for Business and Policy Studies. Download from www.sns.se.

For presentations of the Eurosystem, see:

★ **The European Commission** (http://ec.europa.eu/economy_finance/the_euro/index_en.htm?cs_mid=2946).

★ **Padoa- Schioppa, T.** (former member of the Executive Board of the ECB) An Institutional Glossary of the Eurosystem. Download from www.ecb.int/press/key/date/2000/html/sp000308_1.en.html.

On Taylor rules, see: 'Monetary policy in the Eurozone has been looser than critics think', *The Economist*, 14 July, 2005. Download from www.economist.com/finance/displayStory.cfm?story_id_4174785.

On diverging inflation rates in the Eurozone, see: **ECB** (2005) 'Monetary policy and inflation differentials in a heterogeneous currency area', *Monthly Bulletin*, May: 61–78.

Useful websites

The ECB website: www.ecb.int.

The Treaty of Maastricht: http://europa.eu.int/eurlex/en/treaties/index.html.

The President of the ECB reports every quarter to the Committee of Economic and Monetary Affairs of the European Parliament. The transcripts of the meetings, gentlemanly called 'Monetary Dialogue', as well as background reports can be found at: www.europarl.eu.int/comparl/econ/emu/default_en.htm.

Public opinion on the euro: http://europa.eu.int/comm/dg10/epo/euro_en.html.

A website dedicated to EONIA and interest rates in the Eurozone: www.euribor.org/default.htm.

Annual reports on the ECB by academic observers, *Monitoring the European Central Bank*, published by the Centre for Economic Policy Research, can be found at www.cepr.org.

References

Aucremanne, L., M. Collin and T. Stragier (2007) *Assessing the Gap between Observed and Perceived Inflation in the Eurozone: Is the Credibility of the HICP at Stake?*, Working Paper No. 112 , National Bank of Belgium.

Blinder, A., C. Goodhart, P. Hildebrand, D. Lipton and C. Wyplosz (2001) 'How do central banks talk?', *Geneva Reports on the World Economy* 3, Centre for Economic Policy Research, London.

Burda, M. and C. Wyplosz (2009) *Macroeconomics*, 5th edition, Oxford University Press, Oxford.

Crowe, C. and E. Meade (2008) 'Central bank independence and transparency: evolution and effectiveness', *European Journal of Political Economy*, 24 (4): 763–77.

ECB (2003) 'The ECB's monetary policy strategy', Press release, 8 May. Download from www.ecb.int.

Chapter 18

Fiscal policy and the Stability Pact

Economic prosperity and the viability of the monetary union cannot be sustained without tackling past fiscal policy failures, i.e. a trend towards increasing government expenditure and taxation levels combined with high structural budget deficits and government debt accumulation.

European Commission (2001)

I know very well that the Stability Pact is stupid, like all decisions which are rigid.

Romano Prodi (EU Commission President), *Le Monde*, 17 October 2002

Chapter contents

18.1 Fiscal policy in the monetary union	*520*
18.2 Fiscal policy externalities	*524*
18.3 Principles	*528*
18.4 The Stability and Growth Pact	*532*
18.5 Summary	*542*

Introduction

The monetary union implies the loss of monetary policy as a macroeconomic stabilization instrument, which seems to enhance the role of fiscal policy. However, national fiscal policies affect other countries. Do these spillover effects also call for sharing the fiscal policy instrument? This chapter first reviews how fiscal policy operates across national boundaries and presents the principles that can help to decide whether some limits in national decisions are in order. This lays the ground for an understanding of the Stability and Growth Pact. The chapter next examines the Pact's impact on policy choices and the controversies that have arisen in the early years of its implementation.

18.1 Fiscal policy in the monetary union

18.1.1 An ever more important instrument?

When joining a monetary union a country gives up one of its two macroeconomic instruments – monetary policy – but retains full control of the other – fiscal policy. Does this mean that fiscal policy has to do double work? As explained in Chapter 9, in the simple Keynesian *IS–LM* world, monetary and fiscal policy are nearly substitute tools to stabilize output and employment fluctuations. It means that, in the Eurozone, fiscal policy becomes even more important. In the event of asymmetric shocks – identified by the optimum currency area theory in Chapter 11 as the main source of costs in a monetary union – fiscal policy is the only available macroeconomic instrument. This is a good departure point to keep in mind but, in practice, some important differences imply that the two instruments are not as easily substitutable as suggested by the *IS–LM* analysis. In particular, fiscal policy is more difficult to activate and less reliable than monetary policy.

A common problem with both instruments is that they affect spending largely through expectations. For monetary policy, as explained in Chapter 10, the central bank can only control very short-term interest rates while private spending is financed through long-term borrowing. For fiscal policy, changes in spending and/or taxes impact on the budget balance, which immediately raises the question of the financing of the public debt. Consider, for instance, a cut in income taxes that creates a budget deficit. The government will have to borrow and increase the public debt, but how will this new debt be reimbursed? If, as is plausible, taxes are eventually raised, the policy action is properly seen as the combination of a tax reduction today and a tax increase later. This is an action unlikely to wildly boost consumption.[1]

Fiscal policy faces a major additional drawback: it is very slow to implement. A central bank can decide to change the interest rate whenever it deems necessary, and can do so in a matter of seconds. Not so for fiscal policy. Establishing the budget is a long and complicated process. The government must first agree on the budget, with lots of heavy-handed negotiations among ministers. The budget must then be approved by the parliament, a time-consuming and highly political process. Then spending decisions must be enacted through the bureaucracy, and taxes can only be changed gradually as they are never retroactive. For example, income taxes can only affect future incomes, implying long delays. On the other hand, once implemented, fiscal policy actions tend to have a more rapid effect on the economy (six to 12 months) than does monetary policy (12 to 24 months).

As a result, fiscal policy is like a tanker; it changes course very slowly. The delay may even be such that, when fiscal policy finally affects the economy, the problem that it was meant to solve has disappeared. In principle, macroeconomic policies are meant to be countercyclical, i.e. to slow down a booming economy or speed up a sagging economy. Fiscal policy has occasionally been found to be pro-cyclical: an expansionary action designed to deal with a recession hits the economy when it has already recovered. If this is the case, it actually speeds up the economy when it is already desirable to slow it down.

18.1.2 Borrowing instead of transfers

Another way of looking at fiscal policy is that the government borrows and pays back on behalf of its citizens. During a slowdown, the government opens up a budget deficit that is financed through public borrowing. In an upswing, the government runs a budget surplus which allows it to pay back its debt. A government that borrows to reduce taxes now and raises taxes later to pay back its debt is, in effect, lending to its citizens now and making them pay back later. Individual citizens and firms could, in principle, do it on their own, borrowing in bad years and paying back in good years. This would have the same stabilizing effect as fiscal policy. Is fiscal policy a futile exercise or, worse, a bad political trick? Not quite.

To start with, it is true that, in the previous example, the government simply acts as a bank vis-à-vis its citizens. The reason why it may make sense is that, when the economy slows down, lending becomes generally riskier and banks become very cautious. Many citizens and firms cannot borrow in bad times, or can only borrow at high cost. Indeed, workers who lose their jobs are considered by their banks as bad risk, and so are firms that face sagging profits or even losses. When governments are considered a good risk, which is generally the case in Europe, they can borrow at all times at reasonably low cost. This is why countercyclical fiscal policy can be effective.

An additional reason is related to one of the optimum currency area criteria examined in Chapter 11, the desirability of substantial inter-country transfers. In that dimension, Europe was found to do very poorly. Can this problem be alleviated? Fiscal policy is part of the answer.

---

[1] The extreme case where consumers save all of the tax reduction to pay for future tax increases is called Ricardian equivalence. It is explained, and its empirical validity assessed, in, for example, Burda and Wyplosz (2009).

When a country faces an adverse asymmetric shock, its government can borrow from countries that are not affected by the shock. This is the equivalent of a transfer: instead of receiving a loan or a grant[2] from other Eurozone governments or from 'Brussels', the adversely affected country's government borrows on international private markets. In this way fiscal policy makes up for the absence of 'federal' transfers in a monetary union.

18.1.3 Automatic stabilizers and discretionary policy actions

Automatic stabilizers

Fiscal policy has one important advantage: it tends to be spontaneously countercyclical. When the economy slows down, individual incomes are disappointingly low, corporate profits decline and spending is rather weak. This all means that tax collection declines: income taxes, profit taxes, VAT, etc. are less than they would be in normal conditions. At the same time, spending on unemployment benefits and other subsidies rises. All in all, the budget worsens and fiscal policy is automatically expansionary. These various effects are called the automatic stabilizers of fiscal policy. Table 18.1, which displays estimates of the size of the stabilizers, shows that, on average, a 1 per cent decline in growth leads to a deterioration of the budget balance of about 0.5 per cent of GDP. There are some differences from one country to another, which reflect the structure of taxation and of welfare payments.[3]

Discretionary fiscal policy

The automatic stabilizers just happen. Discretionary fiscal policy, on the contrary, requires explicit decisions to change taxes or spending. As noted above, such decisions are slow to be made and implemented. This is why, in some countries, the budget law sets aside some funds

Table 18.1 Automatic stabilizers: sensitivity of government budget balances to a 1 per cent decline in economic growth

Country	%	Country	%	Country	%	Country	%
Germany	0.5	Austria	−0.5	Greece	−0.6	Portugal	−0.4
France	−0.5	Belgium	−0.5	Ireland	−0.4	Spain	−0.5
Italy	−0.4	Denmark	−0.7	Netherlands	−0.6	Sweden	−0.5
UK	−0.6	Finland	−0.5				

Source: Economic Outlook, OECD 1997

[2] A grant is not to be reimbursed, but a collective system of grants implies that any country is supposed to be alternately giving and receiving, the total averaging zero over the long run. This is no different from long-term borrowing–receiving now, paying back later.

[3] For example, the more progressive are income taxes, the more tax collection declines during a slowdown, hence the greater the stabilization effect. Similarly, the automatic stabilizers are stronger the larger are the unemployment benefits.

that can be quickly mobilized by the government if discretionary action is needed. Even then, the amounts are small and their use is often politically controversial.

Because of the automatic stabilizers, the budget figures do not reveal what the government is doing with its fiscal policy. The budget can change for two reasons. It can improve, for example, because the government is cutting spending or raising taxes, or because the economy is booming. In order to disentangle these two factors, it is convenient to look at the cyclically adjusted budget. This procedure is based on the output gap concept, which is presented in Chapter 9. Remember that, for instance, a negative gap indicates that the economy is under-performing, that it operates below its potential. The cyclically adjusted budget balance is an estimate of what the balance would be in a given year if the output gap were zero. The actual budget balance is lower than the cyclically adjusted budget balance when output is below potential, i.e. when the output gap is negative, and conversely when the output gap is positive. The difference between the evolution of the actual and cyclically adjusted budget balances is the footprint of the automatic stabilizers.

The cyclically adjusted budget balance is a reliable gauge of the stance of fiscal policy since it separates discretionary government actions from the cyclical effects of the automatic stabilizers. An improvement indicates that the government tightens fiscal policy whereas an expansionary fiscal policy worsens the cyclically adjusted budget balance. If the government never changed its fiscal policy, the cyclically adjusted budget balance would remain constant, at least to a first approximation.[4] Box 18.1 illustrates this point in the case of the Netherlands. These two issues – the role of the automatic stabilizers and the distinction between the actual and cyclically adjusted budgets – play a crucial role in what follows.

Box 18.1 The automatic stabilizers in the Netherlands

Figure 18.1 displays the output gap along with the actual and cyclically adjusted budget balance of the Netherlands. We can see that the actual balance generally moves in tandem with the output gap, an indication that the automatic stabilizers are at work. Note also the steady improvement in the budget that occurred during the convergence years 1995–99. It is due partly to government efforts to meet the Maastricht conditions, as shown by the reduction of the cyclically adjusted deficit, and partly to a rising output gap that made it easier to meet the Maastricht entry condition. It is also interesting to observe that the sharp deterioration of the budget over 2001–05 – which brought the Netherlands into violation of the Stability and Growth Pact – is the consequence of a serious slowdown, and occurred in spite of visible government efforts to avoid this outcome.

Note that the cyclically adjusted budget, which is a measure of discretionary actions, also tends to move in the same direction as the output gap. This shows that in good years, when the output gap rises, the government conducts restrictive fiscal policies, while its policy is expansionary when the output gap declines. Put differently, fiscal policy tends to be used in a countercyclical way, which dampens the business cycle. Looking carefully at the figure shows numerous exceptions, however.

▶

---

[4] Why to first approximation? Because as the economy grows, more people climb the income ladder and face higher tax rates. Also, the structure of the economy changes, possibly changing the way taxes are collected.

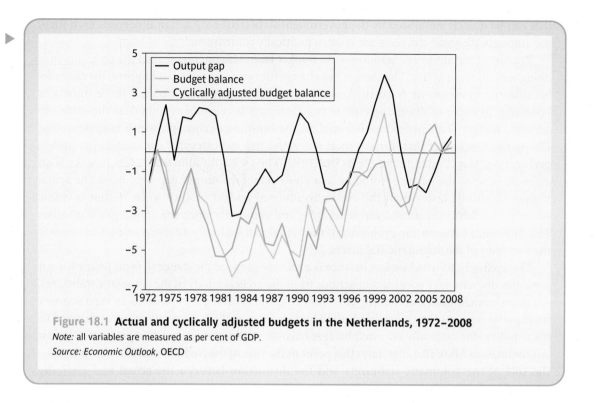

Figure 18.1 Actual and cyclically adjusted budgets in the Netherlands, 1972–2008
Note: all variables are measured as per cent of GDP.
Source: Economic Outlook, OECD

18.2 Fiscal policy externalities

18.2.1 Spillovers and coordination

So far, the discussion has concerned individual countries. But fiscal policy actions by one country may spill over to other countries through a variety of channels, described below: income and spending, inflation, and borrowing costs. Such spillovers, called externalities, mean that one country's fiscal policy actions can help or hurt other countries. In such a situation, when one country decides what to do, it cannot ignore the effect on its partners and, conversely, it also has to take into account policy decisions taken elsewhere. This implies that countries subject to each other's spillovers stand to benefit from coordinating their fiscal policies. In principle, all concerned countries could agree on each other's fiscal policy to achieve a situation that befits them all. This is what policy coordination is about.

While, formally, fiscal policy remains a national prerogative, it is natural to ask whether the deepening economic integration among Eurozone countries calls for some degree of coordination. On the one hand, the setting up of a monetary union strengthens the case for fiscal policy coordination as it promotes economic integration. On the other hand, fiscal policy coordination requires binding agreements on who does what and when. Such detailed arrangements would limit each country's sovereignty, precisely at a time when the fiscal policy instrument assumes greater importance. The question is whether sharing the same currency increases the spillovers to the point where some new limits on sovereignty are desirable and justified. To

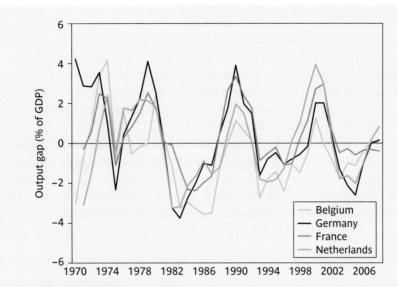

Figure 18.2 Income spillovers, 1972–2005
Source: Economic Outlook, OECD

answer this question, we review the channels through which spillovers occur and examine what difference the Eurozone makes.

18.2.2 Cyclical income spillovers

Business cycles are transmitted through exports and imports. When Germany enters an expansion phase, for instance, it imports more from its partner countries. For these partner countries, the German expansion means more exports and more incomes, and the expansion tends to be transmitted across borders. Figure 18.2, which displays output gaps for a number of countries, confirms that business cycles are highly synchronized in Europe, and were so long before the adoption of the euro. Quite obviously, the spillover is stronger the more the countries trade with each other, and the larger is the country taking action.

What does this mean for fiscal policy? Consider, first, the case when two monetary union member countries undergo synchronized cycles, for example both suffer from a recession. Each government will want to adopt an expansionary fiscal policy, but to what extent? If each government ignores the other's action, their combined action may be too strong as each economy pulls the other one from the recession – an effect of the Keynesian multiplier. If, instead, each government relies on the other to do most of the work, too little might be done. Consider next the case when the cycles are asynchronized. An expansionary fiscal policy in the country undergoing a slowdown stands to boost spending in the already booming country. Conversely, a contractionary fiscal policy move in the booming country stands to deepen the recession in the other country. The risk, in this case, is too much policy action.

18.2.3 Borrowing cost spillovers

A fiscal expansion increases public borrowing or reduces public saving. As the government is usually the country's biggest borrower, large budget deficits may push interest rates up. Once they share the same currency, Eurozone member countries share the same interest rate. One country's deficits, especially if the country is large and its deficits sizeable, may impose higher interest rates throughout the Eurozone.[5] As high interest rates deter investment, they affect long-term growth. This is another spillover channel.

As stated, the argument is weak. Europe is fully integrated in the world's financial markets so any one country's borrowing is unlikely to make much of an impression on world and European interest rates. On the other hand, heavy borrowing may elicit capital inflows. This could result in an appreciation of the euro, which would hurt the area's competitiveness and cut into growth. Borrowing costs thus represent another channel for spillovers.

18.2.4 Excessive deficits and the no-bailout clause

The question of debt sustainability cannot be taken lightly in Europe in view of the near-tripling of public debts as a share of GDP since 1970, as Fig. 18.3 shows.[6] In the distant past, public debts have occasionally risen but only in difficult situations, and mostly during wars. The recent

Figure 18.3 Public debt of the Eurozone, 1970–2008
Source: Economic Outlook, OECD

---

[5] Jürgen Stark, a high-level German official who was influential in designing the Stability and Growth Pact, writes: 'The state's absorption of resources which would otherwise have found their way into private investments results in higher long-term interest rates' (Stark, 2001, p. 79).

[6] This is the debt for the whole zone, but the situation differs from country to country. Two countries, Belgium and Italy, have a debt in excess of 100 per cent of GDP. These debts are seen as the weak elements of the chain.

generalized debt build-up is partly related to the oil shocks of the 1970s and 1980s, but this is not the only reason. The figure illustrates what is sometimes called the 'deficit bias', a disquieting tendency for governments to run budget deficits for no other reason than political expediency. Does it call for a specific collective measure?

In principle, it is in each country's interest to resist the deficit bias, so fiscal discipline does not call for any collective measure unless spillovers can be identified. What happens when a public debt becomes unsustainable? As noted in Chapter 17, financially hard-pressed governments may be tempted to call upon the central bank to finance their deficits. Debt monetization, as this is called, is the traditional route to inflation. But this door is explicitly closed by the Maastricht Treaty, which forbids the Eurosystem from providing direct support to governments.

Heavy public borrowing by one country is a sign of fiscal indiscipline that could trouble the international financial markets. If markets believe that one country's public debt is unsustainable, they could view the whole Eurozone with suspicion. The result would be sizeable capital outflows and euro weakness. This is another potential source of spillover.

There is still another potential spillover. If a government accumulates such a debt that it can no longer service it, it must default. The experience with such defaults is that the immediate reaction is a massive capital outflow, a collapse of the exchange rate and of the stock markets, and a prolonged crisis complete with a deep recession and skyrocketing unemployment. Too bad for the delinquent country, but being part of a monetary union changes things radically. It is now the common exchange rate that is the object of the market reaction. The spillover can further extend to stock markets throughout the whole monetary union.

A further fear is that the mere threat of one member country's default would so concern all other member governments that they would feel obliged to bail out the nearly bankrupt government. This last risk has been clearly identified in the Maastricht Treaty, which includes a no-bailout clause. The clause states that no official credit can be extended to a distressed member government. In spite of the no-bailout clause, it remains that, in the midst of an emergency, some arrangement could still be found to bail out a bankrupt government. For example, the ECB could be 'informally' pressed to relax its monetary policy to make general credit more abundant at a lower cost, which would result in inflation. More generally, it is feared that a sovereign default would badly affect the Eurozone and undermine its credibility, with seriously adverse effects on the euro.

These spillovers do not rely on standard fiscal policy income effects but on the risk of excessive, and potentially unsustainable, deficits. They point to a catastrophic event. Defaults, however, do not occur in blue skies – it takes years to accumulate large debts. The implication is that a preventive procedure is required to avoid the need to deal with an emergency.

18.2.5 Collective discipline

Why do governments seem to have a deficit bias, and why does this bias seem to differ from country to country, as can be seen in Table 18.2? Deficits allow governments to deliver goods and services today without facing the costs, passing the burden of debt service to future governments or even to future generations. It is tempting to do so, especially when elections are near; but adequate democratic accountability should prevent governments from indulging. Even though future generations are not here to weigh in, the current generation may reasonably

Table 18.2 Public debts in Europe, 2009

Austria	Belgium	Bulgaria	Cyprus	Czech Rep.	Denmark
63.3	90.1	13.0	52.6	28.0	21.6
Estonia	Finland	France	Germany	Greece	Hungary
4.2	32.8	75.9	69.5	102.1	76.7
Ireland	Italy	Latvia	Lithuania	Luxembourg	Malta
32.9	118.9	12.8	19.0	8.6	68.7
Netherlands	Poland	Portugal	Romania	Slovakia	Slovenia
44.1	49.7	74.0	17.4	31.6	25.7
Spain	Sweden	UK		EU27	Eurozone
39.3	37.2	60.2		66.9	73.3

Source: AMECO, European Commission

expect to be called upon to service the debt, and anyway most people care about the next generation. So a debt build-up often reflects a failure of democratic control over governments. Why has this been happening in Europe's democracies?

Public spending often favours narrow interest groups (civil servants, the military, public road contractors, etc.), while the debt service is diffused and borne by an unstructured majority, and interest groups are well organized and influential with the government. The time of reckoning should come when elections are held, but the electoral process is not always effective at imposing budgetary discipline. Indeed, some political regimes – typically parliamentary regimes which involve large coalitions – seem to be doing less well at keeping deficits and debts in check.

Changing the democratic regime (the form of democracy, how elections are organized) could help, but it is a rather intractable endeavour. This is why some governments find it appealing to seek external restraint and to invoke 'Brussels' as a scapegoat that can be blamed when resisting interest groups and political friends. Collective discipline, even if not necessarily justified by spillovers, can be used as a substitute for adequate domestic institutions.

18.3 Principles

The existence of spillovers is one argument for sharing policy responsibilities among independent countries. It is not the only argument, however, and there are powerful counter-arguments. The broader question is, at which level of government – regional, national, supranational – should policies be conducted? The theory of fiscal federalism deals with this question. The principle of subsidiarity is another way of approaching the issue. Both approaches have been presented earlier, in Chapter 3, and are briefly recalled in this section.

18.3.1 Fiscal federalism

The theory of fiscal federalism asks how, in one country, fiscal responsibilities should be assigned between the various levels (national, regional, municipal) of government. It can be transposed to Europe's case, even though Europe is not a federation, by asking which tasks should remain in national – possibly regional in federal states – hands and which ones should be a shared responsibility, i.e. delegated to Brussels. There are two good reasons to transfer responsibility to Brussels and two good reasons to keep it at the national level. An additional concern is the quality of government at the national and supranational level.

Two arguments for sharing responsibilities: externalities and increasing returns to scale

As noted before, spillovers, also called externalities – when one country's actions affect other countries – lead to inefficient outcomes when each country is free to act as it wishes. Sometimes too much action is taken, sometimes not enough. This is the case of tariffs (see Chapter 4) and fiscal policy. The other argument is that some policies are more efficient when carried out on a large scale. Increasing returns to scale can be found in the use of money,[7] in the design of commercial law or in defence (army, weapons development and production), among others.

One solution is coordination, which preserves sovereignty but calls for repeated and often piecemeal negotiations, with no guarantee of success. Another solution is to give up sovereignty, partly or completely, and delegate a task to a supranational institution. In Europe, some important tasks have already been delegated to the European Commission (the internal market and trade negotiations) and to the Eurosystem (monetary policy).

Two arguments for retaining sovereignty: heterogeneity of preferences and information asymmetries

Consider the example of common law concerning family life (marriages and divorces, raising children, dealing with ageing parents, etc.). Practices and traditions differ across countries, sometimes to a considerable extent. In this domain, preferences are heterogeneous and a supranational arrangement is bound to create much dissatisfaction.

Now consider the decisions of where to build roads, how large to make them, where to set up traffic lights, etc. These require a good understanding of how people move, or wish to move, in a geographic area: it is a case of information asymmetry, since it is likely that the information is more readily available at the local level than at a more global level.

Heterogeneity of preferences and information asymmetries imply that it would be inefficient to share competence at a supranational level. Much of the criticism levelled at 'Brussels' concerns cases where either heterogeneity or information asymmetries are important: deciding on the appropriate size of cheese or the way to brew beer is best left to national governments, or even local authorities, no matter how important the externalities or increasing returns to scale.

The quality of government

An implicit assumption so far is that governments always act in the best interest of their citizens. While this may generally be the case, there are numerous instances when governments either pursue their own agendas or are captured by interest groups. Indeed, like any institution, governments often wish to extend their domain of action, possibly in order to increase their own power or because they genuinely believe that they can deal with important problems. In

---

[7] Chapter 11 argues that this is a key benefit from a large currency area.

addition, there is no such thing as 'the best interest of citizens': some citizens favour some actions, others do not. Governments exist in part to deal with such conflicts and do so under democratic control but, as noted in Section 18.2.5, elections cannot sanction every one of the millions of decisions that favour well-connected interests. In spite of all the good things that can be said about democracy, it is not a perfect system, and it often fails.[8]

Once this fact of life is recognized, the principles from the theory of fiscal federalism need to be amended. There is no general rule here, only the need to always keep in mind that a good solution may turn out to be bad if the government is misbehaving. In particular, the quality of government and of democratic control ought to be brought into the picture. The question here is whether Brussels performs better than the national governments.

18.3.2 The principle of subsidiarity

It should be clear by now that in most cases the four arguments for and against centralization at the EU level are unlikely to lead to clear-cut conclusions, and the warning about the quality of government further complicates the issue. In each case, one has to weigh the various arguments and trade off the pros and cons. This is often mission impossible, hence another question: where should the burden of proof lie?

The EU has taken the view that the burden of proof lies with those who argue in favour of sharing sovereign tasks. This is the principle of subsidiarity (presented in Chapter 3) and it is enshrined in the European Treaty:

> In areas which do not fall within its exclusive competence, the Community shall take action, in accordance with the principle of subsidiarity, only if and insofar as the objectives of the proposed action cannot be sufficiently achieved by the Member States and can therefore, by reason of the scale or effects of the proposed action, be better achieved by the Community.
>
> (Article 5)

18.3.3 Implications for fiscal policy

A key distinction: micro- vs. macroeconomic aspects of fiscal policy

It is crucial to separate two aspects of fiscal policy. The first aspect is structural, that is, mainly microeconomic. It concerns the size of the budget, what public money is spent on, how taxes are raised, i.e. who pays what, and redistribution designed to reduce inequalities or to provide incentives to particular individuals or groups. The second aspect is macroeconomic. This is the income stabilization role of fiscal policy, the idea that it can be used as a countercyclical instrument.

Here, we focus on the macroeconomic stabilization component of fiscal policy, ignoring the structural aspects. To simplify, we look at the budget balance and ignore the size and structure of the budget and the resulting evolution of the public debt. We apply the principles of fiscal federalism to ask whether there is a case for limiting the free exercise of sovereignty on national budget balances and debts.

---

[8] Churchill is rumoured to have said: 'Democracy is the worst possible system, except for all others.'

The case for collective restraint

Section 18.2 identifies a number of spillovers: income flows, borrowing costs and the risk of difficulties in financing runaway deficits, possibly leading to debt default. Some of these spillovers can have serious effects across the Eurozone. In addition, some countries have not established political institutions that are conducive to fiscal discipline so it may be in their own best interest to use Brussels as an external agent of restraint. On the other hand, it is difficult to detect a scale economy.

These externalities call for some limits on national fiscal policies, and such limits can take various forms, ranging from coordination and peer pressure to mandatory limits on deficits and debts.

The case against collective restraint

Working in the opposite direction are important heterogeneities and information asymmetries. Macroeconomic heterogeneity occurs in the presence of asymmetric shocks. A common fiscal policy, on top of a common monetary policy, would leave each country without any counter-cyclical macroeconomic tool. Heterogeneity can also be the consequence of differences of opinions regarding the effectiveness of the instrument. Some countries (e.g. France and Italy) have long been active users of fiscal policy whereas others (e.g. Germany) have a tradition of scepticism towards Keynesian policies. Finally, national political processes are another source of heterogeneity. In some countries, the government has quite some leeway to adapt the budget to changing economic conditions, whereas in others the process is cumbersome and politically difficult.

Information asymmetries chiefly concern the perception of the political implications of fiscal policies. Each government faces elections, and economics is often an important factor shaping voter preferences. Whether and how to use fiscal policy at a particular juncture is part of a complex political game, which makes national politics highly idiosyncratic. While governments have a lot of understanding for each other's electoral plight, they have a hard time absorbing all the fine details of foreign national politics.

Overall

It is far from clear that the macroeconomic component of fiscal policy should be subject to external limits. Quite clearly, a single common fiscal policy is ruled out, but what about some degree of cooperation? The debate is ongoing and is unlikely to be settled in the near future. The subsidiarity principle implies that, as long as the case is not strong, fiscal policy should remain fully a national prerogative. On the other hand, the spillover that could result from *excessive* deficits is important, as it forms the logical basis for the Stability and Growth Pact.

18.3.4 Fiscal policy coordination

As a country joins the monetary union, it gives up monetary policy but retains the fiscal policy instrument. For the monetary union as a whole, in contrast, the fact that the euro is floating means that monetary policy is effective, hence the importance of the task attributed to the Eurosystem. On the other hand, the overall fiscal policy stance of the monetary union may matter for the euro's value, but it is likely to be ineffective as a collective instrument. This analysis suggests that fiscal policy should continue to be exerted at the national level (where the exchange rate is irremediably fixed), while there is little to be gained by aiming at a high level of coordination, beyond the spillover aspects studied in Section 18.2.

18.3.5 What does it all mean for fiscal policy?

Applying the principles of fiscal federalism to the macroeconomic fiscal policy instrument leaves us with few uncontroversial conclusions. There are valid reasons for jointly imposing discipline and for policy coordination. There are equally valid arguments in the opposite direction. All in all, the case for further transfers of sovereignty is weak. This conclusion is challenged by some who attach much importance to spillovers and think that macroeconomic coordination is both promising and relatively easy to implement. It is also challenged from the opposite end of the spectrum by those who see coordination as a collusion of self-interested governments. Sceptics tend to conclude that, given the weakness of the case, subsidiarity should be applied and fiscal policy left entirely in national hands. The debate has been around for a decade and is not likely to disappear for some time.[9] For a while, it seemed to have been partly settled by the adoption of the Stability and Growth Pact, but the Pact itself has been highly controversial and has encountered serious difficulties.

18.4 The Stability and Growth Pact

18.4.1 From convergence to the quest for a permanent regime

As explained in Chapter 17, admission to the monetary union requires a budget deficit of less than 3 per cent of GDP and a public debt of less than 60 per cent of GDP, or declining toward this benchmark. But what about afterwards, in the permanent monetary union regime? Could countries achieve the two fiscal criteria, join the monetary union and then freely relapse in unbridled indiscipline? This would be against the spirit of the convergence criteria and it would raise the fears detailed in Section 18.2.4. The founding fathers of the Maastricht Treaty were keenly aware of this risk and, indeed, Article 104 unambiguously states that 'Member States shall avoid excessive government deficits' and goes on to outline a detailed 'excessive deficit procedure'. The Treaty left the practical details of the procedure to be settled later – and this is the task fulfilled by the Stability and Growth Pact (SGP).[10]

As adopted in 1997, the SGP was meant to be strictly enforced. However, because fiscal policy remains a national competence, final word had to be given to ECOFIN, the council of Finance Ministers of the Eurozone, acting on proposals from the Commission. The Commission

---

[9] Some references are provided in the further reading section at the end of this chapter.

[10] The initiative was taken by Germany in 1995 and the Pact adopted in June 1997 by the European Council. Informed by its own inter-war history, Germany was always concerned that fiscal indiscipline could lead to inflation. This is why it insisted on a clear and automatic procedure. It wanted to make full use of the provisions of the Maastricht Treaty, which allowed for fines in the case of excessive deficits. The other countries were less enthusiastic but Germany was holding the key to the Eurozone. France, in particular, was unhappy with the German proposal. It obtained the symbolic addition of the word 'growth' to what Germany had initially called the Stability Pact.

has assumed the responsibility of 'tough cop', but ECOFIN has been loath to make decisions that would strongly antagonize its members, especially the Finance Ministers from the large countries. In November 2003, France and Germany were to be sanctioned. Under pressure from the French and German Finance Ministers, ECOFIN recanted and put the SGP 'in abeyance'. The Commission took ECOFIN to the Court of Justice of the European Communities for violation of the Pact, an unprecedented action. In June 2004, the Court decided that ECOFIN had indeed breached the law but only because of the phrasing of its decision (the SGP cannot be put in abeyance). A new resolution quickly corrected the error, without changing the fact that France and Germany had not been sanctioned. This episode confirmed the view that the SGP was not well designed. Recognizing that it was too rigid to be enforceable, governments and the Commission prepared a reformulation of the Pact. The new version was adopted in June 2005.

The reasoning of Section 18.3 explains the difficulties of the SGP. The benefits from coordination are limited, the collective need for discipline is high but collectively enforced discipline clashes with sovereignty. This conflict is unavoidable. Discipline cannot be enforced without the threat of sanctions. In the same spirit as nuclear deterrence – the cost of an attack would be so great that no attack will be undertaken – the initial version of the SGP sought to make sanctions automatic to avoid a situation where sanctions would be needed. Some small countries were put on the spot, as is explained further below, but the two largest countries called its bluff and the Pact caved in. The crisis exposed a latent rift between large and small countries, which complicated subsequent negotiations. The revised SGP does not solve the logical conflict that lies at its heart, as it keeps the principle of sanctions; instead it seeks to avoid a situation where sanctions have to be applied.

18.4.2 The Pact

The SGP consists of four elements:

1 A definition of what constitutes an 'excessive deficit'.
2 A preventive arm, designed to encourage governments to avoid excessive deficits.
3 A corrective arm, which prescribes how governments should react to a breach of the deficit limit.
4 Sanctions.

The SGP applies to all EU member countries but only the Eurozone countries are subject to the corrective arm.

Excessive deficits

The SGP considers that deficits are excessive when they are above 3 per cent of GDP. In order to leave room for the automatic stabilizers to play their role, the Pact also stipulates that participants in the monetary union commit themselves to a medium-term budgetary stance 'close to balance or in surplus'. The medium term is understood to represent about three years.

The SGP recognizes that serious recessions, beyond any government control, can quickly lead to deepening deficits. Trying to close down deficits during a recession implies adopting a contractionary policy, which may deepen the recession, with potentially disastrous consequences. Consequently, the Pact defines exceptional circumstances when its provisions are automatically suspended. A deficit in excess of 3 per cent is considered exceptional if the country's GDP declines by at least 2 per cent in the year in question. The SGP also identifies an intermediate situation, when the real GDP declines by less than 2 per cent but by more than 0.75 per cent. In that case, if the country can demonstrate that its recession is exceptional in terms of its abruptness or in relation to past output trends, the situation can also be deemed exceptional. When output declines by less than 0.75 per cent, no exceptional circumstance can be claimed.

As could be expected from experience, these exceptional circumstances are truly exceptional, to the point of being unlikely to occur. The experience of 2001–03 showed that shallower but longer-lasting slowdowns can gradually deepen the deficit, unless the automatic stabilizers are prevented from operating by tightening up the structurally adjusted budget. In that case, however, the risk is that a restrictive fiscal policy turns a shallow slowdown into a serious recession; this may allow a country to invoke an exceptional circumstance, but it is really no justification for the pain imposed by a pro-cyclical fiscal policy, i.e. a policy that deepens an ongoing recession.

This is why, in its revised version, the SGP introduces two elements of flexibility. First, it admits that a negative growth rate or an accumulated loss of output during a protracted period of very low growth may be considered as exceptional. Second, it suggests taking account of 'all other relevant factors'. In contrast with the 3 per cent limit and the −2 and −0.75 per cent definition of exceptional circumstances, these new elements are vaguely specified. In particular, the notion of 'all other relevant factors', presented in Box 18.2, opens the door to a very flexible interpretation of the SGP.

Box 18.2   What are 'all the other factors'?

The definition of 'all the other factors' pitted against each other is those who wanted to keep the SGP unchanged and those who wished to make it more flexible.

One part concerns the definition of excessive deficits. A number of countries wanted some 'good' expenditures that particularly matter to them to be excluded from the deficit calculation. France was keen to spend more on research and obtained a reference to the Lisbon Strategy. Germany claimed that its unification with East Germany was still a drain on its budget and obtained a reference to 'the unification of Europe'. The UK is committed to providing aid to the poor countries and obtained a reference to 'fostering international solidarity'. The other countries' wishes were recognized through mention of 'achieving European policy goals'.

The other part concerns the preventive arm. The idea is that budget consolidation is easier in good times, when a restrictive fiscal policy is indeed countercyclical. The new SGP stipulates that judgement on whether a country is in an excessive deficit – no longer a simple matter given the vagueness of the definition of good spending – will take into account the efforts made in good times.

It will take time to see how this new concept is implemented. Clearly, the flexibility camp, which included most of the large countries, has won, and this has alarmed the ECB:

> The Governing Council of the ECB is seriously concerned about the proposed changes to the Stability and Growth Pact. It must be avoided that changes in the corrective arm undermine confidence in the fiscal framework of the European Union and the sustainability of public finances in the Eurozone Member States.

(ECB statement, 21 March 2005)

The preventive arm

The SGP's aim is to ensure that member countries will conduct disciplined fiscal policies. As explained in Section 18.2.4, the premise is that governments exhibit a deficit bias because of domestic pressure and political expediency. The SGP can exert counter-pressure in the form of peer pressure, called mutual surveillance. The preventive arm is designed to submit Finance Ministers to a collective discussion of each country's fiscal policy in the hope that this will be enough to deliver budgetary discipline. Prevention is meant to prevent the need for correction.

Formally, each Eurozone government submits early each year a Stability Programme. The document presents the government's budget forecast for the current year and the next three years. If the deficit is expected to exceed 3 per cent of GDP, the programme also explains what actions will be taken to correct this violation of the SGP. The Commission examines each programme, including its detailed technical aspects, and submits its individual assessments to ECOFIN. Each assessment must include an evaluation of whether the planned budgets are consistent with the SGP and whether previous commitments have been honoured. The Commission may also point out technical errors, for instance overoptimistic forecasts.

ECOFIN then delivers an opinion, adopted by qualified majority. The opinion can only be approval, but it can also include recommendations that form the corrective arm. All these documents are made public.[11]

EU member countries that are not part of the Eurozone must still submit Convergence Programmes. The content of these programmes and the procedure is the same as in the case of the Stability Programmes, with the difference that ECOFIN cannot impose sanctions, it can only issue recommendations. However, for the countries that are aiming to join the monetary union, failure to comply with the SGP implies a violation of the budgetary criteria.

The corrective arm

When a country does not meet the requirements of the SGP, ECOFIN applies gradually increasing peer pressure. The process starts with an 'early warning'. Early warnings are issued when ECOFIN concludes that a country is likely to see its deficit become excessive. A country given an early warning is also presented with recommendations – which may or may not be made public – which it is expected to follow in order to prevent being in a situation of excessive deficit. An early warning can be seen as a political hand grenade.

The next step is the excessive deficit procedure (EDP). The procedure is triggered by an ECOFIN opinion stating that a country's budget is in excessive deficit, as defined above. ECOFIN simultaneously issues recommendations – following a recommendation from the Commission – which the country must follow. The country must soon present a set of prompt corrective measures, which are examined by the Commission. The Commission submits its assessment to ECOFIN, which may or may not be satisfied with the proposed measures. A mandatory recommendation can be seen as a political conventional bomb.

What follows is a set of evaluations of the measures taken by the delinquent country and of the budget outcome. More recommendations can be issued, increasingly pressing and tight. In the end, if the country remains in excessive deficit, sanctions are to be imposed by ECOFIN, as

---

[11] The stability programmes are available at: http://ec.europa.eu/economy_finance/sg_pact_fiscal_policy/sg_programmes9147_en.htm.

explained below. Whereas the initial SGP established a precise set of deadlines, the revised Pact allows for quite some flexibility, at the discretion of ECOFIN.

Sanctions

If a country fails to take corrective action and to bring its deficit below 3 per cent by the deadline set by the Council, it is sanctioned. A sanction can be seen as a political nuclear bomb. The sanction takes the form of a non-remunerated deposit at the Commission. The deposit starts at 0.2 per cent of GDP and rises by 0.1 of the excess deficit up to a maximum of 0.5 per cent of GDP, as shown in Table 18.3. Deposits are imposed each year until the excessive deficit is corrected. If the excess is not corrected within two years, the deposit is converted into a fine, otherwise it is returned.

Table 18.3 **Schedule of fines**

Size of deficit (% of GDP)	Amount of fine (% of GDP)
3	0.2
4	0.3
5	0.4
6+	0.5

Several aspects of the SGP are noteworthy. First, formally, it does not remove fiscal policy sovereignty. Governments are in full control; they only agree to bear the consequences of their actions. Second, the intent is clearly pre-emptive since there is a lengthy procedure between the time a deficit is deemed excessive and the time when a deposit is imposed, with two more years before the deposit is transformed into a fine. Third, while a fine is politically a nuclear bomb-shell, the declaration that a country is in violation of the Pact is a more conventional bombshell, meant to elicit prompt corrective action. Finally, all decisions are in the hands of the Council, a highly political body that can exploit many of the 'ifs' included in the Pact.

18.4.3 The Pact and countercyclical fiscal policies: how much room to manoeuvre?

Early experience with the Stability and Growth Pact has revealed some problems, as Box 18.3 recalls. These early difficulties raise the question of whether the Pact leaves enough room for countercyclical fiscal policies. The answer requires consideration of the two aspects of fiscal policy mentioned in Section 18.1.3: the automatic stabilizers and discretionary policy.

Box 18.3   Ten years of the Stability and Growth Pact

Over the first ten years of monetary union, the Excessive Deficit Procedure (EDP) has been triggered 15 times, including seven cases concerning Eurozone members, which are subject to sanctions (see Table 18.4). Yet, sanctions have never been imposed. This can be seen as proof that the SGP has been effective at reigning in restraining fiscal indiscipline with a soft touch. Given the small number of cases

Table 18.4 History of GDP actions

| Year | Early Warning Recommended | | EDP |
	Issued	Not issued	
2001	Ireland		
2002		Portugal	Portugal
2002		Germany	
2003			Germany
2003	France		France
2004		Italy	
2004			Netherlands
2004			Greece
2004			Czech Republic
2004			Cyprus
2004			Hungary
2004			Malta
2004			Slovakia
2005			Portugal
2005			Italy
2005			UK
2008			UK
2008	Romania		

Source: http://ec.europa.eu/economy_finance/sg_pact_fiscal_policy/excessive_deficit9109_en.htm

and the short history, it is too early to draw firm conclusions. A few odd episodes, which spurred considerable controversies, are recalled here.

Ireland

In early 2001, Ireland was the first country to be formally warned. Strangely enough, its 2000 budget sported a surplus of 4.7 per cent of GDP and the Commission recognized that its debt level was low. The 2000 Stability Programme announced a budget surplus of 4.3 per cent for 2001, continuing high surpluses for the following years and a further decline in the debt ratio. But the 2001 budget ended up with a surplus of 1.7 per cent, much lower than the commitment. ECOFIN detected this upcoming slippage and reacted with an early warning. The year 2001 was an election year and the outgoing government relaxed its virtuous stance. Since the Irish economy was booming, the Council concluded that an expansionary fiscal policy was not adequate because it was pro-cyclical at a time when inflation was rising. The Irish government and citizens were infuriated and saw the heavy hand of Brussels invading their national sovereignty.

Germany

The Stability Programme presented by Germany at the end of 2000 anticipated a deficit of 1.5 per cent of GDP for 2001; the final figure was 2.7 of GDP. Following pledges from the German government,

ECOFIN decided not to follow the Commission's recommendation of an early warning. But then, contrary to the government's previous promises, the 2002 budget deficit stood at 3.8 per cent of GDP. The German government argued that this was the result of an unforeseeable exceptional event, floods in eastern Germany. This explanation did not cut much ice with the Commission and ECOFIN, and Germany, the promoter of the SGP, became the second country to be put under the EDP in January 2003.

France

For 2001, France had announced a deficit of 1.4 per cent of GDP, the outcome was 2.7. In 2002, the deficit reached 3.2 per cent of GDP. The Commission recommended issuing an early warning, which was issued in January 2003 by ECOFIN. By June 2003, a further deterioration was visible, partly because income taxes were reduced in both years following an election campaign promise by President Chirac. ECOFIN accepted the Commission recommendation to trigger the EDP.

France and Germany escape the SGP

By November 2003, it became clear that France and Germany were not heeding the recommendations made earlier by ECOFIN. Their 2003 deficits, not yet known, turned out both to reach 3.7 per cent of GDP, and forecasts for 2004 and 2005 did not envision a return to below 3 per cent. This led the Commission to issue mandatory recommendations, the last step before sanctions. After intense lobbying by France and Germany, ECOFIN decided by qualified majority to 'hold the excessive deficit procedure for France and Germany in abeyance for the time being'. This decision was subsequently annulled by the Court of Justice of the European Communities, mostly on legal technical grounds.

The Netherlands

In 2003, the Dutch deficit stood at 3.2 per cent, the result of a long slowdown (see Fig. 18.1). As it was expected to fall below 3 per cent in 2004 and afterwards, no action should have been taken. But the Dutch government, which had led the resistance against the French and German whitewash in November 2003 and was keen to restore credibility to the SGP, asked to be put under the EDP.

The automatic stabilizers

The automatic response of budget balances to cyclical fluctuations is a source of difficulty for the SGP. The Pact's strategy is that, in normal years, budgets should be balanced to leave enough room for the automatic stabilizers in bad years. A simple example illustrates the idea. Table 18.1 shows that, on average, a 1 per cent decline in GDP growth tends to worsen the budget deficit by 0.5 per cent of GDP. Using this rough estimate, the left-hand panel of Fig. 18.4 shows how much, depending on the initial budget position, the GDP can decline before the automatic stabilizers bring the budget to a deficit of 3 per cent. Obviously, if the budget is already at the 3 per cent limit (the leftmost point on the horizontal axis), there is no room available and the stabilizers must be blocked – fiscal policy becomes pro-cyclical – independently of the size of the slowdown (the zero on the vertical axis). If, instead, the budget is initially balanced (the zero on the horizontal axis), it would take a fall of 6 per cent of GDP (read off the vertical axis) to reach a deficit of 3 per cent. In comparison, the GDP decline that has led France and Germany to breach the limit in 2003 was about 2 per cent.

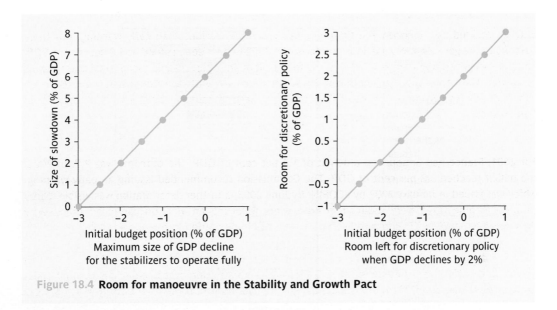

Figure 18.4 **Room for manoeuvre in the Stability and Growth Pact**

Discretionary policy

This reasoning assumes that countercyclical fiscal policy – the use of the budget to cushion business cycles – relies only on the automatic stabilizers. However, having abandoned the monetary policy instruments, governments may consider that it is not enough to rely only on the automatic stabilizers when the economic situation worsens. Forsaking discretionary fiscal policy can prove to be politically unacceptable for real-life governments, especially if they face elections.

The promoters of the SGP have an easy response. Governments can avail themselves of much more room to carry out discretionary policy by running a budget surplus, possibly a large one, in normal years. This idea is illustrated in Fig. 18.4. The right-hand panel asks the following question: Suppose that the GDP declines by 2 per cent of GDP, what is left for a further discretionary fiscal expansion over and above the automatic stabilizers? Using the same rule of thumb as in the left-hand panel, we know that the stabilizers worsen the budget by 1 per cent of GDP. The remaining room for manoeuvre depends again on the initial budget position. The graph shows that if the budget was, for instance, in a surplus of 1 per cent (to be read on the horizontal axis), the government can voluntarily increase spending, or cut taxes, to the tune of 3 per cent of GDP (the top reading on the vertical axis).

Bringing budgets to the safe zone? Staying there?

Thus the SGP intentionally provides a strong incentive to bring the budget to a position of balance, or even surplus. According to their promoters, when this is achieved, monetary union member countries will have recovered almost all the required room for manoeuvre. Only deep recessions will prevent the countercyclical use of fiscal policy, and deep recessions will qualify as exceptional. The main challenge, therefore, lies in the early years, when a number of countries still run deficits. It is bad luck, in this view, that the early years have been characterized by a protracted slowdown, thus delaying the time when all budgets are in balance or surplus. There is no reason to give up, especially as some countries have now fully adjusted.

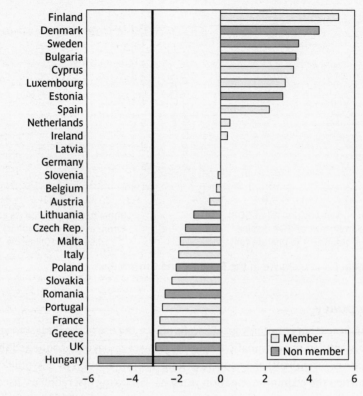

Figure 18.5 **Budget balances (percentage of GDP) in 2007**
Source: AMECO, European Commission

Figure 18.5 shows the situation in 2007, at the end of a period of rapid growth that preceded a serious slowdown in the wake of the oil shock of 2006–07 and the financial crisis that started in 2007. It shows that few countries had comfortable margins to meet a serious downturn and that many countries are close to the 3 per cent limit. The figure also suggests that the Eurozone member countries are not systematically more virtuous than the other EU countries.

To this, the SGP critics make two objections. Maybe, they say, Europe's poor economic performance since 1999 is partly due to the SGP, which has prevented a more dynamic counter-cyclical use of fiscal policies. Figure 18.1 shows how the Dutch government, an ardent supporter of the SGP, has exercised a countercyclical fiscal policy from 2001 onwards. Not only may this policy have deepened and prolonged the slowdown, it did not even prevent the Netherlands from being (self) declared in breach of the SGP (see Box 18.3). This is like shooting yourself in the foot.

In addition, SGP critics observe that, if the budget is in surplus in normal years, it means small deficits in bad years and big surpluses in good years. On average, therefore, the budget will be in surplus. This may sound good, but what does it mean for the public debt? Surpluses, year in and year out, imply that the public debt will be on a declining trend. Looking at Fig. 18.3 and Table 18.1, this seems exactly what Europe needs. But there remains a question: How far will the debt decline? As long as the budget remains on average in surplus, the debt will decline, so one day it will be zero. And after? The debt will become negative, which means that the government will start lending to the private sector, at home or abroad. Put differently, the government will raise taxes to make loans, competing with private banks. This makes little sense, critics argue.

Of course, the promoters of the SGP have answers to these counterarguments, and the debate is raging. The SGP has been and will remain controversial. The next section takes a step backwards and looks at the principles presented in Section 18.2 that lie behind the debate.

18.4.4 Limits of the Pact

The SGP is meant to serve two main useful purposes: to counteract the deficit bias and to reduce the odds of a debt default within the monetary union which, as noted in Section 18.2.4, could result in highly painful spillover effects. Yet, it does not come without a number of weaknesses, as its tumultuous history illustrates. The economic rationale is weak and the political conditions of its implementation are bound to be contentious.

Economic issues

The 3 per cent limit is artificial. In the face of economic and political difficulties – rising unemployment, for instance – governments may find it hard to justify a particular number. Those who stand to suffer from a rigorous application of the Pact may ask: Why 3 per cent and not 2 or 3.5 per cent? In addition, targeting the budget balance is like shooting at a moving duck: it changes all the time as economic conditions evolve, and it is therefore beyond government control. This opens the door to endless discussions on whether a government should be blamed, possibly even sanctioned, for an excessive deficit.

One frequently made suggestion is to target the cyclically adjusted budget balance since it captures discretionary actions. Requiring, for instance, that the cyclically adjusted budget always be in balance allows the full use of the automatic stabilizers. Allowing it to be balanced on average over a business cycle additionally permits the countercyclical discretionary use of fiscal policy. This makes good economic sense. There is a serious difficulty, however. If the SGP is to have any influence on governments subject to the deficit bias, it must be backed by credible sanctions. If sanctions are imposed, the conditions under which they are triggered must be clear and uncontroversial. The problem is that computing the cyclically adjusted budget balance is more art than science. There exist many methods to do so, each of which leads to different results. It is easy to foresee a country threatened with sanctions produce its own cyclically adjusted estimates, which cannot be dismissed.

Is there a better measure than fiscal discipline? Yes, there is, and it is rooted in good economics. Why do we care about fiscal discipline in the first place? Section 18.2.4 provides the answer: because lack of discipline eventually leads to a debt default. The natural implication is that the SGP should target the debt-to-GDP ratio. As long as it declines or remains at a moderate level, there is no threat of default. The EDP, as described in the Maastricht Treaty, refers to both the annual deficit (limit set at 3 per cent of GDP) and to the public debt (limit set at 60 per cent of GDP). The SGP makes a passing reference to the debt but chose instead to focus on the deficit figure. One possible reason is that the 60 per cent reference is unrealistic given the situation of many countries. Instead of jettisoning this other arbitrary number, the

SGP de-emphasized the debt. The Commission proposed reintroducing it, but it has not been followed by ECOFIN. Yet such a step would dispose of most of the controversies that currently plague the Pact. Targeting the public debt over the medium term – not the budget balance year after year – would leave governments free to use fiscal policy as they see fit in the short term, while anchoring their actions to the need to pay back previous borrowing.

Political issues

Imposing fiscal discipline from outside has the obvious advantage of protecting governments from domestic interest groups. On the other hand, using Brussels as a scapegoat may be good politics in the short term but, if invoked too often, it can undermine general support for European integration. In particular, the imposition of fines could be met with popular rejection. But, without fines, the SGP is unlikely to have enough teeth and could be overlooked when it is politically convenient to do so, which in effect means that there is no pact.

When the SGP was under discussion, one view was that it should be entirely automatic, with each step, including sanctions, to be decided by the Commission on the basis of a transparent and unambiguous roadmap. The opposite camp pointed out that fiscal policy remains an element of national sovereignty. In every country, budgets are set by the government and the parliament in a procedure that has a deep justification. In every democracy, deciding who will pay taxes and how much, and how the public money is to be spent, is in the hands of elected officials. An automatic application of the SGP, including detailed mandatory recommendations, would clearly violate this basic principle of democracy. This is why, in the end, the final say on whether to issue an early warning, on the imposition of the EDP and its associated recommendations, and of course on sanctions, is in the hands of ECOFIN, which brings together representatives of democratically elected governments. Yet, seen from the angle of a particular country, ECOFIN is not an institution which enjoys domestic democratic legitimacy. This feature perhaps helps explain why the SGP could not be applied to France and Germany once their governments strenuously objected.

Yet, leaving the final decision in the hands of ECOFIN has a serious drawback. Finance Ministers are, by definition, politicians. As such, they make elaborate calculations involving tactical considerations often far away from the principles discussed here. This has been made clear by the surprising early warning addressed to small Ireland, while France and Germany were spared the rigour of the EDP (see Box 18.3).

We face a serious contradiction. The budget is firmly identified as a sovereign prerogative, and time-honoured democratic principles vest the budget with democratically elected officials. On the other hand, domestic politics often give rise to a deficit bias and all Eurozone countries have an interest in preventing fiscal indiscipline in any of its members. The SGP tries to deal with this contradiction, but the magic formula remains to be found.

18.5 Summary

The loss of national monetary policy leaves fiscal policy as the only macroeconomic instrument. Budgets can be seen as a substitute for the absence of intra-Eurozone transfers, one of the OCA criteria not satisfied in Europe.

Fiscal policy operates in two ways:

★ The automatic stabilizers come into play without any policy action because deficits increase when the economy slows down, and decline or turn into surpluses when growth is rapid.

★ Discretionary policy results from willing actions taken by the government.

The main arguments in favour of some collective influence on national fiscal policies are:

★ The presence of spillovers, the fact that one country's fiscal policy affects economic conditions in other Eurozone countries. The main spillover channels are: income flows via exports and imports; and the cost of borrowing as there is a single interest rate.

★ The fear that a default by a government on its public debt would badly affect the common exchange rate and generally hurt the union's credibility.

The theory of fiscal federalism provides arguments for and against the sharing of policy instruments. The presence of spillovers and of increasing returns to scale argues for policy sharing. The existence of national differences in economic conditions and preferences, and of asymmetries of information, argues against policy sharing. Finally, the quality of government matters.

The Stability and Growth Pact (SGP), an application of the excessive deficit procedure envisioned in the Maastricht Treaty, is based on four organizing principles:

★ A definition of excessive deficits. In principle, deficits should not exceed 3 per cent of GDP. Special circumstances correspond to deep recessions. The 2005 revision allows for a number of 'other factors', a step designed to introduce flexibility.

★ A preventive arm, which is designed to encourage, through peer pressure, governments to resist the deficit bias. Prevention rests on annual Stability Programmes. These programmes are evaluated by the Commission, which issues a recommendation to ECOFIN. ECOFIN, in turn, expresses an opinion.

★ A corrective arm, which is triggered when a country is found to have an excessive deficit. This triggers increasingly binding recommendations by ECOFIN, based on suggestions from the Commission. A milder procedure, called early warning, can be triggered when ECOFIN determines, on the basis of a recommendation from the Commission, that a country may soon run an excessive deficit.

★ When a country has not followed the recommendations and remains in excessive deficit, sanctions may apply. Sanctions take the form of fines.

The difficulties encountered in the implementation of the SGP can be traced to both economic and political considerations:

★ From an economic viewpoint, targeting the annual budget deficit can lead to pro-cyclical policies, i.e. policies that reinforce either a slowdown or a boom. The revised SGP intends to encourage countercyclical policies in good times.

★ From a political viewpoint, the SGP faces a formidable contradiction. Fiscal policy is a matter of national sovereignty, in the hands of democratically elected governments and parliaments. At the same time, fiscal policy is recognized as a matter of common concern.

Self-assessment questions

1. What is the difference between actual and cyclically adjusted budgets? Why are discretionary actions visible only in changes of the cyclically adjusted budget balance?

2. In Fig. 18.1, identify years when fiscal policy is pro-cyclical, and years when it is countercyclical.

3. What are externalities or spillovers? How do they operate in the case of fiscal policy?

4. Explain the no-bailout clause.

5. What is the intended purpose of the Stability and Growth Pact?

6. Why is fiscal policy useful at the country level in the monetary union and not at the overall EU level?

7. When can ECOFIN impose fines in the framework of the Stability and Growth Pact?

8. If the SGP required the cyclically adjusted budget to be balanced every year, explain why fiscal policy would be strictly confined to the automatic stabilizers. What difference would it make if the cyclically adjusted budget had to be balanced on average over business cycles?

9. Why are fines under the Stability and Growth Pact sometimes described as pro-cyclical fiscal policy?

10. Why is there a contradiction between the Stability and Growth Pact and sovereignty in the matter of budgets?

Essay questions

1. How would you reform the Stability and Growth Pact?

2. Imagine that a Eurozone member country is running budget deficits and accumulating a large public debt. What scenario can you envision when financial markets refuse to further finance the deficits? In your story, consider the reaction of domestic citizens as well as that of the Commission and ECOFIN.

3. When the Stability and Growth Pact was being negotiated, some countries wanted it to be a fully automatic procedure, others wanted decisions to be interpreted by the Finance Ministers. Why is this distinction important? How does the agreed-upon pact reflect this difference of opinions?

4. Some countries argue that the monetary union needs a common fiscal policy to match the common monetary policy. Evaluate this view.

5. With the Stability and Growth Pact and its limits on fiscal policy, what is left for governments to do in the monetary union?

6. As part of its decision on whether to join the Eurozone, the UK Treasury has studied the Stability and Growth Pact and states:

   Where debt is low and there is a high degree of long-term fiscal sustainability, the case for adopting a tighter fiscal stance to allow room for governments to use fiscal policy more actively is not convincing. Provided that arrangements are put in place to ensure that discretionary policy is conducted symmetrically, then long-term sustainability would not in any way be put at risk.

(Fiscal Stabilization and Eurozone, HM Treasury, May 2003)

Interpret and comment.

Further reading: the aficionado's corner

An excellent collection of readings is Part III in:

De Grauwe, P. (ed.) (2001) *The Political Economy of Monetary Union*, Edward Elgar, Cheltenham.

For a presentation and a defence of the Stability and Growth Pact, see:

Brunila, A., M. Buti and D. Franco (eds) (2001) *The Stability and Growth Pact*, Palgrave, Basingstoke.

For a detailed and critical presentation of the Stability and Growth Pact, see:

Eichengreen, B. and C. Wyplosz (1998) 'The Stability Pact: more than a minor nuisance?', *Economic Policy*, 26: 65–104.

On the tendency of governments not to always serve their citizens' interests and what it means for the EU, see:

Persson, T. and G. Tabellini (2000) *Political Economics*, MIT Press, Cambridge, MA.

Vaubel, R. (1997) 'The constitutional reform of the European Union', *European Economic Review*, 41 (3–5): 443–50.

Fiscal policy

On the cyclical behaviour of fiscal policy, see:

European Commission (2001) 'Fiscal policy and cyclical stabilization in Eurozone', *European Economy*, 3: 57–80.

Hallerberg, M. and R. Strauch (2002) 'On the cyclicality of public finances in Europe', *Empirica*, 29: 183–207.

Melitz, J. (2000) 'Some cross-country evidence about fiscal policy behaviour and consequences for Eurozone', *European Economy*, 2: 3–21.

For analyses on the politico-economic aspects of fiscal policy, see:

Alesina, A. and R. Perotti (1995) 'The political economy of budget deficits', *IMF Staff Papers*, 42 (1): 1–37.

Persson, T., G. Roland and G. Tabellini (2000) 'Comparative politics and public finance', *Journal of Political Economy*, 108 (6): 1121–61.

von Hagen, J. and I.J. Harden (1994) 'National budget processes and fiscal performance', *European Economy Reports and Studies*, 3: 311–408.

For an introduction to the theory of fiscal federalism, see:

Oates, W. (1999) 'An essay in fiscal federalism', *Journal of Economic Literature*, 37 (3): 1120–49.

Reform of the Stability and Growth Pact

The view of the Commission:
http://ec.europa.eu/economy_finance/publications/publication_summary7558_en.htm.

The view of the ECB: www.ecb.int/press/key/date/2005/html/sp051013.en.html.

Academic analyses and alternative proposals:

Calmfors, L. (2003) 'Fiscal policy to stabilise the domestic economy in the EMU: What can we learn from monetary policy?', *CESifo Economic Studies*, 49 (3): 319–53.

Wolff, G. (2007) 'Budget institutions to counteract fiscal indiscipline in Europe?'. Download from www.uni-bonn.de/~guntram/papers%5CPittsburghNewsletter022007.pdf.

Useful websites

The official texts can be found on the Commission's website at
http://ec.europa.eu/economy_finance/other_pages/other_pages12638_en.htm.

Euractiv's overview of the SGP, with many references, is at
www.euractiv.com/Article?tcmuri=tcm:29-133199-16&type=LinksDossier.

References

Burda, M. and C. Wyplosz (2009) *Macroeconomics: A European Test*, 5th edition, Oxford University Press, Oxford.

European Commission (2001) *Communication from the Commission to the Council and the European Parliament*, ECFIN/581/02-EN rev.3.

OECD (1997) *Economic Outlook*, OECD, Paris.

Stark, J. (2001) 'Genesis of a pact', in A. Brunila, M. Buti and D. Franco (eds) *The Stability and Growth Pact*, Palgrave, Basingstoke.

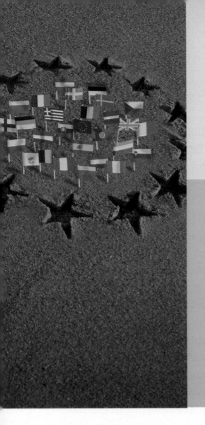

Chapter 19

The financial markets and the euro

*The big payoff on the Euro is, of course, in the capital
markets. [. . .] It will move from the dull bank-based
financing structure to big-time debt markets and markets
for corporate equities that offer transparency for the
mismanaged or sleepy European companies.
Capital markets are good at kicking butt.*

Rudi Dornbusch (2000), p. 242

Chapter contents

19.1	The capital markets	548
19.2	Microeconomics of capital market integration	553
19.3	Financial institutions and markets	559
19.4	The international role of the euro	572
19.5	Summary	579

Introduction

This chapter looks at the integration of European financial markets. Following the single market, adoption of the euro is expected to encourage further integration of Europe's capital markets, providing savers and borrowers alike with more and better opportunities. This, in turn, is expected to improve the overall productivity of the European economy and could also affect the way monetary policy works.

The chapter starts by outlining what is special about the financial services industry, distinguishing between banks and financial markets. It shows that financial markets can be at the same time very efficient and yet subject to some important failures. The next section, 19.2, presents the microeconomic analysis of capital market integration. It establishes the basic result that capital market integration raises economic efficiency and welfare. Yet, some gain and some lose from capital market integration, which explains why it is controversial.

Section 19.3 provides a review of the situation before and after the adoption of the single currency. An important aspect of this evolution is that financial institutions and markets have been shaped by centuries of national traditions. The single market (presented in Chapter 4) has already deeply modified the financial markets, but important differences remain. The single currency might well usher in a new era of transformation, exposing many limitations of the single market and calling for further actions, which are examined here. This leads to an evaluation of the unfinished business of adapting the national regulation and supervision of financial activities to the new challenges of the common currency.

Finally comes the question of whether the euro will become a currency used worldwide alongside the US dollar, why it matters and what has happened so far.

19.1 The capital markets

19.1.1 What are financial institutions and markets?

Because they support the accumulation of capital, the capital markets are central to long-term growth, as explained in Chapter 7. Their task is to collect savings and to provide producers with the financial means that they need to invest in productive equipment and new operations. There are many different forms of capital market and institution that cater to different customers with varied and sometimes complex requirements. At a very general level, the capital market performs three main functions:

1 *It transforms maturity.* Savers typically do not like to part with their 'money' – we call it their assets, because money is just one type of asset – for too long. Borrowers, on the other hand, typically prefer to obtain stable resources. The markets therefore mostly borrow short and lend long.

2 *It performs intermediation.* Savers and borrowers do not meet face to face. Savers deposit their funds in financial institutions that re-lend them to borrowers. The trip may be long, going through many financial institutions and across many national borders.

3 *It deals with inherent risk.* A loan implies giving out money against the promise of future repayment. In the meantime, the borrower may face difficulties that make repayment partly or totally impossible, and some borrowers may simply be dishonest.

The best-known financial institutions are banks: they receive deposits, in effect borrowing from their customers; they offer loans; and they often provide assistance for managing portfolios. In contrast to these universal banks, investment banks specialize in managing portfolios; they do not even accept deposits and sometimes cater only to wealthy customers. Many fund management firms do not even deal with individuals; they offer 'wholesale' services to banks and insurance companies. Insurance companies are also considered to be financial institutions. Part of their activity is to provide insurance, which, strictly speaking, is not a financial service. Yet, in order to face potentially high payments, they accumulate large reserves, which they want to manage in order to obtain returns as high as possible. In effect, they take 'deposits' – the insurance premia paid by their customers – that they use to 'make loans' as they invest in financial assets. In addition, many insurance companies propose pension schemes and life insurance, which can be seen as deposits with very long maturities. In fact, recent years have seen the emergence of financial conglomerates that combine classic universal banking, investment banking and insurance.

The bond and stock markets represent the other component of the financial system. Like banks, they are designed to collect savings and lend them back to borrowers, with the crucial difference that the end users – lenders and borrowers – 'meet' each other on the markets. Bonds are debts issued by firms and governments for a set maturity at an explicit interest rate, which can be indexed and therefore variable. Stocks (also called shares) are ownership titles to firms: they have no maturity since they last as long as the firm itself and the returns are determined by the firm's performance. Lenders (also called investors) usually operate through intermediaries – brokers, investment banks – which they instruct to buy or sell assets on their behalf on the markets. Most small investors, and many large ones too, in fact purchase funds, which are ready-made baskets of shares and bonds managed by financial intermediaries. Each fund has particular characteristics: the relative importance of bonds and stocks, the industry or country where they invest, the degree of risk and associated guarantees, as explained in the next section.

Financial institutions come in all shapes and sizes. A few huge international banks coexist with small, strictly local ones. Some financial markets attract lenders and borrowers from all over the world (New York's Wall Street and the City of London are the two largest), whereas others deal in a very narrow range of local assets. As will be explained below, financial markets are more efficient the larger they are.

19.1.2 What do financial markets do?

Matching lending and borrowing needs: maturity

The function of financial markets is to make savers and borrowers meet and to offer each saver and each borrower the best possible deal. This not only includes returns but also the available menu of size and maturity of assets, as well as the ability to sell or buy any amount at any time.

Imagine an individual who wants to put aside a given amount. She can always deposit this amount with her bank on a chequing account and withdraw whenever she wants whatever she wants, but the interest rate offered is quite low. She can do better by choosing term deposits; in that case she will have to pay a penalty if she needs to withdraw before the maturity is reached. On the other hand, term deposits offer more attractive interest, which grows with the maturity.

The bank thus encourages its customers to choose longer-term deposits. Why? Because the bank will re-lend the deposit to another customer who will be ready to pay a higher interest for loans of longer maturity. Time has a value, and the market sets its price.

Bank deposits are not the only way to save. She could buy bonds, with various maturities, or stocks, which are of unlimited duration. In that case, she would lend directly – albeit via her broker and the market – to the borrowers who issue bonds and stocks. The returns will be higher than bank deposits of the same maturity because these bonds and stocks are riskier than bank deposits. Risk is another issue that we now examine.

Matching lending and borrowing needs: risk

Bonds are issued by governments, banks and firms. Their maturities range from the very short term – 24 hours or less – to the very long term – 10, 20 years or more. Stocks are issued by firms; the holder owns a share of the firm and is entitled to the corresponding portion of profits. Bonds and shares are risky: if the issuer goes bankrupt, they are probably worth nothing, at best a fraction of their face value.[1] How do financial markets deal with risk?

Consider the return to investing in a particular project, say a new factory. When the investment is made, there is usually no way of knowing for certain whether the project will yield profits. And even if the venture proves profitable, the future profit level is uncertain. Tastes, exchange rates, prices and the level of competition can all change unexpectedly, thereby altering profits. Of course, one can make a reasonable guess as to what the profit will be, i.e. calculate what the profit should be, on average, but in deciding whether to invest, the best-guess average is not enough. The owner of the investment must also consider uncertainty. If two projects have the same average return (i.e. expected value), but the profit flow is more variable (i.e. riskier) for one than the other, then savers should judge the riskier project to be worth less. 'A bird in the hand is worth two in the bush' is the colloquial way of expressing the commonsense principle that people tend to discount the expected value of a risky project more than that of a risk-free project.

But what has this to do with financial markets? Bonds and shares are issued by firms that plan new investments. Bondholders and shareholders thus bear the investment risk. For them to be willing to buy a risky asset, there must be a reward. This is why the rate of return is adjusted for risk by incorporating a risk premium. The premium is set so that borrowers can convince savers to bear the risk. Savers obviously prefer no or little risk, but they may be attracted by a higher return. They face a trade-off between return and risk. This is why the risk-adjusted return typically rises with the risk of the asset, as shown in Fig. 19.1. Depending on her appetite for risk and return, the saver will choose where on the curve she would like to be.

Different savers will pick different points on the risk–return trade-off schedule because they have different degrees of aversion to risk. Financial markets allow every saver to find an asset that meets its preference and therefore every borrower to find the resources that he needs.[2] Markets balance demand and supply by setting the risk premium. Put differently, the markets put a price tag on risk and all assets fit nicely on the same risk–return schedule shown in

---

[1] Bonds issued by solid governments are considered riskless, which really means the least risky.

[2] Well, not every borrower. Very risky borrowers are usually unable to raise funds.

Fig. 19.1. The risk–return schedule reveals the price of risk, and financial markets allow everyone to trade off a higher return for more risk, or the converse, depending on personal preferences.

Diversification

Markets do not just price risk, they also allow for diversification. The basic issue can be illustrated by an example. Ask yourself, 'How risky is it to bet on red at the roulette table?' You might answer that you win almost half the time since on a roulette wheel all numbers, except 0 and 00, are either red or black. This is

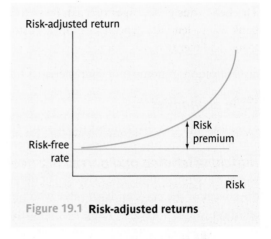

Figure 19.1 **Risk-adjusted returns**

the correct answer if you consider the bet-on-red 'project' in isolation. But there is a more complete answer. For instance, suppose you add a bet-on-black 'project' to your 'portfolio' of projects. That is, in addition to betting on red with each roll of the ball, you also bet on black with each roll. Now the effective risk of this betting venture is much reduced. You always win and always lose, except for when the ball lands on 0 or 00, in which case you lose both bets to the house.[3]

The point to note here is that the average loss from either 'portfolio' – the only-on-red portfolio and the both-red-and-black portfolio – is the same. In both cases, you lose on average 2 out of every 38 rolls of the ball (there are 38 numbers on the wheel – 18 red numbers, 18 black and the two zeros). However, the more 'diversified' portfolio (the both-red-and-black portfolio) provides less variation because one element of the portfolio does well when the other does badly. Clearly, the both-red-and-black betting strategy would take all the fun out of betting, but when we apply the same reasoning to a more serious investment – say a worker's pension fund – then the reduced volatility is highly valued.

The lesson to be learned from this example is that the risk of a particular project must be evaluated from the perspective of the investor's total portfolio of projects. Typically, some projects will do well when others do badly, so the average return to the portfolio is less risky than any individual project. Or, to put it in terms of the 'risk-adjusted rate of return' phraseology, the risk adjusted return on a diversified portfolio is higher than that on an undiversified portfolio of investment projects.

Financial markets can offer almost unbounded possibilities for diversification, the more so the bigger they are. By increasing the variety of projects, i.e. assets, large financial markets allow savers to hold relatively riskless portfolios composed of very risky assets. Both savers and borrowers stand to benefit from the situation. Because the portfolios bear little risk, the risk premium is reduced and this reduction is shared among savers, who receive higher returns, and borrowers, who face lower borrowing costs.

---

[3] In finance jargon, the red and black 'projects' are perfectly negatively correlated (their correlation coefficient is −1). More generally, risk diversification is higher the more negatively correlated are the assets that make up a portfolio.

19.1.3 Characteristics of financial markets

Financial markets are shaped to deal with the functions previously described, that is, matching the needs and preferences of borrowers and lenders, pricing risk and allowing for risk diversification. A number of characteristics follow.

Scale economies

Matching and risk diversification are both easier when there is a large number of borrowers and lenders. The finance industry is subject to massive scale economies which affect banks and financial markets. Where small banks and markets survive, it is not difficult to find some barriers to competition. The existence of different currencies is one such barrier. Indeed, before the advent of the euro, an Irish saver who purchased Portuguese assets faced currency risk in addition to the normal lending risk, and this made Irish assets more attractive to her. The creation of a single currency removes this particular barrier to competition.

Networks

One response to scale economies is the emergence of large financial institutions and markets. Another response, which goes hand in hand with the first, is the building of networks. When a financial firm receives funds from a saver, it needs to re-lend these funds as soon as possible since 'time is money'. With some luck, it will find among its customers a borrower with matching needs and preferences, but more often not. The solution is to re-lend the saver's money to another financial firm which may have spotted a borrower or identified another financial firm which may have spotted a borrower, etc. This is why financial markets operate as networks. Indeed, money passes quickly from firm to firm until it finds a house – a suitable borrower – somewhere in the network, and quite possibly in a very different corner of the world.

A financial firm is like a telephone hook-up: if you are the only one with a hook-up, it is of no use. A telephone is more useful the more people are connected to the network. This effect is called a network externality. A financial firm can offer better deals when it is in contact with a large number of other firms which deal with many customers, savers and borrowers alike. Network externalities exploit increasing returns to scale: the larger the network, the better it works. The best network could well be the whole world, hence the tendency towards the globalization of financial services.

Asymmetric information

A fundamental characteristic of financial activities is that the borrower always knows more about his own riskiness than the lender. This information asymmetry carries profound implications. Borrowers may intentionally attempt to conceal some damning information for the sake of obtaining a badly needed loan. As a consequence, lenders are very careful, not to say suspicious. They may simply refuse to lend rather than take unbounded risks. Alternatively, they may set the price of risk very high, i.e. they ask for very large risk premia. This, in turn, may discourage low-risk borrowers who cannot convincingly signal their true riskiness, while desperate borrowers are willing to pay any premium. If this process goes unchecked, only bad risks are present in the market and, knowing that, lenders withdraw.[4] At best, the price of risk is excessive, at worst the financial market dries up. Box 19.1 illustrates this phenomenon.

Box 19.1 Asymmetric information at its worst: the Great Crisis of 2007–08

House prices started to fall in the USA in late 2006. Why should that destroy a year or two later some well-established banks in New York, London and Frankfurt? Because a bank that lent money to a home-owner in Nebraska had resold this loan to a bank in, say, New York, which resold it to another bank in, say, Frankfurt, which could have resold it to a bank in New York. In the end, many banks were indirectly lending a little bit to the Nebraskan home-owner. This is risk-diversification at its best: if the home-owner defaults on his loan, every bank will suffer a minute loss. This is also information asymmetry at its worst: what does a big international bank in Paris know about this borrower? Worse, these loans were not just cut into small pieces, the small pieces were repackaged together. So a bank in Brussels could hold a package of portions of loans to tens of thousands of totally unknown American home-owners. It would not really know, or even care to know, what it owned. In fact, it could not investigate the long chain of slicing and repackaging that had produced the assets that it had bought. When the housing market turned down and tens of thousands of home-owners stopped paying for houses that were worth less than the loans they owed, banks around the world abruptly discovered that these packages had become toxic. Too late.

Then a new information asymmetry hit the markets. Bank A knew that it had a pack of toxic assets. It would suspect that Bank B was in the same or a worse situation. Not knowing the situation for sure, and already worried about its own situation, Bank A stopped doing business with Bank B, which anyway would not lend anything to Bank A or Bank C, or any bank. The interbank markets, where banks lend to each other, seized up. The interbank markets are often referred to as the mother of all financial markets, since this is where liquidity is being redistributed. With liquidity frozen, the crisis was on its way.

Asymmetric information is unavoidable and it tends to undermine the development of financial institutions and markets. This phenomenon explains many features of the financial services industry presented below. One general response is regulation, i.e. legislative measures that aim at reducing the overall riskiness.

19.2 Microeconomics of capital market integration

19.2.1 EU policy on capital market integration

Until the 1986 Single European Act and the 1988 directive that ruled out all remaining restrictions on capital movements among EU residents, EU capital markets were not very integrated. Although the free movement of capital is in the Treaty of Rome, the Treaty provided several large loopholes that EU members eagerly exploited. The basic problem was that, until recently,

---

[4] This phenomenon is called adverse selection. Borrowing in a desperate situation is sometimes called 'gambling for resurrection'.

EU nations just did not believe that unrestricted capital mobility was a good idea. They saw capital flows as responsible for repeated balance-of-payment crises and banking crises. As a result, the Treaty of Rome did not impose any formal requirements concerning capital market liberalization. The only stricture was a general one against capital restrictions that inhibited the proper functioning of the Common Market. The European Commission advanced capital flow liberalization only modestly, with directives in 1960 and 1962. These promoted partial liberalization but included numerous opt-out and safeguard clauses, which were in fact extensively used by EU members.

The main goal of EU capital market liberalization prior to the 1980s was to facilitate real business activities. For example, national policies should not hinder a company based in one Member State from setting up business in another Member State. This so-called right of establishment covered international transfers of capital that may be necessary to set up business. Likewise, national policies were not supposed to hinder the repatriation of profits or wages among Member States to the extent that such hindrances act as restrictions on the free movement of goods and workers.

Chapter 1 explains that the Single European Act 1986 instituted the principle that all forms of capital mobility should be allowed inside the EU. The actual liberalization was implemented by a series of directives which ended with the 1988 directive that ruled out all remaining restrictions on capital movements among EU residents. The resulting integration was raised to the level of a Treaty commitment by Article 56 of the Maastricht Treaty. This banned all national restrictions on the movement of capital except those required for law enforcement and national security reasons.

The costs of international capital mobility are macroeconomic. The impossible trinity principle introduced in Chapter 10 explains the necessity to give up monetary policy independence while keeping exchange rates fixed and the associated risk of financial instability. The benefits of allowing capital to move across national boundaries are microeconomic. They fall into two categories: allocation efficiency and diversification, which we consider in turn.

19.2.2 Economics of capital mobility: allocation efficiency

The normal functioning of a market economy requires capital to be invested in the activities that yield the highest rewards. To the extent that capital market barriers inhibit this efficient allocation, capital controls lower the allocative efficiency of the European economy. To understand this point, we start with the simplest analytic framework that allows us to organize our thinking about the economic consequences of capital market integration. Specifically, we suppose that there are only two nations (Home and Foreign) and that, initially, capital flows are not allowed between them. We also assume that these nations initially have different returns to capital. To keep things simple, we suppose that there is only one good and it is produced by both nations using capital and labour.

The framework can be depicted with the diagram shown in Fig. 19.2. This will eventually allow us to look at the international distribution of capital and impact of capital flows, but to get started we focus on Home, ignoring capital mobility. The *MPK* curve in the diagram shows how the 'marginal product of capital' (the amount of output produced by an extra unit of capital) declines as the total amount of capital employed increases. The marginal product of

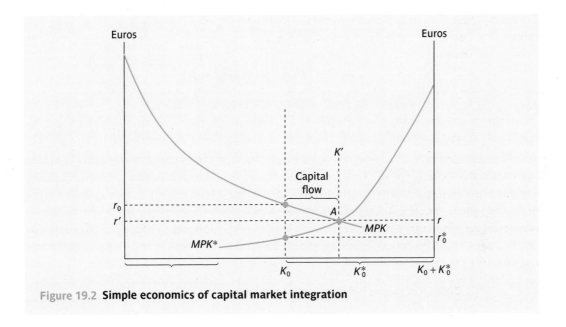

Figure 19.2 **Simple economics of capital market integration**

capital is declining in this diagram for exactly the same reason that the *MPL* curve was convex in Fig. 8.12. Holding constant the amount of labour employed in Home, the addition of more capital increases the overall output, but each additional unit of capital adds less output than the previous one.

If the capital stock in Home is given by K_0, then the equilibrium marginal product of capital in Home will be r_0, assuming that the capital market is competitive. The idea is that firms competing for Home's capital supply force the 'price' of capital, r, up to the point where the price they pay for capital just equals its marginal product. By the usual logic of competition, the outcome is that competitive firms pay r_0 and all capital is employed.

Next consider the situation in the other nation, Foreign. To keep everything in one diagram, we add the Foreign capital stock to that of Home's to get the total two-nation supply of capital. This is shown as $K_0 + K_0^*$ on the horizontal axis. We also draw the marginal product curve for foreign capital, but we reverse it since we measure the amount of capital employed in Foreign from right-to-left (Home employment of capital is measured from left-to-right). Following the same competitive logic as for Home, we see that the foreign return to capital will be r_0^* since this is the *MPK** where all of the capital is employed in Foreign. (This way of depicting the Home plus Foreign capital stock makes it easy to study partitions of the total between the two nations; each point on the horizontal axis between zero and $K_0 + K_0^*$ shows a different partition.)

Analysis of capital market integration

As the diagram is drawn, capital earns a higher return in Home than it does in Foreign. If we now allow international capital flows and, for the sake of simplicity, assume that such flows are costless, it is clear that capital will leave Foreign and move to Home in search of a higher reward. Such capital flows raise the level of capital employed in Home and lower it in Foreign, thus narrowing the gap between r_0 and r_0^*. Indeed, under our assumption that capital flows are

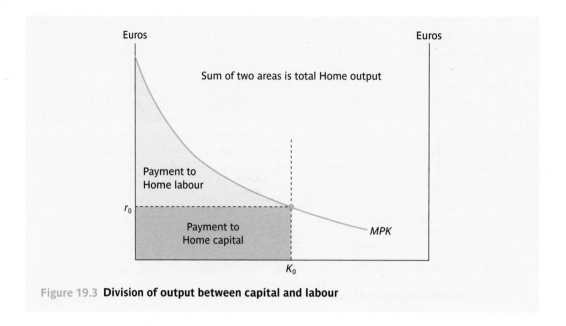

Figure 19.3 **Division of output between capital and labour**

costless, capital moves from Foreign to Home until the returns are equalized. This occurs at point A, where the two MPK curves intersect. The resulting capital flow and the common reward, r', are illustrated in the diagram. Notice that the capital movement has raised the return in the sending nation and lowered it in the receiving nation.

Winners, losers and net welfare effects

Who wins and who loses from this capital movement? What are the overall effects on native workers and capital owners?

To answer these questions, we need to show how one determines the impact of capital movements on the earnings of labour (we have already seen the impact on the reward to capital). Looking at Fig. 19.3, we note that the area under the MPK curve gives total Home output. The reason follows directly from the definition of the marginal product of capital. The first unit of capital employed produces output equal to the height of the MPK curve at the point where $K = 1$. The amount produced by the second unit of capital is given by the level of MPK at the point where $K = 2$, and so on. Adding up all the heights of the MPK curve at each point yields the area under the curve.

The total earnings of Home capital is just the equilibrium reward, r_0, times the amount of capital, K_0. And, since we are assuming that capital and labour are the only two factors of production in this simple world, labour receives all the output that is not paid to capital. Graphically, this means that capital's income is the grey rectangle shown in the diagram, while labour's income is the blue area between the MPK curve and the r_0 line. With this in hand, we turn now to the welfare effects of capital flows.

In our simple, no-capital-mobility-to-free-capital-mobility policy experiment, the 'native' capital owners in Home lose since their reward has fallen from r_0 to r' (see Fig. 19.2). The amount of the loss is measured by the rectangle A in Fig. 19.4 (the A in this diagram is unrelated

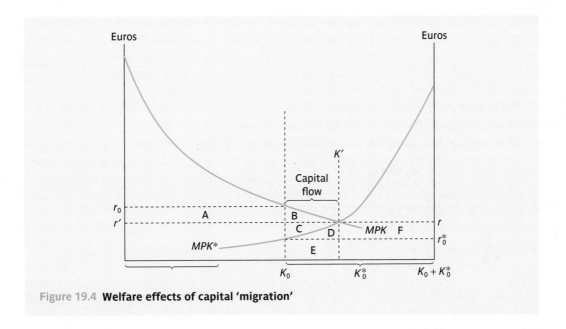

Figure 19.4 **Welfare effects of capital 'migration'**

to the A in Fig. 19.2). Home labour increases its earnings by area A plus the triangle B. Thus the total economic impact on Home citizens is positive and equal to the triangle B. Another way of seeing that Home gains from capital mobility is to note that the extra capital that flows in raises total output in Home by the areas B + C + D + E, but the payments to the new capital only equal the areas C + D + E (i.e. r' times the capital flow).

Correspondingly, Foreign output drops by D + E, while the capital remaining in Foreign sees its reward rise from r_0^* to r'. The size of this gain is shown by rectangle F, which is the change in r times the amount of capital left in Foreign after the integration (this is illustrated by point A). Foreign labour sees its earnings drop by D + F. Combining all these losses and gains, the Foreign factors of production that remain in Foreign lose overall by an amount measured by triangle D. However, if we count the welfare of Foreign factor owners, including the capital that is now working in Home, the conclusion is reversed. Total gains to Foreign capital are C + D + F, while the loss to Foreign labour is D + F. Foreign gains from the capital outflow by an amount equal to the triangle C.

In short, while capital flows create winners and losers in both nations, collectively both nations gain from the movement of capital. The deep reason for this has to do with efficiency. Without capital mobility, the allocation of productive factors was inefficient. For example, on the margin, Foreign capital was producing r^*, while it could have been producing r_0 in Home. The capital flow thus improves the overall efficiency of the EU economy and the gains from this are split between Home and Foreign. Foreign gets area C; Home gets area B.

The result that both countries benefit from capital market integration is the basis for the single market and the Commission directive. It underpins the view that, by further encouraging capital mobility, adoption of the euro will raise economic efficiency and welfare.[5] It is important,

---

[5] It is also the rationale for financial globalization, but that is another story.

however, to remember the assumptions that were made in reaching this result, in particular that the capital market itself is functioning perfectly well. This assumption is not warranted. Section 19.1.3 explains the many specificities of this market, including asymmetric information, which makes it difficult to deal with inherent risk, and network externalities, which skew competition. When the perfect market assumption is removed, the result no longer holds: capital market integration may or may not be beneficial; it all depends on the details of the deviations from perfection and on a host of other features.

Does it mean that capital market integration is a bad idea? Probably not. The presumption is that, as long as competition is strong enough, integration is beneficial. Yet, things can go wrong and this is why the authorities have to be vigilant and, when needed – and only when needed – regulate the markets to ensure that the expected benefits from integration are reaped. This issue is taken up in Section 19.3.4.

19.2.3 Economics of capital mobility: the diversification effect

Section 19.1.3 explains how financial markets facilitate investment by matching borrowers and savers and by pricing risk. Capital market integration (and the exchange rate stability that comes with the euro – see next section) reduce the risk premium and therefore lower the borrowing costs of firms while offering better returns to savers. This makes Europe a better place to invest. In this way, financial market integration can raise the investment rate and growth, as explained in Chapter 7.

Since European integration is rather gradual and since many things affect the risk-adjusted rate of return, it can be difficult to figure out exactly how financial market integration affects the investment climate in Europe as a whole. The same logic, however, applies to individual nations joining the EU. Since the financial markets in some nations – for example, a small nation like Estonia – are relatively undeveloped, getting access to the European financial markets by joining may have a big impact on their risk-adjusted rate of return and thus a big impact on their investment rate.

19.2.4 Effects of the single currency on financial markets

The adoption of the euro eliminates the currency risk within the Eurozone. In principle, therefore, savers do not have to worry about where the asset is issued as long as it is denominated in euros, and borrowers can tap the whole area by taking on euro-denominated debt. There is no longer any reason for financial markets to be Finnish, Greek or German.

A single financial market first means more competition as national currencies that used to act as non-tariff barriers are eliminated.[6] Rents associated with dominating positions should disappear and the need to retain and attract new customers should push financial institutions to constantly improve their performance. A unified financial market should also allow a better exploitation of scale economies, with the emergence of large financial institutions and markets. Table 19.1 shows a ranking by the magazine *The Banker* of the largest banks in the world,

---

[6] Chapter 3 presents non-tariff barriers, i.e. restrictions to trade that are designed to protect local firms by such means as specific regulation, standards, administrative authorizations and controls, etc.

Table 19.1 The top ten commercial banks in 2005 and 2008 (ranked by total assets)

	2005			2008	
Rank	Bank	Country	Rank	Bank	Country
1	UBS	Switzerland	1	Royal Bank of Scotland	UK
2	Citigroup	USA	2	Deutsche Bank	Germany
3	Mizuho	Japan	3	BNP Paribas	France
4	HSBC	UK	4	Barclays Bank	UK
5	Crédit Agricole	France	5	HSBC	UK
6	BNP Paribas	France	6	Crédit Agricole	France
7	JP Morgan Chase	USA	7	Citigroup	USA
8	Deutsche Bank	Germany	8	UBS	Switzerland
9	Royal Bank of Scotland	UK	9	Mitsubichi	Japan
10	Bank of America	USA	10	Bank of America	USA

Source: The Banker, July 2005 and July 2008

according to their total assets. In 2005, there were only three Eurozone banks in the top ten league.[7] In 2008, the situation has not changed much in this respect, although these banks have climbed up the ladder. The 2007–08 crisis has taken its toll of US banks and British banks are, for the time being, the great winners. The situation mirrors the situation of stock markets: Eurozone stock markets (Frankfurt, Paris, Milan, etc.) are small in comparison with Wall Street and the City of London.

One possible negative aspect of the euro, however, is that the potential for diversification shrinks. Before the advent of the euro, a Belgian saver could diversify her portfolio by acquiring German, Italian and other European assets. Now these assets are less diverse as they all share the same currency and as cyclical conditions become more homogeneous (as shown in Chapter 17). To achieve a high degree of diversification, these assets may have to move further, to less well-known parts of the world.[8] All in all, however, the positive effects of scale economies in a wider unified market are likely to outweigh the negative effects of reduced diversification.

Finally, the fact that the US dollar is a world currency gives US citizens and firms some advantages. The potential emergence of the euro as another world currency, and the expected benefits, are examined in Section 19.4.

19.3 Financial institutions and markets

19.3.1 Banking: What is special about banking?

The banking industry is special in three respects. First, banks are naturally fragile, and bank failures can be systemic, as explained in Section 19.3.4 below. As a consequence, banks are

[7] The situation was similar in 2005 and in the first edition of this book in 2002, except that the top ten list included one French and two German banks.

[8] This is not a serious concern. As globalization develops, so do the possibilities of diversification. Over the past few years, Chinese and Indian assets have joined Brazilian and Korean assets in well-diversified portfolios.

highly regulated and supervised. Second, the information asymmetry problem is acute since banks earn profits primarily from their lending activities. Banking does not conform to the perfect market model.

One implication is that long-term relationships are important as they provide banks with track records of their customers and help to build up confidence, breaking somewhat the information asymmetry. The downside is that well-established customers have little incentive to quit their banks. While this attachment alleviates the information asymmetry problem, it also reduces competition.

That aspect is further reinforced by the fact that it is plainly painful to change bank. Many payment orders are automated, some payments and receipts are always under way, and so it is never the right time to shift to another bank. Proximity of the branch also often discourages switching. For these reasons, most banking relationships tend to be long-lasting, much longer than in most other service industries, and competition is less severe.

The starting point

These features explain why banks started to develop at the local level, which allowed them to know their customers reasonably well, thus minimizing information asymmetries. Scale economies next led to a process of growth and mergers as banks sought to become ever bigger, but so far this process has generally taken place within national boundaries. Figure 19.5 shows that the number of banks has declined in the Eurozone recently, and a large part of this decline is explained by mergers and acquisitions. However, Fig. 19.6 indicates that a vast majority (77 per cent for the Eurozone as a whole) of these mergers and acquisitions take place within countries. The figure also reveals that there are big differences across countries. Quite clearly, mergers and acquisitions in the big countries are predominantly conducted internally.

There exists further evidence that the euro has not led banks to operate at the Eurozone level. For instance, loans by Eurozone-based banks to customers located elsewhere in the area remain a small (6 per cent) and unchanged proportion of total bank loans.

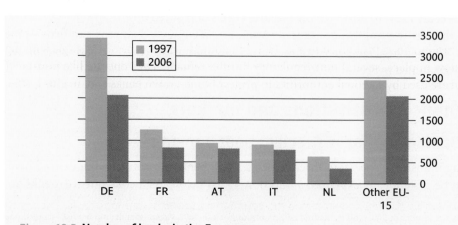

Figure 19.5 Number of banks in the Eurozone
Source: Euro Monitor 4, Deustche Bank Research, 22 April 2008

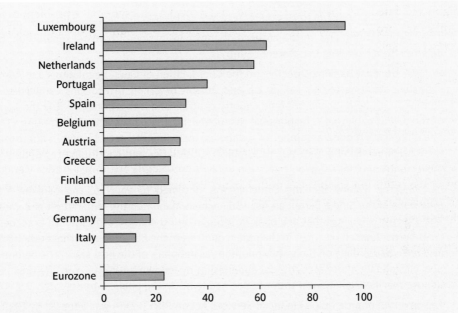

Figure 19.6 Percentage of mergers and acquisitions of EU banks carried out across countries within the Eurozone, 1995–2004
Source: Monthly Bulletin, ECB, May 2005

National or pan-European concentration

The fact that each country had its own currency – the exception being the Belgium–Luxembourg currency union – and that many restrictions to capital movements were in place until the late 1980s, explains why the concentration process initially took place within, and not across, countries. The advent of the euro could change all that, but little has happened so far. Several reasons have been advanced to explain the continuing apparent parochialism of banks in contrast with other industries.

First, local regulations still differ. This has long been recognized and has led to a succession of harmonization efforts, described in Box 19.2. In addition, while in theory a 'single banking market' is now in place, several non-regulatory hurdles remain. They operate like non-tariff barriers and are used by national authorities to protect home-grown banks and, in effect, stifle competition.

Box 19.2   **Harmonization of banking regulation in Europe**

Efforts at building a unified banking market in Europe go far back in history. The main steps are as follows:

★ In 1973, a directive on the Abolition of Restrictions on Freedom of Establishment and Freedom to Provide Services for self-employed Activities of Banks and other Financial Institutions established the principle of national treatment. All banks operating in one country are subject to the same

▶ non-discriminatory regulations and supervision as local banks. Yet, widespread capital controls limited competition and, in the absence of any coordination of banking supervision, banks were deterred from operating in different countries.

★ In 1977, the First Banking Directive on the Coordination of Laws, Regulations and Administrative Provisions Relating to the Taking Up and Pursuit of Credit Institutions established a gradual phasing in of the principle of home country control. Under this principle, it is the home country of the parent bank that is responsible for supervising the bank's activities in other EU countries. The directive left open a number of loopholes, including the need to obtain authorization from the local supervision authorities to establish subsidiaries and continuing restrictions on capital movements.

★ In 1989, the Second Banking Directive was designed to apply to the banking industry the provisions of the Single European Act 1986, which mandated the elimination of capital controls. The directive stipulates that any bank licensed in an EU country can establish branches or supply cross-border financial services in the other countries of the EU without further authorization. It can also open a subsidiary on the same conditions as nationals of the host state. The parent bank must now consolidate all its accounts for supervision by its own authority. Yet, the host country can impose specific regulations if they are deemed to be 'in the public interest'.

★ Facing a lack of progress, a Financial Services Action Plan (FSAP) was adopted in 1999. This plan called for the harmonization of prudential rules, the establishment of a single market in wholesale financial services and efforts to unify the retail market.

★ Limited results led to the adoption in 2001 of the Lamfalussy process.[1] The process involves four steps: (1) the adoption of common core legal values; (2) the adoption of detailed proposals at the national level: (3) the consolidation of these measures at the European level, including the creation of a Committee of European Securities Regulators (CESR), which brings together a newly created regulator, the European Securities Committee (ESC), and the national regulators; (4) enforcement of the agreements by the European Commission.

The 'single banking market' is not limited to the EU members. When the EFTA countries, with the exception of Switzerland, joined the European Economic Area (EEA) in 1992, they accepted the European banking legislation.

[1] Called after Alexander Lamfalussy, former Chairman of the European Monetary Institute (the predecessor of the European Central Bank), in his capacity as Chairman of a Committee of Wise Men.

Second, for several centuries, banks have developed along diverse lines, leading to different traditions in banking. While acquiring a foreign bank could be the easiest way of adjusting to that country's practices, problems with integrating personnel seem to deter mergers and acquisitions.

Third, the tax treatment of savings differs from country to country. Thus the choice of where to bank may be driven by tax purposes rather than by the quality of banking services. Tax evasion may well have become as strong an incentive to scout the European banking scene as the search for better service or risk diversification, thus undermining the very purpose of financial integration. In 2005, a new agreement came into effect to combat tax evasion; all EU-based banks must now report their foreign customers to their tax authorities.

Finally, protectionism is suspected. The fact that mergers and acquisitions in the large countries are predominantly within-borders (see Fig. 19.6) may simply be a size effect, but it

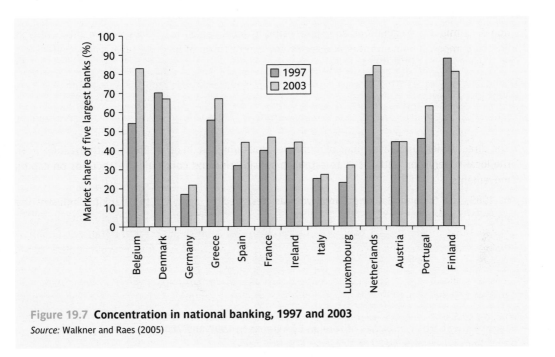

Figure 19.7 **Concentration in national banking, 1997 and 2003**
Source: Walkner and Raes (2005)

may also be the result of protectionism. For instance, in 2005, the Governor of the Bank of Italy was officially warned by the EU Commission not to interfere in attempted purchases of two large Italian banks by a Spanish and a Dutch bank; yet, these attempts failed and the matter has been sent to the courts.

The evidence so far is that, through mergers and acquisitions, banks have been consolidating at the national level. Their strategy seems to be, first, to reach a size that is large enough to enable them to engage in foreign purchases. Meanwhile, as banks merge at the national level, concentration increases (Fig. 19.7), which may result in less, not more, competition. Thus, in contrast with the effects expected from the Single European Act as laid out in Chapter 3, it could be that the early impact of the monetary union is to reduce competition. This could be the perverse effect of combining partial integrative measures with continuing NTB protectionism. There is some recent evidence, though, that competition has not declined. More optimistically, we may just be on the eve of a wave of pan-European mergers and acquisitions that will eventually make the single banking market a reality.

Trade in services

While banks do not consolidate at the pan-European level, they could still offer services across borders. This form of competition is exactly what the Second Banking Directive was meant to promote, and the elimination of exchange risk should reinforce it. They can open new branches and move close to their customers to circumvent the information asymmetry. Figure 19.8 shows the percentage of local branches of banks from the European Economic Area.[9] With few exceptions,

---

[9] The EEA includes the old EU15 member countries as well as Iceland, Liechtenstein and Norway which have accepted the European banking legislation.

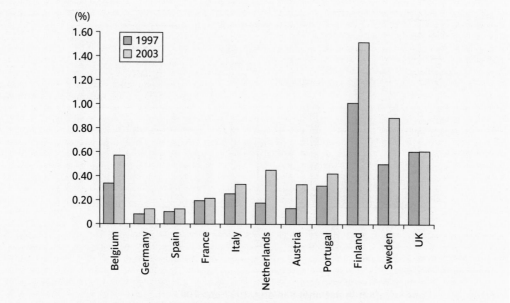

Figure 19.8 Share of branches of foreign EEA banks in 1997 and 2001
Source: Structural Analysis of the EU Banking Sector, ECB, November 2002

there is not yet any sign of a powerful euro effect that would prompt banks to move into other countries. They may expect that it will be very hard to win away customers because of the large fixed costs involved in changing banks. The limited extent of cross-border competition is further confirmed by bank charges for bank transfers from one Eurozone country to another, which have been kept so high (some €17 on average for a €100 transfer in 2000, about ten times the cost of a domestic transfer) that the Commission stepped in and imposed a new regulation which prohibits banks from charging a different fee for within-Eurozone transfers from the one they apply to domestic transfers.

19.3.2 Bond markets

We first look at the market for bonds issued by national governments. Most governments are believed to be highly trustworthy, financially at least. This is why interest rates on public debts are often considered risk-free and therefore directly comparable, without having to adjust for risk.

Figure 19.9 shows the evolution of interest rates on government short-term bonds. For decades, interest was lowest on German bonds. Since the other currencies were perceived as being weaker than the Deutschmark, other governments had to pay higher rates to compensate for currency risk.[10] This is called the currency risk. As the date of launching the single currency drew nearer and more certain, the currency risk declined and gradually became irrelevant. The

---

[10] This is the interest parity principle, which is presented in Chapter 9. It can be stated as: Interest rate in Italy − Interest rate in Germany = Expected depreciation of the lira vis-à-vis the Deutschmark.

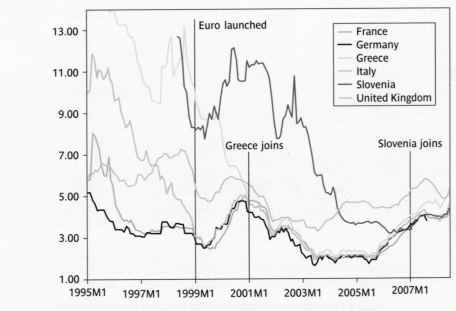

Figure 19.9 Interbank (3 month) interest rates, January 1995–June 2008
Note: For Greece, 12-month interest rate.
Source: IMF

figure shows an impressive convergence of the French and Italian rates towards the German level by January 1999. The convergence becomes complete as time passes, an indication that the short-term compartment of the bond market is fully integrated. Note the evolution of the Greek interest rate since Greece joined the Eurozone in January 2001; this is when convergence occurs. Much the same happens in the case of Slovenia. It is also interesting to observe that the UK rate does not converge since the UK has decided not to adopt the euro.

The long-term compartment of the bond market is examined in Fig. 19.10. The picture is broadly similar, with two differences. The convergence occurs earlier, before the launch of the euro. This is logical. Long-term rates can be seen as the average of current and future short-term rates, all the way to maturity. If markets expect the short-term rates to converge in the future, the weight of the not-yet-converged short-term rates declines as time passes by. The early convergence therefore reveals that the financial markets have been convinced ahead of time that the monetary union would start as planned. Yet a keen eye will detect that convergence is not complete. This may reflect differences in the perceived quality of governments as borrowers,[11] or less than full integration because of remaining institutional differences in this market segment. Most observers conclude that full integration has been achieved on the interbank market, not on the government bond market, and much less on the market for private bonds issued by large corporations.

---

[11] This could reflect different public debt size or varying degrees of compliance with the Stability and Growth Pact (Chapter 18). The fact that interest rates on the German debt remain the lowest while Germany's deficit is excessive suggests that this is not the explanation.

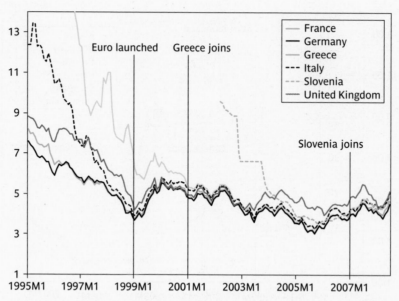

Figure 19.10 Interest rates on long-term government bonds, January 1995–June 2008
Source: IMF

19.3.3 Stock markets

The stock market is where large – and some medium-sized – firms raise the financial resources that they need to acquire capital and generally develop their activities. They issue shares which are held by individuals or by large institutional investors, such as pension funds and insurance companies. Increasingly, individuals buy shares from collective funds designed to offer good risk–return trade-offs through extensive diversification, as explained in Section 19.1.2. Yet, for all the hype about globalization, it is striking that stock markets are characterized by a strong home bias: borrowers and savers alike tend to deal mostly on domestic markets and to hold domestic assets.

One reason for the home bias is information asymmetry: investors know more about domestic firms. This is unlikely to change. Another reason is currency risk. This obstacle to capital mobility has been eliminated within the Eurozone, so we would expect less of a home bias. Is it happening? Apparently, yes. The continuous line in Fig. 19.11 shows that the proportion of assets held by Eurozone-based investing funds that report pursuing a Europe-wide strategy has sharply increased following the adoption of the euro in 1999. Could it just be part of the globalization trend? The dotted line, which shows the proportion of the same funds that have followed worldwide investment strategy, confirms the plausibility of a euro effect.

Another piece of evidence is provided by the evolution of stock exchanges, the marketplace where shares are traded. Most European countries long had one stock exchange, or more. This was natural when currency risk was segmenting the various national markets. Will things change with the advent of the euro? In the USA, which is similar to the Eurozone in economic and geographic size, there are 15 stock exchanges, but only two or three significant ones, all

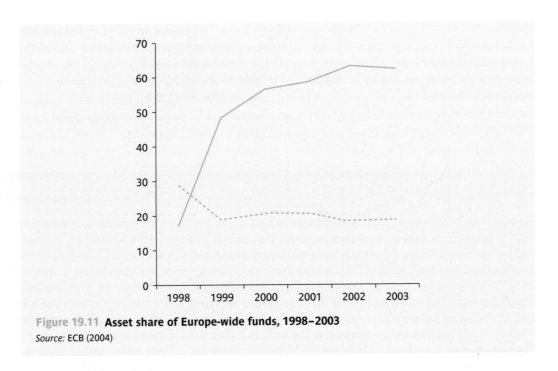

Figure 19.11 **Asset share of Europe-wide funds, 1998–2003**
Source: ECB (2004)

dominated by the New York Stock Exchange (NYSE). Because stock exchanges display strong scale economies, the perception is that the Eurozone is evolving in this direction, towards one major centre and a handful of secondary exchanges. The question is where will they be? Each country seems to be keen to retain its stock exchange, for reasons of prestige and because it can be a major activity.

Table 19.2 displays the sizes of the European exchanges as well as those of the NYSE and Tokyo, measured by market capitalization, i.e. the total valuation of all the firms listed on the exchange. In comparison with the NYSE, European exchanges remain small, and therefore likely to suffer from limited scale economies. London dominates, and seems to have taken advantage of the creation of the euro by attracting many corporations from the Eurozone. For

Table 19.2 Size of stock markets (total capitalization), June 2005

Exchange	€ bn	% GDP	Exchange	€ bn	% GDP	Exchange	€ bn	% GDP
New York	10 729	112.7	OMX	593	90.6	Luxembourg	40	145.3
Tokyo	2 850	76.5	Milan	592	42.0	Budapest	26	28.8
London	2 284	131.3	Oslo	134	58.9	Prague	25	27.4
Euronext	1 910	78.0	Athens	100	57.5	Cyprus	4	35.7
Frankfurt	936	42.1	Vienna	93	37.9	Bratislava	4	11.3
Madrid	769	91.8	Dublin	89	55.7	Malta	2	56.7
Zurich	667	221.5	Warsaw	57	25.7			

Note: Euronext is Paris, Brussels and Amsterdam; OMX is Copenhagen, Helsinki, Stockholm, Tallinn, Riga and Vilnius.
Source: European centres: Federation of European Securities Exchanges; New York and Tokyo: NYSE; GDP estimates from *Economic Outlook*, OECD and IMF

a while it was thought that Frankfurt would benefit from the location of the ECB, but this has not happened. In fact, London and Frankfurt tried to merge in 1998, but this attempt failed for reasons explained in Box 19.3. In order to challenge both London and Frankfurt, a number of exchanges have merged. Euronext was created in 2000 by the exchanges of Paris, Brussels and Amsterdam, keeping physical operations in each city. In 2003, Stockholm and Helsinki merged into OMX, which has since linked up with Copenhagen and the Baltic States (Riga, Tallinn and Vilnius), also keeping physical operations in each of these cities. The process of consolidation is slowly under way.

Box 19.3 Consolidation of stock markets

Some consolidation is taking place among traditional stock markets. The most noticeable example has been the creation of Euronext in September 2000, the result of a merger of the Amsterdam, Brussels and Paris stock exchanges. Euronext is subject to Dutch legislation and has a subsidiary in each of the participating countries. Each subsidiary holds a local stock market licence that gives access to trading in all the participating countries. Euronext achieved consistency in some, but not all, of the institutional characteristics of its predecessor markets. Single quotation and a common order book are guaranteed, as well as price dissemination systems, a unified trading platform and one clearing and settlement system, Euroclear. Nevertheless, the local markets are not legally merged, which implies, for example, that the regulatory body in each of the participating countries retains its prerogatives. From the beginning, Euronext was not intended to be a closed structure and was eager to finalize agreements with other stock exchanges. In 2001, this resulted in the acquisition of Liffe, the London derivatives trading platform, and the agreement to integrate also the Portuguese exchanges of Lisbon and Porto.

Before Euronext, another, even larger merger between stock exchanges was tried. In 1998, the Deutsche Börse (DB) and the London Stock Exchange (LSE) were planning to merge in an attempt to gain a leadership position in Europe. The creation of iX ('international Exchange') was officially announced on May 2000. The DB and the LSE planned to participate in equal measure as shareholders of the new exchange, which would be subject to British legislation. It was envisaged to quote the 'blue chips' of both exchanges in London and the technology stocks in Frankfurt. The trading system would have been the German one (Xetra), considered to be the more modern and reliable. While the negotiations between the two stock exchanges were still in process, the OM Gruppen, owner of the Stockholm stock exchange, made an unexpected public offer and tried to take over the LSE. This event critically affected the projected merger between DB and LSE, which was subsequently rejected by the LSE board.

Several reasons led to the failure of the merger. In general, there were some doubts that the merger would create value added and would consistently exploit economies of scale. First, contrary to Euronext, where companies belonging to the same sector retained the freedom to choose the location of their listing, iX required the 'blue chips' to be traded in London and the technology stocks in Frankfurt. This solution would have implied costs for both exchanges. Second, some of the companies would have had to move from one exchange to the other and deal with the change in regulations and supervisory authorities. Finally, the new entity did not include the creation of a common clearing and settlement system, hence it would have failed to provide lower settlement costs.

In 2005, there were again rumours of a possible purchase of the LSE by DB.

Source: Adapted from Hartmann et al. (2003)

19.3.4 Regulation and supervision

The rationale

Section 19.1 identified a number of characteristics specific to financial markets: these markets display important scale economies, they operate as networks and they suffer from information asymmetries. These characteristics imply that financial markets suffer from 'market failures', i.e. deviations from the textbook description of perfect markets. In the presence of failures, markets may malfunction, which justifies interventions by the authorities. Indeed, in every country, financial markets are regulated and the financial institutions are closely supervised.

The presence of scale economies implies that a few large firms eventually dominate the market. The tendency for competition to become monopolistic challenges the perfect competition assumption.[12] It also means that financial markets are vulnerable to difficulties suffered by one or two of these important players. This vulnerability is sharpened by the two other characteristics. The network feature means that all large financial institutions are continuously dealing with each other, and routinely borrowing and lending huge amounts among each other. If one of these institutions fails, all the others may be pulled down. Failures tend to be systemic.

The third characteristic, the presence of information asymmetries, means that all financial firms routinely take risks. Every asset represents the right to receive payments in the future, be it 24 hours or 15 years. It is trivial to observe that the future is unknown, but this feature has deep implications for financial markets. Today's value of an asset represents the best collective judgement by financial market participants of the likely payments that the asset holder may expect to receive upon maturity. But one thing is sure: the future will differ from today's expectations. The asset may yield better returns than expected, but can also be revealed as catastrophic and its value can deeply deteriorate. When this happens, asset holders see their wealth decline, and the decline is typically sudden. This is why financial systems are inherently fragile and prone to panics and crises.

As the financial institutions are central to modern economies, systemic failures immediately provoke severe disruptions that leave no firm or citizen unharmed. When declines in asset values are widespread, those who hold large amounts of assets can become insolvent. Many financial institutions (banks, pension funds, insurance companies) that hold large amounts of assets may then fail, spreading the hardship to the whole economy as numerous examples – from the Wall Street crashes of 1929 and 2007–08 to Korea in 1998 or Argentina in 2002 – remind us.

Regulation and supervision

To reduce the incidence of such catastrophic events, and possibly even eliminate them, financial institutions are regulated. Over the years, regulation has changed and become more sophisticated. The general thrust is to ensure that financial institutions adopt prudent strategies. This is done by requiring them to hold enough high-quality assets, for example bonds issued by respectable governments or by solid corporations.

Regulation, in turn, requires supervision. It is not enough to pass down good rules; it is essential to make sure that they are respected. Since financial conditions can quickly deteriorate,

---

[12] As explained in Chapter 6, monopolistic competition describes the situation where a small number of large firms dominate the market.

supervision must be continuous. Given the complexity of modern finance, and the possibility of hiding emerging problems, supervisors must be as sophisticated as the financiers themselves, and they need to exercise their duties with great diligence and firmness.

Adapting regulation and supervision to the single currency

Regulation – the establishment of rules – is largely designed at the EU level[13] whereas supervision – the implementation and enforcement of regulation – continues to be carried out at the national level. This assignment of tasks is understandable. The EU's central aim is often described as 'the four freedoms': free mobility of goods, services, assets and people. For financial services to move freely, financial institutions need to be allowed to operate throughout the EU if they so wish. If national regulations differed, financial institutions would have to register in each and every country where they wished to operate. This would greatly hamper the mobility of financial services. Savers, unsure about the quality of foreign regulations, would prefer to keep their money at home.

What about supervision? One argument for keeping supervision at the national level is the existence of another kind of information asymmetry, this time between supervisor and supervisee. Obviously each financial firm knows more about its business, and the risks that it is taking, than its supervisor. Quite likely, most firms wish to hide their difficulties, especially if their disclosure would lead to fines or outright closure. It is argued that these information asymmetries are lower at the national than at the union level. National supervisors know their financial institutions well, and over the years have developed a relationship that allows for a smooth process. Another argument is subsidiarity: unless proved impossible or inefficient, supervision should remain at the national level.

National supervisors differ in important ways. Their legal briefs vary and their level of expertise is not uniform. This can be problematic if and when financial crises suddenly occur, because, at that stage, in an effort to stunt systemic effects, prompt reaction is of the essence. The authorities must decide whether to bail out – at taxpayers' expense – failing institutions or let them fail. Given the networking among financial institutions, the bailout decision is unlikely to concern a single country.[14] A proper reaction therefore calls for instantaneous and extensive sharing of information, based on an intimate knowledge of the institutions and their managers.

The current solution relies on cooperation among national supervisors, but there is no presumption that all can be told quickly enough. More ominously, national supervisors may be sensitive to the interests of their national financial institutions and wish to protect them. Proximity may reduce information asymmetries but it can also nurture nationalistic senti-ments. If that is the case, cooperation is unlikely to develop into a fully trusted partnership. Finally, the national agencies in charge of supervision have an obvious interest in not being closed down. Some of them are actually part of the national central banks which have already lost their monetary policy-making role and are highly reluctant to be deprived of their last important function, supervision.

---

[13] More precisely, EU-level regulation sets minimum standards, leaving individual countries free to establish more stringent – but not more lenient – rules. Within this principle, national-level rules are subject to the principle of mutual recognition, i.e. foreign rules are recognized as substitutes for domestic ones.

[14] Small banks are typically not operating internationally, so the problem concerns larger banks, precisely those that are important for systemic contagion.

National resistance to establish a single European supervisor has been effective. After all, this is also about jobs in Amsterdam, Helsinki and Madrid, and old, possibly cosy, links between supervisors and supervisees. The Second Edition of this text included the following: 'so far, in the absence of any major shake-up, it is impossible to prove that national-level supervision is inadequate. Yet most observers believe that this is the case and that the true reason for retaining national-level supervision is a lack of interest.' The crisis of 2007–08 has brutally shown how important this issue really is.

19.3.5 Channels of monetary policy

The link between a financial system and monetary policy is tight. Monetary conditions deeply affect the daily functioning of financial markets. Financial systems cannot blossom unless the currency is reasonably stable and monetary policy cannot operate without a well-functioning financial market. Because most of what we call money is in the form of bank deposits, the good functioning of the banking and financial systems is crucial to the trust that underwrites any money. This is one reason why central banks have a direct interest in the quality of the financial system.

Another reason is that monetary policy decisions are transmitted via financial markets through the availability and cost of credit. The financial system is the channel through which monetary policy affects the economy, its growth and its inflation rates. The fact that the euro is the currency of different countries, each with its own financial system, creates a novel situation.

The main question is whether a given policy decision can have different and unwanted effects in different countries. There are many reasons why this can be the case:

★ The ECB sets the short-term interest rate (EONIA), as described in Chapter 17. In most countries, loans depend on longer-term interest rates, which typically move less than short-term rates and whose movements depend on the reaction of the financial market. In these countries, the effect of central bank actions is both muted and somewhat uncertain. In some countries, however, the interest rate that applies to loans is indexed on the short-term rate and central bank actions have a stronger impact.

★ The effect of the interest rate largely depends on the importance of bank credit. In some countries, bank credit is the main source of financing for most firms and households, but in other countries, firms make more important use of stock markets. Monetary policy will have a more direct effect in the first group of countries than in the latter, where the evolution of share prices will become an important, yet uncertain, channel.

★ Monetary policy also operates through the exchange rate. With a common exchange rate, those countries that have a higher share of external trade with the non-Eurozone countries stand to be more strongly affected.

EMU countries differ on all these dimensions, which raises the possibility that monetary policy could be a source of asymmetric shocks, precisely what the OCA theory suggests is the main drawback of a monetary union (see Chapter 11). Whether all these differences add up to a serious problem, however, is another question, so far with no clear answer. A further issue is whether, over time, the existing structural differences will fade away. Early indications are that it is the case.

19.4 The international role of the euro

The classic attributes of money apply to its international role. Externally, a currency can be a medium of exchange used for international trade, a unit of account used to price other currencies or widely traded commodities, and a store of value used by foreign individuals and authorities. Domestically, these attributes are underpinned by the legal status of money; internationally, they have to be earned.

In the nineteenth century, sterling was the undisputed international currency. It was displaced by the US dollar in the twentieth century. Clearly, only large economies can expect their currency to achieve an international status, a condition that the Eurozone fulfils. Currently, some 320 million people live in the Eurozone, and new membership could eventually bring this number to 470 million, to be compared with 280 million people living in the USA. The EU's GDP is 75 per cent of that of the USA. Another condition is that the currency must be stable. The Eurosystem's commitment to price stability further suggests that, eventually, the euro can aspire to having a large international role. Will it, and if so, when? Would it be a good thing? These are the issues that we consider in this final section.

19.4.1 Medium of exchange: trade invoicing

Whenever an export takes place, there must be an agreement on the currency that will be used to set the price and then carry out the payment. Will it be the exporter's, the importer's or a third currency? Each side of the trade would rather use its own currency to avoid exchange costs and uncertainty. In that sense, the Eurozone stands to benefit from a wider acceptability of its currency.

There is some evidence that European firms are increasingly able to invoice trade in euros, as shown in Fig. 19.12. Yet the bulk of primary commodities (oil, gas, raw materials) are priced in

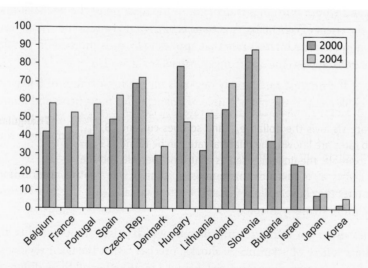

Figure 19.12 Share of exports invoiced in euros (% of total exports)
Notes: For European countries: exports outside the Eurozone. For France, Japan and Korea: 2003 instead of 2004.
Source: Kamps (2006)

US dollars in specialized markets, and this is unlikely to change in the foreseeable future. Even if European firms can now more often avoid exposure to currency risk by using the euro, the dollar is and will remain the currency of choice among countries which are in neither the USA nor the euro currency areas. The exception seems to be countries on the periphery of the EU, mostly those in Europe that will join the EU in the coming years.

19.4.2 Unit of account: vehicle currencies on foreign exchange markets

The foreign exchange market is a network of financial institutions that trade currencies among themselves. This is a huge market where, on any average day, some US$ 3000 billion worth of exchanges take place (this amounts to almost a quarter of US GDP). Most of the world currencies are not really traded, as explained in Box 19.4. The bulk of transactions involve a vehicle currency. Table 19.3 reports the percentage of trades that involve, on one side or another, the three main world currencies (the sum for all currencies would be 200 per cent since each transaction involves a pair of currencies). The share of the euro in 2001 is much smaller than the sum of the shares of its constituent currencies. This simply reflects the elimination of exchange rate transactions among the currencies that joined the Eurozone. Overall, the table reveals considerable stability. The pre-eminence of the dollar remains unchallenged.

Box 19.4   Vehicle currencies

Each transaction must involve two currencies. Since there exist more than 180 currencies in the world, there are about 16 000 bilateral exchange rates.[1] If all these bilateral rates were traded, most of them (think of the exchange rate between the Samoan tala and the Honduran lempira) would involve very few trades, resulting in a host of shallow, hence inefficient and volatile, markets. This is why foreign exchange markets use the property of triangular arbitrage to considerably reduce the number of currency pairs that are traded.

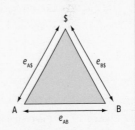

Figure 19.13
Triangular arbitrage

The idea is simple and illustrated in Fig. 19.13. Consider two currencies, A and B, and their bilateral exchange rate, e_{AB}. Currency A has an exchange rate vis-à-vis the dollar, $e_{A\$}$, and so does currency B, $e_{B\$}$. Once these two rates are known, the bilateral rate can be found as $e_{AB} = e_{A\$}/e_{B\$}$. In this example, the dollar is used as a currency vehicle and the implied bilateral rate e_{AB} is called a cross-rate. In practice, cross-rates are rarely traded and very few currencies are internationally used.

[1] With n currencies, there exist $n(n-1)/2$ bilateral exchange rates. Here, $16\,110 = (180 \times 179)/2$.

19.4.3 Store of value: bond markets

Large firms and governments borrow on the international markets by issuing long-term debt, bonds. This is an enormous market. Figure 19.14 shows that the share of bonds issued in euros

Table 19.3 **Currency composition of exchange trading volume (%)**

	US dollar	Euro	Yen	Deutschmark	French franc	ECU and other ERM currencies	Pound sterling	Swiss franc
1992	82		23.4	39.6	3.8	11.8	13.6	8.4
1998	87.3		20.2	30.1	5.1	17.3	11.0	7.1
2007	86.3	37.6	22.7				16.5	6.8

Note: If all currencies were listed, the sum would be 200 per cent since each exchange involves two currencies.
Source: Triennial Central Bank Surveys, BIS

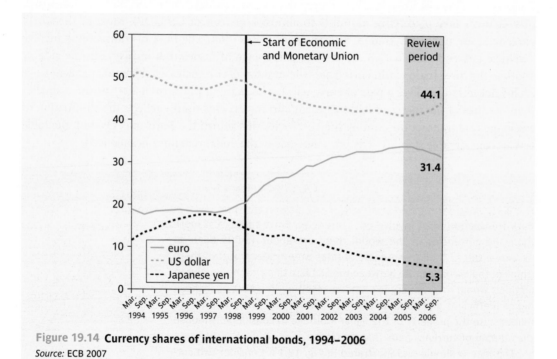

Figure 19.14 **Currency shares of international bonds, 1994–2006**
Source: ECB 2007

has taken off following the launch of the euro. This is not very surprising when we look at Figs 19.9 and 19.10. The national bond markets have been promptly unified into a single euro market whose depth does not differ markedly from that of the dollar bond market. As a result, Europe can now claim its fair share of the market, and is increasingly doing so. Interestingly, the City of London has become the leading marketplace for this instrument whereas New York seems disinterested.

19.4.4 Store of value: international reserves

All national central banks hold foreign exchange reserves to underpin trust in their currencies and, if need be, to intervene on foreign exchange markets. Currencies appropriate for this

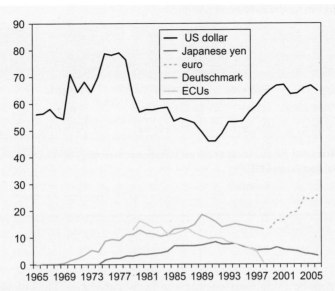

Figure 19.15 Foreign exchange reserves: shares of main currencies (1965–2007)
Source: Chinn and Frankel (2005) and ECB (2007)

role as a store of value must be widely traded and be perceived as having long-term stability. Figure 19.15 shows that the euro has made some progress since its creation, but the dollar seems firmly entrenched as the leading currency.

European countries at the periphery of the Eurozone (including the UK) are gradually replacing dollars with euros. A number of developing countries have also announced their intention to do so, largely for political reasons. Recently, various Asian authorities, who accumulated vast reserves in dollars, have signalled that they could be diversifying into the euro. This would be an important step.

Why should the euro eat into the dollar's market share? Besides politics, central banks are traditionally unwilling to change the currency composition of their reserves. In particular, large-scale sales of dollars could precipitate a depreciation of the US currency with two adverse effects: the depreciation would alter international competition in trade and it would create losses for dollar-holders, including for the central banks themselves. This is why, even if the euro may be an attractive store of value, a major shift would require a serious deterioration in the dollar's own quality as a store of value. For example, Fig. 19.15 shows that the dollar's share dropped in the late 1970s when inflation rose in the USA. It may be that the financial crisis that originated in 2007 in the USA will eventually dent the dollar's supremacy.

19.4.5 The euro as an anchor

When a country does not let its exchange rate float freely, it must adopt an anchor, a foreign currency to which its own currency is more or less rigidly tied. The anchor, which works as

Table 19.4 Countries using the euro as an anchor

ERM 2	Peg to euro	Peg to basket incuding the euro	Managed floating with euro as reference currency	Euro-based currency boards	Unilateral euroization
Denmark	Hungary	Botswana	Croatia	Bulgaria	Kosovo
Estonia	CFA Franc Zone	Lybia	Czech Rep.	Estonia	Montenegro
Latvia	Cape Verde	Morocco	Macedonia	Lithuania	Micro-states
Lithuania	Comoros	Russia	Romania	Bosnia-Herzegovina	
		Seychelles	Serbia		
		Tunisia			
		Vanuatu			

Note: The micro-states are: Republic of San Marino, Vatican City, Principality of Monaco, Andorra.
Source: ECB 2007.

a unit of account, can be a single currency or a basket of currencies. The link can be deliberately vague – known as a managed float – or quite explicit, ranging from wide crawling bands to the wholesale adoption of a foreign currency (for details, see Chapter 10).

In 2007, out of some 100 currencies not classified as freely floating, 18 used the euro as an anchor in one way or another. Adding the countries of French-speaking countries that form their own currency unions and countries that use as anchor currency baskets that include the euro, a total of some 40 countries use the euro one way or another when they set their exchange rate policies. The situation is presented in Table 19.4. Most of the countries listed in the table are geographically close to the Eurozone (central and eastern Europe, northern Africa) or have historical ties to one of its constituent legacy currencies (e.g. French-speaking Africa). Two former members of the Yugoslav Federation, Kosovo and Montenegro, have 'euroized', i.e. they have unilaterally adopted the euro as their own currency but are not part of the Eurosystem. Four countries operate a currency board tied to the euro, including two Baltic States (Estonia and Latvia) that are ERM members.

19.4.6 Parallel currencies

Foreign currencies are also sometimes used alongside the domestic currency, fulfilling all three functions of means of payment, unit of account and store of value. Parallel currencies, as the phenomenon is called, emerge in troubled countries where the value of domestic currency is eroded by very rapid inflation or political instability. In most cases, the parallel currency circulates in cash form, but a number of countries also allow bank deposits.

The dollar is the universal parallel currency of choice, but the Deutschmark used to be used in central and eastern Europe and in Turkey, and the French franc used to circulate widely in northern Africa and parts of sub-Saharan Africa. In all these countries the euro has replaced the Deutschmark and the franc. The problem with the use of parallel currencies is that little is known about it, if only because this is highly informal and not captured by official statistics. Box 19.5 discusses some indirect evidence.

19.4.7 Does it matter?

In the minds of some Europeans, launching the euro also means challenging the supremacy of the dollar. Indeed, the dollar reigns supreme: it is the currency of choice for international trade; it is the first foreign currency that is held by individuals, corporations and central banks; and it is also the currency most widely used to denominate financial assets. The wish to displace the dollar is no doubt driven by political sentiment, but what about the economic advantages?

Box 19.5   Some indirect evidence of the use of the euro as parallel currency

The parallel use of a currency takes place abroad, by definition, and is not tracked down by foreign authorities. Any attempt to measure the phenomenon starts with asking whether there are 'too many' banknotes floating around. Central banks know very precisely how much currency is in circulation, but they are at a loss to define what a 'normal' level is. Figure 19.16 shows the amount of currency in circulation in the Eurozone after 2003 (when banknotes and coins were introduced), and in the EU12 countries beforehand. Based on previous trends, there is a clear indication that after a dip associated with the changeover, currency in circulation has increased at a very fast clip. The ECB estimates that some 100 billions of euros are circulating outside the Eurozone. As a comparison, the Federal Reserve estimates that 450 billions of dollars are circulating outside the USA.

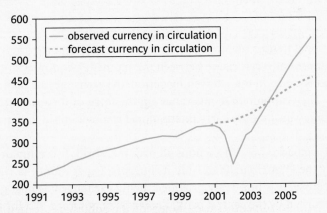

Figure 19.16 Currency in circulation (billions of euros)
Source: ECB (2007)

Another 'parallel' use of banknotes concerns illegal activities, both within and outside the country. A distinguishing feature of euros is that they exist in very large denominations, which makes it easy to pack vast amounts of money in a small suitcase. Figure 19.17 shows the use of available denominations of euros and dollars. The banknote of choice in the Eurozone (e.g. in ATMs) is the €50 denomination, larger than the $20 denomination that dominates in the USA. The figure also shows that large denominations represent a large share of total currency denomination in both the Eurozone and the USA.

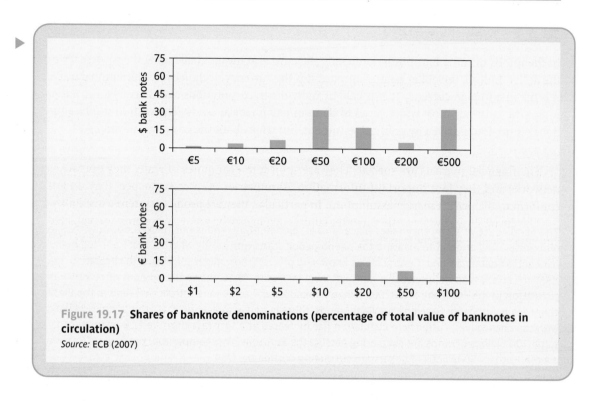

Figure 19.17 Shares of banknote denominations (percentage of total value of banknotes in circulation)
Source: ECB (2007)

When international trade is invoiced in a foreign currency, importers and exporters face an exchange risk. Many months can elapse between the moment a commercial contract is undertaken and payment is made. In the intervening period, the exchange rate may change, imposing a risk on traders. They can purchase insurance (in the form of forward exchange contracts), but at cost. US firms, which mostly carry international transactions in dollars, thus enjoy some advantage.

In addition, 'greenbacks' are conspicuous all over the world. It is estimated that half of the dollars printed by the USA circulate outside its borders. Paper money is virtually costless to produce but, of course, it is not freely provided, being exchanged against goods, services or assets. The profit earned by the central bank, known as seigniorage, is a form of tax. When it is levied on residents, it is just one form of domestic taxation, but when levied on foreigners, it represents a real transfer of resources. The value of expatriate dollars is about 3 per cent of the US GDP – a nice sum. However, once we realize that it has been accumulated over several decades, it is not really a significant source of revenue.

All in all, the economic benefits of having a world currency are quite modest. This explains why the ECB considers that a possible international role for the euro is something that it should neither encourage nor discourage. Beyond some legitimate pride, it does not really care.

19.5 Summary

Financial markets allow savers and borrowers to 'meet' to their mutual benefit. They also set a price on risk and offer ways to reduce exposure to risk via diversification. The presumption is that market integration improves the allocation of saving and borrowing, thus raising the overall economic performance. Not all factors of production benefit from capital market integration, however.

The financial markets are special. They are subject to economies of scale, they operate as networks and they face important information asymmetries. As a consequence, they do not conform to the perfect market assumption. In particular, they are prone to systemic instability.

This instability, as well as other market failures, explains why financial systems are regulated and supervised. For the most part, regulation has been fully harmonized throughout the EU but supervision remains at the national level. This is unlikely to be a lasting solution, but further centralization faces stiff opposition.

Banks share these characteristics, which explains why competition does not take the form implied by the perfect market assumption. In particular, large switching costs and information asymmetries explain why the adoption of the euro has not been followed by a deep restructuring of the banking industry. So far, bank mergers and acquisitions have occurred mostly at the national level; only a few banks have succeeded in expanding across borders. Differences in national regulations and some degree of protectionism on the part of supervisors also seem to limit changes. Plans have been drawn up to break this log-jam.

The effects of the launch of the euro are still under way, and depend on which market segment is considered. Bond markets have been promptly unified. Stock markets, on the other hand, remain small. Some consolidation is taking place, but the largest European exchanges, including Europe's largest – London – remain undersized relative to New York or Tokyo.

The euro has the potential for challenging the US dollar as an international currency, but old habits die hard and, despite some changes, the dollar's supremacy has not been seriously dented. The euro has made some progress in trade invoicing and bond issuance. At the periphery of the Eurozone, it plays a dominant role as anchor for local currencies and, possibly, parallel currency.

Self-assessment questions

1. What is depth in financial markets? What is breadth? What are network externalities?

2. What is the phenomenon of information asymmetry? How can it explain why banks refuse credit to some customers? How can it contribute to systemic risk in financial markets?

3. List the reasons why banks are subject to increasing returns to scale. Why do fixed switching costs matter for competition among banks?

4. How do we know that bond markets have been unified in the Eurozone upon the launch of the euro? Why has this not happened for stock markets?

5. Explain how the three functions of money apply at the international level.

6. What is the phenomenon of gambling for resurrection? Why can it be lethal to financial markets?

7. What is the difference between regulation and supervision? What are the dangers of decentralized supervision in the Eurozone? Why is centralization resisted?

8. What is the difference between a parallel and a vehicle currency?

Essay questions

1. Banks can expand through either organic growth (winning new customers) or mergers and acquisitions. How does this distinction matter for the single European banking market?

2. 'The real reason why Eurozone countries can't agree on a single supervising agency is that each one wants to protect its own financial institutions.' Evaluate this view.

3. 'The Great Crisis of 2007–08 has exposed the high degree of coordination of central banks and the division of governments.' Evaluate and comment.

4. In which ways can the existence of different national financial systems complicate monetary policy in the Eurozone? What kinds of measures could help the ECB?

5. The largest dollar banknote denomination is $100, the largest euro denomination is €500. This has led some to suspect that Europe wants to capture the market of currencies used for illegal transactions. What is your view of this motive?

6. Comment on the quote from Rudi Dornbusch at the head of this chapter.

7. Finance is a major industry in the UK, accounting for some 5 per cent of its GDP. Does this characteristic make membership of the Eurozone rather more or rather less appealing?

8. 'Will the euro displace the dollar as the world's leading currency over the next twenty years? Nah, the Chinese currency (the yuan) will.' Comment.

Further reading: the aficionado's corner

Baltzer, M., L. Cappiello, R. De Santis and S. Manganelli (2008) *Measuring Financial Integration in New EU Member States*, Occasional Paper No. 81, ECB.

Bush, C. and G. DeLong (2003) 'Determinants of crossborder bank mergers: is Europe different?', in H. Herrmann and R.E. Lipsey (eds) *Foreign Direct Investment in the Real and Financial Sector of Industrial Countries*, Springer Verlag, New York.

Gaspar, V. and P. Hartmann (2005) 'The Euro and money markets: lessons for European financial integration', in A. Posen (ed.) *The Euro at Five: Ready for a Global Role?*, Institute for International Economics, Washington, DC.

Kazarian, E. (2006) *Integration of the Securities Market Infrastructure in the European Union: Policy and Regulatory Issues*, Working Paper 241, International Monetary Fund.

Coeurdacier, N. and P. Martin (2007) *The Geography of Asset Trade and the Euro: Insiders and Outsiders*, Discussion Paper No. 6032, CEPR, London.

The Lamfalussy Report (a 2001 report on measures to take to support further integration of European financial markets). Download from http://europa.eu.int/comm/internal_market/en/finances/general/lamfalussyen.pdf.

Schildbach, J. (2008) 'European banks: the silent (re)volution', EU Monitor 4, Deustche Bank Research. Download from www.dbresearch.com/PROD/DBR_INTERNET_EN-PROD/PROD0000000000224371.pdf.

Walkner, C. and J.P. Raes (2005) 'Integration and consolidation in EU banking – an unfinished business', Economic Papers 226, *European Economy*. Download from http://europa.eu.int/comm/economy_finance/publications/economic_papers/2005/ecp226en.pdf.

On the international role of the euro, see:

Chinn, M. and J. Frankel (2005) *Will the Euro Eventually Surpass the Dollar as Leading International Reserve Currency?*, NBER Working Paper 11510. Download from www.nber.org/papers/w11510.

Lim, E.-G. (2006) *The Euro's Challenge to the Dollar: Different Views from Economists and Evidence from COFER (Currency Composition of Foreign Exchange Reserves) and Other Data*, Working Paper 06/153, International Monetary Fund.

Portes, R. (2008) 'The international role of the euro: a status report', *European Economy Economic Papers* 317, European Commission.

Useful websites

Websites concerned with regulation and supervision:

The Basel Committee on Banking Supervision: www.bis.org/bcbs/aboutbcbs.htm.

Financial Stability Institute (FSI): www.bis.org/fsi/index.htm.

The ECB–CFS research network: www.eu-financialsystem.org.

The Financial Services Action Plan website, full of reports and legal texts: http://europa.eu.int/comm/internal_market/en/finances/actionplan/.

References

Chinn, M. and J. Frankel (2005) *Will the Euro Eventually Surpass the Dollar as Leading International Reserve Currency?*, NBER Working Paper 11510. Download from www.nber.org/papers/w11510.

Dornbusch, R. (2000) *Keys to Prosperity, Free Markets, Sound Money and a Bit of Luck*, MIT Press, Cambridge, MA.

ECB (2004) *Measuring Financial Integration in the Eurozone*, Occasional Paper No. 14, April.

ECB (2007) *Review of the International Role of the Euro*, European Central Bank, Frankfurt.

Hartmann, P., A. Maddaloni and S. Manganelli (2003) 'The Eurozone financial system: structure, integration and policy initiatives', *Oxford Review of Economic Policy*, 19 (1): 180–213.

Kamps, A. (2006) *The Euro as Invoicing Currency in International Trade*, Working Paper No. 665, ECB.

Walkner, C. and J.P. Raes (2005) 'Integration and consolidation in EU banking – an unfinished business', Economic Papers 226, *European Economy*. Download from http://europa.eu.int/comm/economy_finance/publications/economic_papers/2005/ecp226en.pdf.

INDEX

A

accountability, Eurosystem 504–5
AD curve
  aggregate demand and supply
    diagram 268–9
  IS-LM interpretation 278–9
Adenauer, Konrad 8
adverse shocks, OCAs 317–19
agglomeration 394–403
  agglomeration diagram 416–18
  agglomeration forces 394–403
  circular causality 401
  cost-linked 395–8
  demand-linked 395–8
  dispersion forces 394–401
  economic geography 393–401
  EE-KK diagram 418–23
  empirical evidence 412
aggregate demand and supply
    diagram
  AD curve 268–9
  macroeconomics 268–76
  neutrality of money 269–72
  PPP 273–6
aggregate welfare effects, CAP
    357
agricultural levies, revenue, EU
    88
agriculture, common policy
    54–5
airlines
  state aid 446
  subsidies, EU-wide 446
allocation effects
  liberalization 221–3
  medium-run growth bonus
    221–3
allocation efficiency
  capital market integration
    554–8
  capital mobility 554–8
allocation of spending, EU
    regional policy 406, 410–11
allocation, political, EU regional
    policy 410–11

Amsterdam Resolution
  EMS 482, 483
  ERM 482
Amsterdam Treaty 33
animal welfare, CAP 364–5
anti-competitive behaviour 52–3,
    426–40
  see also competition; EU
    competition policy
  antitrust practices 433, 435–6
  Article 81 (formerly Article 85)
    442
  Article 82 (formerly Article 86)
    443
  BE-COMP framework 427–32
  cartels 432–4
  collusion 427–32
  EU law 441–3
  exclusive territories 432–4
  M&As control 436–7, 443–4
  Microsoft 435–6
  partial collusion 430–2
  perfect collusion 429–30
  state aid 437–40
anti-dumping measures, EU trade
    policy 458–9
anti-subsidy measures, EU trade
    policy 458–9
antitrust practices 433, 435–6
  see also anti-competitive
    behaviour
approximation of laws,
    competition 52–3
Article 81 (formerly Article 85),
    anti-competitive behaviour
    442
Article 82 (formerly Article 86),
    anti-competitive behaviour
    443
assent procedure, legislative
    processes 78
asymmetric information
  financial markets 552–3
  fiscal federalism 529
  toxic assets 553

asymmetric monetary policy
    effects, Eurosystem 512–13
asymmetric shocks
  effects 337–8
  OCAs 319–21, 330–1, 337–8
asymmetries, Eurosystem 510–11
automatic stabilizers
  fiscal policy 522–4
  monetary unions 522–4
  Netherlands 523–4
  SGP 538–9
autonomy, legal system 68

B

Balassa–Samuelson effect
  inflation differentials 511
  PPP 275–6
banks/banking
  concentration 561–3
  ECB 495–8, 501–2
  financial markets 559–64
  harmonization, regulation
    561–2
  interbank interest rates 564–5
  M&As 560–1
  national concentration 561–3
  pan-European concentration
    561–3
  regulation 561–2
  services 563–4
  starting point 560–1
  top ten banks 559
  trade in services 563–4
barriers to mobility, migration
    257–9
barriers to trade see tariffs
BE-COMP diagram 192–5,
    427–32
  closed economy 198–200
  imperfect competition 192–5
  monopoly 192–5
BE-COMP framework
  anti-competitive behaviour
    427–32
  collusion 427–32

BE curve 199–200, 209–10
benefits distribution, CAP
     358–9
'Big-5' institutions 68–77
     institutional changes 99–103
     Lisbon Treaty 99–103
bond markets 564–6
     euro 573–4
     store of value 573–4
border effect, OCAs 342
border price changes
     discriminatory liberalization
        166–7
     domestic price change 166–7
border price effects, import
        demand curve 146–7
borrowing cost spillovers 526
borrowing/lending, capital
        markets 548–51
borrowing/transfers
     fiscal policy 521–2
     monetary unions 521–2
Bretton Woods, exchange rates
        307
budget deficit, convergence
        criterion 491–2, 494
budget, EU 83–93
     contributions 86–90
     expenditure 83–6, 87
     milestones 87–8
     process 92–3
     revenue 86–90
     SGP 539–41
     summary 106
     UK rebate 91–2
budget problem, CAP 361

C
California, OCAs 315–16
CAP see Common Agricultural
        Policy
capital market integration 54,
        553–9
     see also capital markets
     allocation efficiency 554–8
     analysis 555–6
     diversification effect 558
     EU policies 553–4
     losers 556–8
     microeconomics 553–9
     welfare effects 556–8
     winners 556–8

capital markets 548–59
     see also capital market
        integration; financial
        markets
     borrowing/lending 548–51
     diversification 551
     functions 548
     intermediation function 548
     lending/borrowing 548–51
     maturity function 548–50
     risk function 548, 550–1
capital mobility 27
     allocation efficiency 554–8
     diversification effect 558
     economics of 554–8
     exchange rates 289–90
     losers 556–8
     welfare effects 556–8
     winners 556–8
cartels
     anti-competitive behaviour
        432–4
     vitamin cartels 433
cases
     discriminatory liberalization
        185–8
     legal system 66–7
     small country case,
        discriminatory liberalization
        185–8
Cassis de Dijon, frictional barriers
        157
Central Banks see European
        Central Bank (ECB)
CET see Common External Tariff
Charter of Fundamental Rights,
        Lisbon Treaty 104–5
chronology, 1948–2007; 44–6
Churchill, Winston, 'United
        States of Europe' 3, 7
citizens' right of initiative, Lisbon
        Treaty 104
closed economy, BE-COMP
        diagram 198–200
co-operation procedure
     enhanced co-operation 79–80
     legislative processes 78
codecision procedure, legislative
        processes 77–8
Cohesion Fund, EU regional
        policy 409
Cold War 8–9

collective discipline, spillovers
        527–8
collective negotiations
     economics 240–2
     labour markets 240–2
     unemployment 240–2
collective restraint
     fiscal policy 531
     spillovers 531
collusion
     anti-competitive behaviour
        427–32
     BE-COMP framework 427–32
     long-run economic costs 432
     partial collusion 430–2
     perfect collusion 429–30
colonies, former, preferential
        arrangements, EU trade
        policy 462–3
Commission 72–4, 99–101
     Commissioners 72–3
     composition 72–3
     decision making 74, 126
     EU competition policy 440–1
     executive powers 74
     institutional changes 99–101
     legislative powers 73–4
     Lisbon Treaty 99–101
Common Agricultural Policy
        (CAP) 353–80
     aggregate welfare effects 357
     animal welfare 364–5
     benefits distribution 358–9
     budget problem 361
     changed circumstances 359–66
     consequences, unintended
        360–1
     cross-compliance 372
     decoupled payments 367–9
     developing nations 366
     disposal problem 361–2
     distribution of farmer benefits
        358–9
     dumping 362
     economic logic 366–9
     efficiency 358–9
     'factory farming' 364–5
     farm income problem 363
     farm size 358–9
     first pillar 371–3
     food mountains 361–2
     food stores 359

food tax and subsidy interpretation 356–7
funding 374–7
'Green' revolution 360–6
impact, world food markets 362
importers, net 355–7
industrialization of farming 364–5
international objections 362
MacSharry reforms 369–71
mountains, food 361–2
Mozambique, CAP's sugar policy 366
net importers 355–7
new economic logic 366–9
old simple logic 355–9
paradox 363–4
payments 363–4, 374–7
pillars 371–4
politics 372–3
pollution 364–5
price-floor diagram 355–7
price floor liberalization 367–9
price supports 355–9
problems 359–66
problems, remaining 374–7
reforms 369–73
rural development 373–4
scandals 374–7
social inequality 374–7
sugar policy 366
supply control attempts 369
surplus food 361–2
tariffs 357
tax-and-subsidy 356–7
today's CAP 371–4
unintended consequences 360–1
variable levy 357
welfare effects 357
world food markets impact 362
Common External Tariff (CET)
  EU trade policy 464–6
  revenue, EU 88
common policy
  agriculture 54–5
  trade 51
communism, collapse 28–30
COMP curve 198–200, 208–9
comparative advantage 390–3
  empirical evidence 412

Heckscher–Ohlin comparative advantage 392–3
  specialization 391–3
competences, Lisbon Treaty 97–9
competition
  see also anti-competitive behaviour; EU competition policy
  approximation of laws 52–3
  EU competition policy 440–6
  EU regional policy 407–9
  harmonization 52–3
  regional competitiveness and employment 407–9
  state aid prohibited 52
  taxes 52
  undistorted 52–3
complementarity vs. substitutability, labour market integration 254
'Conclusions of the Presidency', European Council 72
Constitution difficulties
  Lisbon Treaty 94–5
  summary 106
Constitutional Treaty 35–7
  EU trade policy 458
consultation procedure, legislative processes 78
consumer surplus, welfare analysis 144–5
control mechanism, democracy as 119
convergence criteria
  budget deficit 491–2, 494
  ERM membership 491
  Eurosystem 513–14
  inflation 490–1
  long-term nominal interest rate 491
  Maastricht Treaty 490–3
  non-Eurozone members 513–14
  public debt 492–3, 494
convergence, EU regional policy 407–9
coordination
  fiscal policy 524–5, 531–2
  spillovers 524–5, 531–2
  corrective arm, SGP 535–6
  cost-linked agglomeration forces 395–8

Council see Council of the European Union; European Council
Council of Europe 12–14
Council of Ministers see Council of the European Union
Council of the European Union 68–70, 101
  decision-making rules 70
  Lisbon Treaty 101
  Presidency of the EU 70
countercyclical fiscal policies, SGP 536–41
Cournot–Nash equilibrium 195–7
crawling pegs, exchange rates 294, 295
currency boards, exchange rates 295–6
currency crises, exchange rates 297–9
currency unions, exchange rates 296
customs union 172–9
  vs. free trade agreements 177–9
  frictional barriers 175–7
  political integration 178–9
  preferential liberalization 172–9
  price effects 173
  quantity effects 173
  rules of origin 177–8
  second-order terms of trade changes 175
  three-nation trade pattern 173
  trade deflection 177–8
  welfare effects 174–5
cyclical income spillovers 525

D

DCR barriers see domestically captured rent barriers
de Gaulle, Charles 20
debt, public see public debt
decentralization, diversity 114–15
decision making 110–37
  Commission 74, 126
  democratic legitimacy 133
  economical view 121–6
  efficiency 123–6
  EU ability to act 123–6

European Parliament 126
legitimacy 132–3
Nice Treaty 125, 127–8, 132
Normalized Banzhaf Index
(NBI) 130–1
passage probability 123–5
power distribution 126–32
qualified majority voting
(QMV) 122–3
subsidiarity 111–13
task allocation 111–13
decision-making rules
codecision procedure 77–8
Council of the European Union
70
legislative processes 77–8
decoupled payments, CAP 367–9
defragmentation
industrial restructuring 190–2
liberalization 190–2
Delors, Jacques 25
demand curves, marginal utility
142–3
demand, labour markets 237–40
demand-linked agglomeration
forces 395–8
demand side, aggregate demand
and supply diagram 268–9
democracy, as control mechanism
119
democratic control, European
Parliament 75–6
democratic legitimacy, decision
making 133
Deutschmark
EMS 476–8
Germany 476–8
developing nations, CAP 366
'direct effect', legal system 67
discretionary fiscal policy
monetary unions 522–4
SGP 539
discriminatory liberalization
see also liberalization;
preferential liberalization
analysis of unilateral 163–72
border price changes 166–7
cases 185–8
domestic price change 166–7
free trade equilibrium 164–5
MFN tariff analysis 165
NICNIR framework 163–4

preferential liberalization
163–72
price effects 165–8
PTA (Preferential Trade
Arrangement) Diagram
164–5
quantity effects 165–8
small country case 185–8
supply switching 167–8
trade creation 171–2
trade diversion 171–2
Viner's ambiguity 171–2
welfare effects 168–71
dispersion forces 394–401
agglomeration 394–401
disposal problem, CAP 361–2
distribution of farmer benefits,
CAP 358–9
distributional consequences
tariffs 153
welfare effects 153
diversification
capital markets 551
OCAs 333–4
diversification effect
capital market integration 558
capital mobility 558
diversity
decentralization 114–15
local informational advantages
114–15
divorce
enhanced co-operation 79
legislative processes 79
dollarization, exchange rates 296
domestic price change
border price changes 166–7
discriminatory liberalization
166–7
domestically captured rent (DCR)
barriers, tariffs 155–6
domino effect 18–21, 25–7
dumping, CAP 362
duopoly 195–7

E

early post-war period 4–11
see also post-war European
growth
Cold War 8–9
death toll 5–6
EPU 10–11

GDP 5, 6
hunger 6
ideologies 6–7
Marshall Plan 9
OEEC 9–11
political instability 6
refugees 6
east/west Europe, unification
31–2
eastern enlargement 32–9
ECB see European Central Bank
economic geography
agglomeration 393–401
divergence within nations
386–9
Europe 382–90
evolution 386–9
integration 389–90
peripherality 383–6
production specialization
389–90
economic integration
EU 48–59
impact 423
summary 105
economic issues, SGP 541–2
economic logic, CAP 366–9
economical view, decision
making 121–6
economies of scale
financial markets 552
location decision 396
task allocation 116–17
ECSC see European Coal and
Steel Community
ECU see European Currency Unit
EDP see Excessive Deficit
Procedure
EE-KK diagram, agglomeration
418–23
efficiency, CAP 358–9
EFTA see European Free Trade
Association
empirical evidence
agglomeration 412
comparative advantage 412
economic activity 412
EU regional policy 412
empirical measures, power
distribution 128–9
empirical studies
NICNIR framework 179–80

preferential liberalization
179–80
employment
see also labour markets;
unemployment
EU regional policy 407–9
regional competitiveness and
employment 407–9
'empty chair' policy 22
EMS *see* European Monetary
System
EMU *see* European Monetary
Union
energy market
state aid 444–5
subsidies, EU-wide 444–5
enhanced co-operation
divorce 79
legislative processes 79–80
enlargement
2004; 35–7
eastern enlargement 32–9
EPU *see* European Payments
Union
equilibrium, labour markets
239–40
equilibrium prices
output 199–200
size of firm 199–200
ERM *see* Exchange Rate
Mechanism
EU
economic integration 48–59
founding principles 96–7
income disparity 385–9
law 64–8
legal system 64–8
EU ability to act, decision making
efficiency 123–6
EU competition policy 440–6
see also anti-competitive
behaviour; competition
Commission's power 440–1
institutions 440–1
EU law 64–8
anti-competitive behaviour
441–3
EU members, power distribution
126–32
EU or EC? 64
EU policies, capital market
integration 553–4

EU practice
proportionality 112
subsidiarity 112
task allocation 111–12
EU regional policy 405–11
allocation of spending 406,
410–11
allocation, political 410–11
Cohesion Fund 409
competition 407–9
convergence 407–9
empirical evidence 412
employment 407–9
European territorial
cooperation 407–9
guiding principles 406–10
instruments 406–10
objectives 406–10
political allocation 410–11
'poor four' 405–6
priorities, spending 409–10
regional competitiveness and
employment 407–9
spending allocation 406
spending priorities 409–10
Structural Funds 409
EU trade policy 449–68
anti-dumping measures 458–9
anti-subsidy measures 458–9
colonies, former, preferential
arrangements 462–3
Common External Tariff
(CET) 464–6
Constitutional Treaty 458
differences among Member
States 452–4
Euro-Meds 460–1
European Mediterranean trade
area 459–62
exports/imports statistics
450–2
external trade composition
454–6
external trade policy 459–66
facts: pattern of trade 450–6
former Soviet republics 461–2
GSP 463–4
GSP treatment plus 461–2
institutions 456–9
non-regional FTAs 464
pan EuroMed cumulation
system 461

pattern of trade: facts 450–6
poor nations 463–4
tariffs 457–8, 464–6
trade in goods 456–7
western Balkans 461–2
euro 29–30
anchor 575–6
bond markets 573–4
foreign exchange markets
573–5
international reserves 574–5
international role 572–8
parallel currencies 576–8
store of value 573–5
trade invoicing 572–3
UK 329–30
vehicle currencies 573
Euro-pessimism 21–5
euroization, exchange rates 296
Europe
economic geography 382–90
optimum currency area?
329–45
Europe Agreements 31
European Central Bank (ECB)
see also Eurosystem
differences 501–2
EMU 495–8
European Coal and Steel
Community (ECSC)
12–14
European Commission *see*
Commission
European Convention 35–7
European Council 71–2, 102–3
'Conclusions of the Presidency'
72
Lisbon Treaty 102–3
European Court of Justice 76–7
Lisbon Treaty 103
European Currency Unit (ECU),
EMS 473–4
European Free Trade Association
(EFTA) 16–21
European integration
growth relationship 214–18
locational effects 396–401
'poor four' 223–7
European Monetary System
(EMS) 471–87
1979–85; 475–6
1986–92; 476–8

1992–3; 478–80
Amsterdam Resolution 482, 483
arrangements 472–5
assessment 474–5
crisis: 1992–3; 478–80
Deutschmark 476–8
ECU 473–4
EMS-1; 475–81
EMS-2; 482–3
exchange rates 308–10
exchange rates, joint management 473
flexible/cohesive arrangement 474–5
Germany 476–8
impossible trinity 474–5, 484
inflation 475–6, 478–80
inflation, non-Eurozone 484–5
lessons 481
mutual support 473
new EU member states 483–5
parity grid 472
re-engineered 481–5
softer 481–2
European Monetary Union (EMU) 488–518
  see also Eurosystem
Central Banks 495–8
ECB 495–8
Eurosystem 495–515
Maastricht Treaty 489–95
European Parliament 74–6, 103
  decision making 126
  democratic control 75–6
  Lisbon Treaty 103
  location 75
  organization 74–5, 105
European Payments Union (EPU) 10–11
European territorial cooperation, EU regional policy 407–9
Eurosystem
  accountability 504–5
  asymmetric monetary policy effects 512–13
  asymmetries 510–11
  convergence criteria 513–14
  EMU 495–515
  exchange rates 509–10
  growth 506–9
  independence 502–4, 505

inflation 506–9
inflation differentials 511–12
instruments 499–500
more members? 513–14
non-Eurozone members 513–14
objectives 498–9
one money, one policy 510–13
strategy 500–2
transparency 505
Eurozone
  Germany 319
  Italy 328
  Portugal 328
  UK 329–30
Excessive Deficit Procedure (EDP), SGP 536–8
excessive deficits
  SGP 533–4, 536–8
  spillovers 526–7
Exchange Rate Mechanism (ERM) 290, 294–5, 308–10
  see also European Monetary System (EMS)
  Amsterdam Resolution 482
  convergence criterion 491
exchange rates
  Bretton Woods 307
  capital mobility 289–90
  choices 291–9
  co-ordination 54
  crawling pegs 294, 295
  currency boards 295–6
  currency crises 297–9
  currency unions 296
  dollarization 296
  EMS 308–10, 473
  euroization 296
  Eurosystem 509–10
  fixed 284–5
  fixed and adjustable 294–5
  flexible 292–4
  floating 283–4
  France 304–5
  freely floating 292–3
  Germany 306, 319
  impossible trinity 289–90
  inflation differential 273–6
  inter-war period 304–6
  joint management, realignments 473

macroeconomics 273–6
managed floating 293–4
monetary policies 283–5, 571
monetary unions 296, 299–303
price-specie mechanism 301–3
real exchange rates 319
realignments, joint management 473
Snake 307–8
target zones 294
UK 304
exclusive territories, anti-competitive behaviour 432–4
executive powers, Commission 74
expenditure, EU 83–6, 87
  by area 83–6
  by member 86, 87
export supply curve
  supply and demand analysis 147–8
  welfare analysis 148
exports
  see also EU trade policy
exports/imports statistics, EU trade policy 450–2
external trade composition, EU trade policy 454–6
external trade policy, EU trade policy 459–66
externalities
  see also spillovers
  fiscal policy 524–32

F

'factory farming', CAP 364–5
failed integration 15, 23–4
farm income problem, CAP 363
farm size, CAP 358–9
FCR barriers see foreign captured rent barriers
federalism 11–18
Feldstein, Martin 344
financial institutions
  banks/banking 559–64
  bond markets 564–6
  financial markets 559–71
  stock markets 566–8
financial markets 547–82
  see also capital markets
  asymmetric information 552–3
  banks/banking 559–64

characteristics 552–3
economies of scale 552
financial institutions 559–71
networks 552
regulation 569–71
scale economies 552
single currency 558–9, 570–1
single currency effects 558–9
stock markets 566–8
supervision 569–71
toxic assets 553
fiscal federalism
asymmetric information 529
heterogeneity of preferences 529
increasing returns to scale 529
quality of government 529–30
spillovers 528–30
task allocation 113–21
theory to practice 120–1
trade-offs 113–20
fiscal policy 519–46
automatic stabilizers 522–4
borrowing/transfers 521–2
collective restraint 531
coordination 524–5, 531–2
discretionary 522–4
externalities 524–32
IS-LM interpretation 279–80
micro vs. macroeconomic aspects 530
monetary unions 520–4
SGP 532–42
spillovers 524–32
transfers/borrowing 521–2
fiscal transfers, OCAs 326–7, 337, 344
fixed and adjustable exchange rates 294–5
fixed exchange rates 284–5
flexibility, Lisbon Treaty 98–9
flexible exchange rates 292–4
floating exchange rates 283–4
food stores, CAP 359
food tax and subsidy interpretation, CAP 356–7
foreign captured rent (FCR) barriers, tariffs 156–7
foreign exchange markets
euro 573–5
vehicle currencies 573
founding principles, EU 96–7

France
exchange rates 304–5
neutrality of money 269–71
free trade agreements
vs. customs union 177–9
rules of origin 177–8
trade deflection 177–8
free trade equilibrium, discriminatory liberalization 164–5
free trade in goods 51
labour markets 247
non-tariff barriers 51
tariffs 51
freely floating exchange rates 292–3
frictional barriers
1992 programme 175–7
Cassis de Dijon 157
customs union 175–7
price effects 176
quantity effects 176
tariffs 157–9, 175–7
trade creation 176
trade diversion 176
Viner's ambiguity 176
welfare effects 176, 177
funding, CAP 374–7

G
GDP
see also output
early post-war period 5, 6
growth 214–17
prices 266–8
geography *see* economic geography; real geography
Germany
Deutschmark 476–8
EMS 476–8
Eurozone 319
exchange rates 306, 319
four-way division 7
institutional reform process 38
output gap 319
real exchange rates 319
unification 29–30
GNP based revenue, EU 89
Greece, medium-run growth effects 227
'Green' revolution, CAP 360–6
growth 211–32

1950–1973; 216–17
accession growth 216–17
European integration relationship 214–18
Eurosystem 506–9
GDP 214–17
logic of growth 212–18
phases of European growth 213–14
post-war European growth 213–14, 215
growth effects 211–32
induced capital formation 218–27
long-run effects 212–13
long-run growth 227–30
medium-run effects 212–13, 217–27
Solow's analysis 218–27
GSP, EU trade policy 463–4
GSP treatment plus, EU trade policy 461–2
guiding principles, EU regional policy 406–10

H
harmonization
banks/banking regulation 561–2
competition 52–3
VAT 117–18
Heckscher–Ohlin comparative advantage 392–3
heterogeneity of preferences, fiscal federalism 529
High Representative of the Union for Foreign Affairs and Security Policy, Lisbon Treaty 101–2
homogeneity of preferences criterion, OCAs 327, 337–9
homogeneous preferences, OCAs 327, 337–9
Hume, David 301
hunger, early post-war period 6

I
ideologies, early post-war period 6–7
immigration *see* migration
imperfect competition

BE-COMP diagram 192–5
monopoly 192–5
import demand curve
border price effects 146–7
supply and demand analysis
145–7
trade volume effects 146–7
welfare analysis 146–7
importers, net, CAP 355–7
imports
see also EU trade policy
imports/exports statistics, EU
trade policy 450–2
impossible trinity
EMS 474–5, 484
exchange rates 289–90
income disparity, EU 385–9
incomes/populations 80–2
increasing returns to scale, fiscal
federalism 529
independence, Eurosystem
502–4, 505
indices
European economic
integration 58–9
OCAs 330–1
trade dissimilarity 333–4
induced capital formation
growth effects 218–27
Solow's analysis 218–27
industrial restructuring
defragmentation 190–2
liberalization 190–2
industrialization of farming, CAP
364–5
inflation
convergence criterion 490–1
EMS 475–6, 478–80
Eurosystem 506–9
public opinion 507–9
inflation differentials
Balassa–Samuelson effect
511
Eurosystem 511–12
exchange rates 273–6
macroeconomics 273–6
information, asymmetric *see*
asymmetric information
institutional changes
'Big-5' institutions 99–103
Commission 99–101
Lisbon Treaty 99–103

institutional effects, trade
integration 244–5
institutions
'Big-5' 68–77, 99–103
Commission 72–4, 99–101
Council of the European Union
68–70, 101
EU competition policy 440–1
EU trade policy 456–9
European Council 71–2, 102–3
European Court of Justice
76–7, 103
European Parliament 74–6, 103
summary 105–6
instruments, EU regional policy
406–10
inter-war period, exchange rates
304–6
interbank interest rates 564–5
interest rate parity condition
macroeconomics 280–3
open economy 280–3
interest rates
interbank interest rates 564–5
macroeconomics 279–83
monetary policies 571
intergovernmental policy, three-
pillar structure 60–4
intergovernmentalism 11–18
intermediation function, capital
markets 548
international objections, CAP 362
international reserves
euro 574–5
store of value 574–5
investment rate, medium-run
growth effects 223
Ireland, medium-run growth
effects 226–7
IS-LM interpretation
AD curve 278–9
fiscal policy 279–80
monetary policies 279–80
short-run 276–80
Italy
Eurozone 328
Eurozone membership 514–15
windfall gain 514–15

J

jurisdictional competition
119–20

K

Kenen criterion, OCAs 325
Kenen, Peter 323
knowledge creation/absorption,
long-run growth effects
227–30
Krugman, Paul 198

L

labour market integration 54
complementarity vs.
substitutability 254
economics 252–5
migration 252–5
labour markets 233–62
characterization 234–7
collective negotiations 240–2
concepts 235–6
demand 237–40
equilibrium 239–40
free trade in goods 247
Mundell criterion 322–4
OCAs 322–4, 342–4
principles 237–42
'social dumping' 245–8
supply 237–40
trade integration 242–8
unemployment 234–7, 240–4
wage rigidity 242
labour mobility
Mundell criterion 322–4
OCAs 322–4, 334–7
law
anti-competitive behaviour
441–3
EU 64–8, 441–3
sources 64–5
summary 105
types 65
legal system 66–8
autonomy 68
cases 66–7
'direct effect' 67
EU 64–8
European Court of Justice
76–7, 103
primacy of EC law 67–8
principles 66–8
legislative powers, Commission
73–4
legislative processes 77–80
assent procedure 78

co-operation procedure 78
codecision procedure 77–8
consultation procedure 78
decision-making rules 77–8
divorce 79
enhanced co-operation 79–80
Lisbon Treaty 104
legitimacy
    decision making 132–3
    democratic 133
lending/borrowing, capital
    markets 548–51
liberalization 190–2
    see also discriminatory
        liberalization; preferential
        liberalization
    allocation effects 221–3
    defragmentation 190–2
    impact 200–4
    industrial restructuring 190–2
    long term effects 202–3
    medium-run growth bonus
        221–3
    no-trade-to-free-trade
        liberalization 200–3
    price/cost effects 203–4
    short term effects 202
    welfare effects 203
Lisbon Treaty 37–9, 93–105
    'Big-5' institutions 99–103
    changes to Treaty of Rome
        57–8
    Charter of Fundamental Rights
        104–5
    citizens' right of initiative 104
    Commission 99–101
    competences 97–9
    Constitution difficulties 94–5,
        106
    Council of the European Union
        101
    EU powers extension 98–9
    European Council 102–3
    European Court of Justice 103
    European Parliament 103
    flexibility 98–9
    founding principles, EU 96–7
    High Representative of the
        Union for Foreign Affairs
        and Security Policy 101–2
    institutional changes 99–103
    legislative processes 104

national parliaments' roles
    103–4
organization 95–6, 105
passerelle clause 98–9
power shifts 131–2
two-pillar structure 95–6
local informational advantages,
    diversity 114–15
location decision, scale
    economies 396
locational effects, European
    integration 396–401
long-run
    macroeconomics 269–76
    neutrality of money 269–72
    purchasing power parity (PPP)
        273–6
long-run economic costs,
    collusion 432
long-run growth effects 212–13,
    227–30
    European integration effects
        229–30
    knowledge creation/absorption
        227–30
    Solow-like diagram 228–30
long term effects, liberalization
    202–3
long-term nominal interest rate,
    convergence criterion 491
long-term unemployment 240–2
Luxembourg
    power distribution 129–30
    vote shares 129–30
Luxembourg Compromise 22

M

M&As *see* mergers and
    acquisitions
Maastricht Treaty 29–30, 63–4
    components 489–90
    convergence criteria 490–3
    EMU 489–95
    EMU timetable 489
    ratification 490
    ratification difficulties 30
    three-pillar structure 60–4
    two-speed Europe 493–5
McKinnon criterion, OCAs
    325–6
McKinnon, Ronald 323
macroeconomic co-ordination 54

macroeconomics 265–87
    aggregate demand and supply
        diagram 268–76
    Balassa–Samuelson effect
        275–6
    exchange rates 273–6
    fiscal policy 530
    inflation differential 273–6
    interest rate parity condition
        280–3
    interest rates 279–83
    IS-LM interpretation 276–80
    long-run 269–76
    micro vs. macroeconomic
        aspects, fiscal policy 530
    money market 276–80
    neutrality of money 269–72
    open economy 280–3
    output 266–8
    PPP 273–6
    prices 266–8
    short-run 276–80
    tools 265–87
MacSharry reforms, CAP
    369–71
managed floating exchange rates
    293–4
marginal costs, supply curves
    143–4
marginal utility, demand curves
    142–3
market accessibility, real
    geography 403–5
Marshall Plan 9
maturity function, capital
    markets 548–50
MD-MS, supply and demand
    analysis 148–9
Meade, James 172
medium-run growth bonus
    allocation effects 221–3
    liberalization 221–3
medium-run growth effects
    212–13, 217–27
    Greece 227
    investment rate 223
    Ireland 226–7
    'poor four' 223–7
    Portugal 225–6
    Spain 225–6
Members of European Parliament
    (MEPs) 74–5

MEPs *see* Members of European Parliament
mergers and acquisitions (M&As) 191–2
  anti-competitive behaviour 436–7, 443–4
  banks/banking 560–1
  control 436–7, 443–4
MFN tariff analysis 149–55
  discriminatory liberalization 165
micro vs. macroeconomic aspects, fiscal policy 530
microeconomics, capital market integration 553–9
Microsoft, anti-competitive behaviour 435–6
migration 248–59
  1950–2010; 248–52
  barriers to mobility 257–9
  complementarity vs. substitutability 254
  labour market integration 252–5
  OCAs 322–4, 334–7
  unemployment 255–7
monetary integration, failure 23
monetary policies
  channels 571
  effects 571
  exchange rates 283–5, 571
  interest rates 571
  IS-LM interpretation 279–80
  nominal interest rates 280
  real interest rates 280
monetary unions
  automatic stabilizers 522–4
  borrowing/transfers 521–2
  discretionary fiscal policy 522–4
  exchange rates 296, 299–303
  fiscal policy 520–4
  transfers/borrowing 521–2
money market, macroeconomics 276–80
Monnet, Jean 13–14, 15
monopoly 192–5
  BE-COMP diagram 192–5
  imperfect competition 192–5
most favoured nation tariff *see* MFN tariff analysis

Mozambique, CAP's sugar policy 366
Mundell criterion
  labour mobility 322–4
  OCAs 322–4
Mundell, Robert A. 323

N
Nash equilibrium 195–7
Nash, John 195
national parliaments' roles, Lisbon Treaty 103–4
nationalism vs. solidarity, OCAs 327–9, 339–41
NBI *see* Normalized Banzhaf Index
net importers
  CAP 355–7
  price-floor diagram 355–7
Netherlands, automatic stabilizers 523–4
networks, financial markets 552
neutrality of money
  aggregate demand and supply diagram 269–72
  France 269–71
  long-run 269–72
  macroeconomics 269–72
  Switzerland 269–71
Nice Treaty 33–4
  decision making 125, 127–8, 132
  reforms 125, 127–8
NICNIR framework *see* no imperfect competition and no increasing returns framework
no-bailout clause, spillovers 526–7
no imperfect competition and no increasing returns (NICNIR) framework 163–4
  empirical studies 179–80
no-trade-to-free-trade liberalization 200–3
nominal interest rates, monetary policies 280
non-Eurozone members
  convergence criteria 513–14
  Eurosystem 513–14
non-regional FTAs, EU trade policy 464

non-tariff barriers, free trade in goods 51
Normalized Banzhaf Index (NBI), decision making 130–1

O
objectives, EU regional policy 406–10
OCAs *see* optimum currency areas
OEEC *see* Organization for European Economic Cooperation
oligopoly 197
omitted integration
  social policy 55–7
  tax policy 56–7
one money, one policy, Eurosystem 510–13
open economy
  interest rate parity condition 280–3
  macroeconomics 280–3
open-economy supply and demand analysis 145–9
openness, OCAs 325–6, 331–3
optimum currency areas (OCAs) 314–49
  adverse shocks 317–19
  asymmetric shocks 319–21, 330–1, 337–8
  border effect 342
  California 315–16
  criteria 322–9
  desirability 316–17
  diversification 333–4
  Europe? 329–45
  fiscal transfers 326–7, 337, 344
  homogeneity of preferences criterion 327, 337–9
  homogeneous preferences 327, 337–9
  index 330–1
  Kenen criterion 325
  labour markets 322–4, 342–4
  labour mobility 322–4, 334–7
  logic 316–17
  McKinnon criterion 325–6
  migration 322–4, 334–7
  Mundell criterion 322–4
  nationalism vs. solidarity 327–9, 339–41

openness 325–6, 331–3
politics 344–5
production diversification
    325
Rose effect 342
solidarity criterion 327–9
solidarity vs. nationalism
    327–9, 339–41
symmetric shocks 321–2
theory 345–7
trade dissimilarity 333–4
trade effects 341
transfer criterion 326–7
UK 329–30
organization
    European Parliament 74–5,
        105
    Lisbon Treaty 95–6
    summary 105
Organization for European
    Economic Cooperation
    (OEEC) 9–11
output
    see also GDP
    equilibrium prices 199–200
    macroeconomics 266–8
    prices 266–8
    size of firm 199–200
output gap
    Germany 319
    real exchange rates 319

P

parallel currencies, euro 576–8
Parliament, European *see*
    European Parliament
parliaments' roles, national
    103–4
partial collusion, anti-competitive
    behaviour 430–2
passage probability, decision
    making 123–5
passerelle clause, Lisbon Treaty
    98–9
pattern of trade, EU trade policy
    450–6
perfect collusion, anti-
    competitive behaviour
    429–30
peripherality
    economic geography 383–6
    real geography 403–5

policy, EU competition *see* EU
    competition policy
policy, EU regional *see* EU
    regional policy
political allocation, EU regional
    policy 410–11
political instability, early post-war
    period 6
political integration, customs
    union 178–9
political issues, SGP 542
politics
    CAP 372–3
    OCAs 344–5
pollution, CAP 364–5
'poor four'
    EU regional policy 405–6
    European integration 223–7
    medium-run growth effects
        223–7
poor nations, EU trade policy
    463–4
populations/incomes 80–2
Portugal
    Eurozone 328
    medium-run growth effects
        225–6
post-war European growth
    213–14, 215
    see also early post-war period
power distribution
    decision making 126–32
    empirical measures 128–9
    EU members 126–32
    Luxembourg 129–30
    vote shares 129–30
power shifts, Lisbon Treaty
    131–2
PPP *see* purchasing power parity
preferential liberalization 162–88
    see also discriminatory
        liberalization; liberalization
    customs union 172–9
    discriminatory liberalization
        163–72
    empirical studies 179–80
    WTO rules 179
Presidency of the EU 70–2
    'Conclusions of the Presidency'
        72
    Council of the European Union
        70

preventive arm, SGP 535
price/cost effects
    liberalization 203–4
    Single Market Programme
        (1986–92) 192
price effects
    customs union 173
    discriminatory liberalization
        165–8
    frictional barriers 176
    tariffs 150–1
price-floor diagram
    CAP 355–7
    net importers 355–7
price floor liberalization, CAP
    367–9
price-specie mechanism,
    exchange rates 301–3
price supports, CAP 355–9
prices
    macroeconomics 266–8
    output 266–8
primacy of EC law, legal system
    67–8
priorities, spending, EU regional
    policy 409–10
producer surplus, welfare analysis
    144–5
production diversification, OCAs
    325
production specialization,
    economic geography
    389–90
proportionality, EU practice
    112
protection types, tariffs 155–9
PTA (Preferential Trade
    Arrangement) Diagram,
    discriminatory liberalization
    164–5
public debt
    convergence criterion 492–3,
        494
    spillovers 526–8
public opinion, inflation 507–9
purchasing power parity (PPP)
    aggregate demand and supply
        diagram 273–6
    Balassa–Samuelson effect
        275–6
    long-run 273–6
    macroeconomics 273–6

Q

qualified majority voting (QMV), decision making 122–3
quality of government, fiscal federalism 529–30
quantifying European economic integration 58–9
quantity effects
customs union 173
discriminatory liberalization 165–8
frictional barriers 176
tariffs 150–1

R

real exchange rates
Germany 319
output gap 319
real geography
market accessibility 403–5
peripherality 403–5
real interest rates, monetary policies 280
rebate, UK 91–2
reform, task allocation 113
Reform Treaty *see* Lisbon Treaty
reforms
CAP 369–73
Nice Treaty 125, 127–8
refugees, early post-war period 6
regional competitiveness and employment, EU regional policy 407–9
regional policy, EU *see* EU regional policy
regional unemployment 402–3
regulation
banks/banking harmonization 561–2
financial markets 569–71
revenue, EU 86–90
agricultural levies 88
CET 88
GNP based 89
by member 89–92
VAT resource 89
risk function, capital markets 548, 550–1
Robinson, Joan 193
Rose effect, OCAs 342
rules of origin

customs union 177–8
free trade agreements 177–8
rural development, CAP 373–4

S

Samuelson, Paul 172
sanctions, SGP 536
scale economies
financial markets 552
location decision 396
task allocation 116–17
Schuman, Robert 12, 13
second-order terms of trade changes, customs union 175
Second World War, early post-war period 4–11
services
banks/banking 563–4
unrestricted trade 52–3
SGP *see* Stability and Growth Pact
short-run
IS-LM interpretation 276–80
macroeconomics 276–80
short term effects, liberalization 202
single currency
financial markets 558–9, 570–1
supervision 570–1
single currency effects, financial markets 558–9
Single Market Programme (1986–92) 25–7
price/cost effects 192
size, EU economies 82–3
size of firm
equilibrium prices 199–200
output 199–200
ski instructors, unrestricted trade in services 53
small country case, discriminatory liberalization 185–8
Snake, exchange rates 307–8
'social dumping'
economics 245–8
labour markets 245–8
unemployment 245–8
social harmonization 55–6
social inequality, CAP 374–7
social policy, omitted integration 55–7

solidarity criterion, OCAs 327–9
solidarity vs. nationalism, OCAs 327–9, 339–41
Solow-like diagram, long-run growth effects 228–30
Solow, Robert 219
Solow's analysis
growth effects 218–27
induced capital formation 218–27
Spain, medium-run growth effects 225–6
specialization
comparative advantage 391–3
trade effects 341–2
spending allocation, EU regional policy 406, 410–11
spending priorities, EU regional policy 409–10
spillovers
borrowing cost 526
collective discipline 527–8
collective restraint 531
coordination 524–5, 531–2
cyclical income 525
excessive deficits 526–7
fiscal federalism 528–30
fiscal policy 524–32
no-bailout clause 526–7
principles 528–32
public debt 526–8
subsidiarity 530
task allocation 117–18
VAT 117–18
Stability and Growth Pact (SGP) 532–42
automatic stabilizers 538–9
budget, EU 539–41
corrective arm 535–6
countercyclical fiscal policies 536–41
discretionary fiscal policy 539
economic issues 541–2
EDP 536–8
elements 533–6
excessive deficits 533–4, 536–8
fiscal policy 532–42
limits 541–2
political issues 542
preventive arm 535
sanctions 536

state aid
  airlines 446
  anti-competitive behaviour
    437–40
  energy market 444–5
  EU policies 444–6
  subsidies, EU-wide 438–40,
    444–5
state aid prohibited, competition
  52
stock markets 566–8
  consolidation 568
store of value
  bond markets 573–4
  euro 573–5
  international reserves 574–5
Structural Funds, EU regional
  policy 409
structure, EU, three-pillar
  structure 59–64
subsidiarity
  decision making 111–13
  EU practice 112
  principle 530
  spillovers 530
subsidies, EU-wide
  airlines 446
  anti-subsidy measures 458–9
  energy market 444–5
  state aid 438–40, 444–5
  unfair competition 439–40
  welfare effects 438–9
substitutability vs.
    complementarity, labour
    market integration 254
sugar policy, CAP 366
supervision
  financial markets 569–71
  single currency 570–1
supply and demand analysis
  export supply curve 147–8
  import demand curve 145–7
  MD-MS 148–9
  open-economy 145–9
supply and demand diagrams
  142–5
supply control attempts, CAP 369
supply curves, marginal costs
  143–4
supply, labour markets 237–40
supply side, aggregate demand
  and supply diagram 268

supply switching, discriminatory
  liberalization 167–8
supranational policy, three-pillar
  structure 60–4
surplus food, CAP 361–2
Switzerland, neutrality of money
  269–71
symmetric shocks, OCAs 321–2

T
target zones, exchange rates 294
tariffs
  see also customs union; free
    trade agreements
  CAP 357
  CET 88
  cheats, stopping 177–8
  Common External Tariff
    (CET) 464–6
  common trade policy 51
  DCR barriers 155–6
  distributional consequences
    153
  EU trade policy 457–8, 464–6
  FCR barriers 156–7
  free trade in goods 51
  frictional barriers 157–9,
    175–7
  MFN tariff analysis 149–55
  price effects 150–1
  protection types 155–9
  quantity effects 150–1
  taxing foreigners 154–5
  TBTs 157–9
  welfare effects 151–4
task allocation
  decision making 111–13
  economies of scale 116–17
  EU practice 111–12
  fiscal federalism 113–21
  proportionality 112
  reform 113
  scale economies 116–17
  spillovers 117–18
  subsidiarity 112
  theory to practice 120–1
  three-pillar structure 112–13
  trade-offs 113–20
  VAT 117–18
tax-and-subsidy, CAP 356–7
tax policy, omitted integration
  56–7

taxes
  competition 52
  VAT 89, 117–18
taxing foreigners, tariffs 154–5
technical barriers to trade (TBTs),
  tariffs 157–9
theory, OCAs 345–7
theory to practice
  fiscal federalism 120–1
  task allocation 120–1
three-nation trade pattern,
  customs union 173
three-pillar structure
  EU 59–64
  intergovernmental policy 60–4
  superceded 95–6
  supranational policy 60–4
  task allocation 112–13
toxic assets
  asymmetric information 553
  financial markets 553
trade barriers see tariffs
trade creation
  discriminatory liberalization
    171–2
  frictional barriers 176
trade deflection
  customs union 177–8
  free trade agreements 177–8
trade dissimilarity, OCAs 333–4
trade diversion
  discriminatory liberalization
    171–2
  frictional barriers 176
trade effects
  OCAs 341
  specialization 341–2
trade in goods, EU trade policy
  456–7
trade in services, banks/banking
  563–4
trade integration
  economic effects 243–4
  failure 23–4
  institutional effects 244–5
  labour markets 242–8
  unrestricted trade in services
    52–3
trade invoicing, euro 572–3
trade-offs
  fiscal federalism 113–20
  task allocation 113–20

trade policy
  see also EU trade policy
  common 51
trade volume effects, import
    demand curve 146–7
transfer criterion, OCAs
    326–7
transfers/borrowing
  fiscal policy 521–2
  monetary unions 521–2
transparency, Eurosystem 505
Treaty of Rome 14–16, 63–4
  additions 57–8
  Articles 1, 2 and 3; 49
  fountainhead of integration
    48–50
  Lisbon Treaty changes 57–8
two-pillar structure, Lisbon
    Treaty 95–6
two-speed Europe, Maastricht
    Treaty 493–5

U
UK
  euro 329–30
  Eurozone 329–30
  exchange rates 304
  OCAs 329–30
UK rebate 91–2
undistorted competition 52–3
unemployment
  collective negotiations 240–2
  labour markets 234–7, 240–4

long-term 240–2
migration 255–7
regional 402–3
'social dumping' 245–8
unification
  east/west Europe 31–2
  Germany 29–30
'United States of Europe',
    Churchill, Winston 3, 7
unrestricted trade in services
    52–3

V
variable levy, CAP 357
VAT
  harmonization 117–18
  spillovers 117–18
  task allocation 117–18
VAT resource, revenue, EU 89
vehicle currencies
  euro 573
  foreign exchange markets 573
Viner, Jacob 172
Viner's ambiguity
  discriminatory liberalization
    171–2
  frictional barriers 176
vitamin cartels 433
vote shares
  Luxembourg 129–30
  power distribution 129–30
voting, qualified majority voting
    (QMV) 122–3

W
wage rigidity
  cyclical impact 242
  labour markets 242
war *see* early post-war period;
    inter-war period; post-war
    European growth; Second
    World War
welfare analysis 144–5
  consumer surplus 144–5
  export supply curve 148
  import demand curve 146–7
  producer surplus 144–5
welfare effects
  CAP 357
  capital market integration
    556–8
  capital mobility 556–8
  customs union 174–5
  discriminatory liberalization
    168–71
  distributional consequences
    153
  frictional barriers 176, 177
  liberalization 203
  subsidies, EU-wide 438–9
  tariffs 151–4
world food markets impact, CAP
    362
WTO rules, preferential
    liberalization 179